Anonymus

Secretary of the Treasury

Annual Report, 1865

Anonymus

Secretary of the Treasury
Annual Report, 1865

ISBN/EAN: 9783741136566

Manufactured in Europe, USA, Canada, Australia, Japa

Cover: Foto ©Thomas Meinert / pixelio.de

Manufactured and distributed by brebook publishing software
(www.brebook.com)

Anonymus

Secretary of the Treasury

REPORT

SECRETARY OF THE TREASURY

ON

THE STATE OF THE FINANCES

FOR

THE YEAR 1865.

―――――

WASHINGTON:
GOVERNMENT PRINTING OFFICE.
1865.

INDEX TO REPORT ON THE FINANCES.

FINANCE REPORT.

LETTER

THE SECRETARY OF THE TREASURY,

TRANSMITTING

His annual report for the year 1865.

DECEMBER 5, 1865.—Laid on the table and ordered to be printed.

TREASURY DEPARTMENT, *December* 5, 1865.

SIR : I have the honor to transmit to the House of Representatives the annual report of the Secretary of the Treasury, as required by law.

With great respect,

HUGH McCULLOCH,
Secretary of the Treasury.

Hon. SCHUYLER COLFAX,
Speaker of the House of Representatives.

REPORT

OF

THE SECRETARY OF THE TREASURY.

TREASURY DEPARTMENT,
Washington, December 4, 1865.

In conformity with law, the Secretary of the Treasury has the honor to submit to Congress his annual report.

Next in importance to the great questions involved in the restoration of the federal authority over the southern States, and the re-establishment of civil government therein under the Constitution, are the financial questions, embracing—

The currency;

The public debt; and

The revenue;

all of which demand the early and careful attention of Congress.

In presenting these important subjects, with their various connexions, the Secretary is painfully conscious of his own inability properly to discuss them, difficult as they are, and involving as they do the national honor and the pecuniary interests of thirty millions of people. He will, however, offer as clearly and definitely as he can his own views in relation to them, not doubting that Congress will sustain and carry out by appropriate legislation those that are approved by their superior wisdom, and reject those which are regarded as either impracticable or unsound.

The fact that means have been raised, without foreign loans, to meet the expenses of a protracted and very costly war, is evidence not only of the great resources of the country, but of the wisdom of Congress in passing the necessary laws, and of the distinguished ability of the immediate predecessors of the present Secretary in administering them. It is hardly necessary to suggest, however, that the legislation which was proper and wise during the progress of hostilities may not be appropriate or even justifiable in a time of peace.

The right of Congress, at all times, to borrow money and to issue obligations for loans in such form as may be convenient, is unquestionable; but their authority to issue obligations for a circulating medium as money, and to make these obligations a legal tender, can only be found in the unwritten law which sanctions whatever the representatives of the people, whose duty it is to maintain the government against its enemies, may consider in a great emergency necessary to be done. The present legal-tender acts were war measures, and while the repeal of those provisions which made the United States notes lawful money is not now recommended, the Secretary is of the opinion that they ought not to remain in force one day longer than shall be necessary to enable the people to prepare for a return to the constitutional currency. It is not supposed that it was the intention of Congress, by these acts, to introduce a standard of value, in times of peace, lower than the coin standard, much less to perpetuate the discredit which must attach to a great nation which dishonors its own obligations by unnecessarily keeping in circulation an irredeemable paper currency. It has not, in past times, been regarded as the province of Congress to furnish the people directly with money in any form. Their authority is "to coin money and fix the value thereof;" and, inasmuch as a mixed currency, consisting of paper and specie, has been found to be a commercial necessity, it would seem also to be their duty to provide, as has been done by the National Currency act, that this paper currency should be secured beyond any reasonable contingency. To go beyond this, however, and issue government obligations, making them by statute a legal tender for all debts, public and private, is not believed to be, under ordinary circumstances, within the scope of their duties or constitutional powers.

The reasons which are sometimes urged in favor of United States notes as a permanent currency are, the saving of interest and their perfect safety and uniform value.

The objections to such a policy are, that the paper circulation of the country should be flexible, increasing and decreasing according to the requirements of legitimate business, while, if furnished by the government, it would be quite likely to be governed by the necessities of the treasury or the interests of parties, rather than the demands of commerce and trade. Besides, a permanent government currency would be greatly in the way of public economy, and would give to the party in possession of the government a power which it might be under strong temptations to use for other purposes than the public good— keeping the question of the currency constantly before the people as a political question, than which few things would be more injurious to business.

But the great and insuperable objection, as already stated, to the direct issue of notes by the government, as a policy, is the fact, that the government of the United States is one of limited and defined powers, and that the authority to issue notes as money is neither expressly given to Congress by the Constitution, nor fairly to be inferred, except as a measure of necessity in a great national exigency. No consideration of a mere pecuniary character should induce an exercise by Congress of powers not clearly contemplated by the instrument upon which our political fabric was established. The government, in the great contest which has been recently closed, has not sought to increase its own powers, nor to interfere with the rightful powers of the States. The questions decided by the war are, that the Union is indissoluble; that whatever is essentially opposed to it must be removed; that the federal authority, within its proper sphere, is supreme; and that the validity of acts of Congress not to be determined by the States, but by that tribunal which the complex character of the government made a necessity. It is the crowning glory of the Constitution that this great war has been waged and closed without the powers of the government being enlarged or its relations to the States being changed.

The issue of United States notes as lawful money was a measure expedient, doubtless, and necessary in the great emergency in which it was adopted, but this emergency no longer exists, and however desirable may be the saving of interest, and however satisfactory these notes may be as a circulating medium, these considerations will not, it is respectfully submitted, justify a departure from that strict construction of the Constitution given to it previous to the war by patriotic men of all parties, and which is essential to the equal and harmonious working of our peculiar institutions. The strength of the government has been proved by the manner in which it has carried on the greatest war of modern times; it only remains, for the vindication of its excellence and the perfection of its triumphs, that all powers exercised for its preservation, but not expressly granted by the Constitution, be relinquished with the return of peace. While, therefore, the Secretary is of the opinion that the immediate repeal of the legal-tender provisions of the acts referred to would be unwise, as being likely to affect injuriously the legitimate business of the country, upon the prosperity of which depend the welfare of the people and the revenues which are necessary for the maintenance of the national credit, and unjust to the holders of the notes, he is of the opinion that not only these provisions but the acts also should be regarded as only temporary, and that the work of retiring the notes which have been issued under them should be commenced without delay, and carefully and persistently continued until all are retired.

In speaking of the legal-tender acts, reference has only been made to those which authorized the issue of United States notes. The interest-bearing notes which are a legal tender for their face value were intended to be a security rather than a circulating medium, and it would be neither injurious to the public, nor an act of bad faith to the holders, for Congress to declare that, after their maturity, they shall cease to be a legal tender, while such a declaration would aid the government in its efforts to retire them, and is therefore recommended.

The rapidity with which the government notes can be withdrawn will depend upon the ability of the Secretary to dispose of securities. The influences of funding upon the money market will sufficiently prevent their too rapid withdrawal. The Secretary, however, believes that a decided movement towards a contraction of the currency is not only a public necessity, but that it will speedily dissipate the apprehension which very generally exists, that the effect of such a policy must necessarily be to make money scarce and to diminish the prosperity of the country.

It is a well-established fact, which has not escaped the attention of all intelligent observers, that the demand for money increases (by reason of an advance of prices) with the supply, and that this demand is not unfrequently most pressing when the volume of currency is the largest and inflation has reached the culminating point. Money being an unprofitable article to hold, very little is withheld from active use, and in proportion to its increase prices advance; on the other hand, a reduction of it reduces prices, and as prices are reduced the demand for it falls off; so that, paradoxical as it may seem, a diminution of the currency may in fact increase the supply of it.

Nor need there be any apprehension that a reduction of the currency—unless it be a violent one—will injuriously affect real prosperity. Labor is the great source of national wealth, and industry invariably declines on an inflated currency. The value of money depends upon the manner in which it is used. If it stimulates productive industry, it is a benefit, and to the extent only to which it does this is it a benefit. If, on the other hand, it diminishes industry, and to the extent to which it diminishes it, it is an evil. Even in the form of the precious metals, it may not prove to be wealth to a nation. The idea that a country is necessarily rich in proportion to the amount of gold or silver which it possesses, is a common and natural but an erroneous one, while the opinion that real prosperity is advanced by an increase of paper money beyond what is absolutely needed as a medium for exchanges of real values, is so totally fallacious, that few sane men entertain it whose judgment is not clouded by the peculiar financial atmosphere which an inflation is so apt to produce.

An irredeemable paper currency may be a necessity, but it can scarcely fail, if long continued, to be a calamity to any people. Gold and silver are the only proper measure of value. They have been made so by the tacit agreement of nations, and are the necessary regulator of trade, the medium by which balances are settled between different countries and between sections of the same country. As a universal measure of value they are a commercial necessity. The trade between different nations and between sections of the same country is carried on by an exchange of commodities, but is never equally balanced by them; and unless credits are being established, the movements of coin unerringly indicate on which side the balance exists.

If the United States buy of other nations—as they now and too generally do—more than they sell to them, it is evident that a balance is thus created which must either be settled in coin or continued as a debt.

That balances between nations should be promptly paid is the dictate of wisdom, because by prompt payment the adverse current is checked before the debtor nation becomes seriously involved; while, on the other hand, if they are permitted to accumulate, they may, when the day of payment can no longer be deferred, prove not only disastrous to the debtor, but greatly disturb the business of the creditor nation. Even with the vast increase of gold and silver which has taken place within the last quarter of a century, the specie which is possessed by commercial nations is a very inconsiderable sum in comparison with their foreign and domestic property exchanges; and no nation can afford to continue a traffic which leaves it with a heavy debt to be paid in the precious metals, unless these metals are a part of its productions, and then only to the extent that they are productions. When there are no artificial obstacles in the way, and balances between nations are promptly settled, the flow of coin from one to the other produces but little embarrassment to the debtor nation. The nation that loses coin either diminishes its purchases, or, by a reduction of the prices of its commodities which the loss occasions, becomes a more inviting market than before, and, by attracting purchasers, reverses the current and draws again to itself the coin of which it had been deprived.

All this is well understood; and if trade between nations were carried on by an exchange of products and a prompt payment of balances in specie, no nation would ever become indebted to another to an extent seriously to affect its prosperity.

All serious embarrassment growing out of commercial intercourse between the people of different nations results from failure in the prompt payment of balances, and the carrying forward of these balances by extensions of credits.

The trade between the different sections of the United States is subject to the same laws. If one section, in the course of trade, becomes a debtor to another, the balances must be carried in the form of debt—always expensive, and generally dangerous to the debtor section—or settled with money. If the measure of value is a convertible currency, and trade and exchanges are left to the natural laws that govern them, settlements take place promptly and without embarrassment to business. The banks of the debtor section are drawn upon by their depositors and note-holders for coin or exchange. This return of notes and withdrawal of deposits, if considerable in amount, produce a contraction of discounts; and this contraction either checks overtrading, or so reduces the price of products as to increase the demand for them until the current changes and the equilibrium is restored.

This brief statement of the well-known laws of trade not only illustrates the necessity of prompt payment of balances between the United States and foreign nations and between the different sections of the United States, but the necessity of having everywhere the same standard of value.

It is admitted that on a coin basis there will be periods of expansion. Times of the greatest expansion and speculation in the United States have been, indeed, when the banks were nominally paying specie. This was the case prior to the revulsions of 1837 and 1857, the expansion of credits having, in both instances, preceded suspension; but this does not militate against the theory just stated.

The great expansion of 1835 and 1836, ending with the terrible financial collapse of 1837, from the effects of which the country did not rally for years, was the consequence of excessive bank circulation and discounts, and an abuse of the credit system, stimulated in the first place by government deposits with the State banks, and swelled by currency and credits until, under the wild spirit of speculation which pervaded the country, labor and production decreased to such an extent that the country which should have been the great food-producing country of the world became an importer of breadstuffs.

The balance of trade had been for a long time favorable to Europe and against the United States, and also in favor of the commercial cities of the seaboard and against the interior, but a vicious system of credits prevented the prompt settlement of balances. The importers established large credits abroad, by means of which they were enabled to give favorable terms to the jobbers. The jobbers, in turn, were thus, and by liberal accommodations from the banks, able to give "their own time" to country merchants, who, in turn, sold to their customers on an indefinite credit. It then seemed to be more reputable to borrow money than to earn it, and pleasanter, and apparently more profitable, to speculate than to work; and so the people ran headlong into debt, labor decreased, production fell off, and ruin followed.

The financial crisis of 1857 was the result of a similar cause, namely, the unhealthy extension of the various forms of credit. But, as in this case the evi had not been long at work, and productive industry had not been seriously di minished, the reaction, though sharp and destructive, was not general, nor were the embarrassments resulting from it protracted.

Now, in both these instances the expansions occurred while the business of the country was upon a specie basis, but it was only nominally so. A false system of credits had intervened, under which payments were deferred, and specie as a measure of value and a regulator of trade was practically ignored. Everything moved smoothly and apparently prosperously as long as credits could be established and continued, but as soon as payments were demanded and specie was in requisition, distrust commenced, and collapse ensued. In these instances the expansions preceded and contractions followed the suspensions, but it will be recollected that while the waves were rising specie ceased to be a regulator, by reason of a credit system which prevented the use of it.

The present inflation, following the suspension of 1861, is the result of heavy expenditures by the government in the prosecution of the war and the introduction of a new measure of value in the form of United States and treasury notes as lawful money. The country, as a whole, notwithstanding the ravages of the war, and the draught which has been made upon labor, is, by its greatly developed resources, far in advance in real wealth of what it was in 1857, when the last severe financial crisis occurred. The people are now comparatively free from debt; the banks, with their secured circulation and large investments in government securities, although not in an easy condition, and doubtless too much extended, are, it is believed, generally solvent; but the same causes are at work that produced the evils referred to. There is an immense volume of paper money in circulation—under the influence of which prices, already enormously high, are steadily advancing, and speculation is increasing—which must be contracted if similar disasters would be avoided.

If the war could have been prosecuted on a specie basis, there would doubtless have been a considerable advance in the prices of those articles which were in demand by the government; but inasmuch as, in the condition of our political affairs, extensive credits could not have been established in Europe, the tendency in this direction would have been kept within reasonable check by the outflow of coin to other nations, which would have been the natural result of the advancing prices in the United States. On a basis of paper money, for which there was no outlet, all articles needed for immediate use, of which it became the measure of value, felt and responded to the daily increase of the currency; so that rents and the prices of most articles for which there has been a demand have been, with slight fluctuations, constantly advancing from the commencement of the war, and are higher now, with gold at forty-seven per cent. premium, than they were when it was at one hundred and eighty-five. Even those which were affected by the fall of gold upon the surrender of the confederate armies, or by the increased supply or diminished demand, are advancing again to former if not higher rates. The expansion has now reached such a point as to be absolutely oppressive to a large portion of the people, while at the same time it is diminishing labor, and is becoming subversive of good morals.

There are no indications of real and permanent prosperity in our large importations of foreign fabrics; in the heavy operations at our commercial marts; in the splendid fortunes reported to be made by skilful manipulations at the gold room or the stock board; no evidences of increasing wealth in the facts that railroads and steamboats are crowded with passengers, and hotels with guests; that cities are full to overflowing, and rents and the prices of the necessaries of life, as well as luxuries, are daily advancing. All these things prove rather that a foreign debt is being created, that the number of non-producers is increasing, and that productive industry is being diminished. There is no fact more manifest than that the plethora of paper money is not only undermining the morals of the people by encouraging waste and extravagance, but is striking at the root of our material prosperity by diminishing labor. The evil is not at present beyond the control of legislation, but it is daily increasing, and, if not speedily checked, will, at no distant day, culminate in wide-spread disaster. The remedy, and the only remedy within the control of Congress, is, in the opinion of the Secretary, to be found in the reduction of the currency.

The paper circulation of the United States on the 31st of October last was substantially as follows:

1. United States notes and fractional currency $454,218,038 20
2. Notes of the national banks 185,000,000 00
3. Notes of State banks, including outstanding issues of State banks converted into national banks 65,000,000 00

704,218,038 20

The amount of notes furnished to the national banks up to and including the 31st of October was a little over $205,000,000, but it is estimated that $20,000,000 of these had not then been put into circulation.

In addition to the United States notes, there were also outstanding $32,536,900 five per cent. treasury notes, and $173,012,140 compound interest notes, of which it would doubtless be safe to estimate that $30,000,000 were in circulation as currency.

From this statement it appears that, without including seven and three-tenths notes, many of the small denominations of which were in circulation as money and all of which tend in some measure to swell the inflation, the paper money of the country amounted, on the 31st of October, to the sum of $734,218,038 20, which has been daily increased by the notes since furnished to the national banks, and is likely to be still further increased by those to which they are entitled, until the amount authorized by law ($300,000,000) shall have been reached, subject to such reduction as may be made by the withdrawal of the notes of the State banks.

The following is a statement of the bank note circulation of the country at various periods of highest and lowest issues prior to the war:

January, 1830		$61,324,000
"	1835	103,692,495
"	1836	140,301,038
"	1837	149,185,890
"	1843	58,564,000
"	1856	195,747,950
"	1857	214,778,822
"	1858	155,208,344
"	1860	207,102,000

It will be noticed by this statement that the bank note circulation of the United States increased from $61,324,000 to $149,185,890 between the 1st of January, 1830, and the 1st of January, 1837, in which latter year the great financial collapse took place; fell from $149,185,890 in 1837, to $58,564,000 in 1843, and rose to $214,778,822 on the 1st of January, 1857, in which year the next severe crisis occurred; falling during that year to $155,208,344, and rising to $207,102,000 on the 1st of January, 1860.

The following is a statement of bank deposits and loans in the same years:

Years.	Deposits.	Loans.
January 1, 1830	$55,560,000	$200,451,000
" 1835	83,081,000	365,163,000
" 1836	115,104,000	457,506,000
" 1837	127,397,000	525,115,000
" 1843	56,168,000	254,544,000
" 1856	212,705,000	634,183,000
" 1857	230,351,000	684,456,000
" 1858	185,932,000	583,165,000
" 1860	253,802,000	691,945,000

On the 30th of September, the date of their last quarterly reports, the deposits and loans of the national banks (the Secretary has no reliable returns of these items from the few remaining State banks) were as follows:

Deposits, individual and government......................... $544,150,194
Loans.. $485,314,029

To which should be added—
Investments in United States bonds and other
United States securities.................. 427,731,600
                                        ——————————
                                        913,045,629

These figures are a history in themselves, exhibiting not only the past and present condition of the country in matters of exceeding interest, but indicating unerringly the dangerous direction in which the financial current is sweeping.

On the 1st of January of the memorable year 1837 the bank note circulation of the United States was $149,185,890, the deposits were $127,397,000, the loans $525,115,000. In January, 1857, the year of the next great crisis, the circulation was $214,778,822, the deposits were $230,351,000, the loans, $684,456,000. There are no statistics to exhibit the amount of specie actually in circulation in those periods, but it would be a liberal estimate to put it at $30,000,000 for 1837, and $50,000,000 for 1857.

These were years of great inflation, the effects of which have been already referred to—the revulsion of 1837 not only producing great immediate embarrassment, but a prostration which continued until 1843, at the commencement of which year the bank note circulation amounted only to $58,564,000, deposits to $56,168,000, loans $254,544,000—flour having declined in New York from $10 25 per barrel on the 1st of January, 1837, to $4 69 on the 1st of January, 1843, and other articles in about the same proportion.

The reaction in 1857 was severe, but, for the reason before stated, less disastrous and protracted.

On the 30th of September last the deposits of the national banks alone amounted to $544,150,194; their loans—estimating their national securities as a loan to the government—to $913,045,629; both of which items must have been increased during the month of October; while on the 31st of that month the circulation, bank and national, had reached the startling amount of upwards of $700,000,000. Nothing beyond this statement is required to exhibit the present inflation or to explain the causes of the current and advancing prices. If disaster followed the expansions of 1837 and 1857, what must be the consequences of the present expansion unless speedily checked and reduced?

It is undoubtedly true that trade is carried on much more largely for cash than was ever the case previous to 1861, and that there is a much greater proper demand for money than there would be if sales were made, as heretofore, on credit. It is also true that there is a larger demand than formerly for money on the part of manufacturers for the payment of operatives. But, making the most liberal allowances for the increased wholesome demand arising from these causes and from the advance of the country in business and population, it is apparent from the foregoing statements, if the advance in prices did not establish the fact, that the circulating medium of the country is altogether excessive.

Before concluding his remarks upon this subject, it may be proper for the Secretary, even at the expense of repetition, to notice briefly some of the popular and plausible objections to a reduction of the currency :

First. That by reducing prices it would operate injuriously, if not disastrously, upon trade, and be quite likely to precipitate a financial crisis.

To this it may be replied, that prices of articles of indispensable necessity are already so high as to be severely oppressive to consumers, especially to persons of fixed and moderate incomes and to the poorer classes. Not only do the interests, but the absolute necessities of the masses, require that the prices of articles needed for their use should decline.

Nor is there any reason to apprehend, by any policy that Congress may adopt, so rapid a reduction of prices as to produce very serious embarrassment to trade. The government currency can only, to any considerable extent, be withdrawn by a sale of bonds, and the demand for bonds will be so affected by the state of the market that a rapid contraction will be difficult, if not impossible, even if it were desirable. There is more danger to be apprehended from the inability of the government to reduce its circulation rapidly enough, than from a too rapid reduction of it. It is, in part, to prevent a financial crisis, that is certain to come without it, that the Secretary recommends contraction. Prices are daily advancing. The longer contraction is deferred, the greater must the fall eventually be, and the more serious will be its consequences. It is not expected that a return to specie payments will bring prices back to the standards of former years. The great increase of the precious metals and high taxes will prevent this; but this consideration makes it the more important that all improper and unnecessary influences in this direction should be removed.

Again it is urged, that a contraction of the currency would reduce the public revenues.

It is possible that this might be the immediate effect, but it would be temporary only. The public revenues depend upon the development of our national resources, upon our surplus productions; in other words, upon labor. The revenues derived from transactions based upon a false standard of value, or from interests that can only flourish in speculative times, are not those upon which reliance can be placed for maintaining the public credit. What a healthy and reliable business requires is a stable basis. This it cannot have as long as the country is inflicted with an inconvertible currency, the value of which, as well as the value of the vast property which is measured by it, is fluctuating and unreliable, and may be, in no small degree, controlled by speculative combinations.

It is also urged that the proposed policy would endanger the public credit, by preventing funding; and that it would compel the government and the people, who are in debt, to pay in a dearer currency than that in which their debts were contracted.

The Secretary is unable to perceive any substantial ground for this objection. He cannot understand how the process of funding is likely to be aided by the continuance of prices on their present high level, or how the credit of the government is to be restored by the perpetuation of an irredeemable currency, especially as that currency consists largely of its own notes. While it is hoped that early provision will be made for the commencement of the reduction of the national debt, an early payment of it is not anticipated. Nor is it understood that those who are apprehensive of the effects of contraction entertain the opinion that the present condition of things should be continued until any considerable portion of this debt shall be paid.

So far as individual indebtedness is regarded, it may be remarked that the people of the United States, if not as free from debt as they were six months ago, are much less in debt than they have been in previous years, and altogether less than they will be when the inevitable day of payment comes round, if the volume of paper money is not curtailed. A financial policy which would prevent the creation of debts and stimulate the payment of those already existing, so far from being injurious, would be in the highest degree beneficial.

It is further urged that a reduction of the government notes would embarrass the national banks, if it did not force many of them into liquidation.

To which it may be said that it is better that the banks should be embarrassed now than bankrupted hereafter. Their business and their customers are now under their control. What will be their condition in these respects if the expansion continues and swells a year or two longer it is not difficult to predict. While there has been no unhealthy expansion of credits in the United States for which the banks have not been largely responsible, there has been none by which they have not been ultimately the losers. Unless their sentiments are misunderstood by the Secretary, the conservative bankers of the country are quite unanimously in favor of a curtailment of the currency, with a view to an early return to specie payments.

Again, it is said that the excessive bank deposits have as much influence in creating and sustaining high prices as a superabundant currency. This is unquestionably true; but it is also true that excessive deposits are the effect of excessive currency, and that whenever the currency is reduced there will be, at least, a corresponding if not a greater reduction of deposits.

The last objection which will be noticed to the measure recommended is that it would, by reducing the rate of foreign exchanges, reduce exports and increase imports.

It is doubtless true that a high rate of exchange did for a time increase the exportations of our productions, and diminish the importation of foreign articles, but this advantage was much more than counterbalanced by the largely increased expenses of the government and of the people resulting from the very cause that produced the high rate of exchange. Besides, this apparent advantage no longer exists. The advance of prices in the United States, notwithstanding the continued high rate of European exchange, is now checking exports and inviting imports, and is creating a balance in favor of Europe that is likely to be the greatest obstacle in the way of an early resumption of specie payments. Nor must it be forgotten, that while the export of our productions was stimulated by the high rate of exchange, this very high rate of exchange enabled Europe to purchase them at exceedingly low prices.

Unless an unusual demand for our products is created in Europe by extraordinary causes, it will be ascertained, by reference to the proper tables, that our imports increase, and our exports diminish, under the influence of a redundant currency. But reference to figures is hardly necessary to substantiate this proposition. It is substantiated by the statement of it. A country in which high prices prevail is an inviting one for sellers, but an uninviting one for purchasers. Such a country is unfortunately the United States at the present time. In order, however, that there may be no misapprehension on this point, the attention of Congress is respectfully called to a clear and interesting paper from Dr. Elder, statistician of this department, accompanying this report.

Every consideration, therefore, that has been brought to the mind of the Secretary confirms the correctness of the views he has presented. If the business of the country rested upon a stable basis, or if credits could be kept from being still further increased, there would be less occasion for solicitude on this subject. But such is not the fact. Business is not in a healthy condition; it is speculative, feverish, uncertain. Every day that contraction is deferred increases the difficulty of preventing a financial collapse. Prices and credits will not remain as they are. The tide will either recede or advance; and it will not recede without the exercise of the controlling power of Congress.

The Secretary, therefore, respectfully but earnestly recommends—

First. That Congress declare that the compound interest notes shall cease to be a legal tender from the day of their maturity.

Second. That the Secretary be authorized, in his discretion, to sell bonds of the United States, bearing interest at a rate not exceeding six per cent., and redeemable and payable at such periods as may be conducive to the interests of the government, for the purpose of retiring not only compound interest notes, but the United States notes.

It is the opinion of the Secretary, as has been already stated, that the process of contraction cannot be injuriously rapid; and that it will not be necessary to retire more than one hundred, or, at most, two hundred millions of United States notes, in addition to the compound notes, before the desired result will be attained. But neither the amount of reduction, nor the time that will be required to bring up the currency to the specie standard, can now be estimated with any degree of accuracy. The first thing to be done is to establish the policy of contraction. When this is effected, the Secretary believes that the business of the country will readily accommodate itself to the proposed change in the action of government, and that specie payments may be restored without a shock to trade, and without a diminution of the public revenues or of productive industry.

At the close of a great war, which has been waged on both sides with a vigor and energy, and with an expenditure of money, without a precedent in history, the people of the United States are incumbered with a debt which requires the immediate and careful consideration of their representatives.

Since the commencement of the special session of 1861, the most important subject which has demanded and received the attention of Congress has been that of providing the means to prosecute the war; and the success of the government in raising money is evidence of the wisdom of the measures devised for this purpose, as well as of the loyalty of the people and the resources of the country. No nation within the same period ever borrowed so largely, or with so much facility. It is now to be demonstrated that a republican government can not only carry on a war on the most gigantic scale, and create a debt of immense magnitude, but can place this debt on a satisfactory basis, and meet every engagement with fidelity. The same wisdom which has been exhibited by the national councils in providing the means for preserving the national unity, will not be wanting in devising measures for establishing the national credit.

The maintenance of public faith is a national necessity. Nations do not and cannot safely accumulate moneys to be used at a future day, and exigencies are constantly occurring in which the richest and most powerful are under the necessity of borrowing. The millennial days, when nations shall beat their swords into ploughshares and their spears into pruning-hooks, and learn war no more, are yet, according to all existing indications, far in the future. Weak and defaulting nations may maintain a nominally independent existence, but it will be by reason of the jealousies, rather than the forbearance, of stronger powers. No nation is absolutely safe which is not in a condition to defend itself; nor can it be in this condition, no matter how strong in other respects, without a well-established financial credit. Nations cannot, therefore, afford to be unfaithful to their pecuniary obligations. Credit to them, as to individuals, is money; and money is the war power of the age. But for the unfaltering confidence of the people of the loyal States in the good faith of the government, the late rebellion would have been a success, and this great nation, so rapidly becoming again united and harmonious, would have been broken into weak and belligerent fragments.

But the public faith of the United States has higher considerations than these for its support. It rests not only upon the interests of the people, but upon their integrity and virtue. The debt of the United States has been created by the people in their successful struggle for undivided and indivisible nationality. It is not a debt imposed upon unwilling subjects by despotic authority, but one incurred by the people themselves for the preservation of their government—by the preservation of which, those who have been leagued together for its overthrow are to be as really benefited as those who have been battling for its maintenance. As it is a debt voluntarily incurred for the common good, its burdens will be cheerfully borne by the people, who will not permit them to be permanent.

The public debt of the United States represents a portion of the accumulated wealth of the country. While it is a debt of the nation, it becomes the capital of the citizen. The means of the merchant, the manufacturer and farmer, and also those of the workingman and the soldier, have been liberally invested in it; and it is an interesting fact—a practical evidence of the great resources of the country—that so large an amount of their wealth could be loaned by the people to the government without embarrassing industrial pursuits. Notwithstanding more than two thousand millions of dollars of the means of the people of the United States have been thus loaned, no branch of useful industry has suffered by the investment. It is undoubtedly true, that, if the wealth which has been invested in United States securities could have been employed in agriculture, in commerce, in mining and manufactures—in opening farms and the better improvement of those already under cultivation, in building railroads and ships, in working the mines, and in increasing the variety and amount of our manufactures—the nation would have been far in advance of what it now is in

material prosperity. But it is also true, that, notwithstanding the large investments by the people of the United States in the securities of their government ;
notwithstanding, also, more than two millions of men, in the northern States
alone, were, for longer or shorter periods, in the military service, and at least
seven hundred thousand for a good part of the time the war continued were
constantly under arms ; and notwithstanding the immense waste of life, consequent upon operations so extensive and battles so sanguinary as characterized
this memorable struggle, the larger part of the country has still, since eighteen
hundred and sixty, progressed both in wealth and population. The loyal
States have advanced in material prosperity in spite of the great drain that has
been made upon them ; and now that the war is closed, the Union is no longer
in peril, and the men that made the armies on both sides so effective and formidable are to be again employed in profitable pursuits, the onward march of the
country—even if a temporary reaction, as a result of the war, and the redun-
dancy of the currency, shall be experienced—will be decided and resistless.

The debt is large; but if kept at home, as it is desirable it should be, with
a judicious system of taxation it need not be oppressive. It is, however, a
debt. While it is capital to the holders of the securities, it is still a national
debt, and an incumbrance upon the national estate. Neither its advantages
nor its burdens are or can be shared or borne equally by the people. Its influences are anti-republican. It adds to the power of the Executive by increasing
federal patronage. It must be distasteful to the people because it fills the
country with informers and tax-gatherers. It is dangerous to the public virtue,
because it involves the collection and disbursement of vast sums of money, and
renders rigid national economy almost impracticable. It is, in a word, a national
burden, and the work of removing it, no matter how desirable it may be for
individual investment, should not be long postponed.

As all true men desire to leave to their heirs unincumbered estates, so should
it be the ambition of the people of the United States to relieve their descend-
ants of this national mortgage. We need not be anxious that future genera-
tions shall share the burden with us. Wars are not at an end, and posterity will
have enough to do to take care of the debts of their own creation.

Various plans have been suggested for the payment of the debt; but the
Secretary sees no way of accomplishing it but by an increase of the national
income beyond the national expenditures. In a matter of so great importance
as this, experiments are out of place. The plain, beaten path of experience is
the only safe one to tread.

The first step to be taken is, to institute measures for funding the obligations
that are soon to mature. The next is, to provide for raising, in a manner the
least odious and oppressive to taxpayers, the revenues necessary to pay the
interest on the debt, and a certain definite amount annually for the reduction of
the principal. The Secretary respectfully suggests that on this subject the
expression of Congress should be decided and emphatic. It is of the greatest
importance, in the management of a matter of so surpassing interest, that the
right start should be made. Nothing but revenue will sustain the national
credit, and nothing less than a fixed policy for the reduction of the public debt
will be likely to prevent its increase.

On the 31st day of October, 1865, since which time no material change has taken place, the public debt, without deducting funds in the treasury, amounted to $2,808,549,437 55, consisting of the following items:

Bonds, 10-40's, 5 per cent., due in 1904,	$172,770,100 00	
Bonds, Pacific Railroad, 6 per cent., due in 1895	1,258,000 00	
Bonds, 5-20's, 6 per cent., due in 1882, 1884, and 1885	659,259,600 00	
Bonds, 6 per cent., due in 1881	265,347,400 00	
Bonds, 5 per cent., due in 1880	18,415,000 00	
Bonds, 5 per cent., due in 1874	20,000,000 00	
Bonds, 5 per cent., due in 1871	7,022,000 00	
		$1,144,072,100 00
Bonds, 6 per cent., due in 1868	8,908,341 80	
Bonds, 6 per cent., due in 1867	9,415,250 00	
Compound interest notes, due in 1867 and 1868	173,012,141 00	
7-30 treasury notes, due in 1867 and 1868	830,000,000 00	
		1,021,335,732 80
Bonds, Texas indemnity, past due	760,000 00	
Bonds, treasury notes, &c., past due	613,920 09	
		1,373,920 09
Temporary loan, ten days' notice	99,107,745 46	
Certificates of indebtedness, due in 1866	55,905,000 00	
Treasury notes, 5 per cent., December 1, 1865	32,536,901 00	
		187,549,646 46
United States notes	428,160,569 00	
Fractional currency	26,057,469 20	
		454,218,038 20
		2,808,549,437 55

The following is a statement of receipts and expenditures for the fiscal year ending June 30, 1865:

Balance in treasury agreeably to warrants, July 1, 1864,		$96,739,905 73
Receipts from loans applicable to expenditures	$864,863,499 17	
Receipts from loans applied to payment of public debt	607,361,241 68	
		1,472,224,740 85
Receipts from customs	84,928,260 60	
Receipts from lands	996,553 31	

2 F

Receipts from direct tax $1, 200, 573 03
Receipts from internal revenue......... 209, 464, 215 25
Receipts from miscellaneous sources.... 32, 978, 284 47
                                        ————————————— $329, 567, 886 66

                                                      1, 898, 532 533 24

EXPENDITURES.

Redemption of public debt............................ $607, 361, 241 68
For the civil service................ $44, 765, 558 12
For pensions and Indians 14, 258, 575 38
For the War Department........... 1, 031, 323, 360 79
For the Navy Department 122, 567, 776 12
For interest on public debt 77, 397, 712 00
                                     ————————————— 1, 290, 312, 982 41

                                                    1, 897, 674, 224 09

Leaving a balance in the treasury on the 1st day of July,
    1865, of...................................... $858, 309 15

The following statement exhibits the items of increase and decrease of the
public debt for the fiscal year 1865 :

Amount of public debt June 30, 1865 ...:............ $2, 682, 593, 026 53
Amount of public debt June 30, 1864 .... 1, 740, 690, 489 49

        Total increase 941, 902, 537 04

Which increase was caused as follows, by—
Bonds, 6 per cent., act July 17, 1861..$29, 799, 500 00
Bonds, 6 per cent., act February 5, 1862. 4, 000, 000 00
Bonds, 6 per cent., act March 3, 1863.. 32, 327, 726 66
Bonds, 6 per cent., act June 30, 1864.. 91, 789, 000 00
                                        ————————————— $157, 916, 226 66
Bonds, 5 per cent., act March 3, 1864............... 99, 432, 350 00
Bonds, 6 per cent., acts July 1, 1862, and July 2, 1864,
    issued to Central Pacific Railroad Company, interest
    payable in lawful money........................ 1, 258, 000 00
Treasury notes, 7-30, acts June 30, 1864, and March 3,
    1865, interest payable in lawful money........... 671, 610, 400 00
Compound interest notes, 6 per cent.,
    act June 30, 1864............... $178, 756, 080 00
Temporary loan, 6 per cent., act July
    11, 1862............................ 17, 386, 869 96
                                       ————————————— 196, 142, 949 96

United States notes, acts February 25, 1862, July 11, 1862,
   and January 17, 1863............................ $1,509,295 16
Fractional currency, act March 3, 1863................   7,363,098 85

        Gross increase.......................... 1,135,232,320 63
From which deduct for payments—
Bonds, 6 per cent., act July 21, 1842.... $1,400 00
Treasury notes, 6 per cent., acts December
  23, 1857, and March 2, 1861..........   158,800 00
Bonds, 5 per cent., act September 9, 1850,
  (Texas indemnity)................   1,307,000 00
Treasury notes, 7-30, act July 17, 1861.. 30,212,300 00
Certificates of indebtedness, 6 per cent.,
  act March 1, 1862.................. 44,957,000 00
Treasury notes, 5 per cent., one and two-
  year, act March 3, 1863............111,132,740 00
United States notes, acts July 17, 1861,
  and February 12, 1862..............   308,396 25
Postal currency, act July 17, 1862......   5,252,147 34
                               193,329,783 59

      Net increase.......................... 941,902,537 04

In the report of the Secretary for the year 1864, there was excluded from the public debt the sum of $77,897,347 02, which amount had been paid out of the treasury, but had not been reimbursed to the Treasurer by warrants, and was not reimbursed until after the commencement of the next fiscal year. This explains the difference between $18,842,558 71, assumed in that report as the balance in the treasury July 1, 1864, and $96,739,905 73, the balance according to the warrant account, as above stated.

The following is a statement of the receipts and expenditures for the quarter ending September 30, 1865:

Balance in treasury, agreeable to warrants, July 1, 1865.. $858,309 15
Receipts from loans applicable to expendi-
  tures............................ $138,773,097 22
Receipts from loans applied to payment
  of public debt.................... 138,409,163 35
                               277,182,260 57
Receipts from customs................ 47,009,583 03
Receipts from lands.................. 132,890 63
Receipts from direct tax............. 31,111 30
Receipts from internal revenue........ 96,618,885 65
Receipts from miscellaneous sources.... 18,393,729 94
                               162,186,200 55

                               440,226,770 27

EXPENDITURES.

For the redemption of public debt......	$138, 409, 163 35
For the civil service.................	10, 571, 460 99
For pensions and Indians.............	6, 024, 241 86
For the War Department.............	165, 369, 237 32
For the Navy Department.............	16, 520, 669 81
For interest on the public debt........	36, 173, 481 50

$373, 068, 254 83

Leaving a balance in the treasury on the 1st day of October, 1865, of.................................... $67, 158, 515 44

The Secretary estimates that the receipts for the remaining three quarters of the year ending June 30, 1866, will be as follows:

Balance in treasury October 1, 1865....................		$67, 158, 515 44
Receipts from customs................	$100, 000, 000 00	
Receipts from lands.................	500, 000 00	
Receipts from internal revenue........	175, 000, 000 00	
Receipts from miscellaneous sources....	30, 000, 000 00	

305, 500, 000 00

372, 658, 515 44

The expenditures, according to the estimates, will be:

For the civil service..................	$32, 994, 052 38	
For pensions and Indians	12, 256, 790 94	
For the War Department.............	307, 788, 750 57	
For the Navy Department...........	35, 000, 000 00	
For interest on public debt...........	96, 813, 868 75	

484, 853, 462 64

Deficiency............................. 112, 194, 947 20

The receipts for the year ending June 30, 1867, are estimated as follows:

From customs.....................$100, 000, 000 00		
From internal revenue............... 275, 000, 000 00		
From lands...................... 1, 000, 000 00		
From miscellaneous sources........ 20, 000, 000 00		

$396, 000, 000 00

The expenditures, according to the estimates, will be:

For the civil service:..............	$42, 165, 599 47
For pensions and Indians...........	17, 609, 640 23

For the War Department........... $39,017,416.18
For the Navy Department.......... 43,982,457 50
For the interest on the public debt.... 141,542,068 50

$284,317,181 88

Leaving a surplus of estimated receipts over estimated
expenditures, of................................. 111,682,818 12

The debt of the United States was increased during the fiscal year ending June 30, 1865, $941,902,537 04, and during the first quarter of the present fiscal year $38,773,097 22. The Secretary has, however, the satisfaction of being able to state that during the months of September and October the public debt was diminished to the amount of about thirteen millions of dollars.

If the expenditures for the remaining three quarters of the present fiscal year shall equal the estimates, there will be a deficiency, to be provided for by loans, of $112,194,947 20, to which must be added $32,536,901 for the five per cent. treasury notes, (part of the public debt,) which become due the present month, and are now being paid out of moneys in the treasury, and all other payments which may be made on the public debt.

The heavy expenditures of the last fiscal year, and of the months of July and August of the present fiscal year, are the result of the gigantic scale on which the war was prosecuted during a portion of this period, and the payment of the officers and men mustered out of the service. The large estimates of the War Department for the rest of the year are for the payment of troops which are to remain in the service, and of those which are to be discharged, and for closing up existing balances.

The statement of the probable receipts and expenditures for the next fiscal year is, in the highest degree, satisfactory. According to estimates which are believed to be reliable, the receipts of that year will be sufficient to pay all current expenses of the government, the interest on the public debt, and leave the handsome balance of $111,682,818 12 to be applied toward the payment of the debt itself.

By the statement of the public debt on the 31st of October, it appears that, besides the compound interest, the United States, and the fractional notes,

The past-due debt amounted to................. $1,373,920 09
The debt due in 1865 and 1866, to............. 187,549,646 46
The debt due in 1867 and 1868, to............. 848,323,591 80

During the month of October about $50,000,000 of the compound interest notes were funded in 5-20 six per cent. bonds under the provisions of the act of March 3, 1865.

The Secretary would be gratified if the treasury could be put at once in a condition to obviate the necessity of issuing any more certificates of indebtedness, or raising money by any kind of temporary loans; but he may, for a short period, be obliged to avail himself of any means now authorized by law for meeting current expenses and other proper demands upon the treasury.

Of the debt falling due in 1867 and 1868, $830,000,000 consist of 7 3-10 notes. It may be regarded as premature to fund any considerable amount of these notes within the next year; but in view of the fact that they are convertible into bonds only at the pleasure of the holders, it will be evidently prudent for Congress to authorize the Secretary, whenever it can be advantageously done, to fund them in advance of their maturity.

The Secretary has already recommended that he be authorized to sell bonds of the United States, bearing interest at a rate not exceeding six per cent., for the purpose of retiring treasury notes and United States notes. He further recommends that he be authorized to sell, in his discretion, bonds of a similar character to meet any deficiency for the present fiscal year, to reduce the temporary loan by such an amount as he may deem advisable, to pay the certificates of indebtedness as they mature, and also to take up any portion of the debt maturing prior to 1869 that can be advantageously retired. It is not probable that it will be advisable, even if it could be done without pressing them upon the market, to sell a much larger amount of bonds within the present or the next fiscal year than will be necessary to meet any deficiency of the treasury, to pay the past-due and maturing obligations of the government, and a part of the temporary loan, and to retire an amount of the compound interest notes and United States notes sufficient to bring back the business of the country to a healthier condition. But no harm can result from investing the Secretary with authority to dispose of bonds, if the condition of the market will justify it, in order to anticipate the payment of those obligations that must soon be provided for.

When the whole debt shall be put in such a form that the interest only can be demanded until the government shall be in a condition to pay the principal, it can be easily managed. It is undeniably large, but the resources of the country are even now ample to carry and gradually to reduce it; and with the labor question at the south settled on terms just to the employer and to the laborer, and with entire harmony between the different sections, it will be rapidly diminished, in burden and amount, by the growth of the country, without an increase of taxation.

The following estimate of the time which would be required to pay the national debt (if funded at five per cent. and at five and one-half per cent.) by the payment of two hundred millions of dollars annually on the interest and principal, and also of the diminution of the burden of the debt by the increase of productions, may not be without interest to Congress and to taxpayers.

The national debt, deducting moneys in the treasury, was, on the 31st of October, 1865, $2,740,854,750. Without attempting a nice calculation of the amount, it may reach, when all our liabilities shall be accurately ascertained, it seems safe to estimate it, on the 1st of July, 1866, at three thousand millions of dollars. The amount of existing indebtedness yet unsettled, and the further amount that may accrue in the interval, are not now capable of exact estimation, and the revenue of the same period can be only approximately calculated; but it will be safe to assume that the debt will not exceed the sum named.

The annual interest upon three thousand millions, if funded at five and one-half per cent. per annum, would be one hundred and sixty-five millions; but if funded at five per cent., it would be one hundred and fifty millions.

Now, if two hundred millions per annum should be applied, in half-yearly instalments of one hundred millions each, in payment of the accruing interest and in reduction of the principal funded at the higher rate of five and one-half per cent., the debt would be entirely paid in thirty-two and one-eighth years. At five per cent. per annum it would be extinguished, by the like application of one hundred millions every six months, in a little over twenty-eight years.

At the higher rate, the sum applied in the first year in reduction of the principal of the debt would be thirty-five millions of dollars; in the last or thirty-second year, when the interest would be diminished to a little over nine millions, about one hundred and ninety-one millions of the uniform annual payment would go to the reduction of the principal.

On the assumption that the debt may be funded at 5 per cent., fifty millions would be applicable to the reduction of the principal in the first year, and in the twenty-eighth or last year of the period—the interest falling to less than eight millions—one hundred and ninety-two millions of the annual payment would go to the principal.

The annual interest accruing upon seventeen hundred and twenty-five millions of the debt on the 31st of October last averages 6.62 per cent. A part of this sum is now due, another portion will be payable next year, and the balance will be due or payable, at the option of the government, in 1867 and 1868. If these seventeen hundred and twenty-five millions shall be funded or converted into five per cents by the year 1869, the average interest of the whole debt will be 5.195 per cent. In the year 1871, if the debt then maturing should be funded at the same rate, the average interest would be reduced to 5.15, and in 1881 to 5 per cent., excepting the bonds for fifty millions to be advanced in aid of the Pacific railroad at 6 per cent., which will have thirty years to run from their respective dates. The interest of these bonds, added to the supposed 5 per cents, would, in 1881, make the average rate of the entire debt five and three one-hundredths of one per cent. until the whole should be discharged.

In these calculations of the average rate of interest upon the funded debt the outstanding United States notes and fractional currency are not embraced. Whatever amount of these four hundred and fifty-four millions may eventually be funded at five per cent. per annum will proportionally reduce the average rates of interest upon the whole debt.

By the terms and conditions of some portion of the debt, the interest on the whole cannot be reduced to exactly five per cent. unless money may be borrowed at some stage of the process at a trifle below 5 per cent. A bonus of one-tenth of one per cent., paid by the bidders for five per cent. loans, would more than cover the excess, the probability of which fully warrants the calculation submitted as to the payment of the total debt at this rate.

It must be observed, also, that the assumed principal of the debt in July, 1866, must undergo some diminution before the funding in 1867, 1868, and 1869 begins. If only one hundred millions shall be paid off in these three years, the principal, thus reduced to twenty-nine hundred millions, would be extinguished by the process already stated in twenty-nine years, if funded at $5\frac{1}{2}$ per cent., and if at 5 per cent. in something less than twenty-seven years. And it is well worthy of attention that one hundred millions less principal at the commencement of the process of payment will save four hundred millions in round numbers in the end if the rate is $5\frac{1}{2}$ per cent., and three hundred millions if 5 per cent.

The burden of a national debt is, of course, relative to the national resources, and these resources are not, strictly speaking, capital, but the current product of the capital and industry of the country. The annual product, however, is found to bear a certain ratio to capital, and this ratio may be conveniently and safely used in computing the probable resources which must in the future meet the national requirement for the payment of interest and extinguishment of the debt.

It has been estimated by one who has made this subject a study, that the products of agriculture, manufactures, mining, mechanic arts, commerce, fisheries, and forests, in the year 1850 were at 28.9 per cent. of the value of the real and personal property of the United States. A similar calculation makes the products of 1860 26.8 per cent. of the wealth of the country in that year, as fixed by the census returns. In the calculation submitted, the annual products of capital and industry are taken, for convenience, at 25 per cent. of the capital wealth of the country, and the capital of each decennial year of the thirty that our national debt may run before its extinguishment by the application of two hundred millions per annum to the payment of its principal and interest, is here estimated upon the basis of its amount and increase as given by the census of 1860. In the year 1860 the real and personal property of the Union was valued (slaves excluded) at fourteen thousand one hundred and eighty-three millions of dollars. Of this amount the States lately in insurrection held three thousand four hundred and sixty-seven millions, being an increase upon the like property in 1850 of 139.7 per cent. The property of the loyal States was valued at ten thousand seven hundred and sixteen millions, an increase of 126.6 per cent. over 1850; together, averaging a decennial increase of 129.7 per cent.

Now, taking the increase of wealth in the loyal States in the ten years from 1860 to 1870 at 125 per cent., we have, as their capital in 1870, twenty-four thousand one hundred and eleven millions; and if we put the wealth of the other States at the same figure as in 1860, without allowing anything for increase, we have a capital for 1870 of twenty-seven thousand five hundred and seventy-eight millions. This sum gives us the product of the year at six thousand eight hundred and ninety-four and a half millions, upon which a payment on the debt of two hundred millions is 2.9 per cent. If we add but 25 per cent. to the wealth of 1860 for the States lately in insurrection, as their probable valuation in 1870, the charge of two hundred millions upon the products of that year will be 2.81 per cent. But, allowing all that can be claimed in this respect, and taking the lowest estimate for 1870 as the basis for calculating the wealth and products of the year 1880, 125 per cent. increase in this period gives a capital of sixty-two thousand and fifty millions, and a product of fifteen thousand five hundred and twelve millions, upon which sum a charge of two hundred millions falls to 1.29 per cent. In 1890, the wealth, estimated at an increase of only 100 per cent. upon that of 1880, gives the year's products at thirty-one thousand and twenty-five millions, upon which two hundred millions amounts to only 0.644 per cent., or less than two-thirds of one per cent., and in the year 1900 the tax upon the products of the year would fall to 0.322 per cent., or less than one-third of one per cent.

To this charge upon the resources of the country if there be added one hundred and forty millions of 1870 for all other expenditures, one hundred and fifty millions in 1880, one hundred and sixty millions in 1890, and one hundred and seventy millions in 1900, the estimated total expenditure will be 4.93 per cent. of the products of capital and industry in 1870, 2.26 per cent. in 1880, 1.17 per cent. in 1890, and barely seven-tenths of one per cent. in 1900. Or, in general statement, the total estimated charges of the national government for the payment of the debt in thirty years, and all other ordinary expenses, begin at less than 5 per cent. of the resources of the country, and end in seven-tenths of one per cent.

These estimates, and the basis upon which they rest, are sustained by the result of English experience upon a debt one-third larger than ours, with ordinary and extraordinary expenses at least one-half larger than ours are likely to reach, and borne through a period of much less wealth-producing power. The government charges for all expenditures fifty years ago took one pound in six of the products of Great Britain, but these charges have now fallen to one pound in nine. We commence our national burdens with resources that, in the very first year, will be required to bear an aggregate of less than 5 per cent., or one dollar in twenty.

It is true that many circumstances may occur to prevent the accomplishment of these anticipated results; but the estimates have been made upon what are regarded as reliable data, and are well calculated to encourage Congress in levying taxes, and the people in paying them.

After careful reflection, the Secretary concludes that no act of Congress (except for raising the necessary revenue) would be more acceptable to the people, or better calculated to strengthen the national credit, than one which should provide that two hundred millions of dollars, commencing with the next fiscal year, shall be annually applied to the payment of the interest and principal of the national debt. The estimates for the next fiscal year indicate that a very much larger amount could be so applied without an increase of taxes.

Before concluding his remarks upon the national debt, the Secretary would suggest that the credit of the five-twenty bonds issued under the acts of February 25, 1862, and June 30, 1864, would be improved in Europe, and, consequently, their market value advanced at home, if Congress should declare that the principal, as well as the interest, of these bonds is to be paid in coin. The policy of the government in regard to its funded debt is well understood in the United States, but the absence of a provision in these acts that the principal of the bonds issued under them should be paid in coin, while such a provision is contained in the act under which the ten-forties were issued, has created some apprehension in Europe that the five-twenty bonds might be called in at the expiration of five years, and paid in United States notes. Although it is not desirable that our securities should be held out of the United States, it is desirable that they should be of good credit in foreign markets on account of the influence which these markets exert upon our own. It is, therefore, important that all misapprehensions on these points should be removed by an explicit declaration of Congress that these bonds are to be paid in coin.

In view of the fact that the exemption of government securities from State taxation is, by many persons, considered an unjust discrimination in their favor, efforts may be made to induce Congress to legislate upon the subject of their taxation. Of course, the existing exemption from State and municipal taxation of bonds and securities now outstanding will be scrupulously regarded. That exemption is a part of the contract under which the securities have been issued and the money loaned thereon to the government, and it would not only be unconstitutional, but a breach of the public faith of the nation to disregard it. It would also, in the judgment of the Secretary, be unwise for Congress to grant to the States the power, which they will not possess unless conferred by express congressional enactment, of imposing local taxes upon securities of the United States which may be hereafter issued. Such taxation, in any form, would result in serious, if not fatal, embarrassment to the government, and, instead of relieving, would eventually injure the great mass of the people, who are to bear their full proportion of the burden of the public debt. This is a subject in relation to which there should be no difference of opinion. Every taxpayer is personally interested in having the public debt placed at home, and at a low rate of interest, which cannot be done if the public securities are to be subject to local taxation. Taxes vary largely in different States, and in different counties and cities of the same State, and are everywhere so high that, unless protected against them, the bonds into which the present debt must be funded cannot be distributed among the people, except in some favored localities, unless they bear a rate of interest so high as to make the debt severely oppressive, and to render the prospect of its extinguishment well-nigh hopeless. Exempted from local taxation, the debt can, it is expected, be funded at an early day at five per cent.; if local taxation is allowed, no considerable portion of the debt which falls due within the next four years can be funded at home at less than eight per cent. The taxpayers of the United States cannot afford to have their burdens thus increased. It is also evident that the relief which local taxpayers would obtain from government taxation, as the result of a low rate of interest on the national securities, would at least be as great as the increase of local taxes to which they would be subjected on account of the exemption of government securities; while if those securities should bear a rate of interest sufficient to secure their sale when subject to local taxes, few, if any of them, would long remain where those taxes could reach them. They would be rapidly transferred to other countries, into the hands of foreign capitalists, and thus at last the burden of paying a high rate of interest would be left upon the people of this country without compensation or alleviation.

The present system of internal revenue is one of the results of the war. It was framed under circumstances of pressing necessity, affording little opportunity for careful and accurate investigation of the sources of revenue. Its success, however, has exceeded the anticipations of its authors, and is a most honorable testimonial to their wisdom, and to the patriotism of the people who have so cheerfully submitted to its burdens.

With the restoration of peace, industry is returning again to its former channels, and a revision of the system now becomes important to accommodate it to the changed and changing condition of the country.

Every complicated system of taxation opens the way to mistakes, abuses, and deceptions. Temptations to dishonesty and fraud are placed before the revenue officers and the taxpayers, and both are often thereby demoralized. Honest men, who pay their taxes in full, are injured, if not ruined, by the ingenuity of those who successfully evade their share of the public burdens.

The multiplicity of objects at present subject to taxation is one of the most serious objections to the present system. Many of these yield little revenue, while its collection is troublesome to the collector, and irritating and offensive to the taxpayers. This multiplicity also involves as many temptations to fraud, and as many difficult questions for decision, as the objects from which large revenue is derived.

To impose taxes judiciously, so as to obtain revenue without repressing industry, is one of the highest and most difficult duties devolved upon Congress. Taxation which in one year may be scarcely felt may the next year be oppressive; and that which may not be burdensome to those who are well established in business may be fatal to those just commencing. Every branch of industry has its infancy, and ought to be encouraged by liberal legislation. Whatever of industry or enterprise is destroyed, by injudicious taxation or otherwise, is a damage to the national welfare.

Heavy taxation may drive capital from our shores, or prevent its employment in the manner most advantageous to the country, and thus prevent that demand for labor which is the best security for its proper reward.

The taxation which is now extremely productive may in a few years become unproductive, or engender a spirit of opposition and discontent which may endanger the national credit.

It is important, therefore, that our revenue system should be frequently and carefully revised, in order that it may be accommodated to the habits and character of the people, to the industry of the country, to labor and capital, to wages at home and wages abroad. It is also of the highest importance that there should be a careful adjustment of our internal to our external revenue system.

That views somewhat similar to these were entertained by Congress, is indicated by the provision in the amendatory act of March 3, 1865, by which the Secretary of the Treasury was authorized to "appoint a commission, consisting of three persons, to inquire and report, at the earliest practicable moment, upon the subject of raising by taxation such revenue as may be necessary in order to supply the wants of the government, having regard to and including the sources from which such revenue should be drawn, and the best and most efficient mode of raising the same."

This subject received the early attention of the Secretary, and under the authority of the act, after careful deliberation, a commission was organized, consisting of Messrs. David A. Wells, Stephen Colwell, and S. S. Hayes, representing, to a certain extent, different sections and interests, and also different political sentiments. The commission was fully organized in June, and has since then been actively engaged in the prosecution of its labors.

An investigation of the character of the revenue, contemplated by the act authorizing this commission, necessarily involves a careful and comprehensive inquiry into the condition of every industry, trade, or occupation in the country likely to be affected by the national revenue system, and, in the absence of nearly all previously compared and exact data, must necessarily be protracted and laborious. From a preliminary report made to the Secretary by the commission, he has reason to infer that enough has already been accomplished by them to indicate the value of an investigation like that in which they are now engaged, and to demonstrate the necessity of the accumulation of a correct and accurate knowledge, properly digested and presented, as a basis for our future revenue legislation.

The plan pursued by the commission has been, to take up, specifically, those sources of revenue which our own experience, and the experience of other countries, have indicated as likely to be most productive under taxation and most capable of sustaining its burdens. In pursuance of this plan, a large number of witnesses have been examined, and much valuable testimony put upon record.

It is understood to be the opinion of the commissioners that it would be inexpedient at once to make any radical and violent changes in the nature and working of the present revenue system, and that we should rather seek, through experience and study, to perfect the present system by degrees, so as to gradually adapt it to the industrial habits and fiscal capacity of the people. The Secretary is also informed by the commissioners that it seems certain to them that, without any increase in the rate of taxation, but by the enactment of some modifications and amendments of the present law, coupled, positively, even with some reduction in the rates, an increase of revenue from comparatively few sources to the extent of some fifty or sixty millions of dollars per annum over and above that now obtained, may be confidently relied on. If this should be the case, an early repeal of a multitude of small taxes which, from the inquisitorial character of their method of collection, have become extremely odious and objectionable, will be advisable.

Although the work of the commission has been thus far mainly directed to the sources likely to be most productive of revenue, the consideration of the subject of the administration of the law has not been omitted by them; and in this department it is believed that some valuable recommendations will be submitted for the consideration of Congress.

As a gratifying feature of their work, the commission report a most cheerful and prompt co-operation on the part of nearly all the representatives of the industrial interests of the country in the procurement of exact information, and a universal expression of ready acquiescence in any demands upon them which the future necessities of the government may require, united, at the same time, with a request that the government should, on its part, seek to equalize, so far as practicable, and fairly distribute the apportionment of its requirements.

In view of the fact that the revision of the whole revenue system has been committed to this commission, the Secretary does not consider it proper for him to present his views upon this important subject in advance of their final report, which it is hoped will be made early in the session.

There are some subjects, however, presented in the report of the Commissioner of Internal Revenue which require the attention of Congress before the report of the commission is received, and in relation to which there should be early action.

In putting into operation the system of internal revenue in the recently rebellious States, it became necessary for the Secretary to decide whether or not an effort should be made to collect the taxes which accrued prior to the establishment of revenue offices therein. After giving the subject due consideration, the Secretary, in view of the facts that there were no federal revenue officers to whom payment of taxes could be made, that the people (many of them involuntarily) had been subject to heavy taxation by the government which was attempted to be established in opposition to that of the United States, and had been greatly exhausted by the ravages of war, issued a circular, under date of the 21st of June, declaring "that, without waiving in any degree the right of the government in respect to taxes which had before that time accrued in the States and Territories in insurrection, or assuming to exonerate the taxpayer from his legal responsibility for such taxes, the department did not deem it advisable to insist, at present, on their payment, so far as they were payable prior to the establishment of a collection district embracing a territory in which the taxpayer resided."

For substantially the same reasons that induced the Secretary to issue this circular, he deemed it to be his duty to suspend all further sales under the direct tax law. Tax commissioners, however, have been appointed for each State, and collections have been made, as far as it has been practicable to make them, without sales of property. Some sales had, however, been previously made in many of the States, and large amounts of property had been purchased for the government. In South Carolina a portion of the lands thus purchased have since been sold under the 11th section of the act of August, 1863.

During the war the laws in regard to stamps have been, of course, in the insurrectionary States, entirely disregarded; and, as a consequence, immense interests are thereby imperilled.

In view, therefore, of the recent and present condition of the southern States, the Secretary recommends—

First. That the collection of internal revenue taxes which accrued before the establishment of revenue offices in the States recently in rebellion be indefinitely postponed.

Second. That all sales of property in those States, under the direct tax law, be suspended until the States shall have an opportunity of assuming (as was done by the loyal States) the payment of the tax assessed upon them.

Third. That all transactions in such States, which may be invalid by the non-use of stamps, be legalized as far as it is in the power of Congress to legalize them.

What action, if any, should be taken for the relief of persons in those States, whose property has been sold under the direct tax law, and is now held by the government, it will be for Congress to determine. The Secretary is decidedly of the opinion that liberal legislation in regard to the taxes which accrued prior to the suppression of the rebellion will tend to promote harmony between the government and the people of those States, will ultimately increase the public revenues, and vindicate the humane policy of the government.

The Secretary is happy in being able to state that the affairs of the Bureau of Internal Revenue are being satisfactorily administered, and the working of the system throughout the country is being gradually improved.

For want of proper accommodations in the Treasury building the bureau has been removed to the large and commodious building on Fifteenth street, which has been secured for such time as the government may require its use, at an annual rent of $23,000.

The reciprocity treaty with Great Britain will expire on the 17th of March next, and due notice of this fact has been given by circulars to the officers of customs on the northern frontier.

There are grave doubts whether treaties of this character do not interfere with the legislative power of Congress, and especially with the constitutional power of the House of Representatives to originate revenue bills; and whether such treaties, if they yield anything not granted by our general revenue laws, are not in conflict with the spirit of the usual clause contained in most of our commercial treaties, to treat each nation on the same footing as the most favored nation, and not to grant, without an equivalent, any particular favor to one nation not conceded to another in respect to commerce and navigation.

It appears to be well established that the advantages of this treaty have not been mutual, but have been in favor of the Canadas. Our markets have been strong, extensive, and valuable; theirs have been weak, limited, and generally far less profitable to our citizens. The people of the Canadas and provinces have been sellers and we buyers of the same productions for which we are often forced to seek a foreign market. It is questionable, in fact, whether any actual reciprocity, embracing many of the articles now in the treaty, can be maintained between the two countries. Even in regard to the fisheries, it is by no means certain that, instead of equivalents having been acquired under the treaty, more than equal advantages were not surrendered by it. But, whatever the facts may be, this subject, as well as that of inter-communication through rivers and lakes, and possibly canals and railroads, are proper subjects of negotiation, and their importance should secure early consideration.

It is certain that, in the arrangement of our complex system of revenue through the tariff and internal duties, the treaty has been the cause of no little embarrassment. The subject of the revenue should not be embarrassed by treaty stipulations, but Congress should be left to act upon it freely and independently. Any arrangement between the United States and the Canadas and provinces, that may be considered mutually beneficial, can as readily be carried out by reciprocal legislation as by any other means. No complaint would then arise as to subsequent changes of laws, for each party would be free to act at all times, according to its discretion.

However desirable stability may be, an irrepealable revenue law, even in ordinary times, is open to grave objections, and in any extraordinary crisis is likely to be pernicious. The people of the United States cannot consent to be taxed as producers while those outside of our boundaries, exempt from our burdens, shall be permitted, as competitors, to have free access to our markets. It is desirable to diminish the temptations now existing for smuggling, and if the course suggested, of mutual legislation, should be adopted, a revenue system, both internal and external, more in harmony with our own, might justly be anticipated from the action of our neighbors, by which this result would be most likely to be obtained.

The attention of Congress is again called to the importance of early and definite action upon the subject of our mineral lands, in which subject are involved questions not only of revenue, but social questions of a most interesting character.

Copartnership relations between the government and miners will hardly be proposed, and a system of leasehold, (if it were within the constitutional authority of Congress to adopt it, and if it were consistent with the character and genius of our people,) after the lessons which have been taught of its practical results in the lead and copper districts, cannot of course be recommended.

After giving the subject as much examination as the constant pressure of official duties would permit, the Secretary has come to the conclusion that the best policy to be pursued with regard to these lands is the one which shall substitute an absolute title in fee for the indefinite possessory rights or claims now asserted by miners.

The right to obtain a "fee simple in the soil" would invite to the mineral districts men of character and enterprise; by creating homes, (which will not be found where title to property cannot be secured,) it would give permanency to the settlements, and, by the stimulus which ownership always produces, it would result in a thorough and regular development of the mines.

A bill for the subdivision and sale of the gold and silver lands of the United States was under consideration by the last Congress, to which attention is respectfully called. If the enactment of this bill should not be deemed expedient, and no satisfactory substitute can be reported for the sale of these lands to the highest bidder, on account of the possessory claims of miners, it will then be important that the policy of extending the principle of pre-emption to the mineral districts be considered. It is not material, perhaps, how the end shall be attained, but there can be no question that it is of the highest importance, in a financial and social point of view, that ownership of these lands, in limited quantities to each purchaser, should be within the reach of the people of the United States who may desire to explore and develop them.

In this connexion it may be advisable for Congress to consider whether the prosperity of the treasure-producing districts would not be increased, and the convenience of miners greatly promoted, by the establishment of an assay office in every mining district from which an annual production of gold and silver amounting to ten millions of dollars is actually obtained.

The attempts at smuggling, stimulated by the high rates of duties on imports, have engaged the attention of the department, and such arrangements have been made for its detection and prevention as seemed to be required by the circumstances, and available for that purpose.

It is quite apparent, however, that, with our extensive sea-coasts and inland frontier, it is impracticable entirely to prevent illicit traffic, though checks at the most exposed points have, doubtless, been put to such practices.

In this connexion it may be remarked that the revenue cutters are diligently and usefully employed in the preventive service, within cruising limits so defined as to leave no point of sea and gulf coasts unvisited by an adequate force.

A similar arrangement will be extended to the lakes on the reopening of navigation, the cutters built for that destination not having been completed in time to be put in commission before its close.

The cutters are an important auxiliary to the regular customs authorities, in the collection and protection of the public revenue, by the examination of incoming vessels and their manifests of cargo; affording succor to vessels in distress; aiding in the enforcement of the regulations of harbor police, and otherwise preventing or detecting violations or evasions of law. A service of this description is unquestionably useful, if not indispensable, to the administration of the revenue system of a maritime and commercial country with such extensive sea, lake, and gulf coasts as our own.

There are now in the service twenty-seven steamers and nine sailing vessels. Of the steamers, seven are of the average tonnage of 350 tons, and draw nine feet of water. These large vessels were constructed during the progress of the late rebellion, and were designed for the combined purpose of a naval force and a revenue coast guard. Their heavy armaments, large tonnage, and crews, however well fitted for such purposes, are not adapted for the revenue service in a time of peace. In consequence of their great draught of water, they must be used mainly as sea-going vessels, and are incapable of navigating the shallow waters of the coasts and their tributaries, which afford the most favorable opportunities for contraband trade. Independently of these considerations, they are so constructed as to be unable to carry a supply of fuel for more than three, or possibly four days, at the furthest.

It is recommended, therefore, that this department be vested with authority to sell the vessels of this description, and expend the proceeds in the purchase of others of a different character and lighter draught, and, on that account, better fitted to accomplish the purposes of a preventive service, and which can be kept in commission at a cost more than one-third less than those of the former class.

For example, the difference in the cost of running for twelve months the "Mahoning," one of the first named class, and the "Nansemond," one of the latter class, is $27,606. The "Mahoning," with twelve tons of coal per diem, can make but eight knots per hour ; while the "Nansemond," with eight tons of coal per diem, will make twelve knots per hour. The "Nansemond," drawing but six feet nine inches, is enabled to cruise in waters entirely inaccessible to the "Mahoning."

To render the service effective and economical, cutters should be of light draught, manned by a small crew, and able to navigate the shoal waters and penetrate the inland bays, rivers, and creeks with which our sea, lake, and gulf coasts abound, but of sufficient tonnage to enable them to perform efficiently and safely the duties of a coast guard at sea, and to furnish succor to vessels in distress ; and at the same time to navigate the interior waters for the prevention of smuggling, and reach readily a port of refuge in the tempestuous weather prevailing at times along our coast, should they be forced to do so.

The working of the marine hospital system, as at present constituted, is not altogether satisfactory. The erection and repair of numerous expensive buildings, and the support of the establishments necessarily connected with their operations, have entailed upon the government a yearly expense far beyond the amount contributed by the seamen, which has been met by large annual appropriations by Congress.

The act of July 16, 1798, by which the system was created, and the rate of contribution fixed at twenty cents per month, confined the action of the government to the simple expenditure, for the benefit of the seamen, of the amounts thus contributed by themselves, and contemplated laying no burden on the public treasury. If it is deemed advisable to continue any system of relief, under control of the government, it is respectfully suggested that the original intent of the law should be carried into effect, and the fund made self-sustaining. With this view, it will be necessary to increase the fund, and to make a material reduction in the expenses.

3 F

Experience has shown, and former Secretaries have at various times, and with entire unanimity, represented to Congress that the system of public marine hospitals, maintained and managed by the government, is the least economical method that has been devised for the administration of this fund, and affords the least comparative benefit to the seamen. The expenses of these establishments are large, independently of the number of seamen received in them. When the patients are numerous, the average rate of expense per man is not unreasonable; but where they are few, as at most of the public institutions, the expense per capita is very largely in excess of the cost of maintaining them under contract at private, State, or municipal institutions, where they would be better accommodated, at an expense exactly proportioned to the services rendered.

Mention may be made, in illustration, of one of these public hospitals, which is maintained at an annual expense of upwards of $4,000, and which accommodates an average of less than a single patient, at a daily cost per capita of more than $14 50; while quite as satisfactory relief can be had under contract for about $1 per day.

There are, moreover, several hospital buildings, erected at great cost, now lying idle, out of repair, and not available for their intended use. Some of these have never been occupied, and one, at least, is situated at a point remote from any port, and where relief is never demanded. Others now occupied are in a condition requiring large and immediate outlay to preserve them.

In view of these facts, it is strongly recommended that authority be conferred by law upon this department to sell such hospitals as experience has shown are not needed; retaining only those situated at important ports where, by the course of commerce, demands for relief are likely to be most frequent and pressing, and where contracts, on favorable terms, cannot be procured with private or municipal institutions. The proceeds should either be returned into the treasury in repayment of their cost, or invested for the benefit of the hospital fund.

In favor of the contract system it may be remarked that it is in operation most successfully at New York, where demands for relief are far the heaviest— at Baltimore, Philadelphia, St. Louis, Louisville, and Cincinnati; and it is believed that quite as advantageous and satisfactory arrangements might be made at other ports where government hospitals are now located. Even at ports where it may be deemed best to retain the ownership of the hospital buildings it might be advisable to lease them to private or municipal hospitals, which would gladly receive the seamen on favorable terms. Such an arrangement was formerly in force at Charleston, South Carolina, much to the advantage of the patients and the fund.

Should these suggestions be adopted, and, at the same time, the rate of contribution fixed at thirty cents a month, instead of twenty, as at present, the proceeds of the tax, thoroughly collected and economically administered, would be ample to meet every demand which a judicious discrimination in affording relief would make upon them; and the seamen would receive far more substantial and efficient benefit than under the present system.

As to the increased rate of contribution, it may be said that the existing rate has stood unchanged through all the fluctuations of prices and wages since 1798; that it is quite disproportioned to the benefit derived by the seamen from the marine hospital system; and that persons of this class are, as a general thing, otherwise free from federal taxation. In this view there can be no hardship or injustice in making the moderate increase suggested.

By the report of the Comptroller of the Currency, it appears that sixteen hundred and one banks had been, on the 31st of October last, organized under the National Banking act. Of these, six hundred and seventy-nine were original organizations, and nine hundred and twenty-two conversions from State institutions.

The Comptroller recommends several amendments to the acts, which will arrest the attention of Congress.

The recommendation that the banks shall be compelled to redeem their notes at one of the three cities named is heartily indorsed. At some future day it may be advisable that redemptions shall be authorized at western and southern cities; but as long as exchange continues to be in favor of the seaboard, it is not expedient to permit banks to redeem at interior points. There are very few country banks or banks in the interior cities that do not keep their chief balances in either Boston, New York, or Philadelphia, there being a regular demand for exchange on these cities. Where the current of trade requires the banks to keep accounts for their own accommodation and that of their customers and the public, there should their redemptions be made. Notes that are par in either of these cities will very rarely be at a discount in any part of the United States, and will be as nearly of uniform value as is, perhaps, ever to be expected in a paper currency.

The Secretary is hopeful that the time is not far distant when redemptions will be something more than nominal. Experience and observation have taught him that frequent redemptions are essential to the solvency of banks of circulation. Nothing so well teaches a bank the necessity of keeping its loans in the hands of prompt customers, and its means under its own control, as the certainty of being frequently called upon to meet its own obligations. It is quite important that inexperienced bankers, under the national banking system, should learn that their notes are not money, but promises to pay it; and the sooner and the more effectively this lesson is impressed upon them, the better will it be for their stockholders and the system.

The national banking system was designed not only to furnish the people with a sound circulation, but one of uniform value; and this is not likely to be fully accomplished until the banks, by compulsion or their own voluntary act, keep their notes at par in the principal money markets of the country.

The establishment of the national banking system is one of the great compensations of the war—one of the great achievements of this remarkable period. In about two years and a half from the organization of the first national bank, the whole system of banking under State laws has been superseded, and the people of the United States have been furnished with a circulation bearing upon it the seal of the Treasury Department as a guarantee of its solvency. It only remains that this circulation shall be a redeemable circulation—redeemable not only at the counters of the banks, but at the commercial cities—to make the national banking system of almost inconceivable benefit to the country.

The present law limits the circulation of the national banks to three hundred millions of dollars; and it is not probable, when the business of the country returns to a healthy basis, that a larger paper circulation than this will be required. Indeed, it is doubtful whether a larger bank note circulation can be maintained on a specie basis. Should an increase, however, be necessary, it can be provided for hereafter. It is, perhaps, unfortunate that a greater restriction had not been placed upon the circulation of the large banks already organized, in view of the wants of the southern States. It is quite likely, however, that the anticipated withdrawal of a portion of the United States notes (not to speak of the effect of the restoration of specie payments) will so reduce the circulation of the northern banks as to afford to the south, under the present limitation of the law, all the paper currency which will be required in that quarter.

The act of March 3, 1865, authorized the Secretary to borrow any sums not exceeding six hundred millions of dollars, and to issue therefor bonds or treasury notes of the United States in such form as he might prescribe.

Under this act there was issued during the month of March $70,000,000 of notes payable three years after date, and bearing an interest payable semi-annually in currency at the rate of seven and three-tenths per cent. per annum, and convertible at maturity, at the pleasure of the holders, into five-twenty gold-bearing bonds.

Upon the capture of Richmond and the surrender of the confederate armies it became apparent that there would be an early disbanding of the forces of the United States, and consequently heavy requisitions from the War Department for transportation and payment of the army, including bounties. As it was important that these requisitions should be promptly met, and especially important that not a soldier should remain in the service a single day for want of means to pay him, the Secretary perceived the necessity of realizing as speedily as possible the amount—$530,000,000—still authorized to be borrowed under this act. The seven and three-tenths notes had proved to be a popular loan, and although a security on longer time and lower interest would have been more advantageous to the government, the Secretary considered it advisable, under the circumstances, to continue to offer these notes to the public, and to avail himself, as his immediate predecessors had done, of the services of Jay Cooke, esq., in the sale of them. The result was in the highest degree satisfactory. By the admirable skill and energy of the agent, and the hearty co-operation of the national banks, these notes were distributed in every part of the northern and some parts of the southern States, and placed within the reach of every person desiring to invest in them. No loan ever offered in the United States, notwithstanding the large amount of government securities previously taken by the people, was so promptly subscribed for as this. Before the first of August the entire amount of $530,000,000 had been taken, and the Secretary had the unexpected satisfaction of being able, with the receipts from customs and internal revenue and a small increase of the temporary loan, to meet all the requisitions upon the treasury.

On two hundred and thirty millions of these notes the government has the option of paying the interest at the rate of six per cent. in coin, instead of seven and three-tenths in currency. The Secretary thought it advisable to reserve this option, because he indulged the hope that before their maturity specie payments would be restored, and because six per cent. in coin is as high a rate of interest as the government should pay on any of its obligations.

The receipts of coin have been for some months past so large that there have been con·tant accumulations beyond what has been required for the payment of the interest on the public debt. The Secretary has, therefore, deemed it to be his duty to sell, from time to time, a portion of the surplus for the purpose of supplying the wants of importers and furnishing the means for meeting the demands upon the treasury for currency. The sales have been conducted by the assistant treasurer in New York in a manner entirely satisfactory to the department and, it is believed, to the public. The sales, up to the first of November, amounted to $27,993,216 11, and the premium to $12,310,459 76; thus placing in the treasury for current use the sum of $40,303,675 87, without which there would have been a necessity for the further issue of interest-bearing notes.

The necessities of the treasury have been such that a compliance with the requirements of the act of February 25, 1862, for the creation of a sinking fund has been impracticable. As long as it is necessary for the government to borrow money, and to put its obligations upon the market for sale, the purchase of these obligations for the purpose of creating a sinking fund would hardly be judicious. After the expiration of the present year the income of the government will exceed its expenses, and it will then be practicable to carry into effect the provisions of the law. The Secretary is, however, of the opinion that the safe and simple way of sinking the national debt is to apply directly to its payment the excess of receipts over expenditures. He therefore respectfully recommends that so much of the act of February 25, 1862, as requires the application of coin to the purchase or payment of one per cent. of the entire debt of the United States, to be set apart as a sinking fund, be repealed.

By virtue of the authority conferred by the fifth section of the act of March 3, 1863, the Treasurer of the United States and the assistant treasurer in New York have been instructed to receive deposits of coin and bullion, and to issue certificates therefor in denominations of not less than twenty dollars.

Instructions were given for the issue of these certificates to promote the convenience of officers of customs and of the Treasurer and assistant treasurers, and for the accommodation of the public. Other considerations also prompted the Secretary to avail himself of the authority referred to. It is expected that the credit of the government will be strengthened by the coin which will be thus brought into the treasury, and that the effect of the measure will be to facilitate to some extent a return to specie payments. If the experiment should be satisfactory in New York, it will be extended to other commercial cities.

For a full explanation of the condition of the mints and their operations during the past year, attention is requested to the report of the director of the mint at Philadelphia.

The total value of the bullion deposited at the mint and branches during the last fiscal year was $32,248,754 97, of which $31,065,349 74 was in gold and $1,183,405 23 in silver. Deducting the redeposits, there remain the actual deposits, amounting to $27,982,849 09.

The coinage for the year was, in gold coin, $25,107,217 50; gold bars, $5,578,482 45; silver coin, $636,308; silver bars, $313,910 69; cents, including the two and three-cent pieces, $1,183,330; total coinage, $32,819,248 64.

Of the bullion deposited, $5,570,371 27 was received at the assay office in New York. Of the gold bars, $4,947,809 21, and of silver bars, $165,003 45, in value, were stamped at the same office.

At the branch mint in San Francisco the gold deposits were $18,808,318 49, and the silver deposits and purchases $540,299 20 in value. The value of the gold coined was $18,670,840; of silver coined, $320,800; and of silver bars, $145,235 58; total coinage, $19,144,875 58.

At the branch mint in Denver the total deposits were $548,609 85, of which $541,559 04 was in gold, and $7,050 81 was in silver.

The survey of the coast, which is under the administrative direction of this department, has been for the past year prosecuted with vigor. Under special assignments most of the field assistants have co-operated with the naval and military forces of the government, and in that way important service was rendered quite up to the close of the war. Since the termination of hostilities the regular operations of the survey have been pushed forward as rapidly as the available means would permit.

The national importance of this work was clearly evinced during the war, and now seems to be generally appreciated. It is therefore recommended that the necessary appropriations be made for the efficient continuance of the work.

The attention of Congress is called to the report of the Solicitor of the Treasury, which exhibits the satisfactory results of the litigation under his supervision; and also the condition of the measures adopted by him and the officers of the customs for the suppression of frauds upon the revenue.

Attention is also specially called to so much of his report as relates to the administration of the fund appropriated to defray the expenses of detecting and bringing to punishment counterfeiters of the securities and coin of the United States. The measures which have been adopted have been attended with important results, and such as to indicate the wisdom of Congress in creating the fund, and the expediency of continuing appropriations. The Solicitor has been requested to cause a thorough revision of the laws relating to counterfeiting to be made, and a bill to be prepared for the consideration of Congress, with a view to remedying defects in existing statutes.

Operations under the several acts of Congress concerning commercial intercourse with the States declared to be in insurrection, the execution of which was confided to this department, have been nearly brought to a close, partly by the restoration of peace, and partly by Executive proclamations. The provisions of those acts were carried out, as far as it was possible in the disturbed condition of the country, under the rules and regulations adopted by the department, with the approval of the Executive, not only without cost to the government, but in such manner as to add considerably to its revenues.

The regulations adopted in conformity with the requirements of the second section of the act of July 2, 1864, relative to abandoned lands, houses, and tenements, and freedmen, were, at the request of the military authorities, and from considerations of public policy, suspended by orders of August 11, 1864. Since then, from time to time, as it was ready to assume the charge of them, the duties appertaining to these subjects have been transferred to the Bureau of Refugees, Freedmen, and Abandoned Lands, according to the provisions of the act of Congress approved March 3, 1865.

By Executive orders, all operations under sections 8 and 9 of the act approved July 2, 1864, authorizing the purchase, by agents of this department, of the products of the insurrectionary districts, were closed, on the east of the Mississippi river, on the 13th of June last, and west of it on the 24th of the same month. The accounts of the different purchasing agents have not been settled, but it is thought that the net profits of the government, by these purchases, will amount to a million and a half dollars.

Since the suspension of purchases by the government the duties of the agents of this department have been confined to securing the property (chiefly cotton) captured by our military forces in pursuance of the acts of March 12, 1862, and July 2, 1864, relative to captured and abandoned property. Up to the 31st of March last there had been received at New York, Cincinnati, and St. Louis, the places designated for sales—including 38,319 bales obtained at Savannah, 4,151 bales at Charleston, and 2,331 at Mobile—about eighty thousand bales.

The general rule under which agents have been acting since the surrender of the forces which had been waging war against the government of the United States, is to collect and forward, as captured property, all cotton described upon the books and lists of the pretended confederate government, or which there was sufficient reason to believe was owned or controlled by it, and that which belonged to companies formed for the purpose of running the blockade, in support of, if not in direct co-operation with, the league which had been formed to overthrow the government of the United States, leaving individual claimants of the property to their recourse before the Court of Claims, as provided by the third section of the act approved March 12, 1863. In the performance of their duties, the agents have had great difficulties to encounter, from the unwillingness of the planters to surrender the captured property in their possession, from extensive depredations upon it after it was collected, and from powerful combinations formed to prevent, under various pretexts, the property fairly captured from coming into the possession of the United States. In spite of all these obstacles, however, it is estimated, from the accounts already received, and from data furnished by the agents, that there will be secured to the government not less than one hundred and twenty-five thousand bales of cotton, including the eighty thousand bales already referred to. What part of the proceeds of this property will ultimately be retained by the government will depend upon the success of the claimants before Congress and the courts. In collecting this cotton, there have been doubtless some instances of injustice to individuals who may be entitled to the consideration of the government; but the Secretary believes that the cotton which has been taken by the agents was rightfully seized, and that no equitable claims for the return of any considerable portion of it or the proceeds thereof can be presented.

It may be proper to add, in this connexion, that many and grave charges of corruption and improper practices have been made against agents employed in this branch of the public service. These charges, however, have been mostly vague in their character, and after such investigation as the Secretary has been able to make, he has concluded that they have been generally instigated by malice or disappointed cupidity, and usually without substantial foundation.

A copy of the several rules and regulations alluded to, which have been put in force since the last session of Congress, is appended hereto as a part of this report.

The various public buildings under the control and management of the Treasury Department are in a favorable condition; and it is to be hoped that only limited appropriations will be necessary for the coming year. On account of the difficulty of providing accommodations for the State Department, it has not been deemed advisable to proceed with the construction of the north wing of the Treasury building during the present year. The granite for the extension has, however, been contracted for and is being prepared, so that during the next season the work can be vigorously prosecuted. The grounds between the Treasury Department and the Executive Mansion are being graded and arranged with as great a regard to convenience and beauty as is practicable, considering the unfavorable location of the edifice, and it cannot be doubted that the Treasury building, when fully completed, will compare favorably, in the simplicity, solidity and beauty of its architectural appearance and proportions, with any structure in this country or in Europe.

The southern custom-houses are reported to be in a damaged and dilapidated condition, and an officer of the department has been sent to inspect them, and report what expenditures are necessary to fit them for the transaction of the public business. The appropriations which will be necessary for the purpose of making the repairs needed will be duly indicated.

By the terms of the lease of the premises occupied as a custom-house in New York, the government had the right, by giving three months' previous notice, to purchase the same at the expiration of the lease for one million of dollars. As the property was regarded as being worth a much larger amount, and was needed for custom-house purposes, it was thought advisable that the government should avail itself of the right to purchase. The property was therefore purchased for the sum named, and conveyed by proper deed to the United States.

The attention of Congress is earnestly called to the necessity of providing for the more adequate compensation of some of the officers connected with the Treasury Department. The salaries of those who are required to furnish bonds with heavy penalties, and who are custodians of large amounts of money, and of others occupying very important positions, are altogether inadequate to the responsibilities which they incur and the services which they render.

For example, the Treasurer, who received and disbursed last year about four thousand millions of dollars, is paid a salary of five thousand dollars per annum. The assistant treasurer in New York, who has in his custody from twenty to forty millions of dollars in coin, and frequently as large an amount in currency, receiving and paying out in the course of the year more than two thousand millions of dollars, receives six thousand dollars. The assistant treasurer in San Francisco receives forty-five hundred dollars in currency, which is an entirely inadequate salary in that State for an officer of character and ability, holding a position of so great responsibility. The Commissioner of Internal Revenue, holding an office which requires in its administration as much executive ability, and as high an order of talent, as any connected with the Treasury Department, receives only four thousand dollars; the Deputy Commissioner twenty-five hundred dollars. The custody of the vast amounts of government securities printed and issued from the Treasury Department is imposed upon the chief of the First Division of the Currency Bureau, who receives an annual compensation of only three thousand dollars. The Comptrollers of the Treasury, whose functions are of supreme importance in the safe transaction of the business of the department, receive salaries which are no just compensation for that business ability and those legal attainments which are indispensable in the places they occupy. Many other officers might also be named whose compensation is entirely inadequate to their talent and services.

The Secretary is aware of the necessity of economy in the expenditure of the public moneys at the present time; but the government, in order to secure the services of competent and faithful officers, must pay salaries equal to those which are paid by private corporations and individuals; and if such salaries are not paid, the result will inevitably be highly injurious to the public service, because incompetent, unfaithful, and irresponsible men will be allowed to fill offices requiring the highest capacity and most reliable integrity.

The duties devolved upon the officers named are too important to be intrusted to persons less able and reliable than those who now hold them; and it is very questionable if the services of such men can be retained, without an increase of compensation. Expensive as living is in Washington and the other cities named at present, and is likely to be for some time to come, there is scarcely one of these officers who can support his family in a manner corresponding to his position, or even comfortably, on the salary which he receives.

It is not asked that there shall be an indiscriminate raising of salaries, but that provision be made for the payment of such salaries as may be necessary to secure the permanent services of the right men in the most important positions in this department. Unless this shall be done, the department will labor under serious embarrassment in the transaction of its vast business during the coming year.

In this connexion the Secretary desires to advert to the disposition that has been made by the appropriation of the last Congress of the two hundred and fifty thousand dollars for compensation to temporary clerks and additional compensation to those permanently employed. Congress having declined to make any general and indiscriminate increase of the salaries of clerks, it was inferred that it was intended that such portion of the appropriation in question as might not be required to pay salaries of temporary clerks should be used carefully in increasing the compensation of those who were performing difficult and important duties, and whose services could not be dispensed with without injury to the government. Upon making the examination necessary to a proper decision as to the use to be made of the fund, it was ascertained that there was no lack of clerks in the lower grades, but that there was a scarcity of those of the higher grades competent to perform important and responsible duties. It appeared that many clerks receiving the highest salary allowed by law had resigned because they could obtain greater compensation elsewhere. The Treasurer's office had suffered largely in this manner, many of his most valuable clerks having left to accept situations in banks and commercial establishments where they could obtain permanent employment and higher pay. There were indications, also, that many others would do the same unless additional compensation should be made to them. Under these circumstances it was decided to use a part of the fund in slightly increasing the salaries of clerks of this description until the intention of Congress in relation to its disposition should be more clearly indicated. The amount of the fund already expended in this way is about twenty-five thousand dollars. If the disposition which has been thus made of it is not in accordance with the intention of Congress, it is, of course, competent for them to provide a different expenditure of it. The Secretary, however, deems it to be his duty to say that the interests of the service imperatively require that the salaries of clerks who are acting as heads of divisions, or are employed in duties requiring in their performance a high order of ability, as well as the salaries of the officers referred to, should be considerably increased. It would doubtless be a true economy to diminish the number of clerks, and to increase the compensation of those who may be retained.

For information in regard to the condition and operations of the various bureaus of this department, reference is made to the accompanying reports of the proper officers, all of whom, with the Assistant Secretaries, merit the thanks of the country for the efficient manner in which they are discharging their onerous and responsible duties.

HUGH McCULLOCH,
Secretary of the Treasury.

Hon. SCHUYLER COLFAX,
Speaker of the House of Representatives.

No. 1.

Receipts and expenditures for the fiscal year ending June 30, 1865.

The receipts into the treasury were as follows:

From customs, viz:

During the quarter ending September 30, 1864	$19,271,091 96	
During the quarter ending December 31, 1864	15,123,926.78	
During the quarter ending March 31, 1865	20,518,852 54	
During the quarter ending June 30, 1865	30,014,387 32	
		$84,928,260 60

From sales of public lands, viz:

During the quarter ending September 30, 1864	342,185 84	
During the quarter ending December 31, 1864	287,835 26	
During the quarter ending March 31, 1865	162,010 47	
During the quarter ending June 30, 1865	204,521 74	
		996,553 31

From direct tax, viz:

During the quarter ending September 30, 1864	16,079 86	
During the quarter ending December 31, 1864	843,380 34	
During the quarter ending March 31, 1865	52,714 81	
During the quarter ending June 30, 1865	288,398 02	
		1,200,573 03

From internal revenue, viz:

During the quarter ending September 30, 1864	46,562,859 92	
During the quarter ending December 31, 1864	55,129,731 76	
During the quarter ending March 31, 1865	65,262,803 28	
During the quarter ending June 30, 1865	42,508,820 29	
		209,464,215 25

From miscellaneous and incidental sources, viz:

During the quarter ending September 30, 1864	9,020,171 44	
During the quarter ending December 31, 1864	9,295,852 44	
During the quarter ending March 31, 1865	4,159,223 73	
During the quarter ending June 30, 1865	10,503,036 86	
		32,978,284 47

Total receipts, exclusive of loans		329,567,886 66

From loans, viz:

From 6 per cent. 20-year bonds, under act of July 17, 1861	108,573,524 55	
From United States notes, under act of February 25, 1862	4,159,830 00	
From 5-20-year bonds, under act of February 25, 1862	252,657,15	
From temporary loans, under acts of February 25 and March 17, 1862	131,478,072 86	
From certificates of indebtedness, under acts of March 1 and 17, 1862	130,975,200 63	
From fractional currency, under act of March 3, 1863	14,614,563 15	
From 6 per cent. 1881 bonds, under act of March 3, 1863	32,175,805 23	
From 6 per cent. compound interest notes, under acts of March 3, 1863, and June 30, 1864	180,214,140 00	
From 10-40-year bonds, under act of March 3, 1864	99,558,400 01	
From 7 3-10 three-year treasury notes, under acts of June 30, 1864, and March 3, 1865	675,556,297 02	
From 6 per cent. 5-20-year bonds, under act of June 30, 1864	94,706,250 25	
		1,472,224,740 85

Total receipts		1,801,792,627 51
Balance in treasury on July 1, 1864		96,739,905 73
Total means		1,898,532,533 24

The expenditures for the year were as follows:

For civil, foreign intercourse, and miscellaneous		44,765,558 12
For pensions and Indians		14,258,375 38
For war		1,031,323,360 79
For navy		122,567,776 12
For interest on the public debt, including treasury notes		77,397,712 00
		1,290,312,982 41

For redemption of stock, loan of 1842	1,400 00	
For redemption of Texas indemnity stock, under act of September 9, 1850	1,631,899 38	
For reimbursement of treasury notes, acts prior to December 23, 1857	400 00	
For payment of treasury notes, under act of December 23, 1857	1,100 00	
For payment of treasury notes, under act of March 2, 1861	43,550 00	
For redemption of United States notes, under act of July 17, 1861	370,599 00	
For redemption of United States notes, under act of February 25, 1862	4,335,133 47	
For redemption of 7 3-10 three-year coupon treasury notes, under act of July 17, 1861	136,411,050 00	

For redemption of postage and other stamps, under act of July 17, 1862..	$4, 739, 367 34
For redemption of temporary loans, under acts of February 25 and March 17, 1862	118, 488, 838 19
For redemption of certificates of indebtedness, under acts of March 1 and 17, 1862	174, 827, 000 00
For redemption of fractional currency, under act of March 3, 1863	6, 676, 364 30
For redemption of one-year 5 per cent. treasury notes, under act of March 3, 1863	38, 473, 320 00
For redemption of two-year 5 per cent. treasury notes, under act of March 3, 1863	113, 957, 250 00
For redemption of three-year 6 per cent. compound interest treasury notes, under acts of March 3, 1863, and June 30, 1864	1, 458, 060 00
For redemption of three-year 7 3-10 treasury notes, under act of June 30, 1864	3, 945, 900 00
	$600, 977, 169 83
Total expenditures	1, 897, 674, 224 09
Balance in treasury July 1, 1865	858, 309 15

No. 2.

Receipts and expenditures, as estimated for the year ending June 30, 1867.

RECEIPTS.

From customs	$100, 000, 000 00	
From internal duties	275, 000, 000 00	
From lands	1, 000, 000 00	
From miscellaneous sources	20, 000, 000 00	
		$396, 000, 000 0

EXPENDITURES.

For the civil service	42, 165, 599 47	
For pensions and Indians	17, 609, 640 23	
For War Department	39, 017, 418 18	
For Navy Department	43, 982, 457 50	
For interest on the public debt	141, 542, 068 50	
		284, 317, 181 88
Leaving a surplus of estimated receipts over estimated expenditures of		111, 682, 818 12

No. 3.

Statement of duties, revenues, and public expenditures during the fiscal year ending June 30, 1865, agreeably to warrants issued, exclusive of trust funds.

The receipts into the treasury were as follows :

From customs, viz :

During the quarter ending September 30, 1864	$19, 271, 091 96	
During the quarter ending December 31, 1864	15, 123, 928 78	
During the quarter ending March 31, 1865	20, 518, 852 54	
During the quarter ending June 30, 1865	30, 014, 387 32	
		$84, 928, 260 60

From sales of public lands, viz :

During the quarter ending September 30, 1864	342, 165 84	
During the quarter ending December 31, 1864	287, 835 26	
During the quarter ending March 31, 1865	162, 010 47	
During the quarter ending June 30, 1865	204, 541 74	
		996, 553 31

From direct tax, viz :

During the quarter ending September 30, 1864	16, 079 86	
During the quarter ending December 31, 1864	843, 380 34	
During the quarter ending March 31, 1865	52, 714 81	
During the quarter ending June 30, 1865	288, 398 02	
		1, 200, 573 03

From internal revenue, viz :

During the quarter ending September 30, 1864	46, 562, 859 92	
During the quarter ending December 31, 1864	55, 129, 731 76	
During the quarter ending March 31, 1865	65, 262, 803 28	
During the quarter ending June 30, 1865	42, 508, 820 29	
		209, 464, 215 25

From miscellaneous and incidental sources, viz:

During the quarter ending September 30, 1864	$9,020,171 44	
During the quarter ending December 31, 1864	9,295,852 44	
During the quarter ending March 31, 1865	4,159,223 73	
During the quarter ending June 30, 1865	10,503,036 86	
		$32,978,284 47
Total receipts, exclusive of loans		329,567,886 66

Receipts from loans, viz:

From 6 per cent. 20-year bonds, per act July 17, 1861	108,573,524 55	
From United States notes, per act February 25, 1862	4,159,830 00	
From 5-20-year bonds, per act February 25, 1862	232,657 15	
From temporary loans, per acts February 25 and March 17, 1862	131,436,072 86	
From certificates of indebtedness, per acts March 1 and 17, 1862	130,975,200 63	
From fractional currency, per act March 3, 1863	14,614,363 15	
From 6 per cent. 1881 bonds, per act March 3, 1863	39,175,805 23	
From 6 per cent. compound interest notes, per acts March 3, 1863, and June 30, 1864	180,214,140 00	
From 10-40-year bonds, per act March 3, 1864	99,558,400 01	
From 7 3-10 three-year treasury notes, per acts June 30, 1864, and March 3, 1865	675,556,297 02	
From 5-20-year 6 per cent. bonds, per act June 30, 1864	94,706,250 25	
		1,472,204,740 85
Total receipts		1,801,792,627 51
Balance in the treasury on July 1, 1864		96,739,905 73
Total means		1,898,532,533 24

The expenditures for the year were as follows:

CIVIL.

For Congress, including books	$3,585,171 86	
For executive	4,993,329 03	
For judiciary	1,612,502 36	
For government in Territories	260,469 44	
For assistant treasurers and their clerks	140,820 50	
For officers of the mint and branches, and assay office at New York	91,714 88	
For supervising and local inspectors, &c	72,462 44	
For surveyors general and their clerks	77,475 37	
Total civil list		$10,833,944 87

FOREIGN INTERCOURSE.

For salaries of ministers, &c	295,378 36	
For salaries of secretaries and assistant secretaries of legation	35,458 82	
For salaries of consuls general. &c., including loss by exchange	406,381 62	
For salaries of secretaries of legation to China, Japan, and Turkey, as interpreters	1,181 39	
For salaries of interpreters to the consulates in China and Japan	1,810 56	
For interpreters, guards, and other expenses of consulates in the Turkish dominions	1,749 49	
For contingent expenses of all missions abroad	55,474 85	
For contingent expenses of foreign intercourse	136,722 61	
For office rent for consuls not allowed to trade	39,545 59	
For purchase of blank books, stationery, &c., for consuls	54,320 59	
For salaries of marshals of consular courts in Japan, China, &c	5,471 58	
For relief and protection of American seamen	125,476 00	
For bringing home from foreign countries persons charged with crime	865 49	
For expenses of acknowledging the services of masters and crews of foreign vessels in rescuing American citizens from shipwreck	5,178 30	
For prosecution of work, including pay of commissioner, per first article o freciprocity treaty with Great Britain	8,000 00	
For rent of prisons for American convicts in Japan, China, Siam, and Turkey	8,229 80	
To carry into effect convention between the United States and the republic of Peru of January 12, 1863, for settlement of claims	500 00	
For defraying expenses consequent upon carrying into effect the act of Congress relating to "habeas corpus," and regulating judicial proceedings in certain cases	2,650 00	
For an act to encourage immigration	13,000 00	
For expenses incident to an act to carry into effect a treaty for the settlement of claims of the Hudson Bay and Puget Sound Agricultural Companies	7,570 00	
For expenses incident to an act to carry into effect convention with Ecuador for the adjustment of claims	267 50	
For the payment of the first annual instalment towards capitalization of the Scheldt dues	55,584 00	
For consular receipts	7,001 53	
Total foreign intercourse		1,260,818 08

MISCELLANEOUS.

For mint establishment...	$746,313 93
For contingent expenses under the act for safe-keeping the public revenue...	160,450 23
For compensation to persons designated to receive and keep the public money..	7,835 30
For compensation to special agents to examine books, &c., in the several depositories..	5,128 75
For building vaults as additional security to the public funds in sixty-six depositories..	34,135 19
For compensation to receiver at Santa Fé, acting as depository.........	2,000 00
For salary of clerk, watchman, and porter in office of depositary at Santa Fé..	2,484 02
For survey of the Atlantic and Gulf coasts of the United States..........	201,900 00
For survey of the western coast of the United States..................	127,500 00
For survey of the Florida reefs and keys...........................	6,000 00
For publishing the observations of the survey of the coasts of the United States..	3,000 00
For repairs of steamers used in the coast survey.....................	4,000 00
For pay and rations of engineers for seven steamers used in the coast survey...	8,600 00
For running a line to connect the triangulation on the Atlantic coast with that on the Gulf of Mexico, across the peninsula of Florida..........	5,000 00
For the services of the California central route......................	250,000 00
For facilitating communication between the Atlantic and Pacific States by electric telegraph...	39,917 65
For collection of agricultural statistics.............................	20,000 00
For payment for horses and other property lost or destroyed in the military service of the United States...............................	754,390 32
For expenses of the Smithsonian Institution........................	30,910 14
For the continuation of the Treasury building.......................	485,240 83
For constructing fire-proof vaults and file-cases for the collector and assistant treasurer at New York....................................	3,570 55
For building vaults and fitting up offices in the custom-house at Philadelphia, for receipt and custody of such public money as may be deposited therein...	50,000 00
For building post offices, court-houses, &c., including purchase of sites..	68,758 83
For expenses incident to the issue and disposal of $200,000,000 United States bonds...	68,825 90
For compensation to prize commissioners, and other expenses connected therewith...	300 00
For salaries of commissioners in insurrectionary districts in the United States...	53,782 45
For contingent expenses of commissioners of direct taxes in insurrectionary districts in the United States............................	8,996 22
For Department of Agriculture......................................	86,304 05
For expenses incident to carrying into effect national loans...........	6,588,641 81
For expenses incident to an act to provide a national currency.........	59,682 72
For expenses of engraving, printing, preparing, and issuing United States treasury notes, fractional notes, and bonds......................	14,592 03
For detection and bringing to trial persons engaged in counterfeiting coin, &c..	46,595 59
For plates, paper, special dies, and the printing of circulating notes, and expenses necessarily incurred in procuring said notes, including miscellaneous items..	441,250 00
For allowance or drawback on articles on which internal duty or tax has been paid..	670,428 31
For lighting and ventilating the Treasury building...................	715 11
For constructing bridges and market-house in Georgetown.............	13,000 00
To pay taxes on lands owned by the United States....................	3,749 67
For payment of messengers of the respective States for conveying to the seat of government the votes of electors of said States for President and Vice-President of the United States.................................	19,401 00
For a gold medal for Major General Grant...........................	2,843 00
For a gold medal for Cornelius Vanderbilt...........................	3,000 00
For expenses of collecting the revenue from customs..................	5,437,490 48
For repayment to importers of excess of deposits from unascertained duties..	2,283,313 97
For debentures or drawbacks, bounties, or allowances.................	968,815 77
For refunding duties, under the act extending the warehouse system.....	2,425 85
For debentures and other charges..................................	21,638 54
For salaries of special examiners of drugs..........................	5,748 18
For additional compensation to collectors, naval officers, &c..........	246,134 81
For support and maintenance of light-houses, &c.....................	409,836 09
For building light-houses, &c., for beacons, buoys, &c................	466,969 97
For light-boats, compensation of keepers of stations, &c..............	359,471 86
For marine hospital establishment..................................	348,472 82
For building marine hospitals, including repairs, &c..................	6,172 71
For building custom-houses, including repairs, &c....................	1,069,362 18
For annual repairs of marine hospitals and custom-houses.............	17,831 75
For unclaimed merchandise...	1,393 48
For proceeds of sale of goods, wares, &c............................	402 07
For purchase of steam or sailing revenue cutters....................	393,197 12
For purchase of products of States in insurrection..................	2,462,653 29

For rents of offices for surveyors general	$13,149 70
For repayment of lands erroneously sold	9,117 89
For indemnity for swamp lands sold to individuals	·216,186 33
For surveys of public lands	62,720 72
For surveys of public lands and private land claims in California, &c.	26,084 15
For services of special counsel, &c., in defending the title to public property in California	4,200 00
For suppression of the slave trade	48,074 17
·For expenses of taking the eighth census	28,979 02
For salaries and other expenses of the Metropolitan Police	116,680 88
For repairs, &c., for the President's House	12,000 00
For rebuilding the President's stable	2,000 00
For lighting the President's House, the Capitol &c., with gas	63,500 00
For fuel for the President's House	2,400 00
For alterations and repairs of buildings in Washington, improvement of grounds, &c.	450,402 58
For compensation of public gardener, gate-keepers, laborers, watchmen, &c.	23,857 55
For penitentiary in the District of Columbia	1,981 89
For Columbia Institute for Deaf, Dumb, and Blind in the District of Columbia	40,925 00
For completing the Washington aqueduct	144,612 67
For Potomac and Eastern Branch bridges, compensation of draw-keepers, &c.	1,232 00
For support of transient paupers in the District of Columbia	6,000 00
For coal for the library of Congress	962 85
For expense of packing and distributing congressional journals and documents	·6,000 00
For purchase of libraries for the Territories of Colorado, Dakota, and Nevada	6,275 27
For patent fund	259,217 88
For Patent Office building	63,800 00
For support of insane paupers of the District of Columbia, and army and navy of the United States	48,000 00
For preservation of collections of the exploring expedition	2,600 00
For drawings to illustrate the report of the Commissioner of Patents	6,000 00
For purchase of United States Statutes	2,765 00
For roads and canals, State of Michigan	9,445 44
For relief of the State of Wisconsin	225,276 63
For the relief of sundry individuals	70,930 33
For deposits by individuals for expenses of surveys of public lands	13,131 75
For compiling and supervising the Biennial Register	500 00
For purchase of gold coin, act of March 17, 1862, 1st section	5,072,960 11
	32,673,545 69
From which deduct repayments on account of appropriations under which there were no expenditures during the year	2,750 52
Total miscellaneous	$32,670,795 17

UNDER THE DIRECTION OF THE INTERIOR DEPARTMENT

·For the Indian department	3,802,393 60	
For pensions, military	9,139,167 36	
For pensions, naval	152,443 12	
For relief of sundry individuals, including payments on account of depredations by Indians	1,164,571 30	
Total Interior Department		14,258,575

UNDER THE DIRECTION OF THE WAR DEPARTMENT.

For the Pay department	351,573,554 62	
For the Adjutant General	118,686 33	
For the Surgeon General	19,584,634 38	
For the Commissary General	147,085,231 32	
For the Provost Marshal General	10,676,267 27	
For the Quartermaster's department	446,565,474 54	
For the Ordnance department	46,774,634 23	
For the Engineers' department	6,183,587 15	
For the Secretary's office, (army expenditures)	2,733,823 96	
Relief of sundry individuals	7,246 99	
Total War Department		1,031,323,360 79

UNDER THE DIRECTION OF THE NAVY DEPARTMENT.

For pay of the navy	27,500,997 92
For prize money to captors	5,740,909 21
For miscellaneous	283,539 50
For provisions and clothing	10,566,882 75
For construction and repair	34,411,258 30
For ordnance	7,199,135 05
For equipment and recruiting	15,475,440 23
For yards and docks	4,046,506 07

For medicine and surgery	$474, 504 01	
For marine corps	1, 762, 539 61	
For navigation	566, 729 47	
For steam engineering	14, 464, 597 48	
For relief of sundry individuals	30, 116 52	
Total Navy Department		$122, 567, 776 12
To which add—		
For interest on the public debt, including treasury notes		77, 397, 712 00
Total expenditures, exclusive of principal of the public debt		1, 290, 312, 982 41

PRINCIPAL OF THE PUBLIC DEBT.

For redemption of stock, loan of 1842	1, 400 00	
For redemption of Texan indemnity stock, act of September 9, 1850	1, 631, 889 39	
For reimbursement of treasury notes, per acts prior to December 23, 1857	400 00	
For payment of treasury notes, act December 23, 1857	1, 100 00	
For payment of treasury notes, act March 2, 1861	43, 550 00	
For redemption of United States notes, act July 17, 1861	370, 599 00	
For redemption of 7 3-10 3-year coupon bonds, act July 17, 1861	138, 411, 050 00	
For redemption of postage and other stamps, act July 17, 1862	4, 739, 387 34	
For redemption of United States notes, act of February 25, 1862	4, 335, 133 47	
For redemption of temporary loans, acts of February 25 and March 17, 1862	118, 488, 836 19	
For redemption of certificates of indebtedness, acts March 1 and 17, 1862	174, 827, 000 00	
For redemption of fractional currency, act March 3, 1863	6, 676, 364 30	
For redemption of 1-year 5 per cent. treasury notes, act March 3, 1863	38, 473, 390 00	
For redemption of 2-year 5 per cent. treasury notes, act March 3, 1863	113, 957, 230 00	
For redemption of 3-year 6 per cent. compound interest treasury notes, acts March 3, 1863, and June 30, 1864	1, 456, 060 00	
For redemption of 3-year 7 3-10 coupon treasury notes, act June 30, 1864	3, 945, 900 00	
Total principal of the public debt		607, 361, 241 68
Total expenditures		1, 897, 674, 224 09
Balance in the treasury July 1, 1865		858, 309 15

TREASURY DEPARTMENT, *Register's Office, November 24, 1865.*

S. B. COLBY, *Register.*

No. 4.

Statement of the receipts and expenditures of the United States for the quarter ending September 30, 1865, exclusive of trust funds.

RECEIPTS.

From customs	$47, 009, 583 03	
From sales of public lands	132, 890 63	
From direct tax	31, 111 30	
From internal revenue	96, 618, 685 65	
From incidental and miscellaneous sources	18, 393, 729 94	
Total receipts, exclusive of loans		162, 186, 200 55
From loans:		
From 6 per cent. 20-year bonds, per act July 17, 1861	$10, 000 00	
From United States notes, per act February 25, 1862	2, 322, 615 00	
From temporary loans, per acts February 25 and March 17, 1862	50, 045, 576 12	
From certificates of indebtedness, per acts March 1 and 17, 1862	26, 054, 799 37	
From fractional currency, per act March 3, 1863	4, 950, 163 75	
From 6 per cent. 1881 bonds, per act March 3, 1863	149, 370 00	
From 10-40-year bonds, per act March 3, 1864	5 00	
From 6 per cent. compound interest notes, per acts March 3, 1863, and June 30, 1864	26, 400, 000 00	
From 5-20-year bonds, (5 per cent.,) per act June 30, 1864	9, 211, 000 00	
From 7 3-10 3-year treasury notes, per acts June 30, 1864, and March 3, 1865	158, 068, 731 33	
		277, 182, 260 57
		439, 368, 461 12

EXPENDITURES.

Civil, foreign intercourse, and miscellaneous..	$10,571,460 99
Interior, (pensions and Indians)...	6,024,241 86
War	165,369,277 32
Navy	16,820,669 81
Interest on the public debt, including treasury notes.......................................	36,173,481 50

Total expenditures, exclusive of principal of public debt 234,659,091 48

Principal of public debt:

Reimbursements of treasury notes, issued prior to December 23, 1837.......	$200 00	
Payment of treasury notes, per act of March 2, 1861	1,200 00	
Redemption of Texas indemnity stock, per act September 9, 1850	94,000 00	
Redemption of United States notes, per act July 17, 1861..................	80,533 25	
Redemption of 7 3-10 3-year coupon bonds, per act July 17, 1861	25,150 00	
Redemption of stock loan of 1842..	10,100 00	
Reimbursement temporary loan, per acts February 25 and March 17, 1862..	33,677,413 29	
Redemption certificates of indebtedness, per acts March 1 and 17, 1862......	80,044,000 00	
Redemption United States notes, per act February 25, 1862	6,365,700 00	
Redemption portage and other stamps, per act July 17, 1862..............	1,003,257 02	
Redemption fractional currency, per act March 3, 1863	2,897,980 79	
Redemption 5 per cent. 2-year treasury notes, per act March 3, 1863.	5,000,000 00	
Redemption 5 per cent. 1-year treasury notes, per act March 3, 1863	7,000,000 00	
Redemption 3-year 6 per cent. compound interest notes, per act March 3, 1863...	2,149,629 00	
		138,409,163 35
		373,068,254 83

S. B. COLBY, *Register,*

TREASURY DEPARTMENT, *Register's Office, November 24,* 1865.

4 F

REPORT ON THE FINANCES.

No. 5.—*Statement of the indebtedness*

	Acts authorizing loans, and synopsis of same.
Act of July 21, 1841, and April 15, 1842.	Authorized a loan of $12,000,000, bearing interest at a rate not exceeding 6 per cent. per annum, and reimbursable at the will of the Secretary, after six months' notice, or at any time after three years from January 1, 1842. The act of April 15, 1842, authorized the loan of an additional sum of $5,000,000, and made the amount obtained on the loan after the passage of this act reimbursable after six months' notice, or at any time not exceeding twenty years from January 1, 1843. This loan was made for the purpose of redeeming outstanding treasury notes, and to defray any of the public expenses.
Act of Jan. 28, 1847....	Authorized the issue of $23,000,000 in treasury notes, bearing interest at a rate not exceeding 6 per cent. per annum, with authority to borrow any portion of the amount, and issue bonds therefor, bearing interest at a rate not exceeding 6 per cent., and redeemable after December 31, 1867. The 13th section authorized the funding of these notes into bonds of the same description. The act limited the amount to be borrowed or issued in treasury notes and funded as aforesaid to $23,000,000, but authorized the funding of treasury notes issued under former acts beyond that amount. The excess of the $23,000,000 is made up of treasury notes funded under the 14th section.
Act of March 31, 1848 ...	Authorized a loan of $16,000,000, bearing interest at a rate not exceeding 6 per cent. per annum, and reimbursable at any time after twenty years from July 1, 1848. Authority was given to the Secretary to purchase the stock at any time.
Act of Sept. 9, 1850	Authorized the issue of $10,000,000 in bonds, bearing 5 per cent. interest, and redeemable at the end of fourteen years, to indemnify the State of Texas for her relinquishment of all claims upon the United States for liability of the debts of Texas, and for compensation for the surrender to the United States of her ships, forts, arsenals, custom-houses, &c., which became the property of the United States at the time of annexation.
Old funded and unfunded debts.	Consisting of unclaimed dividends upon stocks issued before the year 1800, and those issued during the war of 1812.
Acts prior to 1857	Different issues of treasury notes..
Act of Dec. 23, 1857....	Authorized an issue of $20,000,000 in treasury notes, bearing interest at a rate not exceeding 6 per cent. per annum, and receivable in payment of all public dues, and to be redeemed after the expiration of one year from the date of said notes.
Act of June 14, 1858....	Authorized a loan of $20,000,000, bearing interest at a rate not exceeding 5 per cent. per annum, and reimbursable at the option of the government at any time after the expiration of fifteen years from January 1, 1859.
Act of June 22, 1860....	Authorized a loan of $21,000,000, bearing interest at a rate not exceeding 6 per cent. per annum, and reimbursable within a period not beyond twenty years, and not less than ten years, for the redemption of outstanding treasury notes, and for no other purpose.
Act of Dec. 17, 1860....	Authorized an issue of $10,000,000 in treasury notes, to be redeemed after the expiration of one year from the date of issue, and bearing such a rate of interest as may be offered by the lowest bidders. Authority was given to issue these notes in payment of warrants in favor of public creditors at their par value, bearing 6 per cent. interest per annum.
Act of Feb. 8, 1861......	Authorized a loan of $25,000,000, bearing interest at a rate not exceeding 6 per cent. per annum, and reimbursable within a period not beyond twenty years, nor less than ten years. This loan was made for the payment of the current expenses, and was to be awarded to the most favorable bidders.
Act of March 2, 1861....	Authorized a loan of $10,000,000, bearing interest at a rate not exceeding 6 per cent. per annum, and reimbursable after the expiration of ten years from July 1, 1861. In case proposals for the loan were not acceptable, authority was given to issue the whole amount in treasury notes bearing interest at a rate not exceeding 6 per cent. per annum. Authority was also given to substitute treasury notes for the whole or any part of the loans for which the Secretary was by law authorized to contract and issue bonds at the time of the passage of this act, and such treasury notes were to be made receivable in payment of all public dues, and redeemable at any time within two years from March 2, 1861.
Act of March 2, 1861 ...	Authorized an issue, should the Secretary of the Treasury deem it expedient, of $2,800,000. in coupon bonds, bearing interest at the rate of 5 per cent. per annum, and redeemable in twenty years, for the payment of expenses incurred by the Territories of Washington and Oregon in the suppression of Indian hostilities during the years 1855 and 1856.
Acts of July 17, 1861, and August 5, 1861.	Authorized a loan of $250,000,000, for which could be issued bonds bearing interest at a rate not exceeding 7 per cent. per annum irredeemable for twenty years, and after that redeemable at the pleasure of the United States; treasury notes bearing interest at the rate of 7.30 per cent. per annum, payable three years after date, and United States notes without interest, payable on demand, to the extent of $50,000,000, (increased by act of February 12, 1862, to $60,000,000,) the bonds and treasury notes to be issued in such proportions of each as the Secretary may deem advisable. The supplementary act of August 5, 1861, authorized an issue of bonds bearing 6 per cent. interest per annum, and payable at the pleasure of the United States after twenty years from date, which may be issued in exchange for 7.30 treasury notes, but no such bonds to be issued for a less sum than $500; and the whole amount of such bonds not to exceed the whole amount of 7.30 treasury notes issued.

of the United States, June 30, 1865.

Title.	Length of loan.	When redeemable.	Rate of interest.	Price of emission.	Amount authorized.	Amount issued.	Amount outstand'g June 30, 1865.
Loan of 1842....	20 years	After Dec. 31, 1862	6 per ct. per annum.	Par ..	$17,000,000	$8,000,000	$105,406 45
Loan of 1847....	20 years	After Dec. 31, 1867	6 per ct. per annum.	Par ..	23,000,000	28,207,000	9,415,250 00
Loan of 1848....	20 years	After July 1, 1868.	6 per ct. per annum.	Par ..	16,000,000	16,000,000	8,908,341 80
Texas indemnity	15 years	After Dec. 31, 1864	5 per ct. per annum.	Par ..	10,000,000	5,000,000	842,000 00
Old funded debt.	Demand	On demand.......	3 & 6 per ct.	Par ..	....	....	114,115 48
Treasury notes.	....	On demand.......	1 m. to 6 p. ct.	Par ..	....	....	104,511 64
Treasury notes..	1 year..	1 year after date ..	5 to 5½ pr. ct.	Par ..	20,000,000	....	8,800 00
Loan of 1858....	15 years	Dec. 31, 1873......	5 per ct. per annum.	Par ..	20,000,000	20,000,000	20,000,000 00
Loan of 1860....	10 years	After Dec. 31, 1870	5 per ct. per annum.	Par ..	21,000,000	7,022,000	7,022,000 00
Treasury notes..	1 year..	1 year after date ..	6 & 12 per ct. per ann.	Par ..	10,000,000	10,000,000	600 00
Loan of Feb. 8, 1861.	20 years	After June 1, 1881.	6 per ct. per annum.	Par ..	25,000,000	18,415,000	18,415,000 00
Treasury notes.	2 years.	2 years after date }	6 pr.ct. per annum. }	Par ..	22,468,100	22,468,100	5,800 00
	60 days.	60 days after date }		.....	12,896,350	12,896,350	....
Oregon war.....	20 years	After July 1,1881..	6 per ct. per annum.	Par ..	2,800,000	1,090,850	1,016,000 00
20-year sixes..	20 years	After June 30, 1881	6 p.ct. p. ann.	.....	....	50,000,000	50,000,000 00
7.30 notes.....	3 yrs. {	After Aug. 19, 1864	7.30 per ct. per ann. }	.....	....	139,999,750	139,155,650 00
(two issues.)		After Sept. 30, 1864					
Demand notes.	Payable on demand.	Demand..........	None......	.....	....	60,000,000	472,603 00
20-year sixes..	20 years	After June 30, 1881	6 per ct. per annum.	Par ..	Exchang'able for 7.30 treasury notes.	....	431,300 00

No. 5.—*Statement of the indebtedness*

	Acts authorizing loans, and synopsis of same.
Act of Feb. 25, 1862....	Authorized the issue of $500,000,000 in 6 per cent. bonds, redeemable after five years, and payable twenty years from date, which may be exchanged for United States notes. Also, on
March 3, 1864..........	Authorized the issue of not over $11,000,000 additional of similar bonds, to meet subscriptions already made and paid for.
June 30, 1864........ ⎰ January 28, 1865.... ⎱	On hand unsold in the United States or Europe..................................
Act of Feb. 25, 1862....	Authorized the issue of $150,000,000 in legal-tender United States notes, $50,000,000 of which to be in lieu of demand notes issued under act of July 17, 1861.
Act of July 11, 1862....	Authorized an additional issue of $150,000,000 legal-tender notes, $35,000,000 of which might be in denominations less than five dollars; $50,000,000 of this issue to be reserved to pay temporary loans promptly in case of emergency.
Resolution of Congress, January 17, 1863.	Authorized the issue of $100,000,000 in United States notes, for the immediate payment of the army and navy, such notes to be a part of the amount provided for in any bill that may hereafter be passed by this Congress. (The amount in this resolution is included in act of March 3, 1863.)
Act of March 3, 1863....	A further issue of $150,000,000 in United States notes, for the purpose of converting the treasury notes which may be issued under this act, and for no other purpose. And a further issue, if necessary, for the payment of the army and navy, and other creditors of the government, of $150,000,000 in United States notes, which amount includes the $100,000,000 authorized by the joint resolution of Congress, January 17, 1863.
Act of Feb. 25, 1862....	Authorized a temporary loan of $25,000,000 in United States notes, for not less than thirty days, payable after ten days' notice, at 5 per cent. interest per annum. (This was increased to $100,000,000 by the following acts.)
March 17, 1862..........	Authorized an increase of temporary loans of $25,000,000, bearing interest at a rate not exceeding 5 per cent. per annum.
July 11, 1862........'...	Authorized a further increase of temporary loans of $50,000,000, making the whole amount authorized $100,000,000.
Act of June 30, 1864....	Authorized the increase of temporary loans to not exceeding $150,000,000, at a rate not exceeding 6 per cent.
Act of March 3, 1863....	Authorized a loan of $300,000,000 for this, and $600,000,000 for the next fiscal year, for which could be issued bonds running not less than ten, nor more than forty years, principal and interest payable in coin, bearing interest at a rate not exceeding six per cent. per annum, payable in bonds not exceeding $100 annually, and on all others semi-annually, the whole amount of bonds, treasury notes, and United States notes, issued under this act, not to exceed the sum of $900,000,000. And so much of this act as limits the loan to the current fiscal year is repealed by act of June 30, 1864, which also repeals the authority to borrow money conferred by section 1, except so far as it may affect $75,000,000 of bonds already advertised.
Act of June 30, 1864....	
Act of March 3, 1863....	And treasury notes to the amount of $400,000,000, not exceeding three years to run, with interest at not over 6 per cent. per annum, principal and interest payable in lawful money, which may be made a legal tender for their face value, excluding interest, or convertible into United States notes.
Act of March 3, 1864....	Authorizes the issue of bonds not exceeding $200,000,000, bearing date March 1, 1864, or any subsequent period, redeemable at the pleasure of the government after any period not less than five years, and payable at any period not more than forty years from date, in coin, bearing interest not exceeding six per cent. yearly, payable on bonds not over one hundred dollars annually, and on all other bonds semi-annually, in coin.
Act of March 1, 1862....	Authorized an issue of certificates of indebtedness, payable one year from date, in settlement of audited claims against the government. Interest 6 per cent. per annum, payable in gold; and by
Act of March 3, 1863....	Payable in lawful currency on those issued after that date. Amount of issue not specified.
Act of July 17, 1862....	Authorized an issue of notes of the fractional parts of one dollar, receivable in payment of all dues, except customs, less than five dollars, and exchangeable for United States notes in sums not less than five dollars. Amount of issue not specified.
Act of March 3, 1863....	Authorized an issue not exceeding $50,000,000 in fractional currency, (in lieu of postage or other stamps,) exchangeable for United States notes in sums not less than three dollars, and receivable for any dues to the United States less than five dollars, except duties on imports. The whole amount issued, including postage and other stamps issued as currency, not to exceed $50,000,000. Authority was given to prepare it in the Treasury Department, under the supervision of the Secretary.
Act of June 30, 1864....	Authorized issue in lieu of the issue under acts of July 17, 1862, and March 3, 1863, the whole amount outstanding under all these acts not ¦to exceed $50,000,000.

of the United States, June 30, 1865—Continued.

Title.	Length of loan.	When redeemable.	Rate of interest.	Price of emission.	Amount authorized.	Amount issued.	Amount outstanding June 30, 1865.
Five-twenties.	5 or 20 years.	After April 30, 1867.	6 per cent..	Par ..	$515, 000, 000	$514, 780, 500	$514, 780, 500 00
United States notes, new issue.	....	....	None	Par ..	450, 000, 000	....	432, 687, 966 00
Temp'y loan..	Not less than 30 days.	After ten days' notice.	4, 5, and 6 per ct.	Par ..	150, 000, 000	....	89, 717, 061 40
Loan of 1863..	....	After June 30, 1881.	6 per ct....	Pr'm. 4. 13 p. c.	75, 000, 000	75, 000, 000	75, 000, 000 00
Treasury notes.	2 years.	2 years after date.	5 per ct....	Par ..	....	} 211, 000, 000	42, 336, 710 00
	1 year..	1 year after date.	5 per ct....	Par ..	} 400, 000, 000		
Treas'y notes.	3 years	3 years after date.	6 p.c. comp. interest.	Par ..	....	17, 250, 000	15, 000, 000 00
Ten-forties	10 or 40 years.	After Feb. 28, '74.	5 per ct....	Par ..	200, 000, 000	172, 770, 100	172, 770, 100 00
Certificates of indebtedness.	1 yr..	1 year after date.	6 per ct....	Par ..	Not specified.	....	115, 772, 000 00
Postal currency	....	....	....	Par ..	Not specified.	20, 192, 456	9, 915, 408 66
Fractional currency.	....	....	....	Par ..	50, 000, 000	....	15, 090, 420 10

No. 5.—*Statement of the indebtedness*

	Acts authorizing loans, and synopsis of same.
Act of June 30, 1864....	Authorized the issue of $400,000,000 of bonds redeemable at the pleasure of the government after any period not less than five nor more than thirty years, or, if deemed expedient, made payable at any period not more than forty years from date. And said bonds shall bear an annual interest not exceeding 6 per centum, payable semi-annually in coin. And the Secretary of the Treasury may dispose of such bonds, or any part thereof, and of any bonds commonly known as five-twenties, remaining unsold, on such terms as he may deem most advisable, for lawful money of the United States, or, at his discretion, for treasury notes, certificates of indebtedness, or certificates of deposit, issued under any act of Congress.
	Also, authorizes the issue of and in lieu of an equal amount of bonds authorized by the first section, and as a part of said loan, not exceeding $200,000,000 in treasury notes of any denomination not less than $10, payable at any time not exceeding three years from date, or, if thought more expedient, redeemable at any time after three years from date, and bearing interest not exceeding the rate of 7 3-10 per centum, payable in lawful money at maturity, or, at the discretion of the Secretary, semi-annually; and such of them as shall be made payable, principal and interest, at maturity, shall be a legal tender to the same extent as United States notes, for their face value, excluding interest, and may be paid to any creditor of the United States, at their face value, excluding interest, or to any creditor willing to receive them at par, including interest; and any treasury notes issued under the authority of this act may be made convertible, at the discretion of the Secretary of the Treasury, into any bonds issued under the authority of this act, and the Secretary may redeem and cause to be cancelled and destroyed any treasury notes or United States notes heretofore issued under authority of previous acts of Congress, and substitute in lieu thereof an equal amount of treasury notes, such as are authorized by this act, or of other United States notes; nor shall any treasury note bearing interest issued under this act be a legal tender in payment or redemption of any notes issued by any bank, banking association, or banker, calculated or intended to circulate as money.
Act of Jan. 28, 1865.....	Whole amount may be issued in bonds or treasury notes, at the discretion of the Secretary.
Acts of July 1, 1862, and July 2, 1864.	Bonds issued to the Central Pacific Railroad Company in accordance with these acts.
Act of March 3, 1865....	Authorized an issue of $600,000,000 in bonds or treasury notes; bonds may be made payable at any period not more than forty years from date of issue, or may be made redeemable at the pleasure of the government, at or after any period not less than five years, nor more than forty years from date, or may be made redeemable and payable as aforesaid, as may be expressed upon their face, and so much thereof as may be issued in treasury notes may be made convertible into any bonds authorized by this act, and be of such denominations, not less than fifty dollars, and bear such dates, and be made redeemable or payable at such periods as the Secretary of the Treasury may deem expedient. The interest on the bonds payable semi-annually, on treasury notes semi-annually, or annually, or at maturity thereof, and the principal or interest, or both, be made payable in coin or other lawful money; if in coin, not to exceed 6 per centum per annum; when not payable in coin, not to exceed 7 3-10 per centum per annum. Rate and character to be expressed on bonds or treasury notes.

of the United States, June 30, 1865—Continued.

Title.	Length of loan.	When redeemable.	Rate of interest.	Price of emission.	Amount authorized.	Amount issued.	Amount outstanding June 30, 1865.
Five-twenties.	5 or 20 years.	After Nov. 1, 1865.	6 per cent..	......	....	$91,789,000	$91,789,000 00
Treasury notes.	3 years.	3 years after date.	6 per cent. comp. int.	......	Substitute red'd 5 p.c. notes.	168,661,290	178,756,080 00
Treasury notes.	3 years.	3 years after date.	6 per cent. comp. int.	......	....	10,094,790	
....	....	....	....	......	$400,000,000		
7.30 treasury notes.	3 years.	3 years after Aug. 15, 1864.	7.30 per c.	Par..	....	234,400,000	234,400,000 00
Central Pacific R. R. Co. bonds.	30 yrs..	'After Jan. 15, 1895.	6 per cent..	Par..	....	1,258,000	1,258,000 00
7 3-10 treasury notes, three issues.	3 yrs.	After Aug. 14, '67. After June 14, '68. After July 14, '68.	7 3-10 per cent.	Par..	600,000,000	437,210,400	437,210,400 00
							2,682,593,026 53

No. 6.

Paper money circulation and domestic exports.

TREASURY DEPARTMENT, *November* 29, 1865.

An unprecedented increase in the quantity of breadstuffs and provisions exported from the loyal States to foreign countries in the fiscal years 1861, '62, '63 and '64, concurring with a vast increase in the amount of currency in circulation, and a consequent enhancement of the premium upon foreign bills of exchange, as measured by the currency, has been taken to prove that the increase of these exports is due to the excess of paper money in use, or to the high currency price of foreign bills corresponding to its rate of depreciation in gold value.

The history of our domestic exports and bank issues during thirty-five years preceding the outbreak of the rebellion affords no evidence that high prices at home, or an over-abundance of paper money, whether redeemable or irredeemable, ever had the effect of stimulating exportation. The official tables of domestic exports show a seeming concurrence of the kind in the years 1854, '55, '56 and '57, but other causes are readily found for the very considerable growth of our foreign commerce in this period, showing that it had no dependence upon the accompanying increase of paper money circulation.

For the purpose of presenting the facts as they bear upon this question, our export trade in domestic products with the cotemporaneous movements in bank circulation are here given in groups of years, which most clearly exhibit their respective fluctuations. In this statement the exports of breadstuffs and provisions, those of cotton wool, all other than these, and the totals, exclusive of specie, are distinguished. The bank circulation of each period is stated in its average amount *per capita*, for the purpose of showing its relative supply, as well as this method of measuring the business requirements of the time can do; and the percentage of increase and decrease serves for a readier apprehension of the movements in the several divisions of commerce here adopted, and in the paper money circulation of the same periods.

Statement showing the fluctuations of bank note circulation in the United States, the exports of domestic produce, exclusive of specie, and the rates per cent. of increase and decrease in each, in periods, from the year 1825 to 1860.

GROUPS OF YEARS.	Breadstuffs and provisions.	Per cent. increase or decrease.	Cotton.	Per cent. increase or decrease.	All other exports.	Per cent. increase or decrease.	Total exports.	Per cent. increase or decrease.	Average circulation in capita.	Per cent. increase or decrease.
1825–'32, 8 years	12.9	....	28.4	....	16.4	....	57.7	....	$4 74	....
1833–'36, 4 years	12.1	— 6.0	55.5	+ 95.0	21.8	+ 33.0	89.4	+ 55.0	7 10	+ 49.0
1837–'38, 2 years	9.6	— 20.0	62.4	+ 12.0	22.9	+ 5.0	94.9	+ 6.0	8 35	+ 17.0
1839–'45, 7 years	16.2	+ 68.0	54.6	— 12.0	17.0	— 26.0	87.8	— 7.0	5 16	— 38.0
1846–'47, 2 years	48.2	+200.0	42.6	— 22.0	35.3	+108.0	126.1	+ 43.0	5 08	— 1.0
1848–'53, 6 years	30.4	— 37.0	85.0	+100.0	36.1	+ 2.0	151.5	+ 20.0	5 34	+ 5.0
1854–'57, 4 years	64.1	+111.0	110.4	+ 30.0	63.7	+ 76.4	238.3	+ 57.3	7 30	+ 36.7
1858–'60, 3 years	44.7	— 43.5	161.5	+ 46.3	75.8	+ 19.0	282.0	+ 18.3	6 08	— 16.7

Exports of breadstuffs and provisions in connexion with the supply of bank currency.

During the eight years 1825–'32 the bank circulation never exceeded sixty-one millions, or an average *per capita* of the total population of $4 74, and the average export of breadstuffs and provisions was twelve and nine-tenths millions of dollars. In the next four years (1833–'36) the circulation rose to $7 10, an increase of 49 per cent.; but these exports fell to twelve and one-tenth millions, a decline of 6½ per cent. In the years 1837–'38 the circulation varied from $9 46 to $7 20, averaging $8 35, an increase of 76 per cent. upon the first-mentioned period; yet these exports fell to nine and six-tenths millions, a decrease of above 25 per cent. The average exports of the next following seven years (1839–'45) were sixteen and two-tenths millions, an increase of 68 per cent. over the immediately preceding period; but the circulation averaged only $5 16 *per capita,* a decrease of 38 per cent.

In the years 1846–'47 our exports of breadstuffs and provisions, under the great demand occasioned by the scarcity in Europe, which commenced in 1846 and amounted to a famine in Ireland in 1847, rose to forty-eight and two-tenths millions, or quite 200 per cent. above those of the next previous period, although the circulation declined 1 per cent.; and the next six years (1848–'53) show a decline of 37 per cent. in these exports, with an increase of 5 per cent. in the circulation.

The four fiscal years 1854–'57 present the first and last concurrence of an excessive currency and enhanced exports of food in any period previous to the rebellion, the former rising nearly 37 per cent. and the latter 111 per cent. upon the average of the preceding six years. But it must be recollected here that the Crimean war actually commenced in March, 1854, with preparation made in the preceding winter, and ended in April, 1856. France, England, Sardinia, Turkey, and Russia were all involved in it, which sufficiently accounts for the very considerable enhancement of all branches of our foreign commerce, except in cotton, the regular increase in which was naturally checked during the period. In 1857 these exports fell off about three millions, but were still at twenty-five millions, or 50 per cent. above those of the next following year, and during this year our chief customer had a war in Persia, another in China, and the great mutiny in India upon her hands. All this very well accounts for an increase of thirty-four millions a year in our provision exports over the undisturbed previous period from 1848 to 1853. In September, 1857, a general bank suspension showed that the circulation had been during four years in excess of legitimate business requirements, standing in the first three at full 40 per cent. above the safe average *per capita,* and rising to 43 per cent. nearly in the year of the explosion.

In the three years 1858–'60 the prices of American breadstuffs and provisions fell in the English market 33 per cent. below those of 1854–'57, and our exports declined 43½ per cent., although the currency was still at least 17 per cent. *per capita* above the safe supply, and tending again, as shown by its still further increase of about 3 per cent. more on the 1st of January, 1861, to an early revulsion, if the rebellion had not brought with it a release of the banks from the obligation to redeem their notes in any better currency.

It will be noticed that from 1839 to 1853, inclusive, the average circulation did not vary more than 26 cents *per capita,* standing very uniformly through these fifteen years at about $5 20. Now, in this period our domestic exports, exclusive of specie and cotton, rose from forty and four-tenths to eighty and four-tenths millions, or 100 per cent., while in the seven years, 1854 to 1860, when the circulation ranged near two hundred millions, and full 30 per cent. *per capita* above the average of the fifteen preceding years, the same kinds of exports rose only from one hundred and twenty-one and a half to one hundred and twenty-four and a half millions, or $2\frac{3}{8}$ per cent. Moreover, the exports of food included in these amounts fell from near sixty-six milliohs in 1854, the first year of the Crimean war, to forty-five and a quarter millions in 1860. It is true that cotton rose in the same time from ninety-three and a half to one hundred and sixty-two millions, swelling the total exports materially; but it will not be claimed that the state of the currency is to be credited with this result. A common cause could not have operated so unequally upon these different branches of our commerce, and the inquiry may be settled, after a fair exami- nation of all the facts, in the clear conclusion that in all the fluctuations of our foreign commerce and bank circulation, occurring in thirty-five years before the rebellion, no fact sustains the notion that an excessive or depreciated currency favors exportation. The real causes of extraordinary increase in the exports we have found in an increased demand in the foreign markets, occasioned either by failures of their own crops or the increased demand of their wars, helped sometimes by the decline of prices arising from our own superabundance of agri- cultural products.

During the period of the rebellion our exports have been reported in irre- deemable currency prices. Any calculation made upon the figures in which the values are expressed, and any efforts made to ascertain the concurrent quantities of paper money in active circulation at the several stages of change in the pro- duce movements, would be at once very difficult and unreliable; still, we have command of such data as may throw some light upon the question with which we are here concerned.

In the fiscal years 1862, '63, and '64 the exports of cotton have no proper bearing upon this inquiry. The leading manufactures, which, from their variety of kinds, have no common measure but their aggregate value, stood very evenly at thirty-five millions in each of the three years, the currency prices of 1863 and 1864 being reduced to the gold standard. In the years 1858, '59, '60, and '61 they averaged forty-one millions—so there was no increase in the quantity of these exports, but a falling off of about 15 per cent.

In the three years 1858, '59, and '60 all exports, other than specie, cotton, and breadstuffs and provisions, ranged from sixty-nine to seventy-nine millions in the year, averaging seventy-five and eight-tenths millions. In 1862, '63, and '64 they varied from sixty-one to seventy-two millions, giving an average of sixty-five and a half millions a year, the currency prices of 1863 and 1864 being, as before, reduced to the gold standard. Here again there is no increase of quantity, measured by values, but a decrease of over 13 per cent. These points settled, our question is cleared of its disturbing elements. The inquiry is now limited to the exports of breadstuffs and provisions, and the supposed effect of an enormously inflated currency upon them. We will take of these wheat and wheat flour, and hams and bacon, as the chief and the fair representatives of the whole.

In the fiscal years 1854, '55, '56, and '57 the exports of wheat, in grain and flour, amounted to ninety-four millions of bushels, and of hams and bacon to one hundred and sixty-nine and three-quarters millions of pounds. In 1858, '59, and '60 the wheat export was fifty-eight and three-quarters millions bushels; the hams and bacon fifty-eight and three-quarters millions of pounds. In the four fiscal years 1861, '62, '63, and '64 our total exports of wheat and wheat flour, reduced to wheat, rose to 214,135,710 bushels—an increase of 128 per cent., or two and a quarter times the quantity exported in the European war period, 1854, '55, '56, and '57; and of hams and bacon, 520,607,108 pounds— an increase upon the same period of $206\frac{1}{2}$ per cent., or more than three times the quantity. If the first three of these years be compared with 1858, '59, and '60— three years of ordinary causes of demand in Europe—the wheat export rises to two and three-quarter times, and the hams and bacon to nearly eight times.

Once before, in the Irish famine year, we increased our total exports of bread-stuffs and provisions in a single year 148 per cent., or two and a half times their value in the next preceding year. And again, in 1854, we doubled them in one year, and sustained them at this proportion for four years together, under the demand created by European wars on the continent and in Asia. But these instances only serve to show our ability to answer any demand that the rest of the world is occasionally compelled to make upon us. They do not explain the immense consumption of American food in the years under consideration.

Without looking to other causes, the prices at which these commodities were sold in the foreign markets show reasons for a largely increased consumption there. Great Britain and Ireland in the five years 1860-'64 took 71½ per cent. of our total exports of wheat and flour, and 84 per cent. of the hams and bacon. The prices at which these were sold in the United Kingdom may therefore be taken to indicate the gold value of the whole export of the period to foreign countries.

In the following table we give the imports of wheat, and wheat flour in its equivalent in wheat, with the computed real value, and the prices of hams and bacon, imported from the United States, as they are found in the publications of the British Parliament:

Calendar years	Wheat.	Price per quarter.	PRICE PER CWT.	
			Hams.	Bacon.
	Cwt.	*s. d.*	*s. d.*	*s. d.*
1854, '55, '56, and '57	20,771,740	71 0	66 1	49 6
1858 and '59	5,213,289	47 8	57 9	46 9
1860	9,315,123	57 8	68 9	53 5
1861	15,610,472	55 2	47 0	48 2
1862	21,765,087	50 3	35 5	35 1
1863	11,869,179	43 9	33 2	26 11
1864	10,077,431	38 0	....	....
1865, (6 months)	907,224	37 3	....	....

NOTE.—The wheat may be approximately rendered into bushels by multiplying the hundred-weights by two, and into quarters by dividing the same figures by four. The changes in the quantities of hams and bacon correspond sufficiently well with those of flour and wheat for our purpose. The prices of these for 1864 and 1865 cannot be obtained with precision, but they seem to have fallen nearly in the same ratio as wheat and flour.

Previous to the year 1860, whenever wheat fell to forty-one or forty-two shillings per quarter in England, our exports to the United Kingdom were merely nominal. In 1859, the price being so low as forty-three shillings and tenpence, our exports fell off to 861,000 bushels. In 1858 the price was forty-eight shillings, and our exports were nine and a half millions of bushels. The price has ranged from forty-one to seventy-one shillings in an interval of four years. Among all the leading commodities of commerce, scarcely one can be found so variant in price as wheat and wheat flour, and very few whose prices so greatly affect the consumption in Europe. There are twenty millions of people in Great Britain and Ireland whose necessary expenditures are so near their income, that they must economize closely when prices rule but little higher than the lowest rates. These people can easily increase their consumption of wheat thirty millions of bushels per annum, when its cost declines as much as the above statement shows, in the period of the prodigious increase of our exports, which supplied two-thirds of the excess of consumption of the four years 1861, '62, '63, and '64.

The prices of nineteen years of peace, from 1829 to 1847, give fifty-seven shillings and tenpence as their average. We may therefore take 57.8 as it stood in 1860 for the medium or fair and moderate rate, and from it estimate the constant and rapid decrease of price which we assume as the true cause of the inordinately large consumption in the four following years. Thus measured, the decrease of price is 4½ per cent. in 1860, 12¾ in 1862, 24 in 1863, and nearly 34 in 1864; four years in which the aggregate American exports of wheat and wheat flour went to the prodigious figure of one hundred and eighteen and a half millions of bushels, or twenty-nine and a half millions per annum. The thing to be explained, however, is, how our farmers could afford to sell such enormous quantities of their produce at prices so much lower than they ever before touched in the foreign market, without either greatly diminishing or entirely stopping exportation.

The solution is found in the fact that while they sold at a very low price in gold, they were paid in an unusually high price in the currency in use at home, which, being a legal tender, was worth its face value, without any discount or depreciation, in the payment of debts contracted before this period at the gold standard of prices. A vast amount of such debt is known to have been discharged in this way. In 1864, when the foreign price of wheat went down to about four shillings and ninepence per bushel, covering freight, insurance, commissions, and all intermediate charges and profits, which still further reduced the gold price to the producers, they could still afford to send to England twenty million bushels, the premium upon gold, due to the depreciation of our currency, ranging from 51 to 185 per cent., and all that premium going dollar for dollar, to the extent so applied, in the discharge of old debts. Roughly averaged, the varying premiums of the year were equal to 104 per cent., which quite doubled the farmer's share of the four and ninepence per bushel paid for his wheat in England, when converted into currency at home.

But the agriculturists, owning the farms which they cultivated, and the stock and machinery which they used, had another advantage in the premium, whether they had debts to pay or not. They held their lands, buildings, stock, and implements of husbandry at the gold price of the previous period, and had no expenses of husbandry to meet in the high currency prices of the time, except wages, improvements, repairs, and taxes. These are but a small portion of their investment, and upon all the rest of it its proportion of the premium was clear gain, but in currency, whose purchasing power was measured by the ruling prices, unless invested in government bonds bearing gold interest. Farmers breeding their own stock had a similar profit on the premium to those who owned the lands which they cultivated. The same reasoning applies also to miners, in the proportion that their mines and machinery bear to their total outlay. But to manufacturers the profit of the premium upon foreign sales would only accrue in the proportion of their real estate and machinery bought at the gold prices of the preceding period; all other elements of production to them cost currency prices; and these are so considerable that their exports would bear but little reduction in gold prices—certainly not enough to make or command a foreign market, as we have already seen in the fact that the exports of the leading manufactures of the country actually fell off, while the products of agriculture so greatly increased.

It is held by the authorities on this subject that enhancement of the nominal exchange, or that portion of the expressed rate which is due to depreciation of the currency, can have no effect upon foreign trade, for the reason that where such depreciation exists, the premium which the exporter of commodities derives from the sale of a bill of exchange on a foreign customer is only equivalent to the increase of the price to the exporter occasioned by such depreciation. This is true, doubtless, where all the elements and the whole cost of production are equally enhanced and in equal proportion to the depreciation of the currency; but the facts of our recent history require a modification of this general proposition.

There is a limit, also, to the operation of the causes which we find stimulating exportation of our breadstuffs and provisions. When the foreign gold price falls below a given mark, the premium must hold a relatively high rate, or the trade is checked. In the first eight months of the current calendar year (1865) the imports of wheat, in grain and flour, from the United States into England, fell to a trifle more than one-eighth of the quantity imported in 1864, and to one-sixteenth of the year 1862. The British prices had gone down in these eight months to thirty-seven shillings and three pence per quarter, and the average premium on gold had fallen from 104 to 65 per cent.

The foreign market gorged, and the currency at home recovering itself, tend together to level exchange to its real rate, and as soon as the rate of premium fails to carry the foreign prices up to the actual cost of production exportation must stop.

Respectfully submitted :

WILLIAM ELDER.

Hon. HUGH McCULLOCH,
    Secretary of the Treasury.

REPORT OF COMPTROLLER OF THE CURRENCY.

OFFICE OF THE COMPTROLLER OF THE CURRENCY,
Washington, December 4; 1865.

SIR: I have the honor to transmit to the House of Representatives the annual report of the Comptroller of the Currency, as required by the 61st section of the national currency act.

I have the honor to be, very respectfully, your obedient servant,
FREEMAN CLARKE,
Comptroller of the Currency.

Hon. SCHUYLER COLFAX,
Speaker of the House of Representatives.

REPORT.

Since the last annual report from this office two hundred and eighty-three new banks have been organized, and seven hundred and thirty-one State banks converted into national associations, making the total number organized to November first sixteen hundred and one; of which six hundred and seventy-nine were new banks, and nine hundred and twenty-two were conversions from State banks.

A statement of the respective States and Territories in which each bank is located, the paid-in capital, the currency delivered to each, and the bonds deposited with the Treasurer to secure their notes is herewith submitted; also a detailed statement of the affairs of each bank on the first Monday of October last, with an abstract of their condition on that day, an abstract of the condition of all the banks on the first days of January, April, and July, 1865; together with the names and compensation of the clerks and other employés, and the total expenses of the bureau, for the fiscal year ending June 30, 1865.

One bank has voluntarily gone into liquidation, and has been closed under the provisions of the law, viz:

First National Bank, Columbia, Mo.:

Circulation outstanding	$11,990
Circulation redeemed	78,010

Lawful money has been deposited with the Treasurer for the redemption of the outstanding notes of the above-named bank, and the bonds withdrawn.

The First National Bank of Attica, N. Y., has failed, and a receiver has been appointed to close up its affairs. Its outstanding circulation, none of which has been presented for redemption, is $44,000, secured by $31,500 of six per cent. and $18,500 of five per cent. bonds.

By section 44 of the national currency act any bank incorporated by special law, or banking institution organized under a general law of any State, is permitted, on the performance of certain specified requirements, to be converted into a national association, with the same powers and privileges, and subject to the same duties, responsibilities, and rules as are prescribed for the associations originally organized under that law.

By the seventh section of the act amending the "Act to provide internal revenue to support the government," approved March 3, 1865, the privilege of conversion on the part of State banks was extended, so as to give a preference to those which should apply prior to the first day of July, 1865, over new associations applying for the privileges of the national currency act.

The result has been that nearly all of the State banks have voluntarily changed into national associations, and it is a gratifying fact that this transformation has been accomplished without deranging the business of these institutions, or affecting essentially the volume of bank note circulation. Since the amendment of the act, no national currency has been delivered to a converted State bank, until the circulation issued by it under State laws, had been reduced below the amount to which its capital as a national bank would have entitled it under the law; and as many of the converted banks had a greater amount of State notes in circulation than they were entitled to under the national act, the result has been to diminish rather than increase the volume of bank note circulation.

This restrictive course in reference to State bank circulation, has been the cause of great complaint on the part of many of the banks, more so, perhaps, for the reason that in several States the enabling acts giving consent to the conversion of the State banks to national associations, contain provisions nominally giving the right to converted banks to continue the issue of their State circulation for a limited time, after the conversion is completed.

It is, however, very clear that it is not the spirit or intent of the law to allow any national bank to have a greater circulation than the amount prescribed in the act, and that after a bank becomes a national association it is, as provided in the 44th section of the law, subject to and bound to observe all its provisions. A converted State bank is unquestionably bound to redeem its State circulation and discharge all the obligations of the State institution, while any State enactments granting privileges or imposing restrictions in conflict with or repugnant to the United States laws are necessarily void.

The national currency act permits the conversion of State into national institutions without reference to State laws, and it must be conceded that the laws of the United States are paramount to State enactments. The 23d section of the act prohibits national banks from issuing or circulating as money any notes other than such as are authorized by the provisions of the national currency act. If a national bank converted from a State institution pays out and circulates the notes of the State bank which it is bound to redeem, it certainly issues notes prohibited by the act.

If the rights of converted banks to reissue the notes of the State bank, and also to receive national notes to the amount that their capital entitled them to were recognized they would have had a double circulation, and the aggregate at this time would probably have been two-fold the amounts of their present issues.

The amount of national bank notes in actual circulation on the
1st day of October last, was $171, 321 903

The amount of State bank notes in circulation at the same date, as appears by returns to the Commissioner of Internal Revenue, was 78, 867, 575

Making the bank circulation on the 1st day of October last...   250, 189, 478

The amount of legal-tender notes and fractional currency issued and outstanding on the 1st of October, 1865, was.........   704, 584, 658
National bank notes in the hands of banks not yet issued....   19, 525, 152
National currency yet to be issued to banks 109, 152, 945

Making the aggregate amount of legal-tender and bank notes in circulation as authorized to be issued to and by the banks*.   1, 083, 452, 233

---

* All statements and comparisons in this report are made up to the 1st of October last, that being the date of the last quarterly return from the banks.

From which sum should be deducted, State
bank circulation now outstanding that will be
retired about as fast as national currency is
issued to converted banks.................. $78,867,575
Also the amount of "compound interest notes"
converted into 5·20 bonds since the 1st of
October last........................... 44,417,329
                                                            ──────────── 123,284,904

The amount then left as the available currency of the country
is   960,167,326

In order to ascertain the amount of actual
active 'circulation on the 1st day of October
last, there should be deducted from the last
mentioned sum—
The amount of national currency delivered to
banks, and not then in circulation........ $19,525,152
National circulation not delivered to banks ... 109,152,945
Amount of legal-tender notes held by banks, including $74,261,847 compound interest notes, 193,094,365
Compound interest notes, other than those held
by banks, mostly held as investments by insurance and trust companies and savings banks,
less say $10,000,000 in actual circulation... 121,314,195
Currency in the treasury of the United States, 56,236,440
                                                            ────────────
        Total...................................   499,323,097

Which will show the actual circulation to be...............   460,844,229

This favorable exhibit of the amount of paper in actual circulation, is owing
in a great degree to the accumulation of currency in the hands of the banks, in
the absence of the great demands of the government for currency since the close
of the war.

As an erroneous impression may prevail as to the aggregate amount of lawful money that banks are required to hold, it is thought proper to state that as
the liabilities stood on the first day of October the required sum was $74,261,847
over the amount that banks were permitted to have to their credit, and count
as part of the same, in banks acting as redeeming agents. The banks held at
that time $14,966,143 in coin, which, deducted from $74,261,847, leaves
$59,295,704, the sum that they should have held in legal-tender notes to fulfil
the requirements of the law.

It will be seen, therefore, that the sum held, in lawful money, in excess of
the required reserve, was $170,045,896.

It cannot be necessary to dilate upon the inevitable consequences which must
result from this excessive amount of irredeemable currency, if left uncontrolled
by the action of government in respect to the reduction of its own issues, and
in enforcing a system of redemption which shall curtail by its operations the
power and tendency to expansion. So far as bank issues are concerned it is
believed that the most efficient check would be found in its compulsory redemption in the great financial and commercial centres of the country—New York,
Boston, or Philadelphia. Under such a system, properly enforced, many insti-

tutions established chiefly for the advantage arising from the issue of their own promises, without the expectation of being called upon to redeem them, would find that they had exceeded the requirements of legitimate business, and obtain relief in the abatement of their issues. The circulation thus withdrawn from sections where it is not required, could be dispensed to other portions of the country as yet but partially supplied with banking institutions.

In this manner, also, would a remedy be furnished for the unequal distribution which has resulted from the act of the 3d of March last, giving the preference to the conversion of State banks over applications for new national associations, without reference to the amount of currency which by such conversion has been concentrated in localities where the former institutions were the most numerous.

The national banks already organized embody a capital sufficient to entitle them to receive $309,672,992 of circulation on the deposit of the requisite securities in government bonds. It is not anticipated, however, that more than three hundred millions will be called for by banks now organized, as many of them, located in large cities of the northern States, will not ask for the amount of circulation to which their capital entitles them. Bonds have been deposited to entitle the banks now organized to $244,754,125 of circulation only. In no event will the limit of the act be exceeded.

Whatever may have been the intention of the framers of the federal constitution in respect to the measure of value to be used in the transaction of business during a time of peace, and in the ordinary flow of events, there is ample justification for a departure from a metallic currency and a bank circulation redeemable in specie on demand, in the necessities of the country as superinduced by the unparallelled civil war through which the nation has been called to pass. Now, however, that the emergency which called for this departure from first principles has happily been surmounted, it would seem to be the dictate of sound policy to return as speedily as the financial condition of the government and the business interests of the country will allow to a more normal condition of the currency, so that the pecuniary relations subsisting between ourselves and other nations may be placed upon a more harmonious basis of value.

The evils resulting from an irredeemable currency are too well known to require enumeration. They should be tolerated no longer than absolute necessity requires. The funding, and the consequent retirement of a portion of the inactive circulation shown to be now held in reserve, and liable to be called out as increased speculations and additional enhancement of prices may demand, and the consequent reduction of the same to the amount required by the actual necessities of business would seem to constitute one of the first steps towards that sound condition of finance under which alone a permanent prosperity can be secured. By such a course only can we place the manufacturing and producing interests of the country in a position to compete successfully with other nations, prevent an excess of imports over exports, and thus prevent a drain upon our resources, which must otherwise postpone to an indefinite period the resumption of specie payments.

Under the present inflation of prices the cost of labor and of all the elements entering into the production of staple commodities, whether in agriculture, mechanics, or manufactures, is such as to invite the direct competition of all other countries in our own markets. It is this which makes our market the best to sell in and the worst to buy in on the part of foreigners, and which, in the consequent absence of an adequate export demand, must eventuate in the denuding us of the precious metals and the creation of a debt abroad that will be a greater drain upon our resources than our present national debt.

By a gold valuation of our imports and exports, the balance that has accrued

5 F

against this country during the four years previous to the 30th day of June last, including the interest on American securities held abroad purchased within that time, and also taking into due consideration the difference between the standard of our own and that of foreign gold, (nine and three-eighths per cent.,) has been $308,000,000 of dollars.

By reason of the probable falling off in the export of coin, and the increased amount of interest to be paid abroad, it is estimated that the accruing balance during the present fiscal year will amount to $120,000,000, making a total for five years of $428,000,000.

Our only resource to pay this gold balance against us has been and still is the sale of our securities abroad. The amount required, if sold at an average discount of forty per cent., will be $713,000,000, and the annual interest at six per cent. will be $42,780,000. The discount of forty per cent. will amount to $285,200,000; every dollar of which will be an entire loss to the country.

The almost exclusive use and demand for gold now is for the payment of custom duties to be paid out again for the interest on the public debt; this is followed by the sale of the surplus beyond the amount required to pay the interest, which surplus again accumulates to go repeatedly through the same process. If one-half of the differences between our imports and exports were paid in gold as they occur, the price of gold and foreign exchange would have long since reached a rate sufficiently high to have materially checked our imports and increased in a corresponding ratio our exports. The price of gold is now governed by the demand for the purposes stated, and the foreign balances against us are paid as before shown, by the sale abroad of government and other securities at a discount of about forty per cent.; thus instead of paying, creating an additional indebtedness to the extent of the difference between the amount received for our securities and their par value, every fraction of which we shall ultimately have to pay in gold, in addition to the interest. It may be said that our exports will be increased by the addition of southern productions. This will undoubtedly be so; but to no greater extent than our imports will increase. The south will need more than all the goods her surplus crops will purchase, and if we cannot compete in the open market with other nations, our relative position in reference to imports and exports will not be improved.

In view of our position, prudential considerations would seem to point to such an adjustment of the tariff, intermediate to the resumption of specie payments, as to discourage inordinate importations; this can be done by increasing the rate of duties just in proportion as the price of gold and foreign exchange may recede, thus keeping up the cost of importations as high as they now are, including the present rate of foreign exchange. This could be followed by a graduated reduction of such increase, say ten per cent., at the expiration of each six months, until brought down to the original rate. Imports would be held back in view of such reduction, and there would be no overwhelming crash resulting from a sudden fall of prices, but business would adjust itself to the present and prospective condition in which it would be placed under the legislation indicated. In the mean time, by a steady reduction of the volume of irredeemable currency and consequent reduction of prices, we would be able once more to place our manufactured and agricultural productions on a footing that would enable them to enter into successful competition with those of other nations in the markets of the world.

As the first step to be taken towards a reduction of the government issues used as currency, sound policy would indicate the conversion of all the interest-bearing legal-tender notes into 5-20 six per cent. bonds. It is believed that the slight contraction caused by such conversion would be scarcely perceptible, more especially at this time, as it is not probable that more than five per cent.

of the whole issue is now in active circulation. It would be simply exchanging one security held as an investment for another.

The national banks alone, as shown by their reports, held on the first of October last $193,094,365 in legal-tender notes, or $22,772,462 more than the whole amount of their national bank circulation at that time; they also held in notes of other banks $16,247,241, and of their own notes not in circulation $19,526,152, making a total of unemployed circulation in the hands of national banks $228,966,758, which is several millions more than the entire paper circulation of the country on the first of January, 1861, or at any previous period.

In view of the urgent demand that will undoubtedly be made for an increase of the national bank circulation, and as a gentle mode of further reducing the volume of legal-tender notes, it is suggested that the national currency act be so amended as to allow an increase of the limit to four hundred millions of dollars, on conditions only, that all the banks be required to redeem their notes in New York, Boston, or Philadelphia; and also that an issue of six per cent. 5-20 bonds be authorized to the amount that it will require to secure the additional circulation under the provisions of the act, which bonds the banks, when organized, shall purchase as each may require of the Secretary of the Treasury at such fair rate as he may from time to time prescribe, but not less than their par value, and pay for the same in the United States legal-tender notes, and all notes so received shall be cancelled and destroyed. The bonds so issued would not affect the price or demand for other bonds, as they would be held as security for the circulation, and only offered in market in the event of the failure or closing of a bank.

With the requirement to redeem at the central and accessible points mentioned, there would be but little danger of bank issues exceeding the limits prescribed by the demands of legitimate business.

Under the action indicated, it is believed that the balance of trade with other nations would within a reasonable time be again turned in favor of this country; whenever that point is reached, with the perfect confidence which would ensue in the convertibility of legal-tender notes and the stability of sound bank circulation, the return to and maintenance of specie payments would be rendered comparatively easy, and the demand for gold be confined to the healthful and legitimate adjustment of balances with foreign countries.

Although of comparitively recent origin, and yet in the infancy of its development, the national banking system has become thoroughly interwoven with all the business and interests of the country. Not only the stockholders in the national banks, but every member of the community has an immediate interest in the stability of a currency which forms the medium of exchange and value, not in isolated sections of the country between particular classes, but throughout the length and breadth of the land, and by every citizen of the republic. And this system, so ramified and so essential to the prosperity of all classes, is based upon the national faith and credit as its chief corner-stone, and can only exist as that credit is maintained intact.

Nobly have our citizens battled for the preservation of our institutions; freely have they poured out their blood and treasures to sustain the government in its contest with ruthless treason, and now that success has crowned their exertions and sacrifices, the maintenance of the national honor, through an unsullied public credit, becomes a no less imperative and solemn duty; nor can it be doubted that all just measures calculated to sustain the faith and integrity of the government will find a ready response from the patriotic masses.

The resources of the country are great beyond enumeration, the development of wealth rapid beyond precedent, and it requires only a judicious application of means to the end proposed to enable the government not only to meet all its pecuniary obligations with entire promptitude, but without imposing exactions that shall be unduly burdensome or give just cause of complaint to the people.

It is believed that from a few sources a revenue can be raised sufficient to meet the interest on the public debt, pay the ordinary expenses of government, and contribute thirty millions of dollars annually to a sinking fund that will pay the national debt in thirty-two years and a half.

The tariff can be so adjusted as to produce one hundred and twenty millions of dollars; one hundred millions can be raised on whiskey, malt liquors, and domestic wines; fifteen millions on tobacco; one hundred and twenty-five millions on cotton; fifteen millions from stamps; from licenses twenty millions, and from the premium on the surplus of gold, after paying interest on bonds, ten millions, making, in the aggregate, four hundred and five millions of dollars, a sum probably one hundred millions in excess of the amount that will be required under an economical administration of the government, leaving a large margin on the above estimate for reduction. The estimates, however, of the revenue derivable from the several sources indicated are not the result of loose conjecture, but each is founded upon a careful inquiry in reference to past productions and revenue under the existing law.

It is estimated that the cotton crop the next year will amount to between two and a half and three millions of bales; a tax of ten cents per pound on two and a half millions will produce one hundred and twenty-five millions of dollars. It is reasonable to suppose that the annual crop of cotton, after two or three years, will equal in amount the average of the crop for a few years previous to 1861, which was about four and a half millions of bales. A tax of eight cents per pound on that quantity would produce one hundred and eighty millions of dollars, a sum more than sufficient to pay the interest on the public debt after the entire amount is funded. The license and stamp duties could be dispensed with after the next fiscal year, and it is to be hoped that after that period no more income will be derived from premium on gold.

Three-fourths of the crops of cotton and tobacco are exported; that proportion therefore of the tax on those articles would be paid by foreign countries, and to that extent contribute to the liquidation of the public debt and relief of our own people.

A tax on cotton of eight or ten cents per pound would neither diminish the domestic production or foreign demand for that staple. Our means of production, natural and applied, are such as to enable us to furnish the article at a less price, including the tax proposed, than any other country. Even at half the price which this product now commands in New York and Liverpool it can be grown and sold at a large profit, including the proposed tax, in its cost. Nor would the imposition of a tax on the staple production of the southern States prove injurious to that section of the Union. It will of necessity be a large purchaser of northern manufactures, and if by the proposed measure the north and south be relieved almost entirely from other taxation for government purposes, as they would be if cotton is taxed to the extent proposed, their purchases would be made at a correspondingly less price, and both north and south derive a benefit from the operation.

By thus restricting the subject of revenue to a few articles of general production the cost of collection would be greatly reduced by the discharge of a whole army of assessors, collectors, &c., to the manifest advantage of the public treasury; nor would the least of the benefits to result from this action be found in the fact that such an adjustment of the system of taxation would leave no ground for public complaint, and consequently preclude *dishonest and disloyal politicians* from uniting with the *enemies of the Union* in assailing the public credit and repudiating the national obligations.

There is no question which more vitally concerns the national banking system than the power of the States to tax the government securities which form the invested capital of the banks organized under that system. Not only have their investments been made upon the solemn pledge of the national faith, held out to corporations and individuals, that their stocks should be "free from taxation by or under State authority ;" but the option of refraining from such investment was denied to the national banks, as it was by law made a fundamental condition to their existence that one-third of their capital should at all times be held in the form of national securities by the Treasurer of the United States ; and, in addition, every dollar of their circulating notes must be secured by a like deposit. Hence, while individuals might have refrained at their pleasure from placing confidence in the good faith of the government, these institutions were deprived of such liberty of action ; and now, while the right of individuals to immunity from taxation on government stocks is generally conceded, the like privilege is sought to be withdrawn from the national banks by their taxation for State, municipal, and local expenses. The constitutional ægis, which the Supreme Court of the United States has hitherto extended over the national securities, no matter by whom or for what purpose held, is now sought to be wrested from its hands upon the theory of State jurisdiction ; a flagrant violation of the contract entered into with the public creditors under the clearest enactments of law, and the most binding obligations of public faith. It is conceded for the most part by the advocates of State taxation, that the United States stocks in the hands of individuals cannot be assessed for State and municipal purposes. But a discrimination against the stocks held by banks is sought to be established, on the ground that a tax imposed upon the shares in a bank is not a tax upon the securities represented by those shares. That the position assumed by those who favor this hypothesis will be found, upon critical examination, to be fallacious can scarcely admit of a doubt ; that the discrimination in favor of one class of creditors and against another, both having complied with the same conditions, is grossly unjust, must be obvious to all. That exemption from State taxation was intended to apply to the stock issued, no matter in whose hands it might be found, cannot be questioned. No exception was made in favor of individuals ; no discrimination was attempted against banks. If the shares of a bank whose capital is invested in United States stocks be taxable, to whose benefit does the exemption from taxation guaranteed to those stocks inure ? Does the principle of immunity pledged by Congress become inoperative because an association has loaned to the government the money for which it holds those obligations ? Surely, the exemption belongs to some person, and to whom can it be assigned but to the respective stockholders, whose scrip simply represents the proportionate share which each has contributed to the purchase of the government securities. Upon the theory propounded, an individual who purchases one hundred thousand dollars of government stock for a specific purpose, may plead, and receive, the exemption from State taxation which the act of Congress pledges ; but if four persons purchase the like amount for a similar purpose, and each receives a certificate of the amount he has paid towards the gross investment, they lose all benefit of the immunity attached to the securities in hand. The injustice, if not the absurdity, of such discrimination must be sufficiently obvious.

Nor will the impropriety of the proposed taxation of national banks be less apparent, when it is borne in mind that they are already taxed by the general government to a greater extent than any other corporations or class of business. The law of their creation requires them to perform certain duties, and authorizes them to exercise certain privileges, yet for this they must pay a license. It imposes, also, a tax of one-half of one per cent. on their deposits, one per cent.

on their circulation, one per cent on their capital beyond the amount invested in government securities, and five per cent. on their income or earnings. All this is paid from the ordinary earnings of a bank, and reduces its profits to the extent of the taxes paid, whereas all other corporations, manufacturers, &c., are permitted to increase their rates and charges to a sum more than adequate to cover the amount of taxes paid, thus preserving their profits intact, and casting their burdens upon the public, in the capacity of consumers, travellers, &c.

It is not through palpable injustice to vested interests, and by a disgraceful violation of public faith, that the subject of State taxation should be reached If public policy demands a contribution to State and local expenses at the hands of these institutions, there is a mode of attainment not distant which can be reached without a breach of national honor. Nearly three-fourths of the public debt is either not funded, or matures at the option of the government, within a short period, and almost the whole amount within the next eight years. It is within the power of the government at such time, without violence to its engagements, to try the experiment of issuing bonds subject to State taxation, or of borrowing at a less rate of interest than is now paid, thus extinguishing its present obligations to its creditors. But every dictate of expediency and justice, its character and credit at home and abroad, demand that Congress and the highest judicial tribunal of the nation shall frown upon all attempts to override the constitutional functions indispensable to the preservation of the credit and stability of the government.

But as neither public policy nor constitutional right can at present allow the taxation of national banks for State and local purposes, it would be equitable that these institutions should pay, say one per cent., on their capital, (irrespective of the amount invested in public stocks,) in lieu of all present taxation for revenue purposes, and one-half of one per cent. on their circulation as an indemnity to the government for the expense incurred in furnishing the banks with circulating notes, and meeting the expenditures incidental to the administration of this bureau. Perhaps a preferable method in relation to the expenses thus incurred for circulation and supervision would be found in waiving the tax on circulation, and meeting the expenditures required by such direct assessment on the banks as should be equitable.

There are some amendments to the national currency act suggested by the experience of its practical workings, which, if adopted, would prove of great utility, the most important of which has already been alluded to—requiring banks to redeem their issues at par in either of the cities of New York, Boston, or Philadelphia, as the only certain method of securing for national bank notes a uniform par value in every section of the country, and prevent an excess of issues beyond the legitimate demands of business.

A penalty should be imposed upon banks for issuing notes with the engraved and printed signatures of the officers. The greatest protection against counterfeiting is found in the written signatures of those through whom the bills are uttered. The fact that they are written and not printed renders it incumbent on the counterfeiter to attempt an imitation through the same instrumentality on each note. He may make a fac simile of the signature once, but in the very next attempt make such a variation as to disclose the spurious character of the note. But a printed signature being once correctly imitated, the same result is produced at each revolution of the press with mechanical accuracy. Just as safely might the merchant send his notes to an engraver to have his signature and those of his indorsers stamped thereon, as for banks to have their notes executed through this process. Unless all possible guards which ingenuity can devise be thrown around the currency, it will soon be difficult to distinguish the spurious from the genuine issue, and banks will be as likely to redeem the former as those of their own promulgation.

By the first section of the national currency act, the bureau under which its operations were to be carried into effect, is made an adjunct of the Treasury Department, and of course located at Washington. During the incipiency of the measure there were many reasons rendering contiguity to the treasury desirable and proper; but now that the system has become operative, and what was theory at the first has been reduced to practice, there are many reasons which render it expedient that the operations of the currency bureau should be transferred to the great financial and business emporium of the country, the city of New York. Not only would the convenience of those concerned in the business of banking be promoted by the change of location, but a great saving in expense would thus be effected. Nearly two hundred thousand dollars per annum in express charges alone would be saved to the government and the banks by the change of location proposed; while the risk, loss of time, and personal expenses, which would thus be obviated, are large in the extreme. When the circulation now in use by the banks shall have become worn, and require renewal by exchange of old for new, the inconvenience, loss of interest, and expense, will be increased to a manifold extent.

The government already owns the buildings in New York which a transfer of the office would require for its accommodation, that are now rented for about the sum the Treasury Department is paying for an equal amount of room outside of the treasury building that would be vacated by the removal of the bureau. I am satisfied, therefore, that both the interests of the government, the public and the banks would be subserved by a transfer of the bureau to New York at an early day.

With a system of redemption properly enforced, the banks located out of the cities named as redeeming points, should be relieved from the obligation to keep a reserve equal to fifteen per cent. of their circulation and deposits constantly on hand. It would be a hardship to require banks to be prepared to redeem both at home and at one of the points indicated, and in addition to keep an idle reserve of fifteen per cent. against contingencies.

There is no real strength or safety derived from the provision as it exists. When a bank fails, neither money nor reserve in any shape would be found on hand, and the sooner those that are improperly conducted or are organized for other than a legitimate banking business are closed up, the better will it be for the system and the public.

By the 32d section of the act it is provided "that every association formed or existing under the provisions of this act shall take and receive at par, for any debt or liability to said association, any and all notes or bills issued by any association existing under and by virtue of this act."

The provision is anomalous in its character. To compel a bank to respond to the demands of its creditors in *lawful money*, and yet compel it to receive from its debtors such currency as they may choose to offer, does not seem to be warranted by equity or sound policy. It is even questioned whether a national bank is compelled to redeem its circulation at all, in lawful money, if presented by an association organized under the same act, as any "debt or liability" may be discharged by its *own notes* or notes of other national banks, when that "debt or liability belongs to any other association" existing under and by virtue of "the national currency act." The intention and scope of the statute is evidently against such a construction of its provisions, but all ambiguity in reference to it should be removed. All the banks should be required to redeem their notes and pay their balances in lawful money, as well to each other as to the public.

Whatever hostilities the national banking system may have encountered in its first inception, it is no longer denied that it has entrenched itself strongly in the feelings as it has commended itself to the convenience and interests of the whole people. Coming into conflict with local prejudices, and assumed to run counter to private interests, it was natural that its practical operations should have been regarded with jealous suspicions. It is not among the least of the triumphs of the system, that in a period of war, amid monetary disturbances, caused by the gigantic requirements of the government, it has stood the test of practical experiment in the most satisfactory manner, vindicating the partialities of its friends, and overcoming by its beneficial effects the hostilities of its most determined enemies.

In a country already celebrated for its commercial, manufacturing, and agricultural activity, no want could be more sensibly felt than that of a homogeneous currency, of equal value at the circumference, as well as at the commercial centres of our extended country. This could not be obtained under the restricted operations of State laws, nor could it be furnished by institutions necessarily circumscribed in their fields of operation, diverse in the extent and character of their liabilities to the public, and without a recognized basis of credit adequate to insure the public confidence in sections remote from the locality where such liabilities were payable It is not denied that the State banks have been of great, if not indispensable service in the development of the resources of the country; it is not designed to underrate their usefulness, to question their patriotism, or assail the integrity of the banking institutions of the States; but as in all enlightened communities there will be progress and improvement it cannot be regarded as invidious to claim for the national banking system a superiority over the more limited system of State institutions, inasmuch as it furnishes a safe and convenient paper circulation, based upon the national credit, and which thus far has been, and with a slight amendment to the act may continue to be, of uniform value throughout the length and breadth of the land. Not only are the regulations by which the national banks are governed of equal applicability; not only are they based upon actual capital and individual responsibility, carefully enforced; but underlying these safeguards there is a foundation of unparalleled security in the government bonds which they are required to hold. A system thus anchored, in which the whole community has a common interest, cannot fail to subserve the highest object of its creation, nor cease to be regarded with favor by an intelligent people.

While, in conclusion, it is allowed me to congratulate Congress and the country on the popularity which the national banking system has achieved, I would add the hope that these institutions may never become subject to the schemes and caprices of political parties, but that in them and through them the public faith and credit may be upheld, and the prosperity of the country greatly promoted.

FREEMAN CLARKE,
Comptroller of the Currency.

Statement of the number of National Banks organized in the several States, with capital stock paid in, bonds deposited by, and circulation issued to, on the 1st of October, 1865.

States.	No. of banks organised.	Capital stock paid in.	Bonds deposited.	Circulation issued to banks.
Maine...............................	60	$8,486,500 00	$7,272,650	$4,751,550
New Hampshire	37	4,606,832 36	4,322,000	2,501,800
Vermont...........................	33	5,077,512 50	5,062,600	3,244,800
Massachusetts	207	79,207,000 00	58,691,850	44,665,180
Rhode Island	59	19,662,500 00	10,045,500	4,837,230
Connecticut	82	23,964,280 00	15,966,800	11,223,360
New York..........................	308	114,872,791 00	62,504,000	37,548,940
New Jersey	54	10,926,534 00	8,591,750	4,763,920
Pennsylvania......................	199	46,684,469 90	37,672,050	29,450,830
Maryland	30	12,155,535 00	6,962,300	2,672,400
Delaware	11	1,378,185 00	1,076,350	434,290
District of Columbia	6	1,585,000 00	1,345,000	1,161,000
Virginia...........................	13	1,162,000 00	981,000	692,100
West Virginia	13	1,620,400 00	1,342,000	441,750
Ohio	136	21,136,675 15	18,540,400	15,479,370
Indiana	70	12,147,332 90	11,369,150	8,893,789
Illinois	79	10,975,850 00	9,781,800	7,885,035
Michigan..........................	38	4,176,310 00	2,755,100	1,798,800
Wisconsin.........................	35	2,666,350 00	2,336,050	1,981,400
Iowa	38	3,263,675 00	2,737,600	2,064,300
Minnesota.........................	12	1,445,000 00	1,293,000	1,046,750
Kansas............................	2	160,000 00	135,000	83,000
Missouri...........................	12	3,699,050 00	1,946,000	1,223,700
Kentucky..........................	11	2,235,675 00	1,764,000	1,293,530
Tennessee	7	965,000 00	745,000	551,940
Louisiana	1	500,000 00	200,000	180,000
Mississippi	1	50,000 00	30,000	25,000
Nebraska...........................	2	115,000 00	60,000	27,000
Colorado	1	200,000 00	70,000	45,000
Georgia	2	150,000 00	74,000	30,000
North Carolina	2	60,000 00	60,000	....
Alabama...........................	2	160,000 00	152,000	....
Nevada	1	155,000 00	155,000	....
Oregon	1	50,000 00	50,000	....
Texas.............................	1	100,000 00	100,000	....
Total	1,566	395,729,597 83	276,219,950	190,847,055

REPORT OF THE COMMISSIONER OF INTERNAL REVENUE.

TREASURY DEPARTMENT, OFFICE OF INTERNAL REVENUE,
Washington, November 30, 1865.

Hon. Joseph J. Lewis having resigned the office of Commissioner, July 1, 1865, and his successor, Hon. William Orton, so lately as November 1, instant, the duty of preparing the annual report of the office unexpectedly devolved upon me at so late a period as, of itself, to preclude the expectation of a voluminous report from me at this time, while the laborious service of the "Revenue Commission," with powers and duties defined in the 19th section of the act of March last, makes it inappropriate that I should present my views upon such subjects as may have come within its consideration before it shall have prepared the report contemplated by the statute. At its request, however, I will at that time, if desired by the Secretary of the Treasury, submit what experience in this office shall have taught me in relation to the several changes it may propose in the law.

In the course of the present report, however, I shall offer a few recommendations affecting mainly the administration of the law, and only those parts of it to which I understand it is not the purpose of the commission to give special attention.

It is a matter of sincere congratulation that, thus far, the people of this country have so patiently borne the burden which has been put upon them, and have so freely contributed of their substance to fill the national treasury. With few exceptions the demand of the tax collector has been met promptly and willingly. And when it is recollected that the present generation only know by tradition, or by reference to obsolete statutes, that taxes have ever been imposed in this country upon articles of their own manufacture, and the objects of internal traffic, or upon the various crafts or professions in which they are employed; and when, too, it is considered that the revenue thus collected for the single year ending June 30, 1865, amounts to a sum nearly or quite equal to all the receipts of this government from whatever sources, except loans and treasury notes, from its organization to the war of 1812; and when it is further considered that this amount was contributed at a time when the commercial marine of the country had been nearly destroyed, and more than a million of hardy men were withdrawn from the productive pursuits of life, we may not only be justly proud that the material strength has been fully equal to the burden imposed, but that it has been borne so quietly and so willingly.

The law requires "that separate accounts shall be kept at the treasury of all moneys received from internal duties or taxes in each of the respective States, Territories and collection districts, and that separate accounts shall be kept of the amount of each species of duty or tax that shall accrue, so as to exhibit, as far as may be, the amount collected from each source of revenue, with the moneys paid as compensation and for allowances to the collectors and deputy collectors, assessors and assistant assessors, inspectors and other officers employed in each of the respective States, Territories and collection districts, an abstract, in tabular form, of which accounts it shall be the duty of the Secretary of the Treasury annually, in the month of December, to lay before Congress."

Tabular statements more specific and comprehensive even than required by statute have been prepared in this office, and are herewith respectfully transmitted. They comprise:

Table A, showing the receipts by collectors from each specific source of revenue, and the amounts refunded in each collection district, State and Territory of the United States, for the fiscal year ending June 30, 1865.

Table B, collections from banks, insurance, railroad, canal, and turnpike companies.

Table C, monthly receipts of internal revenue tax on salaries.

Table D, number and value of internal revenue stamps procured monthly by the Commissioner; and monthly receipts from purchasers of internal revenue stamps, the commissions allowed on the same, and the receipts from agents for the sale of stamps.

Table E, recapitulation of receipts of internal revenue from all sources for the year ending June 30, 1865.

Table F, comparative table showing the territorial distribution of internal revenue, population, and wealth in the United States.

Table G, the gross amounts collected and paid into the treasury, and the amounts expended in the several collection districts, States and Territories, during the year.

Table H, the ratio of the receipts from specific sources to the aggregate of all collections.

AGGREGATE RECEIPTS.

The aggregate receipts of internal revenue for the fiscal year—

*1863 were....................................	$41,003,192 93
1864 were....................................	116,850,672 44
1865 were....................................	211,129,529 17

These amounts are exclusive of the direct tax, or tax of twenty millions of dollars upon the lands of the country, which has been partially paid in various ways, and the duty upon the circulation and deposits of National Banks, which in 1863 was paid to the Comptroller of the Currency, and has since been paid to the Treasurer, but are inclusive of drawback and sums refunded, which in the several years were as follows:

	Drawback.	Amount refunded.
1863	$677,106 40	$57,605 71
1864	687,431 99	237,470 37
1865	698,655 36	422,734 36

RECEIPTS FROM SPECIAL SOURCES.

It may not be unprofitable to present in juxtaposition the amounts received from several of the most important sources of revenue, with brief suggestions in relation to their differences; it should be borne in mind, however, that the law was in operation but ten months for the year ending June 30, 1863.

BANKS, TRUST COMPANIES, AND SAVINGS INSTITUTIONS.

	1863.	1864.	1865.
Dividends and additions to surplus	$766,605 85	$1,577,010 73	$3,987,209 65
Circulation	....	2,056,996 30	1,993,341 89
Deposits	....	780,723 52	2,040,933 26
Capital	....	....	902,835 18

The tax upon dividends was three per cent. until June 30, 1864, after which it was five per cent.

---

*NOTE.—The act of July, 1862, took effect September 1st, and the receipts for the fiscal year 1863 are for but ten months.

A discrepancy exists between these amounts and those from the office of the Secretary of the Treasury. The same receipts are not always reported and entered upon the books of the two offices on the same day. The difference is only one of account.

Other discrepancies of like character may be observed arising from the same source.

"Circulation" and "deposits" were not taxed until October, 1863.

"Capital" was first charged under the act of June 30, 1864, when the duty upon "circulation" was increased.

By the act of March 3, 1865, the tax upon deposits was extended to savings banks having no capital stock.

The taxes upon the "capital," "circulation," and "deposits" of national banks are not received at this office, nor included in the above.

RAILROADS.

	1863.	1864.	1865
Dividends	$338,533 49	$927,393 38	$2,470,816 89
Interest on bonds	253,998 72	596,859 09	847,683 61

The duty was three per cent. until July 1, 1864; afterwards five per cent. The same tax was then imposed upon all profits carried to the account of any fund, or used in construction. The amount received from this source is included in the dividends for 1865.

INSURANCE COMPANIES.

	1863.	1864.	1865.
Dividends and additions to surplus	$225,485 44	$445,366, 17	$764,658 38
Premiums and assessments	321,001 69	523,582 42	961,502 99

Tax upon dividends same as upon dividends of banks.

That upon the gross receipts of premiums and assessments was one per centum until July, 1864, payable quarterly to the Commissioner; after that, one and one-half per cent., payable monthly to the collectors.

SALARIES OF PERSONS EMPLOYED BY THE UNITED STATES GOVERNMENT.

1863	$696,181 71
1864	1,705,124 63
1865	2,826,333 37

This tax is received only from those whose compensation exceeds the rate of $600 per year, and was at the rate of three per cent. until July 1, 1864, and afterwards five per cent.

PASSPORTS.

1863	$8,406 00
1864	11,001 00
1865	27,408 29

Tax three dollars each until July 1, 1864; five dollars since. These amounts were mainly paid through the Department of State. A small sum each year was received from collectors.

REVENUE STAMPS.

1863	$4,140,175 29
1864	5,894,945 14
1865	11,162,392 14

These amounts include the receipts from stamps, required by schedule C as well as schedule B ; upon proprietary articles, matches, photographs, and cards, as well as upon written instruments. The law in respect to these duties has been repeatedly and variously modified, sometimes adding, and sometimes subtracting from the receipts. The large increase of revenue is due in no small degree to the growing observance of the law. After September 1, 1864, stamps were required upon matches, and the receipts from that source for the remaining portion of the fiscal year was probably not less than one million dollars.

ARTICLES IN SCHEDULE A.

1863	$365, 630 93
1864	520, 283 35
1865	779, 901 79

The taxes here are specific upon carriages, yachts, billiard tables, and gold and silver plate kept for use. In 1864 the schedule was increased by the addition of gold watches and piano-fortes, but the change was made after the annual lists, in which the taxes are included, were in the hands of the collectors, and the receipts reported are mainly from the operation of the statute of 1862.

LICENSES.

1863	$6, 824, 178 42
1864	7, 145, 388 71
1865	12, 598, 681 25

The receipts from licenses, like those from income and schedule A, are almost entirely in the report of the year subsequent to their assessment. The reassessment under the act of June, 1864, furnishes the principal exception to this rule. The returns are received in May, but the lists upon which they are entered by the assessors, do not ordinarily reach the collectors until after the 30th of June, or the beginning of another fiscal year. The increase in 1864, in part, from the addition by the act of March, 1863, to the list of persons subject to duty and the increased charge for several descriptions of license ; and that of 1865 from the same source, as well as from a like addition under the act of June 30, 1864, and the increased tax upon wholesale dealers, which, by special provision of the statute, was immediately assessed as additional to that assessed under the prior law.

INCOME.

1863	$455, 741 26
1864	14, 919, 279 58
1865	20, 567, 350 26

This, with licenses, and schedule A, makes up the annual list.

For the reasons just given above, the tax upon the income of 1862, assessed in 1863, is mainly included in the receipts of the fiscal year 1864; less than half a million dollars having been collected in 1863; and the receipts for 1865 consist almost entirely of the tax assessed in 1864 upon the income of 1863.

Most of the tax upon the income of 1864 has been collected since the commencement of the current fiscal year 1866, and will appear in the next annual report from this office. A small part of it is found in the receipts of 1865. Of the amounts collected in 1863, $279,333 76 were returned at five per cent. upon incomes above ten thousand dollars ; $172,770 35 at three per cent. upon incomes of less than ten thousand dollars ; and $3,637 15 upon incomes from United States securities. Of that collected in 1864, $6,913,834 88 were returned at five per cent. ; $7,930,070 77 at three per cent. ; and $75,373 93 at one and one-half per cent. Of that collected in 1865, $801,941 99 were returned at ten per cent. ; $9,934,758 55 at five per cent. ; $9,697,246 96 at three per cent. ; and $133,402 76 at one and one-half per cent.

The receipts from the ten per cent. tax were all from taxes upon the income of 1864. It cannot easily be determined precisely how much of the receipts at five per cent. are due to that year.

The special tax of five per cent. upon all incomes above six hundred dollars, as well from banks, railroads and salaries, as from other sources, brought into the treasury $28,929,312 02.

IRON AND STEEL IN THE VARIOUS FORMS SPECIFICALLY NAMED.

1863.. $1, 862, 826 36
1864.. 3, 694, 168 49
1865.. 9, 218, 808 63

These are the varieties named and described in the seventy-fifth section of the act of July, 1862, amended and somewhat increased by the act of March 3, 1863; still further enlarged with increased rates under the act of June 30, 1864, and twenty per cent. additional to those rates after April 1, 1865. Pig-iron was taxed two dollars per ton by the act of 1864, and during eleven months ending June 30th last, added nearly one and a half million dollars to the public revenue. The additional twenty per cent. to the rate, taking effect April 1, did not increase the receipts until May. Several causes have contributed to secure the tax upon these articles, and it is believed that it has almost universally been paid.

REFINED PETROLEUM AND COAL OIL.

1863.. $649, 962 09
1864.. 2, 255, 328 80
1865.. 3, 047, 212 77

The tax upon petroleum was ten cents per gallon, and upon oil distilled from coal exclusively eight cents until June 30, 1864, after which the rates were twenty and fifteen cents respectively. The increased receipts in 1864, over those of 1863, were owing largely to increased consumption, and to the withdrawal from bond to escape the increased duty. This somewhat overstocked the market, and during the following year checked refining for home consumption.

CIGARS AND CHEROOTS.

1863.. $476, 589 29
1864.. 1, 255, 424 79
1865.. 3, 072, 476 56

Specific taxes, graduated by the different values of the cigars, were imposed by the act of July, 1862. These were largely increased in 1864, but under the act of March 3, 1865, the duty was made uniform at ten dollars per thousand. The anticipation of additional tax largely increased the manufacture in 1864, and the supply at that time has hardly yet been consumed.

TOBACCO—CHEWING AND SMOKING.

1863.. $2, 576, 888 67
1864.. 7, 086, 684 74
1865.. 8, 017, 020 63

Plug and fine-cut tobacco were mainly taxed fifteen cents per pound until June 30, 1864, when the rate was increased to thirty-five cents, and in March, 1865, it was still further increased to forty cents.

The tax upon smoking tobacco was at first five cents, increased to twenty-five cents in 1864, and to thirty-five cents in 1865. Smoking-tobacco made exclusively of stems was taxed at two cents until March, 1863, when it was raised to five cents. In 1864 it was increased to fifteen cents, where it still remains.

The regularity of the manufacture has been largely disturbed by expectation of additional duty, as in the case of cigars.

The tax collected in 1863 represents 23,680,056 pounds; that of 1864 63,372,426 pounds, and that of 1865 only 36,639,020 pounds.

Of the amount charged in 1865, 10,061,163 pounds were manufactured and returned in June, 1864, in anticipation of the increased rates, and the duty paid in the following year. The amounts for the first and the last years were less than the ordinary annual consumption, while the amount for 1864 was greatly in excess. This excess was brought into consumption during the last year at rates with which the regular manufacturers could not compete, except with their old stocks, and the production was, of necessity, largely obstructed. It has also been unfavorably affected by the arrival of large quantities of southern tobacco in northern markets.

The average annual taxable production of the different kinds of manufactured tobacco from September 1, 1862 to June 30, 1865 was 42,809,168 pounds, which at present rates would have produced $15,736,795 65.

FERMENTED LIQUORS.

1863	$1,558,083 41
1864	2,223,719 73
1865	3,657,181 06

From September 1, 1862, to March 3, 1863, the tax was one dollar per barrel, of not more than thirty-one gallons; from that date to April 1, 1864, sixty cents, and since that time one dollar.

The number of barrels upon which tax was received, as nearly as can be ascertained, was 1,765,827 in 1863, 3,459,119 in 1864, and 3,657,181 in 1865.

DISTILLED SPIRITS.

1863	$3,229,990 79
1864	28,431,797 83
1865	15,995,701 66

During the fiscal year 1863 the tax was uniformly twenty cents per gallon. For the fiscal year 1864 the tax was twenty cents until March 7, after which it was sixty cents. From July 1, 1864, until January 1, 1865, it was $1 50 per gallon, and afterwards $2.

Of the amount reported in the year 1865, however, $3,862,820 66, or nearly one-fourth the whole amount, was at twenty or sixty cents per gallon. This resulted mainly from the fact that large quantities of spirits were sold by the distillers within the last ten days of June, 1864, thus escaping the increased duty, while the taxes thereon did not fall due until the following month of July, being the first of the next fiscal year. Considerable quantities were removed from the distilleries, too, under transportation bonds, or under bills of lading, prior to the 1st day of July, under conditions which produced a similar result. Even with this explanation, it may occasion no little surprise that the increase of duty was followed by a decrease of receipts. But I regard the receipts of the past year from distilled spirits as no criterion, if, indeed, even an indication of what would have been received had the tax fallen upon the ordinary, natural consumption of the country. This was checked in some measure, undoubtedly, by the tax, but the distillations in the winter and spring of 1863-'64 were everywhere in advance of consumption, anticipating the increased duty, glutting the market, and thoroughly deranging the customary laws of demand and supply. For a long time the consumption has not been of spirits which have paid the duty current at its date, but always of those taxed, if liable at all, at a previous and lower rate. The increase has never been of advantage to the government, but has swelled the income of manufacturers and speculators. For several months of the past year, when holders were disposing of their adventures, the market price of distilled spirits, even in the Atlantic cities, remote from the place of production, was but little, if any, in advance of the tax. It is no wonder, then, that many distilleries were idle and the revenue small.

The receipts from distilled spirits in

1863 (10 months) were from........................   16, 149, 954 gallons.
1864 were from.... ....,   85, 295, 391   ''
1865 were from....................................   16, 936, 778   ''

Average taxable production per year, from September 1, 1862, to June 30, 1865, 40,537,371 gallons.

From the fact that several of the elements involved are so uncertain and fluctuating, it is very difficult, of course, to determine with confidence how much the consumption is reduced by the present tax, and what will certainly be realized from this source of revenue.. The Revenue Commission has given much attention to this subject, and its report, I have no doubt, will be full and exhaustive. It may not be amiss for me to state, however, that I apprehend there is a prevalent overestimate of this reduction ; and in this belief I am strengthened by the recent "report of the Commissioners of her Majesty's inland revenue," from which it appears that the consumption of distilled spirits in the United Kingdom of Great Britain and Ireland during the year ending March 31, 1852, exclusive of the amount used in the arts and manufactures, was 29,866,260 gallons, while the increase of the excise duty in 1860 to the uniform rate of 10s., or $2 50 per gallon, throughout the kingdom, (at which rate it still remains,) only reduced the consumption during the last year to 26,516,531 gallons. This amount was in addition to 933,649 gallons more employed in manufactures and the arts, methylated and exempt from duty.

In 1852 the tax in England was 7s. 10d. ; in Scotland, 3s. 8d. ; and in Ireland, 2s. 8d.

The population of the United Kingdom in 1852 was 27,500,000, and in 1864, · 29,657,000.

For some years prior to 1860 the rate of duty was uniform throughout the United Kingdom at 8s., or 8s. 1d. per gallon, and in that year it was raised to 10s. From the report of the commissioners for the following year it appears that the domestic production fell off heavily—some nineteen per cent.—immediately after the change in the rate, from 24,985,192 gallons in 1860 to 20,147,824 gallons in 1861, while it will be noticed that the advance in the duty was but slight when compared with that which was imposed under our laws at the commencement of the last fiscal year. The commissioners in the report of 1861, say :

" These figures immediately suggest the question whether the whole of this large decrease is attributable to diminished consumption produced by the addition to the rate of duty. We think that this is not the case. Considerable diminution, indeed, was expected and has doubtless occurred, but various other causes have contributed to the unexpected deficiency above recorded.

"In the first place, we know that unusually large stocks of spirits had been accumulated in February, 1860, in anticipation of an addition to the duty ; and, on the other hand, that since the duty was raised to 10s. the stocks have been uniformly kept as low as possible, and the operations of all persons concerned in the spirit trade restricted to the absolute wants of the moment. Rectifiers, for instance, take ten puncheons at a time, instead of twenty or thirty, as they formerly did, and many of the large retailers who used to replenish their stores · with one hundred gallons at a time, are now careful to limit their purchases to ten or twenty gallons. This is the consequence of the increased cost of the spirits, and may be expected permanently to alter the habits of the trade; operating in combination with the excessive stocks of the year 1859-'60, it has had considerable effect on the relative quantities charged with duty in that and the succeeding year. ·

"Yet, after making allowance for all this, there still remains a large deficiency, which can only be accounted for by diminished consumption ; not, however, wholly produced by the increase of price in spirits, and therefore not necessarily a cause of permanent falling off in revenue.

'We feel justified in assigning to the bad harvest of last year a large share in restricting consumption, both immediately and consequentially.   *   *   *

"On the whole, therefore, we should infer, from a review of the occurrences of the year, · that, although the quantity of spirits brought to charge would in future not reach the same level as in 1859-'60—nearly the highest on record—we should be entitled to reckon with certainty upon charging at the least twenty million gallons in the present year, and might fairly expect, if the country continues in a prosperous state, an addition to that amount of 1,000,000 or 1,500,000 gallons."

By the subsequent reports of the same commissioners it appears that their estimates were fully confirmed.

Upon such experience we can now reasonably base our expectations. Our circumstances are not dissimilar. Our markets are now exhausted of spirits distilled before taxation, or subjected only to the earlier rates. The supplies for consumption must now pay the existing duty, and the receipts for the current year will, I am confident, far exceed the aggregate of all receipts from the same source prior thereto.

It is certain that immense frauds have been perpetrated, for such have been discovered and prosecuted to judgment or to compromise; but the increasing experience and vigilance of our officers, and the appointment of others for special duty at distilleries, will prevent large loss to the government. The Revenue Commission will, I hope, suggest additional checks to be authorized by further legislation; but so long as avarice and falsity are a part of humanity, revenue laws, however thoroughly administered, will be sometimes evaded. The number of illicit distillations detected in the United Kingdom in 1864 was 2,757, and in 1865 3,457; showing that, with all the thoroughness consequent upon careful legislation, long experience, and a more compact population than ours, it was quite impossible to prevent occasional and, undoubtedly, sometimes enormous fraud. It must be the aim and the effort of all persons connected with our revenue laws to insist everywhere and always upon the rights of the government, and, in so doing, the protection of taxpayers who faithfully discharge their duties.

COST OF COLLECTING THE REVENUE.

The cost of collecting the public revenues is naturally a matter of no little solicitude to the Secretary of the Treasury, as it is one of vast importance to the country.

A people heavily subjected to taxation will carefully scrutinize the expenditures of the government, especially so far as they relate to the collection of the revenue they are taxed to produce.

It may not be unsatisfactory to submit, in this connexion, a tabular statement of the costs, from time to time, of collecting the revenues of Great Britain and Ireland, taken largely from the work of J. R. McCulloch, esq., upon "*Taxation and Funding.*"

The percentage cost of collecting inland revenue, after deduction of drawbacks, in the following years, was, (in the £100:)

1840-'41	£5	5s.	1d.	upon....	£26,231.172
1850-'51	4	3	4½	upon....	32,018,825
1860-'61	3	13	7½	upon....	42,019,133

The percentage cost of collecting customs, according to the same authority, before deduction of drawbacks, &c., in the following years, was:

In 1840-'41	£5	8s.	8¾d.	upon...	£26,341,813
In 1850-'51	5	15	8¼	upon...	22,019,784
In 1860-'61	4	6	3	upon...	23,278,250

The actual annual costs to our own government for the collection of its customs for several years cannot be determined with accuracy, because the expenses of revenue cutters, performing the duties of vessels-of-war, have been paid from the appropriations for customs, as have other charges connected with commercial intercourse and abandoned property in insurrectionary districts. They will, however, it is believed, not fall short of three and one-half per centum of the

6 F

receipts—a percentage not above the average for many years past in this country, and, as it will be observed, much below the costs in the United Kingdom for either of the years above given.

I have caused the costs of assessing and collecting the internal revenue of the fiscal year 1865 to be carefully ascertained, including the salaries and authorized expenses of revenue agents, special agents, and inspectors of revenue, the contingent expenses of this office, including its pay-roll, and the costs of revenue stamps, but exclusive of its printing at the office of the public printer, not yet ascertained, and find that the percentage, after deducting drawback and sums refunded as erroneously collected, will not exceed two and seventy-five one-hundredths, $(2\frac{75}{100})$.

This ratio of costs to collections cannot be relied upon for the current year, as the percentage will be greater in the sparsely settled districts of the south. It will not, however, I believe, exceed three and one-half $(3\frac{1}{2})$ per centum of the receipts of the whole country.

ESTIMATE OF RECEIPTS FOR CURRENT YEAR.

As bearing upon the probable amount of revenue for the current fiscal year 1866, I present herewith a statement of the receipts of which certificates of deposit reached this office during July, August, and September, of 1863, 1864, and 1865, respectively:

	1863.	1864.	1865.
July	$5,298,967 18	$16,570,548 39	$21,693,470 75
August	5,604,201 35	15,712,066 84	34,087,539 09
September	6,136,205 43	15,819,770 72	37,939,415 82
Total	17,039,373 96	48,102,385 95	93,720,425 66

I present also the comparative receipts from several large sources of revenue during the first quarter of the fiscal year 1865, and the first quarter of 1866, ending September 30 last:

	1865.	1866.
Fermented liquors	$913,252 53	$1,230,353 69
Refined petroleum and coal oil	302,411 63	810,056 09
Revenue stamps	2,560,509 85	3,010,185 37
Salaries	471,863 07	1,206,878 59
Paper of all descriptions	228,851 60	204,917 76
Cigars and cheroots	526,840 91	600,116 88
Articles in schedule A	316,621 77	981,547 14
Income	13,510,492 98	41,766,016 63
Smoking and chewing tobacco	2,233,926 16	2,078,974 95
Distilled spirits	3,501,071 43	1,085,031 20
Total	24,565,841 93	52,974,028 30

Reports due from several collectors have not been received, although their receipts have been regularly deposited, and the above amounts for 1866 will, in some instances, be considerably increased. The receipts from distilled spirits for the months here reported exhibit no evidence of the amounts consumed, nor of the comparative productiveness of the several rates of duty, as $2,702,257 72 of that reported in 1865 (July, August, and September, 1864) accrued from the imposition of twenty or sixty cents per gallon. The same is true of tobacco, as $1,766,616 79, or more than three-quarters of the whole amount reported in 1865, was derived from the low rates of duty prior to the statute of June 30, 1864.

It will be observed that the increased receipts are largely from the annual list, and especially from income. Not far from sixty per centum of the latter tax was from income in excess of five thousand dollars, and taxable at ten per cent.

At the date of this writing the revenue from the annual list is almost fully collected, and the receipts for the remaining portion of the fiscal year must be mainly from other sources.

The fluctuation in the value of merchandise will, of course, affect the proceeds from whatever bears an *ad valorem* duty. The revenue from the southern States is altogether problematical. From the most reliable data, however, in my possession, with the present law unchanged, I confidently expect that the receipts of this office for the current fiscal year will not be less than $272,000,000.

APPOINTMENT OF ASSISTANT ASSESSORS.

By the amendatory act of March last it was provided that assistant assessors, before that time appointed by the Secretary of the Treasury, should, in case of vacancy, be appointed by the assessors of the several districts, subject to the approval of the Commissioner.

The Attorney General of the United States, to whom the question involved in this change was referred, has given to the Secretary of the Treasury his opinion, that under the second section of article second of the Constitution such appointments can be made only by the President of the United States or the head of a department.

The language of that section is that the President "shall nominate, and by and with the advice and consent of the Senate shall appoint, * * * * all other officers of the United States whose appointments are not herein otherwise provided for, and which shall be established by law. But the Congress may by law vest the appointment of such inferior officers, as they think proper, in the President alone, * * * or in the heads of departments."

It would seem, therefore, that if no other provision of law is made for the appointment of assistant assessors than that which now exists, an undesirable as well as an unintended burden is imposed upon the President and the Senate.

The purpose of the law would seem to be answered as well and more conveniently by giving the power of such appointments immediately to the Secretary of the Treasury, as authorized by the above section of the Constitution; and I respectfully suggest that a modification of the law may be made to that effect.

APPEALS UNNECESSARY.

From the almost universal experience of assessors it seems that the holding of formal appeals from erroneous assessments in the annual list, as required in the nineteenth section, is entirely unnecessary. The public always have access to the assessor at his office, and rarely have actual notice of the advertised time of hearing at any other locality. The result is that in many districts none have ever attended the appeals, which have hence proved of advantage neither to the government nor the taxpayer, while they have been a charge both to the local officers and to the public treasury. Between the assessment and collection there is always opportunity for a hearing if desired, either in person or by correspondence, and after collection this office is always open to the complaints of aggrieved taxpayers.

The system of holding appeals in the several counties is borrowed from the direct tax law, under which a certain amount was apportioned to each county, and the increase or decrease of a single assessment affected every landholder. There was need, therefore, of comparison, and often of personal view. Under the revenue law every assessment is independent, and the machinery referred to seems valueless.

LACK OF UNIFORMITY IN RETURNS.

The singular lack of uniformity in the time when the various returns are due the assessors from different classes of taxpayers is often productive of neglect and irregularities, which the necessary amendments to the law would avoid. There seems to be no reason why the monthly returns, at least, should not all be receivable on the same day and payable at the same time thereafter. The more the statutes are simplified and systematized in their details the less will be the friction engendered in their operation, and the more certain their results.

What I have said of the returns is applicable in its spirit to the penalties of the law. They differ largely in amount for the same grade of offence, while the manner of their recovery is as various, almost, as the forms of proceeding known to the courts. The tax upon slaughtered sheep and lambs is five cents each, and the penalty in case of fraud or evasion is ten dollars, or two thousand per centum, recoverable only by suit, while the penalty for neglect, or refusal to make return and payment of tax upon the gross receipts of certain persons, companies, and corporations, is ten per cent. additional to the duty as estimated by the assistant assessor, to be included in the assessment, and for fraudulent evasion one thousand dollars, without regard to the amount of indebtedness, to be sued for in the courts; and no special penalty whatever is provided for neglect to make return of a succession until after notice from the assistant assessor.

These instances are cited simply for illustration of the variety referred to, and could be made as numerous, almost, as the sources of revenue.

In this connexion I may add that section fourteen, from peculiarities in some parts of its language, is of questionable application to many of the returns required later in the law, which it appears from other parts it was intended to cover, and that the forty-ninth section is so involved in its construction as, thus far, to have been of little practical utility.

INCREASED ALLOWANCE TO ASSESSORS FOR RENT, AND ADDITIONAL COMPENSATION TO ASSESSORS AND ASSISTANT ASSESSORS IN CERTAIN CASES.

Under section 22 the allowance made to assessors for office rent can in no case exceed the rate of $500 per annum. This limit is still much more than sufficient in most districts of the country; but in several of the most populous cities the increase of prices since the passage of the law compels our officers to seek rooms insufficient for themselves and incommodious to the public, or make payment in part therefor out of receipts designed by Congress as compensation for their personal services. It seems but just to them that this limitation be enlarged, and they be allowed sums actually and necessarily expended, subject to the approval now required.

The last proviso of section 22 authorizes the Secretary of the Treasury to fix such additional rates of compensation to assessors and assistant assessors in cases where a collection district embraces more than a single congressional district, and to assessors and assistant assessors, revenue agents and inspectors, in Louisiana, North Carolina, Mississippi, Tennessee, Missouri, California, Oregon and the Territories, as may appear to him to be just and equitable, in consequence of the greater cost of living and travelling in those States and Territories, and as may, in his judgment, be necessary to secure the services of competent officers. The suppression of armed hostility in the insurrectionary districts has brought within the active operation of the revenue law other States neighboring to several of those above named, and in which the cost of living and travelling is nearly the same. To the compensation of revenue officers in those States I respectfully suggest that the authority of the Secretary of the Treasury should likewise be extended.

FRANKING PRIVILEGE.

Assessors and collectors are allowed for postage actually paid on letters and documents received or sent by them relating exclusively to official business. Their communication with this office through the mails is free, and I respectfully suggest that if they were allowed the franking privilege upon official business between their respective offices it would be liable to little abuse, and be a saving of cost to the government.

SAFES.

My predecessors in their reports to the Secretary of the Treasury alike recommended that the purchase of fire-proof safes be authorized for the use of collectors and assessors. In this recommendation I cheerfully concur. Private enterprise of the amount covered by the books and papers of the most unimportant district of the country is seldom left by prudent managers to the dangers to which our offices are now subject. The loss accruing to the government from a single conflagration might almost equal the expenditure necessary for the protection everywhere required.

SALES OF REAL ESTATE FOR TAXES.

Section 30 relates to the seizure and sale at public auction of real estate by the collector when goods and chattels cannot be found sufficient to satisfy the duties imposed.

It provides, among other things, that if no person offers for the estate the amount of the tax to be collected, together with the penalties and charges, the officer shall purchase the same at that sum for the United States, and shall deposit his deed thereof with the district attorney. Although the tax may be large and the realty of disproportionate value, no collection can be made without a full discharge of the duty.

This section is largely copied from the 36th section of the direct tax law of August 5, 1861. The tax to be collected under that law was only that assessed upon the land offered for sale, and the requirement now considered was appropriate. Under the revenue law the land is not assessed, and the requirement is oftentimes embarrassing. I respectfully recommend that the law be so amended that the land may be sold to the highest bidder, and that the United States, through the collector, may be the purchaser.

COMMISSIONER'S CERTIFICATE TO BE REQUIRED IN CERTAIN CASES.

There has been a very general compliance on the part of revenue officers with the requirements of the law and the regulations of this office in preparing and forwarding their various reports. Whenever negligence does occur, however, this office is embarrassed in its operations, and not unfrequently the local officers, who have promptly discharged their duty in this particular, share in the general inconvenience. Sometimes positive damage may result to the government when a person who has neglected to make the returns retires from office. After careful consideration I have concluded to recommend that it be provided by law that no payment shall be made to assessors or collectors on account of salaries or commissions without the certificate of the commissioner that all reports required by law or regulation have been received, or a satisfactory explanation rendered him of the cause of the delay.

REFUNDING TAXES ERRONEOUSLY PAID.

Taxes erroneously or illegally assessed and collected, which, under the 44th section of the act of June 30, 1864, the Commissioner is authorized to refund, subject to the regulations of the Secretary of the Treasury, were, prior to the 30th of June last, by the provisions of the same section, paid by draft drawn on collectors of internal revenue. The 3d section of the act of March last prescribed that after the 30th of June the gross amount of all duties, taxes, and revenues received or collected should be paid, by the officers, collectors or agents receiving or collecting the same, into the treasury of the United States, without any abatement or deduction on account of "salary, compensation, fees, costs, charges, expenses or claims of any description whatever, anything in the law to the contrary notwithstanding."

Such payment, of course, does not allow collectors to honor drafts of the Commissioner, and no little embarrassment has arisen, both to the department and the public, from the want of a clearly authorized method of refunding such taxes. This trouble did not suggest itself during the pendency of the amendatory act, and it is only necessary, I apprehend, to call the attention of Congress to the subject to secure the appropriate legislation.

TAXES IN THE INSURRECTIONARY DISTRICTS.

By circular bearing date June 21, 1865, the Secretary of the Treasury announced that, "without waiving in any degree the rights of the government in respect to taxes which had before that time accrued in the States or Territories in insurrection, or assuming to exonerate the tax-payer from his legal responsibility for such taxes, the department did not deem it advisable to insist at present on their payment, so far as they were payable prior to the establishment of a collection district embracing the territory in which the taxpayer resided."

This office, in pursuance of that circular, commenced and continued the collection of such taxes only as accrued in the several collection districts subsequent to their establishment by the order of the President.

I would respectfully suggest whether or not section 46 of the act of June 30, 1864, which relates to the collection of taxes in States at that time insurrectionary, and referred to in this circular, does not require the careful attention of Congress.

All the instruments enumerated in schedule B of the revenue law, and subject to stamp duty, which were issued for nearly three years in that portion of the United States above referred to, were unstamped and invalid. Immense monetary interests are covered by these instruments, and although much wrong has not yet been suffered by their invalidity, the subject deserves, and will of course receive, special consideration.

PEDDLERS AND SUBSTITUTE BROKERS.

The apparent necessity for two provisions in the act of March last, amendatory of the 79th section of the act of June prior, has passed away with the rebellion. One of them denies license as peddlers to all who are not regularly enrolled for military duty, or physically disabled from service; the other imposes a tax of one hundred dollars upon substitute brokers. Both of them are now useless, while the former, from the discharge of enrolling officers, is liable to produce hardship. They should be repealed.

DEMANDS FOR PAYMENT OF TAXES.

Many complaints have arisen from manufacturers, and no little embarrassment to those charged with the administration of the law, by reason of the amendment to the 83d section, repealing the requirement of demand in writing before the imposition of ten per cent. penalty for non-payment of tax. The purpose of the change was, undoubtedly, to secure punctuality of payment, but neglect is often the result of forgetfulness only, and I believe it but just that written demand notices should be served upon all tax-payers, except when payment accompanies their returns.

DEDUCTIONS BY MANUFACTURERS UNDER SECTION 86.

I would suggest the propriety of amending the 86th section, relative to manufacturers' returns, by striking out so much thereof as relates to deductions.

The law now authorizes the deduction of freight from the place of manufacture to the place of delivery, commission not exceeding three per centum, (except where sales are made at the place of manufacture,) and other expenses of sale *bona fide* paid.

There are so many peculiarities in the method of manufacture and sale of different classes of merchandise in different parts of the country that it has been found impossible to define by any precise and specific rules the deductions allowable as "other expenses of sale *bona fide* paid," while general rules, however carefully drawn, are liable to such a variety of construction that too much diversity of practice has prevailed where it is but just to the honest manufacturer that there should be perfect uniformity. Much time is spent by assessors and assistant assessors in adjusting claims for deductions, and unfortunate differences of opinion often arise between them and the manufacturers, which should be avoided. This diversity of practice has furnished opportunity for numberless short returns, and a large proportion of the manufacturers who have been detected in fraud have urged "expenses of sale" either in extenuation or defence.

It is apparently reasonable to allow for freight, as some manufactories are more remote from the markets than others; but their disadvantage in this respect is, perhaps, fully compensated by the reduced cost of fuel, labor, rents, and motive power. The deductions are allowed only where the tax is *ad valorem.*

The duties upon iron, salt, sugar, molasses, petroleum, and other articles, the freight of which to market is no inconsiderable part of their value, are all specific and without deduction. The amendment proposed would, of itself alone, enhance the burden upon manufacturing; but I believe that a tax of five per centum upon the gross sales of the manufactures in question is preferable to the present rate, with the allowances.

TAX UPON GROSS RECEIPTS OR TONNAGE OF VESSELS.

By section 103 of the act of June 30, 1864, a tax of two and a half per centum is imposed upon the gross receipts of steamboats, ships, barges, canal-boats, or other vessels, employed in the business of transporting passengers or property for hire. The fourth section of the amendatory tariff act of March last relieves vessels paying tonnage duty from the taxation of their receipts. The tonnage duty upon the vessels relieved is but an annual one of thirty cents per ton, and it is respectfully suggested that the amended law imposes unequal burdens upon persons employed in like pursuits.

SECTION ONE HUNDRED AND FIFTY UNNECESSARY.

The peculiar language of section 150 of the act of June 30, 1864, would seem to indicate a purpose at one time of, in some way, collecting the duties upon successions in the insurrectionary districts through the direct tax commissioners. However this may be, there is now certainly no necessity of the section, and I respectfully recommend its repeal.

STAMP DUTIES.

That part of the law which relates to "stamp duties" is not only susceptible of improvement in its details, but is worthy of attention in respect to its general scope, and the objects of taxation.

While the results of its administration are, perhaps, more satisfactory than those of most other parts of the law, yet evasions and violations are frequent, and, though the amount lost to the revenue may be small in the individual instance, it is large in the aggregate. Without asserting that greater vigilance than that heretofore exercised may not secure a more perfect enforcement of the statute, it is yet safe to say that the risk of detection and punishment under the existing system, with the precise phraseology of the law, in respect to violation and punishment, as it is, must always remain so small as to afford too much inducement for its evasion.

Were it not for the inconvenience the change might inflict upon thinly settled districts, it would be wise, it seems to me, to dispense entirely with adhesive stamps, as has been done elsewhere, and substitute stamped parchment or paper, the use of which is its cancellation. Frauds would diminish, but I fear the advantage to the revenue would hardly justify the burden upon the public. Penalty is provided for issuing unstamped instruments only when there is intent to evade the provisions of the law. The instrument itself may be invalid, but there is no punishment of the party who makes or issues it.

Some of the courts have held the government to the proof of fraudulent intention, and thus practically stayed proceedings for neglect to affix or cancel the requisite stamps.

Sufficient time should, undoubtedly, be given the public, whose attention is not specially directed to its obligation in this particular; but as the law has been so long in operation, it is a question worthy of consideration whether or not a reasonable penalty for simple neglect would be oppressive, as it certainly seems necessary.

Every person who sells unstamped articles named in schedule C is subject to penalty; small for neglect alone, larger when there is purpose to evade the law. Similar provisions in relation to unstamped instruments would, I believe, be both just and salutary.

The invalidity of unstamped instruments in the hands of their receiver must always prevent their issue more effectually than the liability of those who sign them to penalty. A more general compliance with the law could therefore be secured, if only those instruments which are of value in the hands of their holder were subjected to stamp duty. The small loss to the revenue from the necessary amendments would, it is believed, be more than compensated by the convenience of the public and the more general observance of the law. It is wise, too, it seems to me, to have few statutes which can easily be violated with impunity. Familiarity with their infringement in their minor details makes it easier for one to forget his obligations when larger sums are in question between himself and the government. Moral as well as bodily diseases are contagious.

A question has frequently arisen concerning the proper rule to be adopted in the case of official papers issuing from the executive departments of the several States, as well as from county and municipal offices. While there is in such cases no express exemption from stamp duty, such as is provided in regard to official documents made or issued by officers of the general government, yet the law has always been most liberally construed in their behalf. It has, however, not always been easy to define the proper limits of such exemption, nor to determine the particular cases to which the rule should apply.

It seems, therefore, desirable that legislation should regulate with its special provisions a matter like this of large and growing importance, and which, it must be confessed, now rests mainly upon the basis of "liberal construction."

In this connexion, it is proper to call attention to the fact that there has arisen in some quarters an attempt, sustained by the judicial decisions of certain State courts, to evade the stamp duty imposed upon "writs or other original process by which any suit is commenced in any court of record."

Neither my predecessors nor myself have been convinced by the arguments upon which those decisions are founded, and this office has not altered nor modified the directions heretofore given requiring such duty to be paid. It has not been deemed advisable, however, to take any steps to bring the question involved before the appellate court for final decision, or to induce others to do so. It is undoubtedly desirable that in such a case an authoritative decision should be reached; but, as in other like cases, it seemed proper that the suit for that purpose should be prosecuted, if at all, by individuals, and in the ordinary way.

The power given to collectors by section 163 of the act of June 30, 1864, to affix exemption stamps, and to determine the rate of stamp duty in certain cases, is one of importance to the revenue, and sometimes of embarrassment to this office in its administration of the law. Without derogating from the intelligence and integrity of those charged with this important duty, it is my conviction that their decisions, under the pressure of other duties, and generally without reference to those made in other districts, must commonly be given with less consideration than if made by those who have larger opportunities for investigation, and whose decisions would produce greater uniformity of practice. The inconvenience of referring such matters directly to this office might in some localities seem, at first, to be an objection to the change; but, if desirable, copies might be forwarded, instead of original papers, and decisions made thereon, in pursuance of which the requisite instructions could be given. Indeed, from a large part of the country inquiries are, even now, constantly presented for consideration, accompanied by documents, or copies, under the impression that the final decision in such cases rests here. It is deemed the duty of this office to give answers to such inquiries; but such answers may encounter or be followed by decisions of subordinate officers based upon opinions directly at variance with those held here, and which are made final by law. It is apparent that such an incongruity in the administration of the law should not exist. Whether the correction should be made in the manner I have suggested, is for the superior wisdom of Congress to determine. As the attention of that body will no doubt be called to the details of the stamp schedules, as well as to other points of the law, it is not necessary that I should refer to all the particulars in which amendments may seem advisable. I would suggest, however, that the difference in the terms applied in different localities to the same kind of instrument, and the various forms of process and modes of proceeding in the several States, have rendered it difficult many times to make a satisfactory application of the provisions of schedule B, as it now exists, to all the cases which are presented for decision. Material advantage, too, might be derived from a more careful and enlarged specification, as in the case of different kinds of conveyance, and from a more definite requirement in the statement of the amount or character of the consideration in cases of conveyance, corresponding in that respect to the approved practice abroad. But these and other amendments can be more particularly pointed out at another time, if desired.

OTHER CHANGES IN THE LAW NOT DEFINITELY STATED, DEEMED NECESSARY.

I purposely omit the consideration of several important changes in the provisions of the law relative to successions and legacies, as well as to tobacco, snuff, cigars, and distilled spirits, which appear to be necessary for the prevention of fraud, the protection of honest taxpayers, and the more uniform and certain collection of the revenue. The patience of the people, burdened as they have been by taxation, is an argument sufficient for their relief from its most annoying and oppressive exactions, so far as is consistent with the public necessities. Unskilled labor contributes in some instances disproportionately to its means, and several requirements of the law are more irritating and burdensome than productive. All these things are, however, being subjected to the thorough scrutiny of the Revenue Commission, and I defer further reference to them for the present.

OPERATIONS UNDER THE DIRECT TAX LAWS.

No appointment of "Commissioner of taxes," authorized by the 56th section of the direct tax law of August 5, 1861, has ever been made; but after the assumption by the loyal States of their apportionment of the twenty millions of dollars thereby imposed, the general superintendence of the collection of the tax in the insurrectionary districts was assigned to the office of internal revenue. For this collection, "a board of tax commissioners" in each of the States in which the insurrection existed was provided by the fifth section of the amendatory act of June 7, 1862. They were appointed, and during the last fiscal year they have been engaged in South Carolina, Virginia, Florida, Tennessee, North Carolina, Louisiana, and, for a portion of the year, in Arkansas.

Since its close they have also been appointed for the States of Georgia, Mississippi, Texas, and Alabama, and have commenced the discharge of their duties.

I herewith submit a statement of the amounts collected by the several commissions prior to June 30, 1865, the amounts received by them from sales of lands, from collections, and other sources, and the quantity or assessed value, or the number of lots purchased by them for the United States, so far as reported to this office, together with their salaries and expenditures:

Districts.	From sales.	Collections.	Other sources, including rents and leases.	No. of acres, assessed value, and number of lots bid in.	Salaries and expenditures.
Florida	$40,414 81	$4,000 00		2,337 lots and 28 blocks.	$27,900 16
South Carolina	170,876 01	99,990 03	$14,654 96	*39,703 acres.	41,412 22
Virginia	131,608 38	119,308 00		8,701 acres, assessed value, $104,645 75	23,816 29
Tennessee	112,366 00	187,634 00		$1,586,882 00	23,637 18
Louisiana	108,203 72				8,447 10
North Carolina	35,986 10				9,175 31
Arkansas	33,537 00	9,729 67		$76,000 00	4,763 08

* This amount is exclusive of lands resold under section 11 of the act of June 7, 1862.

It will be seen that there has been great lack of uniformity in the operations of the several commissions, dependent largely as they were upon the amount of territory protected by the national forces. The quantity of real estate abandoned by disloyal owners, and forfeited to the government, differs in different States, as do the sales of such property, and the amounts of taxes collected.

Of the property purchased for the government at the sales for taxes, leases under section 9 of the act of June 7, 1862, have been made only by the South Carolina commission. In South Carolina, too, and not elsewhere, resales of lands bid in at the sales for taxes have been made by the commission, under section 11 of the same statute. This section provides that purchasers at the sale who shall have faithfully served for the term of three months as an officer, musician, or private soldier, or sailor, in the army or navy or marine service of the United States, as a regular or volunteer, and who shall pay one-fourth part of the purchase money, shall receive a certificate, and shall have the term of three years in which to pay the remainder. The amount which will become due in 1867 and 1868 upon army and navy certificates, issued as above, is $206,994 30. In this State, also, a board of selection, appointed by the President of the United States for that purpose, and comprised in part of the tax commissioners, under his instructions of September 16, 1863, selected and reserved for military, naval, charitable, educational, and police purposes, eighty-one plantations, situated on the several Sea islands of that State.

Under the same instructions the commission made sale of homesteads of ten and twenty acres each to heads of families of African descent.

Since December 10, 1863, there have been 617 certificates of homesteads of this character issued by the commission, most of which were during the last fiscal year.

It is evident from what I have stated that when the duties of the commissioners under the present laws shall be completed, the burdens imposed by it will have fallen unequally upon the people of the districts lately in insurrection. Some will have paid little in addition to their original distributive share of the twenty millions of dollars, while others will have lost their entire estates.

Some States, too, will have paid only the amount apportioned them under the act of August 7, 1861, while others, for the reasons before given, will, through the collections and sales, have contributed largely in excess of such apportionment.

After all the taxes shall have been collected, too, there will remain in several of the States large tracts of land belonging to the general government, bid in at the sales. When the offices of the commissioners shall be vacated there will be no person whose special duty it will be to take charge of these lands, or at least such part of them as shall be subject to redemption, and which, under the opinion of the Attorney General of the United States, referred by the Secretary of the Treasury to this office, the tax commissioners are not bound to turn over to the Bureau of Freedmen Refugees, nor has the Commissioner of the Freedmen's Bureau authority to set them or any portion of them apart for the uses mentioned in the statute of March 3, 1865, or sell them under the same statute.

The direct authority of the commissioners under section 9 of the act of June 7, 1862, to lease lands in any State, extends only until the said rebellion and insurrection in said State shall be put down and the authority of the United States established, and until the people of said State shall elect a legislature and State officers who shall take an oath to support the Constitution of the United States, to be announced by the proclamation of the President, and until the first day of March next thereafter.

Under the law and the proclamation of the President, each and every parcel of land in the States and parts of States lately in insurrection is charged with the payment of so much of the whole tax laid and apportioned upon the State where the same is situated, as shall bear the same direct proportion to the whole amount of the direct tax apportioned to such State as the value of such tract bears to the whole valuation of the real estate of such State, and in addition thereto a penalty of fifty per centum thereon. This charge is a lien upon all lands subject to it from and after the proclamation of the President, on the 1st day of July, 1862. The statutory remedy in default of payment of taxes determined by the commissioners is the sale at public auction of the lands upon which they are a charge.

After the cessation of hostilities, and on the 17th day of May last, the several commissions were directed by this office, in pursuance of the instructions of the Secretary of the Treasury, to suspend all sales of lands for taxes in districts before that time in insurrection until otherwise ordered. Collections, however, have been made in several of the States, because of improved opportunities, with greater success than before, and since the close of the heated term all the boards are at their places of duty.

I submit that the disposition of the lands purchased and now held by the United States, as well as the whole subject of the collection of taxes above referred to, requires the careful consideration of the Secretary of the Treasury and of Congress.

ORGANIZATION OF THE BUREAU.

The Secretary of the Treasury, under the amendment to the first section of the act of June 30, 1864, is authorized only until the 1st day of July, 1866, to assign to this office such number of clerks as he may deem necessary, or the exigencies of the public service may require. Legislative action is therefore indispensably necessary that the requisite clerical force may be provided after June next. And here—were I not aware that all that can be said is already within the knowledge of the Secretary—I would urge the importance of increased compensation, by positive enactments, to a portion, at least, of the officers and employés of this office.

It needs no facts or argument to prove that, in a bureau where the details are so numerous and complicated, the value of one's services increases with experience, almost as much as in the studio or laboratory. Private enterprise is everywhere offering superior inducements to those who are willing to sacrifice their days and nights in its service, and it is not strange that a proper regard for themselves and families compels many of the most deserving to retire from public employment. An organization of this office, somewhat like that of the Treasurer's, was approved and referred to the last Congress by the late Secretary, and I respectfully submit that the necessity of one even more liberal in its provisions was never greater than now.

The correspondence of this bureau is voluminous, and the ladies engaged in its copying, and the discharge of other clerical services assigned them, should be remembered in this organization, and receive compensation more commensurate with their services. There is no reason why they should not be recognized and classed as clerks.

I cannot forbear cheerfully testifying to the punctuality and industry of the persons employed with me in this office, and their compliance with its regulations. Several of those charged with the most important duties, disregarding the customary hours of service, have almost uniformly been at their desks for several hours at night.

The same faithfulness has generally characterized the subordinate officers in the several districts of the country, and I am happy in the belief that at no period since the passage of the revenue law in 1862 have the taxes been more uniformly and thoroughly assessed and collected.

With great respect, your obedient servant,

E. A. ROLLINS, *Commissioner.*

Hon. HUGH McCULLOCH,
        Secretary of the Treasury.

REPORT OF THE TREASURER.

TREASURY OF THE UNITED STATES,
Washington, October 25, 1865.

SIR: In compliance with provisions of statutory law and departmental regulations, the following statements in regard to the moneyed transactions of the treasury of the United States, and of the office in Washington city, and of the necessary business and labor connected with said transactions, during the fiscal year ending with June 30, 1865, are most respectfully submitted.

The books of the various offices of the department, including this office, have been closed as follows:

CASH DR.

Balance from June 30, 1864	$96, 739, 905 73
Repayments	20, 135, 881 21
Trust funds	7, 242, 242 00

RECEIPTS.

Loans	$1, 475, 579, 740 85	
Internal revenue	209, 464, 215 25	
Customs (coin)	84, 928, 260 60	
Miscellaneous	39, 760, 371 03	
Direct tax	1, 200, 573 03	
Lands	996, 553 31	
War Department	6, 160, 524 57	
Navy Department	7, 787, 268 69	
Interior Department	197, 719 81	
		1, 826, 075, 227 14
		1, 950, 193, 256 08

These receipts were carried into the treasury by four thousand nine hundred and eighty-one covering warrants.

CASH CREDIT.

Repayments	$20, 135, 881 21
Trust funds	4, 146, 718 42

PAYMENTS.

Public debt	695, 168, 336 31	
Civil diplomatic, &c	40, 346, 543 63	
War Department	1, 037, 483, 885 36	
Navy Department	130, 400, 213 98	
Interior Department	21, 653, 368 02	
		1, 925, 052, 347 30
Cash on hand to balance		858, 309 15
		1, 950, 193, 256 08

The above payments were made by thirty-one thousand eight hundred and fifty-six drafts, issued on twenty-eight thousand one hundred and ten warrants.
The actual receipts have been as follows:

From customs, in coin	$84, 622, 916 66
From internal revenue	208, 753, 813 52
From loans	333, 694, 397 60

From temporary loans	$147,898,540 95
From seven three-tenths treasury notes	676,610,188 21
From certificates of indebtedness	123,237,000 00
From compound interest notes	191,404,140 00
From legal-tender notes	2,159,830 00
From fractional currency	14,614,563 15
From prize captures	8,206,538 74
From captured and abandoned property	2,427,349 38
From confiscation	187,232 34
From fines, penalties, and forfeitures	436,752 57
From drafts and substitutes	5,321,181 14
From internal and coastwise intercourse	4,020,522 74
From premiums and interest on loans	13,988,143 36
From public lands	919,324 52
From patent fees	278,444 50
From sick and wounded soldiers	393,704 86
From Indian trusts, &c	191,890 89
From National Bank duty	716,081 15
From real estate, direct tax	1,028,679 51
From repayments	4,489,091 59
From conscience money refunded	20,900 65
From fees, licenses, and miscellaneous	10,301,320 88
From War Department	3,602,431 42
From Navy Department	8,504,205 49
	1,848,029,185 82

The receipts on account of the War Department consist, mainly, in repayments into the treasury by disbursing officers, and proceeds of confiscation.

The receipts on account of the Navy Department were, mainly, repayments into the treasury by disbursing officers, and from captures.

The following tables exhibit the movement of the treasury for the five years comprised, in whole or in part, in the period of time between the breaking out and the suppression of the rebellion:

Receipts for the preceding year to June 30.

1861	$88,694,572 03
1862	589,197,417 72
1863	888,082,128 05
1864	1,408,474,234 51
1865	1,826,075,227 14

Payments for the preceding year to June 30.

1861	$90,012,449 79
1862	578,376,242 40
1863	895,796,630 65
1864	1,313,157,872 94
1865	1,925,052,347 30

The receipts and expenditures on account of the Post Office Department were as follows:

Balance from last year	$1,074,294 97
Receipts from postmasters and others	3,445,744 88
Received, but not covered in	3,000 00
Warrants cancelled	25,253 94
	4,548,293 79

There has been paid on 3,148 warrants................... $3,091,025 99
Balance to new account............................... 1,457,267 80

4,548,293 79

The aggregate business transactions, including all necessary entries in the cash accounts on the books, at the principal office in the city of Washington for the last five years, show the following results:

1861.................................. $41,325,339 20
1862.................................. 929,630,814 38
1863.................................. 2,696,059,087 86
1864.................................. 3,889,171,151 00
1865.................................. 4,366,551,844 73

Being more than one hundred times as much in the last as in the first year.

But to give a correct idea of the magnitude of the business of the treasury, in Washington, there should be added to this last named amount of $4,366,551,844 73
The aggregate of receipts and payments, as above...... 3,647,566,764 32
And transfers by letters of instruction, &c............. 1,103,736,403 53

Giving a grand aggregate of...................... 9,117,855,012 58

As the office was open only three hundred and three days, the average is over three million of dollars for every day, and this is exclusive of the agency accounts at all the other offices.

New currency in kinds and amounts as follows has been received, counted, and issued, viz:

Three-years six per cent. compound interest notes........ $215,835,440 00
United States legal-tender notes....................... 5,386,870 00
Fractional currency.................................. 14,618,757 30

Total issues............................... 235,841,067 30

Certificates of indebtedness were issued of the amounts and denominations, as follows:

19,106 certificates of $5,000 each, is.................. $95,530,000 00
33,315 certificates of $1,000 each, is.................. 33,315,000 00

Total issued within the year............... 128,845,000 00

Being over forty-three millions less than the issue of the preceding fiscal year.

Certificates of indebtedness have been redeemed to the amount of....................................... $185,161,077 27

Currency has been redeemed and destroyed as follows:

Old issue United States notes......................... $316,434 00
New issue United States notes......................... 4,242,416 60
One year five per cent. notes......................... 36,052,430 00
Two-years five per cent. notes........................ 8,764,050 00
Two-years five per cent. coupon notes.................. 77,178,900 00
Six per cent. compound interest notes.................. 5,742,670 00
First issue fractional currency....................... 4,903,747 34

Second issue fractional currency........................ $6, 956, 634 30
Third issue fractional currency......................... 49, 530 00
Add discount on mutilated notes......................... 13, 108 09

Total withdrawal of currency.................. 144, 219, 920 33

This redemption involved the separate examination and counting of over seventy million of distinct pieces.

The uncancelled currency of the United States, including time interest notes, and all kinds in the treasury, its various offices and depositories, stood at the close of the fiscal year as follows:

Old issue United States demand notes.................. $472, 603 50
New issue United States legal-tender notes.............. 431, 066, 427 99
Six per cent. compound interest notes.................... 191, 721, 470 00
One-year five per cent. notes........................... 8, 467, 570 00
Two-years five per cent. notes.......................... 7, 715, 950 00
Two-years five per cent. coupon notes.................. 34, 441, 650 00
Fractional currency.................................... 25, 033, 128 76

Total uncancelled currency..................... 698, 918, 800 25

In addition to these, there was held in the reserve fund, legal-tender notes, $16,139,633 51.

National banks had deposited securities in this office preliminary to their organization at the date of the last annual statement to the number of   473
Securities have been deposited during the fiscal year by.............   916

Whole number so depositing June 30, 1865.................. 1, 389

Two of the number have voluntarily discontinued doing business and are winding up their affairs. These have withdrawn their securities Another has failed, and its circulating notes are being redeemed by this office from avails of securities deposited in it, which are amply sufficient to redeem all its outstanding circulating notes at their full face value.

At the date of the preceding annual statement there had been designated of these banks as depositories of public moneys and financial agents of the United States.......................................   204
There have been added during the fiscal year......................   141
And there have been discontinued..................................   15

Leaving the whole number of national banks so designated on the 30th June, 1865, at 330.

These banks have been a great help to this office in the collection of the internal revenue tax, and in the procuring of subscriptions to and the placing of the various government loans. Thus far, with a single unimportant exception, they have all promptly responded to every demand that has been made upon them by this office for the payment of government funds in their custody.

Amount of bonds held for security of circulation at date of last
statement.. $44, 266, 900
Received during last fiscal year.......................... 191, 722, 800

Total amount held for circulation..................... 235, 989, 700

At the date of last report there were held for security of government deposits—

Government securities........................	$10,697,050
Personal bonds.....	19,312,700
Total, June 30, 1864........................	30,009,750

There are now held government securities.............	$32,682,500
Personal bonds.............................	25,000
Total, June 30, 1865........................	32,707,500

Total securities held for national banks, $268,697,200.

Statement of bonds held in security for circulating notes:

Five per cent. coupon bonds........................	$1,104,900
Five per cent. registered bonds.....................	64,283,700
Six per cent. coupon bonds........................	6,282,250
Six per cent. registered bonds.....................	164,318,850
	235,989,700

In security for public deposits:

Five per cent. coupon bonds........................	$3,225,500
Five per cent. registered bonds.....................	2,691,800
Six per cent. coupon bonds........................	3,162,250
Six per cent. registered bonds.....................	5,520,450
Seven three-tenths treasury notes...................	13,817,500
Certificates of indebtedness......................	4,265,000
Personal bonds..............................	25,000
	32,707,500

Total securities held for national banks, $268,697,200.

To facilitate payments at the points where the disbursements must necessarily be made, 5,141 transfer orders have been issued, by which there has been moved from one depository to another, $1,103,736,403 53, being nearly three times as much as was so moved two years ago, and about fifty per cent. more than last year.

There have been issued during the fiscal year upon the offices of New York, Philadelphia, Boston, and San Francisco, 68,138 transfer checks, by which there has been paid at those points $277,371,468 53, of which amount $6,364,922 40 was paid in coin.

There are at the office in Washington 274 open accounts of disbursing officers. There have been received, during the fiscal year, one hundred and five thousand and sixty-four official letters. All of them have received attention; most of them, it is true, by the filling up of printed circulars. But notwithstanding these labor-saving devices, nine thousand eight hundred and seventy-three manuscript letters have been written. This is an increase of more than two thousand over last year, and more than double the number written the year before.

By the tables, wherein are compared the movements of the office for the last five years, it will be seen that the business, labor, and money transactions of the office have again been enormously increased. The tables would not be unaptly represented by a truncated pyramid. It is, however, hoped that the tables representing the business of the office, so far at least as the expenditures are con-

7 F

cerned, for the next five years, will be represented by such a pyramid with its base turned upward.

There is still great difficulty in obtaining, and in retaining when obtained, the services of persons of the talent and proved probity of character required for the safe transaction of the business of the treasury, at the rates of compensation now allowed by law. The assistant receiving teller, three clerks of the fourth class, six of the third class, five of the second class, and quite a number of the best clerks of the first class, have resigned their positions in this office, and have taken employment elsewhere, where their services were better appreciated and rewarded.

The cashier, the assistant cashier, and the chief of the division of national banks, and others, have remained at their places from motives and considerations other than and above mere pecuniary ones. It is, however, doubtful whether, now that the war is over, these patriotic considerations will continue to influence the conduct of this class of officers and clerks.

It is submitted, therefore, that the public interest requires that the pay of most of the employés in this office should be increased, or at least a percentage on their present salaries allowed them, during the continuance of the present high rates of living, and while their services would command better pay elsewhere.

It is also suggested that the female clerks, who in this office incur great responsibilities, should, like the other clerks, be classified, with salaries according to class, ranging from six to nine hundred dollars per annum.

It is again a subject of gratulation that notwithstanding the difficulty of retaining proper persons for want of adequate pay, the immense money transactions of this office have been satisfactorily accomplished without the loss of one cent to the people of the United States.

I have the honor to be, very respectfully, your obedient servant,

F. E. SPINNER,
Treasurer United States.

Hon. HUGH McCULLOCH,
Secretary of the Treasury, Washington, D. C.

SCHEDULE A.

Receipts and disbursements at the office of the assistant treasurer at New York for the fiscal year ending June 30, 1865.

RECEIPTS.

On account of customs	$61,756,729 55
On account of loans	137,314,829 90
On account of internal revenue	9,969,901 54
On account of miscellaneous	415,474,544 53
On account of patent fees	96,540 16
On account of Post Office Department	1,762,940 56
	626,375,486 24

DEBITS.

On account of treasury drafts	$631,223,920 52
On account of Post Office warrants	1,888,265 74
Amount credited to disbursing officers' accounts	587,260,871 61
Amount of checks paid on disbursing officers' accounts	571,742,326 32
Amount paid for interest on the public debt	37,598,390 61
Amount paid on temporary loan	62,683,788 49
	1,882,397,563 29

SCHEDULE B.

Receipts and disbursements at the office of the assistant treasurer at Boston for the year ending June 30, 1865.

	Receipts.	Disbursements.
Temporary loan	$14,000,000	$17,860,000
Five-twenty bonds	319,400	
Loan of 1861, act March 3, 1863	52,600	
Seven-thirty treasury notes	1,253,450	
Internal revenue taxes	2,360,000	
Internal revenue stamps	620,000	
Fishing bounties	400,000	400,000
Disbursing officers' accounts	98,000,000	95,000,000
Post Office Department	432,000	310,000
Customs	10,307,000	
Interest account	9,730,000	9,530,000
Treasurer's general account	....	150,000,000
By transfer and various other sources	130,625,550	
	268,100,000	273,100,000

The amount of fractional currency redeemed is	$1,000,000
The whole number of coupons paid	670,000
The whole number of persons to whom interest is paid	38,000

SCHEDULE C.

Receipts and disbursements at the office of the assistant treasurer at Philadelphia for the year ending June 30, 1865.

RECEIPTS.

From transfer orders	$60,528,185 00
From loans	41,458,405 00
From customs	3,914,028 15
From internal revenue	2,916,440 82
From Post Office	386,090 63
From patent fees	13,143 00
From miscellaneous sources	24,644 81
Total	109,240,937 41

From similar sources the previous year	$120,885,238 11
Deduct	109,240,937 41
Decrease of receipts this year	11,644,300 70

DISBURSEMENTS.

On general treasury warrants	$115,152,815 35
On Post Office warrants	196,234 03
Total	115,349,049 38
Similar payments the previous year	111,651,953 27
Excess of payments this year	3,697,096 11

The payments made on disbursers' checks, numbering 36,350, including those drawn by the Treasurer on his transfer account, amount to	$96,912,506 13
Similar payments previous year	77,573,267 29
Increase of payments on disbursers' checks	19,339,240 84

SCHEDULE D.

*Receipts and disbursements at the office of the assistant treasurer at St. Louis
for the fiscal year ending June 30, 1865.*

Receipts	$177,152,859 19
Disbursements	173,468,565 87

SCHEDULE E.

*Receipts and disbursements at the office of the United States depositary at Cin-
cinnati for the year ending June 30, 1865.*

RECEIPTS.

Loans	$4,048,000 00
Transfers	49,920,000 00
Internal revenue	1,999,569 63
Miscellaneous	9,552,617 40
Deposits by disbursing officers	56,498,173 65
	122,018,360 68

DISBURSEMENTS.

Treasury drafts	$60,032,006 17
Payments on account of temporary loan	4,546,891 00
Interest on public debt	1,647,274 58
Payments to disbursing officers	50,178,692 67
	125,404,864 42

SCHEDULE F.

*Receipts and disbursements at the office of the United States depositary at Louis-
ville for the fiscal year ending June 30, 1865.*

Receipts	$78,795,235 87
Disbursements	80,397,800 57

REPORT OF THE REGISTER OF THE TREASURY.

TREASURY DEPARTMENT,
Register's Office, November, 1865.

SIR: I submit the following report of transactions in this office during the
year ending June 30, 1865.

RECEIPTS AND EXPENDITURES.

The business of this division for the last fiscal year has been greater than in
any previous year.

The number of warrants issued for the civil, diplomatic, miscellaneous, and public debt expenditures was	15,627
In the previous year	12,645
An increase of over twenty per cent	2,982

The number of warrants for receipts from customs, sales of public lands, internal revenue, and miscellaneous for the year 3,764
In the previous year 2,870

An increase of over thirty per cent 894

The number of pay and repay warrants issued during the year in the War, Navy, and Interior (Indian and Pension) Departments was .. 14,019
In the previous year 12,600

An increase of over twelve per cent 1,419

The number of journal pages filled with entries of accounts and warrants relating to civil, diplomatic, miscellaneous, and public debt receipts and expenditures for the year was—
Treasury proper 1,153
Diplomatic 549
Interior, civil, &c 379
Customs 586

2,667

A slight increase over last year.
The number of drafts registered was 33,257.
The number of certificates given for the settlement of accounts was 6,200.

From the First and Fifth Auditor's Offices and the General Land Office there were received 14,047 accounts, an increase over last year of over ten per cent. A majority of these accounts were copied for warrants to issue; all of them were registered, and one-half or more journalized, and posted in the several ledgers. Considerable progress has been made during the year in balancing the ledgers of previous years, and the work is being rapidly brought up to the present time.

There are kept in the division nine ledgers containing personal accounts, and eight appropriation ledgers, an increase of one, arising from the increase in the public debt. It being found impracticable to keep this class of accounts in the civil appropriation ledger, they were transferred to one specially for them. The annual report in detail of the receipts and expenditures has become a work of considerable magnitude, and constantly employs two clerks, and sometimes more. There is much of the work of the division of which account cannot be given that requires time and care.

The care of filing records, copying accounts for suits, preparing the quarterly statement of the receipts and expenditures for the settlement of the Treasurer's accounts, and the copying of warrants, involves much labor, and, to the credit of those whose duty it has been, it has been done with care and celerity.

NOTES AND COUPONS.

This division was organized about the 30th June, 1864, commencing with ten clerks, and has continued under the efficient charge of Mr. Day to the present time. The work devolving upon the division has been constantly increasing, so that on the 30th June, 1865, there were thirty-three (twelve male and twenty-one female) clerks employed. At the present date there are eighty-five (twenty-three male and sixty-two female) clerks in the division.

During the year embraced in this report, the first series of seven-thirty treasury notes, under acts of June 30, 1864, and March 3, 1865, was issued. There were received from the Currency Bureau 1,293,185 notes, each note having five coupons attached, making 6,465,925 coupons. Every note and coupon

was examined and counted previous to issue. Of these notes there were registered and delivered on subscription to the loan branch of the Secretary's
bureau 1,256,808 notes, amounting to $301,693,350. The registering of these
notes covered 2,515 pages. It is a matter of congratulation that this entire
issue was effected without the occurrence of a mistake involving a loss to the
government of a single dollar.

Of treasury notes (upper halves) there have been assorted, counted, and
registered—

Two-years five per cent. coupon treasury notes, act of March 3, 1863, 294,811 notes, amounting to	$100, 445, 150
Two-years five per cent. treasury notes, act of March 3, 1863, 117,409 notes, amounting to	8, 411, 500
One-year five per cent. treasury notes, act of March 3, 1863, 512,662 notes, amounting to	14, 787, 330
Making a total of 924,882 notes, amounting to	123, 643, 980

Of three-years six per cent. compound interest notes, (upper halves,) acts
March 3, 1863, and June 30, 1864, there have been assorted, counted, and
registered 54,820 notes, amounting to $1,596,300. All of the above notes, after
careful examination and comparison, were burned.

Of "seven-thirty" treasury notes, act of July 17, 1861, there have been examined, assorted, counted, and registered 156,836 notes, amounting to $44,437,500.
These notes, after examining the registering of redemption, are packed away
in iron closets in the files-room for future destruction.

The assorting, arranging, counting, and registering of redeemed and mutilated
coupons now employs the larger part of the clerical force of the division. The
number of redeemed coupons assorted, arranged, and counted during the year
is 2,583,117. The number of coupons registered during the year is 1,591,135,
all of which have to be examined after they are registered.

A large amount of miscellaneous work has been performed, incident upon the
commencement of a new division, which cannot be estimated by figures. The
work of examining, arranging, counting, and registering redeemed coupons is
one of great magnitude, and must necessarily require a large clerical force for
many years to come. In this connexion I desire to add my conviction that a
very large share of the work in this division is successfully accomplished by
female clerks; and it is within my observation that there are very many of these
in this bureau receiving a salary of only sixty dollars per month, who are as
capable every way as male clerks who receive $1,200 per annum. It is not
easy to justify this discrimination. The just expenses of ladies are as great as
those of single men. Their sacrifices for the country have gone beyond all
recompense. I therefore believe it to be due from Congress to authorize by
law a classification of female clerks into three or four classes, with salaries
graded from $600 to $1,000 per year.

REDEEMED CURRENCY COUNTED AND DESTROYED.

Of redeemed United States legal-tender notes there have been counted and destroyed in amount	$4, 152, 134
Demand notes	316, 434
Postal currency	4, 688, 588
Fractional currency	6, 418, 722

There has also been counted and destroyed a large amount of surplus bonds,
notes, and fractional currency, never issued by the department, most of which
having been done since the 30th June last, will be more properly stated in my
next report.

COMMERCE AND NAVIGATION.

It is a pleasure to be able to report the work of this division in better progress than for several years past. The statements for the report for the last fiscal year will be in readiness for the printer within the time required by law. This gratifying condition of the work of the division is due to the energetic efforts of the gentlemen employed in it to bring their division to its proper position in the bureau. The statements required for the financial report for 1865 require great *additions*, calling for increased labor beyond any that have preceded it. It embraces summary statements of the imports and exports of foreign merchandise, exports of domestic products, statements of entrances and clearances of vessels in the foreign trade by countries and by districts, statements of the registered, enrolled, and licensed vessels belonging to the United States, by districts, under the new and old admeasurement, in addition to those heretofore required. The work has been resumed upon "imposts," and is now pushed as rapidly as consistent with perfect accuracy in results. Statements are in course of compilation, and will be ready for the report on commerce and navigation for 1865.

The system of book-keeping used in this division, and the successful results effected by the accomplished experts in its application, will justify me in placing on record the fact that the clerks perform the highest character of clerical duty, and deserve the highest clerical compensation.

Since my last report, the annual commerce and navigation report for 1863, as well as that for 1864—both, for causes set forth by my predecessor, considerably delayed—have been issued.

Attached to the former volumes is a series of comparative tables, exhibiting for a period of four years the trade to and from each distinguishable division of every foreign country. The preparation of these tables has been attended with severe labor, and has been the cause of inconvenient delay in the issue of the annual publications from this division. In the succeeding volumes, those for 1864 and 1865, these tables have been, in pursuance of your order, discontinued. For practical use it is quite certain that a comparative exhibit of the leading articles only for a period of four or five years may be all that will be required.

LOANS.

During the last fiscal year the issues of United States stock have been as follows:

Coupon bonds, direct issue.

Loans.	Number of cases.	Number of bonds.	Amount.
1861, acts July 17 and August 5	19,464	113,475	$87,678,050
1862, act February 25, 5-20s......................	12	4,020	4,012,750
1863, act March 3.............................	1,000	70,698	51,380,600
1864, act March 3, 10-40s	6,703	117,869	79,530,300
1864, act June 30, 5-20s.........................	544	111,615	83,300,300
Totals......................	27,723	437,677	305,908,000

Registered bonds, direct issue.

Loans.	Number of cases.	Number of bonds.	Amount.
1861, acts July 17 and August 5	2,023	9,850	$27,026,850
1863, act March 3	345	4,134	17,821 900
1864, act March 3, 10-40s	670	3,975	20,859,900
1864, act June 30, 5-20s	110	1,591	8,519,700
Totals.................................	3,148	19,550	74,228,350

Registered bonds issued for transfers or assignments.

Loans.	Number of cases.	Number of bonds transferred and cancelled.	Number of bonds issued.	Amount.
1847, act January 28...............	164	515	448	$1,237,900
1848, act March 31...............	66	200	167	569,600
1858, act June 14	19	30	30	150,000
1860, act June 22	23	72	84	235,000
1861, act February 8	160	465	405	1,312,000
1861, acts July 17 and August 5....	965	4,205	3,603	14,748,350
1862, act February 25, 5-20s........	1,366	5,978	5,451	17,967,200
1863, act March 3................	493	2,115	1,900	8,311,800
1864, act March 3, 10-40s	741	3,622	2,596	9,959,850
1864, act June 30, 5-20s..........	179	814	766	3,140,950
Totals	4,196	18,016	15,450	57,532,650

Registered bonds issued in exchange for coupon bonds.

Loans.	Number of cases.	Number of bonds issued.	Amount.
1848, act January 28.......................	4	10	$14,000
1858, act June 14.......................	24	84	420,000
1860, act June 22.......................	8	14	62,000
1861, act February 8	109	274	858,000
1861, acts July 17 and August 5......	957	5,668	32,960,150
1862, act February 25	1,352	6,588	39,636,200
1863, act March 3	829	3,937	21,502,000
1864, act March 3	1,260	6,422	41,636,250
1864, act June 30.......................	917	3,876	22,951,450
Totals	5,460	26,873	160,060,050

Total number of bonds signed	497,650
Total number of letters signed..	40,527
Total number of signatures..	536,140
Total amount of bonds issued..	$597,729,050

In addition to the work attending the issue of stock, is that of preparing, semi-annually, schedules of the interest payable on all registered stock, which are sent to each of the United States depositaries.

These schedules contain the names of the creditors, the amount of stock held by each, the rate, date of the commencement, and amount of interest.

The schedules are made out in duplicate, one copy being retained in the office, and one sent to the Treasurer, assistant treasurer, or depositary, who pays the interest.

The number of accounts open for the different loans is, at this date, 18,925.

I present herewith a resumé of the number and amount of bonds issued from this office under the different loans since and including the year 1841.

Statement showing the number and amount of bonds of the following loans issued in the office of the Register of the Treasury to June 30, 1865.

Loan.	Registered or coupon.	Number of bonds issued.	Amount.
1841.................................	....	14, 045	$5, 672, 976 88
1842.................................	Registered ...	9, 721	24, 677, 400 00
1842.................................	Coupon......	2, 415	3, 461, 000 00
1843.................................	Registered ...	6, 848	24, 770, 900 00
1843.................................	Coupon......	2, 186	2, 836, 000 00
1846.................................	Registered ...	7, 510	14, 382, 500 00
1847.................................	Registered ...	36, 912	76, 519, 050 00
1848.................................	Registered ...	8, 296	18, 227, 500 00
1848.................................	Coupon......	7, 011	8, 313, 000 00
Texan Indemnity...................	Coupon......	5, 000	5, 000, 000 00
1858.................................	Registered ...	1, 975	6, 975, 000 00
1858.................................	Coupon......	17, 561	17, 561, 000 00
1860.................................	Registered ...	2, 016	7, 756, 000 00
1860.................................	Coupon......	1, 682	1, 682, 000 00
1861, 8th February	Registered ...	9, 871	25, 748, 000 00
1861.................................	Coupon......	8, 533	8, 533, 000 00
1861, 17th July...................	Registered ...	32, 124	121, 596, 650 00
1861.................................	Coupon......	190, 697	137, 517, 950 00
1862.................................	Registered ...	34, 064	145, 892, 950 00
1862.................................	Coupon......	844, 238	439, 423, 650 00
1863.................................	Registered....	9, 975	47, 637, 300 00
1863.................................	Coupon......	76, 698	57, 178, 100 00
1864, 3d March....................	Registered ...	21, 152	99, 641, 350 00
1864.................................	Coupon......	230, 071	135, 342, 750 00
1864, 30th June...................	Registered ...	6, 178	34, 783, 450 00
1864.................................	Coupon......	111, 615	83, 306, 300 00
Central Pacific Railroad..........	Registered ...	1, 508	1, 508, 000 00
Total..........................	....	1, 699, 302	1, 546, 843, 776 88

This vast amount of highly responsible labor, examining, counting, filling up, signing, entering, and transmitting these masses of bonds, representative of money, with all its temptation to the weak, has been accomplished, I am happy to say, without the loss, in this office, to the government or to any individual, of one dollar. For this success great credit is due to the systematic order of business which has matured under the veteran leading clerks in charge, so many years, of the division and its important subdivisions.

This report would be incomplete without a brief reference to the "files-room." Here is kept the infallible "guide book" to all the accounts coming from various sources through the offices of the First Comptroller and Commissioner of Customs. The perfect system of arranging papers, with exact references of record to each one, has proved adequate to the great increase of vouchers concentrated here by the war. In an office where confusion would be so easy to occur, and yet so intolerable, it is gratifying to feel always sure of order, accuracy, and promptness. It is superfluous to add, what has been for years the impression in your department, that very great credit belongs to Messrs. Smith and Wannall, clerks in charge of the office.

Having reference to your circular of the 1st instant, advising replies to all letters addressed or referred to heads of bureaus to be made on the same day, I am able to say that it has been the invariable custom of this office to reply by next mail to all communications sent to this office requiring answer; and I have no doubt that the general satisfaction of the public with the prompt attention received here is due largely to the observance of this just and salutary rule.

I have the honor to remain, very respectfully, your obedient servant,

S . B. COLBY, *Register.*

Hon. HUGH McCULLOCH,
     Secretary of the Treasury.

REPORT OF THE SOLICITOR OF THE TREASURY.

TREASURY DEPARTMENT, SOLICITOR'S OFFICE,
November 8, 1865.

SIR : I have the honor herewith to transmit eight tabular statements, showing, in part, the operations in charge of this office for the fiscal year ending
June 30, 1865. They are as follows :

1. A statement of suits on transcripts of accounts of defaulting public officers,
contractors, &c., adjusted by the accounting officers of the Treasury Department.

2. Statement of suits for the recovery of fines, penalties, and forfeitures, under the customs revenue laws.

3. Statement of prize cases.

4. Statement of libels filed under the confiscation act of July 17, 1862, and
the non-intercourse act of July 13, 1861.

5. Statement of fines, penalties, and forfeitures, under the internal revenue
laws.

6. Statement of suits in which the United States were interested, not embraced in any of the other tables.

7. Statement of warehouses and transportation bonds reported for suit by
collectors of customs.

8. A general summary or abstract of the foregoing tables.

This summary shows that the whole number of suits, of all descriptions,
brought during the year was 2,348, of which 12 were of class 1, for the recovery of $45,392 57; 345 of class 2, for the recovery of $1,232,725 89; 201
of class 3; 988 of class 4; 476 of class 5, for the recovery of $586,379 20;
254 of class 6, for the recovery of $205,628 99; and 72 of class 7, for the
recovery of $129,400 70. Of these suits 755 were disposed of during the
year, in the following manner, viz: 5 were decided against the United States,
658 for the United States, 57 were settled and dismissed, and 35 were remitted by the Secretary of the Treasury, leaving 1,593 still pending.

Of the suits pending at the beginning of the year, 302 were disposed of in
the following manner, viz: 254 were decided for the United States, 13 were
decided against the United States, and 35 were settled and dismissed.

The total number of suits, of all descriptions, decided or otherwise disposed
of during the year was 1,057. The gross amount for which judgments were
obtained, exclusive of judgments *in rem.*, was $583,039 42, and the whole
amount collected from all sources was $9,558,521 42.

The following table presents, in a compendious form, the results of the litigation of the last year, and also of the year next preceding :

Year.	Total amount reported sued for.	SUITS BROUGHT DURING THE FISCAL YEAR.							
		Total amount of judgments for United States.	Total amount reported collected.	Decided for United States.	Decided against United States.	Settled and dismissed.	Remitted.	Pending.	Total number of suits brought.
1864	$856,644 34	$30,670 82	$4,267,945 65	664	2	43	28	1,866	2,604
1865	2,199,527 35	198,747 98	5,758,497 91	658	5	57	35	1,593	2,348

Year.	SUITS BROUGHT PRIOR TO THE FISCAL YEAR.					Total number of suits disposed of.	Whole number of judgments in favor of U. S.	Whole amount of judgments in favor of United States during the fiscal year.	Whole amount collected from all sources during the fiscal year.
	Amount of judgments in old suits.	Decided for United States.	Decided against United States.	Settled and dismissed.	Amount collected in old suits.				
1864	$37,172 00	340	94	85	$3,717,588 26	1,186	1,004	$67,942 82	$7,985,532 91
1865	343,991 44	254	13	35	3,800,093 51	1,057	912	583,039 42	9,538,521 42

A glance at this table, and a comparison of it with similar ones embraced in former reports, will show a large and constant increase in the business of the office. It will also show that the gratifying improvement noted by me in my last annual report in the proportion of suits decided for and against the United States, respectively, has been sustained during the last year. In the year ending June 30, 1863, of the suits pending at the beginning thereof, there were two hundred and forty decided against the United States, sixty-four settled and dismissed, and only ninety-six decided for the United States; while during the last year, as has been shown, of three hundred and two such suits, two hundred and fifty-four were decided for the United States, thirty-five settled and dismissed, and only thirteen decided against the United States. Similar though not so great improvement is observable in the results of suits brought and determined within the year.

This gratifying result has, in my judgment, been owing to the increased encouragement given to district attorneys by the act of March 3, 1863, and to the efforts put forth by this office, with the sanction of the Secretary of the Treasury, to secure, in all cases, a strenuous prosecution or defence of suits in which the United States has had an interest. The result has been, in my opinion, a saving of hundreds of thousands of dollars directly, and much more indirectly, to the treasury.

In my last annual report I called the attention of the Secretary, at some length, to the measures which had been adopted, in pursuance of the act to which I have just alluded, looking to the prevention or detection of frauds upon the revenue. I do not deem it necessary to enter into a detailed statement of what has since been done in the same direction, but will say, generally, that all the developments which have been since made have served to confirm the views I then expressed, and to demonstrate the wisdom and efficiency of the act in question. A large number of cases of fraud have been discovered by means of the instrumentalities provided by that act, and, as a consequence, penalties and forfeitures to the amount of several hundred thousand dollars have been enforced. The effect cannot but be of the most salutary nature in deterring unconscientious importers from future violations of the law.

Among the measures alluded to was the seizure of a large quantity of Champagne wines, both in the city of New York and in San Francisco; proceedings for the condemnation of which were pending at the time of making my last report, as those instituted in New York still are. In San Francisco sixteen or seventeen cases have been tried, and have resulted uniformly in favor of the government, and I am informed that most of the suits instituted there were made, by agreement, to depend upon the result of those tried. The suits pending in New York involve substantially the same questions as those thus decided. They will be brought to trial at the earliest practicable moment.

It is not improbable that some of the questions involved in these cases may be taken by those interested to the Supreme Court of the United States, but I entertain no doubt of the correctness of the general grounds assumed by the government in regard to them, and I therefore cannot but anticipate a favorable result in their final determination.

The regulations contemplated by the act of 3d March, 1865, in relation to the verification of invoices have not yet been issued by the Secretary of State, owing to causes which it is not necessary here to explain, and our consuls have not generally thought it proper for them, in the absence thereof, to require the evidence contemplated by said act, of the correctness of invoices presented to them for verification; but these regulations will, doubtless, be issued at an early day, and I anticipate from them the most salutary results. This anticipation is fortified by the experience of our consul at Lyons, where for a considerable period it has been usual to demand samples of merchandise, the invoices of which are presented for verification, and, as the consul asserts, with the most signal advantage.

In the administration of the fund appropriated for the suppression of counterfeiting, I have endeavored to accomplish, as far as practicable, the end contemplated in its creation; and the measures which have been adopted have resulted in the arrest and conviction of a large number of offenders, and the seizure of several presses, dies, plates, &c., together with considerable counterfeit money, and a large quantity of paper, ink, and other material for counterfeiting. There was expended, during the year, in the prosecution of these measures the sum of thirty thousand eight hundred and sixty-six dollars and ninety cents.

The special attention which the supervision of these measures has compelled me to bestow upon the statutes relating to counterfeiting the securities of the United States, has revealed to me the fact that the existing laws upon the subject are defective in several particulars, and that for some acts highly prejudicial to the government and the public, no punishment is provided. I therefore respectfully recommend that the department cause a careful revision of these laws to be made by some competent person, and that Congress be asked to remedy such defects as may be found to exist.

I have the honor to be, very respectfully,

EDWARD JORDAN,
Solicitor of the Treasury.

Hon. H. McCulloch,
Secretary of the Treasury.

Statistical summary of business arising from suits in which the United States is a party or has an interest, under charge of the Solicitor of the Treasury, during the fiscal year ending June 30, 1865.

Judicial districts.	Treasury transcripts.		Fines, penalties, and forfeitures under customs revenue laws.		Prize.		Confiscation suits under act July 17, 1862, and suits under act July 13, 1861, &c.		Internal revenue.		Miscellaneous.		Custom-house bonds.		Total amount (reported) sued for.	Total amount (reported) in judgment for United States.
	No.	Amount sued for.	No.	Amount sued for.	No.	Amount sued for.	No.	Amount sued for.	No.	Amount sued for.	No.	Amount sued for.	No.	Amount sued for.		
Maine			67	$2,073 60			1								$2,073 60	$1,000 00
New Hampshire							1		2	$500 00	2	$2,000 00			2,500 00	
Vermont									2	180 00					180 00	
Massachusetts			33	11,867 70	23		11		35	8,716 00	16	72,437 60			93,021 30	479 97
Connecticut											12	300 00			300 00	1,275 00
Rhode Island	1	$3,164 26							3	125 50					3,289 76	5 00
New York, northern district			40	5,050 00			1		45	32,470 00	56	27,304 41			64,824 41	7,593 15
New York, eastern district			1						14	1,896 18					1,896 18	3,350 00
New York, southern district			116		15		26		50	145,193 20	11	31,200 00	41	$44,406 42	220,799 62	25,880 36
New Jersey							6		9	1,100 00	23	3,100 00			4,200 00	2,450 00
Pennsylvania, eastern district			5	400 00	34		2		2	200 00	7	7,000 00			7,600 00	
Pennsylvania, western district									21	120,895 60					120,895 60	
Delaware																
Maryland			2				16		22	12,298 12	1				12,298 12	15,475 00
District of Columbia			1				4		27		29					40,689 48
Virginia									280							7,080 00

uisiana, eastern district			18			69		107		20	21, 040 00			2	32, 000 00	53, 040 00	48, 678
uisiana, western district																
issippi																
xas																
ansas, eastern district								33								5, 369 25
ansas, western district																
souri, eastern district	1	2, 119 14	3	630 00			51		17	3, 430 00	5	4, 600 00			10, 779 14	15, 696 09
souri, western district										1						
nnessee, eastern district							301					3	6, 600 00			6, 600 00	10, 963 10
nnessee, middle district							4									2, 487 00
nnessee, western district	1	436 17					1									
ntucky							50		11	38, 860 00	12	8, 795 00			48, 091 17	13, 151 95
io, northern district			1						15	46, 430 00	20	3, 500 00			49, 930 00	2, 098 56
io, southern district									14	2, 354 50	9	21, 962 50			24, 317 00	1, 250 00
iana							4		51	21, 525 00	2	6, 500 00			28, 025 00	1, 016 94
nois, northern district									35	6, 450 00	1	100 00			6, 550 00	1, 360 00
nois, southern district						10		24		19	22, 600 00					22, 600 00	1, 660 49
chigan, eastern district			19	300 00					2		17	4, 650 00	10	4, 329 48	5	18, 660 28	27, 939 76	1, 851 60
chigan, western district	1	235 28										2	2, 200 00			2, 435 28	3, 106 57
sconsin	1	729 76										2				729 76	
wa	1	11, 897 03									3					11, 897 03	
nnesota	1	3, 988 47									3	345 10			4	9, 627 76	13, 961 33	
nsas	2	18, 890 55							2		34		18			4	18, 890 55	10, 733 50
lifornia, northern district			36	1, 212, 404 59							28	86, 120 00	3	500 00	20	24, 706 24	1, 323, 730 83	125 00
lifornia, southern district			3														
egon																
vada																
ah Territory																
ashington Territory																
braska Territory	3	3, 932 91										4	1, 300 00			5, 231 91	2, 419 65
kota Territory												6	1, 900 00			1, 900 00	
lorado Territory											3						
w Mexico Territory																
izona Territory																
aho Territory																
ontana Territory																
Total	12	45, 392 57	345	1, 232, 725 89	201		988		476	586, 379 20	254	205, 628 99	72	129, 400 70	2, 199, 527 35	198, 747 98

Statistical summary of business arising from suits in which the United States is a party, &c.—Continued.

Judicial districts.	SUITS BROUGHT DURING THE FISCAL YEAR ENDING JUNE 30, 1865.							IN SUITS BROUGHT PRIOR THERETO.					Whole number of judgments returned in favor of the United States during the year.	Total number of suits disposed of.	Whole amount of judgments rendered in favor of the United States during the fiscal year ending June 30, 1865.	Whole amount collected from all sources during the fiscal year ending June 30, 1865.
	Total amount (reported) collected.	Decided for the United States.	Decided against the United States.	Settled and dismissed.	Remitted.	Pending.	Total number of suits brought.	Amount of judgments (reported) in all old suits this year.	Decided for the United States.	Decided against the United States.	Settled and dismissed.	Amount (reported) collected in all old suits this year.				
Maine	$10,249 90	48		3	3	14	68	$15 00	2			$15 00	50	56	$1,015 00	$10,264 90
New Hampshire	2,006 00	2				3	5	1,332 26	1			1,332 26	3	3	1,332 26	3,338 26
Vermont						2	2	396 56	1		3	396 56	1	4	396 56	
Massachusetts	1,831,635 01	32		2	3	81	118	6,179 97	17	1	1	2,446,407 15	49	56	6,659 94	4,278,042 16
Connecticut	750 00	9				3	12		2		2	461 60	11	13	1,275 00	1,211 69
Rhode Island	5 00	1		2		1	4						1	3	5 00	5 00
New York, northern district	38,562 47	60	2		4	66	142		4		1	2,112 12	64	81	7,853 15	40,674 59
New York, eastern district					2	13	15							2	2,350 00	
New York, southern district	2,103,286 15	65	1	18	5	172	261		14	11	8	73,821 69	79	122	25,820 36	2,176,907 84
New Jersey		17				21	38						17	17	2,450 00	
Pennsylvania, eastern district	680,846 18	11				37	48		33		8	513,156 56	44	52		1,174,002 74
Pennsylvania, western district						21	21									
Delaware																
Maryland	17,406 59	14				27	41					21,348 28	14	14	13,475 00	17,406 59
District of Columbia	128,946 22	58				3	61	39,523 40	10				64	66	73,212 88	290,294 57
Virginia	8,921 35	12		3	1	244	260			1		11,000 00	12	16	7,080 00	6,921 35
West Virginia										1		11,000 00	1	1		11,000 00
North Carolina																
South Carolina																
Georgia																
Florida, northern district	14,334 59	27		4		26	57						27	31	10,582 00	14,334 52
Florida, southern district	208,845 29	37		1		9	47		43			494,149 95	80	81	1,920 34	709,088 94
Alabama																
Louisiana, eastern district	455,280 94	67	1		4	144	216	37,382 22	38	1	1	186,060 76	105	113	86,060 22	641,341 72
Louisiana, western district																
Mississippi																
Texas																
Arkansas, eastern district	5,369 25	14		3		16	33						14	17	5,369 25	5,369 25
Arkansas, western district																
Missouri, eastern district	13,397 12	24		3	5	45	77		2			248 70	26	34	15,696 09	13,645 82
Missouri, western district						1	1	2,394 58	1					1	2,394 58	

		17		4	1	279	301						17	21		
nessee, eastern district	10,963 10	3			1	3	7						3	4	10,963 10	10,963 10
nessee, middle district	3,365 83	1					1						1	1	2,487 00	3,365 83
nessee, western district	17,375 57	27				2	45	74				461 09	27	30	13,151 95	17,836 66
tucky	2,614 56	20		4		12	36	3,326 53	18		1	3,326 53	38	43	5,425 09	5,941 09
, northern district	1,117 37	5				18	23	6,037 11	15			4,570 67	20	20	7,287 11	5,688 04
, southern district	1,016 94	18				39	57	2,087 65	23			3,779 62	41	41	3,104 59	4,796 56
ana	1,218 00	6				30	36						6	6	1,360 00	1,218 00
ois, northern district	130,796 32	13				40	53	5,584 62	2		1	8,612 72	15	16	7,945 11	139,409 04
ois, southern district	2,839 03	16		1		36	53	14,671 29	5		4	6,397 84	21	26	16,522 80	9,236 87
higan, eastern district	3,106 57	1				2	2						1	2	3,106 57	3,106 57
higan, western district		1		1		2	3	11,149 51	1				2	2	11,149 51	
consin						3	4	3,330 98	4		1	159 55	4	6	3,330 98	159 55
a						8	8	17,977 54	5			2,190 32	5	5	17,977 54	2,190 32
nesota	226 69	19				37	56		1			23 50	20	20	10,733 50	260 19
sas	13,817 94	11				75	87	107,107 21	7		2	17,691 07	18	20	107,522 21	31,509 01
ornia, northern district						3	3				1			1		
ornia, southern district																
gon																
ada									2			1,000 00	2	2		1,000 00
hington Territory																
a Territory		2				5	7	2,190 10	2			1,903 42	4	4	4,615 75	1,903 42
raska Territory																
ota Territory				3		6	6							3		
rado Territory							3									
Mexico Territory																
ona Territory																
o Territory																
tana Territory																
Total	5,758,497 91	658	3	57	35	1,593	2,348	343,991 44	254	13	35	3,800,023 51	912	1,037	583,039 42	9,558,521 42

REPORT OF THE COMPTROLLER.

TREASURY DEPARTMENT,
Comptroller's Office, November 13, 1865.

SIR: The following report, exhibiting in detail the business of this office for the fiscal year ending on the 30th June, 1865, is respectfully submitted.

Warrants of the Secretary of the Treasury have been examined, countersigned, entered in blotters, and posted as follows:

Diplomatic warrants	2,241
Stock warrants	3,406
Treasury proper warrants	2,014
Quarterly salary warrants	1,042
Treasury Interior warrants	1,785
Treasury customs warrants	2,243
Treasury internal revenue warrants	2,692
War pay warrants	5,100
War repay warrants	446
Navy pay warrants	3,445
Navy repay warrants	549
Interior pay warrants	1,108
Interior repay warrants	78
Treasury appropriation warrants	21
Treasury Interior appropriation warrants	8
Interior appropriation warrants	61
War appropriation warrants	17
Navy appropriation warrants	42
Land covering warrants	325
Customs covering warrants	638
Internal tax warrants	167
Miscellaneous warrants	545
	30,973

The following described accounts reported to this office from the First Auditor, the Fifth Auditor, and the Commissioner of the General Land Office, have undergone revision, and the balances, as then found, reported to the Register of the Treasury.

I. From the First Auditor:

Judiciary.—Embracing the accounts of marshals for expenses of the United States courts; of United States district attorneys; of clerks of the United States circuit and district courts; and of the United States commissioners for per diems and fees 849

Public debt.—Embracing accounts for redemption of United States stock and notes; the interest on the public debt; the United States Treasurer's accounts; United States assistant treasurers' accounts; temporary loans, and all matters in relation thereto 3,276

Mint and branches.—Embracing accounts of gold and silver bullion; of expenses, repairs, salary of employés, &c. 64

Territorial.—Embracing accounts of governors of the Territories for contingent expenses; of the secretaries of the Territories for the legislative and contingent expenses; for the pay of territorial officers, &c. 220

Salaries.—Embracing accounts of salaries of United States and territorial judges; of officers of the executive departments; attorneys, marshals, &c. 583

Public printing.—Embracing accounts for the public printing, binding, and paper... 156
Miscellaneous.—Embracing accounts of the United States coast survey; of the Commissioner of Public Buildings; for horses and other military property lost in the United States service; for the contingent expenses of the executive departments, &c........... 1, 832
Congressional.—Embracing the accounts of the Secretary of the United States Senate, and the Clerk of the House of Representatives.. 72

II. From the Fifth Auditor:

Diplomatic and consular.—Embracing the accounts of foreign ministers; of secretaries and attachés to legations; of consuls general; of consuls and commercial agents for salary and for disbursements for the relief of destitute American seamen; of United States commissioners under reciprocal treaties; of accounts under treaty for foreign indemnity, and of contingent expenses of consuls, &c..... 1, 631
Patent Office.—Embracing accounts for contingent and incidental expenses, for salaries, &c...................................... 12
Agricultural Department.—Embracing accounts for salaries and expenses, &c... 42
Internal revenue.—Embracing accounts for drawback, accounts of United States collectors and assessors, and United States tax commissioners..................................... 3, 765

III. From the General Land Office:

Embracing accounts of receivers of public money, and acting as United States disbursing agents; of surveyors general and deputy surveyors; accounts of the States for percentage of lands sold within their respective limits, of lands erroneously sold, &c........... 1, 314

Aggregate of accounts revised:
From First Auditor 7, 052
From Fifth Auditor.......................... 5, 440
From General Land Office....................... 1, 314
————— 13, 806
Bonds entered, filed, and indexed............................ 326
Letters written upon business of the office................. 5, 181
Letters recorded 3, 422
Letters received, filed, and indexed 10, 819
Internal revenue tax receipts registered, posted, and filed.......... 3, 516

All requisitions made for advances of money to United States disbursing officers of every description have been examined, entered and duly reported upon; and the emolument returns required by law to be semi-annually made by all the United States marshals, district attorneys, and the clerks of the United States courts, have been examined, entered, and properly filed.

The gentlemen connected with the office have, during the year, continued to discharge their respective duties with punctuality and fidelity.

R. W. TAYLER, *Comptroller.*

Hon. HUGH MCCULLOCH,
Secretary of the Treasury.

REPORT OF THE SECOND COMPTROLLER,

TREASURY DEPARTMENT,
Second Comptroller's Office, October 19, 1865.

SIR: I have the honor to submit the following report of the operations of this office for the fiscal year ending June 30, 1865.

For the purpose of making a comparative exhibit of the amount of labor done during this and the preceding year, the work done during the latter period is reproduced from my last annual report.

The aggregate number of accounts of disbursing officers and agents received from the Second, Third, and Fourth Auditors, and finally adjusted in this office, is as follows:

For the year ending June 30, 1864....................................   7,605
For the year ending June 30, 1865....................................   8,755

Thus:

	1864.	1865.
From the Second Auditor...........................	4,866	4,769
From the Third Auditor	2,339	3,497
From the Fourth Auditor...........................	400	489
	7,605	8,755

The aggregate number of certificate accounts received from the Second, Third, and Fourth Auditors, and examined and acted upon in this office, is as follows:

For the year ending June 30, 1864...........................   91,436
For the year ending June 30, 1865...........................   99,568

Thus:

	1864.	1865.
From Second Auditor for arrears of pay and bounty due deceased and discharged soldiers...................	79,496	80,830
From Second Auditor for salaries of contract surgeons...	10,320	14,747
From Fourth Auditor...............................	1,620	3,991
	91,436	99,568

The entire number of prizes adjudicated and prepared for distribution, on reports from the Fourth Auditor, is—

For the year ending June 30, 1864..........................   304
For the year ending June 30, 1865..........................   281

And the number of accounts of discharged and deceased sailors, from the Fourth Auditor, is—

For 1864..   9,489
For 1865..   17,553

The aggregate amount involved in the foregoing accounts is—

1864..   not reported
1865.. $653,826,810

The number of requisitions upon the Secretary of the Treasury examined, countersigned, and recorded in this office, is—

For the year ending June 30, 1864..........................   13,154
For the year ending June 30, 1865..........................   13,750

As follows:

Interior Department—

	1864.	1865.
Pay or advance requisitions	970	1,108
Refunding requisitions	69	81
	1,039	1,189

War Department—

	1864.	1865.
Pay or advance requisitions	8,330	7,946
Refunding requisitions	516	585
	8,846	8,531

Navy Department—

	1864.	1865.
Pay or advance requisitions	2,859	3,463
Refunding requisitions	410	567
	3,269	4,030

The number of official letters written and recorded is—

For 1864 1,860
For 1865 2,551

The number of pages in letter-book occupied in recording official letters is—

For 1864 827
For 1865 951

In addition to this large amount of official correspondence, the number of cases referred to this office, and upon which decisions were made in each individual case, is—

For 1864 .... not reported.
For 1865 3,729

Number of contracts filed and recorded—

In 1864 .... not reported.
In 1865 4,835

Number of charter-parties received and filed—

In 1864 .... not reported.
In 1865 832

Number of bonds of disbursing officers received and filed—

In 1864 .... not reported.
In 1865 1,011

Number of officers reported to Secretary of War as delinquent in the rendition of their accounts, under the act of July 17, 1862—

In 1864 .... not reported.
In 1865 8,290

Number of pensioners whose names have been recorded here upon reports from the Commissioner of Pensions—

In 1864 .... not reported.
In 1865 36,513

The number of referred cases, presented personally, and upon which decisions were made and indorsed, but of which only a brief record is made, is estimated at four thousand.

Their examination employs several clerks necessarily of much experience, and most of them having to be despatched at once, a large share of the time of the Comptroller is occupied in their immediate decision.

A further edition of 2,000 of the Digest of Decisions of Second Comptroller's Office has been issued during the year, and has been much in demand with disbursing and accounting officers of the several departments of the government.

The employment of female clerks in this office has been approved, after proper trial, and is continued not only as a matter of economy, but as opening a field of respectable employment from which women have heretofore been excluded, and as establishing a precedent of great public benefit. A number of the ladies employed, of mature age and considerable experience, have been found fully competent to examine accounts and settle claims of the heirs of deceased officers and soldiers. They report as large a number of accounts adjusted as their male co-laborers engaged on the same class of work, and they have been found, almost without exception, assiduous in the discharge of their several duties, and uniformly observant of the rules and regulations of the department. The increase in the number of those employed will sufficiently measure the increase in the business of the office.

The number of persons employed in 1860 was 18; now the number of persons engaged is 100, and the business of the office requires a still additional force. This will not appear remarkable, however, when it is considered that there are in the Second Auditor's office 131 clerks; in the Third Auditor's office 275 clerks; in the Fourth Auditor's office 105 clerks; in the Pension Office 136 clerks; in the Indian Office 32 clerks; making a total of 679 clerks, whose work is revised in this office; and this condition must necessarily continue, as the accounts which have accrued during the war, and the claims growing out of it will require some years for their final and complete settlement. Many important questions arise in the business of the office, to decide which properly requires time and investigation. To enable the Comptroller to discharge his duties satisfactorily, he should be relieved of some portion of the routine labor of the office, in which so much of his time is now necessarily occupied. The remedy is not easily suggested.

The practice of allowing extended leaves of absence does not prevail as formerly. By this is not meant the ordinary leave given to every employé at least once a year on application, but the reprehensible custom of allowing a substitute to discharge the duties of a desk for long periods of time, while the regular occupant is absent—perhaps engaged in other pursuits. The public business always suffers under such a system, which has no compensating advantages, for the duties of the absentee are rarely capably discharged by his irresponsible substitute. If the ordinary period of absence be exceeded, it would seem to be but justice to require the absentee to submit to a reduction of his pay, or, what perhaps would be better, to the entire loss of it, for the period of his absence beyond the time fixed as the maximum of leave.

Although it is not the intention to give in this report a detail of the decisions of this office, or even any general statement of their import, yet there are two which, in view of the magnitude of the claims affected by them, it is my duty to bring specially to your notice. The first of these is in regard to the pay allowed to officers for their servants, and my own views of the subject will be best understood from the decision itself, which grew out of a law passed on the 20th of June, 1864, increasing the pay of private soldiers to $16 per month.

The question at once arose whether the allowance to officers on account of servants would be increased by the passage of this law; and on the 5th of July, 1864, the Paymaster General submitted the question to this office.

In answer to this, the decision of which I speak was made in a communication addressed to the Paymaster General, as follows:

"SECOND COMPTROLLER'S OFFICE,
"*July* 9, 1864.

"SIR: In answer to your question, submitted on the 5th instant, as to the effect of the recent increase in the pay of soldiers (by act No. 122, June 20, 1864, sections 1 and 12) upon the allowance to officers on account of servants, I am of the opinion it has necessarily no effect on such allowances.

"By law of April 24, 1816, officers are allowed for each private servant actually kept in service, not exceeding the number authorized by regulations, 'the pay, rations, and clothing of a private soldier, or money in lieu thereof, on a certificate setting forth the name and description of the servant or servants in the pay account.'

"On the 6th of August, 1861, the pay of privates was raised by law to $13 per month; and on the 17th of July, 1862, it was enacted that the act of 1861, raising the pay of privates, should not be so construed " as to increase the emoluments of the commissioned officers of the army."

"On the 20th of June, 1864, the pay of privates was raised by law to $16 per month. It is contended that the mere change in the pay of soldiers, by the act of June 20, 1864, operated as a repeal of the restriction in the act of July 17, 1862, which applied only to the pay of privates under the 1st section of the act of August 6, 1861. I do not so regard it. It repealed only what was inconsistent with it, and left untouched, in other respects, both the laws of 1861 and 1862, Congress legislating, not on allowances to officers, but solely in regard to the pay of soldiers; and if we are to imply a repeal of the restriction by force of the act of 1864, we adopt the illogical inference that when the pay of a private was raised from $11 to $13, Congress prohibited a corresponding increase in the allowances for officers' servants because it was *too much*, but intended to repeal the prohibition when the pay of privates was raised to $16.

"So far as any explicit expression of the legislative will can be invoked, it is given in the act of 1862, and is certainly against the allowance; and in the act of 1864, it is the rule in the interpretation of statutes that, " when general words are used which import more than seems to have been within the purview of the law, and those expressions can be restrained to others used in the same law, *or in any other on the same subject,* they ought to be so restrained." (Smith's Comm. § 659.)

"I do not think there is any inconsistency or conflict between the laws of July 17, 1862, and June 20, 1864; but if there is, it is the settled rule that the law which permits must give way to the law which forbids, and that even when an absolute injunctive law cannot be obeyed without violating a prohibitory one the former is powerless.

"The acts of August 6, 1861, July 17, 1862, and June 20, 1864, are all *in pari materia,* and must be construed with reference to each other. In this view, the act of 1864 merely amended the act of 1861, by giving the soldier $16 per month instead of $13, and left in full vigor the restrictive clause in the act of 1862.

"In general, the repeal of a statute cannot be made by implication, if that implication can be avoided. It is very far from being inevitable in this case, and cannot, in fact, be assumed without doing violence to the intent of the legislature, as declared in the only statute expressing the legislative will upon this subject.

"There are some other considerations which may fairly be taken into account in the decision of the question, though they would be of slight avail as an argument against a clear provision of law.

"The increase of pay to soldiers is nearly balanced by the decrease of their rations, and is not therefore objectionable on the ground of a great addition to the public expenditures.

"The state of the public treasury demands all possible economy; and a construction involving the disbursement of millions should not be applied to a statute unless it clearly appears that such was the intent of Congress.

"In making this decision it is a matter of regret to me that it is adverse to the interests of a most meritorious body of men—the officers of our gallant army—who, with comparatively few exceptions, merit both gratitude and a liberal pecuniary recompense from their countrymen.

"The allowance they now receive for servants is manifestly less than they have to pay, except where several officers employ the same servant or servants. But Congress will again convene in a few months, and will doubtless correct any misinterpretation, if such there be, on the part of the accounting officers, by which injustice may be done to officers, and will by positive enactment authorize adequate pay, wherever any augmentation is necessary or proper.

"The Second Auditor, who has primary jurisdiction in the settlement of officers' accounts, has expressed his concurrence with me in the foregoing opinion.

"Your obedient servant,
                                            "J. M. BRODHEAD.
"PAYMASTER GENERAL."

This decision was made July 9, 1864. On the 3d of March, 1865, it was enacted by Congress, "that the measure of allowance for pay for an officer's servant is the pay of a private soldier, as fixed by law at the time." The Senate proceedings when this act was under discussion, and finally passed, show that the House bill was amended for the express purpose of preventing any retroactive construction, thus precluding any increased allowance to officers on account of servants previous to the date of the law; yet, within a fortnight past, a simultaneous and, apparently, organized rush has been made from all quarters; and printed forms of application for difference between $11 and $16 per month, each, for officers' servants, going back to the law of 1862, have been presented in large numbers.

No allowance of any such retrospective claim has been made or will be made by the accounting officers while the laws remain as they are; but the agents who are interested in these claims count upon legislation to effect their object, although any congressional enactment serving their purpose will authorize the distribution of more than a million of dollars.

The other decision to which I have alluded was on the question of bounties to deserters, and, as a fair statement of the question can scarcely be made by abridging my letter on the subject, I transcribe at length the following communication to Judge Advocate General Holt:

"SECOND COMPTROLLER'S OFFICE, May 17, 1865.

"SIR: I beg leave to call your attention to the subject of bounties claimed by deserters, about which I conversed with you some days ago, and which is becoming a matter of great pecuniary importance.

"If I understood you aright, you are inclined to the opinion that the bounty provided by the law of July 22, 1861, is due to a soldier who has been a deserter, if he serves, after his conviction or return to duty, a sufficient time to make up his term of service before desertion the full period of two years.

"I further understand you to hold that when the bounty is payable by instalments, as under General Orders of the War Department Nos. 190 and 191, series of 1863, and the law of July 4, 1864, a soldier sentenced for desertion to a forfeiture of all pay and allowances due or to become due is entitled to the instalments of bounty falling due subsequently to the sentence, unless there be some specific law or order authorizing the bounty which excepts the case of an enlisted man so sentenced, or that of a deserter generally.

"As the construction of the law on this subject may gravely affect the treasury, the accounting officers would respectfully say that they have heretofore arrived at a different conclusion, and would be much gratified if you would review the case, as you intimated your willingness to do in the interview to which I have referred.

' "We have held that by the regulations of the army, having the force of law, a desertion, *ipso facto*, forfeits all pay, &c., due the deserter, and vests the money in the United States; and that even a pardon cannot give him what he has, by his own act, virtually placed in the treasury; that he can claim nothing under the contract of enlistment he violated; that under the act of July 22, 1861, a soldier could have a title to the bounty only on honorable discharge after two years' service, or for wounds received, &c.; that the document itself not saying whether the discharge was honorable or dishonorable, the fact must be determined by proof; that when it fully appeared by the papers in the case that during the time for which he was enlisted he had been guilty of the most dishonorable crime a soldier can commit, viz: desertion, it was *not* an honorable discharge, and bounty could not be paid; that the bounties paid by instalments are subject to the same general conditions as bounty due under the law of 1861, and instalments remaining unpaid at desertion are forfeited and cannot be earned by subsequent return and service; and that even if there be doubt upon the subject, the benefit of the doubt ought not to be given to the man who deserted his flag and the cause of his country in her hour of need.

"The war is now over, and a wretch who three years ago enlisted for three years, deserted a year, returned, and served another year, is now put on an equal footing as to bounty, if this ruling governs, with his comrade who has served faithfully his three years.

"It appears to me that giving to a deserter for *two* years' service the same bounty that is given to a faithful soldier for *three* years' service cannot be sanctioned by justice or sound policy, but is rather a premium upon perfidy, and, relatively, a fine upon fidelity.

"I have written this letter in the utmost haste, for the case is made pressing by the great number of discharges now taking place; and I desire to harmonize with the War Department in the final decision of this important question.

"J. M. BRODHEAD, Comptroller.

"General J. HOLT,
   "*Judge Advocate General.*"

These decisions have governed the Pay department and the accounting officers in the settlement of all accounts to which they are applicable.

They have, however, been controverted. Before they were announced, opinions had been given on these subjects by officers of great ability and integrity, which were so much at variance with my own that the difference to the treasury may be counted by millions.

The sum is so large that great efforts will doubtless be made to influence both executive officers and Congress to make a construction of the present law, or to pass a new one, which will be more clearly in favor of claim agents and deserters.

I am, very respectfully, your obedient servant,
J. M. BRODHEAD,
Second Comptroller.

Hon. HUGH McCULLOCH,
  Secretary of the Treasury.

REPORT OF THE FIRST AUDITOR.

TREASURY DEPARTMENT,
First Auditor's Office, October 16, 1865.

SIR: I have the honor to submit the following report of the operations of this office for the fiscal year ending June 30, 1865.

Accounts adjusted.	No. of reports.	Amount.
Receipts.		
Collectors of customs..............................	1,580	$85,097,939 48
Collectors under the steamboat act................	222	76,191 14
Internal and coastwise intercourse................	170	5,589,504 90
Aggregate receipts.............................	1,972	90,763,635 52
Disbursements.		
Collectors as disbursing agents of the treasury...........	654	4,412,703 07
Official emoluments of collectors, naval officers, and surveyors	769	1,321,435 66
Additional compensation of collectors, naval officers, and surveyors	4	840 09
Excess of deposits for unascertained duties.............	61	620,275 84
Debentures, drawbacks, bounties, and allowances..........	114	569,932 52
Special examiners of drugs...........................	32	4,000 00
Superintendents of lights, &c........................	182	539,477 24
Agents of marine hospitals...........................	504	247,617 56
Accounts for duties and fees illegally exacted...........	299	302,427 29
Fines remitted, judgments satisfied, and net proceeds of unclaimed merchandise paid..............................	15	899 12
Judiciary accounts...................................	1,015	1,456,899 12
Redemption of United States stock loan of 1842...........	2	1,742 00
Redemption of Texan indemnity bonds....................	2	1,641,830 90
Redemption of Oregon war debt........................		
Redemption of 7-30 treasury notes funded...............	438	99,866,800 87
Redemption of certificates of indebtedness..............	56	191,446,674 25
Reimbursement of temporary loans.....................	1,244	115,086,657 50
Redemption of treasury notes received for customs........	29	42,175 53
Interest on the public debt...........................	213	55,941,867 75
Reimbursement of the treasury of the United States for treasury notes, fractional currency, and 5-20 bonds destroyed by burning..	346	142,388,235 24
Property lost in the military service of the United States.......	682	759,230 35
Inspectors of steam vessels for travelling expenses, &c......	106	22,894 76
Superintendent of Public Printing.....................	85	2,196,556 26
Insane Asylum, District of Columbia...................	2	35,004 75
Columbia Institution for the Deaf, Dumb, and Blind........	7	11,999 12
Designated depositaries for additional compensation.........		
Construction and repairs of public buildings............	116	628,895 65
Washington aqueduct.................................	4	135,552 92
Timber agents.......................................	3	1,705 49
Contingent expenses of the Senate and House of Representatives, and of the several departments of the government....	342	1,909,790 77
Mints and assay offices...............................	72	26,362,821 46
Territorial accounts..................................	20	71,440 60
Salaries of the civil list paid directly from the treasury.......	967	398,569 91
Coast survey..	29	389,050 01
Disbursing clerks for paying salaries..................	291	4,718,260 46
Disbursing agent for California land-claims.............	4	4,423 24
Withdrawals of applications for patents, &c.............	4	713 54
Treasurer of the United States for general receipts and expenditures...	3	1,083,339,287 55
Pay and mileage of members of the Senate and House of Representatives...	2	258,306 54

Statement—Continued.

Accounts adjusted.	No. of reports.	Amount.
Commissioner of Public Buildings	158	$216,501 84
Commissioner of Agriculture	37	95,632 31
Capitol extension and new dome	8	397,363 67
Miscellaneous accounts	1,599	12,303,134 00
	10,520	1,755,151,626 75
Accounts recorded	8,524	
Letters written	1,824	
Letters recorded	1,824	
Powers of attorney registered and filed	2,424	
Acknowledgments of accounts written	5,824	
Requisitions answered	484	
	20,904	

T. L. SMITH, *Auditor.*

Hon. HUGH McCULLOCH, *Secretary of the Treasury.*

REPORT OF THE SECOND AUDITOR.

Statement of the operations of the Second Auditor's office during the fiscal year ending June 30, 1865, showing the number of money accounts settled and the amount of the expenditure embraced therein, and, in general, the other duties pertaining to the business of the office ; prepared in obedience to instructions of the Secretary of the Treasury.

The number of accounts settled is 110,774.

Embracing an expenditure of	$158,040,305 05
Viz :	
Pay department	90,094,847 46
Indian affairs	3,231,449 10
Ordnance department	39,102,300 81
Medical and hospital department	3,098,533 19
Quartermaster's department, expended on account of contingencies of the army, &c.	875 39
Supplies, transportation, and care of prisoners of war	101,921 01
Secret service fund	25,090 00
Expenses of the commanding general's office	4,685 09
Contingent expenses of the Adjutant General's department at department headquarters	82 14
Relief of sufferers by a late accident at United States arsenal in Washington, D. C., resolution July 4, 1864	2,000 00
Relief of certain musicians and soldiers stationed at Fort Sumter, act July 24, 1861	574 00
Collecting, drilling, and organizing volunteers	2,865,111 27
Pay of bounty to regulars and volunteers	4,448,685 48
Enrolment and draft	521,747 00
Pay of two and three years' volunteers	16,737 00
Regular recruiting	153,292 46
Refundment of money erroneously taken from soldiers as deserters, and of deposits made by recruits and minors	13,758 35
Arrears of pay, bounty, &c., to discharged and deceased officers and soldiers	14,047,599 35

Contingencies of the army............................ | $311, 016 05

Property accounts examined and adjusted 163, 429
Requisitions registered and posted.....   5, 995, embracing $425, 539, 887 08
Letters, claims, &c., received, briefed and
    registered...................... ..... 170, 340
Letters written, recorded, and mailed.... 126, 569
Paymasters' accounts briefed and posted   2, 073
Certificates furnished Pay department..   27 463
Certificates furnished Pension Office...   11, 441

In addition to the above, various statements and reports have been prepared and transmitted from the office, as follows:

Annual statement of disbursements in the department of Indian affairs for the fiscal year ending June 30, 1864, prepared for Congress.

Statement of the account of the United States with the Chippewa Indians of Lake Superior, from the 23d of February, 1863, to the 1st of January, 1865, under the treaty of 1854, together with a list of the names of persons paid out of the $90,000 provided to pay the debts found due by the above-named tribes, per article 4 of said treaty, with the amount paid to each person, transmitted to the Commissioner of Indian Affairs.

Statement of the account of the United States with the Miami Indians of Kansas, under the treaty of June 5, 1854, from the date of the treaty to June 30, 1864, ten years, transmitted to the Commissioner of Indian Affairs.

Annual statement of the recruiting fund, prepared for the Adjutant General of the army.

Annual statement of the contingencies of the army, prepared in duplicate for the Secretary of War.

Annual statement of the contingent expenses of this office, transmitted to the Secretary of the Treasury.

Annual report of balances on the books of this office remaining unaccounted for more than one year, transmitted to the First Comptroller.

Annual report of balances on the books of this office remaining unaccounted for more than three years, transmitted to the First Comptroller.

Annual statement of the clerks and other persons employed in the office during the year 1864, or any part thereof, showing the amount paid to each on account of salary, with the place of residence, &c., in pursuance of the 11th section of the act of August 26, 1842, and resolution of the House of Representatives of the 13th January, 1846, transmitted to the Secretary of the Treasury.

Monthly reports of the clerks in this office, submitted each month to the Secretary of the Treasury, in compliance with his instructions of the 17th of August and 11th of September, 1861, together with a tabular statement showing the amount of business transacted in the office during the month, and the number of accounts remaining unsettled at the close of the month.

Statement containing the names of the permanent and additional clerks attached to this office, with the rates of compensation, transmitted to the Secretary of the Treasury.

Statement showing the name, place of birth, residence, when appointed, and annual salary of each person employed in this office on the 30th of September, 1865, transmitted to the Register of the Treasury.

Estimate of the expenses of this office for the fiscal year ending June 30, 1865, transmitted to the Register of the Treasury.

All the ledger accounts confirmed by the Second Comptroller have been regularly journalized and posted.

The payments made to officers by paymasters of the army have been entered in the officers' and company pay-books of both the regular and volunteer service.

In addition to the above, a register of attorneys who have presented evidence of being licensed to practice in the departments as claim agents has been kept, and numerous letters, estimated at 200,000 at least, have been written, acknowledging the receipt of claims and embracing correspondence generally with claimants and their agents in relation to claims.

Notwithstanding the very large operations of this office, as shown in part by the foregoing statistics, there has been a heavier accumulation of claims than in any previous year. Those on account of soldiers who were killed or who died in the service are being rapidly disposed of, and in the course of a few months will all be settled, but their place is more than filled by the claims of soldiers who have been mustered out of the service, who believe they have not received all that they were entitled to under existing laws. Thousands of such are received every month that are groundless, yet they must be briefed, filed and examined as well as those of a meritorious character.

One very great embarrassment of the office during the past four years has been the want of room to accommodate its files and a force of clerks large enough to perform the current work. It was never felt more severely than at the present time, and I earnestly ask that some action may be taken to remedy the evil.

The early settlement of paymasters' accounts is of the highest interest to the government. To aid the Paymaster General in making prompt payment to the thousands of our brave soldiers who have been confined in rebel prisons, it has been found necessary to withdraw several of the clerks employed in the settlement of paymasters' accounts, to make the necessary examination of the rolls in this office and report the condition of such soldiers' accounts. This change of work has diminished the expected aggregate of settlements upon this branch from thirty to fifty millions of dollars.

On the 21st of February of the present year a report was made to the then Secretary of the Treasury, at his request, showing the condition of the business in this office on the 31st day of December, 1864, with such recommendations as were deemed to be necessary to secure its proper efficiency and the most speedy disposal of accumulated accounts. As no congressional action was had upon the subject, and as, by the course of events since, the necessity for such action is greater even now than at that time, I have deemed it advisable to make that communication a part of this annual report:

TREASURY DEPARTMENT,
Second Auditor's Office, February 21, 1865.

SIR: In compliance with your request I have the honor to submit herewith the following statement showing the condition of the work in this office on the 31st day of December, 1864, together with the number and classification of clerks necessary to transact the current business and to bring up arrears.

Description of accounts.	Accounts settled in 1864.	Accounts on hand unsettled January 1, 1865.	Clerks employed Dec. 31, 1864.	Clerks required to bring up arrears in 12 months.
Paymasters'	636	3,366	23	140
Indian	906	377	3	3
Ordnance, medical, and disbursing	19,443	1,431	9	10
Arrears of pay and bounty	84,058	76,516	134	170
Recruiting service, enrolment and draft, &c.	2,279	1,821	7	8
Property, (ordnance and quartermaster and ordnance in charge)	73,036	107,798	59	100
Total	180,358	191,309	235	431

Besides the 235 clerks above named, there are 69 employed on other work, as registering and briefing letters, recording and mailing letters, registering and posting requisitions, making examinations of rolls and certificates of such examinations, in answer to inquiries of paymasters, the Paymaster General, and the Commissioner of Pensions, book-keeping, &c., making the aggregate number of clerks employed on the 31st December, 1864, 304. It is proper to mention, however, that this number comprises about 50 clerks appointed in December, leaving the number employed during eleven months of the year about, 256.

It will be observed that the number of paymasters' accounts settled is much smaller in proportion to the number of clerks employed thereon than those of any of the other divisions. This difference is attributable to the nature of these accounts, they being very heavy and voluminous, the settlement of a single one frequently occupying the time of a clerk for months.

In the annual report of this bureau for the fiscal year ending June 30, 1864, attention was called to the condition of the business and the wants of this branch, and reference is now respectfully made to that report. The interests of the government as well as of paymasters require that this class of accounts shall be settled as speedily as possible. The preceding table shows that there were 3,366 unsettled accounts of paymasters on hand January 1, 1865, and the monthly statement for the last month shows that there were on hand on the first of the present month 3,482, making an increase above the number settled of 116. With the present force employed, it will require five years to settle the accounts now in the office. To settle them in one year, an additional force of one hundred and seventeen clerks will be required, allowing each clerk to settle the usual average of a fraction more than two accounts each month. The accounts on hand cover disbursements amounting to over $400,000,000, and each account contains vouchers for many thousands of payments, which require careful scrutiny, as well in regard to their admissibility and the correctness of the payments, under the various laws and regulations, as to the accuracy of computation. The best class of clerical ability is required to examine and adjust them. Mere penmanship, which is so generally supposed to be all that is necessary to fit a man for clerical duty, is of minor importance, and very few who can be obtained for the pay of a first-class clerkship can be useful upon this branch until after a long apprenticeship. Having no doubt that it would be cheaper in the end and more for the interest of the government to secure the services of such experienced, intelligent accountants as cannot be obtained for less than $1,600 per annum than to attempt the settlement of these accounts by gentlemen who are willing to work for $1,200, I respectfully recommend that Congress be requested to authorize the employment of one hundred and seventeen temporary clerks of the third class to be employed in this division, as soon as a suitable building can be procured for the accommodation of the bureau. The difference in expense between settling these accounts in five years with the present force, and settling the same in the manner proposed, is sixty-four thousand dollars. It is a large sum, but is only about one-sixth of one per cent on the disbursements to be examined and settled, and is small compared with the probable loss of the government through long-delayed settlement, or the employment of inexperienced or incompetent clerks.

The foregoing table, together with the following statement for the month of January, exhibits the business of this bureau for the first seven months of the present fiscal year, and shows a very large increase over the corresponding months of last year.

Description of accounts.	On hand January 1.	Received in January.	Settled in January.	Unsettled February 1.	No. clerks employed.
Paymasters'	3,366	191	75	3,482	47
Indian agents'	68	24	42	50	2
Ordnance, medical, and miscellaneous	1,431	2,110	2,025	1,516	9
Bounty, arrears of pay, &c.	76,516	8,570	9,702	75,384	135
Recruiting service, enrolment, and draft	1,612	311	171	1,752	6
Property—ordnance and quartermaster's departments	106,171	15,639	22,052	99,758	59
Property—ordnance in charge	1,627	317	150	1,794	3
Property—Indian agents'	309	20	9	320	1
Deserters' money refunded	209	75	25	259	1
Total	191,309	27,266	34,251	184,324	263

Number of claims registered and briefed, 12,890 ....Clerks employed....	7
Number of letters recorded, mailed, &c., 11,177 .... " "	15
Number of requisitions registered and posted, 562.......... " "	1
Number of certificates issued upon requests of the Paymaster General and Commissioner of Pensions, 3,598..... " "	4
Number of clerks employed on files	14
Number of clerks employed as book-keepers..................................	5
Number of clerks employed otherwise than as above.	3
Total number of clerks employed	312

• By the assignment of the building on the corner of New York avenue and Seventeenth street for the use of the division of this bureau having in charge the examination and adjustment of officers' property accounts, fifty-nine clerks are temporarily employed and the business is now in a more satisfactory condition, but forty more clerks should be employed upon this branch. To accommodate them and the rapidly accumulating files, if that building is retained, another story is required as soon as the weather will permit it to be added. All the room at present assigned to this bureau is now occupied to its utmost capacity, and if the necessary means and facilities for a prompt transaction of the business are to be supplied, *more room* is the first thing required. The present location of the office is unfavorable for the constant necessary communication required with the offices of the Surgeon General and Paymaster General, with which its business is intimately connected, and with the Second Comptroller, by whom all money settlements made in this bureau are revised. The necessary travel at present required between these offices involves the loss of a large amount of time and labor by clerks and messengers, but even this is preferable to risking accounts and vouchers covering seven or eight hundred millions of dollars in buildings separate from each other, or in a building subject to be destroyed by fire.

The proposed increase of clerical force in this office is based upon the presumption that some suitable building will be provided for its accommodation. In the event of such increase, it will be necessary to subdivide the branch in charge of paymasters' accounts and to place one of the most competent of the clerks now employed at the head of each subdivision.

In view of the cares and responsibilities resting upon the chief clerk and heads of divisions, and their necessary increase, if the proposed enlargement of the bureau is carried out, it is respectfully recommended that a temporary increase of the salary shall be made to twenty-five hundred dollars; that a temporary assistant chief clerk shall be authorized, who, with the heads of the divisions, shall receive a temporary increase of salary to twenty-three hundred dollars, and that the heads of subdivisions shall, in like manner, receive eighteen hundred dollars, until it shall be expedient to diminish the force.

With such an organization as is here proposed, the clerical force would consist of—

One chief clerk, at $2,500	$2,500
Seven clerks, at $2,300	16,100
Twenty-seven, at $1,800	48,600
One hundred and seventy-one, at $1,600	273,600
One hundred and nine, at $1,400	152,600
One hundred and eighty-six, at $1,200	223,200

The additions that have been made to the clerical force of this office during the past ten months have mainly been from officers and soldiers who have been wounded and discharged from the military service, and it affords me great pleasure to bear testimony to their general capacity and faithfulness, and further to say that all the gentlemen in this office, with few exceptions, have conscientiously endeavored to perform their duty.

I have the honor to be, very respectfully,

E. B. FRENCH, *Auditor.*

The SECRETARY OF THE TREASURY.

REPORT OF THE THIRD AUDITOR.

TREASURY DEPARTMENT,
Third Auditor's Office, October 20, 1865.

SIR: I have the honor to make the following report of the business and operations of this office for the fiscal year ending June 30, 1865, to wit:

The requisitions drawn on the Secretary of the Treasury in favor of sundry persons for the fiscal year ending June 30, 1865, amounted to	$607,769,067 74
From which is to be deducted the amount of requisitions and drafts returned unpaid and cancelled	1,435,575 00
Total amount of requisitions paid	606,333,492 74

SETTLEMENTS.

Amount of accounts settled of disbursing officers, agents, and States, for advances made	$237,935,303 03
Amount of claims settled and paid	3,223,577 50
Total amount of settlements	241,158,880 53

REGISTRY DIVISION.

During the year there have been received, indorsed, acknowledged, registered, and transmitted to the proper administrative bureaus of the War Department 27,148 money accounts, viz: 12,113 quartermasters'; 11,896 commissaries'; 1,729 engineer; 427 pension agents'; 65 provost marshals'; 33 signal officers'; 27 contraband fund; 19 secret service; 12 confiscation; 2 contraband farms'; 2 hospital tax fund; 2 special scout; 2 rental; 1 sequestration; 1 confederate money; 817 miscellaneous.

And 5,244 officers have been reported to the Second Comptroller as delinquent, in not rendering their accounts in the time required by law. Many of these delinquencies were caused by officers being in the field, remote from the possibility of sending their accounts, and by other causes satisfactorily accounting for the delay.

QUARTERMASTERS' ACCOUNTS.

Money accounts.

On hand June 30, 1865 ....3, 638 accounts, amounting to	$249, 900, 598 28
On hand June 30, 1864 ....2, 977 accounts, amounting to	182, 381, 782 34
Increase of unsettled acc'ts . 661, amounting to	67, 518, 815 94

Property accounts.

On hand June 30, 1865..	12, 786
On hand June 30, 1864..	2, 577
Increase of unsettled accounts	10, 209

During the year 1,513 money accounts were settled, involving $175,122,619 59; and 3,823 property accounts were also settled. 240 special settlements were also made, involving $127,818 10.

Total quartermasters' accounts settled..	5, 336
Total quartermasters' accounts unsettled..	10, 870

SIGNAL ACCOUNTS.

There were received during the year 45 money accounts, involving $137,693 41, and 2,074 returns of signal property; all of which have been settled, except one money account, involving $280 98, and 58 property returns. This branch of the service is pretty well settled up.

COMMISSARIES' ACCOUNTS.

Money.

On hand June 30, 1865, 6, 733 accounts, involving.....	$43,864, 687 85
On hand June 30, 1864, 6, 309 accounts, involving.....	49, 469, 715 27
Increase in number.... 424 Decrease in amount....	5, 605, 027 42

Provision returns.

On hand June 30, 1865.....	7, 256
On hand June 30, 1864.....	6, 270
Increase.....	986

During the year 4,482 money accounts were settled, involving $155,036,222 94; and 4,501 provision returns were also settled.

Total settled.....	8, 983
Total unsettled.....	13, 989

9 F

PENSION AGENTS' ACCOUNTS.

On hand June 30, 1865, 309 accounts, involving........ $5, 146, 744 36
On hand June 30, 1864, 120 accounts, involving........   1, 465, 203 48

Increase......... 189 accounts, involving........   3, 681, 540 88

There were settled during the year 265 accounts, involving $3,454,732 87;
and 201 pension claims, involving $12,621 76.

ENGINEER ACCOUNTS.

On hand June 30, 1865, 449 accounts, involving........ $8, 507, 421 62
On hand June 30, 1864, 162 accounts, involving........   441, 872 32

Increase......... 287 accounts, involving........   8, 065, 549 30

There were settled during the year 351 accounts, involving $1,763,532 83.

STATE WAR CLAIMS.

On hand June 30, 1865, amounting to.................. $5, 656, 930 28
On hand June 30, 1864, amounting to..................   14, 596, 656 04

Decrease 8, 939, 725 76

Claims of this class were settled during the year amounting to $9,579,683 73.

MISCELLANEOUS CLAIMS.

On hand June 30, 1865, 1, 326, amounting to........... $1, 741, 443. 75
On hand June 30, 1864,   891, amounting to...........   413, 444 04

Increase......... 435, amounting to............   1, 327, 999 71

Of this class of claims, 826 were settled and otherwise disposed of during
the year, involving $2,934,775 50. In 436 of those on hand no specific amounts
are stated, the sum named above, $1,741,443 75, indicating only the aggregate
claimed in those wherein specified amounts are stated, the number of which is
890.

OREGON WAR CLAIMS.

The number of claims of this kind received during the year was 220, in 112
of which the aggregate amount claimed was $30,807 68, and in the remainder
no sums were stated. 175 awards were made, amounting to $36,281 56.

STEAMBOAT CLAIMS.

The number of this class of claims received during the year was 97; aggregate amount claimed, $1,583,023 18. The number disposed of during the same
time was 89. Awards were made in favor of 69 of these claims, allowing them
$708,878 22, instead of $820,022 81, the amount claimed, being a disallowance
of $111,144 59. The other 20 cases were rejected, the amount claimed being
$329 065 75.
The number of these cases unsettled on the 30th of June, 1865, was 77.
Amount involved, $739,473; in one claim, however, no amount is stated.

CLAIMS FOR VALUE OF LOST HORSES.

On hand June 30, 1865.... 5, 542 claims, amounting to...... $898, 028 97
On hand June 30, 1864.... 3, 836 claims, amounting to...... 625, 000 00

Increase .... 1, 706 claims, amounting to...... 273, 028 97

During the year 1,344 of these claims were disposed of, to wit: 761 allowed, the awards amounting to $125,768 71; and 583 rejected, the amount thus disallowed being $100,387 36.

RECAPITULATION.

Accounts unsettled June 30, 1865:

Quartermasters', money.............. 3, 638, involving $249, 900, 598 28
Quartermasters', property .... 12, 786.
Signal, money .... 1, involving 280 98
Signal, property .... 58.
Commissaries', money .... 6, 733, involving 43, 864, 687 85
Commissaries', provisions............ 7, 256.
Pension agents'.................... 309, involving 5, 146, 744 36
Engineer officers'.................... 449, involving 8, 507, 421 62

Total...................... 31, 230, involving 307, 419, 733 09

Claims:
State war...,....................................... 5, 656, 930 28
Miscellaneous .... 1, 326, involving 1, 741, 443 75
Steamboats .... 77, involving 739, 473 00
Lost horses .... 5, 542, involving 898, 028 97

Total..................... 38, 175, involving 316, 455, 609 09

The following is the number of accounts received at this office during the fiscal year ending June 30, 1865, and the aggregate of the balances acknowledged by disbursing officers as due the United States at the close of that year, under the following appropriations:

Appropriation.	Number of accounts.	Aggregate of balances.
Quartermasters'	11, 040	$45, 331, 936 94
Commissary......	11, 701	13, 329, 323 38
Engineer	1, 948	952, 945 03
Pension	493	854, 373 40
Provost marshal......	39	74, 889 00
Signal corps......	15	7, 487 29
Contraband fund	19	68, 060 60
Rental fund......	5	13, 063 20
Freedmen's Bureau	1	2, 650 22
Hospital tax fund......	7	35, 226 74
Total	25, 268	60, 669, 955 80

During the same year 23,967 letters were received and registered, 18,971 of which required answers, and were answered, and the answers recorded; and 56,801 circulars were issued. All awards were recorded and letters written for each, and recorded; and every voucher and account has been stamped.

The following statement shows the operations of this office for the quarter ending September 30, 1865, as far as returns have been received, and the great and rapid increase of business :

Accounts on hand, received, and settled at dates mentioned.

	On hand June 30, 1865.	Received to September 30, 1865.	Settled to September 30, 1865.	Number unsettled September 30, 1865.	Amount involved in unsettled accounts.
Quartermasters', money	3,638	695	1,375	2,958	$305,087,760 62
Quartermasters', property	12,786	2,750	1,178	14,358	
Commissary, money	6,733	1,428	1,618	6,543	62,804,886 63
Commissary, provisions	7,256	408	2,013	5,651	
Pension agents'	309	120	131	298	3,986,883 49
Engineer	449	281	51	679	11,586,868 95
Signal money	1	5		6	947 90
Signal property	58	140	104	94	
Total accounts	31,230	5,827	6,470	30,587	383,467,347 59
CLAIMS.					
Pension		228	228		
Horse	5,542	1,620	871	6,291	1,030,830 45
Oregon war		4	109	892	156,255 92
Steamboats	77	13	7	83	771,083 30
State war	8	8	5	11	6,322,684 52
Miscellaneous	1,326	544	279	1,591	2,592,401 26
Total claims	6,953	2,417	1,499	8,868	10,873,255 45
Total accounts and claims				39,455	394,340,603 04

Number of accounts received and referred to military bureaus for administrative examination in quarter ending September 30, 1865, 5,681.

Requisitions drawn in quarter, 624, amounting to $22,988,884 93.

COLLECTION BRANCH.

During the year the operations of this division have been, the writing and recording of 211 letters ; 237 letters have been received, entered, indorsed, and filed away ; 817 special orders from the War Department, notifying the resignation, &c., of officers have been received, examined, registered, indorsed, and filed.

The books have been examined for charges against the officers named in those orders, numbering 1,639 cases. Notices of bonds filed have been received, entered, registered, indorsed, and filed in 615 cases. But one case has been reported for suit, and the necessary papers prepared to accompany said report. The aggregate amount of balances charged against the several parties, in which the above examinations were made, and accruing from June 30, 1864, to June 30, 1865, is $53,396,911 78.

It is probable that in many of these cases the sums which go to make up this aggregate will be largely reduced by the official statements which are to be prepared and sent to the Second Comptroller.

By the act of July 27, 1861, "the Secretary of the Treasury is directed, out of any money in the treasury not otherwise appropriated, to pay to the governor of any State, or his duly authorized agent, the costs, charges, and expenses, properly incurred by such State, for enrolling, subsisting, clothing, supplying, arming, equipping, paying, and transporting its troops employed in aiding to suppress the present insurrection against the United States; to be settled upon proper vouchers, to be filed and passed upon by the proper accounting officers of the treasury."

It will be perceived that the objects for which the "costs, charges, and expenses" were incurred by the State are specifically set forth in the act; and for none others than those thus specified can payment be made. The law also requires that for those costs, charges, and expenses, "proper vouchers" shall be presented.

In the examination of these accounts many suspensions have been made for want of these "proper vouchers;" but quite a number of disallowances have been made because the law, as it now stands, makes no provision for the charges. Among these are:

1. Expenditures made by the several States on account of their troops, *after* they were mustered into the United States service. In all such cases government made full provision for the troops, and expenditures by the States were gratuitous, and cannot be allowed.

2. Expenditures on account of troops not mustered into the United States service. These, of course, could not be refunded.

3. Expenditures on account of officers and employés of the civil departments of the States, and of the military organizations of the States.

4. Expenditures on account of the States solely, and not for raising troops for United States service.

5. Expenditures for damages done to property.

6. Payments made to officers prior to the dates of their commissions and muster into State service.

7. Payments made to troops prior to their acceptance, as companies, into the State service.

8. Personal expenses of commissioned officers in recruiting their companies.

9. Expenditures of States in collecting, transporting, and repairing arms and accoutrements belonging to the several States.

10. Excessive charges for subsisting troops.

11. Payments for drill-masters employed by the States to drill their troops. Officers of companies and regiments are paid to perform that service.

12. Payments for clothing, equipment, and horses furnished commissioned officers. The army regulations require that commissioned officers should furnish themselves with these articles.

13. Expenses for cooking for field officers: not allowed by army regulations.

14. Excessive charges for articles purchased, and services rendered; being higher than is allowed by army regulations.

15. Payments for articles which do not belong to the regular and necessary supply of the army, and are not provided for by the regulations.

16. Double payments; which cannot be allowed.

17. Exchange and interest paid by States in borrowing money, and advertising State bonds for same purpose. Disallowed, not being embraced by the law.

18. Bounties and premiums paid by States to induce men to volunteer. The United States paid bounties to all who enlisted; and those paid by the States were to enable them to raise their quotas, and thus escape the draft. Of course, these expenses were disallowed.

The causes of disallowances in these cases are thus given in detail, that it may be seen that they are radical, and can only be relieved by legislation, if it be the pleasure of Congress to do so. The suspensions are being removed as fast as the agents of the States furnish the necessary evidence for that purpose

When I took charge of this office, in November last, but little had been done towards settling these State war claims. Measures were at once adopted to close them as speedily as possible, and I am happy to say that they are now being rapidly and finally settled.

It is respectfully suggested that the act of July 17, 1862, "to provide for the more prompt settlement of the accounts of disbursing officers," requiring all accounts of disbursing officers to be sent direct to the Treasury Department, might be so modified as to be more effective, and less onerous on this office, if it be determined to perpetuate the present system unchanged.

Instead of sending those accounts to this office, they might be transmitted to the department or bureau under whose authority or direction they originated, where they could have administrative examination, and the balances admitted by the officers regularly entered up. This would give the department to which these officers are directly responsible the balances on hand, as admitted by the officers, and enable them to determine the policy of issuing requisitions on estimates presented.

In the claims' branch of this office many just and equitable claims for the loss of horses while in the military service of the government are rejected, because they are not embraced in any one of the classes specified in the act of March 3, 1849. For instance, an aid on the field of battle, in hurrying from point to point, with orders from the commanding general, has his horse fall dead under him from excessive fatigue. Such would be a most meritorious case, and there are many of them; and yet they cannot be paid for under the law as it now stands.

Again, there is but little doubt that many of these claims are fraudulent, and yet it seems almost impossible to detect those frauds. The agents who present these cases obtain a share of the profits, and should bear their share of responsibilities.

To remedy the former defect, I would suggest that all horses that are killed or die in the military service, without negligence or carelessness on the part of the owner, be paid for, excepting such as die of diseases not consequent on the failure of the government officers to furnish sufficient forage. And, as far as practicable, to guard against frauds, I would suggest that all persons presenting or prosecuting fraudulent claims be held equally guilty, and be made subject to the same punishment as the principals.

In connexion with this subject, I beg leave to call your attention to the incongruity of having in this office a division for the examination and settlement of claims. The duties of that division are onerous and complicated, exceeding eight millions in amount for the past year, and numbering nearly seven thousand cases.

These cases involve almost every question of statute and common law, including marine and insurance decisions, and require for their proper adjudication and decision a high order of talent, and the most incorruptible integrity.

As the law now stands, there is no appeal from these decisions, except to Congress; a matter frequently complained of by claimants when they think injustice has been done. This principle is evidently wrong in itself, for no one person should be clothed with such power, which may be used dishonestly or with prejudice.

In organizing the court of ultimate jurisdiction, (the Supreme Court of the United States,) the framers of the Constitution were particularly careful that not only the services of the most learned jurists should be secured, but that they should be selected from different sections; so that, as a body, they would not be affected by local or personal influences. And yet claims are finally adjudicated by this office ranging from hundreds to hundreds of thousands of dollars.

To remedy this incongruity, and provide proper appellate jurisdiction, I would respectfully recommend that the claims division of this office be separated from it, and organized into an independent bureau, to be called the Bureau of Claims, with commissioner and assistants at proper salaries; and that provision be made that an appeal may be taken to the Court of Claims in all cases involving over two hundred dollars, and that said court be authorized to adjudicate all cases on which action may be refused by the bureau.

This would seem to be eminently proper and necessary at this time, when the claims growing out of the recent rebellion are being pressed on the government for settlement, involving, as they do, immense sums of money, and almost every variety of legal and equitable questions.

Should you deem it expedient to recommend this division, and the establishment of this new bureau, it will afford me pleasure, if you wish it, to submit a programme of its officers, the compensation that should be paid them, and the general provisions of law for organizing it.

The duties of this office, independent of this division, are exceedingly onerous and complicated, and are fully sufficient in themselves to require the constant attention and the exercise of all the abilities of the Third Auditor. By the statements at the beginning of this report it will be perceived that requisitions for over $600,000,000 have been entered at and passed through this office, and that over $300,000,000 of accounts have been settled. These accounts are from the quartermasters', commissaries', pensions, and State war claims divisions; consist of cart-loads of vouchers—every one of which, and each item of which, has to be carefully examined with reference to contracts, laws and regulations; the calculations all revised; suspensions and disallowances carefully noted and entered up, and full statements prepared for the action of the Comptroller. This service requires a thorough knowledge of the general principles of accounts; of the laws, rules, and regulations bearing on them, and the most perfect integrity for the protection and preservation of the public interest. And this service, as a general rule, has been ably, promptly, and efficiently rendered.

For this service, thus rendered, the compensation paid is entirely inadequate, and far short of that in other offices of no higher grade of service. In this office, experience, combined with ability, is of the utmost importance; and yet, so low are the salaries, even of the principal officers, that it is almost impossible to retain their services, as individuals and corporations are constantly striving, by offers of higher pay, to induce them to enter their employ.

As a matter, then, of strict justice, I respectfully recommend the following classification of the clerks in this office, in lieu of all other provisions of law on that subject, to wit:

One chief clerk, at a salary of........................ $2,700 per annum.
Two clerks, chief of quartermasters' and claims divisions,
  each.. 2,500   "
Three clerks, chief of commissaries', pensions, and law or
  collection divisions, each............................ 2,300   "
Three clerks, heads of subdivisions, &c., each.......... 2,000   "
Twenty clerks of fourth class, each..................... 1,800   "
Forty clerks of third class, each....................... 1,600   "
One hundred clerks of second class, each................ 1,400   "
One hundred and twelve clerks of first class, including
  copyists, each.. 1,200   "

This arrangement provides for the chief of division of claims, but, in my opinion, the separation previously suggested is far preferable.

Notwithstanding the vast amount of labor performed in this office, the arrears are very heavy, and will require two or three years' incessant and hard work to bring the accounts up to date. This delay is of serious disadvantage, if not loss, to the government and the disbursing officers, and should never be permitted under any circumstances. Under the system now in force, however, and in view of the sudden and vast increase in the business of the office, this accumulation could not be prevented. The system, therefore, should be changed, not only with reference to the prompt discharge of the duties of the office, but for the safety of the government funds. By the present system large amounts of public money are placed in the hands of disbursing officers, with very inadequate or no security, and the consequence is the long list of defaulters, involving millions of dollars, is constantly increasing. In the following suggestions I do not wish to be considered as recommending a change in the operations of the treasury, as originally devised and arranged by the master-mind that originated the plan of it, but rather to bring the business back to the true intent and meaning of the original system.

Now the different departments in which liabilities originate send forward requisitions for greater or less amounts to be transmitted to disbursing officers, according to the estimates of those officers, without having the means of knowing the balances those officers may have in hand; and those amounts must be transmitted, or the Treasury Department take the responsibility of stopping them, without knowing the particular circumstances that may require such remittances. Thus the public interests may suffer on the one hand by too heavy remittances, and on the other by withholding them. Official courtesy requires that these requisitions be complied with where it can be done consistently with law, and a refusal to do so would naturally cause unpleasant feelings in the department making the requisitions. This substantially makes the Treasury Department the mere fiscal agent of the other departments, instead of the controlling power of the public treasure, as designed by its originator. To obviate this and restore to the treasury its original functions, and at the same time to prevent defalcations and for the more prompt discharge of the public business, I beg leave to recommend as follows, to wit:

That provision be made by law, in all cases of purchases by quartermasters and commissaries, that the original contract or order, approved by the War Department, be sent to this office as a basis for the examination of the accounts that may arise under such contract or order, duplicates of the same to be retained by the War Department, and that those accounts be forwarded to the War Department by the person furnishing the supplies, for administrative examination. When that administrative examination has been made, those accounts to be transmitted to this office, carefully audited, and sent to the Second Comptroller for final action. When that action has been had, the accounts, as at present, to be returned to this office for filing, with a duplicate, however, of the Comptroller's finding, and on that duplicate the Auditor, or some person in his office designated for that purpose, to check on the Treasurer for the amount of the account, with the request that it be sent to the person entitled to receive it, and accompanying that request with the Comptroller's duplicate finding as the authority of the Auditor to draw such check. The Treasurer would be debited with the amounts remitted, and credited with the amounts of the Comptroller's findings. The Comptroller would certify monthly or quarterly to the amount of his findings to the Auditor; and the Auditor would be debited with the amount of his checks and credited with the amount of the Comptroller's findings. Thus there would be a complete check, the First Auditor revising the accounts so far as the aggregates are concerned, which would be a brief and simple labor. This would effectually prevent the possibility of the accumulation of public money in the hands of quartermasters and commissaries, and of course there could be no defalcation on their part; and if this system is adopted, there need be no fear of delay in settling the accounts, as each of them can be readily and finally disposed of and the money remitted within twenty-four hours after the accounts are received in this office.

In relation to the pension accounts, a law might provide that all pensions, as now, shall be paid twice in each year, fractions of times before those periods to be paid up to the first period next after the pension is established; a remittance to be made to each pension agent, on his estimate, of sufficient to pay six months' pensions of his agency; said agent to render his account, charging himself with the amount remitted, and crediting himself with the pensions paid, and a statement also of the pensioners not paid—a general account of the whole, in addition to his monthly accounts, to be sent to this office at least sixty days previous to the next period of payment, with an estimate of the amount required for that next payment. The next remittance would, of course, be only for such an amount as would enable such agent, with the balance he had in hand, to make the next payment. This, of course, would prevent the accumulation of money in the hands of these officers, and would leave it in the treasury till it was absolutely needed. And as security for such remittances, each agent should give bond, with good and sufficient security, owners of real estate, in double the amount of his semi-annual payments, to be increased by the order of the Secretary of the Treasury whenever, in his judgment, the public interests require it; such bond to act as a lien on all the property possessed by the agent or his bondsmen at the time the bond was executed, and on all they might thereafter acquire. And it should be made by law the duty of the Auditor or Comptroller to see that such bonds are duly and properly executed, certified, and filed before signing requisitions or warrants for any money to be sent to any such agents. This branch of business is now heavy, and rapidly increasing; and hence the necessity for this system and these safeguards to be promptly applied. This new system might go into force on the first day of July next, a sufficient force of able and effective men to be detailed to keep it constantly up to date, while the rest of the force could be employed in bringing up the old business.

I have limited these suggestions to the operations of this office, my only object being to secure the prompt discharge of the public business and the safety of the public funds, and I believe, if this system was faithfully carried out, it would secure both these objects. How far it will apply to other bureaus, the able officers in charge of those bureaus can best determine. It proposes, substantially, to pay all debts directly from the treasury to the parties furnishing supplies, so far as that can be established; and where funds must be placed in the hands of disbursing officers, to do so only when and to the amount absolutely needed, and to require the most perfect security for the faithful disbursement of those funds.

All which is respectfully submitted by your obedient servant,

JOHN WILSON, *Auditor.*

Hon. H. McCulloch,
    Secretary of the Treasury.

REPORT OF THE FOURTH AUDITOR.

Treasury Department,
Fourth Auditor's Office, October 14, 1865.

Sir: I have the honor again to comply with your request to furnish the usual annual statement of the transactions of this bureau, and now submit to your consideration a report of the business of the office for the fiscal year ending June 30, 1865. It will be seen, on comparison with previous years, that the operations exceed those of any year since the bureau has been organized.

The number of requisitions drawn on the treasury was three thousand three hundred and forty-six, (3,346,) amounting in the aggregate to $122,670,677 48. The refunding requisitions were three hundred and seventeen, (317,) covering an amount of $1,995,844 91.

There has been paid over to the Secretary of the Navy, as trustee of the naval hospital fund, during this period, the sum of $57,959 96, obtained through the settlements of the accounts of the paymasters of the navy and marine corps, navy agents, and other miscellaneous sources.

To the Commissioner of Internal Revenue has likewise been paid the aggregate sum of $113,488 71, obtained through the same sources as the naval hospital fund.

As these statistics are obtained from the records of the book-keeper of this office, I am reminded to call your attention to another fact which comes from the same source: the accounts of those disbursing officers of the navy now out of service who are delinquent and in some cases really defaulters to the government. Of the latter class there are several who at the commencement of the rebellion chose to cast their aid and sympathy against that government which had bestowed upon them lucrative and important offices, and who "seceded" with large balances against them. If the bondsmen of these men, who are in most instances living south, are men who have available property, the suppression of the rebellion and the restoration of law and order will place them within reach of suits for the benefit of the United States.

The total number of accounts adjusted and settled in this office during the last fiscal year was thirty-two thousand three hundred and sixty-nine, (32,369,) involving no less an amount than $80,367,182 33. The amount of labor, also, involved in the settlement and adjustment of these accounts cannot be adequately estimated by any one not acquainted with the intricacy and difficulty of much the larger number of them. Yet the whole work has been done by a force of seventy-five (75) clerks and thirteen (13) ladies, a portion of whom have, from time to time, been absent more or less from sickness and other necessities. These accounts include those of naval agents, naval storekeepers, agents for the payment of pensions, and the entire body of the numerous disbursing officers of the navy and marine corps.

The correspondence of the office affords a good index to the amount of business transacted by it, and its great and constant increase. The number of letters received during the fiscal year amounts to sixty-six thousand eight hundred and twenty-two, (66,822,) being twenty-one thousand five hundred and sixty-seven (21,567) *more* than were received the previous fiscal year. The number of letters written and sent during the year ending June 30, 1865, was sixty-six thousand three hundred and twenty-one, (66,321,) being seventeen thousand nine hundred and seventy-two (17,972) *more* than were written and sent the year preceding. The following tabular statement gives a view of the letters received, written, and recorded under the heads of the successive months in which the work was done:

CORRESPONDENCE OF THE FOURTH AUDITOR'S OFFICE.

Statement for the fiscal year ending June 30, 1865.

Date.	Letters received.	Letters written.	Letters recorded.
1864—July	3,988	4,072	4,623
August...	4,709	4,523	2,792
September..	4,447	4,932	4,153
October..	5,286	5,075	4,760
November..	5,475	5,260	4,588
December..	6,260	5,809	4,660
1865—January...	5,154	5,852	5,658
February...	5,100	5,745	5,545
March..	6,262	6,440	5,307
April...	5,236	5,048	4,606
May..	7,110	6,938	5,624
June..	7,795	6,627	5,240
Total..	66,822	66,321	57,646

I have continued to have every effort made to distribute the prize money promptly and correctly to the brave sailors and officers who have so daringly earned it, and whose valor, prowess, and efficiency were increased during every year of the war, demonstrating the incalculable naval power of our country as respects stalwart and unconquerable seamen. During the past fiscal year twenty-seven thousand six hundred and ninety-one (27,691) prize claims were received, and twenty-three thousand and seventy-three (23,073) were settled, being nearly *eight-ninths* of the number received; an instance of prompt adjustment and payment, which I am confident no branch of the public service has exceeded. The amount of money so disbursed was $4,759,596 19. When the great variety of amounts paid to so many persons is considered, and the vast number of localities and vessels to which certificates had to be sent, it is surprising and gratifying to find how *very* few errors have occurred. The following table sets forth the details of the distribution of prize-money, as it took place from month to month :

Statement of prize-money disbursed by the Fourth Auditor from July 1, 1864, to July 1, 1865.

Date.	Claims received.	Claims settled.	Amount of claims settled.
1864—July	1,501	1,467	$211,066 21
August...................................	2,422	2,102	236,445 27
September................................	2,120	1,759	541,768 48
October..................................	2,126	1,516	421,225 46
November................................	2,825	1,918	354,085 00
December................................	3,752	2,132	267,239 89
1865—January...............................	2,159	2,250	341,932 58
February.................................	1,441	1,762	491,503 41
March....................................	1,845	1,977	618,525 51
April....................................	1,469	2,149	543,293 81
May......................................	3,723	2,033	371,832 07
June.....................................	2,308	2,008	360,678 50
Total.................................	27,691	23,073	4,759,596 19

The operations of the office in regard to the marine corps, navy pensions, and navy agents, and naval storekeepers residing in foreign countries, is as follows:

The total number of accounts settled is 296, embracing 3,693 minor accounts, and involving disbursements to the amount of $5,192,844 95, viz:

MARINE CORPS.

Accounts of the paymaster, first quarter 1864..................	$105,304 32
Accounts of the paymaster, second quarter 1864..............	90,205 56
Accounts of the quartermaster, first quarter 1864..............	92,699 14
Accounts of the quartermaster, second quarter 1864...........	67,889 83
Accounts of the quartermaster, third quarter 1864............	132,195 35
Accounts of the assistant quartermaster, third quarter 1864....	7,068 50
Accounts of the assistant quartermaster, fourth quarter 1864....	12,758 85
78 accounts (individual) for arrears of pay, bounty, &c........	10,880 06

NAVY PENSION ACCOUNTS.

148 accounts of navy pension agents......................	$215,776 63
24 individual accounts for arrears of pension and unclaimed pensions, under the acts of April 6, 1838, and August 23, 1848...	2,970 10

The number of requisitions registered is 101, viz:

Requisitions drawn by the Secretary of the Interior for advances to pension agents..	57
Requisitions issued in payment of unclaimed pensions................	24
Requisitions, refunding and transfer............................	20

NAVY AGENTS AND NAVAL STOREKEEPERS RESIDING IN FOREIGN COUNTRIES.

Accounts of Baring Brothers & Co., from January 1, 1861 to December 31, 1863..................................	$3,264,517 77
Accounts of same, half year ending June 30, 1864.........	471,686 44
Accounts of same, half year ending December 31, 1864......	516,504 44
Accounts of same, supplemental........................	157,030 72
Accounts of naval storekeepers, (10).....................	45,357 24

The number of letters written in relation to business in this division is 894.

The property accounts of the assistant quartermaster of the marine corps for the 1st, 2d, 3d, and 4th quarters of 1864 have been examined.

The number of pensioners whose names were added to the pension list during the year is 896.

The payment of allotments—the means by which sailors and officers make monthly provisons for their families and creditors, and which is therefore of such great importance, necessity and convenience—has received the most careful attention during the past year, and no effort has been neglected to make it efficient and timely. I annex a tabular statement of the transactions of the office connected with allotments.

Tabular statement of the work performed monthly by the allotment division of the Fourth Auditor's office for the fiscal year ending June 30, 1865.

Date.	Letters received.	Letters written.	Allotments registered.	Allotments discontinued.
1864—July	507	542	557	172
August	523	801	606	324
September	524	874	691	474
October.........................	621	833	754	342
November	616	998	1,049	332
December.......................	524	717	634	367
1865—January	502	641	745	358
February	482	511	711	217
March..........................	552	626	626	475
April...........................	459	466	600	193
May............................	655	595	448	503
June	676	947	507	1,141
Total......................	6,641	8,541	7,930	3,868

I also give a table showing the amount of money paid by the respective navy agents for allotments.

Statement of amount paid for allotments during the year 1864, by navy agents.

New York..	$603,220 07
Philadelphia..	314,563 00
Boston..	446,252 50
Baltimore...	112,662 55
Portsmouth...	56,729 67
Washington...	58,741 68
San Francisco...	1,473 00
	1,593,642 47

The transactions of the office in the settlement of paymasters' accounts are exhibited in the following table:

Total number of accounts received and settled in the paymasters' department from July 1, 1864, to June 30, 1865, with the amount of cash disbursed in those settled, and the number of letters written in relation to the same.

Date.	Accounts received.	Accounts settled.	Cash disbursed.	Letters written.
1864—July	32	14	$484,427 75	208
August	28	25	1,325,263 58	360
September	23	19	2,074,774 37	287
October	32	8	155,621 01	239
November	31	12	532,073 74	239
December	19	21	776,970 76	302
1865—January	37	15	358,010 89	290
February	33	34	4,203,972 32	233
March	36	35	1,725,030 20	388
April	45	49	5,628,467 07	365
May	51	21	4,406,966 91	430
June	54	23	2,107,019 83	377
Total	421	276	23,779,498 43	3,718

A comparison of the foregoing table with that of the previous year shows that one hundred and twenty-nine (129) more accounts were received, and ninety-two more settled, and that the amount involved was $8,146,206 72 more than last year. From the large number of vessels going out of commission it is proper to estimate that for some months to come the receipt of accounts will largely exceed those received for the same period in the past, so that even when the navy is reduced to its permanent footing there will remain quite a large number of accounts to be settled over and above those now on hand, to say nothing of the supplementary settlements to be made in nearly every case of those already and to be settled, growing out of unadjusted allotments at the time of the first settlement. In reference to the number of settled accounts, I would say that the cash disbursements, by which a judgment is usually made concerning accounts, very often do not afford a criterion to estimate their magnitude, as even the smaller accounts are frequently so exceedingly complicated as to require the labor of an experienced clerk for three or four months; others, however, are less difficult and are settled in a much shorter time.

The sudden and rapid increase of the navy within the last few years has rendered necessary a corresponding increase in the clerical force of this office; but the clerks who have been added to it, almost without exception, had no previous acquaintance with paymasters' accounts, and the progress, in the great majority of such cases, has inevitably been slow. Yet, when a view is taken of the labors of the year in this division of the office, and a regard is had to the embarrassments which have been surmounted, there is shown a very satisfactory progress.

During the year ending June 30, 1865, the work performed in the settlement of navy agents' accounts was as follows: Number of accounts settled, 31; amount of expenditures involved, $45,891,499 58; number of vouchers examined, 182,000; average number of clerks employed, 6.

An idea of the amount of labor and care necessary to the proper settlement of these accounts can be obtained by referring to the fact that every one of the above vouchers was critically examined, and that the statement of differences of one of the accounts alone fills a book of 147 pages of foolscap paper. I am gratified to be able to say that there is not now in any of these reconciling statements, which cover such a vast number of entries and are so complicated in their nature, an item of difference between this office and the agents that is not susceptible of full explanation.

It now remains to speak of another very important division of the office, that of general claims. As the arteries permeate the entire structure of the human body, so is the work of this division connected with every individual belonging to the navy, as it adjusts and settles the pay of every person in it, from the gallant Vice-Admiral Farragut down to the obscurest ship-boy, besides including all compensations, bounties, and emoluments of every description except prize-money.

The following table gives an exhibit of the work during the last fiscal year:

Annual report of the general claim division for the fiscal year ending June 30, 1865.

Claims.	No.	Claims adjusted in—	No.	Aggregate amount.
On hand July 1, 1864	942	July, 1864	263	$33,682 92
Received in July, 1864	319	August, 1864	195	21,709 31
" August, 1864	362	September, 1864	260	35,162 99
" September, 1864	274	October, 1864	216	32,686 83
" October, 1864	265	November, 1864	346	62,055 96
" November, 1864	407	December, 1864	466	82,032 08
" December, 1864	533	January, 1865	490	50,244 12
" January, 1865	701	February, 1865	579	51,563 92
" February, 1865	453	March, 1865	557	62,393 11
" March, 1865	658	April, 1865	431	100,986 76
" April, 1865	614	May, 1865	704	127,708 84
" May, 1865	919	June, 1865	789	83,516 34
" June, 1865	726			
	7,173		5,296	743,743 18

Balance remaining on hand June 30, 1865, 1,877.

Of the claims remaining unsettled, there were received in—

January, 1863	51	April, 1864	14
February, 1863	48	May, 1864	0
March, 1863	36	June, 1864	7
April, 1863	29	July, 1864	34
May, 1863	29	August, 1864	65
June, 1863	14	September, 1864	34
July, 1863	24	October, 1864	0
August, 1863	27	November, 1864	27
September, 1863	25	December, 1864	52
October, 1863	6	January, 1865	168
November, 1863	7	February, 1865	61
December, 1863	11	March, 1865	105
January, 1864	19	April, 1865	137
February, 1864	24	May, 1865	265
March, 1864	3	June, 1865	555

Reports have been made upon twenty-two applications for admission to naval asylums, one bounty land, and four pension cases, and sixteen thousand and eighty-six letters written.

A reference to my statement for the previous year will show that more than three times the number of claims were received and adjusted than during the corresponding period of the previous year. A very large number of these claims were for balances due our brave officers and seamen, who had been languishing in rebel prisons, and their accounts were allowed to take precedence of all others. Of claims still remaining on hand unadjusted, many are imperfect in themselves and require corroborative proof from the returns of paymasters, which has not yet been received, although repeatedly applied for. I desire to call particular attention to this evil, as by it many poor and deserving men, or their widows and children, are deprived of the support they so much need, and which they so nobly earned in defending their country in its hour of peril. I allude to this fact thus strongly because the delay thus produced brings blame and censure upon this office which it does not merit. I venture to say that in these cases it will be found, almost without exception, the delay is not chargeable here.

In my last annual report I spoke of the complex nature of these claims, and of the very careful investigation which their adjustment requires, that neither the government nor its creditors may suffer. To the labor heretofore existing has been especially added, within the past year, the adjustment of bounties, a matter abounding with difficulties; to the following, among the many, of which I deem it my duty to call your attention :

The 7th section of the act approved February 24, 1864, provides that "any person now in the military service of the United States who shall furnish satisfactory proof that he is a mariner by vocation, or an able or ordinary seaman, may enlist into the navy under such rules and regulations as may be prescribed by the President of the United States: *Provided*, That such enlistment shall not be for less than the unexpired term of his military service, nor for less than one year. And the bounty-money which any mariner or seaman enlisting from the army into the navy may have received from the United States, or from the State in which he enlisted in the army, shall be deducted from the prize-money to which he may become entitled during the time required to complete his military service."

It will be observed that, by this enactment, the accounting officers are required, in adjusting these cases, to deduct from his prize-money the bounty which the recruit may have received from the State, as well as that paid by the United States. Now, I submit that, in the first place, it is almost if not utterly impracticable to properly determine what amount of bounty was paid by the respective States to each recruit, as the sums were so various. This fact, too, would seem to cause an unjust discrimination, as A, who enlisted in New York, and B, who enlisted in Pennsylvania, may each be entitled to an equal amount of prize-money; but the one may have entered the service under the inducement of a large bounty to save his State from draft, and thus loses a large proportion of what he earned by equal risk with the one not receiving such inducements.

Again : it would seem that this matter of State bounty is one with which the general government cannot properly interfere, as it evidently does by this provision. It thus derives a benefit indirectly from the citizens of such States who are, or have been, taxed to meet the outlays of the State in the payment of large bounties, while it receives the same advantage from those who may not have been so taxed, and thus imposes a discrimination in the expenditures for the support of the war, unless, indeed, it is the intent of the law to refund such amounts deducted from prize-money to the States paying the bounty. In that case much additional labor would be involved in the settlement of these accounts.

One item of additional labor, consequent upon the close of the rebellion, which has devolved upon this office, is that of answering the constant appeals for information in regard to missing relatives and friends who were attached to the naval service. It would seem scarcely just to neglect these appeals, and yet attention thereto absorbs much time. It frequently happens that an industrious and competent clerk may be constantly engaged for hours in determining a proper answer, for which, from those unacquainted with his work, he would receive only the credit of having written a short letter.

I have more than once, in this report, adverted to the vast and constantly increasing transactions of this office. So many seamen are and have recently been discharged, both from vessels still in commission and from those going out of commission—so many men, transferred from the army, are besieging the office for a settlement of their accounts—so many paymasters have closed their connexion with the navy and desire an immediate adjustment of their business, that these, and many others, make a *torrent* of labor. This, with all the accumulations heretofore growing out of the war, rendered it altogether impossible for me, with my regularly appointed force of clerks, to despatch current requirements as fast as the public good and individual necessities imperatively demanded. I therefore informed you of these facts, and requested twenty-five *temporary* clerks to be assigned to this office. The larger portion of that number have been sent, but as business must increase for some time to come, and as it is very important that paymasters' and navy agents' accounts should be settled as soon as possible, in order to detect defaulters, collect balances due the government, commence suits against bondsmen while they can be found, and meet other exigencies connected with these accounts, I trust such force will be granted as will enable me to meet the emergency with all the promptitude which is practicable.

During the past year many new methods of expediting business have been adopted, and a thorough revision given to the various instruments and forms heretofore used, so as to insure economy of time and correctness in result. I have endeavored to carry out your excellent "Rules and Regulations of the Treasury Department," and have considered them to mean *literally* what they say. I do not think this strict interpretation is considered objectionable by any good and desirable clerk. It is my decided opinion that the "Rules" should be enforced, and that employés should be aware that their infraction constituted an offence which surely subjected them to dismissal.

It gives me great pleasure to bear emphatic testimony to the competency, faithfulness, and industry of the clerical force of this office, *taken as a whole*. To their industry and ability the office is indebted for its efficiency, and the amount of work which they have performed during the past year is wonderful, and not exceeded by the same number of clerks anywhere.

The extent of *shirking* in the office, I am happy to believe, is small; but a certain percentage does exist, and when flagrant will be reported to you. In contrast with this disagreeable fact, I repeat my commendation of the diligence and competency of the very great portion of those under my supervision, and such clerks deserve and will secure the good will of the department and bureau. In improving business details, in introducing emendations, in insuring promptitude, and in making the office proceed with despatch and accuracy, I have had the co-operation of the various chiefs of divisions, and especially the constant vigilance, active oversight, and judicious assistance of W. A. Cromwell, esq., my chief clerk, whose attention to his duties has been faithful and untiring.

I spoke in my previous annual report of the ladies who have been detailed to do clerical duty in this office. I can truly repeat what I then said, that they have discharged the duties assigned to them with intelligence, industry, and commendable zeal. Their employment tends to break down that barrier which has so long debarred woman from occupations for which she was as well fitted as man, and from which she was excluded by an unjust prejudice. I can certainly say that those ladies who have been under my supervision have performed their work in the most satisfactory manner. In my judgment, the employment

10 F

of females is advantageous to the government in the way of economy, besides setting a good example in giving occupation to whatever persons are capable of doing the work required. It should, however, be understood by ladies who enter any bureau as clerks, that as sex was disregarded in their employment, so it should not be pleaded for any relaxation or abatement of the customary rules and regulations, and they should take a pride in showing that the department did not misjudge in considering them competent, both physically and mentally, to make efficient and acceptable clerks.

During the past year I have issued a new digest of the "Rules in regard to the transaction of business at the office of the Fourth Auditor of the Treasury." This important work was executed by Mr. A. H. Mechlin, the law clerk of the office, and was performed in an admirable manner. It was essentially a new work, newly arranged and thoroughly indexed, making, when issued, a complete manual of its various subjects.

The increase of the business coming to this bureau, which I have set forth, must inevitably continue for some time; but even when the more immediate influence of the rebellion no longer operates, there will be a great and permanent enlargement in its operations from the extent of the country, the development of new resources, the much larger number of vessels which will always be kept in commission, and those other causes which affect likewise every department of the government. For these reasons I beg leave especially to recommend that the number of clerks now composing the office, in accordance with the "act to supply deficiencies," &c., approved March 14, 1864, be made a permanent organization.

I have the honor to be, very respectfully, your obedient servant,

STEPHEN J. W. TABOR, *Auditor.*

Hon. HUGH McCULLOCH,
   Secretary of the Treasury.

REPORT OF THE FIFTH AUDITOR.

TREASURY DEPARTMENT, FIFTH AUDITOR'S OFFICE,
October 20, 1865.

SIR: During the fiscal year ending June 30, 1865, there have been adjusted in this office six thousand two hundred and forty-five (6,245) accounts, in the settlement of which one hundred and fifty thousand seven hundred and forty-five (150,745) vouchers were examined, involving an amount of two hundred and thirty-six million one hundred and fifty-nine thousand two hundred and forty-two dollars and eighty-four cents ($236,159,242 84;) and six thousand nine hundred and twenty-three letters were written.

I take pleasure in saying that the gentlemen employed in the office have discharged their public duties with intelligence, promptness, and fidelity.

The following schedules are respectfully submitted.

I have the honor to be, respectfully, your obedient servant,

C. M. WALKER, *Auditor.*

Hon. H. McCULLOCH,
   Secretary of the Treasury.

A.—*Statement of expenses of all missions abroad for salaries, contingent expenses, and loss by exchange, from July 1, 1864, to June 30, 1865, as shown by accounts adjusted in this office.*

Mission.	Salary.	Contingencies.	Loss by exchange.	Total.
GREAT BRITAIN.				
CHARLES F. ADAMS, *minister.* From July 1, 1864, to June 30, 1865....................	$16,655 00	$384 83		
CHARLES L. WILLSON, *secretary of legation.* From July 1, 1864, to September 5, 1864	454 03			
B. MORAN, *assistant secretary of legation.* From July 1, 1864, to June 30, 1865....................	2,442 55			
D. R. ALWARD, *assistant secretary of legation.* From November 16, 1864, to March 31, 1865............	543 13			
	20,094 71	384 83	....	$20,479 54
FRANCE.				
WILLIAM L. DAYTON, *minister.* From July 1, 1864, to his death, December 2, 1864......	8,447 63	668 14	$29 82	
WILLIAM L. DAYTON, jr., *ass't secretary of legation.* From July 1, 1864, to May 2, 1865	1,220 58	123 29	3 36	
WILLIAM L. PENNINGTON, *secretary of legation.* From July 1, 1864, to March 31, 1865	2,194 36	732 97	49 86	
JOHN BIGELOW, *minister.* From December 21, 1864, *chargé;* from March 15 to June 30, 1865, minister...........................	6,516 96	1,622 08	1 54	
JOHN HAY, *secretary of legation.* For 12 days, from June 19 to June 30, 1865............	83 18			
	18,462 71	3,146 48	84 58	21,693 77
PRUSSIA.				
N. B. JUDD, *minister.* From July 1, 1864, to June 30, 1865....................	11,430 00	757 00	17 54	
H. KREISSMANN, *secretary of legation.* From July 1, 1864, to June 30, 1865, and chargé from July 5 to September 10, 1864	2,042 29	....	2 17	
	13,472 29	757 00	19 71	14,249 00
AUSTRIA.				
J. L. MOTLEY, *minister.* From July 1, 1864, to June 30, 1865....................	11,430 00	648 45		
G. W. LIPPITT, *secretary of legation.* From July 1, 1864, to June 30, 1865....................	1,740 00			
	13,170 00	648 45	....	13,818 45
JAPAN.				
R. H. PRUYN, *minister.* From July 1, 1864, to December 31, 1864..............	3,577 50	166 55	1,452 00	
A. L. C. PORTMAN, *interpreter.* From July 1, 1864, to December 31, 1864..............	1,202 50			
	4,780 00	166 55	1,452 00	6,398 55
MEXICO.				
THOMAS CORWIN, *minister.* From July 1, 1864, to September 19, 1864	2,584 00			
WILLIAM H. CORWIN, *secretary of legation.* From July 1, 1864, to September 19, 1864	400 50	76 01		
WILLIAM H. CORWIN, *chargé d'affaires.* From September 19, 1864, to June 30, 1865............	4,483 26	182 88		
	7,399 60	258 89	....	7,658 49
BELGIUM.				
H. S. SANFORD, *minister.* From July 1, 1864, to June 30, 1865,....................	7,155 00	1,207 04	19 57	8,381 61

Statement of expenses of all missions abroad, &c.—Continued.

Mission.	Salary.	Contingencies.	Loss by exchange.	Total.
PERU				
C. ROBINSON, *minister.* From July 1, 1864, to June 30, 1865	$9,530 00	$165 37	$12 03	$9,707 40
ITALY.				
GEORGE P. MARSH, *minister.* From March 27, 1861, to September 30, 1864	41,404 16	1,410 70		42,814 86
SWEDEN AND NORWAY.				
J. H. CAMPBELL, *minister.* From July 10, 1864, to March 31, 1865	5,191 26	170 78	72 82	5,434 86
TURKEY.				
E. JOY MORRIS, *minister.* From July 1, 1864, to March 31, 1865	5,366 25	1,701 10	110 21	7,177 56
DENMARK.				
B. R. WOOD, *minister.* From July 1, 1864, to June 30, 1865	7,155 00	431 95		7,582 95
SWITZERLAND.				
G. G. FOGG, *minister.* From July 1, 1864, to June 30, 1865	7,155 00	364 78		7,519 78
NETHERLANDS.				
JAMES S. PIKE, *minister.* From July 1, 1864, to June 30, 1865	7,155 00	529 72		7,684 72
CHINA.				
S. W. WILLIAMS, *secretary of legation.* From July 1, 1864, to March 31, 1865	2,390 00		320 13	2,710 13
PORTUGAL.				
J. E. HARVEY, *minister.* From July 1, 1864, to June 30, 1865	7,155 00	1,210 61	109 99	8,475 60
NICARAGUA.				
A. B. DICKENSON, *minister.* From July 1, 1864, to June 30, 1865	7,155 00	423 25		7,578 25
NEW GRENADA.				
A. A. BURTON, *minister.* From July 1, 1864, to December 31, 1864	3,577 50	225 90	19 36	3,822 76
CHILI.				
T. H. NELSON, *minister.* From July 1, 1864, to June 30, 1865	9,530 00	693 91	1,685 21	
C. S. RAND, *secretary of legation.* From July 1, 1864, to June 30, 1865	1,455 00		129 67	
	10,985 00	693 91	1,804 88	13,483 79
HONDURAS.				
THOMAS H. CLAY, *minister.* From July 1, 1864, to December 31, 1864	3,577 50	86 50		3,663 00
ARGENTINE CONFEDERATION.				
R. C. KIRK, *minister.* From July 1, 1864, to June 30, 1865	7,155 00	61 53	432 70	7,649 23
PARAGUAY.				
C. A. WASHBURN, *minister.* From July 1, 1864, to June 30, 1865	7,155 00	257 38	1,015 82	8,428 10
HAWAIIAN ISLANDS.				
J. McBRIDE, *minister.* From July 1, 1864, to June 30, 1865	7,155 00	559 80	19 18	7,733 98

Statement of expenses of all missions abroad, &c.—Continued.

Mission.	Salary.	Contingen-cies.	Loss by ex-change.	Total.
ECUADOR.				
F. HASSAURECK, *minister*. From July 1, 1864, to June 30, 1865	$7,155 00	$161 52	$453 75	$7,770 27
VENEZUELA.				
E. D. CULVER, *minister*. From July 1, 1864, to June 30, 1865	7,155 00	148 04	....	7,303 04
COSTA RICA.				
C. M. RIOTTE, *minister*. From July 1, 1864, to June 30, 1865	7,155 00	87 15	551 10	7,793 25
SALVADOR.				
J. R. PARTRIDGE, *minister*. From July 1, 1864, to June 30, 1865	6,810 00	437 99		7,247 99
HAYTI.				
B. F. WHIDDEN, *commissioner*. From July 1, 1864, to March 31, 1865	5,366 25	88 75	....	5,455 00
MIXED COURTS.				
CAPE TOWN, SIERRA LEONE.				
CHARLES V. DYER, *judge*. From July 1, 1864, to June 30, 1865	2,405 00			
WILLIAM L. AVERY, *arbitrator*. From July 1, 1864, to June 30, 1865	1,930 00	84 70	26 25	
	4,335 00	84 70	26 25	4,445 95
NEW YORK CITY.				
TRUMAN SMITH, *judge*. From July 1, 1864, to June 30, 1865	2,405 00			
C. BRAINARD, *arbitrator*. From July 1, 1864, to June 30, 1865	980 00			
	3,385 00	....	....	3,385 00
Total	....	....	....	286,546 88

B.—*Statement of the consular returns of salaries, fees, and loss in exchange for the fiscal year ending June 30, 1865.*

No.	Consulates.	Salaries.	Fees.	Loss in ex-change.
1	Antigua, West Indies	$1,500 00	$315 47	$47 46
2	Amoor river			
3	Algiers	1,500 00	28 50	116 95
4	Antwerp	2,500 00	4,614 19	....
5	Amsterdam	1,046 70	364 73	72 64
6	Aix-la-Chapelle	2,500 00	1,691 51	....
7	Ancona	163 64	....	....
8	Alexandria			
9	Athens	250 00	....	....
10	Amoy, China	3,000 00	607 49	....
11	Apia, Navigator's islands	290 75	32 04	290 75
12	Aux Cayes	1,500 00	517 16	141 49
13	Acapulco	2,467 36	892 23	....
14	Aspinwall	1,875 00	3,105 24	....
15	Bristol	1,500 00	660 93	9 81
16	Belfast	2,000 00	5,065 65	....
17	Bay of Islands, New Zealand	750 00	85 91	6 00

Statement of consular returns of salaries, &c.—Continued.

No.	Consulates.	Salaries.	Fees.	Loss in exchange.
18	Barbadoes	$1,609 86	$1,395 08	....
19	Bermuda	1,500 00	860 42	....
20	Balize, Honduras	1,125 00	788 93	....
21	Bordeaux	2,000 00	5,384 13	....
22	Barcelona	1,500 00	225 96	$104 53
23	Brindisi	1,125 00	....	17 83
24	Bilbao	1,500 00	22 06	109 97
25	Batavia	1,000 00	230 64	66 80
26	Bergen	1,500 00	43 25	92 13
27	Bremen	3,000 00	2,029 75	69 49
28	Basle	2,000 00	2,943 00	10 32
29	Beyrut	2,000 00	278 02	22 61
30	Bahia	....	....	....
31	Buenos Ayres	2,000 00	3,432 14	....
32	Bangkok, Siam	1,116 66	200 66	....
33	Cardiff, Wales	1,500 00	2,109 93	....
34	Cork	2,000 00	499 73	27 56
35	Calcutta	5,000 00	1,746 74	863 00
36	Cape Town	1,500 00	335 55	812 16
37	Cadiz	733 51	300 58	1,149 24
38	Curacoa	1,654 90	1,395 11	....
39	Constantinople	5,270 21	236 95	....
40	Cyprus	1,000 00	....	78 25
41	Canton	3,879 57	446 47	103 90
42	Cape Haytien	1,000 00	617 99	....
43	Carthagena	375 00	367 58	....
44	Candia	154 89	....	....
45	Callao	3,166 03	2,102 53	....
46	Cobija	500 00	25 15	....
47	Coaticook, Canada	777 17	393 00	....
48	Chin Kiang	....	....	....
49	Clifton, Canada	550 27	7,449 00	....
50	Dundee	2,000 00	3,085 50	....
51	Demerara	2,173 56	770 03	....
52	Elsinore	1,500 00	2 50	101 74
53	Erie, Canada	504 16	1,029 50	....
54	Funchal	1,622 99	2 96	72 82
55	Fayal, Azores	750 00	499 95	....
56	Frankfort-on-the-Main	3,000 00	1,115 00	24 56
57	Foo-Chóo	3,500 00	691 93	539 50
58	Genoa	1,585 60	424 19	38 67
59	Glasgow	3,125 37	3,978 55	....
60	Geneva	1,500 00	602 00	68 61
61	Gaspé Basin, Canada East	1,500 00	41 67	10 04
62	Guayaquil	750 00	149 83	....
63	Gotteuburg	1,500 00	619 02	127 88
64	Galatz	1,404 30	3 00	11 54
65	Gaboon	1,125 00	3 09	....
66	Guayamas	1,796 28	788 89	120 92
67	Gibraltar	1,500 00	361 14	....
68	Hong-Kong	3,599 36	3,124 29	....
69	Halifax	2,000 00	3,345 96	....
70	Havre	6,000 00	3,933 02	36 28
71	Havana	3,978 26	7,952 12	....
72	Hamburg	2,000 00	6,266 43	....
73	Honolulu	4,000 00	5,412 80	....

Statement of consular returns of salaries, &c.—Continued.

No.	Consulates.	Salaries.	Fees.	Loss in exchange.
74	Jerusalem	$1,500 00	$6 00	$174 77
75	Kingston, Jamaica	2,054 65	1,999 99	2 48
76	Kanagawa	3,000 00	732 21	1,110 44
77	Kingston, Canada West	876 36	1,710 89	
78	London	7,500 00	19,807 44	
79	Liverpool	7,500 00	22,899 76	
80	Leeds	2,613 14	1,463 00	12 39
81	Lisbon	1,500 00	381 28	91 08
82	Lyons	3,486 41	4,328 00	91
83	La Rochelle	1,990 60	178 46	48 49
84	Leipsic	1,668 95	2,911 00	
85	Leghorn	1,746 58	512 19	29 56
86	Lanthala	1,250 00	9 05	425 68
87	La Paz	1,500 00	639 72	
88	La Union	1,125 00	232 40	
89	Laguayra	1,400 00	478 86	
90	Lahaina	3,000 00	260 68	45 36
91	Manchester	3,000 00	8,376 50	13 04
92	Maracaibo	1,125 00	311 25	
93	Melbourne	4,000 00	2,988 87	
94	Malta	1,500 00	382 54	73 20
95	Montreal	4,315 20	7,545 11	
96	Moscow	1,500 00	6 00	200 00
97	Marseilles	2,500 00	1,988 55	26 08
98	Martinique	1,500 00	294 22	
99	Malaga	1,500 00	471 75	74 01
100	Matanzas	2,500 00	4,673 39	
101	Macao	1,500 00	65 62	352 51
102	Munich	326 51	115 50	
103	Messina	1,500 00	776 80	
104	Monrovia	4,857 15	71 73	
105	Mexico	250 00	16 50	
106	Matamoras	593 02	7,701 14	
107	Manzanillo	1,500 00	89 57	
108	Montevideo	1,000 00	1,342 10	
109	Maranham	1,000 00	333 99	56 65
110	Mauritius	2,500 00	184 52	116 29
111	Naples	1,500 00	407 62	24 96
112	Nassau	1,973 46	1,121 27	
113	Newcastle	1,500 00	947 14	8 75
114	Nantes	1,500 00	230 03	58 37
115	Nice	1,500 00	81 00	80 61
116	Nagasaki	3,000 00	425 17	
117	Ningpo	750 00	110 78	
118	Odessa	2,000 00	168 89	211 97
119	Oporto	1,500 00	158 98	110 41
120	Otranto	375 00		
121	Omoa and Truxillo	750 00	46 10	
122	Paris	6,395 92	21,569 98	15 60
123	Prince Edward's Island	1,500 00	840 00	12 61
124	Port Stanley, Falkland islands			
125	Port Mahon	1,500 00	22 00	74 02
126	Ponce, Porto Rico	750 00	232 85	
127	Paramaribo	1,500 00	683 37	
128	Port au Prince	622 25		
129	Passo del Norte	500 00	36 00	

Statement of consular returns of salaries, &c.—Continued.

No.	Consulates.	Salaries.	Fees.	Loss in exchange.
130	Prescott, Canada East	$868 24	$3,673 00	
131	Panama	3,500 00	1,845 51	
132	Pernambuco	2,000 00	630 65	$62 86
133	Para	1,000 00	664 50	
134	Payta	521 00	125 49	
135	Pictou	1,500 00	1,387 15	
136	Palermo	1,500 00	946 04	
137	Piræus	750 00	26 50	29 16
138	Quebec	1,277 65	662 11	4 19
139	Rio de Janeiro	6,000 00	3,918 59	437 79
140	Revel	2,000 00	2 00	1,003 73
141	Rotterdam	2,000 00	1,465 25	
142	Rio Grande	1,062 50	510 43	52 99
143	St. John, New Brunswick	1,500 00	4,449 80	
144	St. John, Newfoundland	1,601 90	578 65	46 00
145	St. Petersburg	2,000 00	479 33	197 55
146	St. Paul de Loando	750 00	58 56	
147	St. Thomas	4,000 00	919 91	53 89
148	St. Domingo	1,980 47	107 33	
149	St. Marc. Hayti	715 31	130 00	
150	St. Catherine	1,000 00	345 35	
151	Santander	1,500 00	19 21	110 13
152	Sarnia, Canada	716 13	2,557 59	
153	St. Lambert, Canada	495 87	539 00	
154	Singapore	1,950 55	354 71	164 61
155	Santiago de Cuba	2,500 00	812 61	
156	San Juan, Porto Rico	2,000 00	832 06	
157	Santiago, Cape de Verde	750 00	66 61	33 72
158	Santa Cruz	1,875 00	190 26	28 67
159	Stockholm	1,500 00	250 50	8 90
160	Stuttgard	2,353 75	665 50	5 17
161	Spezzia	1,000 00	14 44	
162	Smyrna	1,500 00	602 16	126 30
163	Scio	1,500 00	375 00	189 52
164	Shanghai	4,000 00	4,137 41	
165	Swatow, China	3,500 00	361 73	
166	San Juan del Norte and Punta Arenas	2,000 00	738 87	
167	San Juan del Sur	952 94	57 90	
168	Sabanilla	500 00	478 15	
169	Santos, Brazil	1,500 00	55 50	777 98
170	Stettin	1,000 00	153 15	31 09
171	Southampton	2,000 00	137 00	
172	St. Helena	1,500 00	813 09	
173	St. John, Canada East	404 17	614 30	
174	Tehuantepec	1,500 00		
175	Tangiers	3,000 00		296 73
176	Trieste	2,000 00	537 94	15 17
177	Tampico	1,500 00	1,358 54	
178	Tabasco	276 24		801 95
179	Trinidad de Cuba	2,500 00	732 14	
180	Trinidad Island	1,500 00	811 90	
181	Tripoli			
182	Tunis			
183	Turk's Island	2,000 00	576 56	
184	Tumbez, Peru	1,671 30	211 96	
185	Taranto	83 33		
186	Tahiti	1,250 00	493 37	93 03
187	Talcahuano	1,000 00	701 06	

Statement of consular returns of salaries, &c.—Continued.

No.	Consulates.	Salaries.	Fees.	Loss in exchange.
189	Valparaiso.................................	$3,000 00	$2,386 17	....
190	Vienna....................................	1,500 00	1,152 00	$3 57
191	Valencia..................................	1,500 00	116 11	67 94
192	Venice....................................	1,500 00	207 00	73 65
193	Vera Cruz.................................	3,500 00	1,244 28	52 31
194	Windsor, Canada...........................	900 80	12,884 59	....
195	Zurich....................................	....	....	....
196	Zanzibar..................................	1,014 46	119 88	123 87
		345,053 48	287,108 00	13,708 16

Total amount of salaries adjusted and paid for 196 consulates for the year ending
    June 30, 1865 .... $345,053 48
Loss in exchange on same.. 13,708 16

                                      358,761 64
Fees returned from said consulates....................................... 287,108 00

Amount paid by United States treasury................................... 71,653 64

REMARKS.

No.
2. No returns.
5. Including R. G. Barnwell's transit home.
8. Accounts adjusted once a year; no returns.
9. Consulate transferred to Piræus.
10. Second quarter not received.
11. First, 2d, and 3d quarters 1865 not received.
12. Difference due him on draft paid in currency instead of gold.
13. L. S. Ely, transit from his post to San Francisco; G. M. Cole receiving instructions
    and transit to his post.
14. Second quarter not received.
17. Second quarter not received.
18. E. R. Sperry, twenty-nine days receiving instructions; nineteen days transit to his post;
    salary increased to $1,500.
20. Returns incomplete; thirty days transit home.
32. A. J. Westerveld; no returns for 3d and 4th quarters 1864; I. M. Hood, twenty-one
    days, including time receiving instructions.
36. Including loss in exchange on several drafts.
37. Loss in exchange incurred by A. I. Bensusan on account of delay in paying E. S.
    Eggleston's drafts; returns not complete from Eggleston from October 1, 1864, to
    April 5, 1865.
38. James Faxton, twenty days receiving instructions; eighteen days making transit, and
    at his post.
39. C. W. Goddard, one hundred and seventy-seven days making transit from his post;
    John H. Goodenow, thirty days receiving instructions; sixty-two days making transit
    to his post. The account embraces also that of Alexander Thompson, vice-consul,
    whose salary in this report is in addition to the rate of $2,000 per annum.
41. Difference on Mexican dollars and United States currency.
44. No returns.
51. P. S. Figzelmesy, eleven days receiving instructions; thirty-seven days making transit
    to his post.
53. T. N. Blake, eighteen days receiving instructions; twelve days, including transit to his
    post and at his post.
54. Charles A. Leas, thirty-one days receiving instructions.
57. First and 2d quarters 1865 not received.

58. Including fifteen days in October, 1861, waiting his exequatur; W. L. Underwood, seventeen days transit home; J. M. Bailey, including receiving instructions, making transit, and at his post.

64. Returns incomplete. Oscar Malmrós, sixteen days receiving instructions; seventy days making transit.

65. Including 2d quarter 1864; 1st and 2d quarters 1865 not received.

66. Including from December, 1863, to June 30, 1865.

68. Isaac J. Allen, thirty days receiving instructions.

71. W. T. Minor, thirty days receiving instructions, including transit and at his post, from November 30, 1864, to March 31, 1865; 2d quarter not received.

75. J. N. Camp, transit home, thirty-two days.

77. S. B. Hance, twenty days receiving instructions; making transit one day.

80. J. W. Marshall, ninety-one days waiting for his exequatur in 1861 and 1862; twenty days transit home.

82. James Lesley, fifty-four days transit home, including 2d quarter 1864.

83. Including 2d quarter 1864; Thomas P. Smith, receiving instructions twenty-nine days; transit to his post thirty-three days.

84. T. Y. Dickinson, twenty-three days receiving instructions; seventeen days transit to his post.

85. J. Hutchinson, twenty-five days receiving instructions; thirty-four days making transit to his post.

86. Second quarter not received.

88. Second quarter not received.

89. Charles A. Loehr's salary from January 25.

92. Second quarter not received.

95. J. F. Potter, twenty-two days receiving instructions; six days transit to his post.

96. Including 2d quarter 1864; 2d quarter 1865 not received.

102. Three quarters not received; Henry Toomy, twenty-eight days receiving instructions.

104. A. Hanson, forty days transit; 2d quarter not received.

105. Returns incomplete.

106. E. D. Etchinson, twenty-five days receiving instructions; A. Wood, fifteen days receiving instructions; forty days transit to his post.

112. Three quarters not received; T. Kirkpatrick, twenty-six days receiving instructions; six days transit to his post.

115. Including 2d quarter 1864; 3d quarter 1865 not received.

116. Comprising the whole year of 1864; three quarters 1865 not received.

117. No returns from October 1, 1864.

120. Consulate no longer salaried.

121. Second quarter not received.

122. Including the salary of the consular pupil; J. G. Nicolay, twenty-three days receiving instructions.

124. No returns.

126. Two quarters in 1865 not received.

128. H. E. Peck, thirty days receiving instructions.

134. Joseph M. Havens, twenty-seven days making transit to his post; H. T. Whetmore, seventeen days transit home; returns incomplete.

138. W. H. F. Gurley, thirty days receiving instructions; seven days making transit to his post; 3d quarter 1864 not returned.

142. A. Young, twenty days allowed waiting for his exequatur.

144. C. O. Leach, twenty-five days at his post and transit home.

146. Second and 3d quarters 1864, and 2d quarter 1865, not received.

148. Paul T. Jones, three days receiving instructions; forty-nine days transit to his post; no returns from May 31, 1865.

149. No returns since February 24, 1865; J. M. Letts, twenty-three days receiving instructions.

152. J. L. Near, thirty days receiving instructions.

153. W. H. Huestis, twenty days receiving instructions, from December 1 to December 31, making transit and at his post.

154. Including transit to his post; 2d quarter 1865 not received.

157. Comprising the whole year 1864; three quarters 1865 not received.

158. Including 2d quarter 1864.

160. E. Klauprecht, ten days receiving instructions; twenty-four days making transit to his post. This account is from April 1, 1863, to June 30, 1865.

162. Second quarter not received.

167. Third quarter 1864 not received; no returns.

173. G. T. Morehouse, six days receiving instructions.

178. J. H. Mansfield, loss in exchange, difference paid in currency instead of gold; B. H. Sanders, eleven days receiving instructions; fifty-five days transit to his post; returns incomplete.

181. Accounts not adjusted.

182. Accounts not adjusted.
184. Denison Card, forty-one days transit home.
185. A. J. De Zeyk, twenty days salary, now allowed, heretofore suspended; no returns.
186. Including 2d quarter 1864.
188. D. Thurston's salary, commencing January 3, 1865.
194. D. K. Hobard, eighteen days receiving instructions; nine days making transit to his post.
195. Returns incomplete.

C.—*Statement showing the amount expended by the consular officers of the United States for the relief of American seamen at the consulates, the amounts received by them as extra wages and money of discharged seamen, and the amount of loss in exchange incurred by them in drawing for balances due, as appears from the adjustment in the Fifth Auditor's office of the consular accounts for the fiscal year ending June 30, 1865.*

Consulates.	Receipts.	Expenses.	Loss in exchange.
Acapulco	$249 00	$226 00	
Alexandria		28 29	
Alicante	91 44	60 96	
Amoy		39 49	
Antigua		10 08	
Antwerp	1,311 42	583 28	
Apia		182 50	
Aspinwall	72 00	977 65	
Barcelona		203 23	
Batavia	90 00	295 59	
Belfast	819 00	544 00	
Belize	256 17	234 84	
Bermuda	36 00	474 56	
Bombay	60 00	52 45	
Bremen	125 07		
Buenos Ayres	2,466 04	2,218 81	
Cadiz. (Third and fourth quarters 1864 and first quarter of 1865 wanting)		72 60	$6 30
Cork	161 94	381 19	
Curacoa		31 00	
Calcutta	4,391 92	5,065 09	
Callao	1,705 50	5,909 34	
Cardiff	405 73	223 00	
Cape Haytien		36 74	
Cape Town	261 00	1,967 91	18 93
Cobija		22 00	
Constantinople		87 69	14 03
Demerara	48 84	272 47	
Falmouth	114 00	374 44	
Fayal	1,687 95	4,288 83	
Gaspé Basin	36 00	17 60	
Gothenberg		15 25	1 06
Genoa	701 99	456 39	
Gibraltar		43 90	
Glasgow	387 62	184 23	
Guayaquil		177 00	
Guaymas		9 50	
Halifax	98 59	438 84	
Havre		69 35	
Havana. (Third quarter of 1864 wanting)	3,106 10	1,455 50	
Hilo	360 00	284 12	
Hong Kong	2,309 01	753 39	
Honolulu. (Drafts payable in currency)	8,008 23	41,127 66	8,885 07
Kanagawa. (Second quarter 1865 not yet received)	60 00	50 50	30 77
Kingston, Jamaica	14 50	64 64	
Lahaina	468 00	36 40	

Statement—Continued.

Consulates.	Receipts.	Expenses.	Loss in exchange.
Lambayeque...	....	$103 50	....
La Paz..	....	74 45	....
Leeds..	$72 64	13 22	....
Leghorn..	....	63 68	....
Liverpool..	16,570 47	11,233 87	....
London	553 86	688 11	....
Malaga...	120 00	1,700 09	....
Marseilles..	106 36	913 93	....
Matanzas...	112 50	355 39	....
Mauritius...	90 00	70 12	....
Macao	....	15 50	....
Manilla. (Second quarter of 1865 not yet received).	36 00	69 00	....
Martinique..	108 90	72 60	....
Melbourne..	....	1,099 44	....
Monrovia...	....	19 00	....
Montevideo...	1,788 75	1,264 96	....
Nagasaki. (Second quarter of 1865 not yet received)	127 50	85 00	....
Nantes...	363 90	249 50	....
Nassau, Bahamas......................................	....	200 33	....
Newcastle-upon-Tyne	91 07	43 79	....
Odessa...	....	19 04	....
Palermo..	....	113 11	....
Panama..	170 54	626 39	....
Paramaribo...	....	103 20	....
Paris...	....	3 76	....
Payta..	825 70	4,472 75	....
Pernambuco	77 60	2,599 71	....
Pictou	....	245 20	....
Rio de Janeiro..	3,857 31	2,565 41	....
Rotterdam..	259 61	....	....
Singapore	2,089 34	2,966 84	....
Shanghai...	10,154 09	7,963 14	....
Sheffield..	....	90 07	....
Southampton	....	66 46	....
St. Catharine, Brazil	216 00	129 00	....
St. Helena..	1,586 30	1,997 85	....
St. John's, Newfoundland..............................	36 00	67 74	....
St. Petersburg	....	44 29	....
Stettin	....	5 44	....
Stockholm..	....	57 53	....
Swatow..	200 99	....	....
Sydney, Australia. (Third and fourth quarters 1864 and first quarter 1865 wanting).................	....	1,147 14	$202 44
Tahiti..	684 00	4,210 12	235 50
Talcahuano...	1,530 00	9,700 25	....
Tampico	1,800 00	1,270 00	....
Teneriffe	....	58 50	3 47
Trinidad de Cuba	....	25 00	....
Trinidad island	68 73	53 24	....
Tumbez	210 00	1,374 64	250 50
Turk's islands	....	105 99	....
Valparaiso..	9,636 69	11,688 79	....
Victoria, Vancouver's island. (Second quarter of 1865 not yet received)............................	....	1,149 73	....
Total...	83,446 91	143,413 11	9,647 77

Amount of disbursements and loss in exchange $153,060 88
Receipts.. 83,446 91

　　　Excess of disbursements over receipts 69,613 97

D.—*Statement shówing the amount refunded to citizens, seamen, or their representatives, directly from the treasury of the United States, during the fiscal
year ending June 30, 1865; the several sums having been previously received
at the various consulates.*

William M. Henderson, seaman; wages refunded				$90 00
P. Pendleton,	do.	do.		161 00
A. Drake,	do.	do.		28 00
W. & E. Woodbury,	do.	do.		87 12
George Ennis,	do.	do.		34 00
William Petty, citizen, estate of				1,866 48
V. B. Porter,	do.	do.		2,705 62
E. W. Gardner,	do.	do.		201 34
G. H. Miller,	do.	do.		2,165 64
Total				7,339 20

E.—*Statement showing the amount expended by the United States for expenses
incurred on account of seamen charged with crime.*

Fayal	$22 10
Hong Kong	216 96
Malaga	396 34
Matanzas	34 89
Total	670 29

F.—*Statement of the number of destitute American seamen sent to the United
States, and the amount paid for their passage, from the following consulates,
during the fiscal year ending June 30, 1865.*

Consulates.	No. of men.	Amount.	Consulates.	No. of seamen.	Amount.
Apia	1	$10	Cork	1	$10
Aspinwall	91	910	Cardiff, Wales	3	37
Antwerp	1	10	Cadiz	8	80
Antigua	7	70	Cape Haytien	10	310
Acapulco	11	110			
			Demerara	7	70
Baracoa	7	70			
Batavia	2	20	Fayal	95	2,459
Bahamas	9	120	Falmouth	1	10
Bermudas	170	1,186			
			Guayamas	9	90
Calcutta	88	880	Grand Cayman, W. I.	1	10
Cape Town	25	670	Gottenburg	2	20
Cape of Good Hope	2	20	Genoa	2	20
Callao	1	10	Glace Bay, Cape Breton.	1	10
Curacoa	1	10	Guysborough	6	42
Cardenas	7	70			
Cape de Verd island	1	10	Hamilton, Bermudas	1	10

F—Continued.

Consulates.	No. of seamen.	Amount.	Consulates.	No. of seamen.	Amount.
Havana	29	$282	Singapore	11	$110
Honolulu	93	1,160	Santiago, Cape de Verd.	4	50
Havre	4	40	St. John, Newfoundland.	2	20
Halifax	24	181	Shanghai	10	100
Hong Kong	1	10	St. Thomas, W. I.	2	20
			St. Marc, Hayti	1	10
Inagua, Bahamas	5	110	Smyrna	1	10
			St. Helena	24	345
Kingston, Jamaica	2	20	Sagua la Grande	2	20
			St. John, New Brunswick	2	14
London	6	60	Sarnia, Canada West	1	10
Liverpool	13	130	San Juan, Porto Rico	8	115
Lingan, Cape Breton	2	20	St. Michael, Azores	2	20
			Sisal	14	360
Matanzas	2	20	Sierra Leone	2	20
Montreal	1	6	Sydney, New S. Wales.	2	20
Messina	3	30	St. Catherine	2	20
Marseilles	1	20			
Montevideo	1	10	Talcahuano	9	90
Malaga	2	25	Tampico	1	15
Mongonia, New Zealand	1	10	Tahiti	9	90
			Turk's islands	2	20
Nassau	34	310	Trinidad islands	2	20
Norfolk	4	148			
			Victoria	16	135
Palermo	2	20	Vera Cruz	4	40
Paramaribo	12	110	Vancouver's island	26	255
Port Elizabeth	1	10	Valparaiso	3	30
Port au Prince	2	20			
Pernambuco	18	275	Yarmouth, Nova Scotia.	35	350
Panama	1	10			
			Total	1,044	12,820
Rio de Janeiro	12	120			

—Statement showing the amounts paid to assessors of internal revenue in the several districts of the United States for salary and contingent expenses for he fiscal year ending June 30, 1865; the total amount paid assessors for stationery from September 1, 1862, to June 30, 1865; and the number of persons assessed during the fiscal year ending June 30, 1865, not including the special war tax list.

States.	Salary.	Tax.	Net salary.	Clerk-hire.	Stationery.	Printing and advertising.	Postage and express.	Rent.	Total.	Total stationery from Sept. 1, '62, to June 30, '65.	Names assess'd year ending June 30, 1865.
MAINE.											
district	$3,912 46	$165 62	$3,746 84	$1,039 00	$263 35	$72 12	$87 55	$240 00	$5,448 86	$821 13	11,112
district	3,403 55	140 17	3,263 38	499 74	123 32	56 88	81 34	100 00	4,194 66	232 53	*5,776
district	1,983 67	69 18	1,914 49	500 00	55 01	21 00	154 08	75 00	2,719 58	121 16	7,967
district	1,873 25	63 66	1,809 59	845 00	181 35	33 50	163 64	80 00	3,113 08	331 79	6,181
district	1,500 00	45 00	1,455 00	596 00	160 11	30 87	72 11	75 00	2,389 09	355 99	9,756
Total	12,672 93	483 63	12,189 30	3,479 74	783 14	214 37	558 72	570 00	17,795 27	1,562 62	40,792
NEW HAMPSHIRE.											
district	3,454 27	142 70	3,311 57	550 00	134 07	99 75	103 28	75 00	4,275 67	215 36	8,027
district	4,690 35	188 80	4,501 55	781 33	540 80	52 20	301 62	120 00	6,297 50	654 54	9,743
district	2,390 14	86 49	2,300 65	550 00	84 50	46 00	130 02	100 00	3,211 17	270 47	9,654
Total	10,534 76	430 99	10,113 77	1,881 33	759 37	197 95	536 92	295 00	13,784 34	1,140 37	27,424
VERMONT.											
district	2,024 91	71 23	1,953 68	186 41	106 23	38 88	60 07	50 00	2,395 27	180 45	8,780
district	2,073 64	73 67	1,999 97	388 10	56 21	10 00	57 59	73 00	2,586 87	169 71	9,827
district	1,646 83	52 34	1,594 49	313 75	333 35	159 91	191 03	75 00	2,667 53	446 35	5,339
Total	5,745 38	197 24	5,548 14	888 26	495 79	208 79	308 69	200 00	7,649 67	796 51	23,946
MASSACHUSETTS.											
district	4,694 49	189 95	4,504 54	1,187 75	908 15	140 50	315 48	225 00	7,281 42	1,219 35	19,580
district	4,180 10	175 30	4,004 80	1,700 00	601 99	105 76	322 49	250 00	6,985 04	868 27	20,324
district	4,000 00	170 00	3,830 00	3,800 00	2,536 20	87 75	248 05	500 00	11,002 00	3,008 02	41,118
district	4,416 57	182 57	4,236 30	2,631 97	753 32	147 00	21 00	430 00	8,239 65	1,105 57	22,275
district	4,281 72	178 29	4,103 43	1,492 38	581 35	106 50	277 96	212 50	6,774 12	838 87	18,528
district	4,017 32	170 52	3,847 00	1,484 00	674 36	77 25	321 33	262 50	6,666 46	876 48	19,424
district	4,507 76	184 93	4,322 83	1,337 43	635 14	40 75	294 41	100 00	6,730 56	944 79	17,748
district	4,000 00	170 00	3,830 00	1,549 25	960 19	91 75	157 28	300 00	6,886 47	1,136 95	20,768
district	4,485 67	184 18	4,301 49	1,529 45	896 89	116 15	226 96	200 00	6,993 87	845 99	16,205
district	4,039 32	171 17	3,868 15	1,696 00	1,361 43	68 13	282 33	175 00	7,461 08	1,814 13	15,257
Total	42,605 45	1,776 91	40,848 54	18,401 23	9,639 05	981 54	2,477 31	2,675 00	75,022 67	12,658 72	204,227

* No return of names from this district for 1865, and the number given is for year ending June 30, 1864.

States.	Salary.	Tax.	Net salary.	Clerk-hire.	Stationery.	Printing and advertising.	Postage and express.	Rent.	Total.	Total stationery from Sept. 1, '62, to June 30, '65.	Names assess'd year ending June 30, 1865.
RHODE ISLAND.											
1st district	$4,054 82	$171 60	$3,883 22	$2,500 00	$321 92	$16 75	$31 36	$500 00	$7,253 25	$407 85	21,495
2d district	$,305 80	177 02	4,129 78	792 00	30 59	34 00	74 53	148 00	5,208 90	129 87	5,106
Total	8,351 62	348 62	8,013 00	3,292 00	352 51	50 75	105 89	648 00	12,462 15	537 72	26,601
CONNECTICUT.											
1st district	4,000 00	170 00	3,830 00	934 00	474 18	31 20	96 60	133 75	5,499 76	665 40	13,893
2d district	4,000 00	170 00	3,830 00	1,200 00	403 19	33 25	258 92	100 00	5,825 36	635 57	15,975
3d district	4,000 00	170 00	3,830 00	999 99	254 57	13 87	116 03	250 00	5,464 46	402 60	13,846
4th district	3,976 38	108 82	3,807 56	1,037 45	330 40	24 75	185 99	37 50	5,423 65	356 87	13,565
Total	15,976 38	678 82	15,297 56	4,171 44	1,462 34	103 07	657 57	521 25	22,213 23	2,060 44	57,279
NEW YORK.											
1st district	4,125 60	173 76	3,951 84	1,950 00	634 80	59 35	194 94	250 00	7,040 93	796 09	14,891
2d district	4,000 00	170 00	3,830 00	3,500 00	974 40	137 52	80 52	500 00	9,022 54	1,566 04	16,996
3d district	4,750 00	188 00	4,562 00	5,232 50	1,723 71	92*30	83 00	685 00	12,318 51	2,010 42	22,995
4th district	4,000 00	170 00	3,830 00	5,080 00	3,588 52	148 67	123 58	500 00	13,190 77	2,868 64	30,507
5th district	4,000 00	170 00	3,830 00	3,999 97	1,496 59	32 90	90 00	500 00	9,949 46	2,114 34	22,802
6th district	4,000 00	170 00	3,830 00	4,384 17	1,947 48	128 10		500 00	10,489 75	3,076 90	27,392
7th district	4,000 00	170 00	3,830 00	4,000 00	2,323 56	314 16	46 50	625 00	11,139 22	2,587 82	16,435
8th district	4,000 00	170 00	3,830 00	4,200 00	2,676 98	249 29	368 95	750 00	12,075 22	3,392 37	25,892
9th district	4,000 00	170 00	3,830 00	3,812 23	2,706 20	60 95	37 41	485 00	10,931 89	3,149 37	13,165
10th district	4,000 00	170 00	3,830 00	1,800 00	1,202 40	53 00	210 34	400 67	7,496 41	1,586 68	13,954
11th district	4,144 04	164 59	3,979 45	900 00	803 88	51 13	289 16	60 00	6,083 62	920 16	8,738
12th district	3,681 82	154 08	3,527 74	650 00	618 72	34 17	201 60	126 66	5,158 89	648 47	15,835
13th district	2,444 24	92 20	2,352 04	1,000 00	297 96	48 10	208 97	100 00	4,007 07	451 54	10,910
14th district	4,000 00	170 00	3,830 00	3,200 00	1,656 25	97 64	163 56	400 00	9,347 45	2,636 75	20,692
15th district	3,992 62	169 63	3,822 99	1,384 13	802 45	126 25	320 98	195 00	6,651 80	1,392 87	20,089
16th district	1,500 00	45 00	1,455 00	200 00	411 29		122 47	75 00	2,263 76	481 85	5,840
17th district	1,500 00	45 00	1,455 00		47 46	50 25	99 81	50 00	1,702 52	94 86	8,386
18th district	3,887 47	158 53	3,728 94	1,200 00	301 46	71 22	126 42	150 00	5,578 04	529 83	14,468
19th district	1,819 23	60 96	1,758 27	317 00	399 37	117 52	222 78	85 00	2,899 90	730 48	13,590
20th district	3,567 59	136 42	3,431 57	713 00	197 50	46 80	177 65	120 00	4,686 52	267 31	13,944
21st district	3,462 51	143 12	3,319 39	1,800 00	732 14	94 73	-227 12	257 50	6,430 88	1,097 55	*10,576
22d district	3,151 17	127 56	3,023 61	1,000 00	170 99	98 98	102 89	250 00	4,576 47	356 55	12,313
23d district	3,888 15	164 40	3,723 75	-1,800 00	1,083 19	11 05	71 34	250 00	6,919 33	1,157 32	17,411
24th district	3,413 07	140 64	3,272 43	500 00	56 60	38 75	125 67	52 00	4,145 45	149 94	*9,512

District											
i district	2,519 33	95 96	2,423 37	600 00	83 65	85 80	96 88	102 92	3,362 68	199 77	14,973
a district	2,298 99	84 94	2,214 05	949 35	275 25	30 01	90 07	200 00	3,758 73	410 38	11,077
a district	4,000 00	170 00	3,830 00	1,139 84	219 53	94 29	42 81	331 25	5,657 72	307 64	*17,812
a district	3,163 33	125 05	3,038 28	933 33	184 39	11 25	87 48	75 00	4,329 73	409 59	14,783
a district	4,292 77	178 50	4,114 27	2,905 00	665 76	173 15	41 00	500 00	8,399 18	1,173 43	24,322
b district	1,324 09	35 91	1,288 18	155 00	157 82	53 66	113 71	45 00	1,813 37	195 39	9,461
a district	5,500 00	206 00	5,294 00	7,500 00	2,798 75	33 00	56 00	730 00	16,431 75	3,225 96	45,620
Total	111,257 47	4,495 60	106,761 87	67,017 29	30,778 98	2,568 24	4,298 50	9,376 00	220,800 88	40,406 31	544,057
NEW JERSEY.											
district	2,352 57	87 63	2,264 94	600 00	102 34	50 24	79 48	161 94	3,258 94	253 70	8,791
district	3,520 32	146 00	3,374 32	800 00	816 06	64 80	202 39	125 00	5,382 57	1,210 91	12,256
district	3,680 57	154 02	3,526 55	1,350 00	842 79	64 65	164 50	200 00	6,148 49	861 54	17,390
district	3,684 10	154 20	3,529 90	800 00	917 93	111 05	158 69	200 00	5,717 57	1,177 50	*12,064
district	4,000 00	170 00	3,830 00	3,425 00	808 15	63 43	80 95	.387 50	8,595 03	1,147 77	37,382
Total	17,237 56	711 85	16,525 71	6,975 00	3,487 27	354 17	686 01	1,074 44	29,102 60	4,671 42	87,883
DELAWARE	3,551 76	147 58	3,404 18	1,278 58	448 59	32 95	181 89	118 75	5,464 94	801 83	12,566
PENNSYLVANIA.											
district	4,000 00	170 00	3,830 00	4,038 27	912 49	92 11	16 30	500 00	9,389 17	2,007 72	34,571
district	4,000 00	170 00	3,830 00	4,000 00	633 36	66 48	49 50	500 00	9,079 34	2,815 13	19,386
district	4,000 00	170 00	3,830 00	3,996 83	615 35	57 92	114 05	500 00	9,113 75	1,757 04	20,125
district	4,000 00	170 00	3,830 00	3,898 32	836 67	33 35	38 00	500 00	9,136 30	1,686 94	21,948
district	5,296 96	198 61	5,098 35	2,708 33	946 36	43 27	55 25	500 00	9,321 56	1,418 32	14,951
district	2,125 00	76 25	2,048 75	635 89	393 15	27 00	119 93	144 17	3,368 89	646 56	17,790
district	3,510 15	145•50	3,364 65	1,200 00	480 04	5 25	27 99	50 00	5,127 93	532 35	17,212
district	3,462 63	143 13	3,319 50	850 00	166 97	33 50	25 00	256 25	4,651 22	.363 44	14,237
district	3,513 55	145 77	3,369 78	975 00	125 86	53 83	62 56	222 90	4,809 93	329 52	17,703
district	3,546 99	147 34	3,399 65	875 00	235 27	18 75	34 05	100 50	4,683 22	310 52	15,644
district	3,704 47	155 29	3,549 25	1,000 00	234 22	38 50	285 57	150 00	5,257 54	327 40	12,708
district	4,772 07	184 36	4,587 71	969 00	809 91	47 00	341 67	100 00	6,855 29	835 07	11,891
district	2,237 25	83 42	2,173 83	600 00	336 83	14 75	155 15	175 00	3,455 56	424 79	9,412
district	2,687 87	104 39	2,583 48	1,000 00	326 75	64 88	207 60	100 00	4,292 71	690 66	11,211
district	3,289 65	134 48	3,155 17	626 42	.211 40	22 75	105 83	151 75	4,275 32	406 89	12,154
district	1,500 00	45 00	1,455 00	391 25	57 01	28 63	71 05	50 00	2,052 94	98 65	·8,464
di trict	2,734 62	100 93	2,623 87	315 63	128 27	37 50	78 73	50 00	3,231 80	239 45	*6,404
district	1,500 00	45 00	1,455 00	400 00	5 00	40 73	75 16	60 00	2,035 91	78 38	8,081
district	2,632 38	101 62	2,530 76	675 00	249 33	114 25	134 89	40 00	3,744 23	368 41	7,901
district	3,685 81	154 28	3,531 53	800 00	120 07	93 63	193 03	37 50	4,775 76	330 64	16,735
district	3,811 60	154 35	3,657 25	455 00	258 18	27 00	217 31	60 00	4,674 74	378 59	8,507
district	4,000 00	170 00	3,830 00	2,912 33	703 51	208 92	13 50	300 00	7,968 26	1,464 87	17,937
district	3,883 44	164 17	3,719 27	1,200 00	170 83	42 10	68 31	200 00	5,400 51	292 12	15,105
district	2,304 34	80 21	2,224 13	500 00	331 92	20 20	138 75	65 00	3,179 30	380 84	9,261
Total	80,080 78	3,214 05	76,866 73	35,021 27	9,306 01	1,231 92	2,649 18	4,815 07	129,272 18	16,014 61	349,338

* No returns of names from these districts for 1865, and the numbers given are for year ending June 30, 1864.

G.—*Statement showing the amounts paid to assessors of internal revenue, &c.*—Continued.

States.	Salary.	Tax.	Net salary.	Clerk-hire.	Stationery.	Printing and advertising.	Postage and express.	Rent.	Total.	Total stationery from Sept. 1, '62, to June 30, '65.	Names assess'd year ending June 30, 1865.
MARYLAND.											
1st district	$1,500 00	$45 00	$1,455 00	$600 00	$390 14		$74 17	$75 00	$2,594 31	$544 57	*12,112
2d district	3,604 22	150 21	3,454 01	1,200 00	137 96	$96 22	13 00	250 00	5,141 19	271 38	18,248
3d district	4,000 00	169 99	3,830 01	2,465 31	1,224 86	107 28	29 40	525 00	8,181 86	1,719 64	32,156
4th district	3,212 89	118 64	3,094 25	242 00	46 73	61 38	83 27	112 50	3,640 13	134 49	11,615
5th district	3,233 68	131 68	3,102 00	464 00	58 80	40 24	57 20	50 00	3,772 24	143 19	5,537
Total	15,550 79	615 52	14,935 27	4,971 31	1,848 49	305 12	257 04	1,012 50	23,329 73	2,813 27	79,668
DISTRICT OF COLUMBIA	3,802 91	156 62	3,646 29	1,000 00	357 98	95 98	4 50	420 00	5,524 75	477 89	16,587
WEST VIRGINIA.											
1st district	2,868 30	113 41	2,754 89	800 00	106 20	86 20	98 99	60 00	3,906 28	218 63	8,561
2d district, (no returns)											
3d district	1,500 00	45 00	1,455 00	500 00	96 02	27 00	40 80	100 00	2,218 82	147 90	4,417
Total	4,368 30	158 41	4,209 89	1,300 00	202 22	113 20	139 79	160 00	6,125 10	366 53	12,978
VIRGINIA.											
1st district	201 72	6 05	195 67		252 70				448 37	252 70	139
2d district, (no returns)											
3d district	1,500 00	45 00	1,455 00	600 00	169 30	36 93	15 00	300 00	2,576 23	212 01	3,074
4th district	1,500 00	45 00	1,455 00	750 00	78 87	45 20	21 95	144 00	2,495 02	84 77	6,320
Total	3,201 72	96 05	3,105 67	1,350 00	500 87	82 13	36 95	444 00	5,519 62	549 48	9,533
KENTUCKY.											
1st district	3,313 40	130 73	3,182 67	1,650 75	340 58		121 65	135 00	5,430 65	377 84	8,980
2d district	1,964 72	68 23	1,896 49	1,000 00	274 39		191 30	140 50	3,502 58	369 52	16,599
3d district	4,000 00	170 00	3,830 00	1,570 60	308 60	104 30	57 00	275 00	6,145 50	807 17	19,500
4th district	4,000 00	170 00	3,830 00	933 66	351 43	75 75	113 86	250 00	5,554 70	504 73	10,381
5th district	2,474 36	101 37	2,372 99	900 00	189 28	23 55	133 30	210 00	3,829 12	189 28	4,731
6th district	1,279 98	41 50	1,238 48		192 75	16 50	53 15	187 50	1,688 38	192 75	3,861
Total	17,032 46	681 83	16,350 63	6,055 01	1,656 93	220 10	670 26	1,198 00	26,150 93	2,441 29	64,142

MISSOURI.

district	4,000 00	170 00	3,830 00	3,395 83	1,123 88	58 00	39 35	499 99	8,947 05	2,086 62	*32,512
district	1,500 00	45 00	1,455 00	600 00	148 72	21 00	133 09	108 00	2,465 81	306 61	11,284
district	3,481 76	144 68	3,349 08	1,326 00	66 55	40 50	124 88	300 00	5,207 01	214 68	*27,796
district	1,609 78	58 14	1,551 64	297 63	46 75	15 00	33 32	31 00	1,975 54	46 75	5,646
district, (incomplete)	193 68	5 81	187 87		95 15			18 44	43 00	346 46	95 15	
Total	10,797 29	423 63	10,373 59	5,619 66	1,481 05	134 50	349 08	983 99	18,941 87	2,749 82	77,218

OHIO.

district	4,000 00	170 00	3,830 00	3,669 00	1,099 75	34 75		500 00	9,133 50	1,618 60	31,561
district	4,000 00	170 00	3,830 00	1,089 33	157 07	78 50	21 09	300 00	5,475 90	477 58	16,905
district	3,375 00	138 75	3,236 25	1,575 00	456 38	111 65	79 98	100 00	5,539 96	786 99	19,786
district	4,596 70	171 60	4,425 10	588 50	335 89	94 00	59 57	100 00	5,603 06	306 89	*12,764
district	1,747 69	57 38	1,690 31	210 75	403 20	149 25	88 97	85 00	4,627 48	473 80	7,894
district	3,711 23	137 41	3,573 82	500 00	111 75	22 75	189 13	73 33	4,470 78	230 05	7,873
district	3,935 68	166 78	3,768 90	1,030 75	149 47	69 86	206 00	120 00	5,344 98	330 94	18,679
district	1,514 28	45 71	1,468 57	350 00	247 15	20 00	122 73	50 00	2,238 45	333 68	*8,286
district	4,392 41	163 59	4,228 82	883 50	434 51	79 27	147 51	100 00	5,873 61	577 13	*11,896
district	3,422 33	141 10	3,281 23	650 00	260 07		23 91	50 00	4,265 21	263 07	*7,968
district	3,328 40	136 42	3,191 98	105 00	146 40	27 00	29 15	100 00	3,599 54	205 48	6,984
district	4,630 65	174 44	4,456 21	964 13	571 68	77 50	181 20	125 00	6,375 72	921 10	10,962
district	3,431 74	134 92	3,296 82	589 59	237 02	30 45	153 16	92 50	4,399 54	366 32	11,035
district	1,500 00	45 00	1,455 00	328 50	151 79	19 75	292 00	40 00	2,380 04	364 89	11,743
district	1,500 00	45 00	1,455 00	519 02	119 73	31 25	113 97	74 70	2,313 67	189 36	8,197
district	1,500 00	45 00	1,455 00	429 00	146 27	72 00	94 89	36 00	2,233 16	230 46	8,942
district	1,500 00	45 00	1,455 00	400 00	38 53	153 46	51 79	100 00	2,198 78	63 01	*12,620
district	4,000 00	170 00	3,830 00	1,998 99	320 45	20 50	72 00	300 00	6,541 94	527 36	19,584
district	2,308 43	86 92	2,251 51	829 74	257 60	49 50	181 98	127 50	3,697 83	441 12	15,572
Total	58,424 54	2,245 02	56,179 52	16,710 80	5,644 71	1,134 44	2,108 95	2,474 03	84,292 45	8,999 66	248,245

INDIANA.

district	1,500 00	45 00	1,455 00	655 78	444 75	8 00	105 97	106 25	2,775 75	486 44	13,937
district	2,530 39	96 51	2,433 88	570 00	213 40	107 75	121 57	55 26	3,501 86	474 33	9,643
district	3,543 70	144 55	3,399 15	438 47	410 40	93 33	237 20	64 00	4,642 75	604 89	9,108
district	3,732 48	156 61	3,575 87	400 00	465 89	70 50	167 32	84 00	4,765 58	593 76	8,261
district	1,851 99	70 09	1,781 83	302 00	495 78	16 50	113 66	94 10	2,803 81	629 60	13,789
district	3,655 89	147 80	3,508 09	107 40	188 45	47 75	31 00	250 00	4,233 69	221 60	12,686
district	3,047 54	120 90	2,926 64	600 00	296 29	97 30	93 06	37 50	4,050 79	347 74	8,189
district	2,747 59	107 36	2,640 16	816 66	222 73	127 70	50 00	210 00	4,467 25	348 78	11,586
district	1,125 00	33 75	1,091 25	128 63	163 91	21 50	34 79	31 50	c 1,472 98	200 92	13,987
district	1,242 66	37 26	1,205 38	284 53	96 37	65 12	158 87	50 04	1,860 31	177 20	7,909
district	1,125 00	33 75	1,091 25	375 00		16 50	28 00	56 25	1,587 00	44 10	16,105
Total	26,102 10	993 60	25,108 50	4,678 67	2,999 21	671 95	1,141 44	1,038 90	35,638 67	4,182 45	123,920

* No returns of names from these districts for 1865, and the numbers given are for year ending June 30, 1864.

G.—*Statement showing the amounts paid to assessors of internal revenue, &c.*—Continued.

States.	Salary.	Tax.	Net salary.	Clerk-hire.	Stationery.	Printing and advertising.	Postage and express.	Rent.	Total.	Total stationery from Sept. 1, '62, to June 30, '65.	Names assess'd year ending June 30, 1865.
ILLINOIS.											
1st district	$4,000 00	$170 00	$3,830 00	$3,500 00	$996 48	$132 10	....	$500 00	$8,258 58	$1,617 20	$37,682
2d district	3,731 86	129 78	3,602 08	465 00	408 85	65 25	$139 48	125 00	4,805 66	516 74	13,048
3d district	2,370 18	88 50	2,281 68	566 66	114 50	62 00	163 36	122 91	3,311 11	270 64	12,347
4th district	3,412 10	140 59	3,271 51	589 50	69 70	57 50	79 90	60 00	4,128 11	114 22	11,697
5th district	4,000 00	170 00	3,830 00	1,633 00	326 05	153 00	164 99	133 34	6,240 38	462 75	10,848
6th district	2,077 86	73 89	2,003 97	350 00	329 25	21 85	121 49	200 00	3,028 53	465 60	10,935
7th district	1,500 00	45 00	1,455 00	700 00	376 23	27 00	149 81	120 00	2,828 04	436 13	9,980
8th district	3,616 21	150 81	3,465 40	596 00	154 95	87 25	302 31	187 50	4,773 41	227 19	13,951
9th district	2,482 13	92 40	2,369 73	900 00	442 87	90 75	95 89	100 00	3,999 24	496 07	10,297
10th district	2,097 29	74 86	2,022 43	342 00	186 95	3 00	125 29	75 00	2,754 67	246 61	11,311
11th district	1,500 00	45 00	1,455 00	500 00	627 98	82 50	173 12	48 00	2,886 60	691 42	7,675
12th district	3,433 30	139 42	3,293 88	16 34	163 05	82 50	140 91	99 00	3,765 53	329 85	10,906
13th district	2,087 93	74 39	2,013 54	146 00	193 93	25 50	75 74	60 00	2,514 71	253 33	6,521
Total	36,328 86	1,394 64	34,894 22	10,304 50	4,390 79	842 15	1,732 26	1,830 75	53,994 87	6,147 75	167,318
MICHIGAN.											
1st district	4,000 00	170 00	3,830 00	1,624 00	286 32	34 30	76 95	206 25	6,057 82	719 04	20,349
2d district	2,008 69	69 51	1,939 18	519 80	267 80	18 90	314 17	106 25	3,166 20	498 59	14,653
3d district	1,905 72	65 28	1,840 44	600 00	253 90	58 00	122 34	75 00	2,949 68	407 76	14,575
4th district	1,500 00	45 00	1,455 00	280 50	39 40	26 85	145 65	30 00	1,970 40	100 15	7,344
5th district	1,500 00	45 00	1,455 00	666 66	124 47	28 00	108 71	60 00	2,442 84	239 10	11,317
6th district	1,125 00	33 75	1,091 25	450 00	23 29	88 60	46 28	26 25	1,725 67	93 36	*9,988
Total	12,039 41	428 54	11,610 87	4,141 06	988 18	254 65	814 10	503 75	18,312 61	2,058 00	78,226
WISCONSIN.											
1st district	3,928 20	166 41	3,761 79	1,372 97	118 79	65 35	81 11	350 00	5,750 01	290 15	17,527
2d district	1,796 32	59 82	1,736 50	618 00	207 15	50 25	112 93	150 00	2,874 13	431 29	10,174
3d district	1,500 00	45 00	1,455 00	400 00	195 82	32 00	218 77	96 00	2,417 59	341 64	6,734
4th district	1,500 00	45 00	1,455 00	487 50	33 92	20 05	90 58	50 00	2,136 35	72 53	8,192
5th district	1,125 00	33 75	1,091 25	435 00	96 57	54 05	89 47	56 25	1,822 59	312 24	6,182
6th district	1,500 00	45 00	1,455 00	369 00	250 61	79 75	206 48	72 00	2,432 84	468 91	5,506
Total	11,349 52	394 98	10,954 54	3,682 47	902 16	321 45	798 64	774 25	17,433 51	1,916 76	54,305

IOWA.

district	2,888 50	114 42	2,774 08	700 00	418 89	152 00	216 75	93 00	4,354 72	644 19	17,099
district	3,035 83	121 79	2,914 04	440 00	125 21	83 25	158 28	50 00	3,770 78	160 81	10,102
district	3,007 21	120 35	2,886 86	500 00	144 18	62 30	185 94	96 00	3,875 28	319 79	12,371
district	1,500 00	45 00	1,455 00	300 00	409 71	44 00	112 90	48 00	2,369 61	455 98	*9,600
district	1,500 00	45 00	1,455 00	350 00	48 15	27 50	68 70	54 00	2,023 35	89 10	*5,606
district	1,500 00	45 00	1,455 00	422 50	408 63	43 05	91 00	144 00	2,564 18	516 19	3,806
Total	13,431 54	491 56	12,939 98	2,712 50	1,554 77	412 10	833 57	485 00	18,957 92	2,168 06	57,984

MINNESOTA.

district	1,500 00	45 00	1,455 00	445 00	58 50	78 00	93 95	100 00	2,230 55	138 88	*5,112
district	1,499 99	44 99	1,455 00	500 00	415 57	70 37	80 95	112 50	2,634 39	550 52	7,056
Total	2,999 99	89 99	2,910 00	945 00	474 17	148 37	174 90	212 50	4,864 94	689 50	12,168

KANSAS	1,500 00	45 00	1,455 00	1,200 00	250 93	95 95	188 59	240 00	3,430 47	422 90	8,258

CALIFORNIA.

district, (unadjusted)											*6,000
district	3,040 00	122 00	2,918 00	2,250 00	648 44	295 52	179 13	450 00	6,741 19	1,088 44	*1,800
district	3,130 00	126 50	3,003 50	1,934 15	608 41	397 00	172 83	808 25	6,994 14	1,251 23	*1,800
district	3,130 00	126 50	3,003 50	3,116 00	526 36	664 99	307 38	799 00	8,416 51	1,318 72	*2,600
district	3,110 00	125 50	2,984 50	1,062 00	172 88	277 37	106 60	340 00	4,943 35	618 53	*1,500
Total	12,410 00	500 50	11,909 50	8,362 15	1,956 09	1,634 28	765 92	2,397 25	27,025 19	4,276 92	*13,700

OREGON	3,060 00	122 97	2,937 03	1,500 00	227 60	220 00	44 45	510 00	5,439 08	446 54	*6,952
NEBRASKA	1,500 00	45 00	1,455 00	50 00	49 67	31 50	72 61	144 00	1,802 78	74 67	*2,868
DAKOTA											
NEW MEXICO	2,043 47	72 15	1,971 32	999 99	381 55	612 00	63 78	110 00	4,138 64	554 00	

* No returns of names from these districts for 1865, and the numbers given are for year ending June 30, 1864.

G.—*Statement showing the amounts paid to assessors of internal revenue, &c.*—Continued.

States.	Salary.	Tax.	Net salary.	Clerk-hire.	Stationery.	Printing and advertising.	Postage and express.	Rent.	Total.	Total stationery from Sept. 1, '62, to June 30, '65.	Names assess'd year ending June 30, 1865.
UTAH	$2,500 00	$95 00	$2,405 00	$392 00	$319 20	$171 50	$53 92	$300 00	$4,101 62	$596 07	2,316
COLORADO	6,189 50	175 95	6,013 55	1,998 00	579 96	508 95	166 78	525 00	9,792 24	647 21	*4,384
NEVADA	3,080 00	124 00	2,956 00	1,266 45	287 75	466 00	169 14	600 00	5,745 34	422 13	*2,744
WASHINGTON	3,130 00	126 50	3,003 50	450 00	9 75	535 00	28 00	144 00	4,170 25	169 75	*2,816
MONTANA	1,664 40	63 25	1,601 15	....	139 82	13 30	....	245 00	1,999 27	139 82	....
IDAHO	....	....	....	....	....	....	....	....	....	....	....
LOUISIANA	3,571 43	151 78	3,419 65	4,398 47	1,248 11	215 83	2 25	....	9,284 31	1,937 71	17,966
TENNESSEE.											
1st district	4,919 23	192 32	4,726 91	144 00	739 16	84 00	....	480 00	6,174 07	739 16	4,487
2d district	3,441 13	138 14	3,302 99	2,450 93	252 55	233 50	82 30	308 75	6,631 02	319 85	11,743
Total	8,360 36	330 46	8,029 90	2,594 93	991 71	317 50	82 30	788 75	12,805 09	1,059 01	16,230

* No returns of names from these districts for 1865, and the numbers given are for year ending June 30, 1864.

NOTE.—In some of the districts the salary and commissions exceed the limit of $4,000 prescribed by law, the excess being commissions accrued in previous years, and not paid in the adjustment of previous years.

Assessors' bills for stationery paid by collectors are included in the table, so far as they have come to the knowledge of the office.

RECAPITULATION.

States.	Salary.	Tax.	Net salary.	Clerk-hire.	Stationery.	Printing and advertising.	Postage and express.	Rent.	Total.	Total stationery from Sept. 1, '62, to June 30, '65.	Names assess'd year ending June 30, 1865.
....	$12,672 93	$483 63	$12,189 30	$3,479 74	$783 14	$214 37	$558 72	$570 00	$17,795 27	$1,563 62	40,792
Hampshire	10,534 76	450 99	10,113 77	1,881 33	759 37	197 95	538 92	295 00	13,784 34	1,140 37	27,424
out	5,745 38	197 24	5,548 14	868 26	493 79	208 79	308 69	200 00	7,849 67	795 51	23,946
clusetts	42,625 45	1,776 91	40,848 54	18,461 23	9,639 05	581 54	2,477 31	2,675 00	75,022 67	12,658 72	204,227
a Island	8,361 69	348 62	8,013 00	3,292 00	332 51	50 75	105 89	648 00	12,462 15	537 72	26,601
cticut	15,976 38	678 82	15,297 56	4,171 44	1,462 34	103 07	657 57	-521 25	22,213 23	2,060 44	57,279
York	111,237 47	4,495 60	106,761 87	67,017 29	30,778 98	2,568 24	4,208 50	9,376 00	290,800 88	40,406 31	544,057
Jersey	17,237 56	711 85	16,525 71	6,975 00	3,487 27	354 17	686 01	1,074 44	29,102 60	4,671 42	87,883
ware	3,551 76	147 58	3,404 18	1,278 58	448 59	32 95	181 89	118 75	5,844 94	801 83	12,566
sylvania	80,080 79	3,214 05	76,866 73	35,021 27	9,306 01	1,231 92	2,629 18	4,815 07	129,872 18	18,014 61	349,338
land	15,550 79	615 52	14,935 27	4,971 31	1,848 49	305 12	237 04	1,012 50	23,329 73	2,843 27	79,668
ct of Columbia ..	3,802 91	156 62	3,646 29	1,000 00	337 98	95 98	4 50	420 00	5,524 75	477 89	16,567
Virginia	4,368 30	158 41	4,209 89	1,300 00	202 22	113 20	139 79	160 00	6,125 10	366 53	12,978
sia	3,201 72	96 05	3,105 67	1,350 00	500 87	82 13	36 95	444 00	5,519 62	549 48	9,533
ucky	17,032 46	621 83	16,330 63	6,055 01	1,656 93	220 10	670 26	1,198 00	26,150 93	2,441 29	64,142
uri	10,797 22	423 63	10,373 59	5,619 66	1,481 05	134 50	349 08	983 99	18,941 87	2,749 82	77,218
....	38,424 54	2,245 02	56,179 52	16,710 80	5,644 71	1,134 44	2,108 95	2,474 03	84,252 45	8,999 66	248,245
na	26,102 10	993 60	25,108 50	6,678 67	2,999 21	671 95	1,141 44	1,038 90	35,638 67	4,182 45	193,920
is	36,288 86	1,394 64	34,804 22	10,304 50	4,390 79	842 15	1,732 26	1,830 75	53,994 67	6,147 75	167,318
gan	12,039 41	428 54	11,610 87	4,141 06	988 18	254 65	814 10	503 75	18,312 61	2,058 00	78,226
onsin	11,349 52	384 98	10,964 54	3,642 47	902 16	321 45	798 64	774 25	17,433 51	1,916 76	54,305
....	13,431 54	491 56	12,939 98	2,712 50	1,554 77	412 10	853 57	485 00	18,957 92	2,188 06	57,984
sota	2,999 99	89 99	2,910 00	945 00	474 17	148 37	174 90	212 50	4,864 94	689 50	12,168
....	1,500 00	45 00	1,455 00	1,200 00	250 93	95 95	188 59	240 00	3,410 47	422 90	8,258
rais	12,410 00	500 50	11,909 50	8,362 15	1,956 09	412 00	853 00	485 00	27,023 19	4,276 92	13,700
an	3,060 00	122 97	2,937 03	1,500 00	237 60	220 00	44 45	510 00	5,439 08	448 54	6,932
aska Territory ..	1,500 00	45 00	1,455 00	50 00	49 67		31 50	72 61	144 00	1,802 78	74 67	2,888
ta Territory											
tory of New Mexico.	2,043 47	72 15	1,971 32	999 99	381 55	612 00	63 78	110 00	4,138 64	554 00	
Territory	2,500 00	95 00	2,405 00	852 00	319 20	171 50	53 92	300 00	4,101 62	566 07	2,316
ado Territory	6,189 50	175 95	6,013 55	1,998 00	579 96	508 93	160 78	525 00	9,792 24	647 91	4,384
da	3,080 00	124 00	2,956 00	1,266 45	287 75	456 00	169 14	600 00	5,745 34	422 13	2,744
ington Territory.	3,130 00	126 50	3,003 50	450 00	9 75	535 00	28 00	144 00	4,170 25	162 75	2,816
ana Territory	1,664 40	63 25	1,601 15		139 82	13 30	....	245 00	1,999 27	139 82	
Territory											
iana	3,571 43	151 78	3,419 65	4,398 47	1,248 11	215 83	2 25	....	9,284 31	1,937 71	17,966
ssee	8,360 36	330 46	8,029 90	2,594 93	991 71	317 50	62 30	788 75	12,805 09	1,059 01	16,230
Total	572,442 61	22,498 24	549,944 37	229,549 11	86,958 72	15,501 70	23,150 90	37,835 18	942,948 98	128,942 74	2,454,659

H.—*Statement of disbursements for salaries and contingent expenses in collecting taxes, &c., in insurrectionary districts during the fiscal year beginning July 1, 1864, and ending June 30, 1865.*

District.	Salaries.	Tax.	Net salaries.	Stationery.	Office rent.
South Carolina	$10,385 33	$436 04	$9,963 50	$61 00	....
Virginia	9,950 00	385 01	9,567 29	1 20	$40 00
Florida	8,722 82	349 17	8,373 65	132 90	....
Tennessee	10,452 72	397 10	10,055 62	250 80	153 54
North Carolina	8,799 62	331 62	8,468 00	208 57	....
Louisiana	8,100 01	311 32	7,788 69	92 00	....
Arkansas	4,562 08	182 48	4,379 60	317 23	....
Total	60,942 58	2,392 74	58,596 35	1,064 30	193 54

District.	Printing and advertising.	Surveying.	Miscellaneous.	Total.	Tax on survr's salaries.
South Carolina	$371 72	$4,179 98	$68 23	$14,044 43	$44 21
Virginia	395 14	126 70	39 71	10,170 54	2 30
Florida	....	60 00	....	8,566 55	....
Tennessee	27 00	....	608 34	11,095 30	....
North Carolina	....	....	....	8,676 57	....
Louisiana	....	....	566 41	8,447 10	....
Arkansas	....	....	66 25	4,783 08	....
Total	793 86	4,366 68	1,348 94	66,363 67	46 51

REPORT OF THE SIXTH AUDITOR.

OFFICE OF THE AUDITOR OF THE TREASURY
FOR THE POST OFFICE DEPARTMENT,
October 19, 1865.

SIR: In accordance with the uniform custom of this office, I respectfully submit the subjoined statement of the clerical labors performed in this bureau during the past fiscal year.

The forthcoming annual report of this bureau to the Postmaster General will exhibit in detail all that pertains to the financial transactions of the Post Office Department.

SUMMARY OF PRINCIPAL LABORS, VIZ:

The postal accounts between the United States and foreign governments have been promptly and satisfactorily adjusted up to the latest period. Thirty-five thousand three hundred and seventy-four corrected quarterly accounts of postmasters have been re-examined, copied, restated, and mailed; one hundred and three thousand four hundred and twenty-seven letters were received, indorsed, and properly disposed of; eighty-five thousand one hundred and fifty-two letters were answered, recorded, and mailed; fourteen thousand five hundred and ten drafts issued to pay mail contractors; three thousand and six warrants to pay mail contractors. The number of folio-post pages of correspondence recorded, viz: Two thousand six hundred and seventy-two pages in collection book; one hundred and ninety-eight pages in report book; two hundred and forty-three pages in suit book; six hundred and seventy-five pages in miscellaneous book. Forty-nine miscellaneous accounts were reported for payment; one hundred and twelve accounts for advertising were reported and paid; two hundred and fifty-one accounts of special agents were adjusted and paid; two thousand four hundred and seventy letter-carriers' accounts were settled; four hundred and ninety-three thousand four hundred and eight dollars and sixty-four cents was paid to letter-carriers; three thousand two hundred and thirty-seven dollars and eight cents was paid to attorneys, marshals, clerks of the United States courts, &c.

MONEY ORDER DIVISION.

Seven hundred and twenty-four letters were written and mailed; two hundred and ninety-eight of this number were recorded in letter-press book; four hundred and twenty-six of this number were not recorded. The transactions of this branch of the public business involved the amount of two million five hundred and five thousand dollars.

PAY DIVISION.

Sixteen thousand and forty-six accounts of mail contractors were adjusted and reported for payment; fifty-three thousand nine hundred and six collection orders were transmitted to mail contractors; seventy-six thousand three hundred and forty-two postmasters' accounts were examined, adjusted, and registered; two hundred and seventy-six thousand two hundred and fifty-three dollars and sixty-nine cents collected from special and mail messenger offices; two million one hundred and forty-two thousand and ninety-three dollars and five cents aggregate amount of drafts issued to pay mail contractors; two million three hundred and twenty-eight thousand six hundred and one dollars and forty-eight cents received of postmasters by mail contractors on collection orders; two million four hundred and thirty-three thousand three hundred and eighty-six dollars and one cent aggregate amount of warrants issued to pay mail contractors; seventy thousand four hundred and sixteen dollars and eleven cents paid for advertising; fifty-three suits were instituted for the recovery of balances due the United States, amounting to the sum of sixty-four thousand and seventy dollars; sixty-four judgments were obtained in favor of the United States; twenty-five thousand one hundred and ninety dollars and seventy-two cents were collected by suit from late postmasters; forty-one accounts of attorneys, marshals, and clerks of United States courts were reported for payment; sixteen thousand three hundred and six accounts of special mail carriers, mail messengers, and local mail agents were adjusted.

COLLECTING DIVISION.

The collecting division has had charge of the following number of accounts, viz: Twenty-two thousand and fourteen accounts of present postmasters; twenty-eight thousand accounts of late postmasters whose terms of office expired; five thousand eight hundred and ninety-four accounts of postmasters who became late.

The balances ascertained to be due the United States from late postmasters amounted to $1,222,320 27

Of this amount there has been collected $289,239 21
Credited on vouchers 6,372 83
Charged to suspense account 107 71
———————— 295,719 75

Amount remaining for collection 926,600 52

Five thousand four hundred and forty-eight accounts of route agents were settled and reported for payment; seventy-five thousand four hundred and sixteen dollars and ninety-eight cents collected from mail contractors by "collection drafts" for over-collections made by them from postmasters; seven thousand nine hundred and eighty-three accounts of late postmasters having balances due to them in the southern States, and those having credit balances amounting to five dollars and under in the other States, have been closed by suspense, amounting to fifty-five thousand four hundred and one dollars and fifty-one cents; one thousand and fifty-one accounts of late postmasters having balances due to them have been audited and reported to the Postmaster General for payment, amounting to thirty-three thousand nine hundred and thirty-six dollars and seventy-six cents.

The compilation of that portion of the Biennial Register which is prepared in this office, and which has heretofore constituted nearly three-fourths of that document, is now nearly completed, and will be ready for delivery to the public printer on the 31st instant. The preparation of this volume, and the annual report to the Postmaster General at the same time, has imposed great additional labor on this bureau, requiring the services of many of its clerks during extra hours. In addition, many duties of an important character have been discharged requiring much time and labor, which it would not be practicable to particularize in this report.

I have the honor to be, sir, very respectfully,

J. M. McGREW, *Acting Auditor.*

Hon. HUGH McCULLOCH,
     Secretary of the Treasury.

REPORT OF THE COMMISSIONER OF CUSTOMS.

TREASURY DEPARTMENT,
Office of Commissioner of Customs, October, 1865.

SIR : In obedience to your letter of the 10th instant, addressed to me, I have the honor to present my annual report.

The business of this office has been greatly increased during the past year, and especially since the occurrence of the great events brought about by our victorious armies, culminating in the breaking up of the rebellion, the extension of the national laws and authority over the rebellious States, and the reopening of the ports of those States, the appointment of officers of the customs, and the resumption of national commerce. The ports of Norfolk, Richmond, Charleston, Savannah, Mobile, Pensacola, Appalachicola, Galveston and others in Texas, Wilmington, Newbern, Plymouth, and others in North Carolina, were opened soon after the restoration of peace, and officers of customs duly appointed But upon taking possession of the custom-houses at each of these and other ports, it was found that few or none of the records, books, furniture, or property of any kind formerly belonging thereto remained ; everything had been carried away or destroyed. Considerable expense has been incurred in replacing some of this property, though no more has been purchased or supplied than could not be dispensed with.

The appointing of entirely new officers at these several ports, scarcely one of whom had ever had any knowledge derived from experience of the duties of the position he assumed, and which are intricate and perplexing even to one who has had much experience and practical knowledge of them, has thrown much extra care and labor upon this office, and put in requisition no small amount of patience to get these custom-houses into regular, systematic, working order, and to aid the officers to acquire such a knowledge of their duties and of the revenue laws as will enable them to administer the latter with tolerable correctness: perseverance and patience are still required to bring about such a state of things as should exist.

With the restoration of the unity of the nation, and the opening of the southern ports to the commerce of the world, comes the necessity of guarding the whole southern coast against illicit trade, for which our high rates of duties upon foreign goods hold out a very strong temptation, and for which the numerous bayous and inlets of an extensive coast sparsely settled afford such facilities.

Notwithstanding the efforts which have been made to prevent smuggling on the northeastern coast and the northern and northwestern frontier, it has been carried on to a considerable extent, and to that extent lessened the receipts from imports. Several special agents have been employed by the sanction of the department to stop or check this nefarious trade, who, together with most of the collectors on that frontier, as well as on the northeastern coast, have been commendably vigilant, active, energetic, and faithful in their efforts to ferret out, arrest, and punish those thus engaged in defrauding the government. Considerable quantities of smuggled goods have been seized, forfeited, and sold, and the proceeds divided between the government and the officers of customs entitled to shares ; and several persons engaged in this unlawful and demoralizing business have been arrested, tried, convicted, and sentenced to fine and imprisonment under the act of 1842. This act authorizes courts, upon conviction of any one of smuggling, to impose a fine of not over five thousand dollars, or sentence him to imprisonment for a term not exceeding two years, or both.

The impression among those who engage in this reprehensible business has been, that the possible loss of the goods attempted to be smuggled was the only loss or penalty they would incur in case they were detected ; and this was little regarded, since, like blockade-runners, they could well afford to lose two or three ventures out of five, provided they succeeded in running in the other two or three. Under this idea, I blush to record the fact that many, nay, I fear, a majority, of the people living very near the frontier line between this nation and the British Provinces have apparently been disposed not only to give countenance, aid, and assistance to the smuggler, and to conceal him and his goods from the United States officers, but to become partners in the frauds thus practiced against their own government. It may be thought an evidence of superior skill and merit in a community of bandits for one of their number to rob a fellow-being, and evade the clutches of the officers of justice ; and so he who can successfully cheat the government out of a few hundred or a few thousand dollars by evading the revenue laws and those whose duty it is to enforce them, may be looked upon with admiration by those who think it not only no harm, but really an act of merit, to rob the public treasury ; an honest man, however, would not willingly cast his lot in the midst of such a community.

It is vain to think of stopping smuggling by merely seizing and forfeiting the goods smuggled. In the first place, not more than one-tenth, and possibly not more than one-twentieth of the goods attempted to be smuggled are seized, as the facilities of running them in and escaping detection are so great that even with the keenest vigilance and the utmost activity the contrabandist has greatly the advantage of the officer. Something more is necessary, then, to prevent this illicit traffic. The act of 1842, as I have said, imposes a fine or imprisonment, or both ; but while the law fixes the maximum of each, to wit, five thousand dollars and two years' imprisonment, it leaves it discretionary with the courts to impose a merely nominal fine, and to dispense altogether with imprisonment. I would respectfully recommend that the law be so altered as to impose a fine of not less than one hundred dollars, or imprisonment for not less than two months; the maximum of fine to remain as at present, and the maximum imprisonment to be left at two years. Also, to authorize any officer of customs to arrest, and take before some proper officer, any person found in the act of smuggling, or in possession of smuggled goods, or where there is probable cause to believe such person to be engaged in smuggling. With such a law, and with the strenuous co-operation of the courts, smuggling might be made a very hazardous as well as unprofitable business. Some of the courts on the northern frontier have shown a just appreciation of the importance of arresting this illicit traffic, and of teaching wholesome lessons to the smuggler, while others have let him off with a very insignificant fine.

Considerable extra expense has necessarily been incurred in preventing this contraband trade along the northern frontier during the past year, but this has been largely counterbalanced by moneys paid into the treasury arising from the sales of goods seized and condemned on account of being smuggled; the receipts being about five dollars to one of expenses, exclusive of the amount distributed to officers of the customs as their shares of the forfeitures.

In regard to the Atlantic coast I am unable to speak so accurately. Along that coast smuggling is carried on, if at all, more in vessels arriving from foreign ports, or by means of our own coasters which go out to sea, or to some out-of-the-way island, where foreign goods are transferred from vessels from the British provinces or other foreign ports, and by these coasters taken into port, not being subject to the same restrictions on entering as vessels coming from foreign ports. To check and stop this evasion of the revenue laws the department depends, to a considerable extent, upon the efficiency and vigilance of the revenue cutters; but having no control over these, I am not well informed of their operations or success in the preventive service.

Having reason to believe that a more rigid examination of the baggage of passengers and immigrants arriving on steamers and other vessels from Europe, Havana, and other places, than had prevailed, would result in discovering considerable quantities of dutiable goods among, and intended to be passed as, baggage, I took measures, a few months ago, to have this done. The result has shown that I was not mistaken, the duties at a neighboring port collected upon such goods having risen, under this close inspection, from less than one to about six thousand dollars per month. I may be permitted here to remark, that one great stumbling-block in the way of a strict enforcement of the revenue laws is the want of earnestness and conscientiousness in the discharge of their duties by many officers of the customs. They do not feel that the interests of the government are their own, or the obligation of being faithful and vigilant. I do not know whether this is the general rule or the exception; but I am happy to know that there are some the reverse of this, being in every respect zealous and efficient, and ever-watchful of the public interests. It is cause of regret that political conflicts should ever cause the removal of such men from the public service, to be succeeded, it may be, by others of an opposite character. It is my firm conviction that if the most competent, trustworthy, sober, and faithful officers could be retained in the public service, on account of their fidelity and competency, and the incompetent, idle, and worthless discharged, from time to time, on account of their incompetency and worthlessness, the public customs-revenue service would be infinitely better conducted than it has been for forty years past, and at a greatly reduced expense.

The expenses of collecting the revenue have for many years exceeded, and of late years more than doubled, the amount fixed by law in 1849. It may be asked, why has this been allowed? The answer is, because the business of the country has greatly increased, and because various acts of Congress passed since the one above mentioned have thrown large additional burdens upon those expenses. Prices of labor and materials have also been much enhanced, requiring a corresponding increase of compensation; and an increase in the number of inspectors, &c., at the various ports has become necessary by an increase of the duties to be performed.   Formerly the contingent expenses of collectors, surveyors, &c., and their clerk-hire, salaries of deputies, &c., were paid out of the emoluments of their offices—these emoluments arising mainly from fees. But these fees were established when one dollar would purchase more than two will now.   The fees have remained stationary, while labor and materials to be paid for out of them have advanced.   The consequence is, that there is now a deficit where there was formerly a surplus, and this deficit has to be made up by other moneys, which are charged to and go to swell the expenses of collecting the revenue.   I respectfully recommend that Congress be asked to increase the fees at least fifty per cent.

I beg leave to call your attention to the fact that there are now two classes of revenue officers whose services could, in my judgment, be dispensed with without detriment to the public interests.   These are the naval officers and surveyors, both of whom receive large salaries and emoluments, without performing adequate services, or incurring much responsibility.   The naval officer (so called from the fact that similar duties to his were performed under George III, in the colonies, by an officer of the navy designated for that purpose for the time being) was intended to be a check upon the collector; but practically he is no check whatever.   His salary at the seven designated ports is five thousand dollars a year, besides his share of fines and forfeitures, which may or may not amount to a large additional sum.   He has many clerks, besides a deputy, and the work they perform is but a duplication of that performed in the collector's office.   I have not been able to perceive that there is any less accuracy in the accounts of collectors at ports where there are no naval officers, than where there are; and have, therefore, been unable to perceive that it is of the least utility to the government.

The surveyor is next in rank and emolument to the naval officer, his salary being but five hundred dollars a year less, and he sharing with the collector and naval officer a portion of all fines and forfeitures, though his responsibility is very light, and he is wholly subordinate to the collector.   The duties performed by this officer could, I think, be quite as well performed by some one to be designated by the collector, and for a very much less compensation than is now allowed to surveyors.   No naval officer or surveyor has ever been allowed at any of the ports on the northern frontier, nor has it ever been perceived that their services were needed there.   I feel it my duty, looking upon these offices as unnecessary, and only a burden upon the country, to recommend that Congress be asked to dispense with the first entirely, and with the latter at all ports except, perhaps, New York.

In making this recommendation I must disclaim having any unfriendly feeling towards the present incumbents of these offices, for several of whom I have great personal regard; but viewing the offices in the light I do, I am not at liberty to withhold an expression of my opinion.   It is well known to those familiar with custom-house business, and many others, that there have been those who held these offices for many years who were seldom seen in the custom-house, and whose duties were mostly, if not entirely, performed by deputy.

It may be a very antiquated notion that official duties and responsibilities should bear a just proportion to official emoluments; but I cannot but think such a rule is in accordance with the spirit of republican government.

There are a great number of old accounts on the books of this office unclosed, and showing balances for and against collectors and other officers of the customs.   Many of these show equal balances for and against the individuals under different heads: for instance, there may be a balance standing against A in his disbursement account, while a balance of precisely the same amount stands in his favor in his emolument account; and thus, while he owes nothing to the government, his accounts cannot be closed, there being no power under the law, as it now stands, to offset the one against the other, and thus close the accounts on the books. It therefore frequently appears that individuals are defaulters to the government when they are not. I recommend that Congress be asked to pass a law to meet the case.

But there are many balances also standing on the books which are due from former officers; some of them have been, by my direction, looked after and are in a fair way to be collected; the others will be attended to as speedily as possible. Since the date of my last annual report, the labors of the division of "commercial intercourse" and "captured and abandoned property," of this office, have been prosecuted with unremitted attention. To attempt a full exhibit of the work performed, or an enumeration of the difficulties with which the division has had to contend, would require a transcript of the records of the division in detail. It is, however, due to the clerks therein employed, that I should say that, notwithstanding the many, and in many instances insurmountable difficulties, they have faithfully performed their duties, and in a manner, I hope, to meet your commendation, as the statements herewith transmitted will in part show. If these statements are not as complete and satisfactory as could be desired, the cause may be attributed to circumstances not within the control of this office, but, in some degree, to the frequent changes of instructions to the agents of the government, which were deemed necessary; the fact that these agents were scattered over a wide space of country; that they found it difficult to understand their instructions, and to carry them out; and the great difficulty there was in communicating with the department, and the department with them.

There has not been for a great number of years any uniformity in keeping the various accounts required to be kept by collectors of customs. The modes of keeping these are, consequently, almost as numerous as the collectors, each port having books peculiar to itself. As there should be a uniform system at all the ports, I am having prepared such a system, and also forms for various uses, which I shall have the honor to submit for your approval. When such a system and such forms shall be established, I respectfully recommend as a measure of economy, as well as uniformity, that books for these various accounts, and all blanks, be provided by the department for the use of such officers of customs as may require them, to be paid for as they are now paid for, out of the emoluments of the offices to which they are sent. I am quite sure that a very considerable saving might be made by adopting this plan.

The amount of duties refunded since my last report, the papers for which pass through my hands, is two hundred and fifty-five thousand six hundred and ninety-eight dollars and fifty cents, ($255.698 50,) namely: to satisfy judgments recovered against collectors for excess of duties exacted in accordance with instructions from the department, two hundred and thirty-seven thousand and seventy-six dollars and one cent, ($237,076 01;) to satisfy claims in cases where no suits were commenced, eighteen thousand six hundred and twenty-two dollars and forty-nine cents, ($18,622 49.)

I respectfully call your attention to the complexity of the laws relating to revenue from customs. The acts passed by Congress in 1799, relating to this subject, were, it is understood, drawn up with much care by some one or more, fully conversant with the subject, and were, for the circumstances of the country and the condition of our commerce and navigation, as perfect a system as could be devised. But a long period of time has elapsed since then, and most remarkable changes have come over the country, demanding from time to time changes and amendments, which have again and again, perhaps, been changed and amended, until what was once a complete and admirable system, working most harmoniously, has become such a piece of complex and mended machinery as to make it very difficult to comprehend its various parts, and much more to reconcile their incongruities.

To amend these would seem to be but putting patch upon patch without improving them. The task of adapting them to the present condition of the country by amendments is a hopeless one; the whole should be recast in a new code, and this could only be properly done by men who have had much experience in administering these laws, and who have had opportunities to observe and most sensibly to feel their defects, and who have the ability, natural and acquired, to perform the task in a manner creditable and beneficial to a nation second to none in commercial importance and the extent of its navigation. If not thus performed, they had better remain as they are, much as they need codifying.

At the time these laws were chiefly enacted the channels of commerce were confined to bodies or streams of water, and ports were established where vessels arrived; now, commerce breaks away from these channels and sweeps over plains, mountains, and valleys, wherever it listeth; centres of trade and commerce spring up far from water-courses, and it now becomes necessary to establish ports of entry upon those overland commercial highways, and to provide for inspecting foreign goods imported in cars, and treating these in the same manner that we treat foreign vessels laden with merchandise.

I have no occasion to ask for more clerks, but a re-classification of those I have would add much to their efficiency. I have more of the first class and less of the fourth than should be assigned to this office.

The following statement will exhibit, in the briefest space, the amount of work performed in this office during the past year:

Tabular statement of accounts received and passed in the office of the Commissioner of Customs during the financial year 1864–'65.

Period.	Accounts rec'd.	Accounts passed	Letters written.	Letters recorded.	Letters received.	Requisitions.	Amount.	Returns received and examined.	Clerks.
July, 1864	475	213	368	203	315	142	$951,699 83	325	16
August, 1864	273	252	592	115	328	134	769,103 41	368	18
September, 1864....	135	187	596	457	327	175	843,374 82	296	18
October, 1864	203	280	345	335	246	147	936,551 84	295	18
November, 1864	321	344	530	307	318	134	908,795 84	362	19
December, 1864	273	336	992	318	306	185	774,802 51	421	19
January, 1865......	239	201	651	337	238	135	669,366 63	256	18
February, 1865.....	235	291	748	299	446	113	466,220 30	397	18
March, 1865........	212	236	980	388	302	182	734,791 48	575	18
April, 1865........	164	181	619	371	378	135	1,814 758 90	596	19
May, 1865	256	232	929	604	342	149	769,012 99	594	19
June, 1865........	169	178	994	563	433	208	899,710 33	506	19
Total..........	2,955	2,931	8,344	4,297	3,979	1,839	10,538,188 93	4,991	

I have the honor to be, very respectfully, your obedient servant,

N. SARGENT, *Commissioner.*

Hon. H. McCULLOCH,
   Secretary of the Treasury.

P. S.—I herewith transmit a table showing the general results of the receipts and disposal of merchandise within the United States for the year ending the 30th of June, 1865, and a table showing the value of imports and exports in the various collection districts of the nation for the same period.

N. SARGENT, *Commissioner.*

Statement exhibiting the transactions in relation to internal and coastwise commercial intercourse during the fiscal year ending June 30, 1865.

| | COTTON. | | | | TOBACCO. | | | | SUGAR. | | |
| | 4 cents per pound. | | | | $2 per hogshead. | | | | 3 cents per pound. | | |
Port from which shipped.	Bales.	Pounds.	Value.	Fees.	Hhds.	Pounds.	Value.	Fees.	Pounds.	Value.	Fees.
1 Philadelphia, Pa											
2 Delaware, Del											
3 Baltimore, Md											
4 Georgetown, D. C											
5 Alexandria, Va...........											
6 Beaufort, N. C	2,421	1,179,801	$653,028 25	$39,738 88							
7 Beaufort, S. C...........	3,993	297,983	297,983 00	11,920 24							
8 New Orleans, La	93,029	18,742,735	17,494,687 00	703,762 99	39	16,190	$8,419 00	$58 00	8,253,349	$1,402,523 00	$42,075 69
9 Pittsburg, Pa...........											
10 Wheeling, Va											
11 St. Louis, Mo...........	3,851	4,690,764	2,794,518 40	192,742 68	154	....	....	332 00			
12 Louisville, Ky...........	....	5,008,205	2,761,228 80	198,639 23	1,552	....	348,225 00	3,104 00			
13 Paducah, Ky...........	7,075	3,404,691	2,042,814 60	101,426 49	150	264,330	34,950 00	300 00			
14 Nashville, Tenn	2,503	1,149,347	561,505 20	24,818 74	134	195,220	31,771 00	262 00			
15 Memphis, Tenn...........	31,186	19,727,388	8,988,447 20	177,811 61	2	....	200 00	4 00			
16 Cincinnati, Ohio...........	21,561	9,796,380	5,803,900 40	371,420 20	45	....	....	90 00			
17 Evansville, Ind	1,830	877,936	527,266 00	35,042 44	10	9,000	1,220 00	20 00			
18 New Albany, Ind											
19 Madison, Ind											
20 Cairo, Ill...........	15,251	6,838,618	4,115,070 80	259,345 30	308	222,520	105,706 00	616 00			
21 Fernandina, Fla...........	14	4,154	1,731 50	103 25							
22 Norfolk, Va...........	1,270	499,529	418,619 40	19,494 54							
Total.................	183,984	72,237,531	46,430,820 55	2,126,266 59	2,384	707,260	530,491 00	4,786 00	8,253,349	1,402,523 00	42,075 69

Statement exhibiting the transactions in relation to internal and coastwise commercial intercourse—Continued.

which shipped.	MOLASSES.			RICE.				Three per cent. fees.	Gross value of merchandise permitted.
	3 per cent. ad valorem.			3 per cent. ad valorem.					
	Gallons.	Value.	Fees.	Tierces.	Pounds.	Value.	Fees.		
Philadelphia, Pa.								$8,059 67	$3,735,381 95
Delaware, Del.									8,910 36
Baltimore, Md.								269,270 88	17,644,816 26
Georgetown, D. C.								26,212 29	1,091,708 21
Alexandria, Va.								425 06	9,969 81
Beaufort, N. C.								61,036 98	2,843,121 90
Beaufort, S. C.								73,345 02	2,840,454 15
New Orleans, La.	782,776	$573,093 00	$17,192 79	91,623	1,368,410	$127,095 00	$3,812 85	168,929 44	36,131,561 18
Pittsburg, Pa.								4,032 56	178,534 73
Wheeling, Va.								189 00	60,174 31
St. Louis, Mo.								134,588 66	17,160,911 00
Louisville, Ky.								234,398 53	9,811,978 13
Paducah, Ky.								5,245 20	1,265,043 65
Nashville, Tenn.								12,741 93	4,154,654 63
Memphis, Tenn.								8,866 30	4,831,191 35
Cincinnati, Ohio.								465,381 65	20,462,951 21
Evansville, Ind.								10,346 91	1,362,214 00
New Albany, Ind.								1,367 58	225,443 85
Madison, Ind.								664 19	227,496 21
Cairo, Ill.								71,632 52	6,051,887 20
Fernandina, Fla.								1,161 13	44,598 58
Norfolk, Va.								23,004 66	1,047,307 84
Total	782,776	573,093 00	17,192 79	91,623	1,368,410	127,095 00	3,812 85	1,580,863 16	131,189,809 81

Statement exhibiting the transactions in relation to internal and coastwise commercial intercourse—Continued.

	Port from which shipped.	PERMITS GRANTED.					Fees.	All other fees collected.	Total fees collected.	Fines, penalties, and forfeitures collected.	Total receipts.
		At 5 cents.	At 10 cents.	At 15 cents.	At 20 cents.	Total number.					
		Number.	Number.	Number.	Number.						
1	Philadelphia, Pa					14,285	$2,837 00	$568 30	$11,475 97		$11,475 97
2	Delaware, Del					592	592	118 40		118 40		118 40
3	Baltimore, Md	2,118	36		1,083	73,127	76,364	14,897 35	8,182 70	292,350 93		292,350 93
4	Georgetown, D. C					1,739	1,739	347 80	30	26,560 39		26,560 39
5	Alexandria, Va					12	12	2 40	4 10	431 56		431 56
6	Beaufort, N. C					3,171	3,171	634 20	2,928 26	104,308 32		104,308 32
7	Beaufort, S. C			1	111	1,457	1,569	309 90		85,575 16		85,575 16
8	New Orleans, La	5,069	8,399		12,180	19,796	45,374	6,865 55	8,091 09	950,728 40	$18,471 50	969,259 90
9	Pittsburg, Pa		8			213	221	43 40	31 30	4,107 26		4,107 26
10	Wheeling, Va	1				253	254	50 65	25 75	265 40		265 40
11	St. Louis, Mo					13,273	13,273	2,654 60	1,707 30	392,025 94		392,025 94
12	Louisville, Ky	197	250		535	15,056	16,038	3,123 40	5,297 40	444,562 56	3,260 23	447,822 79
13	Paducah, Ky	3,252	1,687		1,430	1,273	7,592	790 40	1,049 05	108,811 14		108,811 14
14	Nashville, Tenn	5,396	2,434		2,013	5,363	15,206	1,686 75	871 80	40,381 22		40,381 22
15	Memphis, Tenn			1,197		11,427	12,624	2,405 10	958 25	190,047 26		190,047 26
16	Cincinnati, Ohio	1,865	984		1,773	18,328	22,950	4,123 20	2,557 30	843,572 35		843,572 35
17	Evansville, Ind	3		3		1,415	1,421	283 05	314 05	46,906 45		46,906 45
18	New Albany, Ind					144	144	28 80	148 17	1,544 55		1,544 55
19	Madison, Ind					124	124	24 80	15 10	704 09		704 09
20	Cairo, Ill					7,902	7,902	1,580 40	1,329 85	334,304 07		334,304 07
21	Fernandina, Fla	......			1	16	17	3 35	6 00	1,973 73		1,973 73
22	Norfolk, Va					767	767	153 40	14 10	42,666 70		42,666 70
	Total	17,901	14,999	19,126		178,613	230,639	43,183 90	34,100 17	3,832,281 15	21,731 73	3,874,012 88

Statement exhibiting the transactions in relation to internal and coastwise commercial intercourse—Continued.

Port from which shipped.	EXPENSES.					Permit fees and assessments refunded.	Fines, penalties, and forfeitures remitted.	Total payments.	Deposits.
	Compensation to—		Rent.	Incidental.	Total.				
	Spec'l agents.	Aids, &c.							
Philadelphia, Pa.		$2,090 26		$705 44	$2,795 70	$257 70		$3,053 40	$9,836 27
Delaware, Del.									
Baltimore, Md.	$60,524 65	32,528 93		14,683 97	107,737 55		1,534 45	109,372 00	218,087 95
Georgetown, D. C.	194 42	400 99		13 00	707 41			707 41	23,849 55
Alexandria, Va.									431 56
Beaufort, N. C.	1,770 40			315 38	2,085 78			2,085 78	54,091 10
Beaufort, S. C.									
New Orleans, La	984 00	76,765 29		4,166 22	81,915 51	12,641 45		94,556 96	869,476 36
Pittsburg, Pa.		3,284 25			3,284 25			3,284 25	881 48
Wheeling, Va.		1,114 20		251 17	1,365 37			1,365 37	126 30
St. Louis, Mo.		13,502 50		216 10	13,718 60	3,465 88		17,184 48	58,855 24
Louisville, Ky		25,930 65		1,593 05	27,683 70			27,683 70	437,214 06
Paducah, Ky		5,483 20	$480 00	532 44	6,495 64			6,495 64	98,209 96
Nashville, Tenn	2,554 44	4,514 32		1,045 25	8,114 01			8,114 01	21,650 99
Memphis, Tenn		16,229 50			16,229 50			16,229 50	
Cincinnati, Ohio	12,425 92	34,240 99	166 66	3,846 41	50,679 98	4,429 07		55,109 05	794,141 52
Evansville, Ind.	180 00	5,361 15		1,171 85	6,713 00			6,713 00	46,006 45
New Albany, Ind.									
Madison, Ind.									
Cairo, Ill.		8,940 90		634 67	9,575 57	960 86		10,536 43	321,082 74
Fernandina, Fla.									
Norfolk, Va.	1,546 20	3,226 80		1,038 42	4,811 42			4,811 42	33,381 12
Total	80,180 03	232,712 93	646 66	30,573 37	344,112 99	23,389 43		367,502 42	2,990,231 95

N. SARGENT, Commissioner

TREASURY DEPARTMENT, Office of Commissioner of Customs, October 31, 1863.

Statement exhibiting the sales of cotton and tobacco made by the several super tions in relation to captured and abandoned pro

COTTON.

QUANTITY RECEIVED.		Date of receipt.	By whom received.	Date of disposition.	QUANTITY SOLD.		Amount of gross proceeds.
Packages.	Pounds.				Packages.	Pounds.	
792 bales		Mar., 1864	Wm. P. Mellen, sup. sp'l agent.	April, 1864	792 bales		$211,973 70
218 bales		...do	......do	May, 1864	218 bales		63,833 92
5 bags and 880¼ bales.		...do	......do	June 1864	5 bags and 880¼ bales.	510,108	166,457 39
49 bags & 1,237½ bales.		May, 1864	......do	July, 1864	1,116 bales.....	87,532	720,670 08
25 bags and 462 bales.	196,599	Aug., 1864	......do	Aug., 1864	11 bags and 199 bales.		130,416 47
326 bales		...do	......do	Sept., 1864	293 bales		168,892 23
618 bales		Sept., 1864	......do	Oct., 1864	618 bales		245,043 94
94 bales		Oct., 1864	......do	Nov., 1864	94 bales		44,453 90
598 bales	{	Nov., 1864 Dec., 1864	} ..do	Dec. 1864	522 bales		234,036 04
155 bales		Jan., 1865	......do	Jan., 1865	155 bales		48,893 50
144½ bales		Feb., 1865	......do	Mar., 1865	144½ bales		27,005 52
45 bales		April, 1865	......do	May, 1865	45 bales		5,599 68
1 bag & 99 bales		May, 1865	......do	June, 1865	1 bag & 99 bales		14,528 61
380 bales		June, 1865	......do	July, 1865	380 bales		67 673 25
680 bales		July, 1865	......do	Aug., 1865	680 bales		90,367 67
8 bags & 81 bales.		July, 1864	B. F. Flanders, sup. sp'l agent.	July, 1864	....		45,684 40
7 bales	2,834	...do	......do	Sept. 1864	....		4,841 50
15 bales	5,249	Sept., 1864	......do	Oct., 1864	....		5,307 84
7 sacks and 17 bales.	6,509	Oct., 1864	......do	Nov., 1864	....		6,609 18
4 bales	1,176	Nov., 1864	......do	Dec., 1864	....		240 20
13 bales	483,233	April, 1865	A. G. Browne, sup. sp'l agent.	June, 1865	13 bales	11,593	1,443 36
1 bag & 10 bales.	4,161	June, 1864	D. Heaton, sup. sp'l agent.	Aug., 1864	10 bales	4,161	6,946 88
1 bale	578	Jan., 1864	......do	...do	1 bale	578	953 26
	1,531		......do	Dec., 1864		1,531	1,806 58
	7,047	July, 1864	......do	Sept., 1864		7,047	12,305 68
61 bales			......do	Dec., 1864	61 bales		25,927 65
10 bales	3,834		......do	April, 1865	10 bales	3,834	2,654 96
17 bales	13,825	Mar., 1865	......do	...do	17 bales	13,825	389 15
4 bales		Jan., 1865	......do	...do	....		589 62

TOBACCO.

14 boxes........		Aug., 1864	Wm. P. Mellen, sup. sp'l agent.	Oct., 1864	4 boxes........		215 10
3 hogsheads		...do	......do	...do	3 hogsheads....		68 00
44 boxes........			B. F. Flanders, sup. sp'l agent.	April, 1864	....		2,268 03
1,041½ dozen....		July, 1864	......do	...do	....		6,074 00
	3,841	Mar., 1865	D. Heaton, sup. sp'l agent.	Sept., 1864	....		1,971 65
	247,741		......do	April, 1865	....		46,867 47

TREASURY DEPARTMENT, *Office of Commissioner of Customs, October* 31, 1865.

*vising special agents of the Treasury Department under the laws and regula-
perty, from January 1, 1864, to April 30, 1865.*

COTTON.

Amount paid for labor, transportation, &c.	Amount paid for auction duties.	Amount paid for assessment.	Amount paid internal revenue tax.	Amount retained for contingent expenses.	Total amount paid.	Amount of net proceeds.	Amount of proceeds released.	Am't on hand subject to decisions of Secretary of Treasury.	Amount deposited.
$16,087 54	$211 86	$13,404 86	....	$3,179 41	$33,483 67	$178,490 03	....	....	....
4,205 00	63 82	3,772 70	$1,886 38	957 47	10,945 43	52,688 49	....	....	....
9,171 19	106 43	5,148 80	2,374 40	2,496 83	....	145,698 74	....	....	....
13,524 23	720 65	20,404 32	10,202 16	10,810 04	55,661 40	665,009 28	$340,000 00	$311,770 13	....
2,709 00	93 41	3,490 28	1,745 14	1,946 23	10,247 06	120,422 37	....	120,422 37	$120,422 37
6,333 33	168 78	4,803 00	2,401 50	2,339 27	16,238 88	152,583 35	27,991 14	194,692 21	152,563 35
11,981 85	244 98	10,910 08	5,435 04	3,675 58	32,267 53	212,776 41	16,063 98	196,712 53	212,776 41
1,433 46	44 42	1,594 92	797 46	566 79	4,537 15	39,916 75	....	39,916 75	39,916 75
11,553 07	234 16	9,407 68	4,703 94	3,513 47	29,412 52	204,823 52	....	204,892 53	....
3,890 60	48 79	2,386 68	1,293 34	732 52	8,551 96	40,341 54	....	40,341 54	....
3,568 51	26 96	2,657 24	1,328 62	405 09	7,986 35	19,019 17	....	19,019 17	....
1,159 81	5 52	769 72	....	82 93	2,017 98	3,512 64	....	3,512 64	....
1,207 37	14 52	1,468 44	....	217 91	2,908 24	11,620 37	....	11,620 37	....
6,553 96	67 65	3,164 56	....	1,015 06	10,801 23	56,872 02	....	56,872 02	....
13,485 64	90 31	5,363 64	....	1,355 48	20,330 07	70,047 60	....	....	....
1,405 50	496 29	1,419 08	709 94	685 27	4,716 08	40,968 39	....	....	40,968 32
93 60	57 42	....	....	79 09	153 64	4,687 95	....	....	4,687 95
102 05	75 89	....	....	79 61	257 48	5,050 36	....	....	5,050 36
1,579 00	88 35	....	....	70 74	1,738 12	4,871 08	1,420 46	3,450 60	....
33 00	19 40	....	....	3 60	56 00	184 20	....	....	....
431 54	23 00	....	....	21 65	476 19	967 17	....	....	....
235 81	201 19	....	....	....	437 00	6,509 88	....	....	6,509 88
32 79	27 92	....	....	....	60 71	904 55	....	....	904 55
49 84	45 16	....	....	....	94 40	1,712 18	....	....	....
498 61	329 14	....	....	....	827 75	11,477 93	....	....	....
261 84	649 19	....	....	....	910 03	25,027 68	....	....	....
65 05	66 37	....	....	....	131 42	2,823 54	....	....	2,823 54
112 38	9 73	....	....	....	122 11	267 04	....	....	267 04
15 50	14 74	....	....	....	30 24	....	....	559 38	....

TOBACCO.

70 77	21	....	....	3 24	74 22	141 88	....	....	....
49 83	07	....	....	1 02	50 92	17 38	....	....	....
4 81	73 63	....	....	34 03	107 47	2,160 76	....	....	....
1,468 42	175 33	....	....	91 10	1,734 85	4,339 15	....	....	4,339,15
61 85	70 79	....	....	....	132 64	1,839 01	....	....	....
1,185 98	1,171 69	....	....	....	2,357 67	44,509 80	....	....	44,509 80

N. SARGENT, *Commissioner.*

Statement exhibiting the sales of miscellaneous articles made by the several supervising special agents of the Treasury Department under the laws and regulations in relation to captured and abandoned property, from October 1, 1863, to August 31, 1865.

By whom received.	Date of disposition.—Sold.	Gross proceeds.	Amount paid.	Net proceeds.	Proceeds released.	Amount on hand.	Amount deposited.	Claimed by Q. M. Dep.
William P. Mellen	April, 1864	$54 17	$59 60	$262 70				
Do	June, 1864	38 60	43 49	354 24				
Do	July, 1864	360 00	168 65					
Do	October, 1864	2,339 19	368 75	2,169 75		*$2,169 75	$2,169 75	
Do	December, 1864	67 83	55 01	68 82		*68 82		
William M. Orme	November, 1864	612 00	612 00	459 40		*452 40	452 40	
Do	April, 1865	5,770 55	5,261 43	5,261 43			5,261 43	
Do	July, 1865	1,313 40	348 08	1,220 43			1,220 43	
Benjamin F. Flanders	May, 1864	8,157 66	717 52	7,440 14			7,440 14	
Do	June, 1864	2,299 23	126 54	2,172 69			2,172 69	
Do	July, 1864	2,067 00	180 85	1,886 15			1,886 15	
Do	September, 1864	27 40	41	26 99			786 04	
Do	October, 1864	854 55	71 54	782 40			782 40	
Do	December, 1864	1,222 75	152 23	575 41				
Do	January, 1865	2,538 45	133 68	3,739 89			3,739 89	
Do	March, 1865	5,001 58	258 35	2,280 18				
Albert G. Browne	November, 1864	69 00	1 40	67 96				
Do	February, 1865	3,276 14	268 94	5,460 31				
Do	March, 1865	3,872 77	126 54	3,746 23				
Do	June, 1865	1,697 70	71 96	1,625 73				
David Heston	October, November, December, 1863; January, February, March, 1864.	5,478 60	92 80	5,358 29			4,533 76	
Do	April, 1864	6,058 94	7 23	575 41				
Do	August, 1864	17,640 25	17,640 25	17,640 25			17,640 25	
Do	September, 1864	20,152 51	1,249 80	18,677 75			18,677 75	
Do	October, 1864	1,300 00	25 00	1,275 00	$485 00		850 00	
Do	November, 1864	7,493 46	379 10	6,813 89			5,898 79	
Do	December, 1864	8,074 46	674 95	7,659 51			7,659 51	
Do	January, 1865	3,626 98	255 29	3,379 62			3,379 62	
Do	February, 1865	9,034 30	561 65	8,477 75			8,221 24	
Do	April, 1865	1,139 65	849 65	3,221 24			4,985 24	
Do	May, 1865	7,987 10	4,363 27	7,475 27			2,860 10	
Do	June, 1865	2,965 55	134 45	2,860 10			2,467 91	$2,467 91
Do	July, 1865	1,553 59	162 05	2,179 64				
Do	August, 1865	1,613 25						
William Silvey	December, 1864	23,164 87	1,118 90	22,179 68			9,000 00	
Do	March, 1865	1,823 78	74 15	1,749 63			1,000 00	

Statement exhibiting the amount received for rent of captured and abandoned property in the several supervising special agencies, from —— to ——.

By whom received.	Number of agency.	Date of receipt.	Am't rec'd.
William P. Mellen.........	First agency.........	April, 1864........	
Do...............	.......do...........	July, 1864	$935 39
Do...............	.......do...........	August, 1864........	1,491 79
Do...............	.......do...........	September, 1864......	769 39
William W. Orne.........	Second agency.......	January, 1865........	5,389 50
Do...............	.......do...........	April, 1865..........	7,674 41
Benjamin F. Flanders......	Fifth agency.........	May, 1864...........	8,495 88
Do...............	.......do...........	June, 1864..........	12,112 35
Do...............	...t....do...........	July, 1864..........	7,154 70
Do...............	.......do...........	August, 1864........	7,155 30
Do...............	.......do...........	September, 1864......	9,694 50
Do...............	.......do...........	October 1864........	9 102 15
Do...............	.......do...........	November, 1864......	11,'955 35
Do...............	.......do...........	December, 1864......	12,474 73
Do...............	.......do...........	January, 1865........	10,220 90
Do...............	.......do...........	February, 1865	12,460 95
Do...............	.......do...........	March, 1865........	9,712 75
Do...............	.......do...........	April, 1865..........	8,597 35
Do...............	.......do...........	May, 1865...........	Missing.
Do...............	.......do...........	June, 1865..........	8,157 68
Albert G. Browne.........	.......do...........	Forms No. —,1864-'65.	No transs'n.
David Heaton............	Sixth agency........	Sep.30,1863 to Dec.1864.	33,557 07
Do...............	.......do...........	For the year 1864....	88,795 87
Do...............	.......do...........	January, 1865........	2,802 04
Do...............	.......do...........	February, 1865	1,137 83
Do...............	.......do...........	March, 1865..........	2,802 79
Do...............	.......do...........	April, 1865..........	2,033 30
Do...............	.......do...........	May, 1865...........	4,489 63
Do...............	.......do...........	June, 1865	2,300 19
Do...............	.......do...........	July, 1865	2,047 03
William Silvey...........	Seventh agency......	May, 1864	25 00
Do...............	.......do...........	June, 1864..........	
Do...............	.......do...........	July, 1864..........	Not fixed.
Do...............	.......do...........	August, 1864	
Do...............	.......do...........	September, 1864	
Do...............	.......do...........	October....	
Do...............	.......do...........	November, 1864......	
Do...............	.......do...........	December, 1864......	36 00
Do...............	.......do...........	January, 1865	
Do...............	.......do...........	February, 1865.......	
B. H. Morse	Second agency.......	Jan., Feb.& Mar., 1864.	3,879 71
Do...............	.......do...........		3,329 74
Do...............	.......do...........		2,692 27
Do...............	.......do...........	April, 1864........ ...	322 50
Do...............	.......do...........	May, 1864............	397 25
Do...............	.......do...........	June, 1864..........	119 00
Do...............	.......do...........	July, 1864..........'..	137 75
C. S. Henry..............	.......do...........	July, 1864............	2 00
E. C. Parkhurst...........	.......do...........	April, 1864..........	158 00
Do...............	.......do...........	August, 1864........	161 35
Do...............	.......do...........	September, 1864......	123 70
Do...............	.......do...........	October, 1864........	107 00
Do...............	.......do...........	January, 1865........	226 20
Do...............	.......do...........	February, 1865.......	382 34
Do...............	.......do...........	March, 1865..........	18 00

N. SARGENT, *Commissioner.*

TREASURY DEPARTMENT,
  Office of Commissioner of Customs, October 31, 1865.

Statement showing the value of imports and exports in the various collection districts in the United States for the fiscal year ending June 30, 1865, and also the aggregate amount.

Ports.	IMPORTS.					EXPORTS.				
	Specie and bullion.	Free goods, exclusive of specie and bullion.	Dutiable entered for—		Total imports.	Merchandise withdrawn for consumption.	Specie and bullion.	Foreign merchandise.		Domestic merchandise.	Total exports.
			Consumption.	Warehouse.				Dutiable.	Free.		
Bath, Me	....	$6,303 00	$3,407 00	$6,607 00	$30,317 00	$34,462 00	....	....	....	$66,160 00	$66,160 00
Bangor, Me	$125 00	5,058 00	6,318 00	98,746 00	110,247 00	116,564 00	....	$93,451	....	672,936 00	696,387 00
Boston, Mass.	138,540 00	3,660,741 00	7,695,874 00	12,636,305 00	24,131,460 00	11,803,547 00	$1,565,460 00	1,600,403	$486,452	17,673,170 00	21,323,485 00
Baltimore, Md	....	89,502 00	1,833,513 00	2,917,306 00	4,840,321 00	3,061,116 00	....	209,122	31,381	11,794,544 00	12,035,117 00
Bristol, R. I.	....	2,072 31	148,100 28	150,173 09	....	160,065 96	....	....	91,197 50	91,197 50
Belfast, Me	....	2,424 00	3,533 00	23,344 00	29,301 00	13,835 00	....	374	5,818	184,685 00	191,077 00
Burlington, Vt	2,255,449 00	6,355,679 00	133,235 00	....	8,744,363 00	....	770,666 00	547,894	....	346,964 00	1,665,524 00
Buffalo, N. Y	....	3,593,520 00	103,435 00	41,799 00	3,738,754 00	48,684 00	....	....	903,885 00	903,885 00
Castine, Me	....	....	669 00	....	669 00	....	....	....	34,198 00	34,198 00
Cleveland, Ohio	....	219,977 00	32,521 00	75,645 00	398,143 00	19,479 00	....	....	505,819 00	505,819 00
Cape Vincent, N. Y	169,822 00	838,770 00	10,328 00	....	1,018,920 00	....	164,298 00	87,575	....	134,594 00	386,467 00
Chicago, Ill	....	193,971 00	119,937 00	7,153 00	321,061 00	102,503 00	....	2,828	....	4,173,617 00	4,176,445 00
Dunkirk, N. Y	....	5,166 39	37 50	....	5,203 89	....	....	300	....	300 00
Detroit, Mich	....	1,350,507 00	84,728 00	13,701 00	1,448,936 00	5,415 00	....	109,386	....	2,767,608 00	2,876,994 00
Ellsworth, Me	1,843 00	1,134 68	....	1,134 00	....	....	....	20,005 00	20,005 00
Erie, Pa	1,843 00	19,503 63	13,250 60	....	34,597 23	....	....	....	237,086 70	237,086 70
Edgartown, Mass	....	65,560 00	....	65,560 00	....	....	....	4,144 20	4,144 20
Fall River, Mass	....	13,952 00	10,699 00	9,076 00	33,727 00	....	....	....	12,094 00	12,094 00
Fairfield, Conn	....	7,356 62	1,794 14	....	9,150 76	....	....	....	1,677 50	1,677 50
Gloucester, Mass	2,000 00	510,852 00	2,589 00	44,631 00	560,072 00	4,295 00	....	739	45	69,162 00	69,946 00
Key West, Fla	8,500 00	1,906 00	11,074 16	16,863 38	37,643 54	....	....	16,029	....	23,819 50	39,849 50

...mouth, N. H	....	15,040 00	....	5,494 00	20,534 00	3,484 00	....	....	....	511 00	511 00
...sburg, N. Y.........	2,819,589 61	2,167,189 00	34,667 40	485,635 00	5,500,074 01	....	1,993,522 50	109,468	5,791	331,260 00	2,430,911 50
...a Amboy, N. J.........	....	400 00	....	....	400 00	....	....	....	....	29,048 00	29,048 00
...ld-nce, R. I.........	....	126,617 00	16,870 00	255,628 00	399,115 00	173,793 00	....	2,008	....	8,182 00	10,190 00
...delphia, Pa	299,366 00	581,137 00	2,035,839 00	5,372,759 00	8,289,101 00	5,355,924 00	....	72,416	....	10,976,430 00	11,048,846 00
...mouth, Mass	....	1,643 00	....	....	1,643 00	....	....	....	....	4,199 00	4,199 00
...ester, N. Y	....	553,495 00	6,683 00	10,671 00	570,849 00	36,548 00	....	1,105	....	357,367 00	358,472 00
...n, Mass	....	35,509 00	57,490 00	122,192 00	215,191 00	54,130 00	25,000 00	38,139	....	71,358 00	134,497 00
...usky, Ohio	....	16,747 00	293 00	....	17,040 00	....	....	....	....	24,023 00	24,023 00
...ension Bridge, N. Y	....	3,231,663 00	40,388 00	32,591 00	3,304,642 00	....	....	9,848	....	139,436 00	149,284 00
...ington, Del	....	1,654 82	38,562 92	....	40,217 74	112 00	....	....	....	63,003 75	63,003 75
...do, Ohio	....	59,490 00	....	12,551 19	72,041 19	....	....	....	....	949,985 00	949,985 00
Total	7,626,421 61	43,028,065 31	80,681,474 63	106,192,412 61	237,528,374 18	97,683,042 46	44,319,796 50	19,273,238	4,992,596	249,370,895 97	317,956,526 47

OFFICE OF COMMISSIONER OF CUSTOMS, *Treasury Department.*

N. SARGENT, *Commissioner of Customs.*

REPORT OF SUPERVISING ARCHITECT.

TREASURY DEPARTMENT,
Office of Supervising Architect, November 11, 1865.

SIR: The operations during the year ending September 30, 1865, on the various public buildings under the direction of the Treasury Department, and committed to the charge of this office, have been limited, and, with some few exceptions, mostly confined to repairs and alterations. No new buildings were commenced, and, in consequence of the failure of appropriations asked for from the last Congress, works had to be stopped; as, for instance, the work of alterations of the Cincinnati, Ohio, Philadelphia, Pennsylvania, custom-houses, and the completion of the Dubuque custom-house.

The following works were completed during the year: the United States court-house at Baltimore, Maryland, the work on the government warehouses and wharves on Staten island, New York, and the new roof of the Windsor, Vermont, court-house.

Proposals were invited for the construction of a new custom-house at Portland, Maine, for which an appropriation of $50,000 had been made, and for the alterations of the Louisville custom-house; but the offers received in both cases exceeded the available means so much that no action was taken.

As stated in the last report of the supervising architect, the marine hospital at Chicago, Illinois, was sold for the sum of $132,000. Many efforts were made to procure another suitable site, and a variety of plans for a new hospital were prepared in this office; but as the negotiations for the purchase of another site have hitherto failed, nothing was done towards the erection of a new hospital.

The various galvanized iron roofs, and the heating apparatus of many of these buildings, have been a source of much serious complaint, perhaps more than ever before. It is to be hoped that the next Congress will grant such means as to gradually remedy these evils.

On the 1st of October, 1864, the aggregate balance of appropriations not withdrawn from the treasury amounted to $1,697,624 04. The appropriations becoming available during the year amounted to $31,911 53; and from proceeds of sale of old Chicago marine hospital, $132,000, making an available amount under the control of this office of $1,861,535 57 for the year ending September 30, 1865. The expenditures during the year amounted to $742,316 16, leaving a balance on the 30th of September, 1865, of $1,119,219 41.

Treasury extension.—In consequence of the failure to provide suitable accommodations for the State Department, no progress was made in the continuation of the north wing of the Treasury extension. A large amount of materials, however, was received in anticipation of the work, and will be on hand, ready, whenever the old State Department may be removed, and Congress provides further means for the prosecution of the same. On account of the pressure for room, an additional attic over the old building was constructed; the old basement rooms remodelled and made available for office purposes; an additional story built on the building on the corner of Seventeenth street and New York avenue; and the building on the corner of Fifteenth and G streets remodelled for the accommodation of the Internal Revenue office. The expenditures for the above work, together with those for furniture, repairs and alterations of the Treasury building generally, were large, and have not as yet been refunded. The temporary diversion of funds from the purposes for which they were appropriated may be justified by the exigencies of the times, but it is to be desired that the same may not occur again. The clerical force of the department is still increasing, and the Treasury building, large as it is at present, does not afford proper accommodations for the whole force; and the early completion of the north wing is not only a desideratum, but a matter of necessity. The construction of that section, with a vast amount of materials, and all the necessary tools and appliances for the work on hand, could be completed in a comparatively short period; and I think that an additional appropriation of $500,000 would be sufficient for the purpose. It is also thought that temporary accommodations for the State Department may be had more readily now than during last winter. The urgent requirements of the department for more room, and the advantages to the work that will result from its early resumption and completion, commend the same to special and favorable consideration.

Buffalo custom-house.—A new hot-water heating apparatus, at a cost of $11,473 75, was put in this building, and completed during last winter. It was tested during several months of the severest winter weather of last year, and proved to be fully and generally satisfactory.

Cincinnati custom-house.—The operations on the work of alterations of this building had to be suspended (as already stated) on account of the appropriation being exhausted. Subsequently an arrangement was made with the former superintendent of the work for completing certain parts of the same, the payment to be deferred and to be dependent on the appropriations that Congress may make for the purpose. This office is not well advised of the present condition of the building, and I am unable to make a detailed statement of the liabilities and requirements of it. I am informed by the late surveyor of Cincinnati that $20,000 will be required to liquidate debts and complete the alterations.

Dubuque custom-house.—For the same reasons as in the foregoing case, the work on this building was suspended. An expenditure of $2,090 from the fund for preservation of public buildings was authorized to complete the first and second stories of this building and render them habitable; by this means a rent of about one thousand dollars for the accommodation of the post office and custom-house will be saved. This work has been carried on well and economically, though it is thought that the business of the place did not require such a large structure as the one erected. No agent of this office having recently visited and inspected the building, I am unadvised of its precise condition at present. The amount required for completing the building, grading, and enclosing the grounds will not exceed $15,000.

Louisville custom-house.—Nothing was done during the past year towards the alteration of this building, for which an appropriation of $15,000 had been made. Proposals for the work were invited, but those received largely exceeded the amount of the appropriation. A new set of plans for remodelling the building was recently submitted by the assistant architect, A. B. Mullett, esq., and approved by the Secretary, and it is confidently expected that its cost will come within the amount of the appropriation, at the same time disposing of the available space of the structure more judiciously and satisfactorily than was done by the former plans.

Philadelphia custom-house.—The alterations of this building have been vigorously prosecuted, and were carried so near to completion that the rooms assigned to the assistant treasurer have been occupied by him. Considerable liabilities were incurred exceeding the appropriation made for the purpose. It will require $30,000 for the payment of the above debts, and for the completion of the building.

Baltimore court-house.—This building has been finally completed and furnished, and proves to be a conspicuous ornament to the city of Baltimore. The work was, throughout, performed faithfully and well. It was begun in the fall of 1860 and suspended in May, 1861, and resumed, by order of the department, in 1862; since then it has been impossible to prosecute it vigorously, partly on account of invasions of the State of Maryland by rebels, partly on account of the scarcity of laborers, and partly on account of the great difficulty of procuring materials. The building was thus constructed during a period when the prices of labor and materials were far higher than at the time when the contract was made—in many instances more than double; and, as both the suspension and resumption of the work were made by order of the government, the Secretary considered that the contractor was entitled to an equitable adjustment of his losses, but as yet has not taken any definite action in the matter.

Windsor court-house.—The new slate roof of this building has been completed, and the building otherwise repaired, at a cost within the amount of the appropriation made for the purpose.

Staten Island.—The work of repairs of the United States government warehouses and wharves has been completed during the current year, and was accepted by the late chief of this bureau, I. Rogers, esq. In consequence of a diversity of opinion as to the character and value of the work furnished by the contractors, different from and adverse to that of the late supervising architect, the Light-house Board refused to pay the amount which they were to transfer in favor of the above work for the cession and improvement of a portion of the revenue depot grounds to the light-house establishment. They contend that the work of improvement on their ground, as well as on all the rest, was not in accordance with the requirements of contracts and stipulations. The examination of the same was submitted to a commission of experts, who reported unfavorably to the opinions of Mr. Rogers, and payment (amounting to $26,599 12) has ever since been withheld from the contractors. I am personally unacquainted with the work, but am confident that the same has been condemned with more severity than the case required. The controversy about the work is mainly due to a neglect in properly recording the changes and deviations from the original contract and specifications, which were found to be necessary. The work has, however, had a severe practical test during the past summer, and, as far as I am aware, has answered the purpose very well.

Appended will be found a table showing the amounts available for each work on the 30th of September, 1864; the additional appropriations made and becoming available; the disbursements made during the year ending September 30, 1865; and the additional appropriations required.

The assistant supervising architect, A. B. Mullett, esq., is at present on a tour of inspection of the southern custom-houses, &c. Until his return it will be impossible to state with accuracy their condition or the amount of repairs required.

All of which is respectfully submitted.

I have the honor to be, very respectfully, your obedient servant,

B. OERTLY,
Acting Assistant Supervising Architect.

Hon. HUGH McCULLOCH,
Secretary of the Treasury.

Tabular statement of custom-houses, marine hospitals, court-houses, post offices, and miscellaneous buildings, showing the amount available for each work September 30, 1864; the additional appropriations made by the 38th Congress, 2d session; the amount available September 30, 1865; and the disbursements made from September 30, 1864, to September 30, 1865.

CUSTOM-HOUSES.

Object.	Balances available September 30, 1864.	Appropriations, 1864-'65.	Balances available September 30, 1865.	Disbursements, 1864-'65.	Additional appropriations required.
annual repair of custom-houses..........................	$4,221 75	....	....	$4,221 75	....
annual repair of custom-houses and marine hospitals......	18,985 87	....	....	18,985 87	....
annual repair and preservation of public buildings........	50,000 00	....	$34,993 79	15,006 21	$50,000 00
angor (Maine) custom-house........................	6,483 00	....	6,237 86	245 15	....
ston (Massachusetts) custom-house...................	135 19	....	135 19	....	....
ffalo (New York) custom-house......................	23,310 40	....	11,836 65	11,473 75	....
arleston (South Carolina) custom-house...............	296 60	....	296 60	....	....
icago (Illinois) custom-house.......................	17,183 33	....	16,056 53	1,126 80	....
iro (Illinois) custom-house.........................	50,000 00	....	50,000 00	....	....
icinnati (Ohio) custom-house.......................	5,000 00	....	....	5,000 00	20,000 00
troit (Michigan) custom-house......................	1,951 83	....	1,719 08	232 75	....
buque (Iowa) custom-house.........................	17,027 80	....	....	17,027 80	15,000 00
orgetown (District of Columbia) custom-house..........	760 79	....	538 35	222 44	....
oxville (Tennessee) custom-house....................	96,568 19	....	96,568 19	....	....
uisville (Kentucky) custom-house....................	15,000 00	....	13,985 00	1,015 00	....
twaukie (Wisconsin) custom-house...................	108 97	....	....	108 97	....
w Orleans (Louisiana) custom-house	8,074 38	....	8,074 38	....	....
shville (Tennessee) custom-house.	104,215 69	....	104,215 69	....	....
w Haven (Connecticut) custom-house.................	1,064 63	....	1,013 50	51 13	....
densburg (New York) custom-house...................	108,858 25	....	108,858 25	....	....
rtsmouth (New Hampshire) custom-house..............	1,660 79	....	988 04	672 75	....
rth Amboy (New Jersey) custom-house.................	20,625 34	....	20,625 34	....	....
iladelphia (Pennsylvania) custom-house..............	50,000 00	....	....	50,000 00	30,000 00
rtland (Maine) custom-house.......................	50,000 00	....	49,010 73	989 27	....
Louis (Missouri) custom-house......................	11,887 15	....	11,887 15	....	....
adusky (Ohio) custom-house........................	1,158 63	....	1,158 63	....	....

CUSTOM-HOUSES—Continued.

Object.	Balances available September 30, 1864.	Appropriations, 1864–'65.	Balances available September 30, 1865.	Disbursements, 1864–'65.	Additional appropriations required.
San Francisco (California) custom-house	$17,410 14		$13,544 21	$3,865 93	
Toledo (Ohio) custom-house	3,409 33		3,409 33		
Wheeling (Virginia) custom-house	309 67		309 67		
Total	685,637 72		555,392 15	130,245 57	$115,000 00

MARINE HOSPITALS.

Object.	Balances available September 30, 1864.	Appropriations, 1864–'65.	Balances available September 30, 1865.	Disbursements, 1864–'65.	Additional appropriations required.
Annual repair of marine hospitals	$19,744 92		$12,418 80	$7,326 12	
Burlington (Vermont) marine hospital	6,475 47		6,475 47		
Chicago (Illinois) marine hospital		*$132,000 00	132,000 00		
Detroit (Michigan) marine hospital	8,582 25		8,582 25		
Evansville (Indiana) marine hospital	4,615 98		4,600 98	15 00	
Galena (Illinois) marine hospital	1,616 66		1,616 66		
Portland (Maine) marine hospital	926 65		926 65		
Pensacola (Florida) marine hospital	20,947 04		20,947 04		
St. Louis (Missouri) marine hospital	25,925 05		25,925 05		
Total	88,834 02	132,000 00	213,492 90	7,341 12	

y West (Florida) court-house	40,908 26		40,908 26		
mphis (Tennessee) court-house	34,856 10		34,856 10		
iison (Wisconsin) court-house	49,870 75		49,870 75		
land (Vermont) court-house	1,631 55		1,631 55		
eigh (North Carolina) court-house					
ingfield (Illinois) court-house	53,866 60		53,866 60		
lahassee (Florida) court-house					
ndsor (Vermont) court-house	10,000 00		1,000 00	9,000 00	
Total	249,434 79		82,762 19	66,672 60	120,000 00

MISCELLANEOUS.

rglar-proof vaults, New York	$6,644 80		$3,074 75	$3,570 05	
e-proof vaults for depositories	51,248 23		14,140 54	37,107 69	$50,000 00
asury extension	474,079 42	$31,911 53	36,857 27	469,133 68	500,000 00
ating Treasury building	15,563 44		2,386 74	13,176 70	10,000 00
ni.ure for public buildings	19,581 57		4,512 82	15,068 75	25,000 00
lt for Philadelphia mint	913 12		913 12		
v Mexico public buildings	52,148 80		52,148 80		
alts for New Mexico public buildings	175 13		175 13		
a Francisco branch mint	45,000 00		45,000 00		
h penitentiary	8,363 00		8,363 00		
ten Island warehouses, &c					29,000 00
Total	673,717 51	31,911 53	167,572 17	538,056 87	614,000 00

[RECAPITULATION.

stom-houses	$685,637 73		$555,392 15	$130,245 57	$115,000 00
rine hospitals	88,894 02	*$132,000 00	213,492 90	7,341 12	
urt-houses	249,434 79		182,762 19	66,672 60	120,000 00
scellaneous	673,717 51	31,911 53	167,572 17	538,056 87	614,000 00
Total	1,697,624 04	163,911 53	1,119,219 41	742,316 16	849,000 00

* Proceeds of sale of old Chicago marine hospital.

REPORT OF THE LIGHT-HOUSE BOARD.

TREASURY DEPARTMENT,
Office of Light-house Board, Washington City, Oct. 26, 1865.

SIR : I have the honor respectfully to submit a report of the operations and condition of the light-house establishment for the fiscal year ending 30th June, 1865.

In the first light-house district, embracing all lights, &c., from the north-eastern boundary of Maine to Hampton harbor, New Hampshire, repairs more or less extensive have been made at the following named stations : Wood island, Goat island, Saddleback Ledge, Deer Island Thoroughfare, Edgemoggin, Mount Desert, Libby island, Little river ; and works of needed renovation are in progress at Seguin, Hendrick's Head, Burnt island, Manheigin, Negro island, and Dice Head ; and it is the opinion of the board that the present condition is such as to warrant the belief that but few large works of repair or renovation need be undertaken in this district during the coming year. There yet remains to be done much that is desirable, but little that is indispensable.

The measures for facilitating the entrance into Portland harbor, viz., increasing the height of the light at Portland Head and substituting a large second-order lens for the fourth-order there in use, thereby greatly augmenting the range of the light, have been completed during the year and have been found to accomplish the desired object. It is believed now that the entrance to this harbor is so completely lighted that navigation in and out is attended with little or no danger. The keeper's dwelling at this station has been thoroughly repaired. In order still further to identify the two lights at Cape Elizabeth as day marks, four broad horizontal red stripes have been painted on the easterly tower, and on the westerly tower one vertical stripe.

The buoyage of the district has been maintained in an efficient condition, a service requiring, in this region of rapid currents and high tides, constant vigilance. The attention of the board having been called to the necessity of additional buoys to mark the dangerous ledges, Grindstone, Sheep Island, and Inner Bay Ledges, in Penobscot bay, the required examinations were made, resulting in the determination of their usefulness, and suitable buoys have accordingly been placed.

The necessity of supplying some more efficient system of fog-signals than at present employed, to aid the navigation of this rock-bound coast, has been seriously impressed upon the board, and careful investigation of the subject has been made. The result has been deemed sufficient to warrant the board in estimating for a sum to cover the expense of substituting the apparatus which may prove to be most effective.

Beacons consisting of casks on masts have been placed on Fiddler's Ledge, Harbor Ledge, and Portersfield Ledge, and spar-beacons have been set at Winslow's Rocks and Ames's Ledge.

A steam buoy-tender has been provided for this district in place of the two sailing-vessels heretofore employed, and which were reported to require extensive and costly repairs.

The second light-house district embraces the coasts from Hampton harbor, New Hampshire, to Gooseberry inlet, Massachusetts. The light-house service in this district has received especial attention, and is now in a satisfactory condition. Repairs and renovations have been made at Cape Cod, (Highlands,) Long Point, Billingsgate island, Nansett, Mayo's beach, Monomoy Point, Bass river, Bishop and Clerks, Great Point, Brant Point, Nobsque, Dumpling Rock, Clark's Point, Hyannis, Sandy Neck, Chatham, Cape Ann, Marblehead, Ten Pound island, Bird island, and other stations.

The structures standing at the discontinued light-house station at Point Gammon, being found to be in a rapid course of demolition from lawless persons, fishermen and others, it was deemed prudent to have them taken down and removed to a place of greater security. Some of the materials, lumber, &c., have been used in the erection of buildings needed at other light-stations.

Repairs are now in progress at Gay Head, Race Point, Sankaty Head, and other stations, which, when completed, will leave the district, in respect to the structures, in a condition requiring but little attention during the next year.

A new spar-beacon, forty-five feet long, bearing a conspicuous day-mark, has been erected at Hardy's Rock, in place of the former structure, carried away by storms.

Extensive repairs have been made to the stone beacon at Great Fawn bar, which the action of ice and storms had rendered insecure.

The various fog-signals in the district have received careful attention, and are now in as good condition as their character will permit.

The last remaining old-style lantern in the district, that at Clark's Point, has been removed and an efficient and modern structure put up, and new and improved lamps have been introduced throughout the district.

The buoyage of the district has been well attended to and kept at all times, so far as circumstances would permit, in an efficient condition.

An inspection has been made of the light-house in the exposed position of Minot's Ledge, and its condition found to be perfectly satisfactory.

A steam-tender has been provided for this district, which is expected to do the work heretofore performed by two sailing-vessels, better, more promptly, and at less expense.

The inspector reports that the light-vessel service of the district during the past year has not been attended with a single casualty requiring the removal of any one of them from its station.

In the third light-house district, embracing the coasts from Gooseberry Point, Massachusetts, to Squam inlet, New Jersey, and including Lake Champlain and Hudson river, much has been done during the past year in the way of repairs and rebuilding, but as many of the structures, which are old, have not been planned on correct principles, much remains still to be done. The extensive commerce, foreign and domestic, traversing this district, demands that the system of lighting and buoyage should be as nearly perfect as possible.

Repairs and renovations, more or less extensive, have been made at the following stations : Newport harbor, New London, New Haven, Esopus Meadows, Saugerties, Stuyvesant, New Baltimore, Schodack channel, Van Wies Point, Block island, Princess bay, Elm Tree, Sandy Hook, West beacon, Fire island, Stratford River beacon, Bridgeport beacon, and Black Rock beacon.

At Rondout and Coxsackie, the light-houses require repairs and the sea-walls to be rebuilt. Special estimates of the cost have therefore been submitted to Congress. Other and less expensive works are required at Beavertail, Four-mile Point, Bergen Point, Passaic river, Black Rock, and Sandy Hook; and it is expected that the current appropriation for repairs and incidental expenses will meet the cost.

Special estimates are submitted to meet the cost of rebuilding the beacons for Norwalk island, Southport and Elbow beacon, which have been destroyed by the action of ice.

The failure of Congress at its last session to act upon the estimates submitted for operations at Warwick, Sands Point, and Nayat Point, in common with all other estimates for the light-house establishment, rendered it necessary to suspend the proposed works, and the estimates are again commended to the attention of Congress.

The beaconage and buoyage of the district have received careful attention, and all damages and losses incurred during the year have been repaired as far and as promptly as practicable.

13 F

The fog-signals of the district have received due attention, and the board, aware of the importance of rendering them as distinctive as possible, have set on foot a series of experiments, in order that the most effective appliances for warning the navigator in thick weather may be adopted.

A steam vessel has been provided for the district to take the place of the two sailing light-house and buoy-tenders now employed, which it is expected will perform the service more effectively, with greater despatch, and at less cost.

The arrangement entered into by which a designated part of the lot of land on Staten island ceded to the United States by the State of New York was to be transferred to the Light-house Board, has not been yet completed. The acting engineer in the service of this board, in a recent report, says: "The grounds are still occupied by the cotton agent. * * * There is a prospect of the premises soon being in our hands again." There is much to be done to these premises to place them in the condition contemplated by the Secretary of the Treasury, and by this board, at the time the arrangement was made. The facilities which the use of this depot will afford the board in its operations, when it shall be placed in the condition contemplated, are much needed, and it is respectfully requested that directions to complete the work may not be delayed longer than is absolutely necessary. (See appendix.)

Congress having made an appropriation of $1,000, approved June 30, 1860, for "a survey to determine the proper site of a light-house at or near the Sow and Pigs, Buzzard bay," the coast survey was requested to do the work. A survey had been made in 1853, and careful measurements show that no change has taken place since. The board has not yet decided that the light-house at Cuttyhunk does not, in conjunction with the system of buoys on the reef itself, subserve all the requirements of commerce.

The fourth light-house district embraces the coasts from Squam inlet, New Jersey, to Metomkin inlet, Virginia, including Delaware bay and tributaries. In this district every essential repair and renovation has been made that the funds at the disposal of the board would allow. The deficiencies and wants of the district have been brought to the attention of Congress, and special appropriations asked for to meet cases which cannot be put off without incurring greater ultimate expense. Among these cases, that of Cohansey light-house is especially urgent. The necessity for providing an effectual protection to the work against the steady encroachment of the water, which has been several times urged upon Congress, is now more pressing than ever. A special estimate is therefore submitted to cover the cost of suitably banking in the site.

The measurements of the beach at Absecum light-house to determine the reported encroachment of the sea at that place have been continued semi-monthly during the past year. The changes in the ordinary high-water line so far have been so slight as not to justify any apprehension of immediate danger to the light-house. The observations, however, will be continued, and all necessary measures which may be required for the protection of the structure will be promptly taken.

Small but essential repairs have been made at Barnegat, Absecum, Cape May, Brandywine, Ready Island, Bombay Hook, and Fenwick's Island light stations.

Under authority of act of Congress a new beacon-light required at Cape Henlopen, in place of the old structure, in consequence of change of shore-line, has been erected. The new beacon-light is a screw-pile structure, built near the point of the cape. The old beacon was taken down, and some of the materials have been used to protect the site of the new structure. The remainder has been sold at public auction.

The increasing dilapidation of the present tower of Assateague has obliged the board to take measures for building a new one, as authorized by act of Congress. The execution of this work has been postponed, however, on account of more pressing wants in other branches of the service. It is now believed that there should be no further delay, and measures are in progress to build a new first class tower for this important sea-coast station. It is found, however, that the sum available for this purpose is insufficient, on account of the rise in the price of materials and labor, and an estimate to cover the additional cost is submitted.

The buoyage and beaconage of the district is in a satisfactory condition.

The fifth light-house district embraces the coasts from Metomkin inlet, Virginia, to New River inlet, North Carolina, including Chesapeake bay and tributaries, and Albemarle and Pamlico sounds.

It was only late in the year that the greater portion of the southern part of this district was brought permanently under the control of the government.

In the northern part the service of the district has been well attended to, and the various aids to navigation maintained in an efficient condition.

In James river the screw-pile light-houses at White shoals, Point of Shoals, and Deep Water shoals, which had been but slightly injured by the enemy, were temporarily put in order, and provided with new fog-bells and illuminating apparatus. The light-house at Jordon's Point, near City Point, was thoroughly repaired and re-established, sundry requisites being provided.

The light has been restored at Stingray Point, after making certain needful repairs to the screw-pile structure, which, though plundered of all movable articles, was but slightly injured. At New Point Comfort light-station the required repairs were much more extensive, and involved much time and expense. A new lens has been provided, and the light re-established.

Owing to the failure of the appropriation for light-house purposes during the last session of Congress, it becomes necessary again to represent the urgent necessity of building a new light-house for Sharp's island, Chesapeake bay. The unusual absence of storm-tides and heavy northwest gales during the past year accounts for the unexpected preservation of the present structure. The sea, however, is gradually but surely undermining the bluff, and has already reached one corner of the building, leaving no doubt as to the result. The estimate of last year for this work is therefore repeated.

The tram-road used in the construction of the new light-house at Cape Charles, being of no further service at that place, has been taken up and the material shipped to Baltimore.

Such slight repairs and renovations as were required in the district have been made, and the disposition of beacons and buoys there met every requirement of commerce.

In the waters of North Carolina the various aids to navigation which, at the date of the last report of the board, were in condition to receive its attention have been put in effective operation.

Immediately upon the close of the rebellion an experienced engineer was sent to those waters to take charge of the work of re-establishing such lights, &c., as the interests of commerce might be found to demand. A large quantity of illuminating apparatus, and other light-house material, which had been abstracted by the enemy, was recovered, and such portions as could be at once made use of were so applied, and the rest sent north for repairs and refitment.

Temporary lights for the accommodation of army transports and navy vessels were, upon the fall of Fort Fisher, established at the entrance to Cape Fear river and at Beaufort, but when the necessity under which they were placed ceased to exist the lights were discontinued.

In view of the fact that commerce has not as yet been re-established as it existed in 1860, the channels in many parts of the coast having, since that time, undergone material changes, it is proposed only to restore such aids to navigation on the southern coast as shall be deemed essential to the trade developed to those ports. It is, moreover, not at all improbable that commerce may seek new channels, involving the necessity of an entirely new arrangement and new kinds of aids.

The work of re-establishing lights of undoubted~utility will be pressed forward as soon as the means are supplied, an estimate of which is submitted.

The excavation of iron ore at Lazaretto Point, near Baltimore, has progressed during the year, but not so rapidly as had been desired, the scarcity of labor having caused the delay. Up to this time some 1,291 tons have been excavated and sold, the net proceeds, $2,013 96, having been deposited in the treasury of the United States. With the present abundance of labor, it is expected that much greater results will be attained during the next year.

An appropriation was made June 20, 1860, for a light-house at the mouth of North river, Albemarle sound, North Carolina, but because that region was open to raids by the enemy it was not deemed prudent to take any steps towards building the structure, and the appropriation was suffered to lapse into the treasury. The necessity for a light-house at that point having been again strongly urged upon the board, an estimate to cover the cost is submitted.

The sixth light-house district embraces the coasts from New River inlet, North Carolina, to Cape Canaveral light-house, Florida, and within its limits the few aids to navigation which had been left unharmed by the enemy have been maintained during the year in useful operation. Measures of renovation have been necessarily confined to such temporary works as would serve the requirements of a recently developed commerce.

The approaches to Charleston were thus' lighted immediately after the occupation of that place by the United States forces, but it was found, upon examination, that an almost total change had taken place, leaving no channel in the harbor as it was in 1860, and opening new ones. Under this altered state of things it became necessary to establish lights temporarily at such places as would be useful guides through existing channels, and to omit all others.

The light-vessel formerly placed off Rattlesnake shoal has been moored at the entrance to Charleston bar, and it is recommended that this position be made permanent, as the vessel will thus answer the double purpose of warning vessels from Rattlesnake shoal, and at the same time form a channel range over Main Ship bar. She will also serve as a guide for vessels approaching from the southward to clear Stono breakers.

A light-vessel equipped from materials collected from Charleston and Port Royal has been placed at the wreck of the monitor Weehawken, which lies directly in the channel way, and a temporary beacon-light has been established on a house on Sullivan's island. These two lights now mark the entrance over the bar and the channel up to the Weehawken. It is recommended that this temporary beacon-light be made permanent, and a suitable structure erected for it.

Temporary structures with steamer lenses occupy the sites (nearly) of the former lights upon Fort Sumter and Castle Pinckney, and answer a good purpose.

The gas-light at White Point Garden (battery) was left by the rebels in tolerably good order, and has been re-established.

The range-lights for Port Royal entrance have been continued. The Bay Point beacon-light (part of this range) is built on a large barrack erected by the rebels in 1861, slightly built, and already beginning to show signs of decay. This important harbor requires a light of the second or third order, and a special appropriation to cover the expense of the establishment of such a light is submitted.

Tybee beacon has been relighted, and temporary beacon-lights established to aid the navigation of Savannah river. The re-establishment of lights at the important stations of Georgetown, Cape Romain, Tybee, St. Augustine and Cape Canaveral, has occupied the consideration of the board, and preliminary steps to this end have been taken. The construction of the iron tower for

Cape Canaveral was suspended at the breaking out of the war, in the contractor's hands, with the understanding that the work should be resumed on notice being given by the board. Notice has been given accordingly, and the contractor has signified his intention to finish the tower as soon as possible.

The entrances to the following places have been buoyed : Winyah bay and Georgetown, (Battle Channel,) Bull's bay, Charleston, Stono river, North and South Edisto, St. Helena sound, Port Royal, Tybee and Calibogue sound, Warsaw sound and Wilmington river, Ossibaw sound and Ogeechee river, Sapelo sound, Doboy sound, St. Simon's sound, Fernandina and St. Mary's, St. John's river, St. Augustine.

In the seventh light-house district, which embraces the coast of Florida, from St. Augustine to Egmont key, the service has been carefully attended, and the lights and other aids to navigation which had been undisturbed by the enemy have been maintained in an efficient condition. Those which had been injured will be re-established as soon as practicable, energetic efforts to this end being in progress.

The important light stations, Cape Florida and Jupiter inlet, have received the especial attention of the board, and an experienced agent has been sent to that district with instructions to use every exertion to re-light those points, and the board has reason to hope that by next spring both of these lights will be again in operation.

The buoyage of the district has been kept up to the standard of efficiency so far as the limited means at the disposal of the board would permit.

In the eighth and ninth districts, embracing the Gulf coast from Egmont to Rio Grande, Texas, the work of re-establishing lights and other aids to navigation discontinued by the enemy has been kept prominently in view, and no effort has been spared to accomplish, so far as the means at the disposal of the board would permit, this desirable result.

The lights, &c., reported last year as having been restored to operation, have been maintained in an efficient manner, but at great cost, in consequence of the peculiar state of the markets in that region, the scarcity of skilled labor and the high price of materials forcing upon the service in these districts an expense entirely disproportioned to that of other districts.

The following stations have been repaired and refitted during the year, and are now in operation: Ship shoal, Shell keys, Southwest reef, St. Joseph's, Round island, (Miss.,) Sand island, Bolivar Point and Padre island ; and others are in course of refitting, and it is expected that in a few months most of those unlighted will be in full course of useful operation.

The buoyage of the district has received careful attention, and the board has great reason to congratulate itself upon having under such difficulties accomplished so much towards a restoration of needed facilities to the commerce of the Gulf.

In the tenth and eleventh districts, which embrace all lights from Lakes Erie and Ontario, and rivers St. Lawrence and Niagara, the various aids to navigation have been kept generally in good order, and the disposition of buoys and beacons leaves but little to be desired. No complaints in this respect have been received. The inspector bears testimony to the general attention to duty displayed by the keepers and assistants.

The work of rebuilding the light-house at Green island (destroyed by fire 1st January, 1864) has been pressed forward, notwithstanding the failure of Congress to provide the funds specially requested for the work, and a light was exhibited from the new structure on the 1st July, 1865. In the erection of this light-house a new and more suitable site was adopted. The expenses of this construction were very heavy; yet, as the work was of imperative necessity, the general fund for repairs was drawn upon to meet the bills. A special estimate

of this work is submitted, out of which it is proposed to reimburse the general
fund for the amounts drawn from it.

The erection of the range-lights authorized by act of Congress for Maumee
bay has not advanced during the year to the extent hoped for by the board.
The delay has been occasioned partly by the difficult and complicated questions
involved, but mainly on account of the impossibility of procuring the necessary
land at private sale at prices warranted by the circumstances of the case. Resort
was necessarily had to a tedious suit at law, which has just resulted in securing
the requisite land to the government at reasonable rates. The work will be
pressed forward to completion.

Upon an examination of the light-house at Mamajuda, it was found necessary
to rebuild it, the present structures not being thought worthy of the repairs required to make them habitable. Temporary measures of protection have been
adopted, and a special estimate to cover the cost of rebuilding is submitted.

The dilapidated condition of the light-houses at Galloo island and Turtle
island has been heretofore reported, and special estimates to cover the cost of
necessary repairs are again submitted. These stations are very important, and
it is desirable that the necessary funds should be provided as soon as possible.

The light-house tower at Presque Isle having been reported to require immediate attention to preserve it from falling, a special examination was made. It
was found to have settled very considerably; the masonry, moreover, being
cracked, with a tendency to further insecurity. It is recommended that this
tower be taken down upon the close of navigation this season, and rebuilt upon
a proper and more suitable site. A special estimate to cover the cost is submitted.

The temporary range-lights at Cedar Point, Sandusky bay, referred to in the
last annual report as having been established, have been continued, and the
importance of rendering these aids permanent is such as to warrant the board in
submitting a special estimate designed to cover the cost of suitable structures.

Many other works of repair in this district of less extent than the foregoing
require attention. It is proposed to complete them as time and opportunity
permit.

The eleventh light-house district embraces Lakes St. Clair, Huron, Michigan, and Superior, and Green bay and tributaries.

The lights and other aids to navigation within its limits have been maintained
in an efficient condition. Various extensive works of renovation have been in
hand during the past year, some of which have been completed. Others are
still in progress; while many, from the large expense involved, must necessarily await congressional action.

The buoys, likewise, have been well attended.

The works of repair at Windmill Point light station, in contemplation at the
date of the last annual report, have been completed, and a new distinctive illuminating apparatus will be put in operation on the opening of the next season
of navigation.

The necessary timber for rebuilding the beacon and pier at Kenosha, Wisconsin, has finally been procured after much delay, and the work will be prosecuted
to insure, if possible, the completion of the structures during the present season
of navigation.

The requisite materials, timber and ballast stone, for the authorized structures at Racine, have been delivered, and the work is being vigorously pushed
in order to secure it before the fall gales set in.

The extensive works reported last year as being in progress at Milwaukie
have well advanced during the year, and it is expected that the light-house will
be nearly completed by the close of navigation.

The light-house at Point Peninsula, between Big and Little Bay de Noquet,

Michigan, for which an appropriation was made by Congress July 2, 1864, has been completed and lighted.

Efforts have been made to establish a light at Sand Point, as authorized by act of Congress of July 2, 1864. A suitable sight was selected, but up to this time the holders of the land have been unable to convey a valid title to the United States. This being, under the law, a pre-requisite, nothing could be done in the matter beyond the preparation of plans and estimates for the work.

A system of range-lights for entering Copper harbor, authorized by act of Congress of June 20, 1860, has been completed and the lights exhibited. The necessary land at Fort Wilkins for the purposes of these range-lights, together with the valuable buildings which occupy it, were, by the courtesy of the War Department, transferred to the Light-house Board.

In the last report reference was made to works then in progress for securing the foundation of the light-house at La Pointe, Michigan. It has been found that the movement of the sand was not arrested by the measures then adopted, and instructions have been given to have the entire surface of the ground covered with broken stone.

The light-house at Minnesota Point having been found to require considerable repairs, prompt measures to this end were accordingly taken.

The special estimates submitted last year for necessary protective works for the light-house at Waugoshance shoal, Straits of Mackinac, having failed to receive the sanction of Congress, nothing could be done toward arresting the increasing dilapidation and decay at this station, which, in point of importance to the interests of navigation, is second to none in the lake region. The pier surrounding the light-house, and designed for its protection, is in course of rapid destruction, and when once destroyed, the light-house must give way. Because of the exposed position, the works required at this point are of a very expensive character, and after a careful study of the whole subject, the board is of opinion that, to carry out the work in a substantial and satisfactory manner, the sum of $200,000 will be required, but has thought it expedient to estimate for only a part of this amount, ($90,000,) to be expended during the year ending June 30, 1866.

A fog-signal is more needed at this point than at any other on the lakes, being the turning point of all vessels passing through the Straits of Mackinac. A special estimate for its establishment is submitted.

The necessity for establishing a system of range-lights at St. Clair Flats has been brought to the attention of the board, and has received careful consideration. Deeming these ranges of manifest usefulness, a special estimate is submitted.

The importance of substituting new and efficient fog-signals at various stations in this district, in place of the bells now in use, has been developed, and a special appropriation is asked to cover the expense.

A light-house at or near old Fort Mackinac is much needed to enable vessels to pass through the straits at night, and McGulpin's Point, about two miles distant, is designated by the engineer of the district as the most suitable location. A special estimate is accordingly submitted.

The most salient point on the eastern shore of Lake Michigan, between Point Betsey and Muskegon, is known as Grand Pointe au Sable, and is unmarked by night. It is a principal landmark for day navigation, and it would seem that the interests of commerce demand that it be suitably lighted. A special estimate is submitted.

The extension of the pier at Chicago during the past summer for a distance of 450 feet into the lake renders it necessary to build a small beacon-light at the end of the pier to mark it.

The light-house tower at Kenosha is found to need extensive repairs. The inner wall is literally crumbling to pieces, and the outer wall also shows several cracks, caused by the action of frost, as in the case of the tower at Presque Isle, Pennsylvania. A special estimate of the cost of these repairs is submitted.

A light-house at Eagle Bluff, on the east coast of Green bay, is much needed to enable steamers plying between lake ports and the port of Green Bay, which use the east channel almost exclusively, to pass between the Little Sister island and the Frying Pan shoals. It is the most prominent bluff on the western shore of Green bay. For the erection of this light a special appropriation is recommended.

The Grand Island light-house was found, upon examination, to be in a wretched condition, on account of the inferior materials employed in its original construction. This structure, which is difficult of access, should be rebuilt in the most substantial manner, so that no further repairs will be required for many years to come.

The existing appropriation of $6,000 for lights at the two entrances of Grand Island harbor, Lake Superior, having been found insufficient to carry on the work, an additional appropriation is respectfully recommended.

A special estimate is also submitted to cover the cost of expensive repairs and renovations found to be necessary at Marquette light-house station.

The Huron islands, Lake Superior, lying as they do in the track of vessels bound to the Portage, are a constant source of anxiety to the navigators, wrecks having frequently occurred at this point. The large and rapidly increasing commerce passing this point warrant the establishment of a suitable light and fog-signal, for which an appropriation is accordingly recommended.

A pier having been built at the mouth of Portage river, and the channel straightened and deepened, a small light is needed to mark the entrance.

A special appropriation is likewise recommended for the establishment of a light-house to mark the channel between Keweenaw Point and Manitou island, Lake Superior, a dangerous passage, at present unmarked by a light, which is deemed very necessary.

Estimates of expense of certain essential works of rebuilding at Copper Harbor and Ontonagon light-stations are submitted.

A special committee of the board was sent to the northwest lakes to ascertain the wants of commerce in that locality. The examination was particularly directed to Green bay and surroundings, and a special estimate to cover the cost of certain necessary aids to navigation, which will comprise a third class light-house on Mahnomah or Chambers island, range-lights at entrance to Fox river, a beacon on Peshtego shoal, &c., is submitted.

The twelfth light-house district embraces the entire Pacific coast of the United States. The various lights and buoys have been kept in an efficient condition, and no complaints on this score have been received.

The failure of Congress to provide at the last session for certain new works for which special estimates had been submitted has confined the engineering work of the district to ordinary repairs and renovations, and preparations for the new works when the necessary special appropriations shall be available.

The buoyage of the district has been well attended to.

The new light-house at Ediz Hook has been completed and lighted.

Having thus given a detailed account of the operations and condition of the light-house establishment in the several districts, there remain but a few matters of general importance to notice.

In anticipation of the ultimate overthrow of the rebellion, and the consequent necessity of providing as promptly as possible for a sudden revival of trade to southern ports, the board took measures to provide ready for use when required, a number of lanterns of the various classes, the lenses having previously been provided as heretofore reported. These, having been constructed, were, after careful inspection, received and stored.

The board has had good reason to congratulate itself on having taken this timely precaution, being thus enabled to hasten materially the re-establishment of lights at many stations where the lanterns had been destroyed by the enemy.

In like manner the board provided for a supply of iron buoys of the several classes and sizes, being thus prepared, on the restoration of trade to any particular port, to re-establish the necessary buoys. These buoys are now in course of construction by contract, at favorable rates to the government.

Upon the close of the war, instructions were given to the acting light-house engineers in the southern districts to inquire for, and recover if possible, the light-house property, comprising illuminating apparatus and other material which had been scattered during the hostilities. This work has been, in a great measure, successfully accomplished, and mainly by the action of the War Department, through which much valuable material has been reclaimed. The apparatus recovered has been forwarded to New York for repairs, being in most instances considerably damaged. That which was fit for immediate use has been either so applied or stored until the towers were in a condition to receive it.

Under sanction obtained from the department an arrangement was made with the Navy Department for the transfer to this board of some small steamers which had been advertised for sale, to be used as light-house and buoy tenders. These steamers, six in number, are to take the place of a larger number of small and inefficient sailing vessels. This arrangement, though attended with some immediate additional expense, will ultimately prove beneficial and economical.

The board has, during the year, given its earnest consideration to the use of lard oil. A large quantity was purchased under contract and distributed to the lights which are fitted with lamps adapted to its use, and the board has yet to record the first case of well-grounded complaint on the part of keepers of the lights so produced, or on the part of mariners. The board is therefore much encouraged in its hope of introducing a cheaper and more certain article of illumination than sperm oil, which has now reached a price far beyond the reach of ordinary appropriations, while the continuance of the supply is a matter of great uncertainty. It is true that lard oil is at present unusually scarce, yet this is only a temporary condition, which, in consideration of the abounding means of supply, cannot long exist.

Very respectfully,

W. B. SHUBRICK,
Rear-Admiral, Chairman.

ANDW. A. HARWOOD,
O. M. POE,
Secretaries.

APPENDIX.

LIGHT-HOUSE OFFICE, 3D DISTRICT,
New York, October 25, 1865.

SIR: In compliance with your instructions of October 3, I have the honor, in connexion with the acting light-house engineer of this district, to make the following report of the condition of the light-house premises, sea-wall, &c., at Staten Island.

The grounds are still occupied by the cotton agent. The closing sales, however, have taken place, and there is prospect of the premises soon being in our hands again.

Referring to my annual report of this year, you will perceive that the boundary fence, dividing the light-house grounds from those of the revenue depot, is about one-half completed, and stands as the contractors left it—thirty feet six inches within the line assigned as the southern boundary of the light-house grounds by order of the Treasury Department, and encroaches to that extent upon our premises, viz., taking away a strip of land 630 feet in length by thirty feet six inches wide.

The only approach to the light-house grounds, except by courtesy, is by water. On the south is the revenue depot; on the north and west are the State lands. Access to the public street can be obtained on the north by the purchase of the strip of land which lies between the light-house grounds and South street, Tompkinsville, twenty-nine feet and one-half inch wide. Negotiations for the purchase of this strip of land have been entered into; and, as the board are aware, the land commissioners of the State have placed it at the disposal of the United States for the sum of $6,000.

The sea-wall, which was intended to protect the whole water front on the east and north, is, and was received, in a very defective condition from the hands of the contractors. It is not high enough by two feet. This wall was thrown down during the first gale after its completion, and rebuilt in the same manner as at first, and is now in a falling condition; the stones are not laid in regular courses as required, nor are they of a suitable size, or well bedded. The wall is entirely unfit to keep the filling from washing out; large quantities of earth have gone through and filled the basin in front, so that the buoy tender cannot enter or leave except at high tide.

The sea-wall bounding the water front on the north, through some error in establishing the boundary, is placed thirty-three feet too far to the south of the true boundary line. This wall, if removed to its proper position, will leave a space to be protected on the east for thirty-three feet by a continuation of the sea-wall on that water front.

The grading of the grounds has not been completed in accordance with the contract. The new filling has not been gravelled, and that portion which has sifted through the walls has not been replaced. The grounds in front of the storehouse need filling in with two feet of earth to bring them to the proper level of the sea-wall when raised.

The stone pyramids supporting the landing wharf were left without repairs by the contractors; some have entirely disappeared—others are in a falling condition, so that it has become a necessity to drive piles to support the wharf. Unless soon repaired the other stone pyramids will likewise fall into decay.

The roadway connecting the landing wharf with the shore is one foot nine inches lower than the former, and an inclined plane is necessary on this account. The roadway, although constructed in accordance with the contract, (excepting the piles which support it, which are from one to three inches less in diameter than called for,) is too lightly built for the heavy buoy service, and not strong enough to withstand the action of the sea and floating ice in winter. No fender-posts have been provided by the contractors, but were supplied by the cotton agency in part, and by the acting engineer.

No boat-house has been built for the service of the light-house establishment, though one was promised by the supervising architect of the Treasury Department in his letter to Professor Joseph Henry, dated June 24, 1863.

Plans and estimates for meeting the requirements resulting from the present condition of the light-house premises, as stated herein, have been made by the acting engineer, and forwarded to the Light-house Board with my approval; and very full reports relating to the above have been sent to the Light-house Board from time to time by the acting engineer and myself, as well as a report of the special commission appointed by the Treasury Department.

I respectfully submit this report of the present condition of the light-house premises, sea-wall, &c.

Very respectfully, your obedient servant,

REPORT OF THE SUPERINTENDENT OF THE COAST SURVEY.

UNITED STATES COAST SURVEY OFFICE,
Washington, October 10, 1865.

SIR : The estimates for the deficiency in appropriations for the survey of the coast for the fiscal year 1865–'66, together with those for the fiscal year 1866–'67, are herewith respectfully submitted ; and I have the honor to request that, if approved, they be included in your estimates for appropriations.

In regard to the existence of a deficiency, it is only necessary to recall the fact that the late Congress failed to pass the general appropriation bill in which the items for the coast survey are included. No appropriation was, therefore, made for the fiscal year 1865–'66. The work has been continued out of the unexpended balances of previous appropriations, and some aid of the same nature afforded by the Treasury Department. The appropriations asked for this work had been approved by both houses during the progress of the bill, and the amounts now estimated for are intended to meet the expenditures for the remainder of the fiscal year, upon the same scale of appropriation.

The following is a brief sketch of the progress made during the past year. While the war continued, a number of parties were connected with, and rendered efficient aid in, naval and military operations, as during the preceding year.

Four parties were attached to the South Atlantic blockading squadron and the military department of the south, by whom a complete resurvey of the entrance to Charleston harbor was effected ; a survey of the inside water passages between St. Helena and Port Royal sounds ; of Broad river and Whale branch to Port Royal ferry ; of Wilmington and Thunderbolt rivers, and the other communications between Savannah and Wassaw and Ossabaw sounds, besides mapping the rebel defences of Charleston and Savannah, and replacing temporary lights, beacons, and buoys, under instructions from the Light-house Board, as fast as the places were reoccupied by the national forces. The entrance to Darien was examined and buoyed, for the transportation of released Union prisoners. Four topographers of the Coast Survey accompanied Sherman's march from Savannah to Goldsboro', and rendered efficient aid in military reconnoissance.

Two parties were connected with the North Atlantic blockading squadron, one of whom, after assisting in the operations against the rebel defences of Wilmington, N. C., made a complete resurvey of both entrances to Cape Fear river, while the other re-lighted and buoyed those channels, as well as that leading into Beaufort harbor, N. C., which at one time was of great importance as a base of supplies. After the close of hostilities the survey of Cape Lookout shoals and the off-shore work on the coast of North Carolina has been continued.

A topographical survey of the north bank of the Potomac river, from the vicinity of Washington to Harper's Ferry, has been made by a party attached to the middle military department, while two others have continued the detailed surveys of approaches to Baltimore and Washington. One topographer was attached to the army operating in the valley of Virginia, and has furnished reconnoissances of the battle-fields of Fisher's Hill and Cedar Creek ; another was on duty with the army in Tennessee, and has mapped Lookout mountain and its approaches.

In connexion with the Mississippi squadron, a party of Coast Survey officers, furnished with a gunboat, have made a very valuable reconnoissance map of over two hundred miles of the Tennessee river, from the Muscle Shoals to its mouth ; of the lower Ohio, from Paducah to Cairo ; and of some ninety miles of the Mississippi river, from Cairo up to St. Mary's. The latter work necessarily ceased when, owing to the reduction of the squadron, a vessel could no longer be assigned to the use of the party. It may be hoped, however, that the great and obvious usefulness, in a national point of view, of a reliable map of the

Mississippi river may lead Congress to make a special appropriation for the further prosecution of that work, the commencement of which involved no public expenditure that would not otherwise have been incurred.

In the regular progress of the survey in the northern sections, parties have been at work, during the summer and autumn, on Passamaquoddy, Goulds-borough, Frenchman's and Penobscot bays, on Muscongus sound, and Medomak, Damariscotta and New Meadow rivers, on the coast of Maine; on Narragansett bay and its dependencies, in Rhode Island; on the coast of New Jersey; and the connexion of the primary triangulation in sections 1 and 2 has been completed by the superintendent's party.

On the western coast, the coast triangulation between San Francisco and Monterey bays has been completed; that of Suisun bay has been continued; the topography between Point Año Nuevo and Point San Pedro, and the off-shore hydrography south of San Francisco, have been continued, and the topography and hydrography of Koos bay have been completed.

An early resumption of the work in the southern sections is contemplated, and is provided for, on a moderate scale, in the estimates herewith presented

The table below gives the amounts estimated to supply the deficiency for the fiscal year 1865–'66 in parallel columns, with the estimates which were originally presented for the whole fiscal year, and were approved by both houses of the last Congress, but failed to become a law before the expiration of its session :

Object.	Estimated for fiscal year 1865–'66, but not appropriated.	Estimated for deficiency for 1865–'66.
For survey of the Atlantic and Gulf coasts of the United States, including compensation of civilians engaged in the work, per act of March 3, 1843..	$181,000	$120,000
For continuing the survey of the western coast of the United States, including compensation of civilians engaged in the work, per act of September 30, 1850..	100,000	75,000
For continuing the survey of the reefs, shoals, keys, and coast of South Florida, including compensation of civilians engaged in the work, per act of March 3, 1849...............................	11,000	11,000
For publishing the observations made in the progress of the survey of the coast of the United States, including compensation of civilians engaged in the work, per act of March 3, 1843..........	4,000	4,000
For repairs of steamers and sailing schooners used in the survey, per act of March 2, 1853......................................	20,000	20,000
For pay and rations of engineers for three steamers used in the hydrography of the Coast Survey, no longer supplied by the Navy Department......	6,000	6,000
Total.........	322,000	236,000

During the continuance of the rebellion the field operations of the coast survey have been unavoidably much restricted. In the southern sections they were carried on only as far as requisite and practicable in connexion with the operations of the naval forces. In most cases where officers of the Coast Survey have served with military or naval commands the working parties have been furnished from the same, and the pay and subsistence of the officers only have been paid from the coast survey appropriations. The coast survey vessels attached to the squadrons have been furnished with coal and kept in repair by the navy.

Under these circumstances a corresponding reduction in the expenditures for the coast survey was made, which, from considerations of economy, was extended to the work on the western coast. The appropriations, which had amounted to over four hundred and fifty thousand dollars in 1860, were reduced, in accordance with the estimates submitted, to about three hundred thousand dollars during the war.

The estimates herewith presented for the fiscal year 1866–'67 approach more nearly to the scale of expenditure before the war. They contemplate the resumption of the work in the southern sections, which, beside being called for to aid in the development of the resources of that part of our country, will be productive of great economy, since it will, as formerly, enable the same parties to be employed in the south during the winter, that are at work in the north during the summer. Without any material increase in the salaries and office expenses the amount of field-work accomplished will be far more than proportionally augmented. Owing to the great increase in the price of labor and supplies of every kind, the appropriations asked for, although the same in amount of the two principal items as those for 1860–'61, will be far from being equivalent to the latter; they are as low as is consistent with an economical prosecution of the work in the several localities where it has been commenced.

The item providing for the continuation of the survey of the Florida reefs and keys has been diminished from forty to twenty-five thousand dollars, because that work is proportionally far advanced towards completion. The item providing for repairs of vessels, on the contrary, is unavoidably increased from ten to twenty thousand dollars on account of the great increase in the cost of such repairs, and because a larger amount of refitting is at present necessary on account of greater wear and tear during the war.

The subjoined table exhibits, in parallel columns, the appropriations made before the war, those during the war, and the estimates now submitted for the fiscal year 1866–'67:

Object.	Appropriated 1860–'61.	Appropriated 1864–'65.	Estimated for 1866–'67.
For survey of the Atlantic and Gulf coasts of the United States, including compensation of civilians engaged in the work, per act of March 3, 1843 ...	$250,000	$178,000	$250,000
For continuing the survey of the western coast of the United States, including compensation of civilians engaged in the work, per act of September 30, 1850 ...	130,000	100,000	130,000
For continuing the survey of the reefs, shoals, keys, and coast of South Florida, including compensation of civilians engaged in the work, per act of March 3, 1849 ...	40,000	11,000	25,000
For completing the line to connect the triangulation on the Atlantic coast with that on the Gulf of Mexico, across the Florida peninsula, including compensation of civilians engaged in the work, per act of March 3, 1843 ...	5,000	....	....
For publishing the observations made in the progress of the survey of the coast of the United States, including compensation of civilians engaged in the work, per act of March 3, 1843 ...	5,000	4,000	5,000
For repairs of steamers and sailing schooners used in the survey, per act of March 2, 1853 ...	10,000	4,000	20,000
For fuel and quarters, and for mileage or transportation, for officers and enlisted soldiers of the army serving in the coast survey, in cases no longer provided for by the quartermaster's department, per act of August 31, 1852.	5,000	....	....
For pay and rations of engineers for steamers used in the hydrography of the coast survey, no longer supplied by the Navy Department ...	12,800	9,000	10,000
Total ...	457,800	306,000	440,000

Respectfully submitted:

For A. D. BACHE,
Superintendent U. S. Coast Survey,
J. E. HILGARD,
Assistant in charge of Office.

Hon. HUGH McCULLOCH,
Secretary of the Treasury.

REPORT OF THE SUPERVISING INSPECTOR OF STEAMBOATS.

SIR: The board of supervising inspectors of steam vessels met in its annual session, in the city of St. Louis, Missouri, pursuant to adjournment, on the 11th day of October, 1865, and having had under consideration various matters of interest arising from the operations of the steamboat laws, have the honor of presenting their thirteenth annual report.

The board, in their annual report of last year, alluded to the evil effects which the act of April 29, 1864, would produce if continued so as to interfere with or supersede the rules of the board of steamboat inspectors upon the inland waters of the United States.

The act of 1864 ignores the use of the steam-whistle, without which it is difficult to conceive how some of the inland waters of the United States can be navigated, without falling back into dangers and fearful collisions, which, before its introduction, continually shocked the public mind. To these waters, especially those of the western rivers, the simple rule that all vessels when meeting shall take the right is not satisfactory nor sufficient; rapid currents and eddies have much to do in determining the proper course of safety. As a general rule, it is proper that vessels in meeting each other should take the right; but it is not, under some circumstances, practicable, and it is in such cases that the rules of the board of inspectors provide a safe and proper remedy by the introduction of the steam-whistle. The rules will themselves best exemplify the nature of the navigation to which they relate, and they are introduced to show how intimately the signals of the whistle are interwoven with the rules of navigation on the waters referred to:

"*Rule 1st.* When steamers are approaching each other the signals for passing shall be one sound made by the steam-whistle to keep to the right, and two sounds made by the steam-whistle to keep to the left. These signals to be first made by the ascending steamer. If the dangers of navigation, darkness of the night, narrowness of the river, or any other cause, render it necessary for the descending steamer to take the other side, she can do so by making the necessary signal, and the ascending steamer must govern herself accordingly. These signals to be observed by all steamers, whether by day or night.

"*Rule 3d.* When two boats are about to enter a narrow channel at the same time, the ascending boat shall be stopped below such channel until the descending boat shall have passed through it; but should two boats unavoidably meet in such channel, then it shall be the duty of the pilot of the ascending boat to make the proper signal, and when answered by the descending boat, to lie as close as possible to the side of the channel the exchange of signals may have determined as allowed by rule first, and either stop the engines, or move them so as only to give his boat steerage way, and the pilot of the descending boat shall cause his boat to be worked slowly until he has passed the ascending steamer."

The act of 1864 requires mast-head lights, where the character of the navigation does not require them, and upon vessels which have no masts abolishes stern lights, where stern lights are quite necessary. In fact, the act seems to supersede that of August 30, 1852, crushing out the beneficial provisions which have been so long and favorably practiced in the navigation of steam-vessels. The board therefore must continue to be embarrassed in the exercise of their official power in relation to signals of sounds or of lights as heretofore, unless the act of 1864 be so construed as to confine its provisions to oceanic waters, or to those on which the navigation of English, French, and Americans are more particularly and mutually concerned, and then not until some guarantee that English navigators on our northern frontier shall more particularly observe the rules they seek to impose upon us.

Remonstrances from the most influential navigators have been presented against the application of any law which shall break up the system of American signals as heretofore established. The continued accumulation of steam-vessels in all the bays, harbors, and rivers, shows there is increasing need of them, notwithstanding the law of 1864 turns back this tide of improvement and throws into confusion the discretionary power, which for twelve years has been usefully exercised in perfecting a system for steamers which is now adopted by common consent as the best means of safety yet devised, for while it concedes the common rule requiring vessels to take the right when the wishes of pilots are not otherwise expressed, yet it also affords the use of a language by which any misunderstanding may be avoided or corrected.

The provisions of the act should therefore be modified so as to confine its operations to ocean navigation, or to exclude its application from the interior waters of the United States. On the western waters mast-head lights are impracticable, no mast being used as at sea; and head-lights upon the stem, or other low positions forward, give a false aspect to the surface of the water, so that pilots cannot well determine the channel or the snags which they are liable to encounter, nor in approaching other boats can they distinguish such lights from the numerous shore lights, which are generally on the same level and usually placed at the several landings. In this case the law should not require head-lights.

Another rule of the board of inspectors seems to be superseded by the act of 1864, by which it is determined, as in former times, that when two steamers are sailing in the same direction the boat ahead shall have the preference. The faster boat, if she would pass, may be prevented by the zigzag course of the boat ahead, and thus, as in former contentions with opposition lines provoked by such continued obstinacy, the faster boat astern drives into the stern or side of the privileged boat, to the great danger of boat and passengers. The rules of the board established a rule which allows the faster boat behind to pass by signals, rendering danger quite out of the question. The vast increase of tonnage of passenger steamers, and the numerous steamers placed under the law of 1852, by the act of Congress approved June 8, 1864, renders it imperative that more time should be devoted to the duty of inspectors than can be done by most of the local inspectors, at the rate of pay now allowed by same. No man can in these times give his whole time to this duty and support his family on the annual pay which the law allows to many districts, after deducting 5 per cent. tax, and this at the same places where common laborers receive $1 75 to $2 per day; and even where local inspectors receive a fair salary, so as to devote their time wholly to the work, they cannot possibly do what the interests of the department demand, so great is the pressure of duty upon some of the districts. The law requires an inspection at least once in each year. The board does not, therefore, hesitate to recommend to your notice the necessity of an act of Congress so fixing the salaries of the inspectors as to enable them to devote their entire time to this service. Underwriters and ship-owners complain that extensive combinations of pilots, especially at the west, are in existence to embarrass the operation of the steamboat law, and to force upon the inspectors their demand for the control of the licensing power, or at least to the limitation of the number of pilots on the rivers, so as to compel the owners of boats to pay exorbitant wages for their services, and they refuse to work as pilots on any boat that has an apprentice on board, and throw every obstacle to advancement in the way of young men desirous to become pilots. They object to licenses being granted except upon the recommendation of two or more of their own number. In that they do all they can to exact wages far beyond the sums paid to officers on steamers requiring equal talent, skill, and fidelity. A law of Congress seems to be called for to secure proper privileges to apprentices and others who may be desirous of becoming pilots.

Freight boats form a class of steamers which seem to have been omitted in the act of 1864 from the list no longer to be exempt from the necessity of inspection under the act of 1852. They should with equal justice be included with tow-boats and ferry-boats. Inspectors seem to feel the importance of a more strenuous effort to sustain the dignity and responsibility of their office, and manifest great zeal in the performance of their duty; but under the increase and increasing amount of service required, the encouraging hand of Congress will be essential to the preservation of able men in the districts, and the promotion of a proper enthusiasm in the performance of official duty.

It is believed the power of the board of supervising inspectors was intended, by the act which established the organization, to have been free to carry out the provisions of the law to the fullest capabilities of the engineering profession of the country, so that it might stand on a par with other boards established for similar purposes of public usefulness upon the coasts and harbors of the United States, and that it was not intended that those rules should be filtered away by rival State or national organizations; yet it is observable that such is the tendency, to the great detriment of its influence upon the public mind.

The large number of accidents reported from some of the districts the past year may be referred to various ruling causes. *Recklessness*, induced by the war, which extends its mischievous tendencies into all branches of trade, is particularly observable among those employed in or on board some classes of steamers. A large number of boats have been used during the war as transports, tugs, and freight boats; these have been depreciated by long and continued use, purchased and put on duty without proper examination, and run without precaution or regard to safety. These will doubtless be found among the most numerous causes of these terrible calamities, which seem to be beyond the reach of official remedy.

The board, at the present session, have revised the rules and regulations according to the suggestions of experience, and have determined to require sealed or locked safety-valves, which are to be taken wholly from the control of all persons engaged in navigating steam-vessels.

The following are statements of the important occurrences which have been brought to the notice of the board during the past year:

Total number of steamers inspected during the year 1865	2, 270
Tonnage of steamers inspected during the year 1865	714, 994
Number of pilots licensed during the year 1865	3, 172
Number of engineers licensed during the year 1865	4, 035
Number of boilers which would not bear hydrostatic test	35
Number of violations of law investigated	28
Number of lives lost by explosion	1, 527
Number of lives lost by foundering or beaching	503
	530
Total number of lives lost	2, 560
Total number of lives saved by life-saving apparatus, as required by law	34
Loss of property by explosion	$110, 000
Loss of property by fire	$148, 550
Loss of property by wreck or foundering	$165, 000
Total loss of property on inspected steamers	$423, 550
Estimated value of steamers inspected in 1865	$221, 016, 800
Estimated value of steamers inspected in 1864	$165, 762, 600
Increase in value from 1864 to 1865	$55, 254, 200
Total number of passengers carried	111, 377, 964

The reports from supervising districts herewith annexed, together with the tabular statements furnished, will show in detail what statistics are upon the records of the several districts.

All of which is respectfully submitted.

P. B. STILLMAN, *President.*

JAMES N. MULLER, *Secretary.*

FIRST SUPERVISING DISTRICT—PACIFIC COAST.

During the year ending August 31, 1865, there have been inspected, in the district of San Francisco, 63 steam vessels, with an aggregate tonnage of 33,686 tons ; 50 pilots and 102 engineers have also been licensed at that port.

There have been inspected in the district of Oregon 25 steam vessels, with an aggregate tonnage of 4,438 tons, and 34 pilots and 17 engineers have been licensed. Aggregate tonnage of steamers inspected on the Pacific coast during the year, 38,124 tons.

Three accidents have occurred to passenger steamers of quite a serious character. The first of these, the explosion of the starboard boiler of the high-pressure steamer Washoe, occurred on the Sacramento river, about forty miles below Sacramento, while on her regular trip from San Francisco. By this accident forty-five passengers lost their lives, also the chief engineer and five of the crew. The Washoe was a new side-wheel steamer of 385 tons, and had four cylinder boilers 32 feet long and forty inches diameter, each containing five flues; these were set on deck, in the same manner usual on the Mississippi and other western rivers. These boilers were made of iron five-sixteenths of an inch in thickness, and stamped as required by law, and were considered when inspected first-class boilers. It was found on examination after the explosion that the shell of the boiler had opened over the furnace for a length of six feet, while the flues remained uninjured. It was testified by one witness connected with the boat, that on other trips he had on three occasions seen the gauge-cocks tried without finding water—showing the most criminal negligence on the part of the engineer in charge, who it appears intrusted the keeping up the supply of water to firemen, without giving the matter sufficient personal attention. There is no evidence, however, that there was a deficiency of water at the time of the explosion, and the cause is somewhat shrouded in mystery; but the local inspectors at San Francisco are of opinion that it resulted from the negligence of the engineer, as above referred to. I must say, however, that I entertain a somewhat different opinion. That the engineer was negligent in the performance of his duties there can be no doubt, but there is another fact which cannot be lost sight of. These boilers had been in use but three months, and although the iron was considered to be of the best quality, certainly as good as it was possible to procure, yet it was found in use that several of the sheets exposed to the direct heat of the furnaces were laminated in their structure, so that they became blistered and cracked, and had to be patched or altogether removed, and new ones substituted, depending on the extent of the injury. From the position of the ruptured portion, as also the fact that the flues remained uninjured, I incline to the opinion that a crack in the sheet had occurred, probably from the boiler not having been properly cleared of scale, and the boiler, thus weakened, was burst simply by the contained pressure extending this crack longitudinally. I believe this is not an unusual cause of the explosion of boilers of this class, where the great shell of the boiler, every part of which is subjected in use to a very severe tensile strain, is directly exposed to the action of the fire; for although the boiler so arranged may withstand any reasonable hydrostatic test when cold, or at moderate temperatures,

14 F

defects may be developed by the application of extreme temperatures, or under such circumstances a local injury may occur from the adherence of scale to the iron, which will endanger the whole structure. For the reasons above stated, I consider the above class of boilers among the most objectionable now in use; and I think it is to be regretted that in the navigation of some of our rivers the character of the water seems to prevent their present abandonment.

In November, 1864, the steamer Sophie McLane exploded her port boiler while lying at her wharf at Suisun city. By this explosion the captain and four of the crew were killed. The accident occurred in the morning before the hour of starting on her voyage had arrived, and there were fortunately but few passengers on board, and none of these were injured. This was a high-pressure side-wheel steamer of 242 tons, and had two boilers in the hold of the vessel 18 feet long and 5 feet diameter, which had been in use only two months. The shell of the boiler gave way, and the boat was torn to pieces and rendered useless. The investigation showed that the explosion occurred from excessive pressure, arising from the criminal negligence and mismanagement of the engineer. He was one of the oldest engineers on the coast, and up to this time had borne an excellent reputation for attention to his duties. His license was revoked, and he immediately left the country to save himself from prosecution.

July 30, 1865, the steamship Brother Jonathan, bound from San Francisco to Portland, Oregon, was lost in a heavy sea by striking upon a sunken rock, bearing about west-northwest from Crescent City, and from eight to ten miles from land. She was a vessel of about 1,200 tons, and had on board when lost, as nearly as can be ascertained, 140 passengers and 50 other persons, being officers and crew, and about 500 tons of freight. She left San Francisco July 28, and experienced very heavy weather all the way up the coast. On the 30th, about 2 o'clock p: m., she was a little to the northward of Crescent City, and was passed at 12 m. by the steamship Sierra Nevada, bound down. The sea was at this time so rough, and the wind blowing so heavy from the north-,west, that it was determined by Captain De Wolf, who was in command of the steamer, to turn back and lie at Crescent City until the storm had abated. The steamer was put about, and had run some ten or fifteen minutes to the southeast when she struck a sunken rock, and was so pierced by it that she remained lodged and could not be backed off. The wind and sea was now beating very heavily on her port quarter, and she swung round and came head to the wind. It appears the rock must have been pointed or wedge-shaped, and when she came head to the wind it was found that in swinging it had burst open the bottom of the ship, and the foremast of the vessel slipped down through the opening until the foreyard lay across the deck. There was an immediate attempt made to get the life-boats cleared from the sinking ship, and the first boat cleared and cast off got away in safety with nineteen persons on board ; these were all the persons saved from the vessel, out of one hundred and ninety. Several of the other boats were got into the water and loaded with passengers, but were stove to pieces against the vessel by the force of the sea running alongside. All the boats were lowered under direction of the officers, every person behaving in the coolest manner, under the assurance of the captain that everything would be done for their safety which was possible. None of the principal officers ever left the deck of the steamer; but when the life-boats had been lost, and all means of escape cut off, they were seen, with the passengers then remaining on board, standing on the after-deck of the vessel until she sunk beneath the waves, which she did in forty-five minutes after striking the rock. During several succeeding days bodies were drifted on shore, all of which had life-preservers secured to them, and many were recognized and taken possession of by their friends, while others were buried where found by the force established to patrol the beach for more than fifty miles to the southward. It is not known with certainty whether the rock upon which the vessel struck had been previously known or not, as it is impossible now to determine the exact position of the steamer at the time, but it is generally believed it was further to sea than any rock or reef now laid down in the charts; and in support of this view, it is hardly possible that a commander so experienced on this route, so constant in his watchfulness, and so eminently correct in all his habits, could have been run on any known danger in broad daylight, and the weather so clear that the position and bearings of the ship must have been fully known to him. The Brother Jonathan was re-built four years since, and was a very stannch vessel, and was very fully sup-plied with boats and all other equipments required by law; she also had very able and experienced officers and a full crew. The public were very deeply im-pressed by this sad calamity, the ship and her officers having the fullest confidence of the people; there has not been heard, in the public press or elsewhere, the least complaint against either; but every one, with a sense of personal bereave-ment in the loss of so many valuable and well-known citizens, seemed, without murmur, to bow in profoundest sorrow to this fearful dispensation of an over-ruling Providence.

There is a practical lesson to be learned from this and similar disasters at sca, which should not be passed by unheeded. It will be observed that the boats of this steamer, with one exception, were dashed to pieces alongside of the vessel, after they had been loaded with passengers, before they could be got clear of the ship. Can this danger be avoided? The difficulty arises from a want of suitable provision by which the boat may be instantly relieved at will from the tackles by which she is lowered into the water. I do not pretend to say that boats in all cases could be got clear of the ship if furnished with such means, but their adoption would, I am fully satisfied, greatly lessen the present danger of disaster from this cause; and I trust Congress will be called upon to require by enactment the application of the best form of boat-disengaging ap-paratus on all our ocean-going steam-vessels.

In conclusion, I feel it to be a duty to call your attention to a subject which, from long experience and observation as an executive officer under the steam-boat act of 1852, I am satisfied has been more destructive to the hopes of the friends of that enactment than all the deficiencies of requirement, the correction of which this board have from time to time recommended. There is no ques-tion but the provisions of the steamboat act above referred to are of the most salutary character, and have been productive in saving to their friends and the country very many and valuable lives, and also much property. To execute this important law, Congress provided a body of officers whose special duty it was made carefully to inspect all passenger steamers at least once in each year, to see that all the provisions of the law were complied with, and that the vessel was otherwise in a condition to warrant the belief that she might be safely em-ployed as a passenger-carrying steamer without peril to life. These officers were also required to visit such vessels arriving or departing to see that their equipment was maintained in good condition, and that they were properly man-aged. They were also charged with the duty of examining, classifying and licensing engineers and pilots of these vessels, and keeping watch over the con-duct of these officers.

By the various salaries paid to the local inspectors ($200 to $2,000) it was evidently contemplated by Congress that they would generally have to give but an insignificant portion of their time to this official duty, and could, without prejudice to the public interests, seek for support mainly, or partially, in some private occupation. In some cases this anticipation was verified, while in many others the imposed public services had been much under-estimated. No one can live without support, and in cases where the salary of a local board of in-spectors was fixed at too low a rate for the time which should be devoted to fully discharging the duties of the office, the public service has correspondingly suffered. I do not say that any of the official acts required by law have not been performed. I am aware that inspectors have done all that could have been done under these circumstances, but there is a great difference between simply doing an act and doing it well and effectively. The inspecting of a steamer annually is no guarantee that she is conducted properly throughout the year; and I believe this continued intermediate examination to be of such vital importance in obtaining the security contemplated, that wherever the business of the port is considerable, all the attention of the inspectors which can be spared from office duties may be given to visiting vessels arriving and departing with a marked change in the record of casualties annually reported. This can only be done by giving these officers remunerative compensation, such as to preclude the necessity of their seeking to eke out by private enterprises the scanty compensation obtained for official services. I trust the board will consider it proper to ask the honorable Secretary of the Treasury to commend this matter to the attention of Congress.

WILLIAM BURNETT, Supervising Inspector.

SECOND SUPERVISING DISTRICT.

An unusual amount of duty has been performed in this district. The local board in Philadelphia report no accidents or any material variation from usual occurrences. The following accidents are reported from the New York district:

On the night of October 18, 1864, the steamer Admiral DuPont, while on her passage from New York to New Haven, and shortly after leaving the wharf, came in collision with the tug-boat Keystone, by which the latter was sunk. An investigation was made in this case, and from the testimony given we find that the Admiral DuPont was in charge of a regular licensed pilot, who used all necessary precautions to prevent a collision, by blowing the steam-whistle, but which was not answered by the tug-boat, and by a sudden change of course by the latter, came across the bow of the Admiral DuPont. No lives lost.

On the night of January 8, 1865, the Jno. V. Melville, on her passage from New York to Port Royal, it being her second day out from port, encountered a heavy gale, was struck by a heavy sea, which stove in the starboard bow, flooded the forward cabin, and broke away the water-tight bulkhead, forward of the engine, and putting out the fires. The engineer reporting the same, a general rush was made by the passengers for the boats, filling them to such an extent as to break away the davits and light rail on the upper deck, by which a large number of persons were precipitated in the water and drowned. The steamer remained afloat about two hours, and then sunk, going down head-foremost, carrying with her all except the mate, third assistant engineer, and two passengers, who were saved. Fifty-three passengers and twenty-three of the crew were lost.

The ship propeller North America left New Orleans December 15, 1864, bound for New York. On the 22d, during a heavy gale of wind, sprung a leak forward, and notwithstanding all the exertions made by the officers and crew, foundered the same night. There were on board 203 sick soldiers, 12 cabin passengers, and a crew consisting of 44 men, making a total of 259 persons, of whom only 62 were saved. Loss of property, including ship, estimated at about $300,000.

On the night of Monday, February 6, 1865, the steamer Empire State, while on her passage from New York to Newport, R. I., was run into by the ship propeller Franconia. An investigation was held, when the following facts were elicited: The vessels were nearly abreast of New Haven light, each bound a different course; the lights of each were distinctly visible for at least twenty minutes before the collision. The vessels continued to steer their proper course until within a distance of about half a mile from each other, when the Franconia suddenly changed her course, bearing down upon the Empire State. The pilot of the latter vessel immediately blew two distinct whistles, but heard no answer from the other vessel. The bell was then rung to slow, stop and back, which was promptly done by the engineer. The Franconia continuing at full speed, struck the Empire State at a right angle, about twenty feet abaft the stern, cutting her through to the keelson, and the vessel was only saved from sinking by having a well-constructed water-tight bulkhead a few feet abaft the fracture. The Franconia, as near as we could find out, was in charge of a Sound pilot, but not licensed by us. No lives were lost.

The ship propeller George Washington was burned to the water's edge on the evening of the 2d of January, 1865, while in this port, having just arrived from sea. The amount of property lost was great, but the valuation was not ascertained by us. No lives were lost.

April 28, 1865, the steamship Ocean Queen, while on her passage from New York to Aspinwall, collapsed the lower flue in the forward boiler; four of the crew were scalded—two fatally, and two slightly. The vessel proceeded on her voyage with one boiler.

On the night of the 7th of June, 1865, the steamer Admiral DuPont left the port of New York for Fortress Monroe, having on board a small detachment of United States troops. On the following morning a dense fog set in. At 4.20 a. m. a sailing vessel was discovered steering nearly in an opposite direction. The engine was immediately stopped and backed, and the wheel thrown hard a-starboard, but, at the rate of speed of the sailing-vessel, a collision could not be prevented by those on board of the steamer, which was struck just forward of the paddle-wheel, and sunk in about three minutes. The greatest part of the passengers and crew were saved by getting on board of the ship, which proved to be the English ship Stadaconda. There were 17 persons drowned, viz: 15 soldiers, one fireman, and a colored woman.

There have been two steamers burned while lying at their respective docks, viz: the tug propeller George O'Vail, on the night of the 4th of August, and the steamboat Chicopee, on the morning of September 16, 1865—the former lying at Brooklyn, N. Y., and the latter at Newark, N. J.; the aggregate loss amounting to about $24,000. No lives were lost.

On the 6th day of August, 1865, the steamboat Arrow, while on her passage from New York to Haverstraw, collapsed one of the lower flues of starboard boiler, scalding fatally one of the firemen no other persons were materially injured by the escaping steam. Four of the passengers were drowned by jumping overboard during the panic. The license of the engineer has been revoked for inattention to his duty and violation of Art. 15, section 9, of the law of 1852.

The Boston board report that they have had five boilers fail, under hydro-static pressure; that no accident has happened, by which life had been lost; that one boat called the Chocoma, on Lake Winnipiseogee, on the night of 3d of July last, was entered by some malicious person, who placed a keg of powder, with a lighted slow-match, in the furnace of her boiler, where it exploded, raising the forward deck and breaking several of the deck-beams. It would no doubt have destroyed the boat and perhaps killed all the crew, who were asleep on board, if the furnace door had been securely shut; but it seems the miscreant was unable to do this, on account of the slow-match, which was laid through the furnace door, so that the principal force of the explosion came out at the door. The boiler, notwithstanding, was found to be uninjured.

On the 7th of February last, about 9 p. m., the steamers Empire State and Franconia collided. The particulars you will find above, with the exception of the loss sustained, which was about $25,000, which was paid by the owners of the Franconia, they admitting the inefficiency of the watch on deck.

As a general thing, the owners and officers of steam vessels continue to comply with all the requirements of the law. We have had but one palpable violation of the law, in the case of the steamer Reindeer, which vessel, without inspection or any other papers, went out with passengers two trips on the 4th of July last. This, in our opinion, was a heedless or wilful violation of the statute, and the case is now pending in the district court.

The inspectors complain of the low salaries allowed, and hope that Congress will see the justice of raising their pay, for the reason that their entire time is required to perform the duties, and also set forth the fact that, when the salaries were made by Congress, in 1852, gold was at par, and the number of steamers was then about one-quarter and the engineers and pilots about one-fifth of what they now are in their districts, and these are rapidly increasing, and that their present salaries of eight hundred dollars, in currency, are entirely inadequate for the services rendered.

The amount of fees received in this district by local board at Boston, in 1853, for licenses was $240; for inspection, $580—total, $820. The amount of fees received for license in 1865 was $2,610; for inspection, $2,682 73—total, $5,292 73.

N. B.—The amount carried out for inspection fees is a close approximation, and very near correct.

THOS. B. STILLMAN,
Supervising Inspector Second District.

THIRD SUPERVISING DISTRICT.

The war having terminated, and business opening and resuming its usual channels, a great number of steamers which were in government employ have entered the various routes upon our coast, bays, and rivers.

The local board at Baltimore have inspected one hundred and forty-two (142) steamers; given license to two hundred and forty-seven (247) engineers and one hundred and eighty-six (186) pilots. Tonnage of steamers, forty-four thousand six hundred and six (44,606) tons.

Inspected at Norfolk and Old Point, Virginia, by supervisor, ten (10) steamers, whose tonnage amounts to fifteen hundred and ninety-six (1,596) tons; licensed sixty-seven (67) engineers and thirty-seven (37) pilots.

At Hilton Head, Charleston, South Carolina, and Savannah, Georgia, inspected four (4) steamers, whose tonnage is eleven hundred and twenty-two (1,122) tons; licensed twenty-three (23) engineers and twenty-six (26) pilots.

At Newbern, North Carolina, five (5) steamers, measuring eleven hundred and thirteen (1,113) tons, were inspected.

At Baltimore, Maryland, thirteen (13) steamers were inspected; tonnage, four thousand six hundred and twenty-one (4,621) tons; granted license to ninety-seven (97) engineers and eighty-seven (87) pilots.

At Norfolk, Virginia, by local board, were inspected twelve (12) steamers, whose tonnage was fifteen hundred and eighty-four (1,584) tons; granted license to sixty-one (61) engineers and twenty-four (24) pilots.

At Charleston, South Carolina, three (3) steamers, measuring seven hundred and seven (707) tons, were inspected.

Total, of steamers inspected in the district, one hundred and eighty-six (186;) tonnage, fifty-four thousand six hundred and forty-two (54,642.) Pilots licensed, three hundred and seventy (370;) engineers, four hundred and eighty-six (486.) Estimated number of passengers carried were four million two hundred and forty-two thousand four hundred and ninety (4,242,490.)

In the month of August, 1865, the supervisor was sent, by special order, to Charleston, South Carolina, Savannah, Georgia, and Mobile, Alabama, to co-operate with the collector of those ports and the United States district judge in the nomination of suitable persons to act as local inspectors of steam vessels for the ports herein mentioned. In consequence of the lateness of the period when they were appointed the supervisor has received no report from them, except Charleston, South Carolina.

The law has been faithfully carried out, with but few exceptions. The local boards are using energetic measures to have it fully complied with, and have determined to punish transgressors. They are attending to their duties faithfully.

There has been some effort made by pilots employed upon the Chesapeake bay, who have derived their license from the State to navigate sail vessels, and who are endeavoring to embarrass steamboat pilots, and in some cases have commenced suits at law against them because they have not procured a State license also, in order to navigate steamers upon the Chesapeake waters, notwithstanding they had a government license.

October 25, 1864.—The steamer Grey Hound, in government employ, while on her way from Bermuda Hundred to Norfolk, Virginia, took fire somewhere near the boiler, by accident, and in a few minutes was in a sheet of flames! Happily no lives were lost. The vessel was burnt to the water's edge and sunk.

March 25, 1865.—The government steamer General Lyon was burned while on her voyage from Hilton Head, South Carolina, to Fortress Monroe, Virginia, having on board at the time some five hundred (500) government troops, nearly all of whom perished by the flames. Vessel entirely destroyed. Reported to have originated by accident.

September 30, 1864.—The steamer Matilda burst her boiler in Hampton creek, Virginia, by which the chief engineer, Thomas Brannan, was so badly scalded that he died.

October 22.—The steamer Mary Washington and schooner Missouri Young collided in the Chesapeake bay. The pilot of the steamer was found inattentive to the duties of his station, and license was suspended for thirty (30) days.

January 10, 1865.—The steamer Georgeanna and schooner John Walker collided on the bay, by which five (5) persons were drowned—one passenger and four of the crew. Upon investigation by the local board they found it purely accidental.

January 7.—The steamers Louisiana and Cambria came in collision off Point No-Point, on Chesapeake bay, but neither vessel was materially damaged. Caused by a thick fog.

April 23.—The steamers Massachusetts and Black Diamond collided on the Potomac river; the former loaded with troops, sixty (60) of whom were drowned. The investigation disclosed the fact that both pilots wholly disregarded the rules established for their government, consequently their licenses were revoked. The opinion given by the local board is, that this lamentable loss of human life has been caused by the present system of carrying signal lights.

May 11.—The tug Mohawk was refused a certificate at Alexandria for want of the equipments required by law.

July 20.—The boiler of the United States revenue cutter Lincoln was subjected to a hydrostatic pressure of forty (40) pounds per square inch. A subsequent examination disclosed a very satisfactory condition of the several parts.

July 31.—The boiler of steamer Carroll gave way under a pressure of thirty-two (32) pounds.

July 27.—The tugs Alpha and Grace Titus collided on the Patapsco river, by which two (2) young men were drowned. The local board decided that the pilot of the Alpha, a naval steamer, was in fault. She left port immediately thereafter, and has not since returned.

August 24.—Steamers George Leary and Sea Gull collided near Cove

Point, on the Chesapeake bay, by which three persons lost their lives The George Leary was cut down to the water's edge. The pilot of the Sea Gull was proved in fault, and his license revoked.

August 30.—Steamers George Appold and Kent collided off Thomas's Point, by which the latter was sunk in a few minutes. In this case, the pilot of the Kent was found in fault, and license revoked.

September 13.—The tugs Atlantic and May Queen collided on the Patapsco river. Little damage was done. The pilot of the Atlantic was found negligent, and his license suspended for thirty (30) days.

There were thirteen steamers and tugs built at Baltimore during the past year, measuring three thousand and four hundred (3,400) tons.

All of which is respectfully submitted.

JAMES N. MULLER, Sr.,
Supervising Inspector Third District.

FOURTH SUPERVISING DISTRICT.

There have been inspected in this district two hundred and six (206) steamers of all classes, ranging from fifty to sixteen hundred tons. The stated tonnage could not be ascertained, as a large number of steamers have not been yet measured by the proper customs officers of this district.

There have been issued in this district seven hundred and twenty (70) pilot licenses and five hundred and eighty (580) engineer licenses.

Several accidents occurred without loss of life, as will be seen by the report of the local boards and the tabular statement appended.

One occurred at Carondelet, near St. Louis, of a more serious nature. The steamer Maria, of two hundred and fifty-four (254) tons burden, exploded one of her boilers, and set the boat on fire. She was burnt and sunk; proved to be a total loss; she was carrying soldiers. The local board at St. Louis held an investigation, found that the engineers had been negligent, and had failed to state correct facts. Their licenses were revoked. The number of lives lost, if any, could not be ascertained.

The steamer Watson, sunk by a snag at the foot of Island No. 76, near the mouth of the Arkansas river. Thirty-four (34) lives were lost.

Disaster of the Sultana. This is perhaps the most frightful disaster ever recorded in the annals of steam navigation. It is stated that over fifteen hundred (1,500) lives were lost. The Sultana was built at Cincinnati, Ohio, in 1863. She was of 660 38-100 tons burden, (old measurement;) had accommodations for seventy-six (76) cabin passengers, and three hundred (300) deck passengers. She had four high-pressure boilers, 18 feet long and 46 inches in diameter, made of iron 17-48 of an inch in thickness ; each boiler had 24 return flues, 5 inches in diameter, made of iron one-eighth of an inch thick. The Sultana was inspected in St. Louis, on the 12th day of April, 1865, by the local board of inspectors, composed of John Maguire and John Shaffer. The boilers were subjected to a hydrostatic pressure of two hundred and ten (210) pounds to the square inch. The working steam pressure allowed was one hundred and forty-five (145) pounds to the square inch. The Sultana had two engines, with cylinders 25 inches in diameter and 8 feet stroke ; had three forcing pumps, six inches stroke, and respectively 5, 6 and 7 inches in diameter ; two of them were worked by hand. The explosion occurred on the 27th day of April, 1865, at about seven miles above Memphis, Tennessee. There was no local board at that time at Memphis. As soon as the news of the terrible occurrence reached St. Louis, by telegraph, I, as supervising inspector of this, the fourth district, considered it my duty, as prescribed by the 22d section of the act of Con--

gress of 1852, to repair immediately to the scene of the calamity. What urged me to take immediate steps is, that on all such occasions the surviving parties leave for parts unknown as soon as they can procure the means to do so. This is especially the case with those that are supposed to be best informed of the probable cause of the accident. Arriving at Memphis, Tennessee, I found that Major General Washburn had instituted a military commission to inquire into the matter. They had made little progress, and had concluded to go to Vicksburg, where they had good ground to believe more information could be gathered. I was invited by General Washburn to join the party, and did so.

At Vicksburg, one of the first witnesses put under oath was R. G. Taylor, an experienced boiler-maker. He stated that he had, at the request of the first engineer, examined and repaired the middle larboard boiler of the Sultana, on her up trip to Memphis. He states that he found, on examination of the larboard boiler, that two sheets were badly bulged out. He was told by the captain that both sheets would be cut out at St. Louis, and he (Taylor) was to cut out only a piece 26 by 11 inches, which he did. He was not permitted to force back the bulge, as he desired, but had to fit his patch to the boiler as it was. *The patch he riveted on was only one-quarter of an inch thick.* To all this the first engineer consented. This was on the part of the engineer a gross violation of the law, the body of the boiler being made of iron 17.48 of one inch, and inspected, and the safety-valves regulated for iron of that thickness, and the pressure allowed was the extreme limit. Had the boiler been inspected after the repairs, the pressure allowed by law would have been 100.43 pounds of working pressure per square inch, as prescribed for boilers 46 inches in diameter, made of iron $\frac{1}{4}$ inch thick.

From Vicksburg to Memphis the Sultana travelled at her usual speed, which shows that the usual pressure of steam was used. The foregoing is sufficient to explain the cause or causes of the explosion. Boilers of a construction not adapted to the water of the Mississippi river, the flues being set in zigzag, which makes them very difficult to clean; the rapid accumulation of sediment renders them easily subject to be burned, or at least overheated; this seems to have been the case of the Sultana. The boilers were imperfectly repaired at Vicksburg, for which the engineer alone can be held responsible.

There is another feature in this disaster that deserves to be mentioned—the large amount of human beings crowded on this boat. The law limits the number of passengers that a vessel is allowed to carry. That law, like many others, has during the war been set aside for military necessities. Civil officers had to be silent, and large numbers of soldiers have frequently been crowded on small crafts. This war was already ended when this inhuman shipment was made, and nobody pretended that there was a necessity. The Sultana left New Orleans with about 250 passengers and crew, and in the hold about 250 hogsheads of sugar. At Vicksburg 2,000 released Union prisoners and 60 horses and mules were shipped on her, while the certificate allowed her only three hundred and seventy-six (376) passengers, all told. The Pauline Carroll, a steamer of the same size, was lying at the wharf at Vicksburg, on her way to St. Louis. The officers of the P. Carroll were anxious to get one thousand (1,000) of those passengers at the regular government rate. The agent of that boat even offered a premium, as he declared himself, but to no avail. It was decided that horse, mule and human freight must be crowded in one heap.

J. J. WITZIG,
Supervising Inspector Fourth District.

Eighty-nine steamboats have been inspected in this district during the year ending October 1, 1865—thirty-five passenger boats, twenty-one freight boats, eighteen ferry-boats, and fifteen tow-boats—with an aggregate tonnage, so far as could be obtained; of nine thousand six hundred and eighty-seven $\frac{70}{100}$ tons. The tonnage of many of the steamers could not be obtained because of the delay in procuring the admeasurement. There have been transported by these steamers two hundred thousand passengers, without loss of life. But one accident has occurred in this district during the year. Steamer John Rumsey exploded her boiler within sight of St. Paul, on the 5th of November, 1864. She was of thirty-nine tons capacity, towing two barges loaded. Some five or six of the men were killed, and others wounded; the boat drifted on to a bar and burned up; cargo and barges saved; loss eight thousand dollars. The engineer says he had water enough in his boiler, and no more steam than he was entitled to carry. We have refused to renew his license since that time. One hundred and twenty-three engineers and one hundred and twenty-three pilots have been licensed; the tabular report will indicate the grade of the same. The local board report that in testing the boiler of the steamer Mankato, on the 9th day of June, at the port of St. Paul, her boiler failed to stand the test pressure, and ordered her to repair the same.

Also, on the 17th day of June, we applied the pressure to the steamer Viola, at La Crosse, Wisconsin, when we discovered a crack in her boiler in connexion with the steam-drum, and ordered her to repair.

On the 23d day of July we tested the steamer New Boston, at Rock island, when the starboard flue of the starboard boiler collapsed; ordered repairs by making and putting in new flues. Same day ordered steamer Jo Parsons to get new steam-pipe.

On the 8th day of September we again applied the test pressure to the steamer Mankato, at St. Paul, which started her boiler-heads. We then condemned the boilers as unfit, and ordered new ones.

Considerable dissatisfaction exists among steamboat owners as to the admeasurement of steamers under the new law; they object to any admeasurement above the main deck on our river steamers as altogether constructive, and without limit. Steamers as at present admeasured cannot carry the number of tons indicated in their register; it would sink them at the landing.

CHARLES L. STEPHENSON,
Supervising Inspector Fifth District.

SIXTH SUPERVISING DISTRICT.

There have been inspected at Louisville, Kentucky, 105 boats, the tonnage amounting to 27,911 tons.

At Nashville, Tennessee, 13 boats, tonnage 12,089, making a total amount of tonnage 40,000; this is an increase of 16,789 tons.

There have been licensed 252 pilots, and original licenses granted to 53, making 305; and to engineers renewals have been given to 260, and original to 44, making 304. Total number of licenses granted 609.

Two boilers were found defective, and two gave way under hydrostatic pressure.

The steamer Ben Levi was sent to Easton, on the Tennessee river, by the United States military authorities, with a regiment of soldiers, about 1st of March, 1865. After performing the trip to Easton in safety, on the return of the boat, when about 150 miles below Louisville, on the Ohio river, on the morning of the 19th of March, her boilers were thrown overboard and torn to pieces, the hull sunk and destroyed. This case was investigated by the local board at Louisville. Their report states that this loss was a clear case of some mischievous or combustible matter which was thrown into the furnace. I have examined the parts of the boilers, and am of the opinion that the conclusion arrived at by the local board at Louisville is correct. The boat was loaded for the trip, and at the time was using the coal that was in her deck-room. I am of the opinion that some combustible matter was mixed in the coal for the express purpose of destroying the soldiers on her trip to Easton. I append the report of the Louisville board to this for the information of the board.

The number of passengers carried in the district for the past year amounts to one million ten thousand.

The number of engineers licensed by original license at Nashville, Tennessee, was ———; number of original pilots, ———; licenses renewed to engineers, ———; licenses renewed to pilots, ———; making a total of ———.

J. V. GUTHRIE,
Supervising Inspector Sixth District.

SEVENTH SUPERVISING DISTRICT.

. One hundred and fifty-one (151) steamers, measuring thirty-two thousand one hundred and sixty-four (32,164) tons, were inspected at Pittsburg, Pennsylvania; forty-seven, (47,) measuring nine thousand and ninety (9,090) tons, were inspected at Wheeling, West Virginia; and one hundred and forty-five, (145,) measuring forty-five thousand one hundred (45,100) tons, were inspected at Cincinnati, Ohio—making, in the aggregate, three hundred and forty-three (343) steamers of all classes, measuring eighty-six thousand three hundred and fifty-four (86,354) tons, being an increase of tonnage inspected over the last year of thirty-three thousand eight hundred and seventy-three (33,873) tons.

The local board at Pittsburg, Pennsylvania, have issued certificates of license to two hundred and ninety-three (293) pilots and two hundred and ninety-two (292) engineers.

The local board at Wheeling, West Virginia, have issued certificates of license to forty-nine (49) pilots and fifty-four (54) engineers.

The local board at Cincinnati, Ohio, have issued certificates of license to three hundred and forty-four (344) pilots and three hundred and fifty-one (351) engineers; making a total number of one thousand three hundred and eighty-three (1,383) officers to whom licenses have been granted. Eighteen (18) applications for license as pilots have been refused, and ten (10) that of engineers. The license of one (1) pilot has been revoked and two (2) suspended. The licenses of two (2) engineers have been revoked and one (1) suspended. Owing to the great demand for the use of steamers for furnishing transportation for military purposes no definite information has been obtained of the number of passengers carried, but the estimated number amounts to one million three hundred and forty thousand and one hundred (1,340,100) passengers.

February 27, 1865.—The steamer W. H. Osborne and tug-boat Collier collided near Sunfish, Ohio; no serious damage. The case was investigated by the local board of Pittsburg, Pennsylvania, and the pilot's license of the latter boat was suspended, he being in fault.

March 20, 1865.—The small steamer Oil City struck a sunken coal barge opposite Wheeling, West Virginia, and sunk to the hurricane deck; no lives lost. She was raised, and is now being repaired. Loss, five thousand (5,000) dollars.

March 22, 1865.—The small steamer David Linch capsized in a gale at

Parkersburg, West Virginia; several passengers on board; passengers and crew all saved by means of life-boat, yawl, and floats, which the boat was amply provided with. Loss, four thousand (4,000) dollars.

March 30, 1865.—The small steamer Malta sunk at the mouth of Muskingum river by striking a sunken barge which obstructed the channel; no lives lost. She was soon raised, and is now running. Loss, three thousand (3,000) dollars.

August 19; 1865.—The steamers Gallatin and Fayette collided on the Monongahela river, twelve (12) miles above Pittsburg, Pennsylvania, causing the loss of one life and the sinking of the latter boat. The case was investigated by the local board at Pittsburg, Pennsylvania, and the license of the pilot of the latter boat revoked, he being found seriously in fault. Loss, twelve thousand (12,000) dollars.

September 9, 1865.—The steamers George Alvree and River Queen were burnt while lying at the wharf at Pittsburg, Pennsylvania. Loss, thirty-six thousand (36,000) dollars. Origin of the fire unknown.

September 23, 1865.—The little steam-tug Nimrod exploded her boiler while lying at the wharf at Pittsburg, Pennsylvania, causing the death of five (5) of her crew. The case is now being investigated by the local board at Pittsburg, Pennsylvania.

RECAPITULATION.

Three hundred and forty-three (343) steamers inspected. Eighty-six thousand three hundred and fifty-four (86,354) tons. Six hundred and eighty-six (686) pilots licensed. Six hundred and ninety-seven (697) engineers licensed. Eighteen (18) applications for pilots' license have been refused, and ten (10) for engineers. Three (3) pilots' licenses have been revoked or suspended, and three (3) engineers. Two collisions, causing a loss of one life and twelve thousand (12,000) dollars' worth of property. One explosion, causing a loss of five (5) lives and four thousand (4,000) dollars' worth of property. Two steamers sunk; loss, eight thousand (8,000) dollars. Two steamers burned; loss, thirty-six thousand (36,000) dollars. One steamer lost in storm; loss, four thousand (4,000) dollars.

The local inspectors of this district have a great amount of labor to perform, requiring their entire time, owing to the increase of tonnage, particularly since the tug-boats, canal propeller, and ferry-boats came under the law of 1852. They are gentlemen fully qualified for the discharge of their duties, and are untiring in their energies in having the law fully complied with.

JNO. S. DEVENNY,
Supervising Inspector Seventh District.

REPORT FROM THE EIGHTH DISTRICT.

There have been inspected in the eighth district during the year ending September 30, 1865, one hundred and ninety-nine steamers, including all classes, passenger, ferry, and tug-boats. There are still remaining something over twenty uninspected, arising from the fact that for a large part of the year there was virtually no local board at the port of Chicago. The salary was so small—being only five hundred dollars—that no competent person could be found who would accept the office, and consequently so much labor was thrown upon me that some of the boats are not yet inspected; but as I have now a board there, these boats will be early attended to.

A large number of steamers in this district have not yet been measured under the new law, but the aggregate tonnage will probably be about twenty-eight

thousand six hundred tons ; the approximate sum of what will be derived from
certificates of inspection of these steamers will be eight thousand six hundred
dollars.

Three hundred and twenty-four pilots and three hundred and nine engineers
have been licensed during the year. For these licenses there has been collected and paid over to the proper authorities the sum of six thousand three
hundred and thirty dollars, making in all, for certificates of inspection of the
steamers and the licenses of engineers and pilots, somewhere close upon fourteen
thousand five hundred dollars. The salaries of two local inspectors at Detroit
at $800 each, at Chicago $500 each, the supervising inspector at $1,500, makes
$4,100 ; after deducting this, together with the necessary travelling and other
incidental expenses; there will still remain a very handsome sum to the credit
of the government over former years and this year's expenses.

Of these inspections and licenses, the local board of Chicago have inspected
fifty-two steamers of all classes, with an approximate tonnage of six thousand
tons, and licensed fifty-three pilots and eighty engineers.

The local board at Detroit have inspected ninety-one steamers, with a tonnage of eighteen thousand tons, and licensed one hundred and seventy pilots
and one hundred and sixty engineers.

The supervising inspector has inspected fifty-six steamers, with about four
thousand two hundred tons, and has licensed one hundred and one pilots and
sixty-seven engineers.

There has been but one accident to passenger steamers in this district the
past year in which the lives of any passengers have been lost; this was in the
propeller Pewabic, on Lake Huron. There have been four explosions of tug-
boats and one propeller, with a loss of ten of the officers and crew ; two steamers
have been totally destroyed by fire while lying at their docks; five or six have
been on fire, but not seriously injured ; two have been sunk, but on these no
lives have been lost. There have been a few collisions, but of no serious moment, and are not reported.

The first accident that occurred after the report of the last annual meeting
was in the explosion of the propeller Tonawanda, in the Chicago river, on the
24th of October, in which three persons were lost—the second engineer, who
was on duty, a fireman, and another person. A very careful investigation into
the causes of the explosion was made by the local board at Chicago, and reported to be from want of sufficient water in the boiler; this was attributed
partially to an improper arrangement of the pipes and valves leading the water
from the forcing pump to the boiler, and also to carelessness or negligence of the
engineer in charge. Believing it to be important that the fullest explanation of
the causes of all accidents should be given to the public, to enable them to
guard against similar ones in future, I shall in my reports be careful to give as
plain explanations as possible. In this instance there were two boilers placed
side by side in the hold of the vessel ; these were supplied with water from one
pump, through a single pipe for a little way, then joining a cross-pipe leading to
either boiler, and through which it is supposed a part of the water will go to
one boiler and a part to the other; upon each branch of this cross-pipe was
placed a regulating valve, under which the water must pass before reaching the
boiler; now, then, the operation would be, if one boiler was receiving more
water than its proportion, the valve would be closed more or less, as the case
may be ; if both valves should be open, and one boiler was fired a little harder
than the other, and even a slight degree of pressure increased in one, which
would always be the case if the steam-pipe should be contracted, the effect
would be to drive the water out of one into the other boiler—one boiler would
be flush, and one scant of water; now, if by a little neglect only one boiler
should be tried, it might be found full, while the other should be empty and already overheated ; then by changing the condition, by firing harder in the other

boiler, or by closing down one of the regulating valves, the water should be driven back and an explosion be the result.

In this instance the boat was only moving from one dock to another to finish up her freight, and it was not deemed necessary to fire but one boiler. The inference of the inspectors was that the engineer thought he had effectually closed the valve leading to the cold boiler, and was deceived, or that he had forgotten it altogether, and that on discovering his mistake, or neglect, he then closed the valve and forced the cold water upon the heated boiler, and that by a sudden generation of steam beyond the safety-valve to discharge, or the boiler to withstand, an explosion followed, and the boat sunk almost immediately. Against the idea of low water, the captain swore that there was so much water that he observed the engine was working water and throwing large quantities out upon the deck. This was explained by the inspectors, that as both boilers were connected by the same steam-pipe to the engine, it was probable enough that one boiler was entirely full, and its water passed over through the engine, as the captain swore.

The inspectors hoped to find, by examining the valves, a verification of their opinion, but they were so much injured that nothing could be determined. Some expected to find the body of the engineer at the valve when the boat was raised, but he was found standing with the starting-bar grasped in his hand. Another defective and reprehensible arrangement was found here: the pipe of the steam-gauge led from the steam-pipe between the throttle-valve and the engine, so that no pressure would be indicated from the boiler while the engines were not running.

It was also found, upon inquiry, that four steamers had been supplied with this arrangement of pipes and valves, and that certainly three of them had exploded in the same manner; and one of them was the ill-fated Globe, that exploded with such terrific violence in Chicago river a few years since, the fragments of which, I believe, this board visited with me soon after.

The local board recommend that no boiler hereafter be passed unless the steam-gauge be open at all times to the pressure in the boiler.

The tug-boat Success exploded her boiler in the Chicago river in May last, by which the engineer and three others lost their lives. The engineer lived to give a full and satisfactory explanation of the cause. He says the water had been getting low for some time from some obstruction to the pump or pipes, but hoping he could find and correct the difficulty before any accident should occur, he ventured to keep running instead of stopping, as he ought, until it was too late; that he knew well enough what the consequences would be if he continued. In the midst of this the bell rang to stop; he then told the captain that his water was low and he dare not stop; but as the captain only wanted to stop to hitch on to a vessel, and it would be but a moment or so, he stopped, and when he started again the explosion came, the boiler leaving the boat and falling into the river some way off. This was a regularly licensed engineer, and was supposed to be competent; but, as it proved, he, like many others, it is feared, had not the ability to say no, though he knew well enough his life was at stake. This boiler has since been taken up, and was found, contrary to the expectation of the board of local inspectors, to have given way down in the lower part of the fire-box, the farthest it could be from the fire, and where, if there had been any water in the boiler, it would have been, and in that part where it would have been overheated it had not given out, and this led the board to doubt the correctness of their former opinion, notwithstanding the statement of the engineer. My attention being called to it, I gave it as careful examination as I could, and found that all the lower part of the boiler near the place which gave way had become much weakened by rust, not being much over one-half of its original thickness, and that this being the weakest part of the boiler, it must of course yield there, without any reference to stronger parts of the boiler, whether weakened by fire or otherwise; and hence it is my opinion that the engineer told the truth, and that the explosion was occasioned from want of a sufficient supply of water until the interior portions had become overheated, and then by some means water was thrown upon the heated plates, and a sudden generation of steam followed, which the safety-valve could not relieve. I am confirmed in this still more by the testimony of the engineer, who stated that he was looking at the steam-gauge, and the hand flew rapidly over as far as it could go, and the explosion followed.

The tug-boat Fanny Stafford exploded her boiler in the Chicago river on the 19th of June. This was the most complete and destructive explosion I have known. Scarcely any vestige of the boat was left. The boiler left the boat, ascending high into the air, passing over a five-story building, across one of the public streets, and down through the roof and two floors, hanging in the third one from the roof; the boiler turned inside out and stripped to pieces in every direction. The engineer and three or four others were lost. The engineer was but a few days before refused a license for incompetency; but, regardless of the law, he still continued to run the boat and the owners to employ him. I had found it out full a week before the accident, and had made the proper complaint for his arrest, and had every day urged the officer to arrest him, but some way it was neglected until too late. By this neglect I have no doubt that three or four lives, and the boat, worth about twelve thousand dollars, were lost.

The tug-boat Fanny White exploded her boiler in Saginaw river, in the State of Michigan, on the 19th of June, by which one or two persons were killed. In this case the boiler had been inspected the year before; but, unknown to the inspectors, it had been materially altered and changed in its construction, and when first fired up it exploded. Supposed cause, imperfect workmanship in putting on the new dome, which blew off.

A collision occurred on the evening of the 9th of August off Thunder bay light, on Lake Huron, between the propellers Meteor and Pewabic, by which the Pewabic was sunk, and thirty-three of her passengers, with seven of the officers and crew, were drowned. This collision, occurring upon a clean, open lake, in a smooth sea, each vessel provided with proper and excellent signal-lights, in full view of each other—and when the lights were first made, if each had kept her proper course, would have passed full a mile away—yet approaching each other and colliding under full steam, at a speed of ten or twelve miles an hour, without ever signalling each other by whistle or otherwise, presents, apparently, a case of most aggravated wrong.

The public very properly called upon the inspectors to give it the most impartial and searching investigation, which was done by the local board of Detroit, and the licenses of Captain George P. McKay and George Cleaveland were revoked for mismanagement, and Mr. Cleaveland arrested and put in prison.

The facts, substantially, are as follows: The two steamers made each other's lights when five or six miles off, and without change of course would have passed full a mile apart; each vessel made the other's green and bright light; the Meteor very properly continued straight forward in her proper course; the Pewabic changes her course a little, but not enough to show her red light, and a little more insensibly crowding up toward the Meteor until within two lengths of her, when she suddenly put her wheel "hard a-port" and showed her red light for the first time, crossing the Meteor's bows; the next instant the collision occurred. On the instant of showing the red light the captain of the Meteor gave one blast of the whistle, that he would go to the right or starboard gang to stop the starboard engine, and put his wheel "hard a-port." The time for all this did not exceed one minute, or perhaps a half. The engineers were both at their posts at the instant the engine stopped, and reversed instantly and without embarrassment; and as soon as it was discovered that the Pewabic was sinking, the life-boats of the Meteor were lowered in good order, and life-preservers thrown over for any who might need them, and, in fact, every-thing was done by the officers and crews of both vessels, after the collision, that coolness and good judgment could do, the Meteor remaining all night in render-ing assistance. The conduct of Captain Wilson and all his officers and crew was highly commended by the board of inspectors, and the course he pursued throughout the whole was approved.

It may be proper to add that these boats were among the very best of their class anywhere, almost new, and supplied with everything required for the safety of passengers—life-preservers, life-boats, fire equipments, pumps, &c. The reason why so many were drowned was that the boat sunk so quick that many were unable to get out of the cabin. Most of those who were taken out of the water had life-preservers on. One or two women were found floating in the water, but dead, showing the efficiency of the preservers—if not in these instances of saving the life, at least floating the body.

Captain McKay, of the Pewabic, whose license had been revoked for mis-management in the case of the collision, appealed to the supervising inspector for a hearing, which was given, and it appearing satisfactorily that he was regularly and properly off watch until within one or two minutes of the collision, and that under the existing circumstances he found a collision inevitable, and that he took the best measures he could to ease off the shock, and save as far as possi-ble his vessel, the decision of the local board was reversed.

The steamer Traveller was burned at the dock in Eagle Harbor, Lake Supe-rior, on the 17th of August. No lives lost. Cause unknown. It was well secured from fire around the boilers.

The steamer J. P. Ward was burned at her dock in Bay City. No lives lost. No cause ascertained. License of the master revoked for not reporting.

The passenger steamer Huron, running from East Saginaw to Goderich, Canada, ran upon a rock at the mouth of Saginaw river, and is a loss, except the engines and boilers, which are being taken out. No lives lost. No report made. License ordered to be revoked for neglect.

The steamer Planet, when within two miles of Mackinaw, about 10 o'clock in the night of the 13th September, was discovered to be on fire in the hold of the vessel and around the boiler. The flames spread so rapidly that the engineer could not reach the pony-engine, which was also in the hold. The pipes conveying the water to the upper decks were put together with soft solder, and were soon melted apart, so as to be entirely useless. The mate immediately got the forward and after pumps at work, throwing water upon the fire where it could be reached. The vessel was stopped on the first alarm, so as not to fan the flames, and a sufficient number of the life-boats were safely lowered into the water, and all the ladies were sent on shore without accident. The engineer, Mr. La Fleur, then turned the steam into the hold, which enabled him to go down far enough with the water hose and direct it upon the flame, until finally it was extinguished. The passengers, in parties, were working with the utmost good will. Mr. La Fleur attributes the saving the vessel mostly to the steam thrown into the hold. He recommends that no pony-engine be placed in the hold, or that the pipe be allowed to be put together with soft solder if it can be avoided.

The steamship Detroit collided with a sail-vessel in the harbor of Milwaukie. No serious injury was done, and no lives lost or persons injured.

The propeller Governor Cusham has been ashore two or three times, and met with some injuries to her machinery; but no lives have been lost, and the in-juries soon repaired.

The boiler of the F. W. Backus, on testing it in the spring, gave way under the hydrostatic test; was ordered to be repaired. When done it stood the test, and she received her certificate.

One license has been refused for writing, or permitting some person to write, upon his license, changing its conditions.

A license was refused to Edward McGlennon by the local board of Detroit, because he was not a citizen of the United States, as required by a resolution of this board. A mandamus was issued by Judge Wilkins, of the United States district court, to the board of inspectors, to appear and show cause why they withheld a license from Edward McGlennon. They appeared in court and pleaded an order by the board of supervising inspectors prohibiting licenses to others than citizens of the United States. After a hearing of the case the judge ordered them to issue immediately the license, as requested by the said McGlennon, with which, I believe, the local board intended to comply; but by some accident McGlennon was drowned immediately after, and before any license was issued.

The propeller Dean Richmond collided with the propeller Illinois, which was reported to the local board at Detroit, and was by them referred to the inspectors at Buffalo.

The propeller Meteor, after the collision with the Pewabic, proceeded on her way to Lake Superior; when arriving at Sault St. Marie, twenty-four hours afterward, she was found to be on fire in the forward hold. Her fire-pumps were immediately set at work to extinguish the flames; but it was found impossible to do so. The hatchways were all fastened down to keep the flames from bursting out, but of no avail, and in order to save the vessel she had to be scuttled and sunk. The local board at Detroit were directed to investigate the case, but were unable to ascertain the cause. They report that she had fifty barrels of unslacked lime in her hold, but the captain, mate and engineer all swear that there was no water near the lime; but I am firmly impressed in the belief that the lime was the true cause, and that some water unknown to them did reach the lime. I recommend that no lime be allowed to be carried in the hold of any steamer hereafter.

The propeller Stockman took fire at her dock and burned to the water's edge—a total loss.

The tug-boat Emerald took fire but was extinguished. Two other tug-boats have been on fire. The frequency of these fires has led some to believe that there is an organized band of boat-burners, but no evidence of it has been adduced. Several of the steamboat owners are keeping extra watchmen on this account.

ALFRED GUTHRIE.

NINTH SUPERVISING DISTRICT.

One hundred and seventy-four steam vessels, of all classes, have been inspected by the supervising and local inspectors of this district during the year ending September 30, 1865, having an aggregate of sixty-nine thousand two hundred and ninety-two tons burden; and showing an increase of inspections in this district for the time above named over the previous year of sixty-four steamers, with an increase of thirteen thousand two hundred and forty-eight tons. In making the above-named inspections, two boilers gave way at Buffalo, New York, under the hydrostatic test; one by the breaking of stay-bolts, and the other by the rupturing of two of the boiler plates in the side of the furnace of same. Both of the above boilers were new, and after being repaired stood the pressure required. One boiler at Cleveland, Ohio, also gave

15 F

way under the hydrostatic test, collapsing one of the main flues of the boiler, which after being repaired by a new flue, the boiler stood the required test; and one boiler also gave way under the hydrostatic test at Burlington, Vermont, which, after repairing same, stood the required pressure.

Three hundred and twenty-eight certificates of license to pilots have been issued by the supervising and local inspectors of this district during the year ending as above, seventy-three of which number were first issues, and two hundred and fifty-five were renewals.

Two hundred and seventy-eight certificates of license to engineers have also been issued as above and during the time named, of which number seventy-one were first issues, and two hundred and seven were renewals.

The licenses of two pilots, issued by the local board at Buffalo, New York, have been suspended by said board for cause; and that of one other pilot, licensed at Cleveland, has been revoked by the board at that port for like reasons.

The local inspectors at Burlington, Vermont, report that no accidents have occurred to any of the steam vessels belonging to their district or inspected by them, nor has any loss of life or injury to person occurred on board the same during the past year.

The local inspectors at Oswego, New York, report that no accidents have occurred during the year to any of the steam vessels belonging to their district or inspected by them, nor has loss of life or injury to persons occurred upon any of said steamers. The said local board also report that complaints have been made to them by masters and pilots of passenger steamers navigating Lake Ontario and the river St. Lawrence of the neglect on the part of British sail vessels, tugs, and towing-boats, to carry the signal lights at night required by the act of Congress of April 29, 1865, "fixing rules and regulations for preventing collisions on the water;" which system is identical with the English laws governing British vessels, and the non-observance of which on the part of British subjects greatly endangered life upon the said waters.

The local inspectors at Buffalo report the investigation of the collision of the steamers Dean Richmond and Illinois, which occurred on Lake Erie, near Point aux Pelee, on the night of June 28, 1865, by which the Illinois was sunk. No lives were lost. The estimated value of vessel and cargo lost, after saving a portion of the cargo, machinery, &c., is forty-five thousand dollars.

The local inspectors at Cleveland, Ohio, report four disasters that have occurred to steam vessels belonging to their district during the year ending September 30, 1865, to wit: The steam-tug Winslow, temporarily employed in the revenue service, and under command of United States revenue officers, in attempting to enter the harbor of Cleveland during a gale, in November, 1864, struck on the outer bar, thereby disabling her screw propeller and carrying away her rudder, and the vessel being unmanageable drifted against the piers and went to pieces. By this disaster six of the crew of the Winslow were drowned. The propeller Prairie State took fire while lying at the wharf at Oswego, New York, on the 21st day of June, 1865. By this accident the vessel was damaged six thousand dollars, and the cargo to the amount of four thousand five hundred and fifty dollars. The propeller City of New York, while lying at the wharf at Milwaukie, Wisconsin, took fire, by which the vessel was damaged two thousand dollars; the damage to cargo not yet ascertained. The propeller Buckeye, bound from Ogdensburg to Toledo, struck a rock near Brockville, Canada West, on the river St. Lawrence, on the 24th of September, 1865, and sunk in seventy feet of water. By this disaster three lives of passengers were lost. The cause of the disaster has not yet been investigated.

The total number of passengers carried by steamers belonging to this district, as near as the same can be ascertained, is as follows:

In the Burlington district...	95,300
In the Oswego district..	34,521
In the Buffalo district, estimated....................................	50,119
In the Cleveland district. estimated.................................	75,000
Ferry-boats upon rivers..	20,000
	274,940

The several local boards of this district report a cheerful willingness on the part of masters and owners of steam-vessels belonging to their respective districts to comply with all the requirements of the inspection laws, and they most respectfully ask that the supervising board will take such action, by its rules and regulations for the guidance of inspectors in their official duty, as will prevent the interference on the part of one local board with the official acts of another, so that harmonious action may generally exist in such boards.

The local inspectors of this district desire to renew their petition of last year that the supervising board will take into consideration the subject-matter of the large increase of labor imposed upon them by recent acts of Congress without a corresponding compensation therefor; and they request that, in view of the corresponding increase of revenue derived by the government from such increase of labor, the supervising board will recommend the passage of an act by Congress that shall equalize the salaries of said inspectors in proportion to the labor performed by them.

A. S. REMIS,
Supervising Inspector Ninth District.

TENTH SUPERVISING DISTRICT.

There have been sixty-five steamers inspected in this district, amounting in tonnage to twelve thousand nine hundred and thirty-seven tons. There have also been licenses granted to two hundred and sixty-one pilots; also to engineers, two hundred and thirty-seven; making a total of four hundred and ninety-eight. This only includes eight months, ending August 30, 1865.

This district has only been under control of the local board since January 1, 1865, and as no supervisor has yet visited it, much information in regard to it is lost.

The following is a list of accidents reported by local board:

Steamboat Gertrude upset, from being too top-heavy; about six lives lost.

Steamboat Bella Donna was run into by the steamer Continental, both boats going up stream at the time. J. Woodard, first engineer of the Bella Donna, lost his life by being knocked overboard. The pilot of the Continental was grossly negligent, and from evidence given we are of the opinion that he ran into the Bella Donna intentionally. His name is H. E. Bixly. We suspended his license for six months. The damage to the Bella Donna was nothing serious.

The steamer Joseph Pierce, a regular liner from here to Vicksburg, and a new boat almost, exploded one of her boilers while lying at a landing a few miles below Vicksburg. There were about twelve or fifteen persons killed and wounded by this disaster. The evidence showed that the second engineer, on watch at the time, J. N. C. Richardson, was to blame, and his license was revoked. The boat took fire and burned, being a total loss.

Steamer Kentucky, a very old boat, sunk in Red river. There were about fifty persons lost, mostly colored troops. No one to blame, as the vessel was leaking to an alarming extent when she left Shreveport, but military necessity said she should go.

Steamers E. F. Dix, Emma, Iowa, and Bella Donna sunk also in Red river, owing to numerous obstructions and wrecks, making navigation very perilous.

Steamer Lelia was totally destroyed by fire in Red river.

Steamer Saratoga was sunk, but was raised, and is now running.

The small steamer Carlotta was sunk opposite this city by coming in collision with the New York steamship Matanza, the great weight of the latter vessel causing the Carlotta to sink to the roof in a few minutes; no lives lost.

The steamship Reindeer exploded her boiler, while on her way to this city from Mobile, by which some six or eight lives were lost. The case will be investigated by the Mobile board.

J. V. GUTHRIE,
Supervising Inspector Sixth District.

Hon. HUGH McCULLOCH,
Secretary of the Treasury.

REPORT OF THE DIRECTOR OF THE MINT.

MINT OF THE UNITED STATES,
Philadelphia, September 29, 1865.

SIR: I have the honor to present the following report of the operations of the mint and its branches for the fiscal year ending June 30, 1865.—The deposits and coinage of the fiscal year just closed exhibit a very satisfactory increase over those of the previous year.

The amount of bullion in value received at the mint and branches during the fiscal year was as follows. Gold, $31,065,349 74; silver, $1,183,405 23; total deposits, $32,248,754 97. From this sum a deduction must be made for re-deposits or bars made at one branch of the mint and deposited at another for coinage. Making this reduction, the amount will be $27,982,849 09.

The coinage for the same period was as follows: Gold coin, $25,107,217 50; unparted and fine gold bars, $5,578,482 45; silver coin, $636,308; silver bars, $313,910 69; cents coined, including the two and three cent pieces, bronze and nickel, $1,183,330; total coinage, $32,819,248 64. Number of pieces of all denominations coined, 87,323,851.

The distribution of the bullion received at the mint and branches was as follows: At Philadelphia, gold deposited, $6,465,212 17; gold coined, $6,436,377 50; fine gold bars, $65,310 24; silver deposits and purchases, $315,943 99; silver coined, $307,508; silver bars, $3,671 66; cents coined, one, two and three-cent pieces, $1,183,330; total deposits of gold and silver, $6,781,156 16; total coinage, $8,016,197 40. Number of pieces, 85,548,735.

At the branch mint, San Francisco, the gold deposits were, $18,808,318 49; gold coined, $18,670,840; silver deposits and purchases, $540,299 20; silver coined, $328,800; silver bars, $145,235 58; total coinage of gold and silver, $19,144,875 58. Number of pieces, 1,775,116.

The assay office in New York received during the year in gold bullion, $5,250,260 04; in silver, $320,111 23; number of fine gold bars stamped at that office, 2,175; value, $4,947,809 21; silver bars, 1,859; value, $165,003 45; total value of gold and silver bullion, $5,570,371 27.

Branch mint at Denver, gold deposits, $541,559 04; silver, $7,050 81; total deposits, $548,609 85. Number of stamped bars, 469; value, $545,363. The report of the superintendent of this branch represents its operations during the year as successful and encouraging. It is engaged in melting, refining, assaying and stamping gold bullion, returning the same to the depositor in the form of unparted bars, bearing the government stamp of weight and fineness.

In my last annual report in reference to this branch mint I remarked that "the efficiency and usefulness of this branch would be greatly increased if a safe and expeditious mode of transportation could be secured. An overland route of six hundred miles is a formidable obstacle in the way of commercial intercourse with our eastern cities and markets. In addition, the hostility of the Indian tribes along the route, doubtless instigated by rebel emissaries and bad white men, has increased the difficulty and dangers of inter-communication, and the transportation of bullion to the Atlantic markets. These difficulties will probably be obviated in due time, and that institution will then assume her proper position as a branch mint.

Efforts have been made to introduce a system of purchases and exchanges, by which the government will assume the risk of transporting bullion from Denver to places where it may be needed for coinage or purchase. The government, by purchasing the bullion at Denver, and paying therefor by draft in specie on the treasurers in the Atlantic States, would relieve the owners of all responsibility, and enable them to convert their bullion into eastern funds with but little expense. The act of Congress establishing a branch mint at Denver provides that "the superintendent of said branch mint at Denver be authorized, under the direction of the Secretary of the Treasury, and on terms to be prescribed by him, to issue, in payment of the gold-dust and bullion deposited for assay and coinage, or bars, drafts or certificates of deposit, payable at the treasury, or any sub-treasury of the United States, to any depositor electing to receive payment in that form."

This provision embodies the true policy of the government in relation to the deposits of bullion in branch mints or assaying offices distant from our great commercial centres. Its accomplishment would not only benefit the hardy miner and the gold regions of Colorado, but also the general commercial interests of the country and government. Renewed efforts ought to be made to introduce this system, and when the difficulties now in the way are removed, and the overland stage route to Denver is in full and successful operation, satisfactory arrangements can be made with that company and others, by which the bullion purchased by the government will be safely brought to the eastern cities and depositories.

The superintendent at Denver constantly urges the necessity for a prompt introduction of the system of purchase and exchange, as contemplated in the act of Congress, to which reference has been made; and, concurring in the necessity for such action, I most respectfully ask the early and favorable consideration of this subject by your department.

Under the efficient management of the superintendent of the branch mint at San Francisco, its operations have been well and successfully performed. The coinage of the past year has been very large. The monthly deposits of bullion are increasing, and it is confidently predicted that the yield of the mines for the current year will largely exceed that of any former period. The past has been a success; the future is full of encouragement.

In this connexion it is gratifying to know that Congress, fully appreciating the magnitude and importance of the mineral wealth of the Pacific States, has made an appropriation for the erection of a new mint-building at San Francisco. The present building is not only unsafe, but wholly inadequate for the increasing business of that branch mint. The new structure should be, in architecture, capacity, machinery, and every particular, adapted to the present and future of California and the Pacific States.

BRANCH MINTS.

The suppression of the rebellion and the anticipated early return of the recusant States to their allegiance present the question, What shall be done with the branch mints at New Orleans, Louisiana; Charlotte, North Carolina; and Dahlonega, Georgia? In my annual report of 1862 it was suggested that the branch mint at New Orleans, after the re-establishment of law and order in

Louisiana, might be successfully operated, and that the branch mints at Charlotte and Dahlonega ought not to be employed again for minting purposes. My opinions on this subject are unchanged. The commercial importance of New Orleans, and the relations of that city to every portion of our country, justified the establishment there of a branch mint; and the amount coined in that institution from its organization, in 1838, to January, 1861, confirmed the propriety of its location at that place. During the period of its active operations, the total coinage was over seventy millions of dollars, as follows: $40,381,615 in gold, and $29,890,037 in silver. The deposits of silver at this branch have always been large; and it is worthy of consideration whether the coinage there should not, for the present, at least, be confined to silver.

The same reasons for re-opening the branches at Charlotte and Dahlonega do not exist. They are away from the commercial centres, inland, and of little commercial importance in themselves. The existence of gold mines in their respective localities may be a reason for re-opening them as assay offices, but not for minting purposes. The results of their operations from their commencement, in 1838, to February, 1861, do not sustain the policy of their original establishment. The coinage of both these branches is limited, by act of Congress, to gold. At Charlotte the total coinage during the twenty-three years of the existence of this branch was only $5,048,641 50; and at Dahlonega for the same period, $6,121,919; an average annual coinage of about $250,000; declining at Dahlonega, from 1857 to 1861, to an annual coinage of about $70,000; and at Charlotte, for the same period, of less than $150,000. These facts seem to be conclusive on the question of re-opening these branches for minting purposes, and particularly when there is no great probability of a large increase in the gold production of those localities.

To meet every commercial want of those places, and also the interests of the miners of gold, the re-opening of these branches for melting, refining, assaying, and stamping gold bullion would be amply sufficient; giving to the superintendent or treasurer of each branch authority to issue, in payment for gold-dust, bullion, or bars deposited for assay, drafts or certificates of deposit, payable in specie at the treasury, or any sub-treasury of the United States, to any depositor electing to receive payment in that form. This provision would wholly supersede the necessity of coining at these branches, or any imaginary benefits resulting therefrom.

The able and interesting report of Professor James C. Booth, appointed, at the suggestion of your department, to examine the condition, &c., of these branch mints, and which has been submitted to you, confirms the views now expressed.

On the subject of assay offices for our gold-mining regions, and the impolicy of multiplying branch mints, my sentiments were fully expressed in my last annual report, to which you are respectfully referred.

GOLD-MINING REGIONS.

The reports from the gold and silver mining portions of the United States are of the most encouraging character. The developments of the past year prove the supply of those minerals to be inexhaustible. With the restoration of the peace and unity of our country and the suppression of the Indian hostilities the production of the precious metals will be greatly increased. The recent discoveries of rich gold deposits have stimulated emigration; capital is hourly seeking investment; the energy of our people has been aroused, and every indication, individual and national, foretells a successful future to this most interesting portion of the United States.

It is not easy to obtain any other reliable statistics than those officially appended to the reports of the director of the mint, but these do not assume to give the amount of the entire production of the precious metals. The shipments to other countries must be large. For example, we are vaguely assured that the silver mines of Nevada average a shipment of one ton daily, which would equal twelve millions of dollars annually. If so, we see but little of this; a small part goes into California circulation, and a large part to China, where it makes one purchase and does no further good to the world, being practically withdrawn from circulation.

We have frequent opportunities for conversation with persons who travel or reside in the various mining regions of the United States and of contiguous provinces, and it is interesting to hear their accounts of the vast developments of wealth and prospects of profitable industry.

Thousands of square miles, made up of snowy mountains, deep cañons, and sterile plains, long supposed to be worthless, and really so for agricultural purposes, are now found to compete in value with the rich garden lands of the cultivated east. Where food cannot be produced, ores and minerals may be dug up to pay for it; if the search disappoints some, it rewards others; and the whole land, tied together politically and socially, feels, or will feel, the beneficent effects of these grand discoveries.

Yet it will be well to guard against exaggeration. It must be remembered that it is not enough to find gold and silver even in considerable quantities; there must be conveniences for living, for mining, and extracting; especially there must be a good supply of wood and water. So important is this, miners tell us that where ore prospects, say, two hundred dollars to the ton, while wood and water can scarcely be had, the mine is really of no value, or of less value than an ore of twenty dollars to the ton, with these adjuvants at hand. On this account, it is said, the silver mines of the famous Humboldt region are, at present, of little practical value. Some of the mining regions will be benefited by the approach of railroad facilities; others, perhaps, must remain forever shut out from the line of profitable labor. But we will not limit the energy or enterprize of the American people.

It is also interesting to observe the incessant efforts to improve the methods of extraction. It is one thing to find where the metals lie, another to bring them to the surface, and still another to get out a paying result, and not leave too large a share lying inextricably in the heap of tailings. Great progress has been made in mining economy within the last fifteen years, judging from the repeated assurance that an ore of gold or silver yielding only fifteen or twenty dollars to the ton, in a good locality, is worth working. In fact, the poor ores are deemed more desirable, all things considered, than the rich ores, which are apt to prove mere pockets.

The advance of the mining art will give new life to our mines at the east and south, where the advantages are so great. Indeed, an experienced capitalist in mines from Nevada, on hearing our report upon a sample of gold ore from a new mine not far from the seat of government, declared "he would rather work it than his mines in the west."

We have also an interesting statement, and one particularly so at this juncture of our national affairs, from a proprietor in the gold region of North Carolina, that "the system of paid labor is likely to show its just and natural effects in the increased return of gold."

There is a published statement that gold mining has been actively recommenced in several counties of Virginia on both sides of the James river, west of Richmond, and with encouraging success. Gold has also recently been found in Maryland, at various points, near the Potomac and Susquehanna. As regards the mines further south, the report of Prof. Booth furnishes the latest and best information.

Outside of our lines, in Canada and Nova Scotia, there are gold workings, and prospects of a most important and satisfactory character. Occasional deposits from those localities are made here and in New York.

With resources illimitable, the precious metals inexhaustible, and our fields rich in the affluance of an abundant production—with a population energetic and enterprising, bold and brave, our country's future is not problematical. National repudiation, even in the presence of a national debt numbered by hundreds of millions, will find no place in the patriotic thought of a reunited and grateful people; and national bankruptcy will only be named in the whisperings of cowardice or the suggestions of treason.

BRONZE AND NICKEL COINAGE.

The coinage of the cent and two-cent piece from the bronze alloy has been very large, but not in excess of the demand. They have been distributed to almost every part of the United States, and many into States, west and south, that heretofore refused to use such coin as currency. The total amount issued during the year will be found in the tables annexed to this report.

As required by law, this bronze and nickel alloy has been regularly assayed and reported by the assayer of the mint, and the legal proportion of the constituent metals found to have been steadily maintained.

By the act of Congress passed March 3, 1865, authority was given to coin a three-cent piece of nickel and copper alloy as a substitute, to some extent, for the fractional paper currency. This coin has been issued and put in circulation. It is neat in appearance, convenient in size, and will become a popular coin. If, in addition to the already prohibited issue of three-cent notes, the five-cent notes of the fractional paper currency were withdrawn, or the circulation limited and gradually reduced, the demand for this new coin would be much increased. Its increased production and circulation would not only furnish a more desirable currency than paper, but would become a source of large revenue to the government. From the profits of the bronze and nickel coinage we have transferred to the treasury of the United States, during the fiscal year just closed, four hundred thousand dollars, ($400,000,) and a few weeks after the expiration of the year the further sum of one hundred thousand dollars ($100,000) was in like manner transferred; the fund remaining being sufficient for all the purposes of this coinage.

From this same nickel alloy a coin of the denomination of five cents, and which would be a popular substitute for the five-cent note, could easily be made. This suggestion, however, is respectfully submitted, in view of the probable withdrawal of the smaller denominations of the fractional paper currency, and as preparative and aid to its accomplishment. This to continue only until the resumption of specie payments, or for a fixed and limited period. In a country abounding in the precious metals, and with silver generally in excess of all demands for coinage, or other purposes, in time of peace, "tokens," or coins of inferior alloy, should not be permitted to take the place permanently of silver in the coinage of pieces above the denomination of three cents.

If the nickel alloy coin of five cents shall be adopted, temporarily or otherwise, provision should be made for its redemption in currency, in sums not less than one hundred dollars, and in manner to suit the convenience of the government, and prevent its becoming troublesome by capricious use. At the proper time similar provision should be made for the redemption of the three-cent piece, in sums not less than sixty dollars. This would secure confidence and circulation for this coin.

MOTTO COINS.

By the fifth section of the act of Congress of March 3, 1865, already referred to, the director of the mint, with the approval of the Secretary of the Treasury, was authorized to place upon all the gold and silver coins of the United States susceptible of such addition, thereafter to be issued, the motto "In God we trust." The direction was at once given to prepare the necessary dies; and it is confidently expected that before the close of the calendar year the gold and silver coins of the mint of the United States will have impressed upon them, by national authority, the distinct and unequivocal recognition of the sovereignty of God, and our nation's trust in Him. We have added to our nation's honor by honoring Him who is "King of kings and Lord of lords."

STATEMENT OF FOREIGN COINS.

The statement of foreign coins required by law to be made annually will be found appended to this report. We have no changes to make in these tables, as no coins differing from those named in the previous report were presented during the year for examination or assay.

The medal department of the mint is in successful operation. A large number of national and other medals have been manufactured during the year. The productions of this department are duly appreciated by the public and approved by the government.

Valuable additions have been made to the cabinet of coins and medals during the year by gift and purchase. It is a place of great resort, and multitudes from every section of our country are daily visitants. The collection of coins is large and valuable. The annual appropriation for the purchase of coins, &c., should be increased. It is now only three hundred dollars.

LIST OF TABLES IN APPENDIX.

A.—Statement of bullion deposited at the mint of the United States and branches during the fiscal year ending June 30, 1865.

B.—Statement of the coinage at the mint of the United States and branches during the fiscal year ending June 30, 1865.

C.—Statement of gold and silver of domestic production deposited at the mint of the United States and branches during the fiscal year ending June 30, 1865.

D.—Coinage of the mint and branches from their organization to the close of the fiscal year ending June 30, 1865.

E.—Gold of domestic production deposited at the mint of the United States and branches, to June 30, 1865.

F.—Statement of the amount of silver coined at the mint of the United States, and branches at San Francisco and New Orleans, under the act of February 21, 1853.

G.—Statement of the amount of silver of domestic production deposited at the mint of the United States and branches, from January, 1841, to June 30, 1865.

H.—Cents of old issue deposited at the United States mint for exchange, for the nickel cent, to April 22, 1864.

I.—Statement of the weight, fineness, and value of foreign gold coin.

J.—Statement of the weight, fineness, and value of foreign silver coin.

Very respectfully, your obedient servant,

JAMES POLLOCK, *Director of the Mint.*

Hon. H. McCulloch,
Secretary of the Treasury, Washington, D. C.

A.—*Statement of deposits at the mint of the United States, the branch mint, San Francisco, assay office, New York, and branch mint at Denver, during the fiscal year ending June 30, 1865.*

Description of bullion.	Mint of the United States.	Branch mint, San Francisco.	Assay office, New York.	Branch mint, Denver.	Total.
GOLD.					
Fine bars	$3,693,237 72				$3,693,237 72
Unparted bars	27,461 26				27,461 26
United States bullion	2,274,530 57	$18,560,100 09	$4,734,388 04	$541,559 04	26,110,577 74
United States coin	53,950 41		2,344 00		56,294 41
Jewellers' bars	246,183 94		223,405 00		469,588 94
Foreign coin	64,865 71		111,097 00		175,962 71
Foreign bullion	104,982 56	248,218 40	179,026 00		532,226 96
Total gold	6,465,212 17	18,808,318 49	5,250,260 04	541,559 04	31,065,349 74
SILVER.					
Bars	180,349 90				180,349 90
United States bullion	45,643 46	500,902 55	68,228 00	7,050 81	621,824 82
United States coin	20,825 62		19,324 00		40,149 62
Jewellers' bars	43,300 61		82,125 00		125,425 61
Foreign coin	22,609 74		136,714 23		159,323 97
Foreign bullion	3,214 66	39,396 65	13,720 00		56,331 31
Total silver	315,943 99	540,299 20	320,111 23		1,183,405 23
Total gold and silver	6,781,156 16	19,348,617 69	5,570,371 27	7,050 81	32,248,754 97
Less re-deposits at different institutions, gold $4,085,555 98, silver 180,349 90					4,265,905 88
Total deposits					27,982,849 09

—*Statement of the coinage at the mint of the United States, the branch mint, San Francisco, assay office, New York, and branch mint at Denver, during the fiscal year ending June 30, 1865.*

Denomination.	Mint of the United States, Philadelphia.		Branch mint, San Francisco.		Assay office, New York.	Branch mint, Denver.	Total.	
	Pieces.	Value.	Pieces.	Value.	Value.	Value.	Pieces.	Value.
GOLD.								
Double eagles	318,820	$6,376,400 00	925,160	$18,503,200 00			$1,243,980	$24,879,600 00
Eagles	675	6,750 00	8,700	87,000 00			9,375	93,750 00
Half eagles	5,215	26,075 00	12,000	60,000 00			17,215	86,075 00
Three dollars	3,355	10,065 00					3,355	10,065 00
Quarter eagles	3,945	9,862 50	8,256	20,640 00			12,201	30,502 50
Dollars	7,225	7,225 00					7,225	7,225 00
Fine bars		85,310 24			$4,947,809 21			5,033,119 45
Departed bars						$545,363 00		545,363 00
Total gold	339,235	6,521,687 74	954,116	18,670,840 00	4,947,809 21	545,363 00	1,293,351	30,685,699 95
SILVER.								
Dollars	32,900	32,900 00					32,900	32,900 00
Half dollars	493,200	246,600 00	613,000	306,500 00			1,106,200	553,100 00
Quarter dollars	88,600	22,150 00	22,000	5,500 00			110,600	27,650 00
Dimes	21,600	2,160 00	150,000	15,000 00			171,600	17,160 00
Half dimes	61,600	3,080 00	36,000	1,800 00			97,600	4,880 00
Three-cent pieces	20,600	618 00					20,600	618 00
Bars		3,671 66		145,235 58	165,003 45			313,910 69
Total silver	715,500	311,179 66	821,000	474,035 58	165,003 45		1,539,500	950,218 69
COPPER.								
Three-cent pieces	3,531,000	105,930 00					3,531,000	105,930 00
Two-cent pieces	26,780,000	535,600 00					26,780,000	535,600 00
Cents	54,180,000	541,800 00					54,180,000	541,800 00
Total copper	84,491,000	1,183,330 00					84,491,000	1,183,330 00
Total coinage	85,545,735	8,016,197 41	1,775,116	19,144,875 58	5,112,812 66	545,363 00	87,323,851	32,819,248 64

C.—*Statement of gold and silver of domestic production deposited at the mint of the United States, branch mint, San Francisco, assay office, New York, and branch mint at Denver, during the fiscal year ending June 30, 1865.*

Description of bullion.	Mint United States, Philadelphia.	Branch mint, San Francisco.	Assay office, New York.	Branch mint, Denver.	Total.
GOLD.					
California	$64,308 07	$11,089,974 52	$2,177,954 04		$13,332,236 63
Idaho	1,400,863 12	3,499,281 14		$71,310 49	4,971,454 75
Montana	453,250 71	3,000 00	1,217,518 00	93,613 01	1,767,381 72
Colorado	308,590 55		938,593 00	375,065 90	1,622,249 45
Oregon	11,491 05	1,103,076 54	9,876 00	1,230 16	1,125,673 75
Washington		22,460 94			22,460 94
Arizona	276 80	20,369 48	707 00	339 48	21,692 76
North Carolina	16,293 25				16,293 25
Georgia	10,450 12		3,422 00		13,872 12
Nevada	576 37	5,400 00			6,925 37
New Mexico			3,924 00		3,924 00
Alabama			2,269 00		2,269 00
Virginia	910 77				910 77
Vermont			316 00		316 00
Refined gold		2,598,601 49			2,598,601 49
Mint bars			364,857 00		364,857 00
Parted from silver	7,519 76	217,935 98	14,003 00		239,458 74
Total gold	2,274,530 57	18,560,100 09	4,734,388 04	541,559 04	26,110,577 74
SILVER.					
Nevada	1,340 50	354,569 92			355,910 42
Lake Superior	9,063 51		4,608 00		13,671 51
California	459 18				459 18
New Mexico	25 84				35 84
Parted from gold	34,754 43	146,332 63	63,620 00	7,050 81	251,757 87
Total silver	45,643 46	500,902 55	68,228 00	7,050 81	621,824 82
Total gold and silver of domestic production	2,320,174 03	19,061,002 64	4,802,616 04	548,609 85	26,732,402 56

D.—*Coinage of the mint and branches from their organization to the close of the fiscal year ending June 30, 1865.*

1. MINT OF THE UNITED STATES, PHILADELPHIA.

Period	GOLD COINAGE							SILVER COINAGE				
	Double eagles.	Eagles.	Half eagles.	Three dolls.	Qr. eagles.	Dollars.	Fine bars. (Value)	Dollars.	Half dollars.	Qr. dollars.	Dimes.	Half dimes.
	Pieces.	*Pieces.*	*Pieces.*	*Pieces.*	*Pieces.*	*Pieces.*	*Value.*	*Pieces.*	*Pieces.*	*Pieces.*	*Pieces.*	*Pieces.*
to 1817		132,592	845,909		29,197			1,439,517	13,104,433	650,280	1,007,151	265,543
to 1837			3,087,925		879,903			1,000	74,793,560	5,041,749	11,854,949	14,463,700
to 1847		1,227,759	3,289,921		345,526			879,873	20,203,333	4,932,073	11,387,995	11,093,235
to 1857	8,132,506	1,970,597	2,280,390	223,015	5,544,900	15,348,608	$33,612,140 46	350,250	10,691,086	41,073,080	35,172,010	34,368,520
	468,504	13,690	19,724	32,633	13,059	113,097	31,088 10	315,530	4,098,000	10,600,000	690,000	4,000,000
	98,126	8,600	20,718	11,524	76,562	206,794	40,298 59	164,000	2,636,000	4,996,000	1,760,000	2,840,000
	188,613	16,013	19,794	13,402	13,731	231,873	170,273 34		349,800	909,800	576,000	870,000
	2,341,921	44,005	56,526	6,079	191,376	78,743	66,434 76	1,750	741,300	3,034,200	1,573,000	2,787,000
	1,022,373	79,299	630,432	5,785		1,709,250	49,421 61	31,400	2,391,300	2,803,750	1,364,550	2,392,550
	150,963	3,658	6,902	39	20,990	1,950	136,030 74	23,170	425,200	412,860	49,460	64,460
	125,962	3,580	300	5,490	474	6,750	307,322 07		319,970	99,970	370	370
	318,820	675	5,216	3,355	3,945	7,295	85,310 24	32,900	490,200	88,600	21,600	61,600
Total	12,869,882	3,500,468	10,245,595	281,741	8,305,940	17,597,067	34,517,318 91	3,313,790	130,177,294	74,632,362	85,437,058	73,160,978

Period	SILVER COINAGE		COPPER COINAGE				TOTAL COINAGE				
	Three cents.	Bars.	Three cents.	Two cents.	Cents.	Half cents.	No. of pieces.	Gold.	Silver.	Copper.	Total value.
	Pieces.	*Value.*	*Pieces.*	*Pieces.*	*Pieces.*	*Pieces.*		*Value.*	*Value.*	*Value.*	
to 1817					29,316,272	5,235,513	52,010,407	$5,610,957 50	$8,266,295 75	$319,340 28	$14,188,563 53
to 1837					46,554,830	2,205,920	158,889,816	17,638,382 50	40,566,897 15	476,574 30	58,682,853 95
to 1847					34,967,663		88,327,378	29,491,010 00	13,913,019 00	349,676 63	43,753,705 63
to 1857	37,778,900	$32,355 55			51,449,979	544,510	244,898,373	256,950,474 46	22,365,413 55	517,222 34	279,833,110 35
	1,266,000	843 37			23,400,000		44,833,707	10,221,676 60	4,671,823 37	234,000 00	15,427,699 97
	1,380,000	9,341 08			30,700,000		44,839,973	2,660,646 59	3,009,241 08	307,000 00	5,976,887 67
	548,000	21,656 30			34,200,000		38,099,346	4,334,576 84	857,076 30	342,000 00	5,553,653 14
	265,000	2,624 37			10,166,000		21,315,255	47,963,145 76	1,601,324 37	101,660 00	49,666,130 13
	606,550	1,797 79			11,600,000		25,951,899	30,036,808 11	2,172,499 29	116,000 00	32,325,307 40
	93,480	5,897 83			47,945,000		49,108,402	3,340,941 74	365,115 53	478,450 00	4,184,507 37
	370	7,655 23	3,531,000	1,822,500	42,735,000		43,114,276	2,898,267 07	208,369 31	463,800 00	3,560,436 40
	20,600	3,671 66		26,780,000	54,180,000		85,546,735	5,521,687 74	311,179 95	1,183,330 00	6,016,197 69
Total	41,960,880	86,843 18	3,531,000	29,602,500	417,114,744	7,985,223	898,932,569	417,679,774 91	98,610,254 48	4,869,053 55	521,179,082 94

2. BRANCH MINT, SAN FRANCISCO.

Period.	GOLD COINAGE.							
	Double eagles.	Eagles.	Half eagles.	Three dollars.	Quarter eagles.	Dollars.	Unparted bars.	Fine bars.
	Pieces.	*Pieces.*	*Pieces.*	*Pieces.*	*Pieces.*	*Pieces.*	*Value.*	*Value.*
1854	141,468	123,826	268	....	246	14,632	$5,641,504 05	$5,863 16
1855	859,175	9,000	61,000	6,600	....	....	3,270,594 93	88,782 50
1856	1,161,750	73,500	94,100	34,800	71,120	94,600	3,047,801 29	122,136 55
1857	604,500	10,000	47,000	5,000	20,000	....	....	....
1858	685,640	27,800	58,600	9,000	49,200	20,000	816,295 65	....
1859	689,140	2,000	9,720	....	8,000	15,000	....	19,871 68
1860	579,957	10,000	16,700	7,000	26,800	13,000	....	....
1861	614,300	6,000	8,000	....	14,000	....	....	....
1862	760,000	18,000	18,000	....	30,000	....	....	....
1863	866,423	9,000	16,500	....	4,000	....	....	....
1864	947,920	5,000	10,000	....	6,800	....	....	....
1865	925,160	8,700	12,000	....	6,256	....	....	....
Total	9,055,151	302,826	351,828	62,100	242,422	87,232	12,775,395 92	236,653 89

Period.	SILVER COINAGE.						TOTAL COINAGE.			
	Dollars.	Half dollars.	Quarter dollars.	Dimes.	Half dimes.	Bars.	No. of pieces.	Gold.	Silver.	Total value.
	Pieces.	*Pieces.*	*Pieces.*	*Pieces.*	*Pieces.*	*Value.*		*Value.*	*Value.*	

D.—*Coinage of the mint and branches, &c.*—Continued.

3. BRANCH MINT, NEW ORLEANS.

Period.	GOLD COINAGE.						SILVER COINAGE.		
	Double eagles.	Eagles.	Half eagles.	Three dollars.	Quarter eagles.	Dollars.	Dollars.	Half dollars.	Quarter dollars.
	Pieces.	*Pieces.*	*Pieces.*	*Pieces.*	*Pieces.*	*Pieces.*	*Pieces.*	*Pieces.*	*Pieces.*
o 1847	.....	1,095,342	709,925	.....	550,328	.....	59,000	13,509,000	3,273,600
o 1857	730,500	534,250	108,150	24,000	546,100	1,004,000	40,000	21,406,000	4,556,000
	47,500	21,500	13,000	.....	34,000	.....	.....	4,614,000	1,416,000
	24,500	4,000	.....	.....	.....	.....	200,000	4,912,000	544,000
	4,350	8,200	.....	.....	.....	.....	*280,000	2,212,000	328,000
(to January 31)	9,600	5,200	.....	.....	.....	.....	395,000	828,000	.....
Total	816,450	1,509,492	831,025	24,000	1,130,628	1,004,000	974,000	47,481,000	10,177,600

Period.	SILVER COINAGE.				TOTAL COINAGE.			
	Dimes.	Half dimes.	Three cents.	Bars.	No. of pieces.	Gold.	Silver.	Total value.
	Pieces.	*Pieces.*	*Pieces.*	*Value.*		*Value.*	*Value.*	
o 1847	6,473,300	2,789,000	.....	.....	28,390,895	$15,189,365	$8,418,700 00	$23,608,065 00
o 1857	5,690,000	8,170,000	720,000	.....	43,328,950	22,934,250	12,881,100 00	35,815,330 00
	1,540,000	2,540,000	.....	.....	10,226,000	1,315,000	2,942,000 00	4,257,000 00
	440,000	1,050,000	.....	$334,996 47	7,184,500	530,000	3,223,996 47	3,753,996 47
	370,000	1,060,000	.....	25,422 33	4,322,550	169,000	1,598,422 33	1,767,422 33
(to January 31)	.....	.....	.....	16,818 33	1,237,800	244,000	925,818 33	1,069,818 33
Total	14,513,500	15,619,000	720,000	337,237 13	94,890,695	40,381,615	29,890,037 13	70,271,652 13

4. BRANCH MINT, DENVER.

d.....................1864	Unparted gold bars	$486,329 97
d.....................1865	Unparted gold bars	545,363 00
	Total	1,031,692 97

D —*Coinage of the mint and branches, &c.*—Continued.

5. BRANCH MINT, DAHLONEGA.

Period.	GOLD COINAGE.					
	Half eagles.	Three dollars.	Quarter eagles.	Dollars.	Total.	* Total.
	Pieces.	*Pieces.*	*Pieces.*	*Pieces.*	*Pieces.*	*Value.*
1838 to 1847....	576, 553	....	134, 101	....	710, 654	$3, 216, 017 50
1848 to 1857....	478, 392	1, 120	60, 605	60, 607	601, 729	2, 607, 729 50
1858..........	19, 236	....	900	1, 637	21, 793	100, 187 00
1859..........	11, 404	....	642	6, 957	19, 003	65, 582 00
1860..........	12, 800	....	1, 602	1, 472	15, 874	69, 477 00
1861, (to Feb. 28).	11, 876	....	....	1, 366	60, 946 00	60, 946 00
Total.	1, 110, 261	1, 120	197, 850	....	1, 381, 780	6, 121, 919 00

6. BRANCH MINT, CHARLOTTE.

Period.	GOLD COINAGE.				
	Half eagles.	Quarter eagles.	Dollars.	Total.	Total.
	Pieces.	*Pieces.*	*Pieces.*	*Pieces.*	*Value.*
1838 to 1847....	269, 424	123, 576	....	393, 000	$1, 656, 060 00
1848 to 1857+...	500, 872	79, 736	103, 899	684, 507	2, 807, 599 00
1858..........	31, 066	9, 056	....	40, 122	177, 970 00
1859..........	39, 500	....	5, 235	44, 735	202, 735 00
1860..........	23, 005	7, 459	....	30, 474	133, 697 50
1861, (to Mar. 31).	14, 116	....	....	14, 116	70, 580 00
Total......	877, 983	219, 837	109, 134	1, 206, 954	5, 048, 641 50

7. ASSAY OFFICE, NEW YORK.

Period,	Fine gold bars.	Fine silver bars.	Total.
	Value.	*Value.*	*Value.*
1854........	$2, 858, 059 18	....	$2, 858, 059 18
1855........	20, 441, 813 63	....	20, 441, 813 63
1856........	19, 396, 046 89	$6, 786 63	19, 402, 832 32
1857........	9, 335, 414 00	123, 317 00	9, 458, 731 00
1858........	21, 798, 991 04	171, 961 79	21, 970, 652 83
1859........	13, 044, 718 43	272, 424 05	13, 317, 142 48
1860........	6, 831, 532 01	222, 226 11	7, 053, 758 12
1861........	19, 948, 728 88	187, 078 63	20, 135, 807 51
1862........	16, 094, 768 44	415, 603 57	16, 510, 372 01
1863........	1, 783, 838 16	158, 542 91	1, 932, 381 07
1864........	1, 539, 751 27	173, 308 64	1, 713, 059 91
1865........	4, 947, 809 21	105, 003 45	5, 112, 812 66
Total	138, 061, 171 14	1, 896, 258 78	139, 957, 429 92

8. SUMMARY EXHIBIT OF THE COINAGE OF THE MINT AND BRANCHES TO THE CLOSE OF THE FISCAL YEAR ENDING JUNE 30, 1865.

Mints.	Commencem't of coinage.	Gold coinage.	Silver coinage.	Copper coinage.	Entire coinage.	
		Value.	*Value.*	*Value.*	*Pieces.*	*Value.*
Philadelphia	1793	$417, 679, 774 91	$96, 610, 254 48	$4, 889, 053 55	898, 939, 569	$521, 179, 082 94
San Francisco	1854	199, 762, 356 81	4, 358, 615 98	....	18, 776, 219	204, 140, 972 80
New Orleans, (to Jan. 31, '61)	1838	40, 361, 615 00	29, 890, 037 13	....	94, 890, 695	70, 271, 652 13
Charlotte, (to March 31, '61)	1838	5, 048, 641 50	....	....	1, 206, 954	5, 048, 641 50
Dahlonega, (to Feb. 28, '61)	1838	6, 121, 919 00	....	....	1, 381, 780	6, 121, 919 00
Assay Office, New York ...	1854	138, 061, 171 14	1, 896, 258 78	....	....	139, 957, 429 92
Denver	1863	545, 363 14	....	....	....	545, 363 00
Total.....................		807, 620, 841 36	134, 755, 166 38	4, 889, 053 55	1, 015, 186, 217	947, 265, 061 29

—*Statement of gold of domestic production deposited at the mint of the United States and branches to the close of the year ending June 30, 1865.*

1. MINT OF THE UNITED STATES, PHILADELPHIA.

Period.	Parted from silver.	Virginia.	N. Carolina.	S. Carolina.	Georgia.	Tennessee.	Alabama.	New Mexico.	California.	Montana.
4 to 1827			$110,000 00							
8 to 1837		$427,000 00	2,519,500 00	$327,500 00	$1,763,900 00	$12,400 00	$45,493 00			
8 to 1847		519,294 00	1,303,636 00	152,366 00	566,315 00	16,499 00	9,451 00			
8 to 1857		534,491 50	467,217 00	55,626 00	44,577 50	6,669 00		$46,397 00	1,379,506 07	
8		18,377 00	15,175 00	300 00	18,365 00				999,191 79	
9		15,780 00	9,305 00		4,675 00	20,190 00	240 00		275 00	663,389 02	
0		17,402 62	8,450 11			7,556 41	595 88	92 76	426,807 61	
1	$68,864 66	7,200 29	7,523 80			15,049 41			244,259 81	
2	3,463 69		81 78		..-©..	135 40			109,778 58	
3	7,896 79	69 00	1,178 84			246 66			514 55	91,663 75	
4			6,093 85						64,306 07	$453,250 71
5	7,519 76	910 77	16,293 25			10,450 12				
Total	87,749 90	1,539,465 18	4,464,474 23	540,467 00	2,446,786 50	36,403 88	55,036 76	49,186 53	230,771,426 53	453,250 71

Period.	Oregon.	Colorado.	Arizona.	Washington Territory.	Idaho.	Dakota.	Nevada.	Other sources.	Total.
4 to 1827								$13,900 00	$110,000 00
8 to 1837								21,037 00	5,063,500 00
8 to 1847								7,218 00	2,624,641 00
8 to 1857	$54,285 00								226,067,473 62
8	3,600 00								1,478,323 07
9	2,660 00	$145 00							1,012,701 79
0	2,780 15	346,604 05	$3,048 37					1,402 01	1,048,180 26
1		607,592 08		$315 70				1,507 96	1,068,892 48
2		1,122,333 50							1,435,890 45
3	7,910 78	1,896,329 87	3,869 75	18,552 88	$1,816 97	$2,198 88	$103 68		2,046,050 11
4	14,182 80	835,146 72	114 72	7,347 97	47,782 50		944 74		1,911,184 04
5	11,491 05	308,590 55	275 80		1,400,863 12		576 37		2,374,530 57
Total	97,219 89	5,216,741 77	7,329 64	26,127 55	2,250,462 69	2,198 68	1,624 79	44,364 97	248,090,297 39

E.—*Statement of gold of domestic production, &c.*—Continued.

2. BRANCH MINT, SAN FRANCISCO.

Period.	Parted from silver.	California.	Colorado.	Nevada.	Oregon.	Dakota.	Washington.	Idaho.	Arizona.	Montana.	Refined gold.	Total.
1854		$10,842,981 23										$10,842,981 23
1855		20,860,437 20										20,860,437 20
1856		29,209,218 24										29,209,218 24
1857		12,596,826 93										12,596,826 93
1858		19,104,369 99										19,104,369 99
1859		14,098,564 14										14,098,564 14
1860		11,319,913 83										11,319,913 83
1861		12,206,382 64										12,206,382 64
1862	$822,823 01	14,029,759 95	$680 00	$13,000 00	$893,000 00							15,754,262 96
1863	1,108,456 57	13,045,711 69	59,472 00	11,250 00	3,001,104 00	$5,760 00	$12,672 00					17,244,436 26
1864	220,900 18	14,643,637 52			2,134,365 00			$1,257,497 50				18,481,350 20
1865	217,935 98	11,089,974 52		5,400 00	1,103,016 54		22,460 94	3,499,281 14	$20,369,48	$3,000 00	$2,598,601 49	18,560,100 09
Total	2,370,115 74	183,197,097 88	60,152 00	29,650 00	7,131,485 54	5,760 00	35,132 94	4,856,778 64	20,369,48	3,000 00	2,598,601 49	200,208,143 71

3. BRANCH MINT, NEW ORLEANS.

Period.	North Carolina.	South Carolina.	Georgia.	Tennessee.	Alabama.	California.	Colorado.	Other sources.	Total.
1838 to 1847	$741 00	$14,306 00	$37,364 00	$1,772 00	$61,903 00			$3,613 00	$119,699 00
1848 to 1857		1,911 00	2,317 00	947 00	15,379 00	$21,606,451 54		3,667 00	21,630,692 54
1858			1,560 00	162 12		448,439 84			450,163 96
1859						93,272 41			93,272 41
1860					661 53	97,135 00	$1,770 39		99,566 92
1861, (to January 31)						19,932 10	1,666 81		21,598 91
Total	741 00	16,217 00	41,241 00	2,883 12	77,943 53	22,265,240 89	3,437 20	7,290 00	22,414,993 74

E.—*Statement of gold of domestic production, &c.*—Continued.

4. BRANCH MINT, CHARLOTTE, NORTH CAROLINA.

Period.	North Carolina.	South Carolina.	California.	Total.
8 to 1847	$1,529,777 00	$143,941 00	....	$1,673,718 00
8 to 1857	2,503,412 68	222,754 17	$87,321 61	2,813,487 86
8	170,560 33	5,507 16	....	176,067 49
9	182,489 61	24,762 71	....	205,252 32
0	134,491 17	....	....	134,491 17
1, (to March 31)	....	65,558 30	....	68,558 30
Total	4,520,730 79	460,523 34	87,321 01	5,068,575 14

5. BRANCH MINT, DAHLONEGA.

Period.	Utah.	North Carolina.	South Carolina.	Georgia.	Tennessee.	Alabama.	California.	Colorado.	Other sources.	Total.
8 to 1847	....	$64,351 00	$95,247 00	$2,978,353 00	$32,175 00	$47,711 00	....	....	$951 00	$3,218,017 00
8 to 1857	....	28,278 82	174,811 91	1,159,420 98	9,837 42	11,918 92	$1,124,712 82	....	....	2,609,931 87
8	....	....	32,342 28	57,891 45	107 33	....	5,293 52	....	....	95,614 58
9	....	2,656 88	4,610 35	57,023 12	....	....	699 19	$82 70	....	65,072 24
0	....	3,485 70	2,004 36	35,588 92	....	....	1,097 37	2,490 86	....	67,085 21
1, (to Feb. 28)	$145 14	812 79	2,066 91	22,182 14	....	....	4,213 79	32,772 28	....	62,193 05
Total	145 14	99,585 19	311,242 81	4,310,459 61	42,119 75	59,629 92	1,236,016 69	57,763 84	951 00	6,117,913 95

E.—*Statement of gold of domestic production, &c.*—Continued.

6. ASSAY OFFICE, NEW YORK.

Period.	Parted from silver.	Virginia.	North Carolina.	South Carolina.	Georgia.	Alabama.	New Mexico.	California.	Montana.
1854		$167 00	$3,916 00	$395 00	$1,342 00			$9,221,457 00	
1855		2,370 00	3,736 00	7,690 00	13,100 00			25,026,896 11	
1856		6,928 00	.605 07	4,052 29	41,101 28	$350 00		16,929,009 90	
1857		1,531 00	1,689 00	2,663 00	20,451 00	233 62	1,545 00	9,898,957 00	
1858		501 00	7,007 00	6,354 00	12,951 00	2,181 00		19,660,531 46	
1859		436 00	20,122 00	700 00	14,756 00		593 00	11,694,872 25	
1860		4,202 00	9,755 00		19,368 00			6,023,628 36	
1861		3,869 00	2,753 00	670 00	6,900 00	818 00	$6,714 00	19,227,658 14	
1862	$241,029 00	316 00	2,232 00	2,065 00	1,460 00		1,543 00	12,580,647 83	
1863	34,928 00		130 00				5,580 00	346,244 60	
1864	7,618 00							116,101 06	
1865	14,003 00				3,422 00	2,269 00	3,924 00	2,177,934 04	$1,217,518 00
Total	296,978 00	20,320 00	32,159 07	24,519 29	134,760 28	7,989 62	17,761 00	132,503,956 75	1,217,518 00

Period.	Idaho.	Colorado.	Utah.	Arizona.	Oregon.	Nevada.	Vermont.	Other sources.	Total.
1854									$9,227,177 00
1855								$1,600 00	25,054,086 11
1856									16,982,129 16
1857									9,917,836 00
1858					$5,561 00			27,523 00	19,732,629 46
1859		$3,944 00			2,866 00			405 00	11,738,694 25
1860		249,981 00	$4,680 00	$1,190 00					6,311,804 36
1861		1,449,166 00	73,734 00	16,871 00	3,181 00			3,293 00	20,739,334 14
1862		912,403 00		391 00	205 00	$40,846 00			13,786,439 83
1863		937,535 00		391 00	7,813 00		$298 00		1,332,319 60
1864	$201,288 00	715,208 00		3,775 00	8,650 00	74 00		117,347 00	1,170,061 06
1865		938,593 00		707 00	9,876 00	949 00	316 00	364,857 00	4,734,388 04
Total	201,288 00	5,205,830 00	78,414 00	23,325 00	38,172 00	41,869 00	614 00	315,025 00	140,370,499 01

7. BRANCH MINT, DENVER.

E.—*Statement of gold of domestic production, &c.*—Continued.

SUMMARY EXHIBIT OF THE ENTIRE DEPOSITS OF DOMESTIC GOLD AT THE U. S. MINT AND BRANCHES TO JUNE 30, 1865.

Mint.	Parted from silver.	Virginia.	North Carolina.	South Carolina.	Georgia.	Alabama.	Tennessee.	California.	Colorado.	Utah.
adelphia ...	$87,749 90	$1,539,465 18	$4,464,474 23	$540,467 00	$2,446,786 50	$55,036 76	$36,403 88	$230,771,426 52	$5,216,741 77	
Francisco...	3,370,115 74							183,197,097 88	60,152 00	
Orleans			741 00	16,217 00	41,241 00	77,943 53	2,883 12	22,255,240 89	3,437 20	
rlotte			4,520,730 79	460,523 34				87,321 01		
lonega			99,565 19	311,242 81	4,310,459 61	59,629 92	42,119 75	1,236,016 69	57,763 84	$145 14
ay office	296,978 00	20,320 00	52,159 07	24,519 39	124,760 28	7,989 62		132,503,956 75	5,205,830 00	78,414 00
ver									861,395 87	
Total.......	2,754,843 64	1,559,785 18	9,137,690 28	1,352,969 44	6,923,247 39	200,599 83	81,406 75	570,051,059 74	11,405,320 68	78,559 14

Mint.	Montana.	Arizona.	N. Mexico.	Oregon.	Nevada.	Dacota.	Idaho.	Washing'n	Vermont	Other sources	Total.
adelphia ...	$453,250 71	$7,309 64	$49,186 53	$97,219 89	$1,624 79	$2,198 88	$2,250,462 60	$26,127 55			$44,364 97	$248,090,297 39
Francisco..	3,000 00	20,369 48		7,131,485 54	29,650 00	5,760 00	4,756,778 64	35,132 94		2,598,601 49	200,208,143 71
Orleans...										7,290 00	22,404,993 74
rlotte											5,068,575 14
lonega.....										951 00	6,117,913 95
ay office....	1,217,518 00	23,325 00	17,761 00		72 00	41,869 00		201,288 00		$614 00	515,025 00	140,370,499 01
ver	93,613 01	339 48		30 16				71,310 49			1,027,889 01
Total......	1,767,381 72	51,343 60	66,947 53	7,268,107 59	73,143 79	7,958 88	7,279,839 82	61,260 49	614 00	3,166,232 46	623,288,311 95

F.—*Statement of the amount of silver coined at the mint of the United States, and branches at San Francisco and New Orleans, under the act of February 21, 1853.*

Year.	United States mint, Philadelphia.	Branch mint, San Francisco.	Branch mint, New Orleans, to Jan. 31, '61.	Total.
1853	$7, 806, 461 00	....	$1, 225, 000 00	$9, 031, 461 00
1854	5, 340, 130 00	....	3, 246, 400 00	8, 586, 130 00
1855	1, 393, 170 00	$164, 075 00	1, 918, 000 00	3, 475, 245 00
1856	3, 150, 740 00	177, 000 00	1, 744, 000 00	5, 071, 740 00
1857	1, 332, 000 00	50, 000 00	....	1, 393, 000 00
1858	4, 670, 980 00	127, 750 00	2, 242, 000 00	8, 040, 730 00
1859	2, 926, 400 00	283, 500 00	2, 689, 000 00	5, 898, 900 00
1860	519, 890 00	358, 500 00	1, 291, 000 00	2, 169, 890 00
1861	1, 433, 800 00	198, 000 00	414, 000 00	2, 045, 800 00
1862	2, 168, 941 50	641, 700 00	....	2, 810, 641 50
1863	326, 817 80	815, 875 00	....	1, 142, 692 80
1864	177, 544 10	347, 500 00	....	525, 044 10
1865	278, 279 66	474, 635 58	....	752, 915 24
Total	31, 826, 154 06	3, 636, 535 58	15, 471, 000 00	50, 933, 689 64

G.—*Statement of the amount of silver of domestic production deposited at the mint of the United States and branches from January, 1841, to June 30, 1865.*

Year.	Parted from gold.	Nevada.	Arizona.	Sonora.	North Carolina.	Lake Superior.	California.	New Mexico.	Total.
1841 to 1851	$768, 509 00								$768, 509 00
1852	404, 494 00								404, 494 00
1853	417, 279 00								417, 279 00
1854	328, 199 00								328, 199 00
1855	333, 053 00								333, 053 00
1856	321, 938 38								321, 938 38
1857	127, 236 12								127, 236 12
1858	300, 849 36					$15, 623 00			316, 476 36
1859	219, 647 34				$23, 398 00	30, 122 13			273, 167 47
1860	138, 561 70	$102, 540 77	$13, 357 00	$1, 200 00	12, 257 00	25, 880 58			293, 797 05
1861	364, 724 73	213, 420 84	12, 290 00		6, 233 00	13, 372 72			610, 011 29
1862	245, 122 47	757, 446 60	103 00			21, 366 38	$8, 294 00		1, 032, 264 45
1863	188, 394 94	856, 043 27				13, 111 32			1, 057, 549 33
1864	166, 791 55	311, 837 01		45 00		2, 765 77			487, 439 33
1865	251, 757 87	355, 910 42				13, 671 51	459 18	$25 84	621, 824 82

H.—*Statement of cents of former issue deposited at the United States mint for exchange for cents of new issue, to June 30, 1864.*

	Value by tale.
1857	$16,602
1858	39,404
1859	47,235
1860	37,500
1861	95,245
1862	53,365
1863	6,185
1864	490
Total	296,026

I.—*A statement of foreign gold and silver coins, prepared by the Direc'or of the Mint, to accompany his annual report, in pursuance of the act of February 21, 1857.*

EXPLANATORY REMARKS.

The first column embraces the names of the countries where the coins are issued; the second contains the names of the coin, only the principal denominations being given. The other sizes are proportional; and when this is not the case, the deviation is stated.

The third column expresses the weight of a single piece in fractions of the troy ounce carried to the thousandth, and in a few cases to the ten thousandth, of an ounce. The method is preferable to expressing the weight in grains for commercial purposes, and corresponds better with the terms of the mint. It may be readily transferred to weight in grains by the following rule: Remove the decimal point; from one-half deduct four per cent. of that half, and the remainder will be grains.

The fourth column expresses the fineness in thousandths, i. e., the number of parts of pure gold or silver in 1,000 parts of the coin.

The fifth and sixth columns of the first table expresses the valuation of gold. In the fifth is shown the value as compared with the legal content or amount of fine gold in our coin. In the sixth is shown the value as paid at the mint after the uniform deduction of one-half of one per cent. The former is the value for any other purposes than recoinage, and especially for the purpose of comparison; the latter is the value in exchange for our coins at the mint.

For the silver there is no fixed legal valuation, the law providing for shifting the price according to the condition of demand and supply. The present price of standard silver is 122½ cents per ounce, at which rate the values in the fifth column of the second table are calculated. In a few cases, where the coins could not be procured, the data are *assumed* from the legal rates, and so stated.

I.—*Gold coins.*

Country.	Denominations.	Weight.	Fineness.	Value.	Value after deduction.
		Oz. Dec.	*Thous.*		
Australia	Pound of 1852	0.281	916.5	$5.32.37	$5.29.71
	Sovereign of 1855–'60	0.256.5	916	4.85.58	4.83.16
Austria	Ducat ,....................	0.112	986	2.28.28	2.27.04
	Souverain	0.363	900	6.75.35	6.71.98
	New Union crown,(assumed).	0.357	900	6.64.19	6.60.87
Belgium	Twenty-five francs	0.254	899	4.72.03	4.69.67
Bolivia	Doubloon	0.867	870	15.59.25	15.51.46
Brazil	20 milreis.................	0.575	917.5	10.90.57	10.85.12
Central America	Two escudos	0.209	853.5	3.68.75	3.66.91
Chili	Old doubloon	0.867	870	15.59.26	15.51.47
	Ten pesos	0.492	900	9.15.35	9.10.78
Denmark	Ten thaler	0.427	895	7.90.01	7.86.06
Ecuador	Four escudos..............	0.433	844	7.55.46	7.51.69
England	Pound or sovereign, new...	0.256.7	916.5	4.86.34	4.83.91
	Pound or sovereign, average	0.256.2	916	4.84.92	4.82.50
France	Twenty francs, new	0.207.5	899.5	3.85.83	3.83.91
	Twenty francs, average	0.207	899	3.84.69	3.82.77
Germany, north.	Ten thaler ......~........	0.427	895	7.90.01	7.86.06
	Ten thaler, Prussian	0.427	903	7.97.07	7.93.09
	Krone, (crown)	0.357	900	6.64.20	6.60.88
Germany, south.	Ducat.....................	0.112	986	2.28.28	2.27.14
Greece.........	Twenty drachms	0.185	900	3.44.19	3.42.47
Hindostan	Mohur	0.374	916	7.08.18	7.04.64
Italy	20 lire....................	0.207	898	3.84.26	3.82.34
Japan ....:....	Old cobang	0.362	568	4.44.0	4.41.8
	New cobang	0.289	572	3.57.6	3.55.8
Mexico .:......	Doubloon, average	0.867.5	866	15.52.98	15.45.22
	Doubloon, new.............	0.867.5	870.5	15.61.05	15.53.25
Naples.........	Six ducati, new	0.245	996	5.04.43	5.01.91
Netherland.....	Ten guilders	0.215	899	3.99.56	3.97.57
New Granada ..	Old doubloon, Bogota.......	0.868	870	15.61.06	15.53.26
	Old doubloon, Popayan.....	0.867	858	15.37.75	15.30.07
	Ten pesos, new.............	0.525	891.5	9.67.51	9.62.68
Peru	Old doubloon	0.867	868	15.55.67	15.47.90
Portugal.......	Gold crown	0.308	912	5.80.66	5.77.76
Prussia........	New Union crown,(assumed).	0.357	900	6.64.19	6.60.87
Rome..........	2½ scudi, new	0.140	900	2.60.47	2.59.17
Russia.........	Five roubles	0.210	916	3.97.64	3.95.66
Spain..........	100 reals	0.268	896	4.96.39	4.93.91
	80 reals..................	0.215	869.5	3.86.44	3.84.51
Sweden........	Ducat	0.111	975	2.43.72	2.22.61
Tunis	25 piastres	0.161	900	2.99.54	2.98.05
Turkey........	100 piastres...............	0.231	915	4.36.93	4.34.75
Tuscany.......	Sequin	0.112	999	2.31.29	2.30.14

J.—*Silver coins.*

Country.	Denominations.	Weight.	Fineness.	Value.
		Oz. Dec.	*Thous.*	
Austria.............	Old rix dollar	0.902	833	$1.02.27
	Old scudo............:	0.836	902	1.02.64
	Florin before 1858	0.451	833	51.14
	New florin	0.397	000	48.63
	New Union dollar.............	0.596	900	73.01
	Maria Theresa dollar, 1780	0.895	838	1.02.12
Belgium	Five francs.........}	0.803	897	98.04
Bolivia	New dollar.......	0.643	903.5	79.07
	Half dollar....................	0.432	667	39.22
Brazil	Double milreis....*...........	0.820	918.5	1.02.53
Canada............	20 cents......................	0.150	925	18.57
Central America....	Dollar	0.866	850	1.00.19
Chili	Old dollar....................	0.804	908	1.06.79
	New dollar	0.801	900.5	98.17
Denmark	Two rigsdaler	0.927	877	1.10.65
England	Shilling, new.................	0.182.5	924.5	22.96
	Shilling, average	0.178	925	22.41
France	Five franc, average	0.800	900	98.00
Germany, north	Thaler, before 1857...........	0.712	750	72.67
	New thaler	0.595	900	72.89
Germany, south	Florin, before 1857...........	0.340	900	41.05
	New florin, (assumed)........	0.340	900	41.65
Greece............	Five drachms	0.719	900	88.08
Hindostan	Rupee ,........*............	0.374	916	46.62
Japan	Itzebu........, ...	0.279	991	37.63
	New itzebu	0.279	890	33.80
Mexico	Dollar, new	0.867.5	903	1.06.62
	Dollar, average...............	0.866	901	1.06.20
Naples............	Scudo	0.844	830	95.34
Netherlands	2½ guild	0.804	944	1.03.31
Norway............	Specie daler.................	0.927	877	1.10.65
New Granada ...:....	Dollar of 1857	0.803	896	97.92
Peru	Old dollar....................	0.866	901	1.06.20
	Dollar of 1858	0.766	909	94.77
	Half dollar, 1835–'38	0.433	650	38.31
Prussia	Thaler, before 1857...........	0.712	750	72.68
	New thaler...................	0.595	900	72.89
Rome	Scudo	0.864	900	1.05.84
Russia............	Rouble	0.667	875	79.44
Sardinia	Five lire	0.800	900	98.00
Spain........,.....	New pistareen	0.166	899	20.31
Sweden ....'.......	Rix dollar....................	1.092	750	1.11.48
Switzerland	Two francs...................	0.323	899	39.52
Tunis	Five piastres	0.511	898.5	62.49
Turkey	Twenty piastres	0.770	830	86.98
Tuscany............	Florin	0.220	925	27.60

No. 7.

Gold, silver, and copper coinage at the mint of the United States in the several years from its establishment, in 1792; the coinage at the branch mints, and the assay office, New York, from their organization to June 30, 1865.

Years.	Gold.	Silver.	Copper.	Total.
1793 to 1795	$71,485 00	$370,683 80	$11,373 00	$453,541 80
1796	102,727 50	79,077 50	10,324 40	192,129 40
1797	103,423 50	12,591 45	9,510 34	125,524 29
1798	205,610 00	330,291 00	9,797 00	545,698 00
1799	213,285 00	323,515 00	9,106 68	645,906 68
1800	317,760 00	224,296 00	29,279 40	571,335 40
	1,014,290 00	1,440,454 75	79,390 82	2,534,135 57
1801	422,570 00	74,758 00	13,628 37	510,956 37
1802	423,310 00	58,343 00	34,422 83	516,075 83
1803	258,377 50	87,118 00	25,203 03	370,698 53
1804	258,642 50	100,340 50	12,844 94	371,827 94
1805	170,367 50	149,388 50	13,483 48	333,239 48
1806	324,505 00	471,319 00	5,260 00	801,084 00
1807	437,495 00	597,448 75	9,652 21	1,044,595 96
1808	284,665 00	684,300 00	13,090 00	982,055 00
1809	169,375 00	707,376 00	8,001 53	884,752 53
1810	501,435 00	638,773 50	15,660 00	1,155,868 50
	3,250,742 50	3,569,165 25	151,246 39	6,971,154 14
1811	497,905 00	608,340 00	2,495 95	1,108,740 95
1812	290,435 00	814,029 50	10,755 00	1,115,219 50
1813	477,140 00	620,951 50	4,180 00	1,102,271 50
1814	77,270 00	561,687 50	3,578 30	642,535 80
1815	3,175 00	17,308 00		20,483 00
1816		28,575 75	28,209 82	56,785 57
1817		607,783 50	39,484 00	647,267 50
1818	242,940 00	1,070,454 50	31,670 00	1,345,064 50
1819	258,615 00	1,140,000 00	26,710 00	1,425,325 00
1820	1,319,030 00	501,680 70	44,075 50	1,864,786 20
	3,166,510 00	5,970,810 95	191,158 57	9,328,479 52
1821	189,325 00	825,762 45	3,890 00	1,018,977 45
1822	88,980 00	805,806 50	20,723 39	915,509 89
1823	72,425 00	895,550 00		967,975 00
1824	93,200 00	1,752,477 00	12,620 00	1,858,297 00
1825	156,385 00	1,564,583 00	14,926 00	1,735,894 00
1826	92,245 00	2,002,090 00	16,344 25	3,110,679 25
1827	131,565 00	2,869,200 00	23,577 32	3,024,342 32
1828	140,145 00	1,575,600 00	25,636 24	1,741,381 24
1829	295,717 50	1,994,578 00	16,580 00	2,306,875 50
1830	643,105 00	2,495,400 00	17,115 00	3,155,620 00
	1,903,092 50	16,781,046 95	151,412 20	18,835,551 65

No. 7.—*Gold, silver, and copper coinage, &c.*—Continued.

Years.	Gold.	Silver.	Copper.	Total.
1831	$714,270 00	$3,175,600 00	$33,603 60	$3,923,473 60
1832	798,435 00	2,579,000 00	23,620 00	3,401,065 00
1833	978,550 00	2,759,000 00	28,160 00	3,765,710 00
1834	3,954,270 00	3,415,002 00	19,151 00	7,388,423 00
1835	2,186,175 00	3,443,003 00	39,489 00	5,668,667 00
1836	4,135,700 00	3,606,100 00	23,100 00	7,764,900 00
1837	1,148,305 00	2,096,010 00	55,583 00	3,299,898 00
1838	1,809,595 00	2,315,250 00	63,702 00	4,188,547 00
1839	1,375,760 00	2,098,636 00	31,286 61	3,505,682 61
1840	1,690,802 00	1,712,178 00	24,627 00	3,427,607 00
	18,791,862 00	27,199,779 00	342,322 21	46,333,963 21
1841	1,102,107 50	1,115,875 00	15,973 67	2,233,957 17
1842	1,833,170 50	2,325,750 00	23,833 90	4,182,754 40
1843	8,302,797 50	3,722,260 00	24,283 20	12,049,330 70
1844	5,428,230 00	2,235,550 00	23,977 52	7,687,757 51
1845	3,756,447 50	1,873,200 00	38,948 04	5,668,595 54
1846	4,034,177 50	2,558,580 00	41,208 00	6,633,965 50
1847	20,221,385 00	2,374,450 00	61,836 69	22,657,671 69
1848	3,775,512 50	2,040,050 00	64,157 99	5,879,720 49
1849	9,007,761 50	2,114,950 00	41,984 32	11,164,695 82
1850	31,981,738 50	1,866,100 00	44,467 50	33,892,306 00
	89,443,328 00	22,226,755 00	380,670 83	112,050,753 83
1851	62,614,492 50	774,397 00	99,635 43	63,488,524 93
1852	56,846,187 50	999,410 00	50,630 94	57,896,228 44
1853	55,213,906 94	9,077,571 00	67,059 78	64,358,537 72
1854	52,094,595 47	8,619,270 00	42,638 35	60,756,503 82
1855	52,795,457 20	3,501,245 00	16,030 79	56,312,732 99
1856	59,343,365 35	5,196,670 17	27,106 78	64,567,142 30
1857, (Jan. 1 to June 30, inclusive)	25,183,138 68	1,601,644 46	63,510 46	26,848,293 60
1858, fiscal year	52,889,800 29	8,233,287 77	234,000 00	61,357,088 06
1859, fiscal year	30,409,953 70	6,833,631 47	307,000 00	37,550,585 17
1860, fiscal year	23,447,283 35	3,250,636 26	342,000 00	27,039,919 61
	470,838,180 98	48,087,763 13	1,249,612 53	520,175,556 64
1861	80,708,400 64	2,883,706 94	101,660 00	83,693,767 58
1862	61,676,576 55	3,231,081 51	116,000 00	65,023,658 06
1863	22,645,729 90	1,564,297 22	478,450 00	24,688,477 12
1864	23,982,748 31	850,086 99	463,800 00	25,296,635 30
1865	30,685,699 95	950,218 69	1,183,330 00	32,819,248 64
	219,699,155 35	9,479,391 35	2,343,240 00	231,521,786 70

No. 7.—*Gold, silver, and copper coinage, &c.*—Continued.

RECAPITULATION OF COINAGE FROM 1793 TO 1865, INCLUSIVE.

Years.	Gold.	Silver.	Copper.	Totals.
1793 to 1800, 8 yrs.	$1,014,290 00	$1,440,454 75	$79,390 82	$2,534,135 57
1801 to 1810, 10 yrs.	3,250,742 50	3,569,165 25	151,246 39	6,971,154 14
1811 to 1820, 10 yrs.	3,166,510 00	5,970,810 95	191,158 57	9,328,479 52
1821 to 1830, 10 yrs.	1,903,092 50	16,781,046 95	151,412 20	18,835,551 65
1831 to 1840, 10 yrs.	18,791,862 00	27,199,779 00	342,322 21	46,333,963 21
1841 to 1850, 10 yrs.	89,443,328 00	22,226,755 00	380,670 83	112,050,753 83
1851 to 1860, 9½ yrs.	470,638,180 98	48,067,763 13	1,249,612 53	520,175,556 64
1861 to 1865, 5 yrs.	219,699,155 35	9,479,391 35	2,343,240 00	231,521,786 70
Total, 72½ yrs.	806,107,161 33	134,755,166 38	4,889,053 55	947,751,381 26

RECAPITULATION OF AVERAGES OF COINAGE FOR EACH DECADE FROM 1793 TO 1865, INCLUSIVE.

Years.	Gold.	Silver.	Copper.	Totals.
1793 to 1800, 8 yrs.	$126,786 25	$180,056 84	$9,923 85	$316,766 94
1801 to 1810, 10 yrs.	325,074 25	356,916 52	15,124 64	697,115 41
1811 to 1820, 10 yrs.	316,651 00	597,081 09	19,115 86	932,847 95
1821 to 1830, 10 yrs.	190,309 25	1,678,104 69	15,141 22	1,883,555 16
1831 to 1840, 10 yrs.	1,879,186 20	2,719,977 90	34,232 22	4,633,396 32
1841 to 1850, 10 yrs.	8,944,332 80	2,222,675 50	38,067 08	11,205,075 38
1851 to 1860, 9½ yrs.	49,561,913 79	5,061,869 80	131,538 16	54,755,321 75
1861 to 1865, 5 yrs.	43,939,831 07	1,895,878 27	468,648 00	46,304,357 34

No. 8.

Statement of the public debt on the 1st day of January in each of the years from 1791 to 1842, inclusive, and at various dates in subsequent years to July 1, 1865.

On the 1st day of January.....1791................. $75,463,476 52
           1792................. 77,227,924 66
           1793................. 80,352,634 04
           1794................. 78,427,404 77
           1795................. 80,747,587 38
           1796................. 83,762,172 07
           1797................. 82,064,479 33
           1798................. 79,228,529 12
           1799................. 78,408,669 77
           1800................. 82,976,294 35
           1801................. 83,038,050 80
           1802................. 80,712,632 25
           1803................. 77,054,686 30
           1804................. 86,427,120 88
           1805................. 82,312,150 50
           1806................. 75,723,270 66
           1807................. 69,218,398 64
           1808................. 65,196,317 97
           1809................. 57,023,192 09
           1810................. 53,173,217 52
           1811................. 48,005,587 76
           1812................. 45,209,737 90

On the 1st day of January.....1813................	$55, 962, 827	57
1814................	81, 487, 846	24
1815................	99, 833, 660	15
1816................	127, 334, 933	74
1817................	123, 491, 965	16
1818................	103, 466, 633	83
1819................	95, 529, 648	28
1820................	91, 015, 566	15
1821................	89, 987, 427	66
1822................	93, 546, 676	98
1823................	90, 875, 877	28
1824................	90, 269, 777	77
1825................	83, 788, 432	71
1826................	81, 054, 059	99
1827................	73, 987, 357	20
1828................	67, 475, 043	87
1829................	58, 421, 413	67
1830................	48, 565, 406	50
1831................	39, 123, 191	68
1832................	24, 322, 235	18
1833................	7, 001, 032	88
1834................	4, 760, 081	08
1835................	351, 289	05
1836................	291, 089	05
1837................	1, 878, 223	55
1838................	4, 857, 660	46
1839................	11, 983, 737	53
1840................	5, 125, 077	63
1841................	6, 737, 398	00
1842................	15, 028, 486	37
On the 1st day of July........1843................	27, 203, 450	69
1844................	24, 748, 188	23
1845................	17, 093, 794	80
1846................	16, 750, 926	33
1847................	38, 956, 623	38
1848................	48, 526, 379	37
On the 1st day of December....1849................	64, 704, 693	71
1850................	64, 228, 238	37
On the 20th day of November..1851................	62, 560, 395	26
On the 30th day of December...1852................	65, 131, 692	13
On the 1st day of July........1853................	67, 340, 628	78
1854................	47, 242, 206	05
On the 17th day of November..1855................	39, 969, 731	05
On the 15th day of November..1856................	30, 963, 909	64
On the 1st day of July........1857................	29, 060, 386	90
1858................	44, 910, 777	66
1859................	58, 754, 699	33
1860................	64, 769, 703	08
1861................	90, 867, 828	68
1862................	514, 211, 371	92
1863................	1, 098, 793, 181	37
1864................	1, 740, 690, 489	49
1865................	2, 682, 593, 026	53

S. B. COLBY, *Register.*

TREASURY DEPARTMENT,
Register's Office, November 22, 1865.

No. 9.—*Statement of the revenue collected from the beginning of the government to the 30th Public Lands, and miscellaneous sources, with the receipts*

	From customs duties, imposts, and tonnage.	From internal revenue.	From direct tax.	From postage.
From March 4, 1789, to Dec. 31....1791	$4,399,473 09			
For the year................1792	3,443,070 85	$208,924 81		
1793	4,255,306 56	337,705 70		$11,020 51
1794	4,801,065 28	274,089 62		29,478 49
1795	5,588,461 26	337,755 36		22,400 00
1796	6,567,987 94	475,289 60		72,909 84
1797	7,549,649 65	575,491 45		64,500 00
1798	7,106,061 93	644,357 95		39,500 00
1799	6,610,449 31	779,136 44		41,000 00
1800	9,080,932 73	809,396 55	$734,223 97	78,000 00
1801	10,750,778 93	1,048,033 43	534,343 38	79,500 00
1802	12,438,235 74	621,898 89	206,565 44	35,000 00
1803	10,479,417 61	215,177 69	71,879 20	16,427 26
1804	11,098,565 33	50,941 29	50,198 44	26,500 00
1805	12,936,487 04	21,747 15	21,882 91	21,342 50
1806	14,667,698 17	20,101 45	55,763 86	41,117 67
1807	15,845,521 61	13,051 40	34,732 56	3,614 73
1808	16,363,550 58	8,210 73	19,159 21	
1809	7,296,020 58	4,044 39	7,517 31	
1810	8,583,309 31	7,430 63	12,448 68	
1811	13,313,222 73	2,295 95	7,666 66	37 70
1812	8,958,777 53	4,903 06	859 22	85,039 70
1813	13,224,623 25	4,755 04	3,805 52	35,000 00
1814	5,998,772 08	1,662,984 22	2,219,497 36	45,000 00
1815	7,282,942 22	4,678,059 07	2,162,673 41	135,000 00
1816	36,306,874 89	5,194,708 31	4,253,635 09	149,787 74
1817	26,283,348 49	2,678,100 77	1,834,187 04	29,371 91
1818	17,176,385 00	955,279 20	264,333 36	20,070 00
1819	20,283,608 76	229,593 63	83,650 78	71 32
1820	15,005,612 15	106,260 53	31,586 82	6,465 95
1821	13,004,447 15	69,027 63	29,349 05	516 91
1822	17,589,761 94	67,665 71	20,961 56	602 04
1823	19,088,433 44	34,242 17	10,337 71	110 69
1824	17,878,325 71	34,663 37	6,201 96	
1825	20,098,713 45	25,771 35	2,330 85	469 56
1826	23,341,331 77	21,589 93	6,638 76	300 14
1827	19,712,283 29	19,885 68	2,626 90	101 00
1828	23,205,523 64	17,451 54	2,218 81	20 15
1829	22,681,965 91	14,502 74	11,335 05	86 60
1830	21,922,391 39	12,160 62	16,980 59	53 13
1831	24,224,441 77	6,933 51	10,506 01	561 02
1832	28,465,237 24	11,630 65	6,791 13	244 95
1833	29,032,508 91	2,759 00	394 12	
1834	16,214,957 15	4,196 09	19 80	100 00
1835	19,391,310 59	10,459 48	4,263 33	393 00
1836	23,409,940 53	370 00	728 79	10 91
1837	11,169,290 39	5,493 84	1,687 70	
1838	16,158,800 36	2,467 27		
1839	23,137,924 81	2,553 32	755 22	
1840	13,499,502 17	1,682 25		
1841	14,487,216 74	3,261 36		
1842	18,187,908 76	495 00		
Half year to June 30...........1843	7,046,843 91	103 25		
Year ending June 30..........1844	26,183,570 94	1,777 34		
1845	27,528,112 70	3,517 12		
1846	26,712,667 87	2,897 26		
1847	23,747,864 66	375 00		
1848	31,757,070 96	375 00		
1849	28,346,738 82	375 00		
1850	39,668,686 42			
1851	49,017,567 92			
1852	47,339,326 62			
1853	58,931,865 52			
1854	64,224,190 27			
1855	53,025,794 21			
1856	64,022,863 50			
1857	63,875,905 05			
1858	41,789,620 96			
1859	49,565,824 38			
1860	53,187,511 87			
1861	39,582,125 64			
1862	49,056,397 62	37,640,787 95	1,795,331 73	
1863	69,059,642 40	109,741,134 10	1,485,103 61	
1864	102,316,152 99	209,464,215 25	475,648 98	
1865	84,928,260 60	209,464,215 25	1,200,573 03	

TREASURY DEPARTMENT, *Register's Office, November 22, 1865.*

of June, 1865, under the several heads of Customs, Internal Revenue, Direct Tax, Postage, from loans and treasury notes; and the total receipts.

From public lands.	From bank stock, dividends, and bonds.	From miscellaneous sources.	Total, exclusive of loans and treasury notes.	From loans and treasury notes.	Total receipts.
....	....	$19,440 10	$4,418,913 19	$5,791,112 56	$10,210,025 75
....	$8,028 00	9,936 65	3,669,960 31	5,070,806 46	8,740,766 77
....	38,500 00	10,390 37	4,652,923 14	1,067,701 14	5,720,624 28
....	303,472 00	23,799 48	5,431,904 87	4,609,196 78	10,041,101 65
....	162,000 00	5,917 97	6,114,534 59	3,305,268 20	9,419,802 79
$4,836 13	1,240,000 00	16,506 14	8,377,529 65	362,800 00	8,740,329 65
83,540 60	385,220 00	30,379 29	8,688,780 99	70,135 41	8,758,916 40
11,967 11	79,920 00	18,692 81	7,900,495 80	308,574 27	8,309,070 07
....	71,040 00	45,187 56	7,546,813 31	5,074,646 53	12,621,459 84
443 75	71,040 00	74,713 10	10,848,749 10	1,602,435 04	12,451,181 14
167,726 08	88,800 00	266,149 15	12,935,330 95	10,125 00	12,945,455 95
188,628 02	1,327,560 00	177,905 86	14,995,793 95	5,597 36	15,001,391 31
163,675 69	....	115,518 18	11,064,097 63	....	11,064,097 63
497,926 79	....	112,575 53	11,826,307 38	9,532 64	11,835,840 02
540,193 80	....	19,039 80	13,560,694 20	128,814 94	13,689,509 14
765,245 73	....	10,004 19	15,559,931 07	48,897 71	15,608,828 78
466,163 27	....	34,935 60	16,306,019 26	....	16,306,019 26
847,939 06	....	21,809 55	17,060,661 93	1,822 16	17,062,484 09
442,253 33	....	23,638 51	-7,773,473 12	....	7,773,473 12
696,548 82	....	84,476 94	9,384,214 28	2,759,992 25	12,144,206 53
1,040,237 53	....	60,098 52	14,423,589 09	8,309 05	14,431,838 14
710,427 78	....	41,125 47	9,801,132 76	12,837,900 00	22,639,032 76
835,655 14	....	236,571 00	14,340,409 95	26,184,435 00	40,524,844 95
1,135,971 09	....	119,399 81	11,181,625 16	23,277,911 79	34,539,536 95
1,267,939 28	....	150,983 74	15,696,916 82	35,384,300 78	50,961,227 60
1,717,985 03	....	123,994 61	47,676,985 66	9,494,436 16	57,171,421 82
1,991,226 06	202,426 00	80,389 17	33,099,049 74	734,542 59	33,843,592 03
2,606,564 77	525,000 00	37,547 71	21,585,180 04	8,765 62	21,585,945 66
3,274,422 78	675,000 00	57,027 10	24,603,374 37	2,291 00	24,605,665 37
1,635,871 61	1,000,000 00	54,872 49	17,840,600 55	3,040,824 13	20,881,493 68
1,212,966 46	-105,000 00	139,072 52	14,573,379 72	5,000,324 00	19,573,703 72
1,803,581 94	297,500 00	452,355 15	20,232,427 94	....	20,234,427 94
915,523 10	350,000 00	141,019 15	20,540,666 26	....	20,540,666 26
984,418 15	350,000 00	127,603 60	19,381,212 79	5,000,000 00	24,381,212 79
1,346,090 56	367,500 00	129,949 25	21,840,858 02	5,000,000 00	26,840,858 02
1,393,785 09	402,500 00	94,088 58	25,260,434 21	....	25,260,434 21
1,495,845 26	420,000 00	1,315,621 83	22,966,363 96	....	22,966,363 96
1,018,308 75	455,000 00	65,106 34	24,763,629 27	....	24,763,629 27
1,517,175 13	490,000 00	112,561 95	24,827,627 38	....	24,827,627 38
2,329,356 14	490,000 00	73,172 64	24,844,116 51	....	24,844,116 51
3,210,815 48	490,000 00	583,563 03	28,526,820 82	....	28,526,820 82
2,623,381 00	639,000 00	101,165 66	31,867,450 66	....	31,867,450 66
3,967,682 55	610,285 00	334,796 67	33,948,426 25	....	33,948,426 25
4,857,600 69	586,649 50	128,412 32	21,791,935 55	....	21,791,935 55
14,757,600 75	560,980 82	696,279 13	35,430,087 10	....	35,430,087 10
24,877,179 86	328,674 07	2,209,891 32	50,826,796 08	....	50,826,796 08
6,776,236 52	1,375,965 44	5,623,479 15	26,954,153 04	2,992,989 15	27,947,144 19
3,081,939 47	4,542,102 22	2,517,552 42	26,302,561 74	12,716,820 86	39,019,382 60
7,076,447 35	....	1,265,086 91	31,482,749 61	3,857,276 21	35,340,025 82
3,292,083 29	1,744,513 80	911,773 82	19,480,115 33	3,589,547 51	23,069,662 84
1,365,627 42	672,769 38	331,985 37	16,860,160 27	13,659,317 38	20,519,477 65
1,335,797 52	....	440,807 97	19,965,009 25	14,808,723 64	34,771,744 89
897,818 11	....	296,335 99	8,241,001 26	12,541,409 19	20,782,410 45
2,059,939 80	....	1,075,419 70	29,320,707 78	1,877,847 95	31,198,555 73
2,077,022 30	....	333,901 78	29,941,853 90	....	29,941,853 90
2,694,452 48	....	274,139 44	29,684,157 05	....	29,684,157 05
2,498,355 20	....	264,444 36	26,531,039 22	28,870,765 36	55,401,804 58
3,328,642 56	....	627,024 13	35,713,109 65	21,293,780 00	57,006,889 65
1,688,959 55	....	338,233 70	30,174,307 07	29,422,585 91	59,796,892 98
1,859,894 25	....	706,059 12	42,234,639 79	5,433,126 98	47,669,766 75
2,352,305 30	266,072 09	991,933 24	52,557,878 55	203,400 00	52,761,278 55
2,043,239 58	1,021 34	438,580 76	49,822,168 30	46,300 00	49,868,468 30
3,667,084 99	....	1,188,104 07	61,787,054 58	16,350 00	61,803,404 58
8,470,798 39	....	1,105,352 74	73,800,341 40	1,950 00	73,802,291 40
11,497,049 07	....	827,731 40	65,350,574 68	800 00	65,351,374 68
8,917,644 93	....	1,116,190 81	74,056,699 24	200 00	74,056,899 24
3,829,486 64	....	1,259,920 88	68,965,312 57	3,900 00	68,969,312 57
3,513,715 87	....	1,352,029 13	46,655,365 96	23,717,300 00	70,372,603 96
1,756,687 30	....	2,163,953 96	53,486,465 64	28,287,500 00	81,773,965 64
1,778,557 71	....	1,068,530 25	56,054,599 83	20,786,808 00	76,841,407 83
870,658 54	....	1,053,515 31	41,476,299 49	41,895,340 65	83,371,640 12
152,203 77	....	93,787 64	51,933,720 76	529,694,460 50	581,628,181 29
167,617 17	....	4,344,139 83	112,687,290 95	776,682,361 87	889,379,652 52
561,313 99	....	51,505,502 26	264,626,771 60	1,121,131,842 98	1,385,758,614 58
996,553 31	....	37,125,002 89	333,714,605 08	1,472,224,740 85	1,805,939,345 93

No. 10.—*Statement of expenditures from the beginning of the government to June 30, 1865,*
Pensions, Indian department, and miscellaneous,

[The years 1862, 1863, and 1864 are from the account of warrants on the treasury

	Civil list.	Foreign intercourse.	Navy Department.	War Department.	Pensions.
From Mar. 4, 1789, to Dec. 31, 1791	$757,134 45	$14,733 33	$570 00	$632,804 03	$175,813 88
For the year..............1792	380,917 58	78,766 67	53 02	1,100,702 09	109,243 15
1793	358,241 08	89,500 00	....	1,130,249 08	80,017 81
1794	440,946 58	146,403 51	61,408 97	2,639,097 59	81,399 24
1795	361,633 36	912,685 12	410,562 03	2,480,910 13	68,673 22
1796	447,139 05	184,859 64	274,784 04	1,260,263 84	100,843 71
1797	483,233 70	669,788 54	382,631 89	1,039,402 46	92,256 97
1798	504,605 17	457,428 74	1,381,347 76	2,009,522 30	104,845 33
1799	592,905 75	271,374 11	2,858,081 84	2,466,946 98	95,444 03
1800	748,688 43	395,288 18	3,448,716 03	2,560,878 77	64,130 73
1801	549,288 31	295,676 73	2,111,424 00	1,672,944 08	73,533 37
1802	296,961 11	550,925 93	915,561 87	1,179,148 25	85,440 39
1803	526,583 12	1,110,834 77	1,215,230 53	822,055 85	62,902 10
1804	624,795 63	1,186,655 57	1,189,832 75	875,423 93	80,092 80
1805	585,849 79	2,798,028 77	1,597,500 00	712,781 28	81,854 59
1806	684,230 53	1,760,421 30	1,649,641 44	1,224,355 38	81,875 53
1807	655,504 55	577,826 34	1,722,064 47	1,288,685 91	70,500 00
1808	691,167 80	304,992 83	1,884,067 80	2,900,834 40	82,576 04
1809	712,465 13	166,306 04	2,427,758 80	3,347,772 17	87,833 54
1810	763,994 69	81,367 48	1,654,244 20	2,294,323 94	83,744 10
1811	644,467 27	264,904 47	1,965,566 39	2,032,828 19	75,043 88
1812	826,271 55	347,703 29	3,959,365 15	11,817,798 24	91,402 10
1813	780,545 45	209,941 01	6,446,600 10	19,652,013 02	86,989 91
1814	927,424 33	177,179 97	7,311,290 60	20,350,806 86	90,164 36
1815	852,247 16	290,892 04	8,660,000 25	14,794,294 22	69,656 06
1816	1,208,125 77	364,620 40	3,908,278 30	16,012,096 80	168,804 15
1817	994,556 17	281,995 97	3,314,598 49	8,004,236 53	297,374 43
1818	1,109,559 79	420,429 90	2,953,695 00	5,622,715 10	*280,719 90
1819	1,142,180 41	284,113 94	3,847,640 42	6,506,300 37	2,415,939 85
1820	1,248,310 05	253,370 04	4,387,990 00	2,630,392 31	3,208,376 31
1821	1,112,292 64	207,110 75	3,319,243 06	4,461,291 78	242,817 25
1822	1,158,131 58	164,879 51	2,224,458 98	3,111,981 48	1,948,199 40
1823	1,058,911 65	292,118 56	2,503,765 83	3,096,924 43	1,780,588 52
1824	1,036,266 84	15,140,099 81	2,904,581 56	3,340,939 83	1,498,326 59
1825	1,330,747 24	371,666 25	3,049,083 86	3,659,914 18	1,308,810 57
1826	1,256,745 48	232,719 08	4,218,902 45	3,943,194 37	1,556,593 83
1827	1,228,141 04	659,311 87	4,262,877 45	3,938,977 88	976,149 86
1828	1,455,490 58	1,001,193 66	3,918,786 44	4,145,544 56	830,573 57
1829	1,327,069 36	207,765 85	3,308,745 47	6,250,230 28	949,594 47
1830	1,579,794 64	294,067 97	3,239,428 63	6,752,688 66	1,363,297 31
1831	1,373,755 99	298,554 00	3,856,183 07	4,846,445 61	1,170,665 14
1832	1,800,757 74	305,181 07	3,956,370 29	5,446,131 23	1,184,422 40
1833	1,562,758 28	955,395 88	3,901,356 75	6,705,092 95	4,589,152 40
1834	2,080,601 60	241,562 35	3,956,260 42	5,698,517 51	3,364,285 30
1835	1,905,551 51	774,750 28	3,864,939 06	5,827,948 37	1,954,711 32
1836	2,110,175 47	533,382 63	5,807,718 23	11,791,208 02	2,882,797 96
1837	2,357,035 94	4,603,905 40	6,646,914 53	13,731,172 31	2,672,162 45
1838	2,688,708 56	1,215,095 58	6,131,580 53	13,088,169 69	2,156,057 29
1839	2,116,982 77	987,667 92	6,182,294 25	9,227,045 93	3,142,750 50
1840	2,736,769 31	683,278 15	6,113,896 89	7,155,204 99	2,603,562 17
1841	2,556,471 79	425,410 57	6,001,076 97	8,042,749 92	2,388,434 51
1842	2,905,041 65	563,191 41	8,397,242 95	6,658,137 18	1,378,931 33
Six months ending June 30, 1843	1,929,429 48	409,566 04	3,727,711 53	3,104,638 48	830,041 18
Fiscal year ending June 30, 1844	2,454,958 15	636,079 56	6,498,199 11	5,193,445 05	2,032,008 99
1845	2,359,652 79	702,637 22	6,297,177 89	5,819,868 50	2,398,867 99
1846	2,532,232 92	409,292 25	6,455,013 92	10,362,374 36	909,739 60
1847	2,570,338 44	405,079 10	7,900,635 76	35,776,495 72	1,742,890 86
1848	2,647,802 87	448,393 01	9,408,476 02	27,834,374 80	1,226,500 92
1849	2,865,196 91	6,908,996 72	9,786,705 92	16,503,843 33	193,695 87
1850	3,027,454 39	5,990,838 81	7,904,724 66	9,687,024 58	886,886 02
1851	3,481,219 51	6,256,427 16	8,880,581 28	12,161,965 11	2,293,377 52
1852	3,439,923 22	4,196,391 59	8,918,842 10	8,521,506 19	2,401,858 78
1853	4,263,861 68	950,871 30	11,067,789 53	9,910,498 49	1,736,262 45
1854	4,620,492 24	17,783,812 31	10,790,096 32	11,722,282 97	1,369,009 47
1855	6,350,875 88	997,007 26	13,327,095 11	14,648,074 07	1,542,933 40
1856	6,452,256 35	3,642,615 39	14,074,834 64	16,963,160 51	1,344,227 70
1857	7,511,547 27	999,177 65	12,651,694 61	19,159,150 67	1,423,770 85
1858	7,116,339 04	1,396,508 72	14,053,264 64	25,679,121 53	1,291,163 14
1859	5,913,281 50	981,946 87	14,690,927 90	23,154,720 53	1,161,190 66
1860	6,077,008 95	1,146,143 79	11,514,649 83	16,472,202 72	1,100,802 32
1861	6,074,141 83	1,147,766 91	12,387,156 52	23,001,530 67	1,034,599 73
1862	5,939,009 29	1,339,710 35	42,674,569 69	394,368,407 36	879,523 23
1863	6,350,618 78	1,231,413 06	63,211,105 27	599,298,600 83	1,031,194 44
1864	8,059,177 23	1,280,681 92	85,733,292 77	690,791,842 97	4,979,632 17
1865	10,833,044 87	1,260,818 08	122,567,776 12	1,031,323,360 79	7,291,610 48

* The first revolutionary pensions.   † Purchase of Florida.
‡ Includes seven millions of Mexican indemnity. The years 1849 to 1852 also embrace large sums paid to Mexico.

TREASURY DEPARTMENT, *Register's Office, November 22, 1865.*

under the several heads of Civil List, Foreign Intercourse, Navy Department, War Department, with the interest and principal of the public debt.

Issued; all previous years are from the account of warrants paid.]

Indians.	Miscellaneous.	Total of ordinary expenditures.	Interest on public debt.	Principal of public debt.	Total debts and loans.	Total expenditures.
$27,000 00	$311,533 83	$1,919,589 52	$2,349,437 44	$2,938,512 06	$5,287,949 50	$7,207,539 02
13,648 85	194,372 32	1,877,903 77	3,201,628 22	4,082,037 76	7,287,665 99	9,141,569 67
27,282 83	24,709 46	1,710,070 26	2,772,242 19	3,047,263 18	5,819,505 29	7,529,575 55
13,042 46	118,248 30	1,500,546 65	3,490,292 32	2,311,285 57	5,801,578 09	9,302,124 74
23,475 69	22,718 50	4,350,658 04	3,189,151 16	2,895,260 45	6,084,411 61	10,435,069 65
113,563 98	150,476 14	2,531,930 40	3,195,054 53	2,640,791 91	5,835,846 44	8,367,776 84
62,396 38	103,880 82	2,833,590 96	3,300,043 06	2,492,378 79	5,792,421 82	8,626,012 78
16,470 09	149,004 15	4,623,223 54	3,033,981 28	937,012 86	3,990,294 14	8,613,517 68
20,302 19	175,111 81	6,480,166 72	3,186,287 60	1,410,589 18	4,596,876 78	11,077,043 50
31 22	180,636 30	7,411,369 77	3,374,704 72	1,203,665 23	4,578,369 95	11,989,739 92
9,000 00	269,803 41	4,981,669 90	4,412,912 93	2,678,794 11	7,291,707 04	12,273,376 94
94,000 00	315,022 36	3,737,079 91	4,125,038 95	5,413,965 81	9,539,004 76	13,276,084 67
60,000 00	203,217 87	4,002,824 44	3,848,828 00	3,407,331 43	7,256,159 43	11,258,983 67
116,500 00	379,358 23	4,452,858 91	4,266,584 85	3,905,204 90	8,171,787 45	12,624,646 36
196,500 00	384,720 19	3,737,079 91	4,148,998 82	3,220,890 97	7,369,889 79	13,727,124 41
234,200 00	445,485 16	6,080,209 36	3,723,407 88	5,266,476 73	8,989,884 61	15,670,093 97
205,425 00	464,546 52	4,984,572 89	3,369,578 48	2,938,141 82	6,307,720 10	11,292,292 99
213,575 00	427,124 98	6,504,338 85	3,438,152 87	6,832,092 48	10,260,245 35	16,764,584 20
337,503 84	337,032 62	7,414,672 14	2,865,074 90	3,586,479 26	6,452,554 16	13,867,226 30
177,625 00	315,783 47	5,311,082 28	2,845,427 53	5,163,476 93	8,008,904 46	13,319,986 74
151,875 00	457,919 66	5,592,604 86	2,465,733 16	5,543,470 89	8,009,204 05	13,601,808 91
277,845 00	509,113 37	6,829,498 70	2,451,272 57	1,998,349 88	4,449,622 45	22,279,121 15
167,358 28	738,949 15	28,082,396 92	3,599,455 22	7,505,698 22	11,106,123 44	39,193,520 36
167,394 86	1,103,425 50	30,127,686 38	4,593,239 04	3,307,304 90	7,900,543 94	38,028,230 32
530,750 00	1,735,731 37	26,933,371 00	5,754,568 63	6,874,353 72	12,628,922 35	39,586,493 35
274,512 16	1,416,995 00	23,371,432 58	7,213,258 69	17,657,804 24	24,871,062 93	48,244,495 51
319,463 71	2,242,384 62	15,454,609 92	6,389,209 81	19,041,824 31	25,432,036 12	40,877,646 04
505,704 27	2,305,849 82	23,808,672 76	6,016,446 74	15,279,784 86	21,296,201 62	35,104,673 40
483,181 39	1,640,917 06	16,300,273 44	5,164,538 11	2,540,388 18	7,703,926 29	24,004,199 73
315,750 01	1,090,341 85	13,194,530 57	5,126,097 90	3,502,397 06	8,628,494 28	21,763,024 85
477,005 44	903,718 15	10,723,479 07	5,087,274 01	3,979,821 61	8,367,083 62	19,090,572 69
575,007 41	644,985 15	9,827,643 51	5,172,578 84	2,676,370 86	7,848,949 12	17,676,592 63
380,781 82	671,063 78	9,784,154 55	4,922,684 80	607,331 81	5,530,016 41	15,314,171 00
429,987 90	678,942 74	15,330,144 71	4,996,562 08	11,571,831 68	16,568,393 76	31,898,538 47
724,106 44	1,045,131 40	11,490,459 94	4,366,769 08	7,728,575 70	12,095,344 78	23,585,804 72
743,447 83	1,110,713 23	13,062,316 27	3,973,480 54	7,067,601 65	11,041,082 19	24,103,398 46
780,624 68	826,123 67	12,653,095 65	3,486,071 51	6,517,596 88	10,003,668 39	22,656,764 04
705,084 24	1,219,368 40	13,296,041 45	3,098,800 50	9,064,637 48	12,163,438 07	25,459,479 52
976,344 74	565,679 08	12,660,490 82	2,542,843 23	9,841,024 55	12,383,867 78	25,044,358 40
622,262 47	1,363,624 13	13,229,533 33	1,913,533 40	9,442,214 82	11,355,748 22	24,585,281 55
926,167 98	1,392,336 11	13,864,067 90	1,383,542 93	14,790,795 27	16,174,338 22	30,038,446 12
1,332,323 40	2,451,202 64	16,516,388 77	772,561 50	17,067,747 79	17,840,309 29	34,356,698 06
1,801,677 08	3,198,091 77	22,713,755 11	303,796 87	1,839,746 51	1,543,543 38	24,257,298 49
1,001,623 07	2,082,565 00	18,425,417 25	202,152 98	5,974,412 91	6,176,565 19	24,601,982 44
1,637,689 80	1,549,396 74	17,514,950 28	57,863 08	308 20	58,191 28	17,573,141 56
4,933,650 11	2,749,721 60	30,868,164 04	*03,389 85	*3,140 32	66,500 17	30,934,664 21
4,299,594 68	2,932,428 93	37,243,214 24		21,822 91	21,822 91	37,265,037 15
5,313,245 81	3,256,868 18	39,445,718 08	14,997 54	5,590,722 73	5,605,720 27	39,455,438 35
2,916,867 18	2,621,340 20	26,496,948 73	399,834 94	10,718,153 19	11,117,987 43	37,614,936 15
2,271,857 10	2,575,351 50	24,139,920 11	174,675 77	3,911,977 93	4,086,613 70	26,226,553 81
2,273,097 44	3,505,899 06	26,196,840 29	288,063 45	5,312,696 99	5,600,689 74	31,797,530 03
1,151,400 34	3,307,791 55	24,361,336 59	778,533 06	7,796,989 88	8,575,539 94	32,936,676 53
282,404 47	1,979,784 48	11,256,508 60	526,584 57	333,011 98	861,596 55	12,118,105 15
1,982,271 00	2,554,146 05	20,650,108 01	1,874,863 62	11,117,039 18	12,991,902 84	33,642,010 85
1,467,774 93	2,839,470 97	21,895,369 61	1,066,085 04	7,528,054 06	8,595,039 10	30,490,408 71
4,080,047 89	3,769,728 42	28,418,459 59	843,228 77	370,594 54	1,213,823 31	27,632,282 90
1,406,008 69	3,910,199 81	53,801,569 37	1,117,830 22	5,601,452 15	6,719,282 37	60,520,851 74
1,100,251 78	2,554,453 37	45,227,454 77	2,391,652 17	13,036,036 25	15,437,688 42	60,655,143 19
504,263 25	3,111,140 61	39,933,542 61	3,554,419 40	12,898,460 73	16,452,880 13	56,365,422 74
1,663,591 47	7,025,450 16	44,049,949 48	3,884,405 95	3,554,321 22	7,438,728 17	44,604,718 26
2,829,801 77	8,146,577 33	44,049,949 48	3,711,407 40	714,947 43	4,426,154 83	48,476,104 31
3,043,576 04	9,867,326 64	40,369,954 56	4,002,014 13	2,320,640 14	6,322,654 27	46,712,608 83
3,900,537 87	12,946,335 03	44,078,156 35	3,665,905 94	6,832,000 13	10,498,905 83	54,577,061 74
1,413,095 08	13,461,450 13	51,142,138 49	3,074,078 73	21,255,902 33	24,335,980 66	75,473,119 08
2,708,347 71	16,738,449 24	56,312,097 72	2,315,996 52	7,536,681 99	9,852,678 24	66,164,775 96
2,586,465 92	15,360,475 94	60,533,636 45	1,954,732 34	10,437,772 76	12,392,505 12	72,726,341 57
4,241,028 60	18,946,189 91	65,032,559 76	1,594,845 44	4,647,182 17	6,242,027 61	71,274,587 37
4,976,871 34	17,847,851 19	72,291,119 70	1,632,774 23	8,118,292 81	9,771,067 04	82,062,186 74
4,551,568 58	16,873,771 68	66,327,405 72	2,637,664 99	14,713,572 81	17,351,237 80	83,678,643 92
2,991,121 54	20,708,183 43	60,010,112 58	3,144,620 94	13,900,362 13	17,045,013 07	77,055,125 65
2,865,481 17	16,026,574 79	62,537,271 62	4,034,157 30	18,813,984 16	22,850,141 45	85,387,313 08
2,203,402 27	14,129,771 52	461,554,453 71	13,190,324 45	96,595,922 09	109,287,246 54	570,841,700 25
1,076,396 35	15,671,830 24	689,980,148 87	24,729,846 61	181,086,635 07	205,816,481 68	895,796,630 65
2,538,297 80	18,155,730 31	811,546,668 57	53,685,421 65	430,197,114 00	483,882,535 72	1,298,144,636 04
4,966,984 90	39,670,795 17	1,212,911,270 41	77,397,713 00	607,361,241 68	684,758,953 68	1,897,674,224 09

* Actual payments on the public debt, but not carried into the totals because of repayments to the treasury.

S. B. COLBY, *Register.*

17 F

No. 11.

Summary statement of domestic produce and manufactures exported from the United States during the fiscal year ending June 30, 1865.

Articles.	Value.	Articles.	Value.
Acids: sulphuric, nitrate, and muriatic	$48,930	Cotton, Sea-island	$296,179
Agricultural implements	1,385,274	Other	5,424,370
Alcohol	358,364	Cotton manufactures:	
Animals, living:		Bleached, printed, and col'd	618,223
Horses	110,270	Brown drills, sheeting, &c.	44,742
Mules	53,115	Duck	101,796
Cattle	159,179	Waste	7,945
Hogs	12,771	All other	2,558,876
Sheep	72,198	Cutlery and steel tools	559,675
Other animals and fowls	17,691	Dental materials	25,803
Animal matter:		Drugs: used in the arts, not specified	51,672
Guts, skins, bladders, &c.	70,189	Medicinal, not specified	1,403,839
Apples:		Dyes, prepared extract of log-	
Green	479,956	wood, &c.	621,142
Dried	99,551	Earthen and stone ware	87,957
Ashes, pot and pearl	727,229	Eggs	51,218
Bark:		Enamelled cloth	57,684
Oak and other, tanners' dyes	158,495	Fancy goods	450,606
Beef	3,304,771	Fertilizers	47,896
Beer, ale, porter, and cider:		Fire-engines and apparatus	28,637
In casks	141,345	Fish, dried or smoked	1,107,767
In bottles	21,806	Fish, pickled	629,966
Bells	53,370	Flax-seed	120,091
Billiard-tables and apparatus	46,672	Fire-works	2,408
Blacking	59,669	Furs and skins	1,036,079
Boats and oars	176,179	Feathers	8,639
Bones	21,267	Flax and tow of flax	42,376
Bone-black	117,846	Fish, fresh	13,890
Books, printed	390,236	Fruit, green, other than apples.	94,427
Books, blank, and pocket-books.	8,844	Fruits, dried and preserved	308,854
Boots and shoes	2,023,210	Gas-metres and pipes	26,492
Bread and biscuit	771,952	Ginseng	547,653
Bricks	60,870	Glassware	1,245,588
Brooms and brushes	180,992	Glue	32,756
Butter	7,234,173	Gold and silver coin and bull'n:	
Cables and cordage	972,348	Gold coin	35,023,856
Candles, sperm and paraffine	8,045	Gold bullion	14,440,865
All other	1,251,123	Silver coin	1,685,676
Carpeting	12,171	Silver bullion	674,880
Carriages and parts, and chil-		Gold-sweepings	8,950
dren's carriages	897,688	Gold manufactures and jew-	
Cars, railroad, and materials	377,969	elry, real and imitation	84,707
Chandeliers and gas-fixtures	56,579	Grass-seed, timothy and other.	2,903
Cheese	11,684,927	Grease	135,442
Chemicals used in the arts	5,537	Gunpowder	30,733
Clay, pipe and pottars'	20,975	Hair and bristles	177,265
Chocolate	11,304	Hams and bacon	10,521,702
Chrome ore	19,078	Hardware	2,061,483
Clocks	905,541	Hats of wool, fur, or silk	190,198
Clothing of wool and cotton	1,456,310	Hats of palm-leaf, straw, &c.	253,025
Clover-seed	446,845	Hay	198,784
Coal	1,348,371	Hemp	259,393
Cobalt and ores of	900	Hemp manufact's, not cordage.	119,738
Combs	74,867	Hides	1,023,596
Confectionery	45,456	Hops	1,348,263
Copper	699,647	Horns and hoofs, and parts	44,701
Copper ore	529,924	Household furniture	2,115,638
Copper and brass, manufactures		Ice	225,825
of, not specified	280,988	India-rubber: man'fs of, shoes	30,935

No. 11.—*Summary statement of domestic produce, &c.*—Continued.

Articles.	Value.	Articles.	Value.
India-rubber, manufactures of:		Oils:	
Goods other than shoes...	$249,171	Spermaceti	$1,511,323
Indian corn..................	3,679,133	Whale and other fish......	816,494
Indian meal.................	1,489,886	Lard, &c., (including tal-	
Maizena or prepared corn.	162,926	low oil)..............	155,454
Ink	16,778	Petroleum, crude..........	6,662,614
Iron and manufactures of:		Refined	8,691,400
Pig......................	32,179	Benzine	173,867
Bar	5,792	Coal.....................	821,088
Railroad bars or rails.....	103,072	Linseed	110,156
Ore	5,463	Of nuts and other edible	
Railroad iron, small; frogs,		and salad oils..........	4,925
&c.......	19,251	Animal—tanners' oil......	2,760
Castings and cast pipe....	61,058	Castor	1,515
Nails....................	935,780	Essential, of all kinds....	107,956
Steam-engines and boilers.	603,552	Onions....	220,694
Locomotive	587,290	Oysters.....................	122,169
Other finished machinery .	2,100,124	Milk	35,738
Machinery furnishings,		Moss....................	3,265
nuts, &c..............	54,629	Oil-cloth	35,962
Boiler-plate and other		Paintings and engravings	84,161
wrought	1,554	Paints, prepared	196,734
Hoops, hoop and band iron	5,415	Paper and stationery	766,428
Railings and furniture....	27,537	Paraffine	37,662
Safes and wrought doors...	58,661	Perfumery and perfumed soaps.	191,388
Manufactures, all other,		Personal effects..........	55,848
not specified...........	938,675	Photographic materials	77,395
Steel	3,907	Pickles and sauces.........	42,553
Steel springs and other man-		Plated ware, silver and other..	34,858
ufactures of, not specified.	56,672	Pork	6,843,135
Jewellers' ashes..............	48,816	Potatoes....	724,593
Lampblack....................	5,485	Printing presses and type.....	295,205
Lamps.......................	384,898	Oakum	29,780
Lard	9,107,435	Quicksilver	979,574
Lead and lead pipe.........	139,201	Rags, woollen.............	130,157
Other manufactures of lead		Rags, cotton and linen	46,822
and of lead and pewter..	28,867	Rice	63,430
Leather and manufactures of		Roots.....................	40,923,
leather....	517,717	Rosin and turpentine.........	157,662
Morocco and other fine....	150,828	Rye meal	32,438
Manufactures other than		Rye and small grains:	
boots and shoes, &c....	190,036	Rye....	133,430
Lime and cement	85,389	Oats....................	256,949
Lumber:		Beans	197,896
Boards, plank, and scantl'g.	4,340,664	Peas	180,060
Laths, pickets, &c........	27,169	Barley	57,651
Box shooks	1,327,593	Bran and shorts...........	20,458
Other lumber and timber		Saddlery and harness	217,312
not specified	2,067,957	Salt......................	355,469
Marble and stone manufactures.	184,512	Sand and other ballast........	12,358
Rough stone.............	69,816	Scales and balances	144,272
Masts and spars...............	139,904	Seeds, garden, and all other,	
Matches	153,590	not specified	187,330
Mathematical and scientific in-		Sewing machines	1,999,274
struments	1,713	Shingles	173,760
Meats, preserved..............	134,981	Shoe-pegs	147,163
Medicines, prepared and patent.	120,455	Silver-ware and manufactures	
Mirrors and gilt frames	9,704	of silver	33,858
Musical instruments: pianos,		Skins other than fur........	612,784
and other	270,511	Skirts, hoop and other........	392,571
Nickel, ore of................	36,710	Snuff....................	39,129
Oil-cake	2,267,393	Silver ore	18,999

No. 11.—*Summary statement of domestic products, &c.*—Continued.

Articles.	Value.	Articles.	Value.
Soap	$983,477	Tobacco and cigars:	
Spermaceti	95,017	Tobacco, manufactured...	$3,439,979
Spirits and liquors, other than		Cigars	140,266
alcohol:		Tree-nails	22,425
Whiskey	196,523	Trunks and valises	207,945
Brandy	63,726	Umbrellas, parasols, and sun-	
Wine	61,276	shades	11,975
Rum	706,134	Varnish	66,982
Cordials, and all other	71,245	Vegetables, preserved or pre-	
Spirits of turpentine	95,747	pared	18,837
Starch	211,102	Vegetables, not specified	73,961
Staves, hoops, and barrels:		Vinegar	46,100
Staves and headings	2,930,915	Wagons, carts, and wheelbar-	
Shooks	2,017,459	rows	333,798
Hoops	778,171	Wax	261,381
Hogsheads and barrels,		Whalebone	493,316
empty	123,668	Wheat	19,397,197
Stearine	28,140	Wheat flour	27,222,031
Stoves and stove furnishings	211,559	Whale foot	6,290
Straw goods	13,264	Window-sashes and blinds	54,812
Sugar and molasses:		Wooden-ware	396,652
Brown	20,617	Wood manufactures, not spe-	
Refined	284,946	cified	858,236
Molasses	16,268	Wool	254,721
Tallow	4,979,135	Woollen cloths and other man-	
Tar and pitch	76,034	factures of wool, not specified.	132,544
Telegraphic instruments and		Zinc	22,509
apparatus	91,576	Zinc, oxide or ore	114,149
Timber, rough and hewn, and		Unenumerated articles:	
all ship timber not specified.	69,699	Manufactured	391,339
Tin ware	100,872	Unmanufactured	149,544
Tobacco and cigars:			
Tobacco, leaf	41,592,138	Total exports, domestic	306,306,758

S. B. COLBY, *Register.*

TREASURY DEPARTMENT, *Register's Office, October* 31, 1865.

No. 12.

Summary statement of goods, wares, and merchandise the growth, produce, and manufacture of foreign countries, exported from the United States during the fiscal year ending June 30, 1865.

Articles.	Value.	Articles.	Value.
FREE OF DUTY.		Corks	$3,597
Animals, living...............	$400	Cotton:	
Articles imported under the re-		Raw	1,816,608
ciprocity treaty.............	2,251,601	All manufactures of, not	
Burrstones, unmanufactured...	487	specified	681,916
Cocoa-nuts...................	170	Cumin seed	694
Dye-woods, in sticks..........	586,362	Diamonds	53,148
Dyes, crude, berries, nuts, and		Drugs, medicinal, not specified	182,582
all others	404,709	All other, not specified	195,781
Indigo......................	256,474	Dyes, not specified...........	82,420
Gold and silver coin and bullion:		Earthenwares and china......	32,657
Gold coin.................	1,799,142	Embroideries of cotton, silk, or	
bullion	1,900	wool	6,877
Silver coin.............	721,865	Engravings, bound or unbound	4,846
bullion		Feathers, crude or dressed....	52,283
Guano	74,568	Flowers, artificial, and feathers	
Junk and oakum	1,319	prepared..................	3,376
Palm-leaf, unmanufactured	21,344	Fire-crackers................	52,662
Ratans and reeds, unmanufact'd	3,884	Fish:	
Seeds, trees, &c..............	5,544	Herring, in barrels........	246
Silk, raw	480,193	All other, not in barrels,	
Wood:		not specified.............	54,547
Mahogany...............	254,582	Sardines and other, in	
Rose	7,890	oil	31,917
All other cabinet.........	35,727	Flax, linens, and all manufac-	
All other articles free of duty.	26,367	tures of..................	123,871
		Fruits:	
Total free of duty........	6,934,528	Green, not specified.......	3,126
		Preserved and dried of all	
PAYING DUTY.		kinds, not specified	10,414
		Currants	2,741
Acids	3,162	Dates	1,959
Arrow-root..................	316	Figs	8,725
Beer, ale, &c.:		Lemons and limes	3,427
In casks.................	8,129	Oranges	12,513
bottles...............	11,229	Plums and prunes	2,697
Books, and all printed matter ..	10,561	Raisins	62,504
Blank	305	Furs:	
Brass, manufactures of, not spe-		Dressed on the skin.......	48,569
cified	1,666	Undressed not on the skin.	25,422
Bristles	42		
Bark, Peruvian or medicinal...	52,261	Ginger:	
Candles, wax and other	15,858	Root	12,032
Caps, gloves, mits, &c., of what-		Preserved or pickled	1,599
ever material composed......	1,238	Glass, all manufactures of.....	31,354
Chalk, of all kinds	2,336	Glue	180
Clothing, of all kinds.........	69,136	Gold and silver leaf, embroide-	
Coal, bituminous....	3,437	ries, and all manufactures of	
Cocoa	163,417	gold and silver	13,903
Tea	1,883,372	Jewelry, real and imitations ..	10,476
Coffee	5,637,856	Gums, copal, arabic, and other.	93,476
Chickory	76	Hair, of the alpaca, and all other	4,220
Combs	2,393	Bracelets, braids, and all	
Copper:		other manufactures of ..	4,405
Ore	75,858		
In pigs	287,153	Hemp:	
Manufactures	2,615	Russian, unmanufactured..	8,222
Sheathing, or yellow metal.	6,666	Manilla and other India ...	1,089

No. 12.—*Summary statement of goods, wares &c.*—Continued.

Articles.	Value.	Articles.	Value.
Hemp:		Oil-cake	$99,969
Jute, Sisal grass, coir, &c..	$13,301	Oils:	
Cables and cordage.......	251,563	Flax-seed, or linseed......	37,510
Gunny cloth, for cotton and		Whale and other fish	48,577
other bagging..........	559,542	Palm and cocoa-nut	66,785
Gunny bags	76,460	Castor	13,660
All other manufactures of		Olive	5,372
hemp, jute, &c	32,151	Petroleum...............	4,386
Hops	14,249	Essential, of all kinds	54,672
Hides and skins.............	614,381	Oil-cloths of all descriptions...	718
Honey	91,363	Opium	119,656
India-rubber:		Paints:	
Unmanufactured.........	57,407	White lead, and all other,	
Manufactures of.........	1	ground in oil	25,676
Gutta-percha and manu-		Dry	494
factures of.............	425	Paper:	
Ink and ink powders	354	Writing................	1,313
Iron :		Printing, sheathing, and	
Pig......................	3,243	other	1,701
Bar......................	4,842	Hangings	1,857
Railroad	30,268	All other manufactures of..	14,835
Rod, hoop, and band	2,140	Perfumery	67,780
Sheet	143	Quinine	3,265
Cables, chains, anchors,		Quicksilver...............	1,102
and wrought flues	19,708	Rags, woollen, and all, not for	
All other forms and manu-		paper	4,280
factures of.............	115,922	Rice	544,268
Steel, in bars and sheets...	1,922	Roman cement	300
Cutlery	49,343	Roots	2,267
Needles	5,697	Saddlery	580
All other manufactures of		Sago and sago flour	1,141
steel....................	18,375	Salt	79,197
Muskets and rifles........	236,171	Sarsaparilla	127,422
Swords and sabres	2,700	Seeds, canary and other........	692
Ivory:		Shell, horn, bone, and all man-	
Unmanufactured	13,981	ufactures of..............	7,915
Manufactures of.........	579	Silk, sewing and twist........	365
Japanned wares of all kinds...	409	Silk:	
Laces of all kinds............	4,106	Piece goods	16,305
Lead:		All other manufactures of.	339,206
In pigs and bars	5,200	Smoking pipes, of clay, brier,	
All other manufactures of.	666	or wood..................	7,360
Leather:		Soap:	
Skins tanned and dressed,		Toilet, and all perfumed...	187
and all upper	110,020	All other	43,525
Bend and sole	18,137	Soda, ash, sal and carb	10,180
Japanned, polished, and		Spices:	
patent	3,093	Cassia	18,372
All manufactures not spe-		Cloves	33,618
cified	17,048	Cinnamon................	11,737
Licorice, paste..............	201	Pepper, black and white..	421,724
Matches	295	Pimento	61,544
Matting..................	20,015	Nutmegs and mace.......	34,175
Metals, platina, and all manu-		Mustard	556
factures of.............	1,680	All other.................	10,322
Musical instruments........	2,082		
Mathematical and philosophi-		Spirits:	
cal instruments...........	509	Brandy	107,012
Nuts:		From grain	13,841
Almonds .... :..........	4,519	other materials	102,983
All other edible	27,875	Cordials, liqeurs, &c.....	20,874
Vegetable ivory...........	43		

No. 12.—*Summary statement of goods, wares, &c.*—Continued.

Articles.	Value.	Articles.	Value.
Wines:		Toys and dolls................	$7,034
In casks, of all kinds.....	$202,919	Umbrellas and parasols.......	915
Champagne, in bottles....	64,817	Vegetables, prepared..........	8,398
All other, in bottles.......	47,466	Vinegar......................	167
Sponges	55,126	Wax	7,738
Straw goods, hats, bonnets, &c.	10,417	Whalebone	20,102
Sugar:		Wood, manufactures of, not	
Brown	2,843,601	specified	45,657
Refined	524,017		
Confectionery	3,254	Wool:	
Molasses	460,919	Unmanufactured.........	3,016
Tar............................	41,041	Cloths of all kinds.......	323,982
Tin:		Blankets	21,953
In blocks or pigs.........	5,223	Carpets and carpeting	1,535
plates or sheets, and		Worsted and mixed piece	
terne tin.............	26,418	goods	48,046
Tin-foil	150	Flannels	64
All other manufactures of .	908	Shawls	40,500
Tonca beans................./...	3,777	Manufactures, not speci-	
Tobacco and cigars:		fied....................	249,358
In leaf, unmanufactured,		Zinc and spelter, and manufac-	
not stemmed............	620,481	tures of	47,327
Manufactures of all kinds,		Unenumerated articles........	162,275
not specified...........	110,556		
Cigars	416,011	Total paying duty	23,455,837

RECAPITULATION.

Free of duty..	$6,934,528
Dutiable	23,455,837
Total exports...	30,390,365

S. B. COLBY, *Register.*

TREASURY DEPARTMENT,
Register's Office, October 31, 1865.

No. 13

*Summary statement of goods, wares, and merchandise, the growth, produce, and
manufacture of foreign countries imported into the United States during the
fiscal year ending June 30, 1865.*

Articles.	Value.	Articles.	Value.
FREE OF DUTY.		Junk, old, and oaknm........	$135,316
		Machinery suitable for the	
Animals of all kinds, living....	$24,023	manufacture of flax and	
Articles imported under the pro-		linen only, and imported for	
visions of the reciprocity trea-		that purpose	130,969
ty with Great Britain.......	30,528,618	Models of invention and im-	
Articles of all kinds for the use		provements in the arts......	6,653
of the United States.........	1,878,962	Oils and other products of	
Articles, the produce of the Uni		American fisheries:	
ted States, brought back.....	2,390,356	Oils, spermaceti, whale	
Books for the library of Congress	17,718	and other fish.........	761,869
Bolting cloths..............	30,223	Other products of fisheries.	416,562
Burrstones, unmanufactured ...	15,192	Paintings and statuary, the	
Cabinets of coins, medals, &c..	145	production of American ar-	
Drugs and dyes :		tists	58,985
Acids used for chemical and		Palm-leaf, unmanufactured...	48,680
manufacturing purposes,		Platina, unmanufactured.....	80,226
not specified............	920	Rags of cotton and linen, for	
Berries, nuts, and other		the manufacture of paper,	
crude dyes, not specified .	48,339	when imported direct.......	995,239
Bismuth.................	10,609	Ratans and reeds, unmanufac-	
Cochineal	343,668	tured.....................	141,156
Indigo.when impor'd direct		Silk, raw, or as reeled from	
from place of production.	601,263	the cocoon, when imported	
Lac dye.................	38,932	direct	1,040,809
Madder :		Specimens of natural history,	
Root	47,399	botany, and mineralogy....	30,026
Ground or prepared ..	392,406	Substances used expressly for	
Nutgalls.................	9,274	manures, not specified......	206
Turmeric....	3,402	Wood, unmanufactured :	
Wood or pastel...........	2,044	Cedar	144,657
Dyewood in sticks :		Lignumvitæ	20,412
Logwood	581,891	Ebony	10,433
Camwood	3,566	Mahogany...............	103,873
Fustic..............	83,173	Rose	136,243
Brazil wood.........	87,426	Box, lancewood, grena-	
Felt, adhesive, for sheathing ves-		dilla, and all cabinet	
sels	12,162	woods, not specified.....	47,680
Gold and silver bullion and coin:		All other articles	200,282
Bullion :			
Gold	27,764	Total free of duty.......	51,061,532
Silver	1,352,077		
Coin :			
Gold	5,092,245	**PAYING DUTY.**	
Silver	753,291		
Guano	273,330	Acids :	
Gypsum or plaster of Paris,		Acetic, acetous, and pyro-	
unground..................	25,739	ligneous	2,874
Household effects, old and in		Nitric and muriatic	1,011
use, of persons arriving from		Sulphuric..............	257
foreign countries, for use and		Alabaster, and manufactures	
not for sale :		of, and spar ornaments.....	9,578
Wearing apparel and per-		Arrowroot	9,760
sonal effects...........	1,508,472	Asphaltum	813
Horse-hair used for weaving,		Beads and bead ornaments ...	243,036
cleaned or uncleaned, drawn		Beer, ale, and porter :	
or undrawn	265,547	In casks...............	17,652
Ice	31,040	In bottles..............	82,913

Summary statement of goods, wares, &c.—Continued.

Articles.	Value.	Articles.	Value.
Billiard chalk	797	Copper:	
Bone black, ivory black, or		Old copper	$105, 936
Frankfort black	2, 164	Copper ore	828, 860
Blacking	4, 030	All manufactures of cop-	
Books, periodicals, pamphlets,		per not specified	14, 286
and all printed matters	289, 310	Cork bark..................	50, 175
Blank books	20, 318	Cork manufactures, all kinds..	157, 539
Brass, and manufacturers of:		Cotton, and manufacturers of	
In pigs and bars	1, 089	cotton:	
Old, and fit only for remanu-		Cotton not manufactured..	14, 772, 668
facture	26, 222	Cottons, plain brown, or not	
Manufactures not specified .	155, 969	bleached:	
Bristles......................	220, 004	Value 16 cents or less per	
Bronze manufactures	27, 944	square yard...........	103, 616
Brushes and brooms	107, 395	Value over 16 cents per	
Butter.......................	42	square yard	1, 292
Buttons and button moulds....	594, 594	Cottons, plain, bleached:	
Canes and walking sticks.....	8, 789	Value 20 cents or less per	
Candles and tapers:		square yard	809, 961
Tallow	2	Value over 20 cents per	
Stearine and adamantine ..	2, 914	square yard	103, 296
Paraffine, sperm, and wax.	1, 641	Cottons, printed or colored, value	
Cards, playing	241	25 cents or less per square	
Carriages and parts...........	5, 670	yard :	
Chalk :		Not over 100 threads per	
White....................	1, 288	square inch, including	
Red, French and all other.	1, 160	warp and filling, and	
Cheese	64, 301	weighing over 5 ounces	
Chicory root	341	per square yard	12, 194
Chicory, ground or prepared..	48, 495	Over 100 and not over 200	
Chloride of lime or bleaching		threads to the square	
powders	598, 147	inch, including warp	
Chronometers, box or ship's,		and filling.............	1, 222, 911
and parts of................	298	Valued over 25 cents per	
Clay, unwrought, pipe clay, fire		square yard.............	63, 425
clay, and kaoline	59, 188	Jeans, denims, drillings,	
Fuller's earth	1, 779	bed-tickings, ginghams,	
Cliff stone	907	cottonades, pantaloon	
Clocks, and parts of...........	49, 938	stuffs, and cotton goods	
Clothing, not elsewhere:		of like description, not	
Clothing, ready-made,		exceeding 20 cents per	
wholly or in part of wool..	50, 679	square yard :	
Balmoral skirts, wholly or		Not bleached or colored:	
in part of wool.........	2, 150	Not over 200 threads per	
Clothing, not of wool......	1, 140, 881	square inch, counting	
Coal :		warp and filling......	32
Bituminous	568, 076	Over 200 threads per	
All other coal	30	square inch, counting	
Cobalt	216	warp and filling......	145
Cocoa and chocolate:		Bleached :	
Not ground	156, 045	Not over 200 threads per	
Ground..................	24	square inch, counting	
Cocoa shells and leaves ...	39	warp and filling......	6, 036
Chocolate	348	Over 200 threads per	
Coffee.......................	10, 966, 541	square inch, counting	
Combs and like, shell and bone,		warp and filling.....	65
manufactures	79, 823	Printed, painted, or colored:	
Copper, and manuf's of copper:		Not over 100 threads per	
In pigs	138, 700	square inch, counting	
Sheathing copper	4, 481	warp and filling......	80, 494
Yellow metal	47, 937	Over 100 and not over	
Sheets, plates, braziers'		200 threads per square	
copper, bottoms, rods,		inch, counting warp	
bolts, nails, and spikes..	169	and filling	264, 019

Summary statement of goods, wares, &c.—Continued.

Articles.	Value.	Articles.	Value.
Cottons:		Drugs and dyes:	
Over 200 threads per sq. in.	$1,445	Borax :	
Jeans, denims, &c., over		Crude or tincal	$1,311
20 cents per square yard :		Refined	1,399
Not bleached, bleached,		Buchu leaves	1,860
or printed	659	Calomel..................	381
Cotton velvet................	57,399	Camphor :	
Cotton thread, in spools of 100		Crude	29,931
yards, or less, excess in pro-		Refined	1,649
portion....................	378,188	Cantharides, or Spanish flies	235
Cotton thread, not on spools ..	230,104	Cardamoms	10,990
Shirts and drawers woven		Carmine lake, dry	3,897
or made on frames wholly		Copperas, green vitriol, or	
of cotton	88,455	sulphate of iron........	1,364
Cotton hosiery................	1,925,362	Coriander seed............	2,122
Laces, braids, trimmings,		Cream of tartar	138,418
gimps, cords, and gal-		Cubebs	25,453
loons	381,851	Cudbear	44,962
All other manuf's, wholly		Cumin seed	6
or in part of cotton, not		Cutch, or catechu, and	
otherwise provided for..	1,506,643	terra japonica..........	128,067
Diamonds and gems, real and		Cuttle-fish bone...........	1,105
imitation:		Dragon's blood	120
Not set....................	647,816	Ergot.....................	1,374
Set	23,880	Ether, fluid not specified..	834
Diamonds, glaziers'	115	Gambier	140,066
Drugs and dyes:		Gelatine	8,682
Acetates :		Glycerine	758
Of lime	15	Fenugreek and fennel seed.	1,378
Of soda..............	72	Indigo, extract of.........	5,295
Acids :		Flowers, leaves, and plants,	
Benzoic..............	2,575	medicinal, not otherwise	
Boracic	11,328	provided for	32,858
Citric	20,847	Iodine :	
Gallic	208	Crude	9,580
Oxalic	20,843	Resublimed	16,424
Tannic or tannin	91	Ipecac	24,549
Tartaric..............	38,067	Jalap	35,533
Albumen................	9,629	Lac, seed lac, and stick lac.	3,554
Alum, alum substitute,		Licorice :	
aluminous cake, and sul-		Root..................	25,435
phate of alumina.......	10,699	Paste or rolls	224,008
Aloes	7,205	Logwood and other dye-	
Ammonia, sal ammonia,		wood extracts..........	7,504
and carbonate of am-		Madder extract and garan-	
monia	59,230	cine	234,832
Analine dyes and colors,		Magnesia :	
roseine, mauve, magenta.	101,521	Carbonate	6,071
Annatto seed or extract. ..	68	Calcined	5,673
Antimony, crude and regu-		Manna....................	3,300
lus of.................	9,401	Morphine and its salts....	421
Argols or crude tartar	185,452	Murexide	105
Arsenic	6,205	Nut-galls	532
Asafœtida	2,486	Nux vomica	840
Balsam copaiva...........	31,225	Opium	373,054
Balsam, Peruvian...........	1,606	Opium prepared for smo-	
Balsam tolu.......,......	10,047	king and opium extract.	127,511
Bark :		Phosphorus	21,643
Peruvian, cinchona, Li-		Rosé leaves..............	329
ma, and calisaya.....	143,489	Safflower	10,180
Quilla bark	1,414	Rhubarb	660
Bitter apples, colocynth or		Santonin	5,399
coloquintida	789	Sarsaparilla..............	78,528

Summary statement of goods, wares, &c.—Continued.

Articles.	Value.	Articles.	Value.
Drugs and dyes:		Flax:	
Senna.....................	$813	Thread lacings and insertings......	$99,715
Smaltz and zaffre, (oxide of cobalt)..............	34	All other manufactures of flax....................	279,385
Sulphate of quinine, and all other salts of........	26,301	Flowers, artifical,and feathers, finished......	120,457
Sulphate of copper, (blue vitriol).................	5,061	Fruits:	
Sulphate of zinc, (white vitriol).................	644	Oranges, lemons, and limes	679,382
Sumac..................	188,733	Olives	4,024
Terra alba................	6,041	Grapes	17,645
Tin oxide, muriate, and other salts of...........	92	Pine-apples, plantains, and bananas..........	111,928
Turmeric	4,242	Cocoa-nuts	53,260
Verdigris	10,279	Fruits in juice, and fruit juice	26,728
Chemical preparations	39,182	Fruits preserved in bottles or jars, in brandy, sugar, &c....................	60,281
Lac dye	4,109		
Medicines prepared, not specified..............	38,020	Green, dry, and ripe fruits, not otherwise provided for	22,475
Drugs and dyes, not specified	72,229		
Earthenwares and china:		Prunes and plums	121,042
Brown earthen and common stone ware	28,296	Dates	42,150
China and porcelain ware, plain white	1,815,719	Currants, Zante, and all other.................	92,322
China and porcelain ware, gilded and ornamented..	186,387	Figs	72,966
Embroideries of cotton, silk, or wool, not otherwise provided for............	521,463	Raisins..................	499,060
		Furs:	
		Undressed on the skin....	1,031,264
Emery: ore or rock and pulverized	30,126	Dressed on the skin	649,426
Engravings and engraved plates.	67,136	Dressed not on the skin ..	11,036
Fans of palm-leaf.............	8,802	Hatters' furs	566,744
Fans, all other	72,895	Fur caps, hats, and all manufactures of furs...	7,048
Feathers, ostrich or other ornamental:		Ginger:	
Crude	188,619	Root or green...........	54,961
Dressed	94,992	Ground	971
Feathers and downs for beds...	5,024	Preserved or pickled	990
Fire-crackers per box of 40 packs	56,707	Glass, and manufactures of glass: cylinder, crown, or common window glass:	
Fish:		Not above 10 by 15 inches.	158,616
Mackerel	152	Above 10 by 15 and not above 16 by 24 inches..	73,263
Herring	30,680	Above 16 by 24 and not above 24 by 30 inches .	84,540
Salmon	188	Above 24 by 30 inches ...	78,475
All other, in barrels......	238	Cylinder and crown glass polished:	
All not in barrels, sold by weight	17,390	Not above 10 by 15 inches..............	3,016
Sardines and anchovies, preserved in oil or otherwise	267,452	Above 10 by 15, and not above 16 by 24 inches.	1,625
Flax, not manufactured	301,829	Above 16 by 24, and not above 24 by 30 inches.	1,320
Tow of flax..............	130,111	Above 24 by 30, and not above 24 by 60 inches.	328
Linens, brown or bleached.	7,113,661		
Brown hollands, burlaps, and all like manufactures, of which flax, jute, or hemp shall be the material of chief value...	1,731,568	Fluted, rolled, or rough plate..............	3,926
		Cast polished plate glass, not silvered:	
Flax or linen yarns for carpets....................	84,758	Not above 16 by 24 inches..............	2,522
Thread, packthread, and twine..	732,365		

*Summary statement of goods, wares, &c.—*Continued.

Articles.	Value.	Articles.	Value.
Glass:		Hair and manufactures of hair:	
Above 16 by 24, and not above 24 by 60 inches.............	$48,822	Hair pencils..............	$2,748
		Hair curled for beds or mattresses.........	6
Above 24 by 60 inches.	129,197	Hair cloth and hair seatings, and other hair manufactures, not specified.	119,978
Cast polished plate glass, silvered:			
Not above 16 by 24 inches.............	121,367	Human hair, not cleaned.	24,189
Above 16 by 24 inches, and not above 24 by 60 inches	114,345	Human hair, cleaned or drawn......	61,403
		Human hair, manufactured......	37,316
Above 24 by 60 inches.	7,525	Hair bracelets, braids, curls and ringlets......	7,289
Glass bottles.............	33,482	Hair of hogs.............	95
Glass bottles containing liquors	77,546	Hats and bonnets of hair or whalebone	5,908
Crystals for watches	30,533	Hats and bonnets of vegetable substance........	170,337
Disks of glass............	4,764	Hemp and manufactures of hemp:	
Glassware:		Russian................	195,264
Plain	50,105	Manilla.................	1,496,311
Cut....................	91,383	Jute and sun hemp......	212,121
Bohemian, porcelain, ornamented, or painted glassware	61,692	Jute buts	5,605
		Sisal grass and like cordage material	36,563
Glass manufactures, not specified	61,350	All other vegetable substances used for like purposes.............	342
Glue......................	1		
Gold and silver manufactures:		Codilla or tow of hemp...	3,126
Gold leaf	208	Hemp yarn.............	27,727
Silver leaf..............	5,174	Jute yarn..............	167,041
Epaulettes, laces, knots, and tassels...........	21,065	Coir yarn	23,996
		Cables and cordage, tarred	17,920
Brooches, bracelets, rings, &c., of gold	32,820	Manilla cables and cordage, untarred	3,274
Silver plated metal and plated wares	579	All other cables and cordage	2,979
Embroideries of gold and silver	1,197	Seines of hemp..........	24,670
All other manufactures of gold and silver.........	22,560	Sheetings of hemp, Russia	82,599
		Sail duck...............	767,197
Grindstones, unwrought.......	12,656	Hemp or jute carpeting ..	33,109
Grindstones or burrstones, wrought or finished	1,571	Gunny cloth and gunny bags	302,796
Gums:		All other manufactures of hemp, jute, &c........	97,536
Arabic, Jedda, and all other sorts of.................	128,427	Grass cloth..............	7,298
Senegal	4,875	Hides and skins, dry.........	2,623,552
Copal, Kowrie, Sandarac and other varnish gums.	160,141	Hides and skins, pickled or green, wet................	252,040
Shellac.................	120,737	Goat skins and baled skins.	1,441,537
Benzoin, or Benjamin.....	444	Horns	64
Myrrh..................	185	Honey	87,954
All other gums..........	29,731	Hops...................	668
Gunpowder..................	38,974	India-rubber:	
Gutta-percha, crude	62,130	Crude or milk of........	1,160,895
Gutta-percha manufactures	2,060	Shoes, boots, webbing, and other manufactures of.	188,245
Gypsum or plaster of Paris, ground or calcined..........	8,956	Manufactures of India-rubber and silk........	76,727
Hair and manufactures of hair:			
Dress goods of mohair, alpaca, &c	84,697	Indigo, imported under 14th section	324,207
Lasting of mohair cloth for shoes or buttons.........	70,981	Ink and ink powders.........	30,014
Manufactures of mohair and goats' hair, not specified.	220,670		

Summary statement of goods, wares, &c.—Continued.

Articles.	Value.	Articles.	Value.
Iron and manufactures of iron:		Steel and manufactures of	
Pig iron	$679,236	steel, in ingots, bars, or	
Bar iron, rolled or ham-		sheets:	
mered	2,173,389	Valued at 7 cents per	
Bar iron, other............	98,127	pound	$582,675
Railroad iron.............	2,806,696	Valued above 7 and not	
Boiler and other plate	21,554	above 11 cents per	
Iron wire, not less than		pound	739,625
No. 16	15,763	Valued above 11 cents per	
Iron wire, less than No. 16.	3,374	pound	107,164
Iron wire, covered	87	Steel wire less than ¼	
Sheet-iron, common, not		inch in diameter	37,543
thinner than No. 20	94,735	Steel in forms not other-	
Sheet-iron, common, thin-		wise provided for.....	215,373
ner than No. 20	114,265	Cross-cut saws	337
Sheet-iron, smooth or pol-		Mill, pit, and drag saws.	409
ished	163,183	Handsaws	23,996
Band and hoop iron, not		Back saws	283
thinner than ¼ inch.....	61,868	Files, rasps, and floats..	311,781
Band and hoop iron, thin-		Skates................	9,553
ner than ¼ inch	127,072	Penknives and pocket	
Slit rods	65,961	knives	548,293
All other rolled or ham-		All other cutlery	368,734
mered	247,872	Needles for knitting and	
Locomotive tire...........	210,385	sewing machines......	1,496
Mill irons and iron for ships		All other needles.......	120,514
and engines, wrought in		Steel squares for meas-	
pieces of 25 pounds or		uring	5
more	7,646	Side-arms	6,171
Anchors and parts of	19,085	Fire-arms, muskets,	
Anvils, cables, and cable		rifles, and other......	131,039
chains	206,482	All other manufactures	
Hammers, sledges, axles,		of steel	619,063
and other wrought	2,228	Istle or tampico fibre	25,594
Trace, halter, and fence		Ivory, not manufactured......	285,949
chains	173,474	Ivory or bone dice or chess-	
Malleable iron in castings.	207	men, or balls	3,400
Wrought-iron, rail'd chairs,		Ivory manufactures, all other..	3,295
and nuts and washers		Ivory nuts, vegetable	38,944
punched	1,938	Japanned wares, all kinds not	
Wrought hinges, bed		otherwise provided for......	12,313
screws, board nails,		Jellies of all kinds	3,056
spikes, rivets, and bolts.	8,944	Jet and manufactures of jet...	27,161
Wrought horseshoe nails..	13,653	Jewelry, real or imitation of...	142,990
Cut nails and spikes.....	506	Lead and manufactures of lead:	
Cut tacks, brads, and sprigs	187	In pigs and bars	1,195,093
Wrought steam, gas, and		In sheets, pipe, and shot..	14,261
water tubes and flues...	87,500	Old and scrap	43,334
Screws for wood	8,425	Lead ore.................	26
Cast-iron vessels, stoves,		Manufactures of lead not	
and stove plates........	6,149	specified	17,092
Andirons, sadirons, tailors'		Leather and manufactures of	
and hatters' irons	11,114	leather:	
Cast butts and hinges	1,607	Bend and sole	10,472
Hollow-ware, glazed or		Tanned calfskins.........	686,629
tinned	3,152	Skins, tanned and dressed,	
Taggers' iron and cast-		and all other upper	
iron not specified.......	6,559	leather................	374,293
All other manufactures of		Japanned, polished or pat-	
iron	928,337	ent	45,910
Old scrap iron	296,726	Gloves of skin or leather..	827,960
Galvanized or coated iron.	1,876	All other manufactures of	
		leather	194,985

Summary statement of goods, wares, &c.—Continued.

Articles.	Value.	Articles.	Value.
Maccaroni and vermicelli	$14,290	Oils, fixed or expressed:	
Marble, white or statuary, in		Olive oil (not salad)......	$54,248
block, rough, or square.....	40	Olive oil (salad, in flasks	
Marble, veined and all other		or bottles).............	90,882
rough.....................	112,844	Mustard oil	42
Marble manufactures not speci-		Croton oil................	2,251
fied.....................	11,067	Oils, volatile or essential:	
Mats of cocoanut, China, and		Bay or laurel	30
all floor mattings	142,032	Almond..................	3,918
Meats:		Anise	1,048
Beef and pork...........	921	Amber, crude and rectified	22
Bacon and hams	3,854	Bergamot	38,452
Meats preserved in cans		Caraway	2,858
or otherwise...........	11,588	Cassia	2,060
Metals:		Cloves...................	1,216
Platina, not manufactured.	22,723	Cinnamon	24
Platina manufactures.....	403	Cajeput	325
Albata, argentine, German		Citronella................	5,436
silver, and all like	17,357	Cognac or œnanthic ether.	175
Britannia and manufac-		Fennel	294
tures of, and pewter	33,826	Juniper	5,636
Dutch or bronze, in leaf ..	46,694	Thyme, white	299
Bronze powders..........	25,492	Orange and lemon	31,736
Nickel	53,692	Origanum................	705
Pewter, old	4,714	Roses, ottar of..........	10,498
All other metals and metal		Valerian	89
compositions not other-		Fruit ethers, essences, or	
wise provided for	41,895	oils, made of fusel oil, or of	
Mineral waters...............	5,197	fruit, or imitation thereof.	33
Mosses, seaweed and other		Brandy coloring	17
vegetable substances used		All other essential oils, not	
for mattresses	1,035	otherwise provided for...	28,606
Music, printed, bound or un-		Paintings in oil, or otherwise,	
bound	12,312	not by American artists, and	
Musical instruments..........	159,536	statuary	252,235
Music strings of animal fibre,		Paints:	
gut strings................	17,346	White lead, red lead, lith-	
Music strings of metal........	3,443	arge, and nitrate of lead.	97,720
Mathematical, philosophical,		Sugar of lead............	3,874
and optical instruments		Whiting and Paris white,	
and apparatus.............	57,258	dry.....................	2,208
Nuts:		Putty...................	715
Almonds, not shelled.....	78,637	Ochres:	
Almonds, shelled.........	17,660	Umber..............	1,517
Filberts and walnuts	88,615	Mineral green, French	
Peanuts and other ground		and Paris green....	18
nuts	118,721	Ultra marine	20,747
All other edible nuts not		All other ochres, dry,	
specified	57,404	not specified.......	12,079
Oil-cloths	33,060	All other ochres ground	
Oils, fixed or expressed:		in oil	122
Flaxseed or linseed	30,736	Prussian blue.	2,527
Hemp or rapeseed	4,050	Vermillion	49,674
Petroleum and coal oil,		Barytes, sulphate of, or	
crude	770	heavy spar	2,343
Petroleum and coal oil,		Blanc fix, satin white, &c.,	
refined	690	of barytes............	774
Seal oil	5,677	Nitrates of barytes	26
Neat's-foot and other animal	5,964	Oxide of zinc...........	4,217
Palm oil	257,267	Water colors, dry or liquid	15,640
Cocoa-nut oil.............	62,660	All other paints and paint-	
Castor oil	18,780	ers' colors............	47,847
Almond oil...............	1,430	Paper and manufactures of paper:	
Oil of mace	103	Writing paper...........	97,510

Summary statement of goods, wares, &c.—Continued.

Articles.	Value.	Articles.	Value.
Paper and manufactures of paper:		Seeds:	
Printing paper, unsized ..	$4,559	Flax-seed or linseed......	$1,228,761
Paper-hangings..........	20,642	Hemp-seed..............	10,702
Paper boxes.............	32,399	Rape-seed..............	2,456
Sheathing paper	1,527	Anise and star anise......	4,807
Manufacture of, not speci-		Canary seed.............	28,805
fied....................	164,666	Caraway................	5,019
Parchment	9,756	Mustard, brown or white..	43,986
Papier-mache, and manu-		Garden and agricultural	
factures of, not specified.	5,393	seeds	52,874
Pens, metallic	47,126	Seeds of flowering plants	
Penholders and pen tips	6,403	and bulbous roots.......	20,354
Pencils, black lead and all other .	59,911	Shell, horn, bone, and vege-	
Percussion caps and fulminates.	48,114	table ivory, manufactures of.	21,862
Perfumeries and cosmetics, all		Silk and manufactures of	
kinds.....................	77,173	silk:	
Philosophical apparatus, and		Silk in the gum	154,920
all articles for schools, reli-		Spun silk for filling in	
gious and other societies....	1,521	skeins or cops	19,448
Philosophical apparatus not for		Silk floss	9,731
schools	13,321	Sewing silk in the gum,	
Photographs and stereoscopes		and purified	10,630
in all forms	12,579	Silk velvets	461,820
Pickles, sauces, and capers ...	50,797	Silk ribbons.............	2,541,812
Pins, all metallic	31,813	Silk buttons	10,100
Plated and guilt ware	16,850	Silk dress goods	3,606,601
Pipes of clay, common or white.	28,002	Silk shawls, scarfs, &c...	337,006
Pipes and bowls, meerchaum,		Silk, raw, from beyond	
lava, &c., not otherwise		Cape of Good Hope....	153,061
provided for	122,827	Silk hosiery..............	205,737
Pipe cases, stems, and all		Silk laces, braids, fringes,	
smokers' articles..........	33,623	and trimmings........	971,094
Plumbago or black lead	151,525	Silk hats, caps, bonnets,	
Potash and salts of potash :		and webbing	14,195
Saltpetre or nitrate of		Silk manufactures, wholly	
potash:		of silk, not specified....	154,478
Crude	548,551	Silk mixed goods, not	
Refined.................	36,435	otherwise provided for .	633,337
Prussiate of potash, yellow.	8,215	Slates, and all other manufac-	
Prussiate of potash, red...	17,355	tures of slate	5,982
Chlorate of potash........	28,974	Soap :	
Potatoes	12,155	Common, Castile, and all	
Pulu	2,285	like	73,385
Quicksilver	65,657	Toilet, and all perfumed..	12,600
Rags, woollen, and all not for		Soda, and salts of:	
paper.......................	27,054	Soda ash................	1,326,273
Rags, cotton or linen, from		Sal soda................	88,593
beyond Cape of Good Hope .	1,819	Caustic soda	206,806
Ratans, from beyond Cape of		Nitrate of soda...........	311,401
Good Hope.................	12,296	Bicarbonate of soda	207,389
Ratans and reeds, manufac-		Epsom salts.............	1,328
tured	650	Rochelle salts	403
Rice:		Spices:	
Cleaned.................	623,035	Cassia and cassia buds...	61,657
Uncleaned	240,460	Cloves and clove stems...	31,599
Paddy..................	63,737	Cinnamon..............	4,067
Rosin.......................	2,181	Black and white pepper,	
Saddlery wares, not otherwise		ground and unground..	208,266
provided for...............	59,946	Cayenne pepper, ground	
Sago and sago flour..........	13,274	and unground.........	9,694
Salt:		Pimento, ground and un-	
In bulk.................	350,492	ground	7,035
In bags or other packages.	381,115	Mustard, in bulk	555
		Mustard, in glass or tin ...	3,901

Summary statement of goods, wares, &c.—Continued.

Articles.	Value.	Articles.	Value.
Spices:		Tobacco, and manufactures of	
Nutmegs and mace.......	$32,585	tobacco:	
Vanilla beans............	13,019	Cigars, valued over $15 and not over $30 per M.	$450,433
Spirits and wines:		Cigars, valued over $30	
Brandy......	155,574	and not over $45 per M.	329,465
Spirits from grain........	58,326	Cigars, valued over $45	
Spirits from other materials.................	51,351	per M..................	128,517
Cordials, liqueurs, and all like beverages	25,449	Toys and dolls..........	343,282
Bay rum	8,888	Trees, shrubs, and plants, for fruit or ornamental	7,405
Wines, value 50 cents per gallon	563,725	Type, type metal, and stereotype plates	2,055
Wines, value over 50 cents and not over $1 per gallon......	174,468	Umbrellas and parasols.......	4,016
		Varnish.................	17,667
Wines, value over $1 per gallon..............	98,232	Vegetables and yams, crude, not specified..............	59,375
Wines sparkling, in bottles	492,720	Vegetables prepared or preserved, not specified........	21,340
All other distilled spirits..	4,849	Vinegar..................	2,496
Spirits of turpentine..........	18,186	Watches and watch materials..	1,269,709
Sponges	45,254	Wax.............	6,414
Starch	129	Wax manufactures..........	262
Straw laces, braids, and chip and palm-leaf ornaments....	438,292	Wheat, grains, flour, and meal:	
Sugar:		Wheat	1,336
All not above No. 12, Dutch standard, in color.	21,391,127	Wheat flour.............	9,630
		Rye and rye flour	1,018
Above No. 12, and not above No. 15.......	3,132,197	Barley	26
		Oats....................	373
Above No. 15, and not above No. 20, not stove-dried	659,582	Oatmeal....	1,239
		Indian corn	131
		Indian meal	8
Loaf and other refined, above No. 20	59,996	Pearl or hulled barley....	70
		Beans and peas...........	275
Sugar candy and confectionery	944	All other grains, bran, shorts, and meals	12,803
Sirup of sugar-cane	207,265	Willow or osier, prepared for use.......................	28,028
Molasses from sugar-cane.	7,264,202	Willow or osier manufactures.	88,803
Sulphur of brimstone, crude...	257,618	Wood, and manufactures of wood:	
Sulphur, flour of	8,360	Rough timber and unmanufactured wood	11,686
Tallow	235		
Tapioca	14,792	Cabinet ware and all manufactures not otherwise provided for :..........	189,748
Tar.........................	43,499		
Tea......	4,702,856	Lumber: Boards, plank, scantling, and hewn timber	118
Tin and manufactures of tin:			
In blocks, pigs, or bars...	541,764	Staves for pipes, hogsheads, &c..............	64,435
In plates, sheets, and terne tin.....	2,711,127	Ebony, from beyond Cape of Good Hope..........	263
Plates, galvanized or coated	30,959	Firewood.....	57
Foil	18,387	Wool and manufactures of wool:	
Manufactures not otherwise provided for......	4,438	Wool on the skin, or wool skins......	108,593
Tobacco, and manufactures of tobacco:		Wool, value 12 cents or less per pound	2,012,175
Leaf....................	480,758		
Stemmed, and all manufactured, not otherwise provided for..........	36,976	Wool, value over 12 cents and not over 24 cents per pound	4,144,262
Snuff...................	1,833		
Cigars, valued $15 or less per M......	105,302		

Summary statement of goods, wares, &c.—Continued.

Articles.	Value.	Articles.	Value.
Wool and manufactures of wool:		Wool and manufactures of wool:	
Wool, value over 24 cents and not over 32 cents per pound	$9,318	Dress goods of wool or worsted, gray or uncolored	$97,414
Wool, value over 32 cents per pound	8,766	Dress goods of wool or worsted, printed or colored	7,719,725
Wool, scoured	26,587	Hosiery, and other knit goods of wool	309,968
Woollen flax, waste or shoddy	410,395	Bunting, and other manufactures of worsted, not otherwise provided for	4,876,590
Woollen cloths, wholly or in part of wool	5,223,524	Felting, and endless belts for paper or printing machines	87,213
Shawls, wholly or in part of wool	34,295	Hats of wool	615
Blankets, wholly or in part of wool	838,741	All other mats of wool and other material	19,239
Flannels, not colored, value 30 cents or less per square yard	12,956	Zinc, spelter, or teutenegue, in blocks or pigs	119,391
Flannels, colored or white, value over 30 cents per square yard	52,219	Zinc, in sheets	200,213
Flannels composed in part of silk	18,154	Zinc manufactures	11,123
Carpets: Wilton, Saxony, Aubusson, velvet, and all jacquard woven	129,613	Unenumerated articles paying ad valorem duties:	
Brussels or tapestry, printed on the warp	217,375	At 10 per cent	93,324
Treble ingrain, three-ply, and worsted chain Venetian	7,520	At 15 per cent	475
		At 20 per cent	75,402
Two-ply, ingrain, and yarn Venetian	86	At 25 per cent	6,890
Druggets, bockings, and felt carpets	18,170	At 30 per cent	49,458
		At 35 per cent	37,487
Carpets, all kinds not specified	98,895	At 40 per cent	6,463
Yarns of wool or worsted	393,130	At 50 per cent	4,046
Balmorals, and all skirtings	192,121	Value of articles paying specific duties not in the preceding form	1,158
		Total imports paying duty	183,258,278
		Total imports free of duty	51,081,532
		Total imports	234,339,810

S. B. COLBY, *Register.*

TREASURY DEPARTMENT,
Register's Office, November 1, 1865.

18 F

No. 14.—*Statement exhibiting the tonnage of American and foreign vessels entered and cleared at each district of the United States during the year ending June 30, 1865.*

Districts.	ENTERED.			CLEARED.		
	American vessels.	Foreign vessels.	Total.	American vessels.	Foreign vessels.	Total.
	Tons.	*Tons.*	*Tons.*	*Tons.*	*Tons.*	*Tons.*
Passamaquoddy, Maine	75,366	8,667	84,033	92,842	9,102	101,944
Machias, Maine	1,399	51	1,450	14,199	1,312	15,511
Frenchman's Bay, Maine	739		739	3,359		3,359
Penobscot, Maine				1,863	132	1,995
Waldoborough, Maine	37	611	648	10,706	551	11,257
Wiscasset, Maine	977		977	259		259
Bath, Maine	2,872	1,964	4,836	9,333	2,226	11,559
Portland and Falmouth, Me.	45,893	88,554	134,447	91,797	96,031	187,828
Saco, Maine				96		96
Belfast, Maine	2,227	791	3,018	15,518	791	16,309
Bangor, Maine	4,245	5,658	9,903	29,719	14,534	44,253
Portsmouth, N. H.	268	4,121	4,389	1,440	4,216	5,656
Vermont, Vt.	26,690	46,082	72,772	19,981	37,229	77,210
Newburyport, Mass.	2,597	3,072	5,669	6,349	4,497	10,846
Gloucester, Mass.	4,391	12,844	17,235	4,887	13,716	18,603
Salem and Beverly, Mass.	2,553	11,447	13,999	3,198	11,103	14,301
Marblehead, Mass.	115	4,063	4,177		3,953	3,953
Boston and Charlestown, Mass.	178,202	476,833	655,035	175,919	489,479	665,398
Plymouth, Mass.		545	545	80	545	625
Fall River, Mass.	3,180	1,685	4,865	2,638	1,421	4,059
New Bedford, Mass.	27,633	3,184	30,817	19,016	3,672	22,688
Edgartown, Mass.	15,158	3,932	19,090	960		960
Nantucket, Mass.	76		76	107		107
Providence, R. I.	9,835	14,724	24,559	6,380	13,894	20,274
Bristol and Warren, R. I.	2,815	502	3,317	2,601	502	3,103
Newport, R. I.	3,434	493	3,927	1,852	392	2,244
Middletown, Conn.	523	139	662	163	139	302
New London, Conn.	3,525	1,358	4,883	3,584	824	4,408
New Haven, Conn.	11,466	4,500	15,966	9,476	2,888	12,364
Fairfield, Conn.	914	2,035	2,949	287	1,238	1,525
Stonington, Conn.	420	214	634	44	214	258
Genesee, N. Y.	27,540	92,016	119,556	76,682	92,197	168,879
Oswego, N. Y.	213,858	222,694	436,552	186,285	221,299	407,564
Niagara, N. Y.	56,378	49,696	106,076	932	49,683	50,615
Buffalo Creek, N. Y.	372,032	88,964	460,996	375,666	86,497	462,163
Oswegatchie, N. Y.		33,665	33,665		33,625	33,625
Champlain, N. Y.	54,306	48,735	103,041	54,727	40,534	95,261
Cape Vincent, N. Y.	144,994	95,601	240,595	144,145	93,189	237,334
Dunkirk, N. Y.	571	1,305	1,876	232	1,305	1,537
Sag Harbor, N. Y.				614		614
New York, N. Y.	774,136	1,301,341	2,075,477	629,186	1,473,729	2,102,915
Perth Amboy, N. J.				2,019	1,186	3,205
Newark, N. J.	952	1,236	2,188		550	550
Philadelphia, Pa.	78,836	80,743	159,579	51,870	90,692	142,562
Erie, Pa.	4,177	14,330	18,507	3,866	14,864	18,730
Delaware, Del.	488	751	1,239	705	531	1,236
Baltimore, Md.	35,006	53,460	88,466	37,906	71,821	109,727
Georgetown, D. C.		77	77	601	77	678
Norfolk and Portsmouth, Va.				2,646		2,646
Alexandria, Va.	1,009		1,009	917		917
Beaufort, N. C.		30	30	677	30	707
Beaufort, S. C.	322	446	768	1,736	365	2,101
Pensacola, Fla.				1,180		1,180
Key West, Fla.	3,954	2,388	6,342	17,921	2,280	20,201
Fernandina, Fla.		12	12	120	12	132
New Orleans, La.	23,508	27,462	50,970	38,726	34,139	72,865
Miami, Ohio	4,904	8,289	13,193	3,310	8,046	11,356
Sandusky, Ohio	3,090	3,936	7,026	2,834	3,936	6,770
Cuyahoga, Ohio	35,939	42,149	78,088	13,279	37,901	51,180
Detroit, Mich.	191,156	188,685	379,841	249,729	328,628	578,157
Michilimackinac, Mich.	19,280	8,712	27,972	137	6,404	6,541
Chicago, Ill.	99,709	49,699	149,408	104,507	50,567	155,074
Milwaukie, Wis.	73,740	10,797	84,537	78,712	19,018	97,730
Oregon, Oregon.	13,854		13,854	38,013		38,013
Puget Sound, Washington T'y.	42,486	10,332	52,818	47,286	24,143	71,429
San Francisco, Cal.	239,907	61,348	321,253	329,505	73,274	402,779
Total	2,943,661	3,216,967	6,160,628	3,025,134	3,595,123	6,620,257

TREASURY DEPARTMENT, *Register's Office, October* 31, 1865.

S. B. COLBY, *Register.*

No. 15.—*Statement exhibiting the tonnage of American and foreign vessels which entered from and cleared to foreign countries, into and from the United States, during the year ending June 30, 1865.*

Countries.	ENTERED.			CLEARED.		
	American vessels.	Foreign vessels.	Total.	American vessels.	Foreign vessels.	Total.
	Tons.	Tons.	Tons.	Tons.	Tons.	Tons.
Russia on the Baltic and White seas	4,592	1,628	6,220	3,236	1,547	4,783
Russia on the Black sea		3,260	3,260			
Asiatic Russia					364	364
Russian possessions in North America	2,536	2,203	4,739	1,359	3,561	4,920
Sweden and Norway	1,536	9,965	11,601		967	967
Swedish West Indies	345	418	763		138	138
Denmark	503		503			
Danish West Indies	7,070	5,494	12,564	7,933	11,534	19,467
Greenland				543	464	1,007
Prussia				442	800	1,242
Hamburg	4,480	76,329	80,809	846	69,236	70,082
Bremen		109,759	109,759	1,787	123,178	124,965
Holland	588	9,173	9,761	1,727	21,876	23,603
Dutch West Indies	8,575	15,390	23,965	1,832	6,724	8,556
Dutch Guiana	3,658	3,599	7,257	4,124	4,313	6,037
Dutch East Indies	2,836	5,006	7,842	2,664	5,304	7,968
Belgium	5,696	19,053	24,749	808	35,126	35,934
England	254,458	645,177	899,635	162,957	627,331	790,288
Scotland	8,826	47,032	55,858	4,913	27,790	32,703
Ireland	248	9,440	9,688	6,042	40,726	46,768
Gibraltar		330	330	4,199	4,878	9,077
Malta				339	553	892
Canada	1,328,477	1,004,409	2,332,886	1,317,978	1,179,067	2,497,045
Other British N. Amer. poss'ns on the Atlantic	258,814	487,868	746,682	308,669	594,354	903,023
British American possessions on the Pacific	102,538	11,087	113,625	123,901	13,783	137,684
British West Indies	49,887	79,543	129,430	41,481	94,138	135,639
British Honduras	3,272	6,779	10,051	3,566	5,322	8,968
British Guiana	6,939	11,317	18,976	5,525	16,932	22,457
British possessions in Africa	5,652	11,925	17,577	6,589	10,977	17,566
British East Indies	21,066	19,806	40,872	19,070	7,189	26,259
Australia	7,915	10,776	18,691	17,121	34,291	51,412
France on the Atlantic	13,371	41,475	54,846	16,183	52,371	68,754
France on the Mediterranean	449	13,659	14,108	7,897	14,871	22,774
French North American possessions		564	564	567	4,802	5,369
French West Indies	1,940	3,145	5,085	4,223	5,447	9,670
French Guiana	234	729	963	860	1,721	2,581
French possessions in Africa	1,382	584	1,966	3,706	906	4,612
Spain on the Atlantic	9,981	4,401	14,382	11,113	18,411	29,524
Spain on the Mediterranean	5,772	6,082	11,854	6,295	5,771	11,997
Canary Islands		1,201	1,201	191	1,006	1,197
Philippine Islands	20,949	5,781	26,630	8,388	1,901	10,289
Cuba	368,954	199,323	568,277	353,001	152,449	505,450
Porto Rico	23,287	30,724	53,011	22,846	23,540	46,386
San Domingo	3,525	3,118	6,643	675	1,659	2,334
Portugal	1,069	6,415	7,484	1,289	9,870	11,159
Madeira				299	699	998
Azores	749	4,140	4,889	1,613	2,429	4,042
Cape de Verde Islands	2,101	422	2,523	316	142	458
Italy—northern ports	6,797	26,646	33,443	2,865	15,658	18,523
Italy—southern ports	15,378	21,950	37,328	3,909	4,878	8,787
Austria		2,437	2,437	384	3,734	4,118
Greece		1,026	1,026			
Turkey in Europe		1,673	1,673		531	531
Turkey in Asia	2,260		2,260	1,946	1,377	3,323
Egypt		1,401	1,491			
Liberia	323		323	818	325	1,143
Other ports in Africa	2,193	2,321	4,514	1,923	550	2,473
Hayti	16,873	31,299	48,172	25,278	38,491	63,769
Mexico	36,091	56,218	92,309	41,603	93,457	135,060
Central America	32,231	1,801	34,032	40,736	4,639	54,375
New Granada	200,546	4,578	205,124	209,252	7,376	216,628
Venezuela	205	14,728	14,933	1,114	16,435	17,549
Brazil	10,508	52,540	63,048	16,128	46,738	62,866
Uruguay, or Cisplatine Republic		3,172	3,172	13,325	16,382	29,707
Buenos Ayres, or Argentine Republic	3,448	17,188	20,636	9,039	24,023	33,062
Chili	4,434	18,681	23,115	19,979	20,954	40,933
Peru	1,351	3,592	4,943	53,061	14,755	69,816
Equador				969		969
Sandwich Islands	20,116	2,167	22,283	22,327	2,445	24,772
Other islands of the Pacific	2,466	704	3,170	4,748	808	5,556
China	17,272	22,372	39,644	34,430	41,047	75,477
Japan	1,811	1,852	3,663	1,037		1,037
Other ports in Asia	2,092		2,092			
Whale fisheries	23,976		23,976	19,755		19,755
Total	2,943,651	3,216,967	6,160,628	3,025,134	3,595,123	6,620,257

TREASURY DEPARTMENT, *October* 31, 1865.   S. B. COLBY, *Register.*

No. 16.

Statement exhibiting a condensed view of the tonnage of the several districts of the United States on the 30th June, 1865, under the old admeasurement.

Districts.	Registered tonnage.	Enrolled and licensed tonnage.	Total tonnage of each district.
	Tons and 95ths.	*Tons and 95ths.*	*Tons and 95ths.*
Passamaquoddy, Maine	1,651 88	4,568 21	6,220 14
Machias, Maine	3,506 45	9,134 86	12,641 36
Frenchman's Bay, Maine	3,839 68	15,584 83	19,424 56
Penobscot, Maine	8,581 72	33,096 52	41,678 29
Belfast, Maine	18,962 46	13,216 19	32,178 65
Bangor, Maine	9,813 81	10,523 67	20,337 53
Waldborough, Maine	39,789 17	131,259 26	171,048 43
Wiscasset, Maine	4,621 56	9,121 67	13,743 28
Bath, Maine	101,902 34	10,821 31	112,723 65
Portland, Maine	53,727 53	12,282 42	66,010 00
Saco, Maine			
Kennebunk, Maine	2,363 88	2,445 03	4,808 91
York, Maine		397 55	397 55
Portsmouth, N. H.	12,952 51	1,317 76	14,270 32
Burlington, Vermont		6,372 56	6,372 56
Newburyport, Mass	11,978 37	1,307 44	13,285 81
Ipswich, Mass			
Gloucester, Mass	2,788 44	12,133 68	14,922 17
Salem, Mass	8,172 69	5,219 00	13,391 69
Marblehead, Mass		1,764 66	1,764 66
Boston, Mass	59,453 42	34,138 32	93,591 74
Plymouth, Mass	908 27	3,351 61	4,259 88
Fall River, Mass	248 18	4,004 60	4,252 78
New Bedford, Mass	63,704 10	2,169 07	65,873 17
Barnstable, Mass	4,921 73	26,229 93	31,151 71
Edgartown, Mass	2,833 86	722 14	3,256 05
Nantucket, Mass	2,371 64	720 31	3,092 00
Providence, R. I	2,593 63	14,199 82	16,793 50
Bristol, R. I	2,005 67	834 74	2,840 46
Newport, R. I	1,198 08	4,312 67	5,510 75
Middletown, Connecticut		6,974 80	6,974 80
New London, Conn	7,191 26	11,588 91	18,780 22
Stonington, Conn	1,712 47	13,666 25	15,378 72
New Haven, Conn	4,059 12	15,044 30	19,103 42
Fairfield, Conn	683 53	7,114 53	7,798 11
Champlain, N. Y		40,510 27	40,510 27
Oswego, N. Y		58,008 57	58,008 57
Niagara, N. Y		316 54	316 54
Genesee, N. Y			
Oswegatchie, N. Y			
Buffalo Creek, N. Y		56,613 89	56,613 89
Sag Harbor, N. Y	1,881 58	523 15	2,704 73
Greenport, N. Y		4,161 93	4,161 93
Dunkirk, N. Y		5,519 91	5,519 91
New York, N. Y	471,473 00	751,791 50	1,223,264 50
Perth Amboy, N. J	1,213 41	22,802 71	24,016 17
Bridgetown, N. J		22,409 33	22,409 33
Burlington, N. J		12,201 62	12,201 62
Camden, N. J	820 75	3,062 64	3,883 44
Newark, N. J		7,727 81	7,727 81
Little Egg Harbor, N. J		4,587 58	4,587 58
Great Egg Harbor, N. J		23,316 33	23,316 33
Philadelphia, Pa	37,258 35	212,014 39	249,272 74
Erie, Pa		2,004 20	2,004 20
Pittsburg, Pa		92,854 79	92,854 79
Wilmington, Del	5,618 77	12,756 47	18,375 29

No. 16.—*Statement, &c.*—Continued.

Districts.	Registered tonnage.	Enrolled and licensed tonnage.	Total tonnage of each district.
	Tons and 95ths.	*Tons and 95ths.*	*Tons and 95ths.*
New Castle, Del................................		2,873 75	2,873 75
Baltimore, Md................................	64,887 58	132,070 51	196,958 14
Oxford, Md..................................		11,263 76	11,263 76
Vienna, Md..................................		....	....
Snow Hill, Md...............................		....	....
St. Mary's, Md..............................		4,382 66	4,382 66
Town Creek, Md.............................		....	....
Annapolis, Md...............................		....	....
Georgetown, D. C............................	673 92	47,133 71	47,807 68
Alexandria, Va..............................	8,029 75	6,628 43	14,658 73
Accomac Court House, Va....................		9,171 85	9,171 85
Wheeling, Va................................		29,333 70	29,333 70
Beaufort, N. C..............................	919 92	539 33	1,459 30
Beaufort, S. C..............................	9,781 83	....	9,781 83
Key West, Fla...............................	6,155 20	312 47	6,467 67
Fernandina, Fla.............................	24 88	....	24 88
Memphis, Tenn..............................		4,938 08	4,938 08
St. Louis, Mo...............................		40,588 84	40,588 84
Chicago, Ill................................	4,223 81	71,220 55	75,444 41
Galena, Ill................................		1,042 07	1,042 07
Sandusky, Ohio..............................		10,436 66	10,436 66
Cuyahoga, Ohio.............................	1,738 48	55,086 13	56,824 61
Cincinnati, Ohio............................		53,103 55	53,103 55
Toledo, Ohio................................		4,237 01	4,237 01
Dubuque, Iowa		2,364 89	2,364 89
Louisville, Ky..............................		72,222 44	72,222 44
Milwaukie, Wis.............................		5,432 74	5,432 74
St. Paul, Minn.............................		3,010 26	3,010 26
Detroit, Mich...............................		54,992 44	54,992 44
Michilimackinac, Mich......................		5,743 88	5,743 88
San Francisco, Cal..........................	34,243 03	32,331 80	66,574 83
Astoria, Oregon	407 65	720 00	1,127 65
Puget Sound, Washington Ter...............	4,413 47	4,458 41	8,871 88
Total......................	1,092,004 13	2,424,783 67	3,516,787 80

S. B. COLBY, *Register.*

TREASURY DEPARTMENT,
   Register's Office, October 30, 1865.

No. 17.

Statement exhibiting a condensed view of the tonnage of the several districts of the United States on the 30th June, 1865, under the new admeasurement.

Districts.	Registered tonnage.	Enrolled and licensed tonnage.	Total tonnage of each district.
	Tons and 100ths.	*Tons and 100ths.*	*Tons and 100ths.*
Passamaquoddy, Maine	6,141 22	3,010 22	9,151 44
Machias, Maine	2,161 22	5,384 21	7,545 43
Frenchman's Bay, Maine	882 00	7,384 47	8,266 47
Penobscot, Maine	1,471 33	11,110 61	12,581 94
Belfast, Maine	3,576 83	10,861 40	14,438 23
Bangor, Maine	3,190 61	6,977 00	10,167 61
Waldborough, Maine	3,084 02	14,947 28	18,031 30
Wiscasset, Maine	678 86	6,930 42	7,609 28
Bath, Maine	11,154 10	5,921 82	17,075 92
Portland, Maine	32,529 14	9,703 80	42,232 94
Saco, Maine		596 99	596 99
Kennebunk, Maine	1,872 08	1,263 35	3,135 43
York, Maine		693 88	693 88
Portsmouth, N. H.	1,065 14	2,657 21	3,722 35
Newburyport, Mass.	2,909 30	2,446 89	5,356 19
Ipswich, Mass.		339 73	339 73
Gloucester, Mass.	324 81	17,648 62	17,973 43
Salem, Mass.	2,579 12	2,575 46	5,154 58
Marblehead, Mass.		2,559 31	2,559 31
Boston, Mass.	61,680 87	34,585 91	96,266 78
Plymouth, Mass.		3,389 20	3,389 20
Fall River, Mass.	690 21	5,227 58	5,917 79
New Bedford, Mass.	8,334 84	2,692 01	11,026 85
Barnstable, Mass.	797 82	32,152 52	32,950 34
Edgartown, Mass.	124 33	382 66	506 99
Nantucket, Mass.	107 05	550 07	657 12
Providence, R. I.	1,099 80	16,148 66	17,248 46
Bristol, R. I.	1,304 39	1,028 19	2,332 58
Newport, R. I.	1,624 26	4,919 19	6,543 45
Middletown, Conn.	145 62	9,685 03	9,830 65
New London, Conn.	1,240 21	15,716 01	16,956 22
Stonington, Conn.		5,971 05	5,971 05
New Haven, Conn.	3,114 15	6,083 46	9,197 61
Fairfield, Conn.		6,315 99	6,315 99
Oswego, N. Y.		39,473 61	39,473 61
Niagara, N. Y.		1,713 28	1,713 28
Genesee, N. Y.		833 48	833 45
Oswegatchie, N. Y.		1,708 46	1,708 46
Buffalo Creek, N. Y.		74,022 48	74,022 48
Sag Harbor, N. Y.		622 13	622 13
Greenport, N. Y.		4,856 91	4,856 91
Dunkirk, N. Y.		7,062 31	7,062 31
New York, N. Y.	192,545 69	200,786 85	393,332 54
Cape Vincent, N. Y.		5,861 96	5,861 96
Perth Amboy, N. J.		12,795 13	12,795 13
Bridgetown, N. J.		4,014 21	4,014 21
Burlington, N. J.		5,276 18	5,276 18
Camden, N. J.		15,111 16	15,111 16
Newark, N. J.	63 01	2,134 48	2,197 49
Little Egg Harbor, N. J.		3,124 43	3,124 43
Great Egg Harbor, N. J.		7,073 98	7,073 98
Philadelphia, Pa.	46,025 76	77,523 77	123,549 53
Erie, Pa.		3,501 26	3,501 26
Pittsburg, Pa.		36,886 99	36,886 99
Wilmington, Del.	2,316 92	8,556 55	10,873 47

No. 17.—*Statement, &c.*—Continued.

Districts.	Registered tonnage.	Enrolled and licensed tonnage.	Total tonnage of each district.
	Tons and 100ths.	*Tons and 100ths.*	*Tons and 100ths.*
New Castle, Del.		1,664 65	1,664 65
Baltimore, Md.	27,840 60	28,008 36	55,848 96
Oxford, Md.		1,725 17	1,725 17
Vienna, Md.			
Town Creek, Md.		325 38	325 38
Georgetown, D. C.	4,346 70	2,731 78	7,078 48
Alexandria, Va.	9,276 03	1,723 12	10,999 15
Norfolk, Va.	1,490 97	4,686 65	6,177 62
Accomac Court House, Va.		1,215 90	1,215 90
Wheeling, Va.		7,021 74	7,021 74
Beaufort, N. C.	2,252 52	1,009 86	3,262 38
Key West, Fla.	6,126 33	707 35	6,833 68
Memphis, Tenn.		2,622 62	2,622 62
St. Louis, Mo.		29,800 66	29,800 66
Chicago, Ill.	1,157 79	61,386 55	62,544 34
Sandusky, Ohio	1,185 72	5,701 18	6,886 90
Cuyahoga, Ohio	1,936 41	26,217 98	28,154 39
Cincinnati, Ohio		40,100 28	40,100 28
Toledo, Ohio		6,392 68	6,392 68
Dubuque, Iowa		54 54	54 54
Milwaukie, Wis.		14,648 58	14,648 58
Detroit, Mich.		42,790 16	42,790 16
Michilimackinac, Mich.		446 05	446 05
San Francisco, Cal.	59,724 34	14,122 97	73,847 31
Astoria, Oregon		1,049 70	1,049 70
Puget's Sound, Washington Ter.	406 65	2,474 59	2,881 24
Total	510,578 78	1,069,415 50	1,579,994 28

S. B. COLBY, *Register.*

TREASURY DEPARTMENT,
Register's Office, October 30, 1865.

No. 18.—*Statement exhibiting the value of domestic and foreign produce and manufactures exclusive of specie, exported from the United States during the fiscal years ending June 30' 1862, 1863, 1864, and 1865, respectively, reduced to gold value; specie exported, and total exports, including specie; amount of reduction, and value of exports in gold for each year.*

DOMESTIC EXPORTS.

Years ending June 30.	Total, exclusive of specie.		Average rate of gold.	Gold value.		Specie.	Total, including specie.	
	For the year.	For 6 mos. to June 30.		For 6 mos. to June 30.	For the year.		Gold value.	Reduction.
1862.......	$182,024,868	$91,012,434	103	$88,361,586	$179,374,090	$31,044,651	$210,418,671	$3,650,848
1863.......	249,891,436	....	137	....	182,402,508	55,993,562	238,396,070	67,488,928
1864.......	217,385,571	....	156	....	139,349,725	64,483,800	203,833,525	79,035,846
1865.......	254,381,491	....	202	....	125,931,426	51,925,277	177,856,703	126,450,055
Total...	903,683,356	91,012,434	......	88,361,586	627,057,679	203,447,290	830,504,969	276,625,677

FOREIGN EXPORTS.

1862.......	$11,026,477	$5,513,238	103	$5,352,658	$10,865,896	$5,842,989	$16,708,885	$160,581
1863.......	9,075,789	....	137	....	6,624,659	7,398,474	14,023,133	2,451,123
1864.......	15,208,500	....	156	....	9,749,042	4,906,685	14,655,727	5,459,463
1865.......	27,867,458	....	202	....	13,795,772	2,522,907	16,318,679	14,071,686
Total...	63,178,222	5,513,238	......	5,352,658	41,035,369	20,671,055	61,706,424	22,142,853

TOTAL.

Years ending June 30.	Currency value, including specie.	Reduction.	Gold value.
1862	$229,938,985	$3,811,429	$227,127,556
1863	322,359,254	69,940,051	252,419,203
1864	301,984,561	83,495,309	218,489,252
1865	336,697,123	142,521,741	194,175,382
Total................	1,190,979,923	298,768,530	892,211,393

N. B.—Until January 1, 1862, the exports were at par value. The reduction is, therefore, upon only one-half the export value for that year.

RECAPITULATION.

```
Domestic exports, exclusive of specie ........................................  $903,683,356
Domestic specie exported .......................................................  203,447,290
        Total domestic ....................................................                    $1,107,130,646
Foreign exports, exclusive of specie ..........................................  63,178,222
Foreign specie exported .........................................................  20,671,055
        Total foreign ......................................................                       83,849,277
        Total exports .....................................................                    1,190,979,923
Reduction on domestic exports ................................................  276,625,677
Reduction on foreign exports ..................................................  22,142,853
        Total reduction ...................................................                      298,768,530
        Total gold value ..................................................                      892,211,393
```

Comparative statement of imports and exports (reduced to gold value) during the fiscal years 1862, 1863, 1864, and 1865, and exhibiting the excess of importations over exportations each year.

Year ending—	Imports.	Exports, gold value.	Excess of imports.
June 30, 1862	$275,357,051	$227,127,556	$48,229,495
1863	252,919,920	252,419,203	500,717
1864	329,562,895	218,489,252	111,073,643
1865	234,339,810	194,175,382	40,164,428
Total........................	1,092,179,676	892,211,393	199,968,283

TREASURY DEPARTMENT, *November* 14, 1865.   S. B. COLBY, *Register.*

No. 19.—*Statement exhibiting the gross value of the exports and imports from the beginning of the government to June 30, 1865.*

Year ending—	EXPORTS			Total imports.	Excess of exports.	Excess of imports.
	Domestic produce.	Foreign merchandise.	Total.			
1790	$19,566,000	$539,156	$20,205,156	$23,000,000	....	$2,794,844
1791	18,500,000	512,041	19,012,041	29,200,000	....	10,187,959
1792	19,000,000	1,753,098	20,753,098	31,500,000	....	10,746,902
1793	24,000,000	2,109,572	26,109,572	31,100,000	....	4,990,428
1794	26,500,000	6,526,233	33,026,233	34,600,000	....	1,573,767
1795	39,500,000	8,489,472	47,989,472	69,756,268	....	21,766,796
1796	40,764,097	26,300,000	67,064,097	81,436,164	....	14,372,067
1797	29,850,206	27,000,000	56,850,206	75,379,406	....	18,529,200
1798	28,527,097	33,000,000	61,527,097	68,551,700	....	7,024,603
1799	33,142,522	45,523,000	78,665,522	79,069,148	....	403,626
1800	31,840,903	39,130,877	70,971,780	91,252,768	....	20,280,988
1801	47,473,204	46,642,721	94,115,925	111,363,511	....	17,247,586
1802	36,708,186	35,774,971	72,483,160	76,333,333	....	3,850,173
1803	42,205,961	13,594,072	55,800,033	64,666,666	....	8,866,633
1804	41,467,477	36,231,597	77,699,074	85,000,000	....	7,300,926
1805	42,387,002	53,179,019	95,566,021	120,600,000	....	25,033,979
1806	41,253,727	60,283,236	101,536,963	129,410,000	....	27,873,037
1807	48,699,592	59,643,558	108,343,150	138,500,000	....	30,156,850
1808	9,433,546	12,997,414	22,430,960	56,990,000	....	34,559,040
1809	31,405,702	20,797,531	52,203,233	59,400,000	....	7,196,767
1810	42,366,675	24,391,295	66,657,970	85,400,000	....	18,742,030
1811	45,294,043	16,022,790	61,316,833	53,400,000	$7,916,833	....
1812	30,032,109	8,495,127	38,527,236	77,030,000	....	38,502,764
1813	25,008,132	2,847,865	27,855,997	22,005,000	5,850,927	....
1814	6,782,272	145,169	6,927,441	12,965,000	....	6,041,559
1815	45,974,403	6,583,350	52,557,753	113,041,274	....	60,483,521
1816	64,781,896	17,138,156	81,920,432	147,103,000	....	65,182,548
1817	68,313,500	19,358,069	87,671,560	99,250,000	....	11,578,440
1818	73,854,437	19,426,696	93,281,133	121,750,000	....	28,468,867
1819	50,976,838	19,165,683	70,142,521	87,125,000	....	16,982,479
1820	51,683,640	18,008,029	69,691,669	74,450,000	....	4,758,331
1821	43,671,894	21,302,488	64,974,382	62,585,724	2,088,658	....
1822	49,874,079	22,286,202	72,160,281	83,241,541	....	11,081,260
1823	47,155,408	27,543,622	74,699,030	77,579,267	....	2,880,237
1824	50,649,500	23,337,127	73,986,657	80,549,007	....	13,562,350
1825	66,944,745	32,590,643	99,535,388	96,340,075	3,195,313	....
1826	53,055,710	24,539,612	77,595,322	84,974,477	....	7,379,155
1827	58,921,691	23,403,136	82,324,727	79,484,068	2,840,659	....
1828	50,669,669	21,595,017	72,264,686	88,509,824	....	16,245,138
1829	55,700,193	16,658,478	72,358,671	74,492,527	....	2,153,856
1830	59,462,029	14,387,479	73,849,508	70,876,920	2,972,588	....
1831	61,277,057	20,033,526	81,310,583	103,191,124	....	21,880,541
1832	63,137,470	24,039,473	87,176,943	101,029,266	....	13,852,323
1833	70,317,098	19,822,735	90,140,443	108,118,311	....	17,977,868
1834	81,024,162	23,312,811	104,336,973	126,521,332	....	22,184,359
1835	101,189,082	20,504,495	121,693,577	149,895,742	....	28,202,165
1836	106,916,680	21,746,360	128,663,040	189,980,035	....	61,316,995
1837	95,564,414	21,854,962	117,419,376	140,989,017	....	23,569,841
1838	96,033,821	12,452,795	108,486,616	113,717,404	....	5,230,788
1839	103,533,891	17,494,525	121,028,416	162,092,132	....	41,063,716
1840	113,895,634	18,190,312	132,085,936	107,141,519	24,944,417	....
1841	106,382,722	15,469,081	121,851,803	127,946,177	....	6,094,374
1842	92,969,996	11,721,538	104,691,534	100,162,087	4,529,447	....
9 mos. to June 30, 1843	77,793,783	6,532,597	84,346,480	64,753,799	19,592,681	....
Year end'g June 30, '44	99,715,179	11,484,867	111,200,046	108,435,035	2,765,011	....
1845	99,299,776	15,346,830	114,646,606	117,254,564	....	2,607,958
1846	102,141,893	11,346,623	113,488,516	121,691,797	....	8,203,281
1847	150,637,464	8,011,158	158,648,622	146,545,638	12,102,984	....
1848	132,904,121	21,128,010	154,032,131	154,998,928	....	966,797
1849	132,666,955	13,088,865	145,755,820	147,857,439	....	2,101,619
1850	136,946,912	14,951,808	151,898,720	178,138,318	....	26,239,598
1851	196,689,718	21,698,293	218,388,011	216,224,932	2,163,079	....
1852	192,368,984	17,289,382	209,658,366	212,945,442	....	3,287,076
1853	203,417,697	17,558,460	230,976,157	267,978,647	....	37,002,490
1854	253,390,870	24,850,194	278,241,064	304,562,381	....	26,321,317
1855	246,708,553	28,448,293	275,156,846	261,468,520	13,688,326	....
1856	310,586,330	16,378,578	326,964,908	314,639,942	12,324,966	....
1857	338,985,065	23,973,617	362,960,689	360,890,141	2,070,541	....
1858	293,758,279	30,886,142	324,644,421	282,613,150	42,031,271	....
1859	335,894,385	20,895,077	356,789,462	338,768,130	18,021,332	....
1860	373,189,274	26,933,022	400,122,296	362,166,254	37,956,042	....
1861	228,699,486	15,271,791	243,971,277	286,598,135	....	42,626,858
1862	213,069,519	16,869,466	229,938,985	275,357,051	....	45,418,066
1863	205,884,998	16,474,256	222,359,254	232,919,920	69,439,334	....
1864	281,869,371	20,115,190	301,984,561	329,562,895	....	27,578,334
1865	306,306,758	30,396,365	336,697,123	234,339,810	102,357,313	....

No. 20.

Statement exhibiting the exports and imports of coin and bullion from 1821 to 1865, inclusive, and also the excess of imports and exports during the same years.

Fiscal year ending—	Imported.	EXPORTED.			Excess of imports.	Excess of exports.
		American.	Foreign.	Total.		
September 30..........1821	$8,064,890	....	$10,478,059	$10,478,059	....	$2,413,169
1822	3,369,846	....	10,810,180	10,810,180	....	7,440,334
1823	5,097,896	....	6,372,897	6,372,897	....	1,275,091
1824	8,378,970	....	7,014,552	7,014,552	$1,366,148	....
1825	6,150,765	....	8,797,055	8,797,055	....	2,646,290
1826	6,880,966	$605,855	4,098,678	4,704,533	2,176,433	....
1827	8,151,130	1,043,574	6,971,306	8,014,880	136,250	....
1828	7,489,741	693,037	7,550,439	8,243,476	....	.753,735
1829	7,403,612	612,986	4,311,134	4,924,020	2,479,592	....
1830	8,155,964	937,151	1,241,622	2,178,773	5,977,191	....
1831	7,305,945	2,056,474	6,956,457	9,014,931	....	1,708,986
1832	5,907,504	1,410,941	4,245,399	5,656,340	251,164	....
1833	7,070,368	366,642	2,244,859	2,611,701	4,458,667	....
1834	17,911,632	400,500	1,676,238	2,076,738	15,834,874	....
1835	13,131,447	729,601	5,748,174	6,477,775	6,633,672	....
1836	13,400,881	345,738	3,978,598	4,324,336	9,076,545	....
1837	10,516,414	1,283,519	4,692,730	5,976,249	4,540,165	....
1838	17,747,116	472,941	3,035,105	3,508,046	14,239,070	....
1839	5,595,176	1,908,358	6,868,385	8,776,743	....	3,181,567
1840	8,882,813	2,236,073	6,181,941	8,417,014	465,799	....
1841	4,988,633	2,746,486	7,287,846	10,034,332	....	5,045,699
1842	4,087,016	1,170,754	3,642,785	4,813,539	....	726,523
9 months, to June 30...1843	22,390,559	307,429	1,413,362	1,520,791	20,869,768	....
Year ending June 30...1844	5,830,429	183,405	5,270,809	5,454,214	376,215	....
1845	4,070,242	844,446	7,762,049	8,606,495	....	4,536,253
1846	3,777,732	423,851	3,481,417	3,905,268	....	127,536
1847	24,121,289	63,020	1,844,404	1,907,024	22,214,265	....
1848	6,360,284	2,700,412	13,141,204	15,841,616	....	9,481,332
1849	6,651,240	956,874	4,447,774	5,404,648	1,246,592	....
1850	4,628,792	9,046,679	5,476,315	7,592,994	....	2,894,202
1851	5,453,592	18,009,580	11,403,172	29,476,752	....	24,019,160
1852	5,505,044	37,437,837	5,236,898	42,674,135	....	37,169,091
1853	4,201,382	23,548,535	3,938,340	27,486,875	....	23,285,493
1854	6,939,342	38,062,570	3,218,924	41,281,504	....	34,342,162
1855	3,659,812	53,957,418	2,280,925	56,247,343	....	52,587,531
1856	4,207,632	44,148,279	1,597,205	45,745,485	....	41,537,853
1857	12,461,799	60,078,352	9,055,570	69,136,922	....	56,675,123
1858	19,274,496	42,407,246	10,225,901	52,633,147	....	33,358,651
1859	7,434,789	57,502,305	6,385,106	63,887,411	....	56,452,622
1860	8,550,135	56,946,851	9,599,388	66,546,239	....	57,996,104
1861	32,314,298	23,799,870	4,364,965	28,164,835	4,149,463	....
1862	16,415,088	31,044,651	5,842,989	36,887,640	....	20,472,552
1863	9,584,105	55,993,562	7,398,474	63,392,036	....	53,807,931
1864	13,115,612	54,483,800	4,906,685	69,390,485	....	56,274,873
1865	7,225,377	51,925,277	2,522,907	54,448,184	....	47,222,807

TREASURY DEPARTMENT, *Register's Office, October* 31, 1865.

            S. B. COLBY, *Register.*

No. 21.

Statement of foreign merchandise imported, exported, and consumed annually, from 1821 to 1865, with the population and rate of consumption, per capita, calculated for each year.

| Years ending— | Value of foreign merchandise. | | | Population. | Consumption per capita. |
	Imported.	Exported.	Consumed and in store.		
September 30......1821	$62,585,724	$21,302,488	$41,923,226	9,960,974	$4 14
1822	83,241,341	22,286,202	60,955,339	10,283,757	5 92
1823	77,579,267	27,543,622	50,035,645	10,606,540	4 71
1824	80,549,007	25,337,157	55,211,850	10,929,323	5 05
1825	96,340,075	32,590,643	63,749,432	11,259,106	5 66
1826	84,974,477	24,530,612	60,434,865	11,574,889	5 22
1827	79,484,068	23,403,136	56,080,939	11,897,672	4 71
1828	88,509,824	21,595,017	66,914,807	12,220,455	5 47
1829	74,492,527	16,658,478	57,834,049	12,545,238	4 61
1830	70,876,920	14,387,479	56,489,441	12,866,020	4 31
1831	103,191,124	20,033,526	83,157,598	13,286,364	6 25
1832	101,029,266	24,039,473	76,989,793	13,706,707	5 61
1833	108,118,311	19,822,735	88,295,576	14,127,050	6 25
1834	126,521,332	23,312,611	103,208,521	14,547,393	7 09
1835	149,895,742	20,504,495	129,391,247	14,967,735	8 64
1836	189,980,035	21,746,360	168,233,675	15,388,079	10 93
1837	140,989,217	21,854,962	119,134,255	15,808,422	7 53
1838	113,717,404	12,452,795	101,264,609	16,228,765	6 23
1839	162,092,132	17,494,525	144,597,607	16,649,108	8 68
1840	107,141,519	18,190,312	88,951,207	17,069,453	5 21
1841	127,946,177	15,469,081	112,477,096	17,612,507	6 38
1842	100,162,087	11,721,538	88,440,549	18,155,561	4 87
9 months to June 30, 1843	64,753,799	6,552,697	58,201,102	18,696,615	4 15
Year end'g June 30, 1844	108,435,035	11,484,867	96,950,168	19,241,670	5 03
1845	117,254,564	15,346,830	101,907,734	19,784,725	5 15
1846	121,691,797	11,346,623	110,343,174	20,327,780	5 42
1847	146,545,638	8,011,158	138,534,480	20,780,835	6 60
1848	154,998,928	21,128,010	133,870,918	21,413,890	6 25
1849	147,857,439	13,088,065	134,769,574	21,956,945	6 13
1850	178,138,318	14,951,808	163,186,510	23,191,876	7 03
1851	216,224,932	21,698,293	194,526,639	23,887,632	8 14
1852	212,945,442	17,289,382	195,656,060	24,604,261	7 95
1853	267,978,647	17,508,460	250,420,187	25,342,388	9 88
1854	304,562,381	24,850,194	279,712,187	26,109,659	10 71
1855	261,468,520	28,448,293	233,020,227	26,885,738	8 67
1856	314,630,942	16,378,578	298,261,364	27,692,319	10 77
1857	360,890,141	23,975,617	336,914,524	28,523,079	11 81
1858	282,613,150	30,886,142	251,727,008	29,376,771	8 57
1859	338,768,130	20,895,077	317,873,053	30,260,134	10 50
1860	362,166,254	26,933,022	335,233,232	....	....
1861	286,598,135	15,271,791	271,326,344	....	....
1862	275,357,051	16,869,466	258,487,585	....	....
1863	252,919,920	15,474,256	236,445,664	....	....
1864	329,562,895	20,115,190	309,447,705	....	....
1865	234,356,810	30,390,365	203,949,445	....	....

S. B. COLBY, *Register.*

TREASURY DEPARTMENT, *Register's Office, October 31,* 1865.

No. 22.

Statement of the value of domestic produce and foreign merchandise, exclusive of specie, exported annually for fiscal years from 1821 to 1865 inclusive.

Year ending—	Value of exports, exclusive of specie.						Specie and bullion exported.
	Breadstuffs and provisions.	Total of domestic produce.	Foreign merchandise.			Aggregate value of exports.	
			Free of duty.	Dutiable.	Total.		
September 30, 1821	$12,341,901	$43,671,894	$986,788	$10,537,731	$10,824,519	$54,496,413	$10,477,969
1822	13,886,856	49,876,079	374,716	11,201,306	11,476,022	61,350,101	10,810,180
1823	13,767,847	47,155,408	1,393,762	19,846,873	21,170,635	68,325,043	6,372,987
1824	15,050,484	50,649,500	1,100,530	17,222,075	18,322,605	68,972,105	7,014,552
1825	11,634,449	66,944,745	1,098,181	22,704,803	23,802,984	90,747,729	8,787,659
1826	11,303,496	52,449,855	1,036,430	19,404,504	20,440,934	72,890,789	4,704,533
1827	11,685,556	57,878,117	813,844	15,617,996	16,431,830	74,309,947	8,014,880
1828	11,461,144	49,976,632	877,239	13,167,339	14,044,578	64,021,210	8,243,476
1829	13,131,858	55,367,307	919,943	11,427,401	12,347,344	67,434,651	4,924,020
1830	12,075,430	58,524,878	1,078,695	12,067,162	13,145,857	71,670,735	2,178,773
1831	17,538,227	59,218,583	642,586	12,434,483	13,077,069	72,295,652	9,014,931
1832	12,424,703	61,726,529	1,345,217	18,448,857	19,794,074	81,520,903	5,656,340
1833	14,209,128	69,950,856	5,165,907	12,411,969	17,577,876	87,528,729	2,611,701
1834	11,524,024	80,623,662	10,757,033	10,879,520	21,636,553	102,260,215	2,076,758
1835	12,009,399	100,459,481	7,012,666	7,743,655	14,756,321	115,215,802	6,477,775
1836	10,614,130	106,570,942	6,534,895	9,232,867	17,767,762	124,338,704	4,324,336
1837	9,588,359	94,280,895	7,756,189	9,406,043	17,162,232	111,443,127	5,976,249
1838	9,636,650	95,560,880	4,951,306	4,466,384	9,417,590	104,978,570	3,508,046
1839	14,147,779	101,625,533	5,618,442	5,007,636	10,626,140	112,251,673	8,776,743
1840	19,067,535	111,660,561	6,202,562	5,805,809	12,008,371	123,668,932	8,417,014
1841	17,196,102	103,636,236	3,953,054	4,228,181	8,181,235	111,817,471	10,034,332
1842	16,902,876	91,799,242	3,194,299	4,884,464	8,078,753	99,876,995	4,813,539
Nine months to June 30, 1843	11,204,123	77,686,354	1,682,763	3,456,572	5,139,335	82,895,689	1,520,791
Year ending June 30, 1844	17,970,135	99,531,774	2,251,550	3,962,508	6,214,058	105,745,832	5,454,214
1845	16,743,421	98,455,330	2,413,050	5,171,731	7,584,781	106,040,111	8,606,495
1846	27,701,921	101,718,042	2,342,629	5,522,577	7,865,206	109,583,248	3,905,268
1847	68,701,121	150,574,844	1,812,847	4,353,907	6,166,754	156,741,598	1,907,024
1848	37,472,751	130,203,709	1,410,307	6,576,499	7,986,806	138,190,515	15,841,616
1849	36,155,507	131,510,081	2,015,815	6,625,276	8,641,091	140,351,172	5,404,648
1850	26,051,373	134,900,233	2,099,132	7,376,361	9,475,493	144,375,726	7,522,994
1851	21,948,651	178,620,138	1,742,154	8,552,967	10,295,121	188,915,259	29,472,752
1852	25,857,027	154,931,147	2,538,159	9,514,925	12,053,084	166,984,231	42,674,135
1853	32,985,322	189,869,162	2,449,539	11,170,571	13,620,120	203,489,282	27,486,875
1854	65,941,323	215,156,304	3,310,907	18,437,397	21,648,304	236,804,608	41,436,456
1855	38,895,348	192,751,135	6,516,550	19,641,818	26,158,368	218,909,503	56,247,343
1856	77,187,301	266,438,051	3,144,604	11,636,798	14,781,372	281,219,423	45,745,485
1857	74,667,852	278,906,713	4,325,400	10,591,647	14,917,047	293,823,760	69,136,922
1858	50,683,285	251,351,033	5,751,850	14,908,391	20,660,241	272,011,274	52,633,147
1859	38,305,991	278,392,080	5,429,221	9,080,050	14,509,971	292,902,051	63,887,411
1860	45,271,850	316,242,423	5,350,441	11,983,193	17,333,634	333,576,057	66,546,239
1861	94,982,693	204,899,616	2,667,456	8,239,360	10,906,826	215,806,442	29,164,635
1862	119,441,596	182,024,868	2,354,818	8,671,659	11,026,477	193,051,345	36,887,640
1863	143,772,421	249,891,436	1,631,605	7,444,177	9,075,782	258,967,218	63,392,036
1864	110,360,840	217,385,571	2,959,287	12,349,218	15,208,505	232,594,076	69,390,485
1865	105,254,620	254,381,481	4,411,621	23,455,837	27,867,458	282,248,939	54,448,184

No. 23.

atement showing the exports of staple productions, breadstuffs, provisions, oils, &c., for the fiscal years ending June 30, 1860, 1861, 1862, 1863, 1864, and 1865.

Articles.	1859-'60.		1860-'61.		1861-'62.		1862-'63.		1863-'64.		1864-'65.	
heat............bushels.	4,155,153	$4,076,704	31,290,133	$38,365,690	37,289,572	$42,573,295	36,160,414	$46,754,195	23,680,669	$31,430,295	9,937,192	$19,397,197
heat flour..........barrels.	2,611,596	15,448,507	4,327,631	24,683,355	4,892,033	27,534,677	4,300,055	28,366,069	3,543,252	25,458,984	2,659,542	27,229,031
Ilnn corn..........bushels.	3,314,155	2,399,808	10,586,029	6,894,808	18,904,858	10,387,383	16,119,476	10,592,704	4,076,789	3,321,526	2,812,726	3,679,133
rn meal...........barrels.	233,709	912,075	203,889	604,306	253,570	778,344	257,948	1,013,273	262,347	1,349,588	199,419	1,489,886
e and other grains........		1,058,304		1,124,504		2,354,625		1,833,757		998,227		825,986
e and other meals......barrels.	11,432	48,172	14,143	55,761	14,463	54,488	8,684	38,067	6,999	37,991	3,035	30,438
ead or biscuit...........		478,740		429,709		490,942		582,268		656,408		771,952
ce...........		2,567,399		1,382,766		156,899		83,404		83,244		63,430
ef...........		2,674,354		1,675,773		2,017,077		2,185,921		3,019,733		3,304,771
tter...........pounds.	7,640,914	1,144,321	15,531,361	2,355,985	26,691,247	4,164,344	35,172,413	6,733,743	30,795,492	6,191,365	21,388,975	7,234,173
eese...........pounds.	15,515,799	1,565,630	32,370,312	3,323,300	34,052,078	2,715,892	49,045,054	4,316,804	47,733,137	5,834,515	53,080,468	11,684,927
rk...........		3,132,313		2,622,420		3,980,153		4,334,775		5,820,648		6,843,135
ams and bacon...pounds.	203,944,610	2,273,708	50,296,382	4,851,627	141,212,780	10,290,572	218,243,609	18,658,980	110,759,485	12,303,729	45,940,712	10,521,702
rd...........pounds.	40,280,519	4,545,231	47,908,911	4,799,297	118,573,307	10,004,921	155,336,596	15,755,570	96,992,144	11,129,533	44,342,295	9,107,435
rd oil...........gallons.	60,209	55,783	85,676	61,763	239,608	148,056	1,230,063	983,349	439,536	376,682	99,250	155,454
allow...........pounds.	15,260,535	1,598,176	29,718,664	2,942,400	46,773,768	4,026,113	63,792,754	6,738,486	55,015,375	6,191,743	30,622,865	4,979,135
ndles...........pounds.	5,033,335	760,508	5,025,667	826,955	6,100,025	981,300	6,836,353	1,187,864	5,578,580	1,406,405	5,018,312	1,259,168
ap...........pounds.	6,859,485	494,405	7,207,240	456,996	9,266,984	636,049	9,097,664	736,524	8,040,382	770,601	7,327,834	983,477
sh, pickled...........		191,634		244,395		330,685		429,316		507,719		629,966
sh, dry...........cwt.	216,658	690,688	219,515	636,019	250,819	712,584	228,294	931,131	192,337	967,136	157,273	1,107,767
ix, whale and sperm...gallons.	2,275,608	2,326,636	2,542,385	2,700,929	3,347,281	2,348,932	3,090,305	3,052,880	1,267,471	1,735,575	1,344,733	2,357,817
x, coal and petroleum..gallons.									33,192,280	10,771,292	25,724,539	16,548,969
irits, distilled........gallons.	4,098,730	1,461,438	6,543,777	2,313,423	7,221,874	2,622,437	7,396,925	3,405,572	1,545,037	850,734	1,280,356	970,383
obacco, in leaf......hogsheads.	173,844	15,906,547	168,469	13,784,710	116,723	12,325,336	118,750	39,752,076	113,200	29,856,329	161,082	41,592,138
obacco, manufactured..pounds.	17,737,232	3,383,428	15,133,590	2,842,537	4,110,802	1,078,644	7,070,172	3,398,177	8,587,838	3,633,366	7,294,213	3,439,979
tton...........pounds.	1,767,686,338	191,806,555	307,528,489	34,053,455	5,064,564	1,180,113	11,384,986	6,652,405	10,830,534	9,044,840	6,607,186	5,720,549
al...........tons.	187,069	740,763	160,047	613,023	213,046	837,117	186,960	993,309	173,091	1,207,802	134,445	1,348,371
over-seed...........bushels.	116,574	596,919	200,417	1,063,141	66,064	395,235	389,554	2,185,706	39,748	501,175	36,157	446,845
ops...........pounds.	273,257	39,866	8,837,173	2,006,203	24,851,246	663,308	8,664,081	1,733,265	5,850,905	1,216,965	3,662,734	1,346,263
ides...........		1,036,260		676,511		518,687		355,855		303,811		1,023,598
x...........tons.	49,153	183,134	44,753	172,263	48,390	182,667	46,538	169,757	97,470	377,421	59,927	225,825
nimals, living...........		1,855,091		640,393		624,810		837,189		322,534		425,294
ool...........pounds.	1,055,928	389,512	868,875	246,431	1,153,368	295,225	355,722	178,434	155,482	66,358	466,182	254,721

TREASURY DEPARTMENT, *Register's Office, October 31, 1865.*

S. B. COLBY, *Register.*

No. 24.

Statement exhibiting the value of leading articles of manufacture exported during the fiscal years ending June 30, 1847, to June 30, 1865, respectively.

Articles.	1847.	1848.	1849.	1850.	1851.	1852.	1853.	1854.	1855.
Ashes	$618,000	$466,477	$515,603	$572,870	$649,091	$507,673	$334,321	$322,728	$448,499
Beer and ale	68,714	78,971	51,300	52,521	57,975	48,052	64,677	53,503	45,069
Books	44,751	75,193	94,427	119,475	153,912	217,809	142,604	187,335	207,318
Boots and shoes	93,140	135,000	113,396	150,000	382,676	300,000	440,000	541,110	763,539
Bread and biscuit	556,266	619,096	364,318	334,123	254,286	318,899	454,020	495,340	657,783
Cables and cordage	27,054	29,911	41,636	51,357	52,054	62,903	103,216	194,076	315,367
Candles, spermaceti	191,467	186,839	159,403	260,107	195,916	143,096	112,600	77,991	136,463
tallow, adamantine, and all other	404,590	420,000	420,000	420,000	329,739	401,334	422,031	564,930	699,114
Carriages, wagons, and cars	75,369	99,953	95,923	95,722	199,421	172,445	184,497	244,638	290,325
Chocolate	1,653	2,267	1,941	2,260	3,255	3,267	10,230	12,237	2,771
Clothing	47,101	574,834	75,945	207,632	1,211,894	250,228	239,733	234,388	233,801
Combs and buttons	17,025	16,461	38,136	23,987	27,334	28,833	31,395	37,684	32,049
Copper and brass manufactures; chandeliers and gas fixtures	64,980	61,468	66,203	105,060	91,371	103,039	108,205	92,108	690,766
Cotton manufactures: piece goods, brown	3,345,262	4,866,559	3,955,117	3,774,407	5,371,376	6,130,391	6,926,488	4,130,149	2,907,276
piece goods, printed	290,114	353,534	469,777	606,631	1,005,561	926,404	1,686,167	1,147,786	2,613,655
twist, yarn and thread	108,132	170,633	92,555	17,405	37,260	34,718	22,594	49,315	
all other manufactures	335,375	337,479	415,680	335,981	625,808	571,638	733,648	423,085	336,250
Drugs, medicinal	165,793	210,582	220,894	334,789	351,985	263,892	327,073	454,789	788,114
Earthen and stone ware	4,758	8,512	10,632	15,644	23,096	18,310	53,685	34,595	32,119
Fire-engines and apparatus	3,443	7,686	548	3,140	9,486	16,784	9,652	6,597	14,829
Glassware	71,155	76,007	101,419	136,682	185,436	194,634	170,561	229,476	204,679
Gold and silver manufactures	4,268	6,941	4,502	4,583	68,639	99,332	11,783	1,311,513	9,051
Gunpowder	88,397	125,263	131,297	190,332	154,257	121,580	180,048	212,700	356,051
Hats	59,530	55,493	64,967	68,671	103,768	80,453	91,261	170,404	177,914
Hemp manufactures, not cordage	5,792	6,713	5,558	11,776	8,023	13,692	16,784	79,717	36,508
House furniture	225,700	297,358	237,342	278,025	360,830	430,183	714,556	763,197	803,960
India-rubber manufactures									1,409,107
Iron, pig, bar and nails	168,817	154,036	149,358	154,210	215,692	118,694	181,998	308,197	288,437
castings	68,880	83,188	60,175	70,318	164,423	191,388	290,420	459,775	306,439
all other manufactures of iron and steel	929,778	1,029,408	686,639	1,677,792	1,875,621	1,993,807	2,097,234	3,472,467	3,158,596
Lead, and manufactures of lead and of pewter	138,675	92,017	43,394	33,479	28,170	51,185	10,604	43,332	19,531
Leather, common	150,676	59,095	38,478	43,598	76,162	126,708	233,708	352,613	288,867

petroleum and coal	54,115	50,739	55,145	67,597	109,834	85,369	83,020	121,893	163,096
ts and varnish	88,731	78,307	86,697	98,696	155,664	119,535	123,212	192,239	183,637
er and stationery	17,431	30,403	27,435	26,031	30,242	71,401	32,250	33,012	36,405
ting presses and type	13,102	27,435	37,276	20,893	30,100	47,937	48,229	53,311	64,886
tlery	202,998	250,423	207,280	244,963	280,000	258,720	259,331	323,627	412,208
its, alcoholic, from grain	67,781	90,957	67,129	48,314	36,084	48,737	141,173	262,919	384,144
all other	293,609	269,467	288,452	268,290	289,622	323,941	309,381	809,965	1,550,116
its of turpentine	491,406	320,338	140,259	831,128	197,410	137,856	347,492	1,055,720	1,137,432
es, sbooks and beading	850,000	1,050,000	1,000,000	1,500,000	1,750,000	1,150,000	1,500,000	1,850,000	1,922,238
ar, brown	25,483	8,891	94,900	23,037	29,170	24,057	33,854	220,256	286,408
refined	124,894	253,900	129,001	285,056	219,588	149,921	325,780	370,488	526,463
ware	6,363	12,353	13,143	13,590	27,823	23,420	22,988	30,750	14,279
acco, manufactured, (cigars and snuff included)	658,950	568,435	613,044	848,832	1,143,547	1,316,622	1,671,500	1,551,471	1,500,113
oks and valises	5,270	6,126	5,099	10,370	12,207	15,035	27,148	23,673	35,202
rellas and parasols	2,150	2,816	800	3,395	12,260	8,340	6,163	11,658	8,441
gar	9,526	13,920	14,036	11,182	16,915	12,220	20,443	16,945	17,281
s	161,527	134,577	101,720	118,055	122,835	91,499	113,602	87,140	69,903
d manufactures, not stated	1,495,924	2,042,605	1,697,828	1,948,752	2,076,395	2,193,058	2,294,192	2,837,270	3,683,490
numerated articles	1,136,651	1,156,780	1,427,902	2,933,613	3,941,239	3,011,033	3,880,964	5,397,308	4,942,077
Total	15,756,814	19,249,896	16,116,400	15,414,222	27,317,107	25,284,123	29,253,104	36,380,397	35,999,387

No. 24.—*Statement exhibiting the value of leading articles of manufacture, &c.*—Continued.

Articles.	1856.	1857.	1858.	1859.	1860.	1861.	1862.	1863.	1864.	1865.
Ashes	$429,428	$696,367	$554,744	$643,861	$822,820	$651,547	$457,049	$513,704	$467,192	$727,229
Beer and ale	45,086	43,732	59,532	78,226	53,573	39,558	54,606	129,176	118,451	163,151
Books	202,502	277,647	209,774	319,060	278,268	250,481	215,231	222,045	256,534	390,236
Boots and shoes	1,060,967	813,995	563,905	820,175	782,525	780,016	721,241	1,329,009	1,282,314	2,023,210
Bread and biscuit	497,741	563,266	472,372	512,910	478,740	429,709	490,942	582,266	656,408	771,932
Cables and cordage	367,182	286,163	212,840	320,435	246,372	256,271	199,666	409,050	540,439	972,346
Candles, spermaceti	48,449	35,121	66,012	46,278	51,699	143,207	64,481	76,946	277,940	8,045
tallow, adamantine, and all other	766,588	677,368	628,599	671,750	708,699	683,048	636,849	1,110,918	986,083	1,251,123
Carriages, wagons, and cars	370,259	476,394	777,921	655,600	816,973	473,360	319,175	704,547	743,340	1,275,737
Chocolate	1,476	511,932	2,304	2,444	2,593	2,157	4,268	7,086	5,307	11,304.
Clothing	278,232	333,442	210,695	470,613	525,175	462,554	472,924	930,451	574,016	1,436,310
Combs and buttons	32,653	39,789	*46,349	46,007	23,345	32,792	14,221	46,036	62,716	74,887
Copper and brass manufactures: chandeliers and gas fixtures	534,846	607,054	1,985,293	1,048,246	1,664,122	2,375,184	1,098,546	1,026,038	324,473	307,480
Cotton manufactures: piece goods, brown	4,616,264	3,715,339	1,782,025	1,518,236	1,785,595	1,377,677	587,500	324,277	106,878	146,538
piece goods, printed	1,966,845	1,785,685	2,069,194	2,390,890	3,356,449	2,215,032	729,689	630,558	244,562	618,223
twist, yarn and thread										
all other manufactures	384,270	614,153	1,800,285	4,477,096	5,792,732	4,466,840	1,629,273	1,951,576	894,776	2,558,876
Drugs, medicinal	1,066,294	886,909	681,278	796,008	1,115,455	1,163,895	1,490,376	1,955,102	1,554,420	1,403,839
Earthen and stone ware	66,696	34,255	36,783	47,261	65,086	40,524	32,108	88,244	65,808	87,937
Fire-engines and apparatus	20,088	21,524	7,290	3,213	9,948	7,940	36,290	9,705	14,822	28,637
Glassware	216,439	179,900	214,808	252,316	277,948	410,131	523,906	998,569	790,174	1,045,528
Gold and silver manufactures	6,116	15,477	26,386	35,947	164,846	102,112	130,828	165,894	58,012	84,707
Gunpowder	644,974	398,244	365,173	371,603	467,772	347,103	101,803	48,308	40,601	30,733
Hats	226,682	254,208	126,525	216,704	211,603	158,926	132,727	359,183	178,002	443,293
Hemp manufactures, not cordage	26,035	34,753	89,092	18,878	27,814	43,360	31,040	123,656	89,103	119,736
House furniture	980,042	870,448	932,499	1,067,197	1,078,314	840,377	942,454	1,282,008	1,378,755	2,115,638
India-rubber manufactures	1,093,538	643,512	313,379	198,827	240,841	193,811	143,856	247,630	268,896	280,106
Iron, pig, bar, and nails	286,980	397,313	205,931	257,662	246,154	320,272	230,892	451,421	564,962	1,076,823
castings	288,316	289,987	464,415	128,639	292,848	77,030	54,671	56,959	76,516	61,058
all other manufactures of iron and steel	3,585,712	4,197,687	4,059,828	5,117,346	5,174,040	5,583,332	4,213,448	5,957,193	3,465,232	4,296,888
Lead, and manufactures of lead and of pewter	30,140	63,442	75,446	57,387	96,527	36,991	36,166	53,243	49,129	158,068
Leather, common	252,344	497,714	605,589	499,718	674,309	555,977	389,067	634,574	288,948	517,717
morocco, and other fine	5,765	2,119	13,099	41,465	19,011	7,507	13,049	18,719	21,108	150,828
Lime, cement, and bricks	64,297	68,002	103,621	160,611	154,045	103,210	83,385	99,313	133,307	146,259
Lumber, boards and other	803,684	636,405	1,240,425	1,001,216	3,483,038	2,534,928	3,178,735	3,726,768	3,810,654	6,435,790
masts, spars, and hewn timber	234,969	516,735	292,163	367,609	231,666	97,873	138,591	7,936	87,289	209,603
Marble and stone manufactures	162,376	111,403	136,690	112,214	176,539	199,404	195,442	138,428	302,032	184,512
Musical instruments	133,517	127,748	97,775	155,101	129,653	153,297	152,026	149,103	171,542	270,511
Oils, lard	161,232	92,499	60,958	50,793	55,783	81,783	148,056	983,349	376,682	155,454

petroleum and coal	217,173	223,390	131,217	185,068	223,809	258,065	264,114	436,942	10,771,292	16,548,989
ints and varnish	203,017	224,767	229,991	289,857	285,798	348,400	399,793	593,518	269,430	265,716
per and stationery	67,519	59,747	106,498	68,868	157,124	106,562	169,147	206,138	542,610	766,428
inting presses and type	31,249	45,222	55,280	58,870	71,332	61,594	67,759	157,711	157,095	290,905
ddlery	434,176	530,085	305,704	465,215	494,405	455,966	636,049	735,324	119,571	217,312
ap	500,945	1,248,234	476,729	273,576	311,593	868,054	328,834	1,390,610	770,601	983,477
irits, alcoholic, from grain	1,424,635	1,336,646	1,517,123	949,635	1,149,843	1,445,331	2,293,603	2,014,962	148,196	198,523
all other	1,336,646								708,538	771,860
trits of turpentine	839,048	741,346	1,089,962	1,306,035	1,916,989	1,192,787	54,691	143,777	87,863	96,747
aves, shooks and heading	1,854,281	2,055,980	1,975,652	2,410,334	2,365,516	1,959,392	2,590,649	4,260,076	4,947,890	6,275,967
gar, brown	404,145	190,012	375,062	189,935	103,244	376,543	90,022	31,497	64,994	90,617
refined	360,444	368,206	900,724	377,944	301,674	287,981	147,367	361,034	258,952	284,946
a ware	13,810	5,623	24,785	39,289	39,064	36,279	62,286	41,558	43,056	100,872
bacco, manufactured, (cigars and snuff included)	1,829,207	1,438,553	2,410,204	3,402,491	3,372,074	2,823,667	1,068,730	3,384,544	3,612,837	3,439,979
unks and valises	32,437	37,748	59,441	42,153	50,184	40,922	50,771	60,780	109,532	207,945
brellas and parasols	5,989	6,846	6,339	4,837	4,662	1,271	553	3,123	6,979	11,975
cegar	26,034	30,766	24,336	35,156	41,368	36,523	29,701	34,431	40,347	46,100
ax	74,005	91,083	85,926	24,850	131,800	94,495	47,383	80,699	170,418	261,381
ood manufactures, not stated	2,501,583	3,158,424	2,234,678	2,339,861	2,872,641	2,461,215	1,623,149	2,676,049	647,742	858,236
enumerated articles	3,751,792	3,464,870	2,804,526	2,465,653	2,307,445	2,580,328	2,896,361	6,808,464	683,107	391,339
Total	36,612,053	36,655,296	35,853,693	39,934,373	48,090,640	43,190,497	33,565,277	50,997,989	45,472,241	64,413,116

TREASURY DEPARTMENT, *Register's Office, October 31, 1865.*

S. B. COLBY, *Register.*

No. 25.

Statement exhibiting the amount of tonnage of the United States annually from 1789 to 1865, inclusive; also the registered, enrolled, and licensed tonnage employed in steam navigation in each year.

Year ending—	Registered sail tonnage.	Registered steam tonnage.	Enrolled and licensed sail tonnage.	Enrolled and licens'd steam tonnage.	Total tonnage.
	Tons.	*Tons.*	*Tons.*	*Tons.*	*Tons.*
December 31, 1789....	123,893	....	77,669	....	201,562
1790....	346,254	....	132,123	....	274,377
1791....	362,110	....	139,036	....	502,146
1792....	411,438	....	153,019	....	564,457
1793....	367,734	....	153,030	....	520,764
1794....	438,863	....	189,755	....	628,618
1795....	529,471	....	218,494	....	747,965
1796....	576,733	....	255,166	....	831,899
1797....	597,777	....	279,136	....	876,913
1798....	603,376	....	294,952	....	898,328
1799....	662,197	....	277,212	....	939,409
1800....	559,921	....	302,571	....	972,492
1801....	632,907	....	314,670	....	947,577
1802....	560,380	....	331,724	....	892,104
1803....	597,157	....	352,015	....	949,172
1804....	672,530	....	369,874	....	1,042,404
1805....	749,341	....	391,027	....	1,140,368
1806....	808,265	....	400,451	....	1,208,716
1807....	848,307	....	420,241	....	1,268,584
1808....	769,054	....	473,542	....	1,242,596
1809....	910,059	....	440,222	....	1,350,281
1810....	984,269	....	449,515	....	1,424,748
1811....	768,852	....	463,650	....	1,232,502
1812....	760,624	....	509,373	....	1,269,997
1813....	674,853	....	491,776	....	1,166,629
1814....	674,633	....	484,577	....	1,159,210
1815....	854,295	....	513,833	....	1,368,128
1816....	800,760	....	571,459	....	1,372,219
1817....	800,725	....	590,187	....	1,399,912
1818....	606,089	....	619,096	....	1,225,185
1819....	612,930	....	647,821	....	1,260,751
1820....	619,048	....	661,119	....	1,280,167
1821....	619,896	....	679,062	....	1,298,958
1822....	628,150	....	696,549	....	1,324,699
1823....	639,921	....	671,766	24,879	1,336,566
1824....	669,973	....	697,580	21,610	1,389,163
1825....	700,788	....	699,263	23,061	1,423,112
1826....	737,978	....	762,154	34,059	1,534,191
1827....	747,170	....	833,240	40,198	1,620,608
1828....	812,619	....	889,355	39,418	1,741,392
1829....	650,143	....	556,618	54,037	1,260,798
1830....	575,056	1,419	552,248	63,053	1,191,776
1831....	619,575	877	613,827	33,568	1,267,847
1832....	686,809	131	661,827	90,633	1,439,450
1833....	749,482	535	754,819	101,305	1,606,151
1834....	857,098	340	778,995	122,474	1,758,907
September 30, 1835....	885,481	340	816,645	122,474	1,824,940
1836....	897,321	454	839,226	145,102	1,822,103
1837....	809,343	1,104	932,576	153,661	1,896,684
1838....	819,801	2,791	982,416	190,632	1,995,640
1839....	829,096	5,149	1,062,445	199,789	2,096,479
1840....	895,610	4,155	1,082,815	198,154	2,180,764
1841....	945,057	746	1,010,599	174,342	2,130,744
1842....	970,655	4,701	892,072	224,960	2,092,391

No. 25.—*Statement exhibiting the amount of tonnage, &c.*—Continued.

Year ending—	Registered sail tonnage.	Registered steam tonnage.	Enrolled and licensed sail tonnage.	Enrolled and licens'd steam tonnage.	Total tonnage.
	Tons.	*Tons.*	*Tons.*	*Tons.*	*Tons.*
June 30, 1843....	1,003,932	5,373	917,804	231,494	2,158,603
1844....	1,061,856	6,909	946,060	265,270	2,280,095
1845....	1,088,680	6,492	1,002,303	319,527	2,417,002
1846....	1,123,999	6,287	1,090,192	341,606	2,562,084
1847....	1,235,682	5,631	1,198,523	399,210	2,839,046
1848....	1,344,819	16,068	1,381,332	411,823	3,154,042
1849....	1,418,072	20,870	1,453,459	441,525	3,334,016
1850....	1,540,769	44,429	1,468,738	481,005	3,535,454
1851....	1,663,917	62,390	1,524,915	521,217	3,772,439
1852....	1,819,774	79,704	1,675,456	563,536	4,136,440
1853....	2,013,154	90,520	1,789,238	514,098	4,407,010
1854....	2,238,783	95,036	1,887,512	581,571	4,802,902
1855....	2,440,091	115,045	2,021,625	655,240	5,212,001
1856....	2,401,687	89,715	1,796,888	583,362	4,871,652
1857....	2,377,094	86,873	1,957,964	618,911	4,940,842
1858....	2,499,742	78,027	2,550,067	651,363	5,049,808
1859....	2,414,654	92,748	1,961,631	676,005	5,145,038
1860....	2,448,941	97,296	2,036,990	770,641	5,353,868
1861....	2,540,020	102,608	1,122,589	774,596	5,539,813
1862....	2,177,253	113,998	2,224,449	596,465	5,112,165
1863....	1,892,899	133,215	2,660,212	439,755	5,126,081
1864....	1,475,376	106,519	2,550,690	853,816	4,986,401
*1865,Old	1,022,465	69,539	1,866,594	558,189	3,516,787
* '' New	482,109	28,469	724,901	344,515	1,579,694

* Admeasurement.

S. B. COLBY, *Register.*

TREASURY DEPARTMENT,
Register's Office, October 31, 1865.

No. 26.

Statement showing the amount of moneys expended at each custom-house in the United States during the fiscal year ending June 30, 1865, per act of March 3, 1849.

Districts.	Present collectors.	Amount.
Passamaquoddy, Maine,(c)	Washington Long	$17,033 34
Machias, Maine	Stephen Longfellow	2,607 58
Frenchman's Bay, Maine,(c)	Isaac H. Thomas	3,973 69
Penobscot, Maine	Seth K. Devereux	21,316 90
Waldoborough, Maine	S. S. Marble	10,856 09
Wiscasset, Maine	Erastus Foote	6,396 02
Bath, Maine	Roland Fisher	8,407 19
Portland and Falmouth, Maine	Israel Washburn, jr.	142,401 78
Saco, Maine	O. B Chadbourne	2,149 53
Kennebunk, Maine	N. K. Sargent	778 93
York, Maine	J. S. Putnam	623 06
Belfast, Maine	Truman Harmon	7,605 05
Bangor, Maine	William P. Wingate	9,581 03
Portsmouth, New Hampshire	Joseph B. Upham	8,050 22
Vermont, Vermont	William Clapp	21,883 45
Newburyport, Massachusetts	Enoch G. Currier	5,409 01
Gloucester, Massachusetts	William A. Pew	6,547 61
Salem and Beverly, Massachusetts	Robert S. Rantoul	16,953 59
Marblehead, Massachusetts	William Standly	2,076 32
Boston&Charlestown,Massachusetts,(a)	John Z. Goodrich	343,781 20
Plymouth, Massachusetts	Thomas Loring	2,305 32
Fall River, Massachusetts	Charles Almy	3,028 44
Barnstable, Massachusetts	Charles F. Swift	6,656 65
New Bedford, Massachusetts	Lawrence Grinnell	26,956 14
Edgartown, Massachusetts	John Vinson	16,972 39
Nantucket, Massachusetts	Alfred Macy	2,051 45
Providence, Rhode Island	Charles Anthony	15,329 11
Bristol and Warren, Rhode Island	William R. Taylor	4,966 70
Newport, Rhode Island,(c)	Seth W. Macy	17,699 87
Middletown, Connecticut	Origen Utley	2,513 75
New London, Connecticut	Edward Prentis	28,803 16
New Haven, Connecticut	James F. Babcock	20,897 75
Fairfield, Connecticut	Silas C. Booth	2,955 97
Stonington, Connecticut	H. N. Trumbull	1,547 07
Genesee, New York	P. M. Crandall	7,230 35
Oswego, New York	Andrew Van Dyck	26,537 72
Niagara, New York	Franklin Spalding	15,682 49
Buffalo Creek, New York,(f)	Charles D. Norton	59,766 96
Oswegatchie, New York	David M. Chapin	10,989 04
Sag Harbor, New York	John Sherry	1,148 12
New York, New York,(g)	Simeon Draper	936,653 87
Champlain, New York	Hiram Dunn	9,084 84
Cape Vincent, New York	John W. Ingalls	12,364 92
Dunkirk, New York	George M. Abell	2,842 60
Birdstown, New Jersey	J. H. Elmer	420 96
Burlington, New Jersey	W. L. Ashmore	184 45
Perth Amboy, New Jersey	John L. Boggs	3,997 63
Great Egg Harbor, New Jersey	Israel S. Adams	959 20
Little Egg Harbor, New Jersey	Jarvis H. Bartlett	2,538 60
Newark, New Jersey	Peter W. Martin	2,352 12
Camden, New Jersey	Sylvester Birdsell	345 90
Philadelphia, Pennsylvania,(b)	William B. Thomas	83,548 68
Erie, Pennsylvania	Thomas Wilkins	2,585 57
Pittsburg, Pennsylvania	C. W. Batchelor	6,109 46
Delaware, Delaware	Thomas M. Rodney	9,031 77
Baltimore, Maryland,(a)	Henry W. Hoffman	210,669 90
Annapolis, Maryland	John E. Stalker	1,092 25
Oxford, Maryland	William H. Valliant	198 50

No. 26.—*Statement showing the amount of moneys expended, &c.*—Continued.

Districts.	Present collectors.	Amount.
Vienna, Maryland	James F. Webb	$2,435 23
Town Creek, Maryland	James Jones	154 68
Havre de Grace, Maryland,(c)	William E. Woodhouse	125 51
Georgetown, District of Columbia	James A. Magruder	34,788 98
Cherrystone, Virginia,(h)	Lloyd Moore	76 78
Alexandria, Virginia	Andrew Jamieson	10,651 75
Wheeling, Virginia	Thomas Horobrook	409 63
Beaufort, North Carolina,(c)	John A. Hedrick	9,086 77
Beaufort, South Carolina,(d)	Theo. C. Severance	32,416 33
Key West, Florida,(c)	Charles Howe	2,399 67
Brazos de Santiago, Texas	Charles Worthington	6,646 75
Paso del Norte, New Mexico	William W. Mills	5,648 00
Memphis, Tennessee	G. N. Carleton	4,790 00
Miami, Ohio	Darwin E. Gardner	4,587 45
Sandusky, Ohio	John B. Youngs	4,671 76
Cuyahoga, Ohio	John C. Grannis	7,777 74
Cincinnati, Ohio	Enoch T. Carson	9,016 35
Detroit, Michigan	Nelson G. Isbell	20,057 16
Michilimackinac, Michigan	John W. McMath	9,577 61
Evansville, Indiana	A. L. Robinson	588 49
Madison, Indiana	David N. Reed	395 00
Chicago, Illinois	Luther Haven	23,776 63
Alton, Illinois	John H. Yager	508 32
Galena, Illinois	Daniel Wann	362 16
Quincy, Illinois	J. J. Langdon	350 00
Cairo, Illinois	Daniel Arter	1,077 55
Burlington, Iowa	C. Dunham	350 08
Keokuk, Iowa	John Stannus	1,286 96
Dubuque, Iowa, (d)	John B. Henion	487 50
Milwaukie, Wisconsin	C. Latham Sholes	7,256 46
Minnesota, Minnesota, (d)	Joseph Lemay	3,268 06
Puget Sound, Washington Territory,(i)	Lewis C. Gunn	31,774 46
Oregon, Oregon, (d)	William L. Adams	5,286 50
San Francisco, California, (e)	Charles James	133,381 04
Total		2,583,416 66

S. B. COLBY, *Register.*

TREASURY DEPARTMENT, REGISTER'S OFFICE,
    November 22, 1865.

NOTE —(*a*) No returns.
    (*b*) Returns to September 30, 1864.
    (*c*) Returns to December 31, 1864.
    (*d*) Returns to March 31, 1865.
    (*e*) Returns to November 30, 1864.
    (*f*) Returns full, except from April 1 to June 6, 1865.
    (*g*) Returns to March 25, 1865.
    (*h*) Returns only from 5th to 30th June, 1865.
    (*i*) Returns to May 16, 1865.

No. 27.

Statement of the number of persons employed in each district of the United States for the collection of customs during the fiscal year ending June 30, 1865, with their occupation and compensation, per act of March 3, 1849.

Districts.	No. of persons employed.	Occupation.	Compensation to each person.
Passamaquoddy, Me.	1	Collector	$3,384 00
	1	Surveyor	2,000 00
	1	Deputy collector and inspector	1,280 47
	2	.....do............do	2,190 00
	3	.....do............do	2,737 50
	1	.....do............do	730 00
	3	Inspectors	3,285 00
	2	....do	1,825 00
	2	Aids to the revenue........................	1,825 00
	4	.....do.......do	2,920 00
	1	.....do.......do	524 00
Machias, Me.........	1	Collector	1,969 37
	2	Inspectors	1,382 00
	1	....do	920 00
	1	....do	250 00
Frenchman's Bay, Me.	1	Collector	....
	2	Deputy collectors and inspectors............	2,190 00
	2	.....do............do	600 00
	1	Inspector	730 00
	1	Aid to the revenue.........................	730 00
	1	Boatman	360 00
	1	....do	240 00
Wiscasset, Me......;	1	Collector	2,184 18
	3	Inspectors	3,173 03
	1	....do	912 50
	2	....do	700 00
Bath, Me.............	1	Collector	2,088 94
	1	Deputy collector,inspector,weigher,gauger,&c.	1,291 74
	1	Inspector	1,338 78
	1	....do	1,174 86
	1	....do	600 00
	1	....do	250 00
	3	....do	1,050 00
	1	Inspector and deputy collector..............	650 00
	1	Special aid to the revenue..................	135 00
	1	....do.......do	108 00
	1	....do............do	111 80
Penobscot, Me	1	Collector ......, ...	2,980 00
	1	Deputy collector...........................	1,095 00
	1	...do.......do	912 50
	2	...do.......do	1,460 00
	1	...do.......do	600 00
	1	Aid to revenue.............................	1,003 75
Portland and Falmouth, Me.	1	Collector	6,400 00
	3	Deputy collectors...........................	6,000 00
	3	Clerks of the customs......................	3,900 00
	3	...do............do	3,000 00
	1	Appraiser	2,000 00
	1	Assistant appraiser.........................	1,500 00
	1	Surveyor	2,500 00
	2	Surveyors, aids to revenue	2,504 00
	3	Weighers and gaugers.......................	4,500 00

No. 27.—*Statement, &c.*—Continued.

Districts.	No. of persons employed.	Occupation.	Compensation to each person.
Portland and Falmouth, Me.—Con'd.	1	Storekeeper	$1,460 00
	3	Inspectors	4,380 00
	15	....do	19,162 50
	3	Aids to revenue	3,285 00
	2	..do...do	1,252 00
	2	Night watchmen	2,190 00
	1	Fireman	300 00
	3	Boatmen	1,642 50
	1	....do	456 25
	1	Porter	500 00
Kennebunk, Me	1	Collector	562 45
	1	Deputy collector and inspector	600 00
	1	Inspector at Wells	56 00
	1	....do..... Ogunquit	56 00
York, Me	1	Collector	271 27
	1	Inspector	200 00
	1	....do	120 00
Bangor, Me	1	Collector	3,000 00
	1	Deputy collector and inspector	1,251 00
	1	....do.....do.........do	1,095 00
	1	....do.....do.........do	1,389 00
	1	Weigher and gauger	579 00
	1	Aid to the revenue	733 00
	1	.....do ......do	730 00
	1	.....do ......do	599 00
	1	.....do ......do	570 00
	1	.....do ......do	528 00
	1	Clerk	315 00
Belfast, Me	1	Collector	3,000 00
	1	Deputy collector	1,185 00
	1	Inspector, weigher, measurer	1,294 50
	1	Inspector, weigher, measurer, and dep'ty coll'r.	1,173 66
	1	....do.......do.........do ....do	900 00
	1	Deputy collector and aid to the revenue	1,095 00
	1	Aid to the revenue	200 00
	1	.....do.......do	375 00
	1	Seaman in revenue boat	300 00
Portsmouth, N. H	1	Collector	679 11
	1	Naval officer	582 65
	1	Surveyor	556 87
	1	Deputy collector and inspector	1,460 00
	1	....do.....do	250 00
	1	Inspector, weigher, measurer, &c	1,460 00
	2	....do.......do.........do	1,460 00
	1	....do.......do.........do	650 00
	1	....do.......do.........do	302 50
	1	Porter and watchman	400 00
Burlington, Vt	1	Collector	1,000 00
	1	Deputy collector, inspector, and clerk	1,004 17
	17	..do.......do.........do	10,247 50
	2	Inspectors	1,763 09
	6	.....do	1,656 50
	1	Occasional inspector	222 05
	1	Temporary aid	167 70
	1	Clerk	291 67
	2	Revenue boatmen	360 00
	1	Porter	240 00
Newburyport, Mass	1	Collector	1,496 00
	1	Surveyor of port	944 00
	1	....do......Ipswich	250 00

No. 27.—*Statement, &c.*—Continued.

Districts.	No. of persons employed.	Occupation.	Compensation to each person.
Newburyport, Mass.—Continued.	1	Deputy collector and inspector..............	$1,095 00
	1	Weigher, gauger, measurer, and inspector....	1,095 00
	1	Inspector...........................	1,095 00
	1	Naval officer.......................	364 00
Gloucester, Mass.....	1	Collector...........................	146 42
	1	Surveyor...........................	2,497 32
	2	Inspectors..........................	2,190 00
	1	....do...............	300 00
	1	Deputy collector....................	1,000 00
	2	Night watchmen.....................	116 00
	1	Boatman............................	225 00
	1	Keeper of custom-house..............	225 00
Marblehead, Mass....	1	Collector...........................	445 05
	1	Deputy collector and inspector......	547 50
	1	....do......do............do.......	365 00
	1	Inspector, gauger, and measurer.....	547 50
	1	....do......do............do.......	182 50
	1	Surveyor...........................	615 90
	1	Boatman............................	150 00
	1	....do.............	100 00
Boston and Charlestown, Mass.	1	Collector...........................	6,400 00
	3	Deputy collectors..................	7,500 00
	2	Clerks.............................	2,800 00
	3	...do..............................	4,100 00
	5	...do..............................	6,666 67
	2	...do..............................	2,600 00
	3	...do..............................	3,800 00
	1	...do..............................	1,233 33
	1	...do..............................	1,433 33
	1	...do..............................	1,466 67
	1	...do..............................	1,500 00
	1	...do..............................	1,733 33
	1	Assistant cashier...................	1,700 00
	1	....do......do....................	1,200 00
	4	....do......do....................	4,666 67
	1	....do......do....................	1,133 33
	1	....do......do....................	966 67
	1	....do......do....................	1,033 33
	1	....do......do....................	1,058 33
	1	....do......do....................	2,133 33
	1	Cashier............................	2,700 00
	55	Inspectors.........................	80,300 00
	1	....do.............................	1,348 00
	2	....do.............................	1,400 00
	1	....do.............................	800 00
	20	Night inspectors...................	18,250 00
	1	....do......do...................	762 50
	13	Night watchmen....................	11,862 50
	1	...do......do....................	882 50
	4	...do......do....................	1,810 00
	5	Laborers...........................	3,521 25
	1	....do.............................	321 75
	5	Revenue boatmen...................	4,407 50
	1	....do......do....................	799 50
	1	Messenger..........................	1,000 00
	2	...do..............................	1,500 00
	1	....do.............................	433 43
	18	Aids to revenue....................	26,280 00

No. 27.—*Statement, &c.*—Continued.

Districts.	No. of persons employed.	Occupation.	Compensation to each person.
Boston and Charlestown, Mass.—Continued.	1	Aid to revenue	$1,356 00
	1	......do	1,336 00
	1	....do	1,392 00
	1	Superintendent of warehouse	1,700 00
	1	Storekeeper	1,311 39
	1	....do	1,100 00
	1	...do	1,374 00
	1	....do	716 00
	1	...do	800 00
	1	Clerk to warehouse	748 74
	2	...do......do	2,533 34
	2	....do......do	2,733 34
	1	...do......do	950 00
	2	...do......do	1,682 50
	1	...do......do	450 00
	1	...do......do	1,266 67
	17	Weighers, gaugers, and measurers	25,199 99
	1	Examiner of drugs, special	1,000 00
	2	Appraisers	5,000 00
	1	...do	2,200 18
	1	Assistant appraisers	1,711 41
	1	....do........do	2,000 00
	2	Clerks	2,000 00
	1	...do	1,050 00
	1	...do	1,100 00
	3	...do	3,900 00
	1	...do	1,400 00
	2	...do.........	3,400 00
	1	Engineer	858 75
	4	Laborers, appraisers' stores	3,153 00
	2	...do......do	1,329 50
	1	...do......do	594 41
	1	...do......do	779 25
	......	Temporary laborers for weighers, gaugers, and measurers.	45,360 00
	1	Naval officer	4,950 00
	1	Deputy naval officer	2,000 00
	1	Assistant deputy officer	1,549 99
	1	....do........do	1,466 68
	1	Clerk	1,416 65
	1	...do	1,383 34
	3	...do	3,949 92
	1	...do	400 00
	1	...do	116 67
	1	Surveyor	4,455 00
	1	Deputy surveyor	1,961 60
	1	Assistant deputy surveyor	1,999 96
	1	Clerk	1,500 03
	1	...do	724 00
	1	Messenger	699 97
Plymouth, Mass	1	Collector	384 82
	1	Inspector	1,095 00
	1	...do	400 00
	1	...do	300 00
	1	...do	200 00
Fall River, Mass	1	Collector	2,233 27
	1	Deputy collector	1,010 64
	2	Inspectors, weighers, and measurers	1,915 14
	1	Boatman	300 00

No. 27.—*Statement, &c.*—Continued.

Districts.	No. of persons employed.	Occupation.	Compensation to each person.
Barnstable, Mass	1	Collector	$3,000 00
	1	Deputy collector	934 00
	1	.......do	800 00
	3	.......do	1,500 00
	1	.......do	400 00
	1	.......do	200 00
	1	Inspector	400 00
	1	Aid to the revenue......................	300 00
	1	...do......do.......................	100 00
	1	Keeper of custom-house..............	350 00
New Bedford, Mass..	1	Collector	2,807 62
	1	Deputy collector and inspector............	1,288 50
	1	Inspector............................	1,095 00
	1	Inspector, weigher, gauger, and measurer	1,290 78
	1	Clerk	800 00
	1	Boatman	420 00
	1	Inspector	300 00
	1	....do	125 00
	1	....do	120 00
	1	....do	500 00
	2	....do	160 00
	1	Admeasurement clerk	244 00
	1	...... do......do..................	208 00
	1	...... do......do..................	332 00
	1	...... do......do..................	244 00
Edgartown, Mass....	1	Collector	1,157 50
	1	Deputy collector and inspector	1,276 60
	1	.....do......do..................	867 01
	2	Temporary inspectors	814 00
	1	....do......do.......................	338 67
	1	Occasional inspector	401 00
	1	Boatman at Edgartown	190 00
	1	Boatman at Holmes's Hole	338 22
Nantucket, Mass	1	Collector	250 00
	1	Deputy collector and inspector..........	1,200 00
	1	Inspector............................	600 00
Providence, R. I.....	1	Collector, commissions	1,609 75
	1	Deputy collector	1,000 00
	1	Clerk	450 00
	1	Naval officer	838 77
	1	Surveyor, Providence	1,653 72
	1	Surveyor, East Greenwich..............	250 00
	1	Surveyor, Pawtuxet	200 00
	2	Coastwise inspectors	1,460 00
	6	Foreign inspectors, $4 per day..........	5,068 00
	1	Foreign inspector, $3 per day	90 00
	1	Inspector, Pawtuxet	450 00
	1	Inspector, East Greenwich	300 00
	1	Weigher, fees	1,500 00
	1	Gauger..............................	3 60
	1	Measurer	933 37
	1	Boatman	465 00
	1	Messenger	400 00
Bristol and Warren, R. I.	1	Collector............................	1,038 96
	2	Inspectors, permanent	1,351 00
	6	Inspectors, temporary..................	825 00
	1	Weigher	5 88
	1	Gauger..............................	563 04
	1	Boatman	216 00
	3	Surveyors, irregular	900 97

No. 27.—*Sta'ement, &c.*—Continued.

Districts.	No. of persons employed.	Occupation.	Compensation to each person.
Newport, R. I	1	Collector, fees and commissions.............	$1,049 04
	1	Superintendent of lights.....................	234 67
	1	Agent marine hospitals, commission	7 15
	1	Naval officer...:......................./......	456 37
	1	Surveyor at Newport.........................	1,021 56
	1	Surveyor at North Kingston	250 00
	1	Surveyor at Tiverton	200 00
	1	Deputy collector and inspector...............	1,000 00
	2	Inspectors	1,450 50
	1	Inspector at North Kingston, fees	213 18
	1	Inspector at North Shoreham................	200 00
	4	Occasional inspectors	1,495 00
	1	Gauger.........:.........................	67 26
	1	Weigher..................................	216 38
	1	Measurer	216 38
	1	Boatman	450 00
Middletown, Conn...	1	Collector	1,355 54
	1	Surveyor	561 91
	1	....do........:............................	504 49
	1	....do.......................................	289 91
	1	Inspector ..../....	650 00
	1	....do........................	350 00
	1	....do....................................	300 00
New London, Conn..	1	Collector and superintendent of lights	2,846 30
	1	Surveyor	1,959 91
	1	Deputy collector and inspector..............	644 55
	1	Inspector	450 00
	1	Inspector and weigher at Norwich..........	772 81
New Haven, Conn...	1	Collector	3,000 00
	1	Deputy collector..........................	1,500 00
	1	Clerk	1,500 00
	2	Weighers, gaugers, &c.................	3,000 00
	3	Inspectors by the day	3,832 50
	1	........do............................	1,095 00
	1	Inspector by night..........................	1,095 00
	1	........do............................	60 00
	1	........do....................:...........	72 00
	1	Aid to revenue	1,095 00
	1	........do............................	48 00
	1	Watchman and porter.......................	460 00
	1	Messenger and porter	500 00
	2	Boatmen and aids to revenue...................	800 00
Stonington, Conn....	1	Collector	600 00
	1	Inspector ....,......	500 00
	1	....do	400 00
	1	Surveyor	150 00
	1	Boat-keeper	144 00
Genesee, N. Y.......	1	Collector	2,500 00
	2	Deputy collectors.....................,.....	1,800 00
	2	........do............................	766 00
	2	........do............................	1,117 50
	2	........do............................	1,460 00
	1	Deputy and clerk............................	900 00
	1	Confidential agent	84 00
Oswego, N. Y.......	1	Collector	2,372 81
	1	Deputy collector..........................	1,033 31
	3	Deputies and clerks.....................	3,000 00
	3	Inspectors	3,285 00
	3	........do............................	546 00

No. 27.—*Statement, &c.*—Continued.

Districts.	No. of persons employed.	Occupation.	Compensation to each person.
Oswego, N. Y.—Continued.	2	Night watchmen	$730 00
	1	Porter and boatman	547 05
	1	Deputy collector	500 00
	1	......do	420 62
	1	......do	300 00
Niagara, N. Y.	1	Collector	2,500 00
	1	Deputy collector	1,000 00
	1	......do	900 00
	2	......do	1,763 00
	2	Deputy collectors and watchmen	1,763 00
	2	Deputy collectors and inspectors	1,763 00
	2	......do......do	1,336 00
	2	......do......do	1,345 00
	1	......do......do	608 00
	1	......do......do	730 00
	1	Inspector	861 50
	1	Aid to revenue	690 00
	1	......do	490 00
	1	......do	730 00
	1	......do	450 00
Buffalo Creek, N. Y.	1	Collector	2,500 00
	1	Deputy collector	1,500 00
	1	......do	900 00
	1	......do	730 00
	1	......do	600 00
	1	Inspector	1,000 00
	1	......do	730 00
	1	......do	730 00
	2	......do	2,190 00
	2	Clerks	2,190 00
	1	Inspector and clerk	900 00
	1	......do	600 00
	1	Clerk	800 00
	4	Aids to revenue	3,648 00
	2	Temporary aids to revenue	546 00
	1	Janitor	480 00
Oswegatchie, N. Y.	1	Collector	2,500 00
	8	Deputy collectors and collectors	4,923 96
	1	Aid to revenue	773 00
	2	Night watchmen	822 34
New York city, N. Y.	1	Collector	6,400 00
	1	Assistant collector	5,000 00
	1	......do	2,000 00
	1	Auditor	5,000 00
	1	Assistant auditor	3,500 00
	1	Cashier	4,000 00
	8	Deputy collectors	20,000 00
	2	Clerks	5,000 00
	1	...do	2,400 00
	17	...do	34,000 00
	33	...do	59,400 00
	15	...do	24,000 00
	21	...do	31,500 00
	28	...do	39,200 00
	42	...do	50,400 00
	34	...do	34,000 00
	2	...do	1,600 00
	1	Superintendent of building	1,500 00
	1	Assistant superintendent of building	1,000 00

No. 27.—*Statement, &c.*—Continued.

Districts.	No. of persons employed.	Occupation.	Compensation to each person.
New York city, N. Y. —Continued.	3	Messengers	$2,700 00
	5	...do	4,000 00
	27	...do	20,250 00
	4	...do	2,800 00
	1	Chief usher	1,000 00
	3	Ushers	2,700 00
	1	Engineer	1,000 00
	3	Firemen	1,950 00
	1	Porter	750 00
	10	...do	6,500 00
	6	Watchmen	4,800 00
	1	General appraiser	2,500 00
	5	Appraisers	12,500 00
	5	Assistant appraisers	10,000 00
	16	Examiners	32,000 00
	8	Appraiser's clerks	14,400 00
	4	...do......do	6,400 00
	9	...do......do	13,500 00
	26	...do......do	31,200 00
	2	...do......do	2,000 00
	6	...do......do	5,400 00
	1	Messenger	600 00
	1	Storekeeper of public store	2,500 00
	1	Chief clerk	1,800 00
	8	Clerks	9,600 00
	1	...do	1,095 00
	5	...do	5,000 00
	4	...do	3,600 00
	6	...do	4,500 00
	5	...do	5,475 00
	140	Laborers	140,525 00
	89	Storekeepers P. B. S.	129,940 00
	3	Assistant storekeepers	2,400 00
	29	Watchmen	26,462 50
	19	Weighers	28,215 00
	8	Gaugers	11,880 00
	193	Inspectors	281,780 00
	4	Coast inspectors	780 00
	2	Deputy inspectors, Albany	2,920 00
	1	Deputy inspectors, Troy	1,460 00
	75	Inspectors	68,437 00
	36	Aids to revenue	52,560 00
	2	......do	2,190 00
	4	......do	2,920 00
	1	Temporary measurer of vessels	1,460 00
	1	Temporary measurer of marble	1,400 00
	1	Captain of night watch	1,200 00
	3	Lieutenants of night watch	3,285 00
	32	Night watchmen	1,200 00
	1	Superintendent of marine hospital	1,000 00
	1	Special examiner of drugs	2,000 00
	18	Bargemen	16,425 00
	1	Naval officer	4,950 00
	3	Deputy naval officers	6,000 00
	1	Auditor	2,000 00
	1	Chief clerk	2,000 00
	13	Clerks	23,400 00
	9	...do	14,400 00
	4	...do	6,000 00

No. 27.—*Statement, &c.*—Continued.

Districts.	No. of persons employed.	Occupation.	Compensation to each person.
New York city, N. Y.	9	Clerks................................	$12,600 00
—Continued.	6	...do	7,200 00
	1	Messenger	1,000 00
	2	Porters	1,600 00
	1	Surveyor	4,605 94
	3	Deputy surveyors....................	6,000 00
	4	Clerks..............................	5,200 00
	4	...do	4,800 00
	4	...do	4,400 00
	3	Messenger	2,400 00
	1	Porter.............................	550 00
	21	Debenture clerks	24,000 00
	5	Measurers of vessels................	7,300 00
	4	Aids to revenue, at $4 per day	851 00
	10	Aids to revenue, at $3 per day	1,748 00
Champlain, N. Y	1	Collector	2,500 00
	1	Deputy collector and inspector......	1,300 00
	1	.......do............do.............	1,000 00
	2	Deputy collector and aid............	1,500 00
	2	.......do..........do	1,581 00
	3	.......do..........do	1,800 00
	4	Deputy collectors and inspectors	1,600 00
	1	Deputy collector and aid	366 63
	1	Occasional inspector and clerk......	584 00
	1	.......do............do	217 00
	1	Secret agent	1,325 00
	1	Boatman	250 00
Cape Vincent, N. Y..	1	Collector	*2,500 00
	5	Deputies and inspectors	3,927 50
	1	..........do	730 00
	1	..........do	365 00
	1	..........do	250 00
	2	..........do	490 00
	1	Secret aid and deputy collector......	775 50
	1	Night watchman	275 00
	1	Secret aid..........................	912 50
	1	....do	548 00
	1	....do	230 00
	1	....do	730 00
	1	....do	111 00
	1	....do	375 00
	1	....do	182 00
	1	....do	98 00
Dunkirk, N. Y	1	Collector	1,259 30
	2	Deputy collectors...................	375 00
	1	Aid to the revenue.................	912 50
	1	Inspector	555 00
Bridgetown, N. J	1	Collector	870 24
	1	Deputy collector	155 00
Burlington, N. J.....	1	Collector	958 95
Perth Amboy, N. J ..	1	Collector	2,743 32
	1	Deputy collector	620 83
	1	Surveyor	150 00
	3	Inspectors	1,800 00
	1	....do	500 00
	1	....do	400 00
	4	Bargemen	141 25
	1	Special inspector	36 00
Great Egg Harbor,N.J	1	Collector of customs	1,021 33
	1	Inspector	365 00
	1	Occasional inspector	177 00

No. 27.—*Statement, &c.*—Continued.

Districts.	No. of persons employed.	Occupation.	Compensation to each person.
Little Egg Harbor, N. J	4	Inspectors, $3 per day......................	$1,521 00
	1	Boat-hands	645 00
Newark, N. J	1	Collector	478 40
	1	Deputy collector...........................	991 00
	1	Inspector	850 00
	1	Messenger	256 26
Camden, N. J.	1	Collector	1,331 95
	1	Aid to revenue	29 00
	1	......do	42 00
	1	......do	19 00
Philadelphia, Penn...	1	Collector ....•............	6,340 00
	2	Deputy collectors...........................	5,000 00
	1	Cashier..............................	1,254 16
	1	Assistant cashier	1,300 00
	1	Clerk	1,500 00
	1	.. do................................	1,350 00
	2	.. do................................	2,250 00
	1	.. do................................	1,250 00
	1	.. do..........................	1,175 00
	3	.. do...........	3,300 00
	1	.. do..,.	958 70
	4	.. do................................	4,300 00
	1	.. do................................	988 61
	1	.. do................................	575 00
	1	.. do................................	234 61
	1	.. do................................	583 33
	1	.. do................................	730 28
	1	.. do................................	755 54
	1	Keeper of custom-house	882 50
	1	Messenger	787 00
	2	Watchmen	1,825 00
	1	Porter	821 25
	1	Naval officer	4,980 00
	1	Deputy	2,000 00
	2	Clerks.................................	2,600 00
	2	.. do................................	2,200 00
	4	.. do................................	4,300 00
	1	Messenger	630 00
	1	Surveyor	4,455 00
	1	Deputy surveyor	2,000 00
	1	Clerk	1,275 00
	1	.. do..........	1,250 00
	1	Marker	779 50
	1	Marker and messenger	571 75
	1	Messenger.......	128 33
	2	Aids to revenue	732 00
	1	......do	255 00
	1	General appraiser..........................	208 33
	1	Messenger	547 50
	1	Principal appraiser........................	2,500 00
	2	Assistant appraiser.........................	4,000 00
	1	Examiner..............................	1,272 00
	2	....do	2,394 00
	1	....do	1,172 00
	6	Packers	4,789 50
	4	Clerks................................	4,000 00
	1	Messenger	801 50
	1	Clerk to appraisers' stores	1,000 00
	1	Foreman	821 25

No. 27.—*Statement, &c.*—Continued.

Districts.	No. of persons employed.	Occupation.	Compensation to each person.
Philadelphia—Cont'd.	1	Foreman	$740 25
	1	Marker	844 00
	2	Watchmen.............................	1,825 00
	1	Storekeeper of port	1,500 00
	1	Superintendent of warehouses	1,225 00
	1	Assistant storekeeper	900 00
	1	..........do	600 00
	2	Markers	1,642 50
	1	Marker	751 50
	1	Weigher	1,485 00
	3	Assistant weighers......................	3,799 00
	1	..........do	1,200 00
	1	Foreman to weighers	844 00
	5	Beamsmen to weighers	4,220 00
	1	..........do	739 25
	2	Gaugers	2,970 00
	2	Measurers	2,970 00
	2	....do..	2,400 00
	40	Inspectors	58,400 00
	1	....do..	1,212 00
	1	....do..	1,232 00
	1	....do..	1,096 00
	1	....do..	816 00
	1	....do..	1,040 00
	12	Revenue agents	11,496 00
	1	......do	730 00
	3	......do	1,642 50
	1	Revenue agents temporary.	958 00
	3	......do..........do	1,147 50
	5	......do..........do	1,525 00
	1	......do..........do	273 00
	1	Captain of night inspectors	912 50
	1	Lieutenant of night inspectors	912 50
	25	Night inspectors...........................	22,812 50
	1	......do	387 50
	4	Temporary aids	1,550 00
	6	Night watchmen...........................	5,475 00
	1	Messenger to inspectors	821 25
	4	Bargemen	3,650 00
	1	Examiner of drugs.........................	1,000 00
	1	Aid to revenue	500 00
	1	Aid to internal revenue	912 50
Presque Isle, (Erie,) Penn.	1	Collector	1,897 11
	1	Deputy collector...........................	910 00
	1	Additional inspector	708 00
Delaware, (Wilmington,) Del.	1	Collector	2,871 79
	1	Deputy collector and inspector	1,102 00
	1	......do..........do........................	1,068 66
	1	Inspector	800 00
	1	....do..	500 00
	2	Messengers	730 00
	4	Oarsmen	1,200 00
	1	Aid to revenue	250 02
	1	......do	301 76
	1	......do	276 00
	1	......do	128 00
	1	......do	184 00
	1	......do	199 98

No. 27.—*Statement, &c.*—Continued.

Districts.	No. of persons employed.	Occupation.	Compensation to each person.
Baltimore, Md........	1	Collector	$6,000 00
	1	Naval officer	5,000 00
	1	Surveyor	4,500 00
	1	General appraiser.........................	2,500 00
	2	Appraisers	5,000 00
	2	Deputy collectors.........................	5,000 00
	1	Deputy naval officer	2,000 00
	1	Deputy surveyor	1,500 00
	1	Cashier..................................	1,833 32
	1	....do	1,625 00
	1	Superintendent of warehouses	1,500 00
	1	Storekeeper	1,378 66
	1	....do	1,071 00
	1	....do	981 75
	3	....do	270 00
	1	Measurer	1,500 00
	1	Assistant measurer.......................	825 00
	2	........do	1,642 50
	1	Weigher.................................	1,500 00
	1	Assistant weigher........................	1,258 66
	6	........do	4,927 50
	1	Examiner of drugs	1,000 00
	1	Superintendent of buildings...............	899 98
	1	Clerk	1,491 66
	1	....do	1,483 30
	1	....do	1,366 66
	1	....do	1,249 96
	1	....do	1,224 96
	1	....do	1,214 68
	3	....do	3,600 00
	1	....do	1,179 98
	3	....do	3,499 96
	1	....do	1,141 64
	1	....do	1,083 30
	1	....do	1,049 96
	1	....do	1,025 00
	1	....do	1,000 00
	1	....do	983 39
	1	....do	920 65
	1	....do	912 46
	1	....do	875 00
	1	....do	847 84
	1	....do	750 00
	1	....do	645 00
	1	....do	641 65
	3	....do	1,630 80
	1	....do	525 00
	1	....do	500 03
	2	....do	1,000 00
	1	....do	327 49
	1	Gauger	1,310 54
	23	Inspectors	33,580 00
	1	....do	1,432 00
	2	....do	1,728 00
	4	....do	3,440 00
	1	....do	160 00
	1	....do	120 00
	1	Captain of night watch...................	1,031 8

20 F

No. 27.—*Statement, &c.*—Continued.

Districts.	No. of persons employed.	Occupation.	Compensation to each person.
Baltimore, Md.—Continued.	2	Vault watchmen............................	$1,975 00
	23	Watchmen.................................	20,987 50
	1	....do	837 50
	2	....do	1,575 00
	1	....do	750 00
	1	....do	702 50
	1	....do	472 50
	6	Boatmen..................................	5,289 00
	3	Messengers	2,415 00
	1	....do	432 00
	2	....do	860 00
	1	....do	75 00
	1	Marker...................................	805 00
	5	Porters...................................	3,837 50
	1	Porter....................................	700 00
Annapolis, Md	1	Collector	470 60
	1	Surveyor, St. Mary's	269 75
	1	Surveyor, Llewellenburg.................	350 00
	1	Surveyor, Nottingham	150 00
	2	Revenue boatmen........................	160 00
Oxford, Md	1	Collector	402 51
Vienna, Md	2	Deputy collectors	1,460 00
Georgetown, D. C...	1	Collector	3,000 00
	1	Deputy collector..........................	800 00
	1	....do....do	1,000 00
	1	Inspector	200 00
	1.	Aid to revenue	817 00
	1	Measurer of vessels......................	540 00
	1	Laborer and assistant measurer	130 00
	1	Laborer at custom-house	346 00
Norfolk, Va.........	1	Chief clerk	275 00
	1	....do	266 66
	1	Clerk	585 44
	7	Inspectors, at $4 each per day	4,708 00
	5	Watchmen, at $2 50 each per day	1,442 50
	2	Boatmen, at $2 each per day	828 00
Alexandria, Va	1	Collector	1,260 67
	1	Deputy collector and inspector............	1,585 00
	2	Inspectors	2,190 00
	1	Surveyor	1,517 28
	1	Boatman	360 00
Beaufort, N. C	1	Collector	1,905 22
	1	Inspector	999 00
	1	Boatman	253 33
Beaufort, S. C.......	1	Collector, acting	1,500 00
	1	Deputy collector	2,000 00
	1	Entry clerk...............................	1,400 00
	2	Clerks....................................	2,000 00
	3	Inspectors	3,285 00
	6	Boatmen	1,800 00
	1	Office boy	120 00
Key West, Fla	1	Collector	1,479 30
	1	Deputy collector	1,095 00
	1	Inspector	1,095 00
	1	Inspector at Cape Florida	416 67
	1	Inspector, temporary, and night watch	81 00
Louisville, Ky	1	Surveyor	3,000 00
	1	Porter, warehouseman	670 00

No. 27.—*Statement, &c.*—Continued.

District.	No. of persons employed.	Occupation.	Compensation to each person.
Cincinnati, Ohio.....	1	Surveyor	$3,000 00
	1	Deputy....................................	2,000 00
	1	2d clerk	1,158 30
	1	Warehouse and permit clerk................	1,340 00
	1	Agency aid	1,134 00
	2	....do	1,815 60
	1	....do	915 40
	1	....do	736 20
	1	....do	767 40
	1	....do	457 98
	1	....do	791 66
	1	....do	549 30
	2	....do	2,250 00
	1	....do	833 40
	1	....do	167 75
	1	....do	540 00
	2	....do	1,257 60
	1	....do	412 00
	1	....do	622 50
	1	....do	42 74
	1	....do	38 35
	1	Janitor	82 66
	1	....do	393 34
	1	Porter.....................................	70 97
	1	Superintendent of heating apparatus.........	211 66
	1	Watchman	96 50
	1	....do	270 00
	1	....do	821 25
	1	....do	443 25
	1	Agency aid on river	449 50
	1	....do........do	500 50
	1	....do........do	572 00
	1	....do........do	396 00
	1	....do........do	182 50
	1	....do........do	575 50
	1	....do........do	643 50
	1	....do........do	447 50
	1	....do........do	702 50
	1	....do........do	661 00
	1	....do........do	107 50
	1	....do........do	734 00
	1	....do.....:..do	541 50
	1	....do........do	422 50
	1	....do........do	450 50
	1	....do........do	40 00
	1	....do........do	622 00
	1	....do........do	454 50
	1	....do........do	69 00
	1	....do........do	115 00
	1	....do........do	162 50
	1	....do........do	40 00
	1	....do........do	335 00
	1	....do........do	250 00
	1	....do........do	270 00
	1	....do........do	67 50
	1	....do........do	87 50
	1	....do........do	20 00
	1	....do........do	2,518 60

No. 27.—*Statement, &c.*—Continued.

District.	No. of persons employed.	Occupation.	Compensation to each person.
Miami, (Toledo,) Ohio.	1	Collector	$1,500 00
	1	Deputy collector	1,000 00
	1	Inspector	900 00
	1	....do	912 00
	1	....do	730 00
	1	Messenger	300 00
Sandusky, Ohio	1	Collector	2,500 00
	1	Deputy collector	1,000 00
	3	....do......do	600 00
	1	....do......do	300 00
	1	Clerk	211 00
	2	Aids to revenue	1,140 00
	1	Porter and watchman	350 00
Detroit, Mich........	1	Collector	2,500 00
	1	Deputy collector and inspector	1,479 96
	1	Deputy collector and entry clerk	1,162 46
	1	Deputy collector and inspector	1,095 00
	4	Deputy collectors and clerks	3,437 50
	1	Deputy collector	730 00
	1	....do......do	600 00
	1	....do......do	321 78
	5	....do......do	1,220 00
	1	....do......do	207 26
	5	....do......do	590 00
	1	....do......do	60 00
	1	....do......do	40 00
	8	Inspectors	7,300 00
	1	....do	360 00
	2	....do	225 00
	1	Deputy collector	999 96
Michilimackinac, Mich.	1	....do......do	1,000 00
	3	....do......do	900 00
	2	....do......do	420 88
	4	....do......do	1,969 87
	7	Aids to revenue	4,302 00
	1	Female inspector	68 00
Evansville, Ind......	1	Surveyor	836 04
	1	Clerk	1,188 00
Chicago, Ill........	1	Collector	2,745 43
	1	Deputy collector	1,350 02
	1	....do......do	1,266 67
	1	....do......do	480 00
	2	Clerks	1,600 00
	1	....do	112 50
	1	....do	144 00
	1	....do	156 00
	1	....do	132 00
	2	....do	140 00
	1	....do	27 50
	1	....do	217 50
	1	....do	320 00
	1	....do	262 50
	1	Inspector	902 50
	2	....do	1,670 00
	2	....do	1,825 00
	1	....do	735 00
	1	....do	877 50
	2	....do	1,225 00
	1	....do	890 00
	1	....do	445 00

No. 27.—*Statement, &c.*—Continued.

Districts.	No. of persons employed.	Occupation.	Compensation to each person.
Chicago, Ill.—Continued.	1	Inspector	$700 00
	1	....do	605 00
	1	....do	665 00
	1	....do	185 00
	1	....do	102 50
	1	...do	12 50
	1	Janitor	730 00
	1	Watchman	638 75
	1	Secret aid of the revenue	100 80
Galena, Ill	1	Surveyor	418 78
Cairo, Ill	1	....do	800 00
	1	Clerk	1,150 00
St. Louis, Mo	1	Surveyor	3,000 00
	1	Clerk	1,800 00
	1	....do	1,500 00
	1	....do	1,000 00
	1	Warehouseman	720 00
	1	Janitor	720 00
	1	Inspector	1,460 00
Milwaukie, Wis	1	Collector	2,500 00
	1	Deputy collector	1,000 00
	2	Inspectors	1,800 00
	6	Deputy collectors	2,400 00
	1	Watchman	480 00
Burlington, Iowa	1	Surveyor	350 00
Keokuk, Iowa	1	Measurer	730 00
Minnesota, Minn	1	Collector	1,000 00
	1	Deputy collector	800 00
	1	Inspector	912 50
	1	Deputy collector	430 00
	1	Occasional inspector	45 00
	3	....do......do	36 00
	1	....do......do	227 00
	1	....do......do	15 00
	1	Deputy cullector	60 00
	1	....do......do	62 00
San Francisco, Cal	1	Collector	6,400 00
	1	Deputy collector and auditor	3,000 00
	2	Deputy collectors	6,000 00
	1	Cashier of the custom-house	3,000 00
	1	Cashier and assistant treasurer	2,500 00
	1	Entry clerk	2,500 00
	1	Assistant auditor	2,250 00
	6	Clerks	13,500 00
	1	Assistant cashier	2,125 00
	2	Clerks	4,200 00
	1	Book-keeper and assistant treasurer	2,000 00
	1	Assistant entry clerk	2,000 00
	2	....do......do	3,750 00
	3	....do......do	5,625 00
	1	Gauger's clerk	1,800 00
	4	....do....do	6,000 00
	2	Assistant liquidating clerks, $8 per day	

No. 27.—*Statement, &c.*—Continued.

Districts.	No. of persons employed.	Occupation.	Compensation to each person.
No returns from the following ports:			
Waldoboro', Me......			
Saco, Me............			
Salem and Beverly, Mass.............			
Fairfield, Conn.......			
Pittsburg, Pa........			
Town Creek, Md.....			
Havre de Grace, Md..			
Wheeling, W. Va....			
Yeocomico, Va.......			
Paducah, Ky........			
Cuyahoga, Ohio			
Madison, Ind.......			
New Orleans, La.....			
Alton, Ill..........			
Quincy, Ill.........			
Peoria, Ill..........			
Hannibal, Mo.......			
Dubuque, Iowa......			
Puget Sound, W. T..			
Port Orford, W. T....			
Cape Perpetua, W. T.			
Sonoma, Cal.........			
San Joaquin, Cal....			
Sacramento, Cal......			
San Diego, Cal......			
Monterey, Cal.......			
San Pedro, Cal......			
Passo del Norte, Tex..			
Oregon, Or..........			

S. B. COLBY, *Register.*

TREASURY DEPARTMENT,
    Register's Office, November 22, 1865.

General result of all receipts and disposal of merchandise within the United States for the fiscal year ending June 30, 1865.

	1864.							
	July.		August.		September.		October.	
	Amount.	Duty.	Amount.	Duty.	Amount.	Duty.	Amount.	Duty.
e of merchandise in warehouse on the first each month	$38,412,944 61	$23,307,477 68	$48,646,117 96	$28,430,214 08	$50,126,932 08	$29,102,518 57	$47,319,456 91	$28,095,846 12
e of merchandise received in warehouse m foreign ports during each month	18,400,597 94	9,520,749 22	13,416,955 05	6,691,669 98	7,327,305 70	3,295,906 42	5,569,326 09	2,746,997 13
e of merchandise received in warehouse imported from other ports during each uth	658,948 64	421,564 93	824,846 66	526,188 28	408,985 00	253,341 93	513,133 00	349,264 12
e of dutiable merchandise entered for consumption from foreign ports during each uth	7,400,574 07	2,478,659 85	8,447,551 61	3,037,676 15	5,716,553 70	1,862,836 76	4,593,672 25	1,331,058 74
e of free merchandise entered for consumption from foreign ports during each nth	2,852,275 95	....	2,969,539 61	....	4,204,467 55	....	5,850,020 50	....
e of merchandise entered for consumption from warehouse during each month	4,702,246 59	2,115,225 16	6,856,602 13	4,631,800 62	8,423,330 63	3,359,097 68	7,111,847 56	3,216,244 50
e of merchandise entered for transportation to other ports during each month	655,671 22	377,270 58	614,502 46	354,831 36	343,826 24	207,313 68	325,149 64	236,746 04
e of merchandise entered for exportation m warehouse during each month	3,468,455 42	2,226,982 01	2,289,883 00	1,558,921 79	1,765,868 00	997,051 41	1,257,189 00	777,100 37
e of merchandise in warehouse at the se of each month	48,646,117 96	28,430,214 08	50,126,932 08	29,102,518 57	47,319,456 91	28,095,846 12	45,797,720 80	26,982,017 06
e of merchandise in transitu at the close each month	1,444,747 00	796,277 97	1,666,066 00	854,809 77	1,488,328 00	855,038 31	1,469,792 00	878,584 84

No. 28.—*General result of all receipts and disposal of merchandise within the United States, &c.*— Continued.

| | 1864. | | | | 1865. | | | |
| | November. | | December. | | January. | | February. | |
	Amount.	Duty.	Amount.	Duty.	Amount.	Duty.	Amount.	Duty.
Value of merchandise in warehouse on the first of each month	$45,707,729 60	$26,962,017 06	$43,343,623 20	$25,980,788 45	$39,992,334 83	$24,793,243 57	$36,540,310 83	$23,436,988 45
Value of merchandise received in warehouse from foreign ports during each month	6,362,750 36	3,024,352 57	5,032,842 23	2,729,562 73	5,179,962 37	2,771,277 65	6,954,891 44	3,343,537 20
Value of merchandise received in warehouse transported from other ports during each month..................................	412,543 42	218,592 43	313,418 50	192,772 69	323,345 00	188,978 27	226,987.00	129,263 23
Value of dutiable merchandise entered for consumption from foreign ports during each month...........	4,165,062 26	1,226,056 54	5,201,528 91	1,385,037 32	6,077,857 69	1,872,394 95	6,094,537 72	2,475,049 01
Value of free merchandise entered for consumption from foreign ports during each month................................	4,683,608 70	....	3,202,723 32	....	2,703,677 00	....	2,423,138 00	....
Value of merchandise entered for consumption from warehouse during each month......	7,664,471 69	3,399,572 82	7,224,147 40	3,249,269 06	7,706,596 00	3,689,070 83	6,924,450 03	3,812,611 54
Value of merchandise entered for transportation to other ports during each month......	262,751 51	173,737 64	228,855 55	134,128 98	227,855 37	143,659 13	204,377 80	105,102 68
Value of merchandise entered for exportation from warehouse during each month........	1,212,177 18	650,863 15	1,244,546 15	726,482 26	1,020,280 00	483,781 08	1,114,116 00	456,617 66
Value of merchandise in warehouse at the close of each month........................	43,343,623 20	25,980,788 45	39,992,334 83	24,793,243 57	36,540,310 83	23,436,988 45	35,470,145 44	23,035,457 00
Value of merchandise in transitu at the close of each month	1,493,379 11	870,473 91	1,315,857 58	773,529 29	1,275,571 58	807,398 00	1,286,999 58	819,941 39

No. 28.—*General result of all receipts and disposal of merchandise within the United States, &c.*—Continued.

	March.		April.		May.		June.	
	Amount.	Duty.	Amount.	Duty.	Amount.	Duty.	Amount.	Duty.
ue of merchandise in warehouse on the first of each month	$35,479,145 44	$23,035,457 00	$37,154,611 54	$24,635,238 85	$35,324,303 55	$24,907,210 66	$28,889,060 09	$29,194,003 32
ue of merchandise received in warehouse from foreign ports during each month	10,259,727 00	5,678,149 55	9,728,654 59	5,933,589 84	7,120,075 81	4,794,186 21	9,770,767 04	6,814,444 60
ue of merchandise received in warehouse transported from other ports during each month	226,224 00	167,576 91	297,362 81	273,833 88	434,167 91	276,708 53	495,374 00	338,096 25
ue of dutiable merchandise entered for consumption from foreign ports during each month	8,944,043 95	3,383,646 17	6,814,026 41	2,896,540 34	8,195,386 03	3,213,399 68	9,672,512 65	4,292,324 67
ue of free merchandise entered for consumption from foreign ports during each month	3,478,809 60	....	4,568,275 15	....	4,330,144 09	....	4,307,761 11	....
ue of merchandise entered for consumption from warehouse during each month	7,483,609 82	3,514,038 50	10,092,462 59	5,193,256 40	12,956,287 76	7,021,857 99	8,475,162 79	5,375,208 58
ue of merchandise entered for transportation to other ports during each month	300,168 08	192,514 85	297,867 56	224,750 58	333,695 42	231,792 88	443,137 07	234,340 25
ue of merchandise entered for exportation from warehouse during each month	1,026,507 00	539,391 26	1,466,395 31	517,494 93	699,504 00	530,451 21	640,040 00	413,456 61
ue of merchandise in warehouse at the close of each month	37,154,811 54	24,635,238 85	35,324,303 55	24,907,210 66	28,889,060 09	22,194,003 32	29,596,861 27	23,324,538 73
ue of merchandise in transitu at the close of each month	1,416,172 58	915,641 34	244,280 58	201,433 71	226,307 58	174,292 87	265,669 58	177,691 98

N. SARGENT, *Commissioner of Customs.*

TREASURY DEPARTMENT, *Office of Commissioner of Customs.*

Statement showing the present liabilities of the United States to Indian tribes under stipulations of treaties, &c.

Names of tribes.	Description of annuities, stipulations, &c.	Reference to laws; Statutes at Large.	Number of instalments yet unappropriated, explanations, remarks, &c.	Annual amount necessary to meet stipulations, indefinite as to time, now allowed, but liable to be discontinued.	Aggregate of future appropriations that will be required during a limited number of years to pay a limited annuity till they expire; am'ts necessary to incidentally effect the payment.	Amount of annual liabilities of a permanent character.	Amount held in trust by the United States on which five per cent. is annually paid; and amounts which, invested at five per cent., would produce permanent annuities.
Chippewas of Lake Superior.	For money, goods, support of schools, provisions, two carpenters, and tobacco; compare 4th article treaty October 4, 1842, and 8th article treaty September 30, 1854.	Vol. 7, page 592, and vol. 10, page 1111.	Twenty-five instalments; one yet to be appropriated.		$9,510 06		
Do..........	Twenty instalments in coin, goods, implements, &c., and for education; 4th article treaty September 30, 1854.	Vol. 10, page 11....	Twenty instalments, at $19,000 each; nine yet unappropriated.		171,000 00		
Do..........	Twenty instalments for six smiths and assistants, and for iron and steel; 2d and 5th articles treaty September 30, 1854.	Vol. 10, page 1109, and vol. 10, page 1111.	Twenty instalments. at $6,300 each; nine yet unappropriated.		56,700 00		
Do..........	Twenty instalments for the seventh smith, &c.	Vol. 10, page 1111..	Twenty instalments, estimated at $1,060 each; eleven yet unappropriated.		11,660 00		
Do..........	For support of a smith, assistant, and shop, and pay of two farmers during the pleasure of the President; 12th article treaty.	Vol. 10, page 1112..	Estimated at $2,260 per annum...	$2,260 00			
Chippewas of the Mississippi.	For money, goods, support of schools, provisions, and tobacco; compare 4th article treaty October 4, 1842, and 8th article treaty September 30, 1854.	Vol. 7, page 592, and vol. 10, page 1111.	Twenty-five instalments; one unexpended.		9,000 00		
Do..........	Two farmers, two carpenters, and smiths and assistants, iron and steel; 4th article treaty October 4, 1842, and September 30, 1854.	Vol. 7, page 592, and vol. 10, page 1111.	Twenty-five instalments; two unexpended; one-third payable to these Indians, $466 66, for two years.		1,400 00		
Do..........	Twenty instalments in money of $20,000 each.	Vol. 10, page 1167..	Third article treaty February 22, 1855; nine unexpended.		180,000 00		
Chippewas, Pilla-	Money, $10,666 67; goods, $8,000; and pur-	Vol. 10, page 1168..	Thirty instalments; nineteen un-		430,666 73		

Do......	For purposes of education; same article and treaty.	Vol. 10, page 1168..	Twenty instalments, of $3,000 each; nine unexpended.	....	27,000 00	....
Do......	For support of smiths' shops; same article and treaty.	...do....	Fifteen instalments, estimated at $2,120 each; four unappropriated.	....	8,480 00	....
ckasaws......	Permanent annuity in goods...................	Vol. 1, page 619....	Act of February 28, 1799, $3,000 per year.	....	$3,000 00	$60,000 00
ppewas, Meno-monees, Winne-bagoes, and New York Indians.	Education during the pleasure of Congress....	Vol. 7, page 304....	5th article treaty August 11, 1827.	1,500 00	....	....
ppewas of Sagi-naw, Swan creek, and Black river.	Two instalments in coin of $18,800 each......	Vol. 7, page 634.	Two instalments yet to be appropriated.	....	37,600 00	....
octaws..........	Permanent annuities.....................	Vol. 7, pages 99, 213, and 236.	2d article treaty November 16, 1805, $3,000; 13th article treaty October 18, 1820, $600; 2d article treaty Jan. 20, 1825, $6,000.		9,600 00	192,000 00
Do....	Provisions for smith, &c...................	Vol. 7, page 212...	6th article treaty October 18, 1820, and 9th article treaty January 20, 1825, say $920.		920 00	18,400 00
Do....	Interest on $500,000; articles 10th and 13th treaty January 22, 1855.	Vol. 11, pages 613 and 614.	Five per cent. for educational purposes		25,000 00	500,000 00
eks.........	Permanent annuities.....................	Vol. 7, pages 36, 69, and 287.	4th article treaty August, 1790, $1,500; 2d article treaty June 16, 1802, $3,000; 4th article treaty January 24, 1826, $20,000.		24,500 00	490,000 00
Do....	Smith's shops, &c...................	Vol. 7, page 287...	8th article treaty January 24, 1826, say $1,110.		1,110 00	22,200 00
Do.........	Wheelwright, permanent...............	Vol. 7, page 287...	8th article treaty Jan. 1826, $600.		600 00	12,000 00
Do	Allowance during the pleasure of the President.	Vol. 7, pages 287 and 419.	5th article treaty February 14, 1833, and 8th article treaty January 24, 1826.	4,710 00	....	....
Do....	Interest on $200,000 held in trust; 6th article treaty August 7, 1856.	Vol. 11, pages 701 and 702.	Five per centum for education............		10,000 00	200,000 00
awares......	Life annuities, &c., two chiefs............	Vol. 7, page 399....	Treaties of 1818, 1829, and 1832..	200 00	....	....
Do.........	Interest on $46,080, at 5 per centum	Vol. 7, page 327....	Resolution of Senate Jan. 19, 1832.		2,304 00	46,080 00
minoles, Florida Indians.	Ten instalments for support of schools; 8th article treaty August 7, 1856.	Vol. 11, page 702...	Two payments of $3,000 each...		6,000 00	....
Do.........	Ten instalments for agricultural assistance; same article and treaty.	...do.....	Two payments of $2,000....		4,000 00	....
Do	Ten instalments for support of smiths and shops; same article and treaty.	...do....	Two payments of $2,200....		4,400 00	....
Do..........	Interest on $500,000, per 8th article treaty August 7, 1856.	...do....	$25,000 annuities....		25,000 00	500,000 00
nas............	Interest on $57,000, being the balance of $157,000.	Vol. 7, page 568, and vol. 10, page 1071.	2d article treaty October 19, 1838, and 9th article treaty May 17, 1854.		2,850 00	57,000 00
naas............	Interest on $200,000...................	Vol. 9, page 842....	2d article treaty Jan. 14, 1846....		10,000 00	200,000 00
knpoos......	Interest on $100,000...................	Vol. 10, page 1079....	2d article treaty May 13, 1854...		5,000 00	100,000 00
Do.........	Gradual payment on $200,000...............	...do....	2d article treaty May 18, 1854; $155,000 heretofore appropriated; due.		48,000 00	....

No. 29.—*Statement showing the present liabilities of the United States to Indian tribes, &c.*—Continued.

Names of tribes.	Description of annuities, stipulations, &c.	Reference to laws; Statutes at Large.	Number of instalments yet unappropriated, explanations, remarks, &c.	Annual amount necessary to meet stipulation, indefinite as to time, now allowed, but liable to be discontinued.	Aggregate of future appropriations that will be required during a limited number of years to pay limited annuities, an'as incidentally necessary to effect the payment.	Amount of annual liabilities of a permanent character.	Amount held in trust by the United States on which five per cent. is annually paid; and amounts which, invested at five per cent., would produce permanent annuities.
Menomonees	Pay of miller for fifteen years	Vol. 9, page 953, and vol. 10, page 1065.	3d article treaty May 12, 1854, $9,000; $6,000 heretofore appropriated; due.		$3,000 00		
Do	Support of smith's shop twelve years	...do	Two instalments of $916 66 unappropriated.		1,833 32		
Do	Fifteen equal instalments to pay $242,686, to commence in 1867.	Vol. 10, page 1065.	4th article treaty May 12, 1854, and Senate's amendment thereto.		242,686 00		
Miamies	Permanent provision for smith's shop, &c., and miller.	Vol. 7, pages 191 and 464, and vol. 10, page 1095.	5th article treaty Oct. 6, 1818; 5th article treaty Oct. 23, 1834; and 4th article treaty June 5, 1854, say $940 for shop and $600 for miller.			$1,540 00	$30,800 00
Do	Twenty instalments upon $200,000	Vol. 10, page 1094.	$130,000 of said sum payable in twenty instalments of $7,500 each; fourteen of each unappropriated.		105,000 00		
Do	Interest on $50,000, at 5 per centum	...do	3d article treaty June 5, 1854; Senate's amendment.			2,500 00	50,000 00
Do	Interest on $221,257 86, in trust	Vol. 10, page 1099.	4th article treaty of 1854			11,062 89	221,257 86
Eel River Miamies	Permanent annuities	Vol. 7, pages 51,91, and 114.	4th article treaty 1795; 3d article treaty 1805; and 3d article treaty Sept. 1809, aggregate.			1,100 00	22,000 00
Navajo Indians	Presents to Indians	Vol. 9, page 975.	10th article treaty Sept. 9, 1849	$5,000 00			
Niaqually, Puyallup, and other tribes	For payment of $32,500 in graduated payments.	Vol. 10, page 1133.	4th article treaty Dec. 26, 1854, still unappropriated.		8,850 00		

lias	Forty instalments, graduated, $240,000, extending for forty years.	Vol. 10, page 1044.	Eleven instalments paid, (see 4th article treaty March 16, 1854,) to be appropriated.		480,000 00		
es and Missou-s.	Forty instalments, graduated, ($385,000,) extending through forty years.	Vol. 10, page 1039..	4th article treaty March 15, 1854, eleven instalments paid, to be appropriated hereafter.		221,000 00		
est............	Interest on $69,120, at 5 per cent; pamphlet copy 1st session 36th Congress.	Vol. 12, page 51....	For educational purposes, Senate's resolution Jan. 19, 1838.			3,456 00	69,120 00
was of Kansas..	Permanent annuities, their portion of	Vol. 7, pages 54, 106, 176, 220.	4th article treaty August 13, 1795; 4th and 5th articles treaty September 17, 1818; 4th article treaty August 29, 1821; and 2d article treaty Nov. 17, 1807.			2,600 00	52,000 00
was and Chippe-a of Michigan.	Interest on $240,000, at 5 per cent	Vol. 7, page 497...	Resolution of Senate May 19, 1836, per year.	8,300 00			
Do............	Education, $5,000; missions, $3,000; medicines, $300, during the pleasure of Congress.	Vol. 7, page 492....	See 4th article treaty March 28, 1836.				
Do........ ...	Three blacksmiths, &c.; one gunsmith, &c.; two farmers and assistants, during the pleasure of the President.	Vol. 7, page 493....	See 7th article treaty March 28, 1826, annually allowed since the expiration of the number of years named in treaty. Aggregate $6,440.	6,440 00			
Do............	$206,000 to be paid after ten years, in not less than four annual instalments.	Vol. 11, page 624 ...	Treaty July 31, 1855............		206,000 00		
Do............ nees........	Interest on $206,000 at 5 per centum............					10,300 00	206,000 00
Do........ ...	Agricultural implements during the pleasure of the President.	Vol. 7, page 488....	See 4th article treaty Oct. 9, 1853..	1,000 00			
Do............	Five instalments in goods and such articles as may be necessary for them.	Vol. 11, page 729..	See 2d article treaty September 24, 1857; first payment of annuities of a permanent character, being the second series.			30,000 00	
Do............	For the support of two manual labor schools..	....do............	3d article treaty; annually, during the pleasure of the President.	10,000 00			
Do............	For pay of two teachers......................	....do........	See 3d article treaty Sept. 24, 1857; annual appropriations required.	1,200 00			
Do............	For purchase of iron and steel and other necessaries for same during the pleasure of the President.	....do............	4th article treaty; annual appropriation.	500 00			
Do............	For pay of two blacksmiths, one of whom to be a gunsmith and tinsmith.	....do........	4th article treaty; appropriation required.	1,200 00			
Do............	For compensation of two strikers and apprentices.	....do........	4th article treaty; annual appropriation required.	480 00			
Do............	Ten instalments for farming utensils and stock.	....do........	4th article treaty; two appropriations 1826 remaining unpaid at the pleasure of the President.		2,400 00		
Do............	For pay of farmer......................		4th article treaty; annual appropriation required.	600 00			
Do............	Ten instalments for pay of miller....		4th article treaty; two appropriations remaining at the discretion of the President.		1,440 00		

Names of tribes.	Description of annuities, stipulations, &c.	Reference to laws; Statutes at Large.	Number of instalments yet unappropriated, explanations, remarks, &c.	Annual amount necessary to meet stipulations, indefinite as to time, now allowed, but liable to limit, to be discontinued.	Aggregate of future appropriations that will be required during a limited number of years to pay limited annuities till they expire; an'n individually necessary to effect the payment.	Amount of annual liabilities of a permanent character.
Pawnees	Ten instalments for pay of an engineer		Two appropriations yet required at the discretion of the President.		$2,400 00	
Do	For compensation to apprentices to assist in working the mill.		4th article treaty; annual appropriation required.	$500 00		
Pottawatomies	Permanent annuity in money	Vol. 7, pages 51,114, 185, 317, 320, and vol. 9, page 855.	4th art. treaty 1795, $1,000; 3d art. treaty 1809, $500; 3d art. treaty 1818, $2,500; 2d art. treaty 1826, $2,000; 2d art. treaty July, 1829, $1,500; 10th article treaty June, 1846, $300.			$29,300 00
Do	Life annuities to surviving chiefs	Vol. 7, pages 379 and 433.	3d article treaty Oct. 16, 1832, $200; 3d art. treaty Sept. 26, 1833, $700.	900 00		
Do	Education during the pleasure of Congress	Vol. 7, pages 296, 318, 401.	3d art. treaty Oct. 16, 1826; 2d art. treaty Sept. 20, 1826; and 4th art. treaty Oct. 27, 1832, $5,000.	5,000 00		
Do	Permanent provision for three smiths	Vol. 7, pages 296, 321.	2d art. treaty Sept. 20, 1828; 3d art. treaty Oct. 16, 1826; 2d article treaty July 29,1829; three shops, at $840 each per year, $2,620.			3,820 00
Do	Permanent provision for furnishing salt	Vol. 7, pages 75, 296, 320.	3d art. treaty 1803; 3d art. treaty Oct. 1826, and 2d article treaty July 29, 1829; estimated $500.			500 00
Do	Interest on $643,000, at 5 per cent	Vol. 9, page 854.	7th article treaty June, 1846; annual interest, $32,150.			32,150 00

...paws	Provision for education, $1,000 per year, and for smith and farmer and smith's shop during the pleasure of the President.	Vol. 7, page 425....	3d art. treaty May 13, 1838; $1,000 per year for education, and $1,660 for smith, farmer, &c., $2,660.	2,660 00			
gue River.......	Sixteen instalments of $2,500 each.	Vol. 10, page 1019..	3d article treaty Sept 10, 1853, four instalments unappropriated.		10,000 00		
ata Section, and mpqua Indians.	$2,000 annually for fifteen years.	Vol. 10, page 1122..	3d article treaty November 18, 1854, four instalments yet to be appropriated.		8,000 00		
Do........	Support of schools and farmer fifteen years...	Vol. 10, page 1123..	Same treaty, 5th article, estimated for schools, $1,200; farmers, $1,000; four appropriations due.		8,800 00		
s and Foxes of istouri.	Interest on $157,400.	Vol. 10, page 544...	2d article treaty October 21, 1837...			7,870 00	157,400 00
s and Foxes of isissippi.	Permanent annuities	Vol. 7, page 85...	3d article treaty November, 1804.			1,000	20,000
Do......	Interest on $200,000, at 5 per cent.	Vol. 7, page 541...	2d article treaty October, 1837...			10,000 00	200,000 00
Do......	Interest on $800,000, at 5 per cent.	Vol. 7, page 596..	2d article treaty October 11, 1842..			40,000 00	800,000 00
ecas........	Permanent annuities	Vol. 7, pages 161 and 179.	4th article treaty September 29, 1817, $500; 4th article treaty September 17, 1817, $500.			1,000 00	20,000 00
Do......	Provision for smith and smith's shops and miller during the pleasure of the President.	Vol. 7, page 349...	4th article treaty February 28, 1831, say $1,660.	1,660 00			
ecas of N. York .	Permanent annuity	Vol. 4, page 442...	Act February 19, 1831..$6,000 00				
Do........	Interest on $75,000.	Vol. 9, page 35....	Act June 27, 1846.... 3,750 00				
Do........	Interest on $43,050, transferred from the Ontario Bank to the treasury of the U. States.	....do	Act June 27, 1846.... 2,150 50			11,902 50	238,050 00
ecas and Shawnees.	Permanent annuity	Vol. 7, page 179...	4th article treaty September 17, 1818.	1,060 00		1,000 00	20,000 00
wnees.	Permanent annuities for education.	Vol. 7, pages 51 and 161, and vol. 10, page 1065.	4th article treaty August 3, 1795; 4th article treaty September 29, 1817; and 3d article treaty May 10, 1854.			5,000 00	100,000 00
Do........	Interest on $40,000.	Vol. 10, page 1065..	3d article treaty May 10, 1854...			2,000 00	40,000 00
Nations of New ork.	Permanent annuities in clothing, &c.	Vol. 7, page 46...	6th article treaty November 11, 1794, $4,500.			4,500 00	90,000 00
ax of the Missis-ppi.	Interest on $300,000.	Vol. 7, page 539...	2d article treaty September 29 1837.			15,000 00	300,000 00
Do	Fifty instalments of interest on $112,000, being ten cents per acre per reservation.	Vol. 10, page 951...	Senate amendment to 3d article; thirty-five instalments to be provided for of $5,600 each.		196,000 00		
Do	Fifty instalments of interest on $1,360,000 at 5 per centum.	Vol. 10, page 950...	4th article treaty July 23, 1851, $68,000 per annum; thirty-five instalments to be provided for.		2,380,000 00		
Do	Fifty instalments of interest on $1,100,000.	Vol. 10, page 955..	4th article treaty August 5, 1851, $58,000 per annum; thirty-five instalments yet to be approp'd.		2,030,000 00		
Do	Fifty instalments of interest on $59,000, being ten cents per acre for reservation.	...do	Treaty August 5, 1851; thirty-five instalments of $3,450 to be provided for.			120,750 00	

Names of tribes.	Description of annuities, stipulations, &c.	Reference to laws; Statutes at Large.	Number of instalments yet unappropriated, explanations, remarks, &c.	Annual amount necessary to meet stipulations, indefinite as to time, now allowed, but liable to be discontinued.	Aggregate of future appropriations that will be required during a limited number of years to pay limited annuities till they expire; am'ts incidentally necessary to effect the payment.	Amount of annual liabilities of a permanent character.	Amount held in trust by the United States on which five per cent. is annually paid; and amounts which, invested at five per cent., would produce the permanent annuities.
Umpquas, Cow Creek band.	Twenty instalments of $550 each..............	Vol. 10, page 1028	3d article treaty Sept. 19, 1853, eight instalments yet due.	....	$4,400 00	....	....
Umpquas, Calapooias, &c., Oregon.	Twenty instalments; payment graduated.....	Vol. 10, page 1126	3d article treaty Nov. 29, 1854, nine instalments to be appropriated under the direction of the President; graduated payments; third series.	....	11,800 00	....	....
Do............	Support of teachers, &c., twenty years........	Vol. 10, page 1127	6th article treaty; estimated at $1,450 per year; nine instalments yet to be appropriated.	....	13,450 00	....	....
Do............	Support of physician fifteen years.............	Vol. 10, page 1127	6th article treaty; estimated at $2,000 per year, four instalments yet to be appropriated.	....	8,000 00	....	....
Willamette Valley bands.	Twenty instalments, graduated payments.....	Vol. 10, page 1144	2d article treaty January 22, 1855, nine instalments yet to be appropriated under the direction of the President	....	53,500 00	....	....

Do	Twenty instalments for an agricultural school and teacher.	Vol. 12, page 929..	14th article treaty Jan. 22, 1855, fourteen instalments yet to be provided for, estimated at $3,000 a year.	....	42,000 00	....	....
Do	Twenty instalments for smith and carpenter shop and tools.	Vol. 12, page 929..	14th article treaty Jan. 22, 1855, fourteen instalments unappropriated, estimated at $500 per year.	....	7,000 00	....	....
Do	Twenty instalments for blacksmiths, carpenter, farmer, and physician.	Vol. 12, page 929..	14th article treaty Jan. 22, 1855, fourteen instalments unappropriated, estimated at $4,600 each year.	....	64,400 00		
Makah tribe........	For beneficial objects $30,000 under the direction of the President.	Vol. 12, page 940..	5th article treaty Jan. 31, 1855, fourteen instalments unappropriated in graduated payments.	....	16,000 00	....	....
Do	Twenty instalments for an agricultural and industrial school and teachers.	Vol. 12, page 941..	11th article treaty Jan. 31, 1855, 14 instalments unappropriated, estimated at $2,500 per year.	....	35,000 00	....	....
Do	Twenty instalments for smith, carpenter shop, and tools.	Vol. 12, page 941..	11th article treaty Jan. 31, 1855, fourteen instalments unappropriated, estimated at $500 each year.	....	7,000 00	....	....
Do	Twenty instalments for blacksmith, carpenter, farmer, and physician.	Vol. 12, page 941..	11th article treaty Jan. 31, 1855, fourteen instalments unappropriated, estimated amount necessary each year, $4,600.	....	64,400 00	....	....
Walla-Walla, Cayuse, and Umatilla tribes.	For beneficial objects, $100,000 to be expended under the direction of the President.	Vol. 12, page 946..	2d article treaty June 9, 1855, fourteen instalments in graduated payments unappropriated.	....	54,000 00	....	....
Do	For two millers, one farmer, one superintendent of farming operations, two school-teachers, one blacksmith, one wagon and plough maker, and one carpenter and joiner.	Vol. 12, page 947..	4th article treaty June 9, 1855, fourteen instalments to be provided for, estimated at $11,200 each year.	....	156,900 00	....	....
Do	Twenty instalments of $500 for mill fixtures, tools, medicines, books, stationery, furniture, &c.	...do	4th article treaty June 9, 1855, fourteen instalments of $3,000 each, unappropriated.	....	42,000 00	....	....
Do	Twenty instalments of $500 for each of the head chiefs of these bands.	...do	5th article treaty June 9, 1855, fourteen instalments yet due.	....	21,000 00	....	....
Do .....?..	Twenty instalments for salary of son of Pio-Pio-Mox-Mox.	...do	5th article treaty June 9, 1855, fourteen instalments of $100 each, yet due.	....	1,400 00	....	....
Yakama nation.....	For beneficial objects $200,000, under direction of the President, in twenty-one instalments in graduated payments.	Vol. 12, page 953..	4th article treaty June 9, 1855, fourteen instalments to be provided.	....	82,000 00	....	....
Do	Support of two schools, one of which to be an agricultural and industrial school, keeping them in repair and providing furniture, books, and stationery.	...do	5th article treaty June 9, 1855, twenty instalments, fourteen of which are yet to be provided for, at an estimate of $500 per year.	....	7,000 00		

ames of tribes.	Description of annuities, stipulations, &c.	Reference to laws, Statutes at Large.	Number of instalments yet unappropriated, explanations, remarks, &c.	Annual amount necessary to meet stipulations, indefinite as to time, now allowed, but liable to be discontinued.	Aggregate of future appropriations that will be required during a limited number of years to pay limited annuities till they expire; am'ts incidentally necessary to effect the payment.	Amount of annual liabilities of a permanent character.	Amount held in trust by the United States on which five per cent. is annually paid; and amounts which, invested at five per cent., would produce the permanent annuities.
Yakama nation....	For one superintendent of teaching and two teachers, twenty years.	Vol. 12, page 953.	5th article treaty June 9, 1855, fourteen instalments yet to be appropriated, estimated at $3,200.	....	$44,800 00	....	....
Do	For one superintendent of farming and two farmers, two millers, two blacksmiths, one farrier, one gunsmith, one carpenter, and one wagon and plough maker, for twenty years.	....do	5th article treaty June 9, 1855, fourteen instalments yet to be provided for, estimated at $9,400.	....	131,600 00	....	....
Do	Twenty instalments, keeping in repair grist and saw mill, and furnishing the necessary tools therefor.	....do	5th article treaty June 9, 1855, fourteen instalments yet to be appropriated, estimated at $300 each.	....	7,000 00	....	....
Do	Twenty instalments for keeping in repair hospital and furnishing medicines, &c.	....do	5th article treaty June 9, 1855, fourteen instalments yet to be appropriated, estimated at $300.	....	4,200 00	....	....
Do	Twenty instalments for pay of physicians.....	....do	5th article treaty June 9, 1855, fourteen instalments yet to be	....	19,600 00	....	....

Do	Twenty instalments for one superintendent of teaching and two teachers.	...do	5th article treaty June 11, 1855; fourteen instalments of $3,200 each yet unappropriated.		44,800 00	
Do	Twenty instalments for one superintendent of farming and two farmers, two millers, two blacksmiths, one tinner, one gunsmith, one carpenter, and one wagon and plough maker.	...do	5th article treaty June 11, 1855; fourteen instalments of $9,400 each to be appropriated.		131,600 00	
Do	Twenty instalments for keeping in repair grist and saw mill, and providing the necessary tools therefor.	...do	5th article treaty June 11, 1855; fourteen instalments of $500 each unappropriated per estimate.		7,000 00	
Do	Twenty instalments for keeping in repair hospital and furnishing necessary medicines, &c.	...do	5th article treaty June 11, 1855; fourteen instalments of $300 (estimated) unappropriated.		4,200 00	
Do	Twenty instalments for pay of physician.	...do	5th article treaty June 11, 1855; fourteen instalments estimated at $1,400 each yet due.		19,600 00	
Do	Twenty instalments for keeping in repair buildings for employés.	...do	5th article treaty June 11, 1855; fourteen instalments estimated at $300 yet due.		4,200 00	
Do	Twenty instalments for salary of head chief.	...do	5th article treaty June 11, 1855; fourteen instalments estimated at $500, appropriated of $500.		7,000 00	
Flathead and other confederated tribes	Twenty instalments for beneficial objects under the direction of the President, $120,000.	Vol. 12, page 976	4th article treaty July 16, 1855; thirteen instalments yet to be appropriated in graduated payments.		50,000 00	
Do	For the support of an agricultural and industrial school, providing necessary furniture, books, stationery, &c.	Vol. 12, page 977	5th article treaty July 16, 1855; fourteen instalments estimated at $300 yet unappropriated.		4,200 00	
Do	For employment of suitable instructors therefor.	...do	5th article treaty July 16, 1855; fourteen instalments yet to be appropriated at $1,400.		19,600 00	
Do	For keeping in repair blacksmith shop, one carpenter shop, one wagon and plough maker's shop, and furnishing tools therefor.	...do	5th article treaty July 16, 1855; fourteen instalments yet to be appropriated of $500.		7,000 00	
Do	For two farmers, two millers, one blacksmith, one gunsmith, one tinner, carpenter, and joiner, and wagon and plough maker.	...do	5th article treaty July 16, 1855; fourteen instalments of $7,400 each yet to be appropriated.		103,600 00	
Do	For keeping in repair flouring and saw mill, and supplying the necessary fixtures.	...do	5th article treaty July 16, 1855; fourteen instalments yet to be made estimated at $500 each year.		7,000 00	
Do	For keeping in repair hospital, and furnishing the necessary medicines, &c.	...do	5th article treaty July 16, 1855; fourteen instalments yet to be appropriated estimated at $300 per year.		4,200 00	
Do	For pay of physician twenty years.	...do	5th article treaty July 16, 1855; fourteen instalments estimated at $1,400 yet due.		19,600 00	
Do	For keeping in repair the buildings of employés, &c., for twenty years.	...do	5th article treaty July 16, 1855; fourteen instalments estimated at $300 each yet to be made.		4,200 00	

Names of tribes.	Description of annuities, stipulations, &c.	Reference to laws; Statutes at Large.	Number of instalments yet unappropriated, explanations, remarks, &c.	Annual amount necessary to meet stipulations, indefinite as to time, now allowed, but liable to be discontinued.	Aggregate of future appropriations that will be required during a limited number of years to pay limited annuities till they expire; and to incidentally necessary to effect the payment.	Amount of annual liabilities of a permanent character.	Amount held in trust by the United States on which five per cent. is annually paid; and amounts which, invested at five per cent., would produce the permanent annuities.
Flathead and other confederated tribes	For $500 per annum for twenty years for each of the head chiefs.	Vol. 12, page 977..	5th article treaty July 16, 1855; fourteen instalments unappropriated, estimated at $1,500 each year.	....	$21,000 00	....	....
Confederated tribes and bands of Indians in Middle Oregon.	For beneficial objects, under the direction of the President, $100,000 in graduated payments.	Vol. 12, page 964..	2d article treaty June 25, 1855; fourteen instalments to be appropriated.	....	54,000 00	....	....
Do	For farmer, blacksmith, and wagon and plough maker for the term of fifteen years.	Vol. 12, page 965..	4th article treaty June 25, 1855; nine instalments yet unappropriated, estimated at $3,500 each year.	....	31,500 00	....	....
Do	For physician, sawyer, miller, superintendent of farming and school teacher fifteen years.	....do	4th article treaty June 25, 1855; nine instalments, estimated at $5,600 each year, yet to be provided for.	....	50,400 00	....	....
Do	Salary of the head chief of the confederated band twenty years.	....do	4th article treaty June 25, 1855; fourteen instalments yet to be appropriated, estimated at $500 each year.	....	7,000 00	....	....
Molel Indians......	For keeping in repair saw and flouring mill, and furnishing suitable persons to attend the same for a period of ten years.	Vol. 12, page 981..	2d article treaty Dec. 21, 1855; four instalments unappropriated, estimated at $1,500 each.	....	6,000 00	....	....
Do	For pay of teacher to manual labor school and for subsistence of pupils and necessary supplies.	....do	2d article treaty Dec. 21, 1855; amount necessary during the pleasure of the President.	$3,000 00	....	....	....
Do	For carpenter and joiner to aid in erecting	Vol. 12, page 982..	2d article treaty Dec. 21, 1855;	....	8,000 00	....	....

-nai-elt and Quil- sil-ute Indians.	For $25,000 to be expended for beneficial ob- jects, under direction of the President.	Vol. 12, page 972..	4th article treaty July 1, 1855; fourteen instalments in gradu- ated payments yet to be provided for.	....	13,700 00	....
Do	For support of an agricultural and industrial school, and for the employment of suitable instructors for the term of twenty years.	Vol. 12, page 973..	10th article treaty July 1, 1855; fourteen instalments unappro- priated, estimated at $2,500 each year.	....	35,000 00	....
Do	For twenty instalments for support of a smith and carpenter shop and tools.	....do	10th article treaty July 1, 1855; fourteen instalments unappro- priated, estimated at $500 each.	....	7,000 00	....
Do	For the employment of blacksmith, carpenters, farmer, and physician, for twenty years.	....do	10th article treaty July 1, 1855; fourteen instalments, estimated at $4,600 each year, to be pro- vided for.	....	64,400 00	....
Do	Twenty instalments in graduated payments, under the direction of the President, for $60,000.	Vol. 12, page 934..	5th article treaty Jan. 26, 1855; fourteen instalments yet to make provision for.	....	32,000 00	....
Jallams........	Twenty instalments for support of an agricul- tural and industrial school and for teachers.	Vol. 12, page 935..	11th article treaty Jan. 26, 1855; fourteen instalments to be pro- vided for, estimated at $2,500 each.	....	35,000 00	....
Do	Twenty years' employment of blacksmith, car- penter, farmer, and physician.	....do	11th article treaty Jan. 26, 1855; fourteen instalments unprovided for, estimated at $4,600 each..	....	64,400 00	....
apahoes and Che- enne Indians of ie Upper Arkan- as river.	For $450,000 in fifteen equal annual instal- ments, under the direction of the Secretary of the Interior, of $30,000 each.	Vol. 12, page 1165	4th article treaty Feb. 18, 1861; ten instalments unappropriated of $30,000.	....	300,000 00	....
Do	For five instalments providing for sawing tim- ber and grinding grain, machine shops, tools, and building purposes, for interpreter, engi- neer, miller, farmer, &c.	....do	5th article treaty Feb. 18, 1861; two instalments to be provided for, estimated at $5,000.	....	10,000 00	....
Do	For transportation and necessary expenses of the delivery of annuity goods and provi- sions.	....do	5th article treaty Feb. 18, 1861; ten instalments unappropriated, es- timated at $5,000 each.	....	50,000 00	....
awa Indians of aachard's Fork, d Roche de Bœuf.	Four equal instalments in money............	Vol. 12, page 1238.	4th article treaty June 24, 1862, one payment yet to be appro- priated of $8,500.	....	8,500 00	....
Do	The accruing interest on the unpaid balance...	....do	4th article treaty June 24, 1862...	....	425 00	....
Do	For this amount, being the last instalment on stocks held in trust by the Department of the Interior.	....do	4th article treaty June 24, 1862...	....	2,849 87	....
stern bands of hoshonees.	Twenty instalments of $10,000 each, to be ex- pended under the direction of the President, 5th article treaty July 2, 1863.	*Page 177, section 5	Eighteen instalments unappropri- ated.	....	180,000 00	....
stern bands of hoshonees.	Twenty instalments of $5,000 each, to be ex- pended under the direction of the President, 7th article treaty October 1, 1863.	Page 557	Eighteen instalments unappropri- ated.	....	90,000 00	....

* The references from this point to the end of the table are to the Pamphlet copy of the laws.

Names of tribes.	Description of annuities, stipulations, &c.	Reference to laws; Pamphlet copy; first and second sessions Thirty-eighth Congress.	Number of instalments yet unappropriated, explanatory remarks, &c.	Annual amount necessary to meet stipulations, indefinite as to time, now allowed, but liable to be discontinued.	Aggregate of future appropriations that will be required during a limited number of years to pay limited annuities till they expire; am'ts incidentally necessary to effect the payment.	Amount of annual liabilities of a permanent character.	Amount held in trust by the United States on which five per cent. is annually paid, and amounts which, invested at five per cent., would produce the permanent annuities.
Northwestern bands of Shoshonees.	Twenty instalments of $5,000 each, to be expended under the direction of the President, 3d article treaty July 30, 1863.	Page 177, section 3	Eighteen instalments unappropriated.		$90,000 00		
Goship bands of Shoshonees.	Twenty instalments of $1,000 each, to be expended under the direction of the President, 7th article treaty October 12, 1863.	Page 177, section 9	Eighteen instalments unappropriated.		18,000 00		
Chippewas of Red Lake & Pembina.	Twenty instalments of $20,000 each, to be paid as annuity.		Eighteen instalments unappropriated.		360,000 00		
Tabequache bands of Utah Indians.	Ten instalments of $20,000 each, March 25, 1864.	Page 25, section 8..	(Goods $10,000, provisions $10,000) eight instalm'ts unappropriated.		166,000 00		
Do	Five instalments of $10,000 each, for the purposes of agriculture and purchase of farming utensils, stock, &c.	Page 75, section 8..	Three instalments unappropriated.		30,000 00		
Chippewas of the Mississippi, Pillagers and Lake Winnebagoshish bands in Minnesota.	Ten instalments of $1,500 each, to furnish Indians with oxen. log chains, &c., 5th article treaty May 7, 1864.	Page 86, section 5..	Eight instalments unappropriated.		120,000 00		
Do	Support of two carpenters, two blacksmiths, four farm laborers, and one physician, ten years.	...do	Estimated at $7,700 per annum, eight instalments to be appropriated.		61,600 00		
Do	This am't to be applied for support of saw mill as long as the President may deem it necessary.	...do	6th article treaty May 7, 1864, annual appropriation.	$1,000 00			
Do	Pay of services and travelling expenses of a board of visitors, not more than five persons, to attend annuity payments to the Indians, &c.	Page 86, section 7..	7th article treaty May 7, 1864....	650 00			
Do	For payment of female teachers, employed on the reservation.	Page 87, section 13	13th article treaty May 7, 1864....	1,000 00			
				60,820 00	10,055,390 98	$533,635 30	$7,427,707 86

No. 30.

Stocks held by the Secretary of the Treasury in trust for the Chickasaw national fund, and deposited for safe-keeping with the Treasurer of the United States.

Description of stock.	Amount.
Six per cent. bonds of the State of Arkansas, due 1868	*$90,000 00
Six per cent. bonds of the State of Indiana, due 1857	†141,000 00
Six per cent. bonds of the State of Illinois, due 1860	‡17,000 00
Six per cent. stock of the State of Maryland, due 1870	§6,149 57
Six per cent. stock of the State of Maryland, due 1890	‡8,350 17
Six per cent. bonds of Nashville and Chattanooga Railroad Co., due 1881	§512,000 00
Six per cent. bonds of Richmond and Danville Railroad Co., due 1876	*$100,000 00
Six per cent. stock of the State of Tennessee, due 1890	§104,000 00
United States six per cent. stock, loan of 1847, due 1867	‖135,250 00
United States six per cent. stock, loan of 1848, due 1868	‖37,491 80
United States six per cent. stock, loan of 1862, due 1867 or 1882	61,000 00
Total	1,212,241 54

* No interest paid by Arkansas since January 1, 1842. ‡ Interest regularly paid.
† Interest only paid by three per cent. fund to 1851. § Interest unpaid from January, 1861.
‖ Interest paid regularly.

SMITHSONIAN FUND.

Statement of stocks now held by the Secretary of the Treasury, and deposited with the Treasurer for safe-keeping, which were purchased for the Smithsonian fund and held as security for moneys paid to the Smithsonian Institution ; showing, also, the amount of interest due on said stocks up to November 30, 1865, together with the amount in the treasury to the credit of the fund.

Description of stock.	Amount.	Interest due up to November 30, 1864.	In the treasury to the credit of the Smithsonian fund.	Aggregate on all accounts.
State of Arkansas	$538,000 00	$686,197 34	....	....
State of Illinois	56,000 00	1,400 00	....	....
United States, loan of 1842	48,061 64	9,852 62	....	....
United States, loan of 1848	33,400 00	635 00	....	....
Total	675,461 64	698,284 96	$298,417 68	$1,672,164 28

No. 31.

REGULATIONS CONCERNING COMMERCIAL INTERCOURSE WITH INSUR-
RECTIONARY STATES, CAPTURED AND ABANDONED PROPERTY, AND
THE PURCHASE OF PRODUCTS ON GOVERNMENT ACCOUNT.

Amended regulation, series of July 29, 1864. [*No. L V.*]

TREASURY DEPARTMENT, *December 22, 1864.*

Regulation LV, concerning commercial intercourse, series of July 29, 1864
is hereby amended as follows :

LV. All existing authorities to purchase products in insurrectionary States
are hereby revoked, except that products purchased in good faith under such
authorities, and paid for in whole or in part, prior to the 29th day of July, 1864,
may be transported to market as before the passage of the act of July 2, 1864,
subject to the following limitations and conditions and included in the following
classes :

1st. Those which have been wholly paid for.

2d. Those upon which part payment has been made, coupled with a legal
obligation to pay the residue, so that the articles purchased are at the risk of
the purchaser, and such payment is in nowise dependent upon their delivery.

3d. Where part payment has been made, without such obligation as to the
balance, so much of the products, alleged to have been purchased, as the amount
actually advanced will pay for at the stipulated price.

The original permits must be produced in such case, and proof furnished to
the satisfaction of a proper permit officer and a supervising or assistant special
agent for the agency or district in which proof is to be made that the property
desired to be moved comes within one of the classes named above, and that the
privilege conferred by the original permit has been in no way violated or abused—
a certificate of which facts must be indorsed upon the permit over their official
signature, which permit, so indorsed, will then be considered as revived and in
full force, to the extent specified in the indorsement, in accordance with this
rule.

W. P. FESSENDEN,
Secretary of the Treasury.

Executive order.

EXECUTIVE MANSION, *December 22, 1864.*

I, Abraham Lincoln, President of the United States, having seen and considered the within amended regulation, numbered LV, prescribed by the Secretary
of the Treasury, do hereby approve of the same; and I further declare and
order that products moving in compliance with the said regulation shall be
exempt from seizure and from confiscation and forfeiture to the United States.

ABRAHAM LINCOLN.

Amended regulation, series of July 29, 1864.

TREASURY DEPARTMENT,
January 4, 1865.

It having been represented to this department that Regulation LV, concerning
commercial intercourse, as amended December 22, 1864, is liable to miscon-
struction, and has been misconstrued as to its intent and meaning, it is hereby

LV. All authorities issued prior to July 29, 1864, to purchase products in insurrectionary States are hereby revoked, except that products purchased in good faith under such authorities, and paid for in part or in whole, prior to the said 29th day of July, 1864, may be transported to market as before the passage of the act of July 2, 1864, subject to the following limitations and conditions, and included in the following classes :

1st. Those which have been wholly paid for.

2d. Those upon which part payment has been made, coupled with a legal obligation to pay the residue, so that the articles purchased are at the risk of the purchaser, and such payment is in nowise dependent upon their delivery.

3d. Where part payment has been made, without such obligation as to the balance, so much of the products alleged to have been purchased as the amount actually advanced will pay for at the stipulated price.

The original permits must be produced in each case, and proof furnished to the satisfaction of a proper permit officer and a supervising or assistant special agent for the agency or district, in which proof is to be made that the property desired to be moved comes within one of the classes named above, and that the privilege conferred by the original permit has been in no way violated or abused ; a certificate of which facts must be indorsed upon the permit over their official signature, which permit, so indorsed, will then be considered as revived and in full force, to the extent specified in the indorsement, in accordance with this rule.

W. P. FESSENDEN,
Secretary of the Treasury.

Executive order.

EXECUTIVE MANSION,
January 4, 1865.

I, Abraham Lincoln, President of the United States, having seen and considered the within amended regulation, numbered LV, prescribed by the Secretary of the Treasury, do hereby approve the same; and I further declare and order that products moving in compliance with the said regulations shall be exempt from seizure and from confiscation and forfeiture to the United States.

ABRAHAM LINCOLN.

Additional regulations concerning commercial intercourse with and in States declared in insurrection, January 26, 1864.

EXECUTIVE ORDER.

EXECUTIVE MANSION,
Washington, January 26, 1864.

I, Abraham Lincoln, President of the United States, having seen and considered the additional regulations of trade prescribed by the Secretary of the Treasury, and numbered LI, LII, LIII, LIV, LV, and LVI, do hereby approve the same; and I further declare and order that all property brought in for sale in good faith, and actually sold in pursuance of said Regulations LII, LIII, LIV, LV, and LVI, after the same shall have taken effect and come in force as provided in Regulation LVI, shall be exempt from confiscation or forfeiture to the United States.

ABRAHAM LINCOLN.

Additional regulations of trade.

TREASURY DEPARTMENT, *January 23, 1864.*

LI. The commanding general having expressed the opinion, in reply to a letter addressed to him by the Secretary of the Treasury on the 16th instant, that restrictions on trade in the States of Missouri and Kentucky may now be safely removed, and the Secretary of War, in his letter of this day, January 23, 1864, having approved that opinion, the twenty-sixth regulation of trade established, with other regulations, on the 11th of September, 1863, is so far modified that all restrictions on trade in the States of Missouri and Kentucky are annulled and abrogated; and all products and goods may be freely taken into and transported within the said States as in time of peace: *Provided, however,* That no products or goods shall be taken from said States, or either of them, into any State declared to be in insurrection, or to any port in said State heretofore blockaded which has been or may be opened, except in compliance with the regulations of September 11, 1863.

Restrictions upon trade in, to, or from other States, and also upon the trade with States in insurrection and parts of said States, especially on the Mississippi and other navigable rivers, will be removed whenever, in the opinion of the President, such removal shall be found compatible with the military measures necessary for the suppression of the rebellion.

S. P. CHASE, *Secretary of the Treasury.*

ADDITIONAL REGULATIONS OF TRADE.

To take effect when promulgated under authority of the President by generals commanding departments.

TREASURY DEPARTMENT, *January 26, 1864.*

LII. All persons being or residing in any of the States declared to be in insurrection, whether within or beyond the lines of national military occupation, may freely bring any goods or products from within the State in which he may reside to any place within such lines where there is a supervising special agent or assistant special agent of the Treasury Department, for sale or other disposition; and so much of any regulation heretofore established as requires the obtaining of any previous authority or permit for bringing goods and products to the place of sale is hereby rescinded.

LIII. In all cases where the owner of the goods and products so brought in for sale shall reside within the lines of national military occupation, and shall take the oath prescribed by the proclamation of the President, dated December 8, 1863, and is not excepted from the amnesty granted by the said proclamation, or proved by affidavits to the satisfaction of the supervising special agent or assistant special agent to be disloyal and hostile to the United States, such owner or his agent may receive the price of his goods and products without deduction, except for dues and fees to the government under the regulations of September 11, 1863, or he may convey such goods and products, having paid said dues and fees, under proper permit, to such other place as he may choose for sale or other disposition; but whenever the owner of said goods and products shall not reside within the lines of national military occupation, such goods and products shall be sold by the supervising special agent or assistant special agent; and all such sales of such goods and products shall take place on Monday of each week at the place of receipt, and shall include all complete lots on hand at the time of sale. And the supervising special agent or the assistant special agent, as the case may be, shall pay to said owner or his agent, if said owner shall have taken said oath, and is not excepted from said amnesty nor proved to be disloyal and hostile, twenty-five per cent. of the gross proceeds of said sales, and shall pay the remainder of such proceeds, after deducting necessary and proper expenses of sale and one per cent. as additional compensation, into the treasury of the United States, and shall give to the owner of each lot sold, or his agent, a receipt or certificate describing the property. But the aggregate compensation of no supervising special agent or assistant special agent shall exceed the sum of five thousand dollars per annum, or at that rate for a less period; and each supervising special agent and assistant special agent charged with the receipt and payment of any money under any regulation of the Treasury Department shall give bond to the satisfaction of the Secretary of the Treasury, in the sum of fifty thousand dollars, for the faithful performance of his duties as such supervising special agent or assistant special agent, and for the punctual payment into the treasury of the United States of all sums by him received and required by law or regulations to be so paid.

LIV. All sales, whether private or public, shall be for notes of the United States or treasury notes, exclusively, and all proceeds of goods and products paid into the treasury under the foregoing regulation shall be restored without interest to the owner of the goods and products sold, in case he shall establish, on the return of peace and the full practical restoration of the authority of the Union, his title to said goods and products, and that since the sale thereof he has conducted himself in all respects as a good and loyal citizen of the United States, and has done nothing inconsistent with the terms of the oath prescribed by the President's proclamation of amnesty.

LV. Nothing in either of the foregoing additional regulations shall authorize the conveyance of supplies beyond the lines of national military occupation, or, except under the regulations of September 11, 1863, within said lines.

LVI. The foregoing regulations, numbered LII, LIII, LIV, LV, shall take effect and be in force within the lines of the several military departments in the insurrectionary States, whenever the generals commanding said departments shall, respectively, under authority from the President, and by proper orders, promulgate the same.

S. P. CHASE, Secretary of the Treasury.

Executive order.

EXECUTIVE MANSION,
Washington, February 2, 1864.

I, Abraham Lincoln, President of the United States, having seen and considered the additional regulation of trade prescribed by the Secretary of the Treasury, and numbered LVII, do hereby approve the same.

ABRAHAM LINCOLN.

Additional regulation of trade.

TREASURY DEPARTMENT, February 2, 1864.

LVII. The Secretary of War having transmitted to this department a letter of the commanding general, expressing the opinion, in reply to a letter addressed to him by the Secretary of the Treasury on the 16th ultimo, that restrictions on trade in the State of West Virginia, within the national military lines, may now be safely removed, the twenty-sixth regulation of trade, established with other regulations on the 11th of September, 1863, is so far modified that all restrictions on trade in the State of West Virginia, within said lines, are annulled and abrogated; and all products and goods may be freely taken into and transported within the above-mentioned portion of said State, as in time of peace: *Provided, however,* That no products or goods shall be taken from said State into any State declared to be in insurrection, or to any port in any such State heretofore blockaded, which has been or may be opened, except in compliance with the regulations of September 11, 1863.

S. P. CHASE, *Secretary of the Treasury.*

Amended regulation, series of July 29, 1864.

TREASURY DEPARTMENT, *February 21, 1865.*

Regulation XVI, concerning abandoned, captured and confiscable personal property, series of July 29, 1864, is hereby amended, as follows:

XVI. Supervising special agents, and such other persons assh all be specially authorized by the Secretary of the Treasury to receive and sell captured, abandoned, and confiscable property, will pay or cause to be paid, out of the general fund arising from the sale of all such property received and sold by him, all expenses necessarily incurred in collecting, receiving, securing, and disposing of the same, including fees, taxes, freights, storage, charges, labor, and other necessary expenses, being careful to avoid all useless or indiscreet expenditures; and will charge each particular lot or parcel with the specific or proportionate amount of all such expenses as can be made specific or proportionate charges to each lot or parcel; and will also, charge and retain out of the proceeds of each lot or parcel one and one-half per centum thereof for the payment of such expenses connected with the collection, transportation, and sale, or other disposition thereof, as cannot be made specific or proportionate charges against each lot or parcel, or are not otherwise provided for, such as rents, compensation to clerks or other employés, auctioneers, printing, and advertising, a carefully stated account of which will be kept by such agents, or other persons, showing in detail all expenses paid out of this fund arising from such charge; and unless unavoidably prevented, they will take vouchers for all expenditures made under this regulation, and transmit the same with their accounts to the Secretary of the Treasury. Out of the balance, if any, of said one and one-half per centum remaining after defraying said expenses the several supervising special agents, or other persons selling as aforesaid, may retain as compensation for extra care and responsibility a sum not exceeding three-fourths of one per centum of the amount of such sales; and with the remainder, if any, may reward extra services in the collection and care of property, rendered by agents and others, in such manner and to such amount as may be approved or directed by the Secretary of the Treasury: *Provided,* That the amount so retained for extra care, responsibility, or services, by any agent or other person, selling as aforesaid, after the date hereof, shall not exceed two thousand dollars per annum, or at that rate for a less period; unless the Secretary shall, for special services and responsibilities, allow a larger sum.

W. P. FESSENDEN, *Secretary of the Treasury.*

EXECUTIVE MANSION, *February 21, 1865.*

Approved:

A. LINCOLN.

Additional regulations to the series of July 29, 1864.

TREASURY DEPARTMENT,
March 21, 1865.

The following additional regulations are hereby prescribed by the Secretary of the Treasury, as supplementary and amendatory to the series of July 29, 1864:

I. The local rules for the first, second, and third special agencies, dated February 1, 1865, made by the general agent of the Treasury Department, for the purpose of carrying out the provisions of the act of Congress approved July 2, 1864, are hereby approved. But neither this approval, nor the local rules, nor any contracts made under them, will be regarded as affecting any right or claim of the United States arising out of the confiscation laws thereof.

II. Rule III, of said local rules, will be amended by inserting the words "loyal and" before the words "well-disposed," so that it will read, "all loyal and well-disposed persons," &c.

III. Products received under the rules relating to the registry of plantations will be disposed of by supervising special agents in the same manner and subject to the same regulations and conditions as provided by Regulation XIII, series July 29, 1864, concerning rents received for abandoned and confiscable lands.

IV. Amended Regulation XVI, concerning abandoned, captured, and confiscable personal property, dated and approved February 21, 1865, is hereby revoked, and the original regulation is restored and stands in the same force and effect as before the amendment. But the same is hereby amended by adding thereto the following proviso, viz: *Provided,* That in special cases of large captures the Secretary of the Treasury may direct different dispositions thereof either through the officers acting under the regulations, or others specially appointed for the purpose, in which cases he will fix such conditions and terms of compensation in each case as he shall think proper.

V. In any special agency district where the duties relating to the several subjects provided for by the regulations, series July 29, 1864, can, with due regard to the public interests, be performed by one assistant special agent, but one will be assigned to duty in such district.

Supervising special agents, before making any changes required by this regulation, will submit their proposed action to the general agent for approval, who will report the action taken to the Secretary.

VI. When the office of a supervising special agent shall be located in the same place where the office of an assistant special agent of a district has heretofore been established, the duties for the district will be merged in the office of the supervising special agent. In such cases an assistant special agent may be assigned to duty as a deputy in the office of the supervising special agent, either by the Secretary, or subject to his approval.

H. McCULLOCH,
Secretary of the Treasury.

EXECUTIVE MANSION, *March 21, 1865.*

Approved:

ABRAHAM LINCOLN.

Amended Regulation IV.

TREASURY DEPARTMENT,
March 30, 1865.

Regulation IV of the "general regulations for the purchase of products of insurrectionary States on government account," dated September 24, 1864, is hereby amended as follows:

IV. The price to be paid for any of the products so purchased shall not exceed the market value thereof at the place of delivery, nor exceed three-fourths of the market value thereof in the city of New York at the latest quotation known to the agent purchasing at the date of delivery of the products, after deducting from such market value: 1st. The internal revenue tax of two cents per pound; 2d, the transportation permit fee of four cents per pound; and 3d, an amount sufficient to cover all actual and estimated expenses of handling, storing, insurance, transportation, commission on sales, &c. Such estimated expenses in no case to exceed an amount for which private parties can secure the performance of the same service.

H. McCULLOCH,
Secretary of the Treasury.

EXECUTIVE MANSION.

The foregoing amended regulation having been seen and considered by me, is hereby approved.

ABRAHAM LINCOLN.

Amended general regulations.

TREASURY DEPARTMENT, April 25, 1865.

The "general regulations" made by the Secretary of the Treasury, dated July 29, 1864, for the purpose of carrying into effect the regulations of that date, and the several acts of Congress authorizing them, are hereby amended as follows, viz:

I. Two additional special agencies are hereby established, distinguished numerically, and respectively designated and described as follows:

The eighth special agency comprises the State of South Carolina and so much of the State of Georgia as lies in and east of the valley of the Ogeechee river, including the city of Savannah.

The ninth special agency comprises the west part of Florida and so much of the State of Alabama as lies south of the Alabama and Mississippi railroad.

II. The boundaries of the fifth special agency as defined by the general regulations, series July 29, 1864, are hereby modified so that it comprises the south and east part of Florida, including Key West, and so much of the State of Georgia as lies south and west of the valley of the Ogeechee river.

III. The boundaries of the third special agency, as defined by the general regulations, series July 29, 1864, are hereby modified so that it comprises so much of the States of Louisiana and Mississippi as lies south of Grand Gulf, and including that place.

IV. In addition to the duties devolved upon the general agent of the Treasury Department by the said regulations he will hereafter be required, under the direction of the Secretary, to cause the regulations concerning the purchase of products of insurrectionary States under the eighth section of the act of Congress approved July 2, 1864, to be properly observed and carried out.

All officers and agents appointed to purchase and sell such products will comply with the instructions of the general agent in regard thereto until otherwise directed by the Secretary of the Treasury.

HUGH McCULLOCH,
Secretary of the Treasury.

Approved April 25, 1865

ANDREW JOHNSON.

Amended regulations for the purchase of products of the insurrectionary States on government account, May 9, 1865.

TREASURY DEPARTMENT, *May* 9, 1865.

I. Agents shall be appointed by the Secretary of the Treasury, with the approval of the President, to purchase for the United States, under special instructions from the Secretary of the Treasury, products of States declared to be in insurrection, at such places as may from time to time be designated by the Secretary of the Treasury as markets or places of purchase.

Agents heretofore appointed for the places designated under previous regulations will continue their agencies as if appointed under these regulations.

II. Before entering upon the discharge of his duty, each of the agents so appointed shall execute a bond, with sureties, in the prescribed form, in a penal sum to be fixed by the Secretary of the Treasury, conditioned for the faithful discharge of his duty, and that he shall not engage, directly or indirectly, in the purchase of products on private account, nor be, in any way, interested in the products purchased by him, or the proceeds or profits arising therefrom.

III. The operations of purchasing agents shall be confined to the single article of cotton; and they shall give public notice, at the place to which they may be assigned, that they will purchase, in accordance with these regulations, all cotton not captured or abandoned which may be brought to them.

IV. To meet the requirements of the 8th section of the act of July 2, 1864 the agents shall receive all cotton so brought, and forthwith return to the seller three-fourths thereof, which portion shall be an average grade of the whole, according to the certificate of a sworn expert or sampler.

V. All cotton purchased and resold by purchasing agents shall be exempt from all fees and all internal taxes. And the agent selling shall mark the same "FREE," and furnish to the purchaser a bill of sale clearly and accurately describing the character and quantity sold, and containing a certificate that it is exempt from taxes and fees, as above.

VI. Purchasing agents shall keep a full and accurate record of all their transactions, including the names of all persons from whom they make purchases, the date of the purchase, a description of the cotton purchased by them, and the quantity and quality thereof, also of the one-quarter retained by them. A transcript of this record will be transmitted to the Secretary of the Treasury on the first day of each month.

VII. Sales of the cotton retained by the purchasing agents under Regulation IV, as the difference between three-fourths the market price and the full price thereof in the city of New York, may be made by such agents at such places and times and in such manner as may be directed in special instructions from the Secretary of the Treasury. Where such sales are not so authorized, the agents shall, without delay, ship it to New York, on the best terms possible, consigned, until otherwise directed, to S. Draper, cotton agent and disbursing officer at that place. Bills of lading in triplicate for such shipment must be taken, one of which shall be sent to the agent at New York, one to the Secretary of the Treasury, and one retained by the purchasing agent.

VIII. Prior to the close of each month, and in sufficient time for the necessary action, the purchasing agent shall prepare and forward to the Commissioner of Customs a full estimate of the probable expenses of his office for the month next ensuing, the amount of which, together with any sum found due from inadequacy of former estimate, or less so much as may remain unexpended from any amount previously sent, will be transmitted to said purchasing agent. Purchasing agents will require receipts in triplicate for all moneys paid by them, one of which receipts shall be forwarded to the disbursing officer, one to the First Auditor of the Treasury with his accounts, and one retained by the agent.

IX. All agents are prohibited from purchasing any product of an insurrectionary State which shall have been captured by the military or naval forces of the United States, or which shall have been abandoned by the lawful owner thereof.

X. These regulations, which are intended to revoke and annul all others on the subject heretofore made, will take effect and be in force on and after May 10, 1865.

HUGH McCULLOCH,
Secretary of the Treasury.

EXECUTIVE CHAMBER,
Washington City, May 9, 1865.

Approved.

ANDREW JOHNSON.

TREASURY DEPARTMENT, *June* 14, 1865.

The following proclamation of the President of the United States, dated the 13th day of June, 1865, removing the restrictions upon internal, domestic, and coastwise intercourse and trade, and upon the removal of products of States heretofore declared in insurrection, except as to articles contraband of war, viz: arms, ammunition, all articles from which ammunition is made, and gray uniforms and cloth, and with certain other exceptions and limitations therein contained, is published for the information and guidance of collectors and other officers of the customs.

H. McCULLOCH,
Secretary of the Treasury.

DEPARTMENT OF STATE.

By the President of the United States of America.

A PROCLAMATION.

Whereas, by my proclamation of the twenty-ninth of April, one thousand eight hundred and sixty-five, all restrictions upon internal, domestic, and commercial intercourse, with certain exceptions therein specified and set forth, were removed "in such parts of the States of Tennessee, Virginia, North Carolina, South Carolina, Georgia, Florida, Alabama, Mississippi, and so much of Louisiana as lies east of the Mississippi river, as shall be embraced within the lines of national military occupation; *   *   * "

And whereas, by my proclamation of the twenty-second of May, one thousand eight hundred and sixty-five, for reasons therein given, it was declared that certain ports of the United States which had been previously closed against foreign commerce should, with certain specified exceptions, be reopened to such commerce on and after the first day of July next, subject to the laws of the United States and in pursuance of such regulations as might be prescribed by the Secretary of the Treasury;

And whereas I am satisfactorily informed that dangerous combinations against the laws of the United States no longer exist within the State of Tennessee; that the insurrection heretofore existing within said State has been suppressed that within the boundaries thereof the authority of the United States is undisputed; and that such officers of the United States as have been duly commissioned are in the undisturbed exercise of their official functions:

Now, therefore, be it known, that I, Andrew Johnson, President of the United States, do hereby declare that all restrictions upon internal, domestic, and coastwise intercourse and trade, and upon the removal of products of States heretofore declared in insurrection, reserving and excepting *only* those relating to contraband of war, as hereinafter recited, and also those which relate to the reservation of the rights of the United States to property purchased in the territory of an enemy, heretofore imposed in the territory of the United States east of the Mississippi river, are annulled, and I do hereby direct that they be forthwith removed; and that on and after the first day of July next all restrictions upon foreign commerce with said ports, with the exception and reservation aforesaid, be likewise removed; and that the commerce of such States shall be conducted under the supervision of the regularly appointed officers of the customs provided by law; and such officers of the customs shall receive any captured and abandoned property that may be turned over to them, under the law, by the military or naval forces of the United States, and dispose of such property as shall be directed by the Secretary of the Treasury. The following articles contraband of war are excepted from the effect of this proclamation: arms, ammunition, all articles from which ammunition is made, and gray uniforms and cloth.

And I hereby also proclaim and declare that the insurrection, so far as it relates to, and within the State of Tennessee, and the inhabitants of the said State of Tennessee as reorganized and constituted under their recently adopted constitution and reorganization, and accepted by them, is suppressed, and therefore, also, that all the disabilities and disqualifications attaching to said State and the inhabitants thereof consequent upon any proclamations issued by virtue of the fifth section of the act entitled "An act further to provide for the collection of duties on imports, and for other purposes," approved the thirteenth day of July, one thousand eight hundred and sixty-one, are removed.

But nothing herein contained shall be considered or construed as in anywise changing or impairing any of the penalties and forfeitures for treason heretofore incurred under the laws of the United States, or any of the provisions, restrictions, or disabilities set forth in my proclamation, bearing date the twenty-ninth day of May, one thousand eight hundred and sixty-five, or as impairing existing regulations for the suspension of the habeas corpus, and the exercise of military law in cases where it shall be necessary for the general public safety and welfare during the existing insurrection; nor shall this proclamation affect, or in any way impair, any laws heretofore passed by Congress, and duly approved by the President, or any proclamations or orders issued by him, during the aforesaid insurrection, abolishing slavery, or in any way affecting the relations of slavery, whether of persons or of property; but, on the contrary, all such laws and proclamations heretofore made or issued are expressly saved, and declared to be in full force and virtue.

In testimony whereof, I have hereunto set my hand, and caused the seal of the United States to be affixed.

Done at the city of Washington, this 13th day of June, in the year of
[SEAL.]   our Lord one thousand eight hundred and sixty-five, and of the independence of the United States of America the eighty-ninth.

ANDREW JOHNSON.

By the President:
WILLIAM H. SEWARD,
    Secretary of State.

22 F

Circular letter of instructions to officers of the Treasury Department relative to commercial intercourse, captured, abandoned, and confiscable property, freedmen, &c.

TREASURY DEPARTMENT,
June 27, 1865.

The various rules and regulations heretofore prescribed by the Secretary of the Treasury in regard to the above-named subjects having been rendered nugatory in whole or in part by the changed condition of affairs in the southern States and Executive orders and proclamations, and the War Department having assumed charge of freedmen, abandoned lands, &c., under the provisions of the act of Congress approved March 3, 1865, the following instructions as to the duties of officers of the Treasury Department in the premises are prescribed, and will be regarded as in full force and effect immediately on the receipt thereof by any officer whose action is in anywise affected thereby:

1. All restrictions on commercial intercourse in and with States and parts of States heretofore declared in insurrection, and on the purchase, transportation, and sale of the products thereof, are removed; *except* as to the transportation thereto or therein of arms, ammunition, articles from which ammunition is made, gray uniforms, and gray cloth; and *except, also,* those relating to property heretofore purchased by the agents or captured by or surrendered to the military forces of the United States. Nor will any fees or taxes be charged or collected, except those imposed by the customs and internal revenue laws. And the supervision necessary to prevent the shipment of the prohibited articles will be exercised only by the regular and ordinary officers of the customs, acting under the revenue laws of the United States.

2. Subordinate officers discharging duties in regard to commercial intercourse, under the regulations referred to, will consider their official connexion with this department as terminating with the 30th instant, without further notice.

3. Agents for the purchase of products of insurrectionary States on government account will close their official business east of the Mississippi with the transactions of the 13th instant, and west of it with the transactions of the 24th instant; returning to sellers all property or money received or collected since those dates respectively, and using such despatch in the premises that their connexion with the department may, if possible, terminate with the 30th instant.

4. Officers of this department charged with the duty of receiving and collecting, or having in their possession or under their control, captured, abandoned, or confiscable personal property, will dispose of the same, in accordance with regulations on the subject heretofore prescribed, at the earliest time consistent with the public interests, and will refrain from receiving such from military or naval authorities after the 30th instant. This will not be construed, however, as interfering with the operations of the agents now engaged in receiving or collecting the property recently captured by or surrendered to the forces of the United States, whether or not covered by or included in the records, &c., delivered to the United States military or treasury authorities by rebel military officers or cotton agents. Those so acting will continue to discharge the duties thus imposed until such property is all received or satisfactorily accounted for, and until the amount so secured is shipped or otherwise disposed of under the regulations on the subject heretofore prescribed. And they will use all the means at their command with the utmost vigor, to the end that all the property so collected, captured, or turned over, shall be secured to the United States with the least possible cost and delay. After the 30th instant the duty of receiving captured and abandoned property not embraced in the above exception will be discharged by the usual and regular officers of the customs at the several places where they may be located, in accordance with regulations relating

to the subject; and officers heretofore performing that duty will give them all the aid and information in their power, to enable them to carry out the same.

5. Officers of this department charged with the care or supervision of or having in their possession or under their control any abandoned or confiscable lands, houses, and tenements, will turn them over to a duly authorized officer of the bureau of refugees, freedmen, and abandoned lands, so far as they may be required or demanded by the same, together with all moneys, books, records, and papers arising from or relating to the property so turned over, taking proper receipts or vouchers therefor. This rule will also govern the action of all agents of this department connected in any way with the care of freedmen, &c., so far as it may be applicable. And all persons asking for any information in regard to the property so turned over, or for the release of the same, or for the release of any proceeds or moneys arising therefrom, will be referred to the commissioner of refugees, freedmen, and abandoned lands, at Washington, to whom communications on the subject should be addressed.

6. Officers of this department having in their possession or under their control any moneys whatever arising from fees collected under the commercial intercourse regulations, (except those collected for the benefit of freedmen, which will be disposed of under section five,) or from the sales of captured, abandoned, or confiscable personal property, will forthwith deposit the same with the nearest assistant treasurer, designated depositary, or deposit bank, (keeping the amounts from the different sources separate,) to the credit of H, A. Risley, esq., supervising special agent, &c., taking therefor receipts in quadruplicate—which receipts must show whence the sums were received—one of which will be retained by the officer so depositing, one forthwith sent to the Secretary of the Treasury, one to the Commissioner of Customs, and one to Mr. Risley, at Washington.

7. All officers above referred to, except proper officers of the customs, acting exclusively under the revenue laws, will, after they have closed their official business, as above directed, and sold at auction, to the highest bidder, the furniture and property remaining on hand, and accounted for the proceeds of the same, forthwith systematically arrange the books, records, papers, &c., of their late office, that they may easily be referred to and examined, pack them in secure and water-proof boxes, and forward the same, so marked as to indicate their contents, together with their respective resignations, addressed to the Secretary of the Treasury, Washington city.

HUGH McCULLOCH,
Secretary of the Treasury.

TREASURY DEPARTMENT, *July* 22, 1865.

It has come to the knowledge of this department that large contracts have been made by some of its agents with various persons for the collection of abandoned or captured or surrendered cotton, authority being generally or in many instances given to the contractors to discover and collect all such cotton within a certain district. While such contracts have been to some extent contemplated or authorized by previous regulations, such action now is not in conformity with the spirit or intention of the Executive proclamation relating to the subject; and if any contracts of that character have been made by you, operations under them should be suspended and closed up at once.

Where agents have not adequate facilities for these purposes at their own command, and the public interest would be prejudiced by delay, no objection exists to the making by them of contracts with reputable and responsible persons, on reasonable and proper terms, for the collection, putting in order and transportation to points accessible for shipment by rail or water of certain specific lots of cotton known to the agent, the locality, quantity, and description of which should be fully and accurately stated in each case; but in view of the manifest evils likely to result from such steps, no arrangement will be sanctioned which contemplates the scouring of any given portions of the country for property of the character herein referred to by persons who are not bonded officers of this department.

As stated above, any existing contract heretofore made by you not in conformity with the spirit of these instructions must be at once modified or closed up, and your future action shaped accordingly.

Respectfully,

H. McCULLOCH.
Secretary of the Treasury.

To the SUPERVISING AND ASSISTANT SPECIAL AGENTS
of the Treasury Department.

TREASURY DEPARTMENT, *August* 18, 1865.

The irregularities, confusion, and conflict growing out of the collection and movement of captured cotton, without an organized system of action governing the whole subject, renders an immediate reform necessary. I have, therefore, determined to establish the following rules governing the first, second, third, fourth, eighth, and ninth agencies:

1. All requirements of the regulations concerning captured and abandoned personal property—series of July 29, 1864—will be strictly observed by all agents engaged in collecting and forwarding captured cotton, except as hereinafter modified.

2. Each agent appointed by me to collect captured cotton will, as soon as practicable after receipt hereof, report in person to the supervising agent of the agency in which he is operating for assignment to duty, and will be directed by him in all his official action.

3. All instructions from this department to assistant agents will be given only through the proper supervising agents.

4. Supervising agents are hereby authorized to make provisional appointments of assistant agents to collect captured cotton in all cases where the public interests will be promoted thereby, subject to my approval.

5. Each assistant agent will make all shipments of cotton collected by him to such supervising agent as he shall be directed to forward to by the supervising agent assigning him to duty, and he will take duplicate receipts for each lot from the supervising agent to whom the same is shipped, one of which he will retain, and the other he will forward to me. Supervising agents will in all cases forward or cause to be forwarded to market all cotton collected by the most expeditious and economical route from the point of collection.

6. Supervising agents will not collect directly, nor make any contract for collecting; but will receive and forward to Simeon Draper, cotton agent, New York, until otherwise ordered, all that shall be sent to them by assistant agents, and will give duplicate receipts for each lot as above indicated.

7. Each assistant agent will be assigned to duty in a well-defined district by the proper supervising agent, and will therein make contracts, in all cases where it can be done with the planter or other person in whose custody the captured cotton shall be found, to prepare in proper packages and condition for transportation, and deliver the same at such place of shipment as shall be agreed upon. The terms of these contracts, when made with planters having custody of the cotton, should be sufficiently liberal to insure fair compensation to them,

and to encourage good feeling on their part. Each contract must be made in writing, and be for the delivery of a specific lot at a designated place, and be made subject to the approval of the supervising agent under whom he is acting. Compensation must be made under such contracts out of the cotton delivered upon them, and must be made only by the supervising agent who receives the cotton.

8. In any case where cotton or other property is moving in the hands of private parties, which a supervising agent has satisfactory reason to believe was captured from the late so-called confederate government, and has been stolen or otherwise wrongfully taken, he will detain the same, and examine fully into the case, and if he shall be satisfied by the proofs submitted that the property was so captured, then he shall seize and forward it as captured property. But if he shall be satisfied that it was not so captured, then he will release it to the party from whom it was taken. Agents shall make a full report to this department of each case, including the testimony. An assistant agent will, in no case, make a seizure of property moving in the hands of private parties, but will inform the proper supervising agent of any facts within his knowledge to show that it has been stolen or otherwise improperly taken, and in case such information results in the seizure and detention of such property it shall be regarded as collected by the agent giving such information.

9. Agency lines will be regarded as heretofore established by the regulations, except when the same are changed by me, or as hereinafter provided, and each supervising agent will confine his action to the agency for which he is appointed, and each assistant agent will confine his action to the district to which he is assigned by the supervising agent.

10. All supervising and other agents engaged in collecting and forwarding captured cotton will be subject to the direction and control of the general agent, who is hereby authorized and directed, in cases where he shall think the public interests require it, to suspend the official action of any supervising or other agent, and temporarily to appoint another to perform his duties; to revoke any contract improperly made, or being improperly executed; to change the lines of agencies; and generally to do, pursuant to the regulations and these instructions, what he shall regard as best for the public interest in the premises, subject to the approval of the department.

It is expected, unless under special circumstances to be determined by the supervising agent, that no more territory will be embraced within a district than the assistant agent, assigned to duty in it, will be able to attend to personally without the appointment of sub-agents.

It is also expected that each supervising agent will keep moving throughout the agency under his charge, personally observing and directing the operations of the assistants by him assigned to duty therein.

It is desired that the captured cotton be secured and forwarded as expeditiously as possible, and that in doing it private interests shall be interfered with as little as possible.

All cotton so collected will, until otherwise directed, be forwarded to Simeon Draper, cotton agent, New York, and the supervising agent forwarding the same will accompany each shipment with a statement to the cotton agent, describing each lot making up such shipment, the marks thereof, and the name of the assistant agent who collected it.

All money required by the supervising agents to defray necessary expenses in collecting will be sent upon their estimates therefor made to me on the first of each month.

H. McCULLOCH,
Secretary of the Treasury.

To the SUPERVISING AND ASSISTANT SPECIAL AGENTS
of the Treasury Department.

TREASURY DEPARTMENT, *November* 21, 1865.

For the information and government of officers of the Treasury Department connected with the collection of captured and abandoned property, the following rules are prescribed, and will be promptly and fully carried out:

1. Hereafter no cotton claimed or recorded by the late so-called Confederate States government as "tithe cotton" or taxes, and which has not been delivered to it or its agents, but remains in the hands of the person assessed, will be taken or collected as captured property.

2. In no case can the title given by or derived from the late so-called Confederate States government be regarded as valid by officers of this department; and cotton in the possession of or claimed by persons under any sale or transfer made by such government will be treated as captured property belonging to the United States.

3. In cases where cotton, formerly belonging to the so-called Confederate government, has been purchased and is held by persons alleging that the same was purchased for the purpose of delivering it to agents of this department authorized to purchase the products of insurrectionary States on government account, in pursuance of contracts made with such agents, it will be taken by agents of this department and treated as captured property.

Persons claiming such property will be advised that, upon presenting to the Secretary of the Treasury any claims they may have in the premises, contracts made by them with the purchasing agents will be respected, and parties who have acted in good faith in the execution of such contracts will be protected.

4. Hereafter, agents forwarding captured cotton will take measures to insure the same while in their possession or *in transit* from place of shipment to New York, being careful to make such insurance in reliable companies, and on the most favorable terms possible to government.

5. In cases where agents have been appointed since the 18th of August last, or shall be hereafter appointed, the commissions of such new agents shall not extend to cotton collected and stored by their predecessors.

Supervising special agents will see that these instructions are at once communicated to all persons acting under and with them, and strictly complied with.

H. McCULLOCH,
Secretary of the Treasury.

To the SUPERVISING AGENTS
of the Treasury Department.